Oil Crops
of
the World

Oil Crops
of
the World
Their Breeding and Utilization

Editors

Gerhard Röbbelen
Institut für Pflanzenbau und Pflanzenzüchtung
Göttingen, Federal Republic of Germany

R. Keith Downey
Agriculture Canada Research Station
Saskatoon, Canada

Amram Ashri
Faculty of Agriculture
Rehovot, Israel

McGRAW-HILL PUBLISHING COMPANY
New York   St. Louis   San Francisco   Auckland   Bogotá
Caracas   Hamburg   Lisbon   London   Madrid   Mexico
Milan   Montreal   New Delhi   Oklahoma City
Paris   San Juan   São Paulo   Singapore
Sydney   Tokyo   Toronto

Library of Congress Cataloging-in-Publication Data

Oil crops of the world.

    Bibliography: p.
    Includes index.
    1. Oilseed plants. 2. Oilseed plants — Breeding.
3. Oilseed products. 4. Knowles, Paulden F.
(Paulden Ford), 1916-   . I. Downey, R. Keith.
II. Röbbelen, Gerhard. III. Ashri, Amram.
SB298.032 1989   633.8'5   89-2546
ISBN 0-07-053081-5

1234567890   HAL/HAL   8965432109

ISBN 0-07-053081-5

The editor for this book was Jennifer Mitchell.

Printed and bound by Arcata/Halliday.

*For more information about other McGraw-Hill materials,
call 1-800-2-MCGRAW in the United States. In other
countries, call your nearest McGraw-Hill office.*

To Paulden F. Knowles

Paul Knowles was born 18 April 1916 in Saskatchewan, Canada where he attended the University of Saskatchewan and received his BSA and MSc. He then began his work on oilseed crops at the University of California at Davis in 1947. After considerable research on flax and other oilseed crops, he turned his attention to safflower, a plant he found to be well-adapted to the environment of California. His work stimulated the introduction of this new crop to California and in 1950 oilseed processors initiated and established production of safflower which continues to this time. Safflower was one of many species Paul Knowles studied as possible new crops for California agriculture, but it is the comprehensive study and practical developments of germplasm of safflower that represents his most important contributions to science and agriculture.

Safflower (*Carthamus* sp.) germplasm was very limited in the USA so he made extensive plant collection expeditions in 1958 and in 1964-1965. These trips through South Asia, the Middle East and North Africa accumulated much of the safflower germplasm in the USDA World Collection, including both cultivated and wild species. These expeditions resulted in many personal friendships with scientists and the respect of representatives of national governments in many countries. At his home base in Davis, he was host and mentor of many M.S. and Ph.D. students. With these students he developed much fundamental knowledge about species relationships and evaluation of cultivated safflower in an extensive series of papers.

v

Paul Knowles recognized very early that there must be genetic bases for the wide range in types and amounts of fatty acids in the safflower seed. He guided students in important studies that discovered major-gene control of oleic, linoleic, and other fatty acids in safflower seed. From this work UC-1, a safflower cultivar with elevated oleic acid in the seed, was developed and grown commercially. UC-1 became the basic germplasm for many breeding programs. Other types were also developed, including intermediate oleic and linoleic acid types, very high linoleic acid, and high stearic acid types.

In 1977 he turned his attention to *Brassica* species as possible rainfed winter crops for California. This followed his two-year assignment as an oilseed crop advisor to the government of Pakistan. During this assignment he made extensive collections of *Brassica* species for Pakistan and USA gene banks. These were grown and evaluated in Pakistan and California. The most promising species were Indian mustard (*B. juncea*) and Ethiopian mustard (*B. carinata*).

In addition to the many studies on safflower and *Brassica*, Paul Knowles contributed much to the information base on flax, sunflower, soybean, and cuphea. Among his more than 160 publications are numerous chapters to books and invited lectures. He coauthored with F. N. Briggs the very successful textbook, *Introduction to Plant Breeding*.

Because of his wide experience and numerous successes in research and the training of scientists he has often been invited to serve as an advisor on oilseed research and development programs. Although he could not accept all of these invitations, he did serve in Egypt, India, Iran, Pakistan, Thailand and Turkey.

He served as Chairman of the Department of Agronomy and Range Science 1970-1975. He has received numerous citations, including Fellow in the American Society of Agronomy and Crop Science Society of America, 1972; Award of Honor, 1983, California Chapter of the American Society of Agronomy; Award of Appreciation from the Western Crop Development Council, 1982; Distinguished Oilseeds Research and Teaching Award, First International Safflower Conference, 1981; Award for Outstanding Service to the Seed Industry, 1983; Special Appreciation Award from Safflower Processors and Growers, 1974; and Distinguished Graduate in Agriculture Award, University of Saskatchewan, 1986.

Upon his retirement in 1982 from active service as Professor of Agronomy from the University of California, Davis, his colleagues, former students, and other friends wished to recognize his many contributions to the advancement of oil crops. This book is a fitting dedication to Paul Knowles. It epitomizes his approach to the integration of agronomy, botany, genetics, chemistry, plant pathology and economics, to the successful use and improvement of oil crops for the world's human population.

P. F. Knowles – Selected Bibliography

Knowles, P.F. 1958. Safflower. Adv. Agron. 10: 289-323.

Ashri, Amram, and Knowles, P.F. 1960. Cytogenetics of safflower (*Carthamus* L.) species and their hybrids. Agron. J. 52: 11-17.

Knowles, P.F. 1960. New crop establishment. Econ. Bot. 14: 263-275.

Schank, Stanley C., and Knowles, P.F. 1961. Colchicine induced polyploids of *Carthamus tinctorius* L. Crop Sci. 1:342-344.

Yermanos, D.M., and Knowles, P.F. 1962. Fatty acid composition of the oil in crossed seed of flax. Crop Sci. 2:109-111.

Knowles, P.F., and Mutwakil, A. 1963. Inheritance of low iodine value of safflower selections from India. Econ. Bot. 17: 139-145.

Knowles, P.F., and Hill, A.B. 1964. Inheritance of fatty acid content in the seed oil of a safflower introduction from Iran. Crop Sci. 4: 596-599.

Knowles, P.F., and Schank, S.C. 1964. Artificial hybrids of *Carthamus nitidus* Boiss. and *C. tinctorius* L. (Compositae). Crop Sci. 4: 596-599.

Schank, S.C., and Knowles, P.F. 1964. Cytogenetics of hybrids of *Carthamus* species (Compositae) with ten pairs of chromosomes. Am. J. Bot. 51: 1093-1102.

Knowles, P.F. 1965. Variability in oleic and linoleic acid contents of safflower oil. Econ. Bot. 19: 53-62.

Harvey, B.L., and Knowles, P.F. 1965. Natural and artificial alloploids with 22 pairs of chromosomes in the genus *Carthamus*. Can. J. Genet. Cytol. 7: 126-139.

Ebert, W.W., and Knowles, P.F. 1966. Inheritance of pericarp types, sterility, and dwarfness in several safflower crosses. Crop Sci. 6: 579-582.

Briggs, F.N., and Knowles, P.F. 1967. *Introduction to Plant Breeding*. Reinhold.

Knowles, P.F. 1967. Processing seeds for oil in towns and villages of Turkey, India and Egypt. Econ. Bot. 2: 156-162.

Knowles, P.F. 1968. Associations of high levels of oleic acid in the seed oil of safflower (*Carthamus tinctorius*) with other plant and seed characters. Econ. Bot. 22: 195-200.

Hill, A.B., and Knowles, P.F. 1968. Fatty acid composition of the oil of developing seeds of different varieties of safflower. Crop Sci. 8: 275-277.

Knowles, P.F. 1968. Registration of UC-1 safflower. Crop Sci. 8: 641.

Knowles, P.F. 1969. Modification of quantity and quality of safflower oil through plant breeding. J. Am. Oil Chem. Soc. 46: 130-132.

Knowles, P.F. 1969. Centers of plant diversity and conservation of crop germplasm: safflower. Econ. Bot. 23: 324-329.

Khidir, M.O., and Knowles, P.F. 1970. Cytogenetic studies of *Carthamus* species (Compositae) with 32 pairs of chromosomes. I. Intrasectional hybridization. Am. J. Bot. 57: 123-129.

Khidir, M.O., and Knowles, P.F. 1970. Cytogenetic studies of *Carthamus* species (Compositae) with 32 pairs of chromosomes. II. Intersectional hybridization. Can. J. Genet. Cytol. 12: 90-99.

Imrie, B.C., and Knowles, P.F. 1970. Inheritance studies in interspecific hybrids between *Carthamus flavescens* and *C. tinctorius*. Crop Sci. 10: 349-352.

Ladd, S.L., and Knowles, P.F. 1970. Inheritance of stearic acid in the seed oil of safflower (*Carthamus tinctorius* L.). Crop Sci. 10: 525-527.

Ladd, S.L., and **Knowles, P.F.** 1971. Interactions of alleles at two loci regulating fatty acid composition of the seed oil of safflower (*Carthamus tinctorius* L.). Crop Sci. 11: 681-684.

Knowles, P.F. 1972. The plant geneticist's contribution toward changing lipid and amino acid composition of safflower. J. Am. Oil Chem. S. 49: 27-29.

Urie, A.L., and **Knowles, P.F.** 1972. Safflower introductions resistant to Verticillium wilt. Crop Sci. 12: 545-546.

Ashri, A., Zimmer, D.E., Urie, A.L., and **Knowles, P.F.** 1975. Evaluation of the germplasm collection of safflower *Carthamus tinctorius* L. VI. Length of planting to flowering period and plant height. Theor. Appl. Genet. 46: 359-364.

Dille, John E., and **Knowles, P.F.** 1975. Histology and inheritance of the closed flower in *Cathamus tinctorius* (Compositae). Am. J. Bot. 62: 209-215.

Knowles, P.F. 1975. Recent research on safflower, sunflower and cotton. J. Am. Oil Chem. Soc. 52: 374-376.

Estilai, A., and **Knowles, P.F.** 1976. Cytogenetic studies of *Cathamus divaricatus* with eleven pairs of chromosomes and its relationship to other *Carthamus* species (Compositae). Am. J. Bot. 63: 771-782.

Knowles, P.F. 1976. Safflower, pp. 31-33. *In* N. W. Simmonds (ed.), *Evolution of Crop Plants*. Longman, London, New York.

Ashri, A., **Knowles, P.F.**, Urie, A.L., Zimmer, D.E., Cahaner, A., and Marani, A. 1977. Evaluation of the germplasm collection of safflower, *Carthamus tinctorius*. III. Oil content and iodine value and their associations with other characters. Econ. Bot. 31: 38-46.

Estilai, A., and **Knowles, P.F.** 1978. Relationship of *Carthamus leucocaulos* to other *Cathamus* species (Compositae). Can. J. Genet. Cytol. 20: 221-233.

Knowles, P.F. 1978. Morphology and Anatomy., pp. 55-87. *In* J. F. Carter (ed.). *Sunflower Science and Technology*. Am. Soc. Agron. Monograph. Madison, Wis.

Heaton, T.C., **Knowles, P.F.**, Mikkelsen, D.S., and Ruckman, J.E. 1978. Production of free fatty acids in safflower seeds by fungi. J. Am. Oil Chem. Soc. 55: 465-468.

Khan, S.A., and **Knowles, P.F.** 1978. A programme for improving the quality of oil and meal in mustard and rape species of Pakistan. Pak. Acad. Sci. 15: 29-35.

Knowles, P.F. 1980. Safflower, pp. 535-547. *In* W. R. Fehr and H. H. Hadley (eds.), *Hybridization of Crop Plants*. Am. Soc. Agron.-Crop Sci. Soc. America. Madison, Wis.

Knowles, P.F. 1983. Genetics and breeding of oilseed crops. Econ. Bot. 34: 423-433.

CONTENTS

Contents

CONTRIBUTORS

D. E. Alexander
Department of Agronomy, Turner Hall, 1102 South Goodwin Avenue, University of Illinois, Urbana, Illinois 61801, U. S. A.

L.-A. Åppelqvist
Department of Food Hygiene, Swedish University of Agricultural Sciences, P.O. Box 7009, S-75007 Uppsala, Sweden

A. Ashri
Genetics and Breeding, Faculty of Agriculture, P. O. B. 12, Rehovot 76100, Israel

D. Atsmon
Department of Plant Genetics, The Weizmann Institute of Science, Rehovot 76100, Israel

M. J. Balick
New York Botanical Garden, Bronx, New York 10458, U. S. A.

H. Belayneh
Highland Oil Crops Improvement Project, Institute of Agricultural Research, Holetta Research Station, P. O. Box 2003, Addis Ababa, Ethiopia

J. M. Bell
Department of Animal and Poultry Science, University of Saskatchewan, Saskatoon, Saskatchewan S7N 0W0, Canada

A. Benzioni
Boyko Institute for Agriculture and Applied Biology, The Institute for Applied Research, Ben-Gurion University of the Negev, P. O. Box 1025, Beer-Sheva 84110, Israel

G. Brousse
Conseil Oleicole International, EME, Juan-Bravo, 10-2'eme, E28008, Madrid 6, Spain

R. Carr
POS Pilot Plant Corporation, 118 Veterinary Road, Saskatoon, Saskatchewan S7N 2R4, Canada

T. A. Coffelt
United States Department of Agriculture, Agricultural Research Service, South Atlantic Area, Peanut Production, Diseases and Harvesting Research Unit, P. O. Box 7099, Suffolk, Virginia 23437, U. S. A.

R. K. Downey
Agriculture Canada Research Station, 107 Science Crescent, Saskatoon, Saskatchewan S7N 0X2, Canada

C. D. Dybing
United States Department of Agriculture, Agricultural Research Service, Northern State Area, Northern Grain Insects Research Laboratory, R. R. 3 Brookings, South Dakota 57006, U. S. A.

W. R. Fehr
Department of Agronomy, Iowa State University, Ames, Iowa 50011, U. S. A.

G. N. Fick
Research Director, Sigco Research, Inc., P. O. Box 289, Breckenridge, Minnesota 56520, U. S. A.

M. Forti
Boyko Institute for Agriculture and Applied Biology, The Institutes for Applied Research, Ben-Gurion University of the Negev, P. O. Box 1025, Beer-Sheva 84110, Israel

J. P. Gascon
Division Sélection, Institut de Recherches pour les Huiles et Oléagineux, Avenue du Val de Montferrand, BP 5035 - 34032, Montpellier cedex, France

J. J. Gottenbos
Unilever Research Laboratory, P. O. Box 114, 3130 AC Vlaardingen, The Netherlands

G. Hatje
Rögeneck 10, D 2000, Hamburg 67, Federal Republic of Germany

F. Hirsinger
Henkel KG a A, Postfach 1100, D-4000 Düsseldorf 1, Federal Republic of Germany

R. Jönsson
Svalöf AB, S-268 00, Svalöv, Sweden

P. F. Knowles
5703 Nakat Way, Birch Bay Village, Blaine, Washington 98231, U. S. A.

R. J. Kohel
United States Department of Agriculture, Agricultural Research Service, Southern Plains Area, Southern Crops Research Laboratory, P. O. Drawer DN, College Station, Texas 77841, U. S. A.

J. Krzymanski
Instytut Hodowli I Aklimatyzacji Roslin, Oddzial Poznansko-Gorzowski, 61-771 Poznan 2, ul. Sieroca 1 a, Poland

C. L. Lay
Genetic Resources, Inc., 2509 S. Neil, Champaign, Illinois 61820, U. S. A.

D. I. McGregor
Agriculture Canada Research Station, 107 Science Crescent, Saskatoon, Saskatchewan S7N 0X2, Canada

J. Meunier
Division Sélection, Institut de Recherches pour les Huiles et Oléagineux, Avenue du Val de Montferrand, BP 5035 - 34032, Montpellier cedex, France

J. M. Noiret
Division Sélection, Institut de Recherches pour les Huiles et Oléagineux, Avenue du Val de Montferrand, BP 5035 - 34032, Montpellier cedex, France

G. Norton
Department of Applied Biochemistry and Food Sciences, University of Nottingham, Sutton Bonington, Loughborough, LE 12 5RD, England

R. Ohlson
AB Karlshamns Oljefabriker, S-292 00 Karlshamn, Sweden

E. H. Pryde (deceased)
United States Department of Agriculture, Agricultural Research Service, Midwest Area, Northern Regional Research Center, 1815 North University Street, Peoria, Illinois 61604, U. S. A.

G. R. Quick
Agricultural Engineering Centre, Roy Watts Road, Glenfield, New South Wales 2167, Australia

K. W. Riley
c/o International Development Research Centre, P. O. Box 8500, 60 Queen Street, Ottawa, Ontario, K1G 3H9

G. Röbbelen
Institut für Pflanzenbau und Pflanzenzüchtung, der Universitat Göttingen, D-34 Göttingen, von Siebold-Strasse 8, Federal Republic of Germany

J. A. Rothfus
United States Department of Agriculture, Agricultural Research Service, Midwest Area, Northern Regional Research Center, 1815 North University Street, Peoria, Illinois 61604, U. S. A.

K. Satyabalan
Ananda Vilas, Opposite Parur Courts, North Parur 683 513, Kerala, India

P. K. Stumpf
Department of Biochemistry and Biophysics, University of California, Davis, Davis, California 95616, U. S. A.

W. Thies
Institut für Pflanzenbau und Pflanzenzüchtung, der Universitat Göttingen, D-34 Göttingen, von Siebold-Strasse 8, Federal Republic of Germany

R. O. Vles
Unilever Research Laboratory, P. O. Box 114, 3130 AC Vlaardingen, The Netherlands

P. Vohra
Department of Avian Sciences, College of Agriculture and Environmental Sciences, University of California, Davis, Davis, California 95616, U. S. A.

PREFACE

Collectively, oil crops and their products are the second most valuable commodity moving in world trade. Production and trade in these commodities has expanded rapidly in response to a growing world population and rising living standard. In addition, technological advances have led to higher production levels and improvements in product quality and versatility. New and different markets have also provided opportunities for new oilseed crops.

Despite these recent advances, the need and opportunity to increase oil crop seed, oil and protein yields is as great today as it has ever been. However, no single publication has been available that deals with oil crop improvement and utilization. The impending retirement of one of the world's leading oilseed researchers helped to focus attention on the need for such a publication. The idea for this book, to be dedicated to Dr. Paul F. Knowles, was initiated in 1983 by Dr. Calvin O. Qualset, Associate Dean of Agriculture and Environmental Sciences at the University of California, Davis. The present editors were contacted and agreed to develop a suitable outline and format, and, with much help, assembled a willing group of authors.

The completion of the project has not been without trial and sorrow. Two of our original authors, Dr. E. H. Pryde and Dr. D. M. Yermanos, passed away before they could complete their tasks. Both have made substantial contributions to the improvement and utilization of oil crops, and their expertise will be sorely missed. The unexpected sale of the Scientific Book Division of Macmillan, the original designated publisher, to McGraw-Hill Publishing Company, also added to the complexity of our task. However, despite these and the usual difficulties of distance and language associated with international authorship, the final product has more than met our expectations.

The original objective of providing a major reference work for those interested or involved with any aspect of the vegetable oil industry, as well as providing a text for undergraduate and graduate classes in plant breeding, crop quality and nutrition, has been achieved. The ten introductory chapters provide general but essential information on the importance of oil crops, their chemical nature and use. The remaining chapters deal with the individual oil crops and their improvement through plant breeding. The subject matter headings for each of the crop chapters are, as far as possible, identical to facilitate comparison between crops. For those who wish to learn more of the agronomy of oilseed production, particularly in the tropics, we would direct the reader to E. A. Weiss's Oilseed Crops (Longman, 1983) as a suitable companion to the present volume.

To produce a book of reasonable length and readability, the number of references that could be included by the authors were restricted. In most chapters, review articles and key references have been cited and should serve as a starting point for readers interested in a more exhaustive review of the subject.

The successful completion of this book would not have been possible without the contribution and cooperation of our many authors. We would also like to acknowledge, with thanks, the contribution of present and past employees of the Agriculture Canada Research Station, Saskatoon, who gave so much of their own time to the preparation of this book. Miss Gladys Hall, former personal secretary to Dr. Downey, read and corrected all the original manuscripts. Mrs. Janet Korven-Stott entered all the chapters into the computer, while Dr. D. Ian McGregor transferred drawings, sketches, formulae and diagrams into his computer to produce the desired readable and uniform product. Finally, we wish to thank Mr. Simon Barber who, despite changing directives for print size and page layout, has produced from his computer an excellent final product. Thanks are also due to many of our colleagues who took the time to review manuscripts and provide useful suggestions and criticism.

R. Keith Downey
Gerhard Röbbelen
Amram Ashri

Chapter 1

World Importance of Oil Crops and their Products

G. Hatje

INTRODUCTION

This book deals in a comprehensive way with the "Oil Crops of the World." It gives a broad view of the many cultivated oil bearing crops, their breeding, nature and utilization. Some oil crops are used directly as a food, such as groundnuts but most are processed by pressing and/or extracting to obtain fat or oil and cake or meal. These joint products are consumed for nutritional purposes and used in technical products. Oils and fats are a vital component of the human diet because they are an important source of energy and act as a carrier of fat soluble vitamins. The required fat intake for good health will vary with the individual depending on the climate and the work performed. Demand for oilcake/meal arises from its high nutritional value as an animal feed as a result of its high content of good quality protein.

The oil crops have been cultivated since antiquity. Sesame seed was already known in ancient times and rapeseed was mentioned in the Indian Sanskrit writings of 2000 BC. In addition, soybeans have been an important staple food in China for thousands of years. However, the dramatic increase in vegetable oil production did not take place until the second half of the present century. Oil crops are now grown all over the world and in many economies they are a vital part of the agricultural sector. There are three distinct groups of oil crops; a) those that are annual or biennial such as soybeans, sunflowers, groundnuts and rapeseed, b) the perennial tree-crops such as coconuts, babassu nuts and oil palms, and c) crops such as cotton and corn germ where the embryo is a by-product.

The palm fruit is an exceptional case in that, unlike other oilseeds, it cannot be transported far for economic and quality reasons. It must be processed locally immediately after harvest from where it is exported all over the world, competing with other vegetable fats and oils. Palm oil has to be regarded as part of the total oilseed sector.

The different oil crops vary in the proportion of oil to meal produced. Soybeans have an oil content of only 18% whereas copra yields about 65% oil. Other oilseeds like rape and sunflower contain about 40% oil. As a result some oil crops are predominantly sources of protein, while others produce primarily oil and fats. More details will be given in the chapters on the individual crop plants.

The present chapter deals with the importance of oil crops in world trade, the nature of the market and the forces which influence it. Oil crops must be regarded as vital part of the world's food supply, especially since animal feeding is an integral part of human nutrition.

There are a number of sources of statistics on oilseeds and their products including the Food and Agricultural Organization of the United Nations (FAO), the United States Department of Agriculture (USDA), and Oil World published by ISTA Mielke GmbH of Hamburg, to name but a few of the most important. Because of the difficulty of consistently recording all data for several decades on a worldwide basis, the figures from the various sources often differ. For this reason Unilever has developed its own system to record statistics from different sources with the data source being consistent and comparable over years. In this chapter statistics presented will be mainly from the Unilever data base but production tables for individual oil crop chapters have been drawn from the 1980 and 1985 FAO Production Year Books.

WORLD OILSEED PRODUCTION

Oilseed Production and Distribution

There are many species of plants in the world whose oil can be used for human consumption. Lennerts (1984) names forty different oilseeds, but only a small number of such crops are significant to the world's food supply and trade (Table 1.1). There are also crops such as palm and olive where the oil is extracted from the fleshy portion of the fruit as well as castor, linseed and tung nuts whose oil is needed for technical purposes.

Table 1.1   Average Annual Production of World Oilseeds for 1935/39, Three
Five Year Intervals, the 1984/85 -1985/86 Period, the Per Cent
Change from 1935/39 to 1984/86 and the Annual Growth Rate from
1957/61 to 1984/86

Oilseed Crop	1935/39	1957/58 -1961/62	1972/73 -1976/77	1984/85 -1985/86	% change 1935: 1986	% Ann. growth 1957/61- 1984/86
	-----------millions of tonnes-----------					
Soybean	12.62	25.67	58.26	94.98	+ 653	+ 5.2
Cottonseed	13.87	18.03	23.59	32.34	+ 133	+ 2.3
Groundnut (shelled)	6.08	9.04	11.24	13.70	+ 125	+ 1.6
Sunflower seed	2.53	5.86	10.52	18.74	+ 640	+ 4.6
Rapeseed	3.82	3.72	7.18	17.83	+ 367	+ 6.2
Sesame	1.62	1.39	1.78	2.07	+ 24	+ 1.5
Copra/palm kernel	3.83	4.05	5.44	6.82	+ 78	+ 2.0
Linseed	3.42	3.26	2.46	2.48	- 27	- 1.0
Castor + tung nut	1.28	1.26	1.56	1.21	- 6	-
World Production	49.07	72.28	122.03	190.17	+ 288	+ 3.8

Source: *Oil World*, Hamburg since 1958, earlier years Unilever (Raw Materials) Ltd.,
London.

Soybeans account for more than 50% of the world's oilseed output while sunflower seed and rapeseed account for a further 19%. The most important tropical
oilseeds are the coconut (copra), palm kernels and groundnuts. These sources
presently contribute only 11% of the world's production against 20% before
World War II.

The major oilseed producing areas are in the temperate zones (Table 1.2).
America and Europe account for 60% of the world production of oilseeds,
whereas in the tropical areas such as Africa, Malaysia and Indonesia less than
6% is grown. These figures relate to the seeds included in Table 1.1.

Other oilseeds are of minor importance in world trade but they do play a significant part in local markets or as raw material for special products. For example safflower seed produces an oil with a high content of polyunsaturated fatty
acids while sheanuts and illipé nuts are the raw materials for producing cocoa-
butter equivalents. In Italy, grape and tomato seed are processed for their oil
while in the USA corn germ, as a by-product of the wet milling industry to produce starch, glucose and high fructose corn syrup, is an oil source of growing
importance.

Table 1.2   Worldwide Distribution of Oilseed Production 1984-1986

Country or region	%world production
USA/Canada	37
Argentine/Brazil	15
China	17
Indian sub continent	6
USSR	6
Europe (East & West)	7
Africa, Malaysia, Indonesia,Philippines	6
Others	6
Total	100

Historical Trends and Growth

Following the Second World War an immense increase in world oilseed production took place (Table 1.1). This increase in production has only been possible because new areas have been used for cultivation and because, thanks to intensive breeding efforts, yields have increased significantly for many crops. The
main growth in production has occurred in countries with high standards of agricultural production but the advanced developing countries such as Malaysia and
Brazil have also contributed to oilseed growth.

Increased soybean production has occurred due to the rising consumption of
livestock products and the concurrent rapid growth in meal demand. Intensive
hog, broiler and egg production requires large quantities of well balanced protein
of which soybean with an 80% meal content is an ideal source. In addition, meal
from rapeseed and to a lesser extent sunflowers have contributed to the growing
need for protein. In the European Community a special support system for rape
and sunflower seed guarantees the farmer a minimum price and the sale of his
total crop. This scheme was the basis for the recent enormous expansion of these
crops.

The production of cottonseed is dependent upon the demand for cotton. Despite the development of synthetic fibers, cotton has continued its own expansion
and cottonseed production has now doubled since the pre-war period. Cottonseed is processed mainly in the regions where it is grown.

In developing countries, where agricultural productivity is rather low, only
limited growth rates of groundnuts and copra have been recorded. For this reason developed countries have acquired a growing dominance in world oilseed
production.

The industrial demand for oilseeds has remained fairly constant over time.
Castor has retained its importance as a raw material for a great many products in
the pharmaceutical and lubricating sector. The decline in the production of

linseed is due to the decrease in the demand for drying oils in the manufacture of paints, varnishes and floorings.

The importance of oilseeds worldwide will continue to increase as population expands and the standard of living improves in developing countries.

OILSEED PROCESSING PRODUCTS

Processing of Oilseeds

Oilseeds are crushed, rolled or flaked before they are pressed in expeller presses or treated with a solvent to remove the oil. The extraction process is used for oilseeds with a comparatively low oil content, such as soybeans. Other high oil content seeds such as sunflower and rape, undergo a pre-expelling process followed by extraction to obtain the oil from the expeller cake (see Chapter 11). The processing method depends on the degree of industrialization in the region concerned. In the tropical oil crop areas expelling is often the only process used while extraction is the chief process in industrialized countries. The quality of the meal can also be improved by de-hulling the seed during processing. This makes for a higher protein content because the crude fiber portion has been removed. The residual oil content in oilmeal is usually about 1 to 2%. Oilcake is the residual from the purely mechanical processing of oilseeds, that is, expelling. More oil is left in the cake than is retained in meal. The oil content of the cake can be 4 to 6% or even more depending upon the seed crop and processing equipment used.

The fact that oilseeds yield two products: oils/fats and oilcake/meal plays an important part in considering the economics of oilseed processing. The proceeds from the sale of oil and meal have to cover the price of the seed, which the oil miller pays, plus the processing costs, including an appropriate yield on capital expenditure. This gross margin between revenues and costs is determined by the crushing capacities in relation to seed supplies and product demand. Oil and meal prices sometimes fluctuate rapidly whereby their prices can actually move in opposite directions. Therefore the ratio of the sales value of meal to that of the oil or fat component changes frequently depending upon the situation in the individual markets. An example from the EEC market will illustrate this situation. In May, 1985 the price of soybean oil and meal in West Germany was 652 and 165 US dollars per tonne. Since one tonne of soybeans yields about 180 kg of oil and 800 kg of meal, the sales value and sales ratios would be as follows:

Product	Value		Ratio
180 kg oil	= US$117	=	47%
800 kg meal	= US$132	=	53%
Total	= US$249	=	100%

The corresponding seed price at that date was US $231 per tonne so the processing margin was positive and amounted to US $18 per tonne from which costs and profit must be recovered. However, by September 1986, the oil/meal sales value ratio had changed to 24:76.

To minimize their risk oilseed processors are obliged to sell both oil and meal at the same time as they buy the seed. This is of course extremely difficult in day-to-day business because they are concerned with three different markets on a world-wide scale namely, the markets for oilseed, for oil/fat and for oilcake/meal. It should also be noted that rapidly changing currency situations in importing and exporting countries are also of great importance in day-to-day trading activities.

OIL AND FAT PRODUCTION

Structure of the World Oil/Fat Market

Why do we talk of oils and fats? The difference is merely a question of consistency. If a substance is normally liquid we speak of it as an oil. If it is normally solid it is known as a fat. Thus the prevailing temperature in a region can influence how an oil or fat is perceived. For example, coconut oil is liquid in its tropical region of origin but in the cooler regions of Western Europe and North America, it becomes a solid fat, even though it is still coconut oil.

The production of oilseeds is shown in Table 1.1 but not all seeds are processed to obtain fat/oil. Part of what is produced is used as sowing seed, fed unprocessed to animals or used directly for human consumption. There are also certain losses in storage and handling. That proportion of oilseed production which is not crushed varies from crop to crop and region to region. In broad terms about 15 to 20% of the seed produced remains unprocessed.

The world oil and fat market can be divided into three main groups; a) consumer products such as butter, lard and olive oil, b) edible-type raw materials such as seed and marine oils, and c) industrial oils and fats including tallow, linseed, tung and castor (Table 1.3).

One special feature of the world oils and fat market is the great number of raw material sources of both animal and vegetable origin. Furthermore there is a high degree of interchangeability among the various vegetable oils and between animal and vegetable sources.

Two thirds of the total fat and oil production is supplied by oilseeds, with soybean supplying about 20% of the total. In the production of vegetable oils three annual crops, soybean, sunflower and rape and one tree crop, palm, predominate accounting for some 73% of all vegetable oils produced.

Table 1.3 Average World Production of Oils and Fats for Selected Five Year Intervals and for 1985/86, in Millions of Tonnes (Visible Oils/Fats Only)

Class and source	1909/ 1913	1935/ 1939	1958/ 1962	1973/ 1977	1985/ 1986
Consumer products					
Butter	2.50	3.80	4.24	5.38	6.45
Lard	2.50	2.44	3.27	4.20	5.46
Olive oil	0.59	0.88	1.32	1.59	1.57
Total consumer prod.	5.59	7.12	8.83	11.17	13.48
Edible-type raw materials					
Seed oils					
Soybean	0.30	0.93	3.28	8.50	14.16
Cotton	0.98	1.23	2.29	2.87	3.57
Groundnut	0.65	1.42	2.45	2.67	3.50
Sunflower	0.12	0.57	1.90	3.71	6.88
Rapeseed	1.08	1.21	1.18	2.50	6.36
Sesame + corn	0.55	0.75	0.57	0.92	1.67
Coconut	0.75	1.94	1.85	2.55	3.25
Palm kernel	0.15	0.36	0.43	0.48	1.04
Palm	0.28	0.99	1.30	2.83	7.72
Seed oils sub total	4.86	9.40	15.25	27.03	48.15
Marine oils					
Fish	0.17	0.44	0.52	1.00	1.53
Whale	0.07	0.49	0.38	0.03	-
Marine oils sub total	0.24	0.93	0.90	1.03	1.53
Total edible group	5.10	10.33	16.15	28.06	49.68
Industrial oils/fats					
Tallow	1.30	1.39	3.43	5.52	6.53
Linseed	0.86	1.04	0.90	0.67	0.68
Castor	0.13	0.18	0.22	0.34	0.39
Tung	0.10	0.14	0.11	0.11	0.10
Sperm	0.01	0.03	0.12	0.09	-
Total industrial oils	2.40	2.78	4.78	6.73	7.70
Total world production	13.09	20.23	29.76	45.96	70.86
World population (10^9)	1.7	2.1	2.9	3.9	4.9
Per capita cons. in kg	7.7	9.6	10.3	11.8	14.8

Source: *Oil World*, Hamburg since 1958, earlier years Unilever (Raw Materials) Ltd., London.

Historic Trends and Growth

Among seed oils, soybean oil output has had an extraordinary growth (Table 1.3). As meal demand generated an expansion of the crop, soybean oil supply automatically increased. A tremendous increase has also taken place in sunflower and rapeseed oil output.

The rapid and continuing rise in palm oil production is also worthy of note. In Malaysia, which is now the largest palm oil producer, the expansion of palm tree cultivation has been an important part of the national economic plan. Because, by the mid 1960s, there were no prospects for natural rubber, the agricultural sector needed to diversify and the government chose palm trees. The steadily increasing Malaysian sales of palm oil on the world market competes directly with the seed oils. Indonesia is now also rapidly increasing its palm oil production.

Since the beginning of this century the percentage of total fat consumption accounted for by vegetable oils rather than animal fats has increased from about 24 to 70%, while the actual quantity consumed has increased some eightfold. It is first and foremost the oils/fats obtained from oilseeds which have met the demand for vegetable oils among the steadily increasing world population. There are, however, considerable differences in fat consumption between individual regions and countries, which result mainly from the differences in purchasing power.

The world production of fats/oils has increased to a greater extent than the world population, making it possible to improve the supply of fat for human consumption. In this century the per capita consumption of fats/oils has almost doubled. But the per capita consumption of edible oils in many developing countries is still well below that recommended for adequate nutrition by the World Health Organization.

PRODUCTION OF OILCAKE AND MEAL

Structure of the World Oilcake/Meal Market

The oilcakes and meals obtained from processing various oilseeds contain high levels of valuable protein. Soybean meal contains 45 to 50% protein while other oilseed meals contain 35 to 40%. Such oilseed meals are therefore referred to as high protein products in contrast to cereals which only contain 10 to 15% protein and are thus regarded primarily as energy sources in animal feeds.

Soybean meal dominates the world meal market (Table 1.4). It is an important component in hog and poultry feeding whereas rape and sunflower meal in Europe tend to be fed to ruminants. However, as low glucosinolate rapeseed meal becomes available in Europe a much larger percentage will enter the hog and poultry feed markets as has been the case in North America. Fish meal, with

Table 1.4   Average World Production of Oilcake and Meal for Selected Five Year Intervals and for 1985/86 in Millions of Tonnes[1]

Crop	1909/ 1913	1935/ 1939	1958/ 1962	1973/ 1977	1985/ 1986
Soybean	1.32	4.19	14.47	37.13	61.95
Cotton	3.13	4.02	7.31	9.44	13.23
Rape	1.77	1.98	1.94	3.94	10.30
Sunflower	0.13	0.64	2.12	3.98	8.06
Groundnut	0.88	2.04	3.31	3.70	4.60
Copra/palm kernel	0.60	1.51	1.54	2.05	3.15
Linseed	1.22	1.48	1.72	1.28	1.28
Sesame	0.61	0.79	0.50	0.50	0.74
Total oilcake/meal	9.66	16.65	32.91	62.12	103.31
Fish meal	0.69	1.79	2.12	4.35	5.93
Total world prod.	10.35	18.44	35.03	66.47	109.24
Total protein equiv.	4.25	7.82	15.28	29.23	47.36

[1] No distinction has been made in the production statistics between oilcake and meal.
Source: *Oil World,* Hamburg since 1958, earlier years Unilever (Raw Materials) Ltd., London.

a protein content of about 65%, is an important competitor to oilcakes and meals from plant sources. However, as fish stocks have declined in recent years, fish meal has become less of a factor in the market place.

Historical Trends and Growth

At the turn of the century farmers in well developed agricultural regions started to feed their animals on compound feeds in addition to farm-produced feedstuffs such as grasses, cereals and potatoes. Compound feeds are mixtures of various components including cereals, molasses, minerals and vitamins with a high proportion of well balanced protein products such as oilcake or meal. Compounded feeds are vital for maximizing livestock gains. Cost-effective livestock production is impossible on the basis of cereals alone. Only in combination with protein feed do the cereal grains yield an optimum feed ration. This is why oilcake/meal is an indispensable supplement to cereals. Increasing consumption of meat, eggs, poultry and milk due to rising living standards has brought about an increase in the demand for animal feeds. According to Oil World statistics (Mielke, 1983), world livestock production almost doubled between 1958 and 1982, increasing from 113 million tonnes to 218 million tonnes.

No statistics on world production of oilcake and meal are available before the Second World War. However it is possible to calculate cake/meal production using as a guide the oil production figures for 1909/13 and 1935/39 given in Table 1.3. In this way the trend of developments can be traced. It was in the second half of this century that there was an explosive increase in the production of oil-cake/meal.

It should be mentioned that primarily in the USA de-oiled soybeans are being used for human consumption in products such as soybean flour, protein concentrates and as a protein isolate which respectively contain approximately 50, 65 and 90% protein. These products are used in a great many texturized protein foods, as ingredients or additives with meat products, in beverages with an enriched protein content and in many other food products. The use of vegetable protein for human consumption is still in its infancy. At present mainly soybean products are used, but proteins from other oilseeds such as rapeseed and sunflower seed are also suitable raw products.

In relation to the total quantity of soybeans produced, the amount used for direct human consumption is very small, about 400,000 to 450,000 tonnes per year, excluding China where large quantities of soybeans are consumed without oil extraction. In some European countries the use of vegetable protein as a substitute or additive for meat or milk is even prohibited by law. The demand for high-protein meal will therefore continue to be confined to livestock production. In the present century the soybean has been the decisive factor in the development of the world animal feed market. The rise in demand, based on a substantial increase in the consumption of livestock products has met with a favorable situation on the supply side which has made it possible to substantially increase the production of soybeans. However, all other oilseed crops have also benefited.

LECITHINS

One by-product which has gained in importance with the enormous increase in soybean production is lecithin. This component of crude oils is obtained when the oilseed is processed. Oils from different crops have different lecithin contents, soybean oil may contain 2 to 3%, cottonseed and sunflower oil 1 to 2% and rapeseed oil a smaller amount. When crude oils are refined, lecithin is usually removed. This is done by adding water to the crude oil followed by centrifuging and dehydration. Phosphatides are the valuable component of lecithin. Only part of the lecithin contained in crude oil is subjected to further processing. No lecithin production statistics are available but it is estimated that of the some 100,000 tonnes produced annually the USA accounts for about 40% while the remaining production is equally divided between Europe and the rest of the world.

Lecithin is, above all, an emulsifier. The crude lecithins obtained from crude oil must be purified and subjected to further processing to make them suitable for various uses. Lecithin uses include pharmaceuticals, foodstuffs (e.g. in the manufacture of margarine, bakery goods and chocolate products), cosmetics, paints and plastics and also in compounds for animal feed.

WORLD TRADE OF OILSEEDS AND THEIR PRODUCTS

Export of Oilseeds

Part of the world's oilseed production is exported from the countries of origin either as seed or as processed products. This is because some industrialized countries in the temperate zones are not self-sufficient and have to import oil-seeds, oils/fats or oilcake/meal. The main exporting regions are North America (USA, Canada), South America (Brazil, Argentina), Malaysia and the Philippines. Europe, Japan and the USSR are the chief importers, but in recent years developing countries have been importing increasing quantities (Table 1.5).

Table 1.5   World Imports of Edible Oils and Oilseeds (on an Oil Equivalent Basis) by Region in 1962/1963 and 1985/1986

Region	Year	
	1962/1963	1985/1986
	--------millions of tonnes--------	
Western Europe	3.50	5.68
Other Developed Countries[1]	1.11	3.51
USSR/East Europe/China	0.34	1.74
Developing Countries	1.11	8.94
Total Imports	6.06	19.87

[1] USA, Canada, South Aftrica, Japan, Australia, New Zealand
Source: *Oil World* , Hamburg since 1958, earlier years Unilever (Raw Materials) Ltd., London.

Parallel to the expansion of oilseed production there has been an increase in crushing capacity both in the developing and industrialized countries. Some countries have even more capacity than is needed to process the local crop. This is why, in most years, soybean exports from Brazil and Argentina have been small and why such seed exports have become a smaller proportion of their total crop production. The world trade in oilseeds has undergone a complete change of structure since the Second World War. While copra, palm kernels, groundnuts and cottonseed used to be exported in their natural state, since the end of the 1960s the main crops entering world trade have been soybean, sunflower and rapeseed (Table 1.6).

The 32 million tonnes of oilseed exports in 1985/86 corresponds to about 17% of the total world production. Soybeans accounted for 79% of the exports (Table 1.6). More than half of these exports went to Europe and almost 20%, mostly soybeans and rapeseed, to Japan. The great proportion of soybeans exported clearly shows that the importing countries are mainly interested in the meal they contain.

Table 1.6   World Exports of Oilseed Crops in Millions of Tonnes for Selected Years

Oilseed Crop	Export by year and percent of total					
	1964	%	1975/76	%	1985/86	%
Soybean	6.28	54.3	19.53	79.4	25.07	78.7
Sunflower seed	0.11	1.0	0.40	1.6	1.80	5.7
Rapeseed	0.34	2.9	1.26	5.1	3.15	9.9
Copra, palm kernel	2.06	17.8	1.60	6.4	0.52	1.6
Groundnut	1.41	12.2	0.99	4.0	0.73	2.3
Others	1.36	11.8	0.88	3.5	0.58	1.8
Total World Exports	11.56	100	24.58	100	31.85	100

Source: *Oil World* , Hamburg since 1958, earlier years Unilever (Raw Materials) Ltd., London

Tropical oilseeds such as copra and palm kernels are now largely processed in the region of origin and the resulting products consumed locally or exported.

Exports of Fats/Oils

Although oilseed crops have expanded in high income countries and in advanced developing countries, these regions have a nearly stable per capita oil consumption and a dropping birth rate. Therefore, all the fats and oils produced in these regions cannot be locally consumed and are exported to meet the worldwide demand. In developing countries, consumption of vegetable oils has risen considerably. For example, in 1982/83 developing countries were importing more fats/oil than Western Europe (Table 1.5). Next to petroleum purchases, edible vegetable oil imports now constitute the largest drain on the hard currency reserves of India and Pakistan. (Gupta, 1985, Anon. 1987). It is also interesting to note that some years ago Russia was an exporter of oil and now has become a large importer.

The amount of vegetable oil moving in world trade has increased over the past few decades (Table 1.7). The considerable rise in rapeseed oil exports is partly due to the growth in Canadian supplies as well as developments in that crop in the European Community. The amount of palm oil moving in world trade has also increased dramatically. In 1985/86 palm oil accounted for 45% of the vegetable oil market with Malaysia being the chief exporting country. The increase in exports of sunflower oil is due to larger quantities originating in Argentina and the USA.

The rise in exports of coconut and palm kernel oils reflects the structural changes in the Asian production regions. New processing capacities have been installed so that copra and palm kernel that used to be exported in the 1950s is now shipped out as crude oil.

Table 1.7   World Exports of Crude and Processed Vegetable Oils and Fats for Selected Years, Per Cent Change, and Annual Growth Rate[1]

Crop Source	Year 1964	Year 1975/76	Year 1985/86	% change 1964-85	% ann. growth 1964-85
	------millions of tonnes------				
Soybean	0.59	0.97	1.52	+158	+4.8%
Sunflower	0.17	0.45	1.37	+706	+10.4%
Rapeseed	0.02	0.27	0.50	+2400	+16.6%
Coconut/palmkernel	0.48	1.27	2.07	+331	+7.2%
Cotton/groundnut	0.68	0.75	0.50	- 26	- 1.5%
Others	0.26	0.24	0.46	+77	+2.7%
Palm	0.57	1.92	5.34	+836	+11.2%
World exports total	2.77	5.87	11.76	+325	+7.1%
World production of vegetable oils/fats	16.71	29.20	48.15	+188	+5.1%
Percent exported	17%	20%	24%	-	-

[1] Olive oil excluded
Source: *Oil World* , Hamburg since 1958, earlier years Unilever (Raw Materials) Ltd., London

In order to obtain a complete picture of the amount of vegetable oil moving in world trade, seeds which are exported in the unprocessed state must be included, based on the oil they will yield at their destination (Table 1.8). These data clearly show that the rising demand for fats and oils on the world market has been met by a dramatic increase in vegetable oil production.

Exports of Oilcake/Meal

Soybeans play a dominant role in the world exports of meal (Table 1.9). Seventy-four percent of the total exports consist of soybean meal, mainly from the USA and South America. The importing regions are countries with high livestock populations with Europe and Japan being the major importers. Approximately one-third of all oilcake/meal produced is exported.

Prices of Oilseeds and Their Products

Exports of oilseeds, oils/fats and oilcake/meal are important trade commodities for the producing countries. Moreover, they are often decisive sources of foreign exchange earnings. This is true of the industrialized countries as well as those developing. On the other hand, the importing countries are dependent on foreign supplies to maintain or improve their standard of living. Considering this

Table 1.8   World Exports of Oils and Oilseeds, on an Oil Equivalent Basis, by Product Group, for Selected Years

Product	Year		
group	1964	1975/76	1985/86
	------------millions of tonnes-----------		
Consumer products			
(butter, lard, olive oil)	1.23	1.26	1.23
Edible-type raw materials			
Seed oils/fats	6.04	11.66	19.02
Marine oils	0.77	0.64	0.72
Industrial oils/fats			
(tallow, linseed, tung			
and castor)	2.04	2.18	2.64
World Total	10.08	15.74	23.61
Edible vegetable oils as % of total	60%	74%	81%

Source: *Oil World* , Hamburg since 1958, earlier years Unilever (Raw Materials) Ltd., London

Table 1.9   World Exports of Oilcake and Meal by Crop, in Millions of Tonnes, for Selected Years[1]

Crop	Exports by year and percent of total					
source	1964	%	1975/76	%	1985/86	%
Soybean	2.53	35.8	10.38	67.1	23.08	73.8
Sunflower seed	0.29	4.1	0.37	2.4	1.93	6.2
Rapeseed	0.15	2.1	0.35	2.3	1.81	5.8
Copra/palm kernel	0.75	10.6	1.24	8.0	2.37	7.6
Groundnut	1.61	22.8	1.55	10.0	0.48	1.5
Others[2]	1.74	24.6	1.58	10.2	1.61	5.1
Total world exports	7.07	100	15.47	100	31.28	100
Fish meal exports	2.42		2.16		2.28	

[1] Includes exports of meal from imported seed
[2] Fish meal excluded
Source: *Oil World* , Hamburg since 1958, earlier years Unilever (Raw Materials) Ltd., London

mutual dependence between exporting and importing regions, world trade in oil-seeds and their products ought really to be as free and unrestricted as possible. However, many factors influence this market.

The prices of oilseeds and their products on the world market are determined on the principle of free trading. In the short term, prices are governed by supply and demand. In the longer term on the supply-side oil crop prices are of course dependent on production costs and the yield obtained per acre. On the demand-side, bids by oilseed processors are governed by the commercial values of the oil and the meal produced, since processors must try and find a margin to cover costs and profit. Thus the combined supply and demand of the oils/fats and the oilcake/meal markets constitutes the demand on the international oilseed market.

Figure 1.1 illustrates in a schematic manner the structure of the vegetable oil crop economy (Augusto and Pollak, 1981). The prices of oilseeds and their products depends on the supply of oilseeds but, conversely, the world oilseed supply reflects the entire price structure on the relevant market. Basically the market is supply orientated, production and stocks fluctuate from year to year, whereas the demand for oils/fats in total tends to steadily rise. The price differentials result-ing from technology, quality and consumer preference as they relate to supply, also influences market development. The interchangeability of the different veg-etable and animal oils and fats results in direct competition among the various products. For example, oils from a number of different crops can be used in the production of margarines, shortenings or salad oils. Certainly the availability of raw-materials, the quality required and the desired properties of the finished product have to be considered in addition to price. Frequently, linear program-ming can be used to find optimal compositions. The degree of interchangeability among oils and fats has increased in recent years through the application of mod-ern technological processes such as hardening, fractionation and interesterifica-tion (Kersten, 1982). Price differentials change as the relative supplies of indi-vidual oils change and provides the mechanism for consumers to shift to the cheaper oil or fat. Therefore all oil/fat prices tend to move together.

The same applies to the use of different kinds of oilcake/meal in the formula-tion of compound feeds. The price of oilcake/meal is governed mainly by its pro-tein content. In the animal feeding sector, however, the intensity of feeding, the price of cereal grains, and the competing products like corn gluten, citrus pellets etc. also have an effect on the price of oilcake and meal. The elevated level of essential amino acids such as lysine, methionine, etc. in oilseed meal are valua-ble components for the livestock producer. They form an important part of the high quality image of this feeding stuff. Finally the livestock product values have a decisive influence on the price the farmer can pay for the feed.

Commodity exchanges and their futures markets are an essential part of the cost discovery mechanism. With futures trading, oilseeds and their products can be bought or sold many months in advance (Turnowsky, 1983). The main center for futures trading in oilseeds and their products is the Chicago Board of Trade where trading in soybeans, soybean meal and oil takes place every working day (Anon. 1978). On the futures market contracts take place on paper to buy or sell a given lot of seed or its products. However, on the contracted delivery date, the last seller has to fulfil the contract terms and deliver the goods. The exchange is an indicator for present and future prices. Prices on the Chicago Board of Trade respond immediately to events and information that encompass politics, economics and weather conditions which may significantly affect future

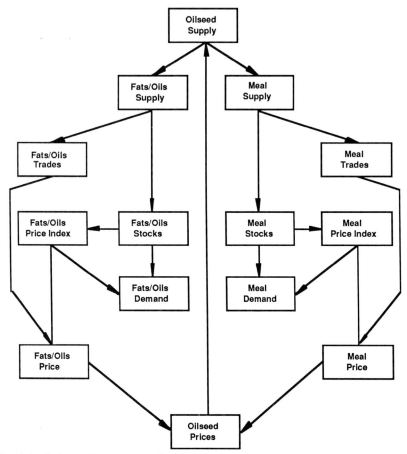

Fig. 1.1 Schematic structure of the vegetable oil crops economy.

supplies, demand and/or price. The prices for soybeans and its products in Chicago in turn influences the pricing of other oils and oilseeds and their meals. As is true of any exchange, there is a speculative element which may influence prices, but futures trading minimizes the risk to both seller and buyer and gives liquidity to the market. Of course, the final trade is done on the physical market by the final seller and buyer for each product.

INDIVIDUAL CONTRACTS IN INTERNATIONAL TRADE

As has been noted, the volume of international trade in oilseeds/oils/fats and oilcake/meal is enormous. Buyers and sellers are located all over the world and often many thousands of miles apart. They frequently speak different languages and operate under different trading regulations. For this reason, organizations which are independent of the interests of a particular country, region or dealer have been formed to establish standard contract terms acceptable to both seller and buyer on a worldwide basis. In 1863 the "Incorporated Oilseeds Association" was founded. In 1910 the "London Oil and Tallow Trades Association" was established, followed in 1913 by the "London Copra Association" and in 1935 the "Seed, Oil, Cake and General Produce Association." In 1971 these London based associations amalgamated to form the "Federation of Oil, Seed and Fats Association Ltd," commonly called FOSFA.

FOSFA has about 1000 members representing 500 different companies in forty-one countries on five continents. FOSFA is first and foremost an organization which publishes standard contracts for the trade. Most contracts are cif or c&f in nature i.e. costs, insurance, freight or costs & freight are paid by the seller for the transport from the port of shipping to the port of destination, where the buyer receives the goods. There are more than fifty different contracts referring to specific products and origins. There are also general contracts which can be applied to various products.

To ensure that these contracts are carried out FOSFA has laid down "rules by which arbitrations and appeals" are to be conducted. For this reason FOSFA also uses standard methods of analyses which are applied in their own laboratory (FOSFA, 1987).

Other organizations in other parts of the world also issue standard contracts but these apply for the most part to fob deliveries, i.e. free on board in the port of shipping, of certain products from the regions concerned.

Quality criteria defined in the contracts are mainly confined to oil content, moisture content, impurities and admixtures. Oilseed processors naturally set great store by the quality of oilseed even if the fatty acid composition of the oil or the protein content of the seed is not specified in the contract. Any buyer or seller is however at liberty to make additions to the standard terms when concluding individual contracts.

Political Framework of the World Oilseed Trade

Since the Second World War there has been several discussions at United Nations Organization as to whether oilseeds and their products could be covered by a worldwide raw materials agreement. The chief objective, as is the case in all international raw material agreements, has been to stabilize prices. From the outset experts from industrialized countries have pointed out that an agreement of this kind could not work due to the number of products involved of both vegetable and animal origin, the interchangeability of the products and the number of countries affected. Oilseeds and their products are not a single commodity such as coffee, cocoa, rubber or olive oil.

At the United Nations Conference on Trade and Development (UNCTAD) an "Integrated Program for Commodities" was signed but vegetable oils were not included among the "core commodities." It is not expected that an international raw materials agreement on oilseeds and their products can be concluded (UNC-TAD, 1977, 1978). There are thus no fixed values for oil crops and their products and prices develop according to circumstances of the market (Schmitz, 1984). Short term production conditions such as weather, quality of plants, area of crops sown and harvested, the quality and quantity of products and long term consumer requirements and purchasing power are the decisive factors in international trade. However, trades take place within a worldwide set of tariff structures. Frequently distortions are brought about by government regulations and interventions. Subsidies and protectionist measures can have a major effect on free trade of oilseeds (Jabara, 1982).

The cultivation of oil crops in the various regions is an extremely important source of income for local farmers. There is a certain inter-crop competition for acreage which will vary from country to country but there are limits imposed by economic and agricultural considerations. In developed regions such as America and Europe farmers have alternative crops which they can grow but this may not be the case in some of the developing countries. As a result oilseed growing and trade form an important part of the political scene in many parts of the world. The FAO Intergovernmental Group on oilseeds, oils and fats of the committee on commodity problems stated (FAO, 1981):

"...Even though a significant portion of the world trade in oilseeds, oils and oilmeals takes place under duty-free conditions, the incidence of protectionist measures affecting international trade in this sector is considerable."

"As regards tariffs, imports of oilseeds and oilseed meals into most developed countries are duty-free, while import duties are generally charged on imports of fats and oils by both developed and developing countries."

Furthermore there are non-tariff barriers, import and export quotas, licensing systems and state monopolies. In centrally planned countries, both in developed and developing ones, state trading practices executed by special state import and export organizations are a normal feature.

Most governments have agricultural programs which, in the interest of sustaining farmers' income, influence the production of agricultural crops (Cracknell, 1968). The USA adminstration, for example, has sought to solve surplus cereal problems by acreage set-aside and payment-in-kind programs. These internal national measures reduce the supply on the world market, thus influencing prices. With a view to eliminating differences in the world trade and import practices on the part of individual countries in international trade in all products, the "General Agreement on Tariffs and Trade" (GATT) was concluded in 1947 and signed by twenty-three nations. Ninety countries had joined GATT by 1983. The purpose of this agreement is to reduce customs duties and stimulate international trade with the ultimate aim of free (liberalized) world trade. Complaints concerning discriminatory measures or restrictions imposed by certain countries can be submitted to GATT headquarters in Geneva.

CONCLUDING REMARKS

The chief significance of the oilseeds and their products is to satisfy the vital demand for oils and fats and for high protein animal feed. Since both are produced at once, situations may arise where there is an excessive supply of one product leading to a drop in price. Such a price change may open possibilities for new uses or even new markets which were previously of no interest. In this century the technological progress in plant processing design and methods have played a decisive part in increasing the value and versatility of oils and fats in the edible and industrial markets of the world (Table 1.10). About 80% of the fats and oils produced is used for edible purposes the rest is processed in the technical sector (Richtler and Knaut, 1984).

Table 1.10   Some Examples of the Wide Use of Vegetable oils.

Edible oil uses	Technical oil uses
salad oils	pharmaceutical products
margarine	soaps
vanaspati	paints and resins, coatings
shortenings	linoleum
cooking oils	cosmetics
fats for the bakery,	lubrication
confectionery industry	chemicals, candles,
and mayonnaise manufacturers	technical products
oils for the fish	plastic coatings
and canning industry	
feed fats	

The list of uses is certainly not complete but it gives some idea of the great variety of possible uses and indeed importance of vegetable oils in the world economy. In recent years competitive products derived from petroleum have been developed for industrial purposes. However this has not led to any radical change in usage. The oilcake and meal remaining after oil extraction is an indispensable raw material for efficient animal feeding. Without such protein there can be no optimal livestock production.

In the second half of this century the production of oil crops in the world has increased immensely. This development has been brought about by the favourable interaction of various factors. The rising demand for meat, eggs and milk has led to an increase in the requirements of high quality proteins which only the oilseeds can provide. This has been coupled with a substantial demand for oils and fats desired by a growing world population in search of a better standard of living. Because the production of oilseeds has increased to a greater extent than the world population, it has been possible to increase the total per-capita consumption of oils and fats, particularly in developing countries.

In parallel to this rise in demand and consumption, there has been an increase in cultivation and in yield per hectare. Agricultural science has made an important contribution to this worldwide balance between demand and supply since increased production would not have been possible without improvements in yield.

In the industrialized countries of the Western world the per-capita consumption of oils/fats has reached a point where no great increase is expected. A comparison of the per-capita consumption in developing countries, however, shows that there is still a substantial latent demand to be met as purchasing power increases.

Further increases in oilseed yields must be obtained if the vegetable oil needs of the world's population is to be met in the coming decades. Improvements in quality are also needed with respect to the optimum utilization of oilseeds and their products.

These requirements represent a challenge to the plant breeders of the world. Despite the high degree of interchangeability, each type of oilseed and its products have special characteristics and advantages and disadvantages for different purposes. These will be considered in details in the following chapters.

REFERENCES

Anonymous, 1987. Annual Report State Bank of Pakistan 1986/87.

Augusto, S., and Pollak, P. 1981. Structure and Prospects of the World Fats and Oils Economy. World Bank Commodity Models. Vol. 1. World Bank Staff Commodity Working Paper No. 6. June 1981.

Chicago Board of Trade. 1978. Action in the Marketplace: Commodity Futures Trading. Board of Trade of the City of Chicago.

Cracknell, N.P. 1968. Fats and oils. The legal framework of the world market. J. World Trade Law 2(4):401-444.

FAO. 1980. Provisional Agenda for the Fifteenth Session of the Committee on Commodity Problems, Intergovernmental Group on Oilseeds, Oils and Fats. Rome. 9-13 March 1981.

——. 1984. Commodity Review and Outlook 1983/1984. FAO Economic and Social Development Series No. 29. Rome.

——. Monthly bulletin of statistics. Rome.

FOSFA. International, Manual, containing all contracts, clauses, arbitration procedures. 24 St. Mary Ave. London EC3A 8ER.

Gupta, H. P. 1985. Mitigating the shortage of edible oils in our national economy. All India Seminar on Rabi Oilseed Crops, 6th. Agra, p 1-5.

Jabara, Cathy L. 1982. Trade Restrictions in International Grain and Oilseeds Markets. USDA. Economics and Statistic Service No. 162. January 1982. Washington, DC.

Kersten, Dr. L. 1982. Der Preiszusammenhang am Weltfettmarkt. Agrarwirtschaft 31(11): 340-351.

Lennerts, Dr. L. 1983. Oelschrote, Oelkuchen, pflanzliche Oele und Fette, Herkunft, Gewinnung, Verwendung. Bonn 1983. Verlag Alfred Strothe, Hannover.

Mielke, S. 1983. The Past 25 Years and the Prospects for the Next 25 in the Markets for Oilseeds, Oils, Fats and Meals. *In* S. Mielke (ed.), *Oil World*. ISTA Mielke GmbH, Hamburg, W. Germany.

Richtler, H.J., and Knaut, J. 1984. Challenges to a mature industry: Marketing and economics of oleochemicals in western Europe. J. Am. Oil Chem. Soc. 61(2): 160-175.

Schmitz, A. 1984. Commodity Price Stabilisation. The Theory and its Application, World Bank Staff Working Papers No. 668. Washington, DC.

Turnowsky, S.J. 1983. The determination of spot and futures prices with storable commodities. Econometrica 51(5): 1363-1387.

UNCTAD. 1977, 1978. TD/B/JPC/Oils/3 and 8. Documents on the "Preparatory meetings" in vegetable oils and oilseeds.

Chapter 2

The Chemical Nature
of Vegetable Oils

L. -A. Åppelqvist

INTRODUCTION

The predominant portion of all commercial vegetable oils but one is a mixture of triacylglycerols. The only exception is jojoba oil which contains almost entirely a mixture of wax esters with 40-44 carbon atoms composed of long chain alcohols esterified with long chain fatty acids (see Chapter 28). Besides triacylglycerols, a large number of constituents are also present to varying degrees depending on the status of the seed or fruit at the time of oil extraction. All vegetable oils contain varying amounts of partial glycerides, mono- and diacylglycerols, as well as unesterified "free" fatty acids. In oils extracted from undamaged fully mature seeds the amount of "partial glycerides" and free fatty acids is generally very low. Oils extracted from high moisture tissues, like immature oilseeds or palm fruits, usually contain considerably higher amounts of free fatty acids due to the action of lipases. Fully mature seeds normally have low amounts of "polar" lipids, phospho- and galactolipids, while in immature or germinated seeds the amounts of "polar" lipids can be significant.

Besides the acyl lipids, mono-, di-, and triacylglycerols as well as phospho- and galactolipids, seed oils also contain small amounts of non-fatty acid lipids. A major component of this group are the sterols of which there are many types. One important variation in the basic structure of the sterol family of compounds is in the sterol ring at position 4 which gives three classes of "sterols," viz 4-desmethyl-sterols, 4-monomethylsterols and 4,4,dimethylsterols. Vegetable oil sterols also contain a number of different side chains. The position of the double bond in the ring may also vary, giving so called Δ-5 sterols and Δ-7 sterols. Thus the number of sterols present in a vegetable oil can be high although, most "sterols" are present in very small concentrations.

Vegetable oils contain pigments of two groups; a) a mixture of carotenoids, which are considered genuine lipids and b) a mixture of chlorophylls and related pigments. These compounds have a polyisoprenoid (lipid) side chain but a non-lipid complex "nucleus." Additional components of a lipid nature, which are generally not considered true lipids, are the tocopherols and tocotrienols which are present in small amounts but are of great importance to oil quality.

The oily materials obtained by pressing and/or solvent extraction of oilseeds or fruits are called oils or fats in industry and commerce but lipids in biochemical and medical research. No strict definition of the term "lipid" seems to exist but it is normally used in one of two ways. The wider frame relates to solubility properties where lipids are considered as those substances which are insoluble in water but soluble in certain organic solvents including hexane, diethyl ether and chloroform or binary mixtures such as chloroform and methanol or hexane and isopropanol. In a more narrow sense, lipids are defined chemically as derivatives of long chain fatty acids and polyisoprenoids. The reader is referred to The Lipid Handbook (Gunstone, Harwood and Padley, 1986) or textbooks (Harwood and Russel 1984; and Christie 1982) for in-depth definitions and nomenclature. Lipids are often divided into the three categories, simple lipids, complex lipids and lipid derivatives. Simple lipids are composed entirely of esters of long chain fatty acids with alcohols, such as triacylglycerols and wax esters. Complex lipids have, in addition to fatty acids and glycerol, some non-lipid components in their molecules, such as phosphoric acid and derivatives of amino acids or a carbohydrate. With this subdivision of the term "lipids," lipid derivatives would also include all the polyisoprenoid-derived compounds, such as sterols.

TRIACYLGLYCEROLS

Nomenclature

Triacylglycerols are the correct name for the components which have different or identical fatty acids esterified to the three OH-positions on the glycerol molecule. Earlier, these components were misnamed triglycerides. However, the name triglycerides is still widely used in the oilseed industry.

The central and outer positions of the glycerol molecule are of course different. According to older nomenclature they are named β and α,α' positions respectively. However, since the two outer positions are often occupied by different fatty acids, triacylglycerols are often asymmetric and a better system of nomenclature is necessary. The stereochemical numbering system agreed upon by a joint nomenclature committee from the International Union of Pure and Applied Chemistry and the International Union of Biochemistry should be used whenever full information on the positioning of fatty acids is available from analytical work (IUPAC-IUB Commission, 1977). The cornerstone of the system is the definition of what is meant by L-glyceraldehyde and D-glyceraldehyde. In a so called Fisher projection of a natural L-glycerol derivative (Fig. 2.1) the secondary hydroxyl group is shown to the left. By definition the central carbon atom becomes sn-2, the carbon atom above sn-1 and the lower carbon sn-3.. The prefix sn-, placed before the stem name of the compound, stands for stereochemical numbering. A triacylglycerol with palmitic acid at sn-1, oleic at sn-2 and stearic at sn-3 should then be named 1-palmitoyl, 2-oleoyl-, 3-stearoyl-sn-glycerol. Litchfield (1972) discusses in detail the stereochemistry of triacylglycerols.

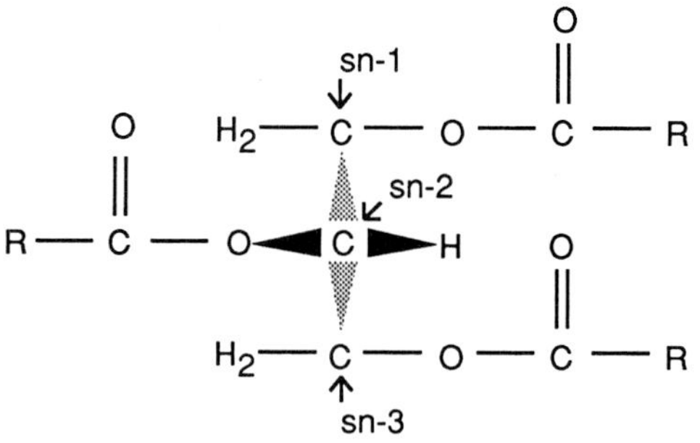

Fig. 2.1 The basic structure of a triacylglycerol, previously named triglyceride. sn-1, sn-2 and sn-3 refers to the carbon numbers of the glycerol according to the stereochemical numbering system.

. Since full structural information is not usually available, simpler names are used. When the stereochemistry of the triacylglycerol is not specified, the primary hydroxyls are still often named α and α' and the secondary named the β position. The same nomenclature is also applied to the naming of diacylglycerols and monoacylglycerols.

Fatty Acids in Triacylglycerols

The triacylglycerols are generally characterized by their overall fatty acid composition which can give a good first estimate of oil quality. Although there are large numbers of fatty acids in vegetable oils, those vegetable oils which predominate in world trade contain primarily palmitic, stearic, oleic and linoleic acids. These are traditional names, derived from the source of the oil or fat from which the fatty acid was originally isolated. Thus palmitic acid is named after palm oil, in which palmitic acid is present in large amounts and oleic acid after olive oil where oleic acid is the major constituent. However there are a large number of fatty acids present in other vegetable oils or fats which are also important on the world market. Trivial names are given to some of these but many have only systematic names. Table 2.1 presents the systematic and trivial names and symbol or short-hand designation for the major saturated fatty acids found in vegetable oils. Fatty acids with an even number of carbon atoms predominate in vegetable oils and normally only trace quantities of odd numbered fatty acids are found. The systematic names are based on the greek words for the number of carbon atoms present. The basis of the shorthand designation is two figures joined by a colon. The first figure indicates the number of carbon atoms and the second one, following the colon, indicates the number of double bonds. Saturated fatty acids are major components of lipids which are solid at room temperature, such as coconut oil and palm kernel oil. Such lipids which are solid at room temperature are often called "fats" whereas "oils" should be liquid at room temperature. However, most vegetable oils are liquid at room temperature and have unsaturated fatty acids as major components.

Table 2.1   The Systematic and Trivial Name and Symbol for some Saturated Fatty Acids of Vegetable Oils

Systematic name	Trivial name	Symbol
Ethanoic	acetic	2:0
Butanoic	butyric	4:0
Hexanoic	caproic	6:0
Octanoic	caprylic	8:0
Decanoic	capric	10:0
Dodecanoic	lauric	12:0
Tetradecanoic	myristic	14:0
Pentadecanoic	-	15:0
Hexadecanoic	palmitic	16:0
Heptadecanoic	-	17:0
Octadecanoic	stearic	18:0
Nondecanoic	-	19:0
Eicosanoic	arachidic	20:0
Heneicosanoic	-	21:0
Docosanoic	behenic	22:0
Tetracosanoic	lignoceric	24:0

Some of the important mono-unsaturated fatty acids, having one double bond, are listed in Table 2.2. In order to fully define a mono-unsaturated fatty acid the position of the double bond in the carbon chain and its geometry has to be stated.

Table 2.2 **The Systematic and Trivial Name and Symbol for Important Vegetable Oil Monoenoic Fatty Acids**

Systematic name	Trivial name	Symbol	
cis-9-dodecenoic	lauroleic	12:1	(n-3)
cis-9-tetradecenoic	myristoleic	14:1	(n-5)
trans-3-hexadecenoic	-	16:1*	
cis-9-hexadecenoic	palmitoleic	16:1	(n-7)
cis-6-octadecenoic	petroselenic	18:1	(n-12)
cis-9-octadecenoic	oleic	18:1	(n-9)
trans-9-octadecenoic	elaidic	18:1*	
cis-11-octadecenoic	cis-vaccenic	18:1	(n-7)
trans-11-octadecenoic	trans-vaccenic	18:1*	
cis-9-eicosenoic	gadoleic	20:1	(n-11)
cis-11-eicosenoic	-	20:1	(n-9)
cis-13-docosenoic	erucic	22:1	(n-9)
cis-15-tetracosenoic	nervonic	24:1	(n-9)

*The (n-x) nomenclature is only used with fatty acids containing *cis* double bonds.

Most unsaturated fatty acids in seed lipids have the double bond in the *cis-* position (see Fig. 4.2 in Chapter 4). There are however some naturally occurring "unusual" fatty acids with *trans* -double bonds and *trans* -fatty acids which are present in substantial amounts in edible oils following hydrogenation. In a systematic name, the position of the double bond is defined by numbering the carbons from the carboxyl end and giving the number of the first unsaturated carbon, preceded by the notation of *cis* - or *trans* -. Oleic acid is thus *cis* -9-octadecenoic acid. However, for reasons explained in Chapter 4, in medical research the distance between the methyl-end of the carbon chain and the first double bond is of utmost importance. Hence this information is included in the shorthand designation of *cis*-monoenes, using the (n-x) symbol, where x is the first unsaturated carbon from the methyl end. The shorthand designation of oleic acid is thus 18:1 (n-9). Among the trivial names gadoleic acid for 20:1 (n-11) is sometimes used in texts for 20:1 (n-9), a significant component of classical rapeseed oil. It is advisable to abstain from use of the name gadoleic acid because of this confusion.

In older literature two different ways of defining the position of the double bond may be found, viz Δ9-octadecenoic acid (position from the carboxyl end) and ω-9 (position from the methyl end) as names for oleic acid.

Many of the important vegetable oils contain so called polyunsaturated fatty acids, which have two or three double bonds separated by a methylene group. The most prevalent are linoleic and linolenic acids (Fig. 2.2 and Table 2.3). Although in everyday use, linolenic stands for all-*cis* 9,12,15-octadecatrienoic acid, there are actually two octadecatrienoic acids in seed oils of commercial interest. The other isomer, all-*cis* 6, 9, 12 octadecatrienoic acid, often called γ–linolenic

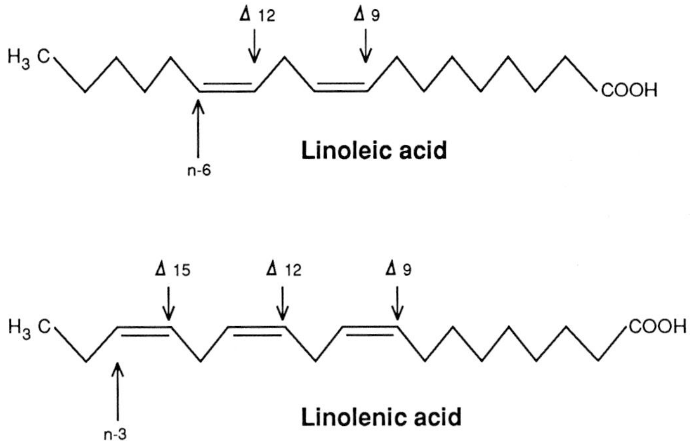

Fig. 2.2 The structure of linoleic and linolenic acids with presentations of the different classification systems for unsaturated fatty acids.

Table 2.3   The Systematic and Trivial Name and Symbol for Three Important Polyunsaturated Fatty Acids of Vegetable Oils

Systematic name	Trivial name	Symbol
cis-cis-9, 12-octadecadienoic	linoleic	18:2 (n-6)
all-cis -9, 12, 15-octadecatrienoic	α -linolenic	18:3 (n-3)
all-cis-6, 9, 12-octadecatrienoic	γ -linolenic	18:3 (n-6)

acid, is found in *Borage officinalis* and various *Ribes* species. This acid has received considerable medical attention. In some seed oil literature the "common" linolenic acid is therefore called α–linolenic acid.

World production of edible oils is predominantly based on seeds or fruits which have only saturated, *cis*-monounsaturated, *cis-cis*-diunsaturated or all-*cis* triunsaturated acids. A general screening of the plant kingdom for seed lipids will indicate that *cis*- fatty acids are rather less common than fatty acids having *trans* -double bonds or hydroxy-groups in their carbon chain. The traditional use of only those seed oils which have the "common" fatty acids for edible purposes probably reflects negative experiences throughout human history in attempts to consume oils from seeds rich in "unusual" fatty acids. However, some of these seed oils are being used or have potential for industrial purposes. Thus castor and tung oils are used in the chemical industry and others have potential as lubricants, ingredients in cosmetics, raw materials for plastics, etc. Table 2.4 presents some examples of unusual fatty acids found in oil-rich seeds. For a fuller picture of the many unusual fatty acids found in seed lipids see Chapter 30 as well as Hilditch and Williams, 1964, and Gunstone et al. 1986 and Smith, Jr. 1970.

Table 2.4   The Structure, Trivial Name and Plant Source of some Unusual Fatty Acids

Structure	Trivial name	Source
$CH_3.(CH_2)_5.CH.CH_2.CH=CH.(CH_2)_7.COOH$ $\quad\quad\quad$ OH $\quad$ *cis*	ricinoleic acid	Castor oil
$CH_3.(CH_2)_4.C=C.CH_2CH=CH.(CH_2)_7.COOH$ $\quad\quad\quad\quad$ *cis*	crepenynic acid	*Crepis foetida*
$\quad\quad\quad$ CH_2 $\quad\quad\quad$ /\\ $CH_3.(CH_2)_7.C=C.(CH_2)_7.COOH$	sterulic acid	Sterculiaceae Malvaceae
$CH_3.(CH_2)_3.CH=CH.CH=CH.CH=CH.(CH_2)_7.COOH$ $\quad\quad$ *trans* $\quad$ *trans* $\quad$ *cis*	α -eleostearic acid	Tung oil
$CH_3.(CH_2)_4.CH-CH.CH_2.CH=CH.(CH_2)_7.COOH$ $\quad\quad\quad$ O $\quad\quad$ *cis* $\quad\quad\quad$ *cis*	(+)-vernolic acid	*Veronia anthelmintica*
$\rightarrow$ — $(CH_2)_{12}.COOH$	chaulmoogric acid	*Hydnocarpus* species

From Christie (1982)

Natural Triacylglycerols

As stated previously, the overall fatty acid composition is a good yardstick of the commercial potential of a given seed oil. However for many applications it is also of considerable interest to know the structure of individual triacylglycerols in the mixture. Normally, the number of different triacylglycerols present in an oil is significantly less than that predicted by assuming all positions were occupied at random by the fatty acids formed in the developing seed. This is because the plant preferentially places unsaturated fatty acids at the 2- position and the 1- and 3- positions normally contain saturated acids, although they often differ in their fatty acid pattern. Nevertheless most vegetable oils are a complex mixture of a large number of individual triacylglycerols. An important exception is cocoa butter, a vegetable fat used in the confectionery industry, which is predominantly 1-palmitoyl, 2-oleoyl, 3-stearoylglycerol and 1,3-distearoyl, 2-oleoylglycerol. For further information see Litchfield (1972).

DIACYLGLYCEROLS, MONOACYLGLYCEROLS AND FREE FATTY ACIDS

In high quality seeds diacylglycerols, monoacylglycerols and free fatty acids are generally present in very low concentrations. Although free fatty acids and diacylglycerols are true metabolites in the biosynthesis of triacylglycerols (Chapter 3) and thus can occur naturally in trace amounts, the presence of larger quantities are generally an indication of lipolytic activity in immature, mechanically damaged or germinated seeds. It should be noted that lipolytic enzymes can be active even at sub-zero temperature and in stored moist tissue, even at -20 °C, may cause lipid degradation.

When the stereochemistry is not fully known 1,2 and 2,3 diacylglycerols, are referred to as α,β-diglycerides and the 1,3-diacylglycerols as α,α' diglycerides. Likewise, 1-monoacylglycerols (or α-monoglycerides) and 2-monoacylglycerols (β monoglycerides) are present in vegetable oils.

PHOSPHO- AND GLYCOLIPIDS

Crude vegetable oils contain, small amounts of phospho- and glycolipids. The phospholipids are chemically characterized by having a polar group, consisting of phosphate joined to either choline, ethanolamine, inositol or serine, attached to the 1 position of the glycerol backbone and one or generally two acyl groups esterified to positions 2 and 3 (Fig. 2.3). The occurrence of elevated levels of phosphatidic acid indicates enzymatic breakdown of the phospholipids during storage and/or extraction. In rare occasions phosphatidyl glycerol and cardiolipin may also be present in vegetable oils.

The phospho- and glycolipids are generally present in the chloroplasts or mitochondria or other membrane-rich organelles of intact seed. The extent of their extraction into the crude oil is dependant on the seed pretreatment and the extraction conditions. Thus careful, cold pressing of oil-rich materials generally releases little of "polar" lipids into the oil whereas a "cooking" followed by pressing and/or solvent extraction will release considerable amounts of phospholipids in the oil phase.

The amphiphilic character of these lipids, with one or two long chain fatty acids as the lipophilic part and the phosphate-linked nitrogenous or sugar part of the molecule as the hydrophilic portion, is the basis for their use as emulsifiers in the food industry. The mixture of crude phospholipids and some other polar lipids, which is obtained as a by-product in the edible oil refining, is called "lecithin." However in a chemical context, lecithin is phosphatidyl choline.

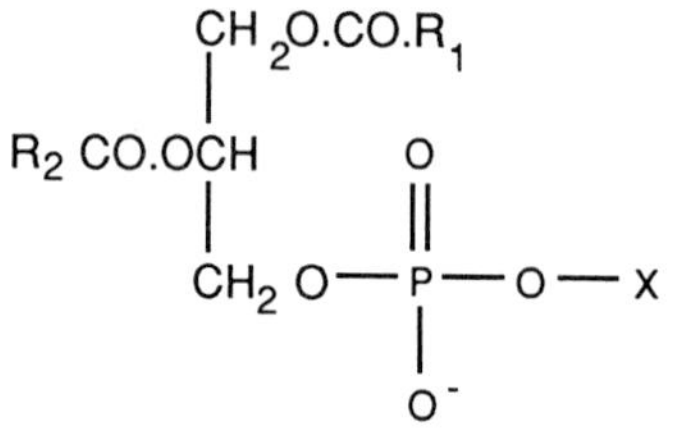

$$CH_2O.CO.R_1$$

R_2 CO.OCH

$$CH_2\ O - P - O - X$$

substituent	phospholipid
X = H	phosphatidic acid
X = serine	phosphatidylserine
X = ethanolamine	phosphatidylethanolamine
X = choline	phosphatidylcholine
X = glycerol	phosphatidylglycerol
X = inositol	phosphatidylinositol
X = phosphatidylglycerol	diphosphatidylglycerol (cardiolipin)

Fig. 2.3 The general structure of some phospholipids. R_1 and R_2 represent fatty acids.

Chloroplast membranes, as well as those of other plastids, contain large amounts of three glycolipids (Fig. 2.4). These lipids are also extracted into the oil, and are then included to some extent in the "crude lecithin" fraction recovered in the edible oil industry. Oils derived from seeds which are rich in green chloroplasts during their development, such as soybeans and rapeseed, can be expected to be richer in these glycolipids than oils from seeds devoid of chlorophyll during development. Phospho- and glycolipids are often rich in polyunsaturated fatty acids, even when the triacylglycerols of the oil are low in such acids.

OTHER ACYL LIPIDS

Besides the phospho- and glycolipids, plant tissue also contains very small amounts of highly complex lipids called phytoglycolipids. A compound called phytosphingosine (2-amino-1,3,4-octadecanetriol) is the main long chain base of phytoglycolipids. It is linked through phosphorylinositol to complex oligosacharides containing a variety of sugars or sugar derivatives (see Christie, 1982).

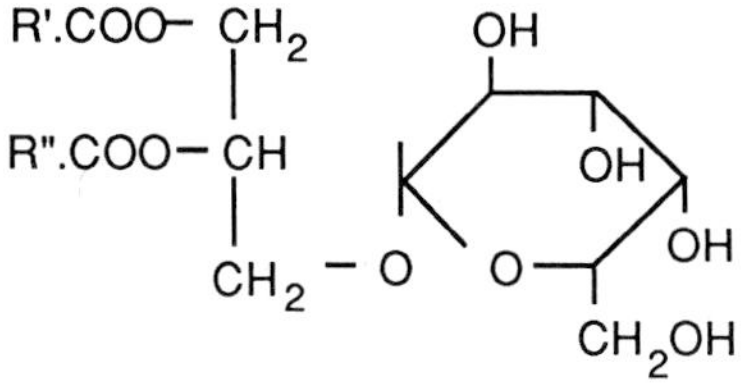

monogalactosyldiacylglycerol

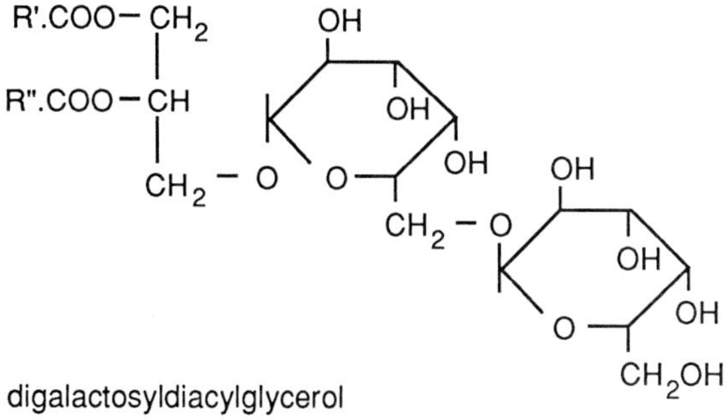

digalactosyldiacylglycerol

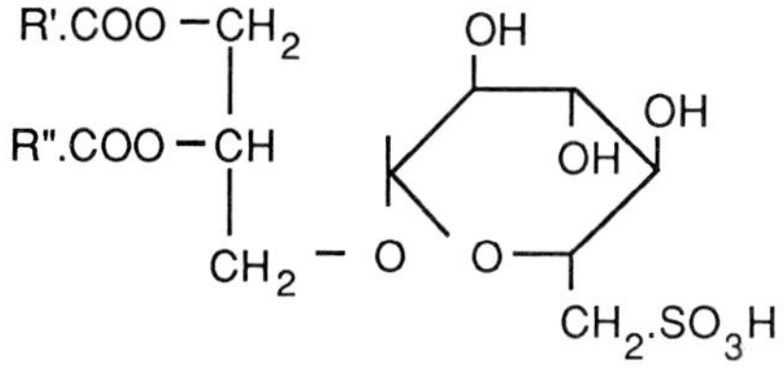

sulphoquinovosyldiacylglycrol

Fig. 2.4 The structures of some glycosyldiacylglycerols.

The surfaces of seed coats are generally covered with cutin, a lipid mixture embedded in polymers. The make up of cutin is largely dihydroxy fatty acids but small molecules also occur (Kolattakody, 1980). Cutin is basically an outer surface covering but it may also occur on special internal structures, such as the embryo (Harwood and Russel, 1986). The composition of cutin will vary depending on the associated plant part. Embedded in the cutin layer are various non-polar lipids. These include true waxes, viz long chain fatty acids (usually 24-28 carbons) which esterify to long chain alcohols (often 26 and 28 carbons), free long chain acids, long chain alcohols (often called "very long chain" compounds), hydrocarbons, aliphatic aldehydes and ketones.

STEROLS AND STEROL ESTERS

Sterols and sterol derivatives are the predominant group of so called polyisoprenoid compounds, derived from the isoprene unit (Fig. 2.5). The carotenoids
are entirely polyisoprenoids and the side chains of tocopherols and chlorophylls
are polyisoprenoid units.

<u>Compound</u>   <u>Structure</u>

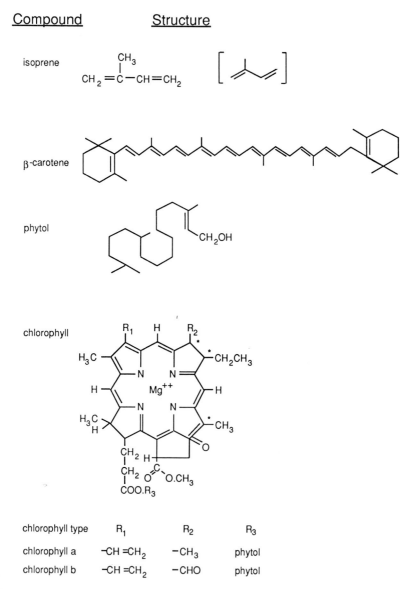

chlorophyll type	R_1	R_2	R_3
chlorophyll a	$-CH=CH_2$	$-CH_3$	phytol
chlorophyll b	$-CH=CH_2$	$-CHO$	phytol

Fig. 2.5 The structures of isoprene, some isoprenoids and the non-lipid
chlorophyll.

In addition to the three classes of sterols, 4-desmethyl, 4-monomethyl and 4,4-dimethyl sterols the oil may contain some compounds with a slightly different sterol "nucleus" with a 4,4,-dimethyl groups present. These are referred to as triterpene alcohols. Whereas most of the plant sterols have a double bond in the 5-6 position, some have a double bond in the 7-8 position. The sterols also differ in carbon number and degree of saturation of the side chain. Some of these structural differences are shown in Figure 2.6. Additional structures are given by Kochhar (1983).

Commonly, the 4-desmethyl sterols are simply called sterols. In most seed oils they comprise ca. 90% of the total sterols but some less common fats and oils, such as rice bran oil and shea butter, have larger proportions of 4-monomethyl and 4,4, dimethyl sterols. Many sterols have a trivial as well as a fully systematic name.

The most common oilseed sterol is sitosterol, (A-3 of Fig. 2.6) with the systematic name of stimast-5-ene-3β-ol. The accepted steroid nomenclature is detailed by the International Union of Pure and Applied Chemistry (1968). Other common sterols are campesterol and stigmasterol (A-2 and A-6 of Fig 2.6 respectively). Rapeseed oil and other oils of Cruciferae have substantial levels of brassicasterol that can be used as a marker of rapeseed oil regardless of erucic acid level (Kochhar, 1983). The patterns of 4-desmethyl sterols and the 4-monomethyl- and 4,4,-dimethylsterols can also be used as "fingerprints" of certain related species (chemotaxonomy) and as markers of edible oils in the trade. Another sterol present in significant amounts in some oils is a compound called Δ-5-avenasterol or iso-fucosterol or 24-etylidene cholesterol (A5 of Fig 2.6). The use of different names for the same sterol is indeed confusing, especially for those not trained in the organic chemistry of natural products. It must also be mentioned that the absolute configuration of branched side chains should be included in the name but this is not always known. There are two ways of expressing the configuration using either the E/Z or R/S systems. The nucleus (D of Fig 2.6) when combined with appropriate side chains forms compounds often referred to triterpene alcohols. Figure 2.6 gives the names and structures of some common des-methyl sterols, 4-monomethyl and 4,4 dimethyl sterols.

The sterols of seed oils occur in free form or as sterol esters of the common long chain fatty acids. In very immature or germinated seeds other forms of bound sterols can be present, viz steryl glucosides and acylated steryl glucosides (see Harwood and Russel, 1984). However, in fully mature seeds only free sterols and sterol esters have to be considered. The concentration of sterols in a seed oil differs between species as does the proportion of free sterols to sterol esters (see Kochhar, 1983). The qualitative and quantitative composition of the sterols is often changed during industrial processing. Generally, the free sterols and sterol esters are analyzed together after release of the bound sterols and therefore only total sterols are usually reported in the literature.

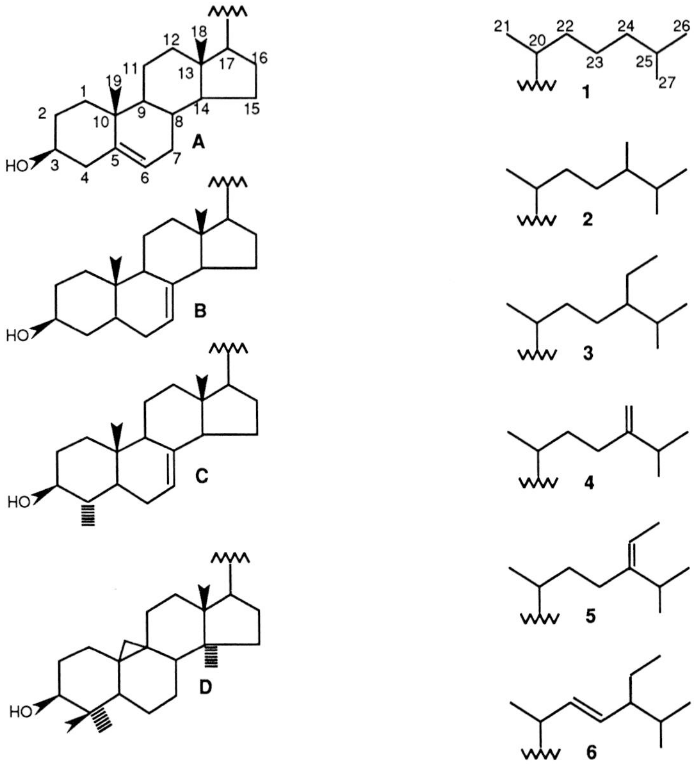

Fig. 2.6 The structures of the steroid rings and the side chains of some major and minor sterols in vegetable oils. Examples are:

A-1   cholesterol   = cholest-5-ene-3βol

A-2   campesterol   = 24-methyl-cholest-5-ene-3βol   = [(24R)ergost-5-ene-3βol]

A-3   sitosterol   = 25-ethyl-cholest-5-ene-3βol   = [stigmast-5-ene-3βol]

A-4   = 24-methylene-cholest-5-ene-3βol

A-5   Δ5-avenasterol   = 24-ethylidene-cholest-5-ene-3βol

A-6   stigmasterol   = 24-ethyl-cholest-5,22-diene-3βol   = [stigmast-5,22,diene-3βol]

B-3   Δ7-stigmasterol   = stigmast-7-ene-3βol   = [24-ethyl-cholest-7-ene-3βol]

B-5   Δ7-avenasterol   = 24-ethylidene-cholest-7-ene-3βol

Examples of 4-monoethylsterols:

C-5   citrostadienol

Examples of 4,4-dimethylsterols

D-1   Cycloartanol

D-4   24-methylene cycloartanol

Both 24R- and 24S- forms are found in vegetable oils.

OTHER LIPIDS AND LIPID SOLUBLE COMPONENTS

Many crude vegetable oils have a yellow, orange or slightly greenish color. The yellow or orange color stems from the carotenoids, which are derivatives of isoprene (Fig. 2.5). There are a number of different carotenoids but one commonly occurring component is β-carotene (Fig. 2.5). The green pigments in crude oil can be a mixture of chlorophylls a and b alone, or together with their breakdown products, pheophytines a and b. The latter lack the central magnesium ion in the complex. The pigments of crude seed oils are removed during industrial refining (see Chapter 11) but it is known that high levels of chlorophylls and/or pheophytins in crude oils always results in greater refining losses and often in a decreased oxidative stability of the refined oils.

An important group of oil components present in low concentration, are traditionally known as tocopherols. These are actually mixtures of tocopherols and tocotrienols (Fig. 2.7). There is a considerable variation, both qualitatively and quantitatively, between different oil seed species in the presence of these compounds (see Harwood and Russel, 1984). The qualitative and quantitative composition of the "tocopherols" in the seed oil is of considerable interest in edible oil production since they retard the rate of oxidation of unsaturated fatty acids and thus extend the maintenance of oil quality (see Gunstone and Norris, 1983 for further information).

CONCLUDING REMARKS

Various attempts have been made in the past by different authors to present the many lipid classes in a logical sequence. The approach used in this chapter has been to start with the predominant portion of any edible seed oil namely the triacylglycerols and their constituent fatty acids followed by other acyl lipids. Waxes, which are mixtures of acyl lipids, are then presented before the sterols and other polyisoprenoid lipids although the former are present in lower concentration than the latter. Other polyisoprenoids or isoprenoid-containing lipid soluble substances are presented last.

It is evident that lipids in a wide sense are a complex mixture of many different compounds. Often lipids are subclassified as either "neutral" or "polar" lipids. A ranking of some of the lipids classes in a sequence from the least polar to the most polar would run as follows; hydrocarbons, wax esters, sterol esters, triacyl glycerols, diacylglycerols and sterols, monoacylglycerols, glycolipids and finally phospholipids. This subclassification is relevant mainly in discussions on lipid class separations by chromatographic techniques (see Christie, 1982).

Another subclassification can be based on the infrastructure of the oil seed, viz storage lipids and membrane lipids. The storage lipids would be mainly, if not exclusively, triacylglycerols or, in jojoba wax, esters. The storage lipids are found in small oil droplets within the cells of the seed.The oil accumulates in these oil bodies during seed development. The phospholipids, glycolipids and

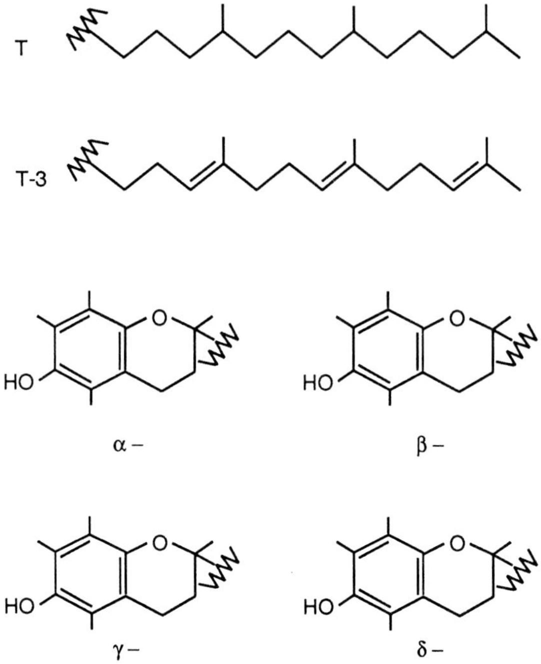

Substitution	Tocopherol (T)	Tocotrienol (T-3)
5,7,8-trimethyl	α – T	α – T – 3(ζ – T)
5,8-dimethyl	β – T	β – T – 3(ε – T)
7,8-dimethyl	δ – T	δ – T – 3(π –T)
8-monomethyl	γ – T	γ – T – 3

Fig. 2.7 The structure of tocopherols and tocotrienols.

sterols occur in membranes of chloroplasts, plastids, mitochondria, the endoplasmic reticuluum and other membraneous organelles. Besides storage lipids and membrane lipids, seeds also contain "surface" lipids. As noted previously this group is composed of a complex mixture of highly apolar lipids such as wax esters, very long chain fatty acids and alcohols (Nature's raincoat). It is intended that this chapter provide the basic understanding of oilseed plant lipid chemistry to facilitate a meaningful dialogue among chemists, breeders and oilseed processors.

REFERENCES

Christie, W. W. 1982. *Lipid Analysis*, 2nd ed., Pergamon Press, Oxford.

Gunstone, F. D., Harwood, J. L. and Padley, F.D. (eds) 1986. *The Lipid Handbook.* Chapman and Hall, London

—— and Norris, F. A. 1983. *Lipids in Foods, Chemistry, Biochemistry and Technology.* Pergamon Press, Oxford.

Harwood, J. L. and Russell, N. J. 1984. *Lipids in Plants and Microbes.* George Allen and Unwin, London.

Hilditch, T. P. and Williams, P. N. 1964. *The Chemical Constitution of Natural Fats.* 4th Ed. Chapman and Hall, London.

IUPAC Commission on the Nomenclature of Organic Chemistry and IUPAC-IUB Commission on Biochemical Nomenclature. 1968. Revised tentative rules for nomenclature of steroids. Biochim. Biophys. Acta Vol. 164 pp 453-486.

IUPAC-IUB Commission on Biochemical Nomenclature (CBN). 1977. The Nomenclature of Lipids. Recommendations, 1976. Eur. J. Biochem. Vol. 79, pp 11-21.

Kochhar, S. P. 1983. Influence of processing on sterols of edible vegetable oils, in: *Progress in Lipid Research.* Vol. 22, pp 161-188, Pergamon Press, Oxford.

Kolattukudy, P. E. 1980. Cutin, Suberin and Waxes *In* (Stumpf, P. K. and Conn, E. E. Eds.) *The Biochemistry of Plants,* Vol. 4; *Lipids: Structure and Function,* pp. 571-645. Academic Press, New York.

Litchfield, C. 1972. *Analysis of Triglycerides.* Academic Press, New York.

Smith Jr, C. R. 1970. Occurrence of Unusual Fatty Acids in Plants *In* (R. T. Holman ed.) *Progress in the Chemistry of Fats and Other Lipids,* pp. 139-177, Vol.11, Part 1, Pergamon Press, Oxford.

Chapter 3

Biosynthesis of Fatty Acids in Higher Plants

P. K. Stumpf

INTRODUCTION

All the major vegetable oils produced from seed or fruit crops contain three main fatty acids, namely palmitic, oleic and linoleic acid. It is the subtle combination of these in the form of triacylglycerols that make them of importance in the food chains of the world population. In addition, specific crops are important in that they yield acids such as lauric, ricinoleic, erucic and α–linolenic acids since these fulfill unique requirements of industry.

It is the purpose of this chapter to describe in some detail how plants synthesize these acids and to speculate on possible mechanisms that might govern the type and composition of fatty acids as they are inserted into the triacylglycerol molecule.

GENERAL CONCEPTS OF PLANT LIPID BIOSYNTHESIS

As illustrated in Figure 3.1, the sole source of carbon required to construct a fatty acid is atmospheric CO_2. In the chloroplast of the leaf cell, carbon dioxide is photochemically reduced by the process of photosynthesis to the immediate end product, phosphoglyceric acid. Phosphoglyceric acid is then photoreduced via non-cyclic photophosphorylation, found in chloroplasts of all green plants, to 3 phosphoglyceraldehyde which is then isomerized to dihydroxy-acetone phosphate (DHAP). DHAP is translocated out of the chloroplast by the phosphate translocator located in the outer envelope of the chloroplast. For each molecule of DHAP transferred out, one mole of inorganic phosphate moves into the chloroplast to fulfill the phosphate requirements of photophosphorylation. In the cytosol, a whole host of enzymes are present that rapidly convert DHAP to sucrose. The reactions are listed as follows:

Triosephosphate isomerase
  Dihydroxyacetone phosphate $\longleftrightarrow$ 3 Phosphoglyceraldehyde
    (DHAP)   (3 PGA)
Aldolase
  DHAP + 3 PGA $\longleftrightarrow$ Fructose 1,6 bisphosphate

Fructose 1,6 bisphosphatase
$$\text{Fructose 1,6 bisphosphate} \xrightarrow{\text{H}_2\text{0}} \text{Fructose-6-phosphate + Phosphate}$$

Phosphoglucoisomerase
  Fructose-6-phosphate $\longleftrightarrow$ Glucose-6-phosphate

Phosphoglucomutase
  Glucose-6-phosphate $\longleftrightarrow$ Glucose-1-phosphate

UDPG Pyrophosphorylase
  Glucose-1-phosphate + UTP $\longleftrightarrow$ UDPG + Pyrophosphate

Sucrose-6-phosphate synthetase
  UDPG + Fructose-6-Phosphate $\longrightarrow$ Sucrose-6-phosphate + UDP

Sucrose-6-phosphatase
  Sucrose-6-phosphate + H_2O $\longrightarrow$ Sucrose + Phosphate

All of these reactions occur in the cytosol of the leaf cell. Recent evidence has shown that these reactions are regulated by a regulator molecule identified as fructose 2,6 bisphosphate (Cseke et al. 1984). Once the sucrose is synthesized it is translocated via the phloem system to a suitable sink as indicated in Figure

3.1. In low lipid containing seeds such as peas and beans, sucrose is converted to starch as the principal storage unit. In high lipid-containing seeds, such as castor bean, soybean, safflower, etc., lipid is the predominant storage unit and in a number of fruits such as oil palm and avocado, the mesocarp is the principal site for lipid storage. Either starch or storage lipid serves as a very important source of carbon during the germination of the seed, however mesocarp tissue, rich in oil, serves no biochemical function for the seed which it encloses. One could speculate, however, that the vigorous bacterial and fungal degradation of the mesocarp tissue, as the fruit lies on the ground, may accelerate the germination process of the seed.

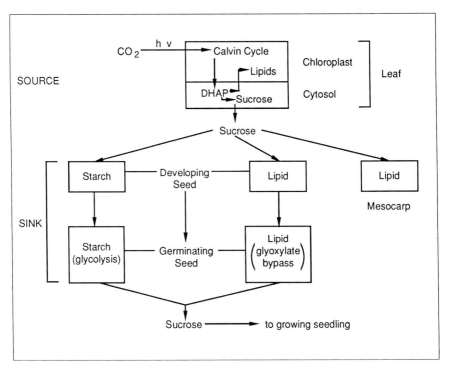

Fig. 3.1 Interacting compartments in plants.

In the developing seed tissue, be it cotyledonous or endosperm tissue, and the developing mesocarp tissue, there is now considerable evidence that special organelles identified as proplastids contain all the necessary enzymes to generate ATP, NADPH, NADH, as well as the enzymes to convert sucrose to acetyl-CoA and the FAS enzymes to utilize acetyl-CoA for oleic acid synthesis (Dennis and Miernyk, 1982). Sucrose, synthesized in the cytosolic compartment of the leaf cell, is transported by the phloem vascular system to the developing seed or mesocarp tissue. There, invertase hydrolyzes sucrose to glucose and fructose. These sugars are then phosphorylated by the proplastid hexokinase to glucose-6-PO_4

and fructose-6-PO_4 which are then converted by glycolytic enzymes to pyruvic acid, generating ATP and NADH. The pyruvate dehydrogenase complex, present in the proplastids of developing seeds and mesocarp tissue, readily converts pyruvate to acetyl-CoA. NADPH is generated by the proplastid pentose PO_4 pathway. Since acetate is also effectively used as a substrate for fatty acid synthesis, acetyl-CoA synthetase is also present in the proplastid.

In summary, in the leaf cell, CO_2 converts to DHAP via the Calvin cycle; DHAP is transported into the cytosol there to be converted to sucrose. In the seed cell and mesocarp, sucrose serves as the source of pyruvate. All the necessary enzymes to convert sucrose to pyruvate and then to acetyl-CoA are found either in the cytosol or in the matrix of the proplastid and later the chloroplast. As we shall see, the complete FAS system is localized in either the proplastid or the chloroplast and the major product of fatty acid synthesis in these organelles is oleic acid, while palmitic acid is the principal saturated fatty acid formed in these organelles.

ANCILLARY ENZYMES

Acetyl-CoA Synthetase

We have already referred to this enzyme which converts acetate to acetyl-CoA:

$$\text{Acetate} + \text{ATP} + \text{CoA} \xrightarrow{\text{Mn}^{2+}} \text{Acetyl-CoA} + \text{AMP} + \text{Pyrophosphate}$$

This enzyme is found both in the cytosol and in the proplastid of the seed cell where it converts free acetate to acetyl-CoA. The enzyme is widespread in all plant tissues and in the leaf cell it is solely localized in the stroma phase of the chloroplast (Stumpf, 1984).

Acetyl-CoA Carboxylase

Acetyl-CoA carboxylase is the enzyme responsible for the synthesis of malonyl-CoA in all plant tissues. In procaryotic organisms, the enzyme consists of three separable proteins, namely biotin carboxylase, biotin carboxyl-carrier protein, and transcarboxylase and these proteins are involved in the following sequence:

$$\text{ATP} + \text{HCO}_3^- + \text{BCCP} \xrightarrow[\text{carboxylase}]{\text{biotin}} \text{CO}_2^- \text{BCCP} + \text{ADP} + \text{Phosphate}$$

$$CO_2^- \, BCCP + Acetyl\text{-}CoA \xrightarrow[\text{transcarboxylase}]{} malonyl\text{-}CoA + BCCP$$

In animal systems, the enzyme exists as a polyfunctional inactive protein with a molecular weight of about 240,000 which consists of three domains representing biotin carboxylase, BCCP and transcarboxylase. These are linked together by an exposed polypeptide chain peculiarly susceptible to attack by endogenous proteases. Very recently, the regulation of this important animal enzyme has been clarified. The rat liver protomer, i.e. the 240,000 mol. wt. protein is readily phosphorylated by ATP and a protein kinase. In the absence of citrate, the fully phosphorylated protein is essentially inactive but the addition of 10 mM citrate fully activates the protomer causing it to polymerize to a large aggregate of several million mol. wt. Partial dephosphorylation of the phosphorylated protomer by a specific protein phosphatase yields a carboxylase that is fully active but is now citrate independent. Thus, there are two levels of activation that are involved in the regulation of this key enzyme.

In plant tissues, acetyl-CoA carboxylase was first identified in 1961 when wheat-germ acetyl-CoA carboxylase was purified some 120-fold and some of its properties were described (Stumpf, 1984). Acetyl-CoA was the most active substrate whereas propionoyl-CoA and butyryl-CoA were progressively less reactive. Unlike the animal system that was markedly activated by the citrate anion, the wheat-germ carboxylase was not affected by a number of mono-, di- and tricarboxylic acids. In 1969, the enzyme was purified some 1000-fold with a mol. wt. of approximately 630,000. More recently, Egin-Buhler et al. (1980) have purified both the acetyl-CoA carboxylase from suspension culture cells of parsley and from wheat germ. Their results indicated that the parsley carboxylase had a mol. wt. of 840,000 consisting of a large subunit of 210,000 and 105,000 dalton, whereas their wheat germ carboxylase had a mol. wt. of 700,000 with a large subunit of 240,000 and a smaller subunit of 98,000 dalton. In both cases, biotin was associated with the larger subunits. The smaller subunits may be proteolytic breakdown products during purification of the enzyme.

Both the maize carboxylase and the avocado mesocarp carboxylase have also been purified. Evidence would suggest that all these carboxylases are oligomeric with a mol. wt. ranging from 6.1 to 6.5×10^5. These enzymes, when kept in solution, rapidly lose their activity and cannot be readily restored. The activity may be stabilized somewhat in the presence of glycerol, citrate, HCO_3^- and bovine serum albumin although the function of all these compounds is not clear.

Eastwell and Stumpf (1983) have examined the regulation of wheat-germ and spinach-chloroplast acetyl-CoA carboxylases. When crude extracts of wheat germ or spinach were preincubated with ATP, and then assayed by the usual procedures, the activity was much lower than when ATP was omitted from the preincubation mixture. In contrast, partial purification of the carboxylase yielded preparations which, on preincubation with ATP, did not show any inhibitory effects by ATP. Further examination indicated that all crude plant extracts contained high levels of adenylate kinase and ATPase. Indeed, the inhibitory component turned out to be ADP which has a K_i of 40 μM with the spinach carboxylase.

Finlayson and Dennis (1984) have recently examined the effects of ADP and ATP with acetyl-CoA carboxylase from developing castor bean seeds. The results suggest three dead-end complexes, namely $E \cdot HCO_3 \cdot ADP$, $E \cdot HCO_3 \cdot P_i$ and $E \cdot PP_i$ which may be involved in the inhibition of the enzyme. Thus, the adenylate charge in the proplastid may participate in the regulation of acetyl-CoA carboxylase and fatty acid biosynthesis in these tissues. There is, however, no evidence to suggest either a phosphorylation-dephosphorylation cycle or an inactive monomer transition to an active oligomer form of the enzyme, both of which mechanisms are of considerable importance in the animal system.

Plant Acyl Carrier Proteins

The demonstration of the presence and requirement of an acyl carrier protein (ACP) in higher plant systems was first reported by Overath and Stumpf (1964) working with extracts of avocado mesocarp tissue. Shortly thereafter, Simoni et al. (1967) isolated, purified and characterized spinach and avocado ACP; Matsumura and Stumpf (1968) elucidated the core amino acid sequence adjacent to the serine residue to which the 4'-phosphopantetheine residue was associated. It is this residue to which acyl groups are attached via a thioester linkage. Although there were marked differences in the composition of the amino acids peripheral to the core amino acid sequence in spinach ACP when compared to the *Escherichia coli* ACP, the core amino acid sequence of -gly-ala-asp-ser-asp-was the same.

A number of investigators have now also confirmed the requirement of ACP for de novo fatty acid synthesis in higher plants. Because *E. coli* ACP is readily available, it is usually employed in experiments dealing with plant fatty acid synthesis. When either *E. coli* ACP or spinach ACP are employed as the component in FAS extracts, the final products are essentially identical. Of course, there always exists the possibility of fine differences in substrate specificity provided by either *E. coli* or the endogenous ACP. Table 3.1 compares some of the characteristics of plant and bacterial ACPs.

There is now considerable evidence that ACP is solely localized in the chloroplasts of the leaf cell and in the proplastid of the seed or mesocarp cell (Ohlrogge et al. 1979). Since the synthesis of the C_{16} and C_{18} fatty acids all involve the participation of ACP as the acyl carrier rather than CoA, it follows that fatty acid synthesis of the C_{16} and C_{18} fatty acids are exclusively a property of these specialized organelles in seeds, mesocarp or leaf cells.

In addition, ACP serves as part of the specific substrate for the conversion of stearate to oleate in that the substrate is stearoyl-ACP, the product is oleoyl-ACP and the enzyme is stearoyl-ACP desaturase all of which is again localized in the proplastid or the chloroplast. We will discuss this enzyme in more detail later in this chapter.

In summary, ACP participates as the thioester moiety in the synthesis of the C_{16} and C_{18} fatty acids, in their transfer to suitable acceptors, and in the introduction of the first double bond in the hydrocarbon chain, namely at the Δ^9 position. Further elongations, modifications and desaturations occur with CoA derivatives and/or complex lipids at appropriate sites in the cell.

Table 3.1   A Comparison of Plant and Bacterial Acyl Carrier Proteins

Source[a]	Mol.Wt.	Amino acid residues	Relative specific activities[a]
Escherichia coli	8700	77	1.0
Arthrobacter sp.	9500	81	1.0
Spinach leaf	9500	88	0.3
Avocado mesocarp	11500	117	0.3

[a] With spinach chloroplast stroma as the source of the fatty acid synthetase assay system.

ENZYMES FOR THE SYNTHESIS OF PALMITIC AND STEARIC ACIDS

Before we discuss in some detail the enzymology of fatty acid synthesis, a brief review of the reactions involved is pertinent. Table 3.2 outlines the several steps involved in the synthesis of a fatty acid. These reactions occur in all cells capable of synthesizing fatty acids. Note the important role of ACP as the substrate-carrier protein. Also note the importance of the ancillary enzymes that catalyze the reactions necessary for the preparation of the substrates.

In prokaryotic cells, fatty acid synthesis occurs in the cytosolic compartment. However, it has been observed that ACP in *E. coli* appeared to be somewhat loosely associated with the inner face of the plasma membrane of the cell. Nevertheless, all the activities associated with the synthesis of palmitic acid from acetyl-CoA were readily separated and assigned to individual proteins. These proteins have been purified and their molecular and kinetic characteristics examined in considerable detail. However, in sharp contrast in yeast, fungi and animal cells, the fatty acid synthetase responsible for the formation of palmitic acid is always found in the cytosolic compartment as very large hetero- or homodimer complexes, respectively (Wakil et al. 1983).

Table 3.2   Reactions for Plant Fatty Acid Synthesis (FAS)

<u>**Ancillary Enzymes:**</u>

A.

$$CH_3COOH + ATP + CoA \xrightarrow[Mg^{2+}]{\text{acetyl-CoA synthetase}} CH_3COCoA + AMP + PP_i$$

B.

$$CH_3COCoA + ATP + CO_2 \xrightarrow[Mg^{2+}]{\text{acetyl-CoA carboxylase}} COOHCH_2COCoA + ADP + P_i$$

C.

$$\text{oleoyl-ACP} + H_2O \xrightarrow{\text{oleoyl-ACP hydrolase}} \text{oleic acid} + ACP$$

<u>**FAS Enzymes:**</u>

1.

$$CH_3COSCoA + ACP{\cdot}SH \xleftarrow{\text{acetyl transferase}} CH_3CO{\cdot}S{\cdot}ACP + CoASH$$

2.

$$HO_2C{\cdot}CH_2COSCoA + ACP{\cdot}SH \xleftarrow{\text{malonyl transferase}}$$
$$HO_2C{\cdot}CH_2CO{\cdot}S{\cdot}ACP + CoASH$$

3.

$$CH_3COS{\cdot}ACP + HO_2C{\cdot}CH_2CO{\cdot}S{\cdot}ACP \xleftarrow{\text{β-ketoacyl-ACP synthetase I}}$$
$$CH_3COCH_2CO{\cdot}S{\cdot}ACP + ACP{\cdot}SH + CO_2$$

4.

$$CH_3COCH_2CO{\cdot}S{\cdot}ACP + NADPH_2 \xleftarrow{\text{β-hydroxyacyl-ACP reductase}}$$
$$D{\text-}CH_3CH(OH)CH_2CO{\cdot}S{\cdot}ACP + NADP^+$$

5.

$$CH_3CH(OH){\cdot}CH_2CO{\cdot}S{\cdot}ACP \xleftarrow{\text{β-hydroxyacyl-ACP dehydratase}}$$
$$CH_3CH\stackrel{trans}{=\!=\!=}CHCO{\cdot}S{\cdot}ACP + H_2O$$

6.

$$CH_3CH\stackrel{trans}{=\!=\!=}CHCO{\cdot}S{\cdot}ACP + NADPH + H^+ \xleftarrow{\text{enoyl-ACP reductase}}$$
$$CH_3CH_2CH_2CO{\cdot}S{\cdot}ACP + NADP^+$$
$$\text{butyryl-ACP}$$

7.
Butyroyl·S·ACP now reacts with a second molecule of malonyl·S·ACP and proceeds through reactions 3-6 to form hexanoyl·S·ACP, etc. until palmitoyl·S·ACP is formed.

8.

$$CH_3(CH_2)_{14}CO{\cdot}S{\cdot}ACP + HO_2CCH_2COSACP \xleftarrow{\text{Enzymes 4,5,6 β-ketoacyl-ACP}}$$
$$\text{Synthetase II}$$
$$C_{17}H_{35}COSACP + CO_2$$

The Plant Fatty Acid Synthetase (FAS) System

In 1953, Newcomb and Stumpf first observed the effective incorporation of [^{14}C] acetate into long-chain fatty acid by plant tissues and five years later, a particulate preparation obtained from avocado mesocarp was the most effective fraction to incorporate[^{14}C] acetate into [^{14}C] palmitic and [^{14}C] oleic acids. In 1958, it was shown that a soluble enzyme extract prepared from an acetone powder of avocado mesocarp particles required HCO_3^- in addition to Mn^{2+}, ATP, CoA and NADPH for the incorporation of [^{14}C] acetate into free [^{14}C] oleic acid. In 1964, Overath and Stumpf showed for the first time that a heat-stable protein was required for the synthesis of fatty acids from [^{14}C] malonyl-CoA. This protein was identified by Overath as a plant ACP. In the meantime, three groups independently demonstrated in 1960-1963 that isolated leaf chloroplasts, in the presence of light, very effectively incorporated [^{14}C] acetate into [^{14}C] palmitic acid and [^{14}C] oleic acid (Stumpf, 1984).

Thus by 1964, the broad outline of de novo plant fatty acid biosynthesis had been laid down. Rather than describe the countless numbers of investigations extending these observations, we shall only describe the current status of the biosynthesis of C_{16} and C_{18} fatty acids in higher plants.

Some years ago, a 10,000 xg particulate preparation was obtained from avocado mesocarp tissue, which synthesized palmitic and oleic acids from [^{14}C] acetate. Later a number of workers demonstrated that chloroplasts from a number of leaf tissues could readily synthesize fatty acids from [^{14}C] acetate, the principal products being palmitate and oleate under aerobic conditions and palmitate and stearate under anaerobic conditions. In 1964, Yamada and Stumpf demonstrated that a 10,000 xg pellet obtained from a homogenate of developing castor bean seeds readily incorporated acetyl-CoA into oleic acid.

Although in the early sixties it was already recognized that a particulate fraction from avocado mesocarp and isolated chloroplasts were active sites of fatty acid synthesis, a precise decision on the actual site of synthesis could not be made. In the isolation of organelles, despite all attempts to preserve the integrity of the structures, disruption of varying extents always occurs. Thus, it was difficult to interpret the observation that supernatant extracts also possessed biosynthetic activity. The question of whether the activity was derived from disrupted organelles or from the cytosolic compartment could therefore not be precisely answered.

Zilkey and Canvin (1969) clarified the earlier observations of Yamada and Stumpf (1964) by isolating large particles by sucrose density gradient centrifugation of homogenates of developing castor-bean endosperm which converted [^{14}C] acetyl-CoA to [^{14}C] oleate and gave these particles the name "oleosomes". In 1975, Weaire and Kekwick reported that plastid preparations obtained by density gradient centrifugation of homogenates of avocado mesocarp or cauliflower bud tissue, incorporated [1-^{14}C] acetate into fatty acids, principally palmitate and oleate, whereas the cytosolic protein fraction was essentially inactive. They concluded that the proplastids were the principal site of fatty acid biosynthesis. In the meantime, Yamada and his group in Japan extended his 1964 observations in a series of papers which carefully documented the capacity of a 10,000 xg particle obtained from developing castor bean endosperm tissue to convert [^{14}C] sucrose to palmitate, stearate and oleate. These studies indicated that proplastids possessed all the enzymes necessary for the conversion of sucrose via a UDPG:fructose transglycosylase to glucose-1-phosphate and then via glucose-6-phosphate into the pentose phosphate pathway and finally to pyruvate and acetyl-CoA. Simcox et al. (1977) extended the Zilkey and Canvin observations on proplastids or oleosomes obtained from developing castor bean endosperm tissue. In essence, they determined that hexose phosphate synthesis from sucrose occurred in the cytosol along with the first oxidative step in the pentose phosphate pathway, namely, the glucose-6-phosphate dehydrogenase reaction. The proplastid contained 6-phosphogluconate dehydrogenase, transketolase, transaldolase and the glycolytic enzymes necessary to convert fructose-6-phosphate to pyruvic acid, pyruvic dehydrogenase and the full complement of fatty acid synthetase enzymes responsible for the formation of oleic acid. Oleic acid then is transported out of the proplastid to the cytosol where the oleoyl hydroxylase is responsible for the conversion of oleoyl to ricinoleoyl moiety; the enzymes for triacylglycerol synthesis were localized on the endoplasmic reticulum membrane.

Further support for the compartmentation concept is obtained from the in vivo work of Ohlrogge et al. (1978) with in vivo incorporation of [^{14}C] acetate and [^{14}C] glucose into fatty acids and alcohols by slices of developing jojoba seed. Specifically, whereas [^{14}C] acetate was used exclusively for the elongation of endogenous oleic acid the ^{14}C from [^{14}C] glucose was uniformly distributed throughout the acyl chain of fatty acids. A reasonable explanation of these entirely different labeling patterns would involve the existence of metabolically separate pools of acetate for de novo synthesis and elongation of acyl chains. These pools could possibly relate to proplastids and to endoplasmic reticulum membranes as two discretely different sites, the first for the de novo synthesis, of stearoyl-ACP, its desaturation to oleoyl-ACP and hydrolysis to free oleic acid, and the second for further elongation, reduction, and condensation of acyl-CoA derivatives for wax ester biosynthesis.

In addition, isolated proplastids from endosperm of germinating castor beans were sites of fatty acid synthesis and chromoplasts from daffodil petals incorporated [^{14}C] acetate into palmitic acid. Proplastids isolated from soybean tissue culture suspension cells were also capable of synthesizing fatty acids from [^{14}C] malonyl-CoA via the ACP pathway.

If the chloroplast can be considered a variant of a proplastid but with a photosynthetic capability, then this organelle should and does have the same complement of fatty-acid-synthesizing enzymes as the proplastid from nonphotosynthetic tissue. Indeed, recent work clearly demonstrated that ACP in a spinach leaf protoplast was exclusively localized in the chloroplast (Ohlrogge et al. 1979). Since antibodies to spinach ACP completely blocked fatty acid synthesis in a spinach leaf homogenate, it followed that ACP was essential for fatty acid synthesis and hence the chloroplast was the specific site for the formation of palmitic and oleic acid in the leaf cell. These acids are then transported from the chloroplast to the cytosolic compartment for further modification, etc.; some of the products of cytosolic modifications (i.e. linoleic and/or α–linolenic acids) are transported back to the chloroplast for final insertion into lamellar membrane lipids (Stumpf, 1984).

Molecular Structure of the FAS System

For a number of years, data suggested that the FAS system was not a high molecular weight polyfunctional protein so characteristic of animal eukaryotic systems. These conclusions were based on the fragmentary evidence that prolonged centrifugation at 100,000 xg did not sediment FAS activity and that ACP had to be added to the reaction mixture for optimal fatty acid synthesis. It was already suggested that the conversion of acetyl-CoA (C_2) to stearic acid (C_{18}) was a 2-step sequence: a de novo system from C_2 -- C_{16} and an elongation system from C_{16}---C_{18}. The conclusions were based on the differential effects of the inhibitor, cerulenin, heat stability, and ammonium sulfate fractionation. The traditional assay of the FAS system was the incorporation of [^{14}C] malonyl-CoA into [^{14}C] C_{16} and -C_{18} acids.

The use of acyl-ACP substrates as intermediates in FAS synthesis was hindered by the technical problem of preparing suitable substrates. Acylated acyl carrier protein substrates could be prepared by chemical procedures but there was considerable evidence to suggest that such acyl-ACP substrates were partially inactive. However, in recent years, the preparation of specific acyl-ACP substrates by mild procedures was developed and these new procedures yielded highly reactive substrates.

Since 1982 laboratories from England, Denmark, Germany and the USA have initiated investigations to elucidate the molecular structure of the FAS system from avocado, barley, safflower, spinach tissues, and parsley suspension culture cells. The results from these laboratories complement each other very well. By appropriate protein fractionation procedures, these workers showed that all these systems are of the non-associated type similar to the FAS system of *E. coli*. Table 3.3 lists the molecular weights of a number of these systems and compares them to the available molecular weight determinations made with the *E. coli* enzymes. While there is some scattering of molecular weights, the order of magnitude appears to be quite similar.

Rather than examine the FAS systems from the various plant tissues, we shall select the safflower FAS system. When crude extracts of developing safflower seeds were fractionated by a number of procedures (Shimakata and Stumpf,

Table 3.3   Molecular Weights of Several Plant FAS Systems

Enzyme	Safflower	Spinach	Barley	Avocado	E. coli
	--------Mol. Wt. x 10^3 (Kilodalton)--------				
Malonyl-CoA:ACP transacylase	22	30	41	40.5	37
β-Ketoacyl-ACP synthetase I	--	56	92	--	66
β-Ketoacyl-ACP synthetase II	--	57	--	--	--
β-Ketoacyl-ACP reductase (NADPH)	83	97	125	40	--
β-Hydroxyacyl-ACP dehydrase	64	85	--	--	170
Enoyl-ACP reductase (NADH)	83	115	--	62.4	90

1982), the following enzyme activities could be separated as discrete proteins and their properties could be individually studied:

Acetyl-CoA + ACP $\longleftrightarrow$ Acetyl-ACP + CoA
Acetyl-CoA:ACP transacetylase

Malonyl-CoA + ACP $\longleftrightarrow$ Malonyl-ACP + CoA
Malonyl-CoA:ACP transacylase

Acyl-ACP + Malonyl-ACP $\longleftrightarrow$ β-Ketoacyl-ACP + CO_2 + ACP
β-Ketoacyl-ACP synthase I

β-Ketoacyl-ACP + NADPH $\longleftrightarrow$ β-OH-acyl-ACP + $NADP^+$
β-Ketoacyl-ACP reductase

β-OH-acyl-ACP $\longleftrightarrow$ Enoyl-ACP + H_2O
β-OH-acyl-ACP hydratase

Enoyl-ACP + NADPH (NADH) $\longleftrightarrow$ Acyl-ACP + NADP (NAD^+)
Enoyl-ACP reductase

Palmitoyl-ACP + Malonyl-ACP $\longleftrightarrow$ β-Ketostearoyl-ACP + CO_2 + ACP
β-Ketostearoyl-ACP synthetase II

A few comments are in order.

(1) Acetyl-CoA:ACP transacetylase has very low specific activity in extracts from developing seeds of *Cuphea lutea*, safflower, rapeseed, and from leaves of pea and spinach. Changing the concentration of this enzyme in a reconstituted system necessary for fatty acid synthesis greatly perturbed the composition of the final products of synthesis in that at low levels of this enzyme, the normal products were 70% stearate and 25 to 30% palmitic but at high levels the

products were now about 80% lauric acid with lesser amounts of the higher homologues. These results suggest that controlling the levels or activities of this enzyme in the cell may have major effects on the fatty acid composition of seed cells(Shimakata and Stumpf, 1983).

(2) β-Ketoacyl-ACP synthetase I has broad specificity for acyl-ACPs up to palmitoyl-ACP. With this substrate, the enzyme has no activity. Furthermore, the antibiotic cerulenin completely inhibits irreversibly this enzyme at 5 μM levels.

(3) β-Ketoacyl-ACP reductase. NADPH is the most effective reductant for this reductase. NADH is essentially inactive.

(4) Enoyl-ACP reductases. In safflower seeds two enoyl-ACP reductases have been observed. Reductase I has an optimum pH of 6.5, it utilizes only NADH, and was able to reduce crotonyl-CoA. Reductase II has a pH optimum of 7.1, it required NADPH rather than NADH and was inert to crotonyl-CoA. Reductase I was active with crotonyl-ACP but less active with 2-decenoyl-ACP whereas reductase II had no activity toward crotonyl-ACP but had high activity with 2-decenoyl-ACP. It would appear that these two reductases interplay with enoyl-ACPs depending on the chain length of the substrate.

(5) β-Ketoayl-ACP synthetase II is the specific condensing enzyme responsible for the conversion of palmitoyl-ACP to stearoyl-ACP. The enzyme is fully active with palmitoyl-ACP but has no activity with stearoyl-ACP thereby guaranteeing the synthesis of C_{18} fatty acid but no higher homologues. It is far less sensitive to cerulenin than is synthetase I.

In summary, C_{16} and C_{18} fatty acids are synthesized in specific organelles identified as proplastids in the seed and mesocarp tissue and as chloroplasts in leaf tissues. The enzymes are non-associated and procaryotic in character. The conversion of $C_2 \rightarrow C_{16} \rightarrow C_{18}$ involves first the formation of palmitoyl-ACP and then its elongation to C_{18} by a highly specific β-Ketoacyl-ACP synthetase II. The role of the proplastid in fatty acid synthesis is presented in Figure 3.2.

BIOSYNTHESIS OF UNSATURATED FATTY ACIDS

Plants are the principal sources of the polyunsaturated fatty acids, linoleic and α–linolenic acids. When we consider that all leaf tissues contain high levels of these acids, it is clear that they are the most abundant unsaturated fatty acids in the world. However, just as the synthesis of cellulose, the most abundant polysaccharide in the world, is poorly understood at present, so the synthesis of these two polyunsaturated fatty acids is not well defined. Oleic acid biosynthesis, in sharp contrast, is quite well documented.

Gurr (1974) has thoroughly reviewed the literature on the biosynthesis of unsaturated fatty acids by both prokaryotic and eukaryotic organisms. Roughan and Slack (1982) have also recently discussed the synthesis of these acids.

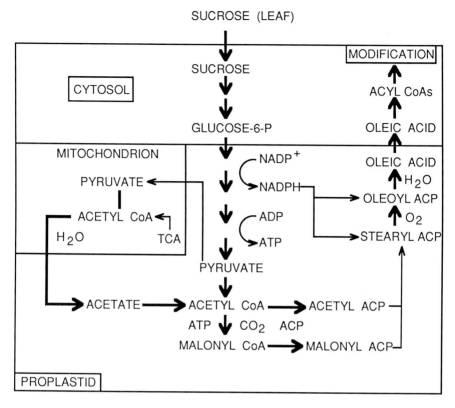

Fig. 3.2 The roles of different compartments of a seed or mesocarp cell in the biosynthesis of fatty acids.

Biosynthesis of Oleic Acid

There are two principal mechanisms for the introduction of a *cis* double bond into a hydrocarbon chain, the anaerobic and the aerobic mechanism. As the name implies, the anaerobic mechanism requires no oxygen because the *cis* double bond is introduced by a highly specific β-hydroxydecanoyl-ACP dehydrase in prokaryotic organisms to form a *cis* -β-γ-decenoyl-ACP. This substrate is then elongated by a series of malonyl-ACP additions until the final product, *cis* - vaccenoyl-ACP, is formed. In contrast, the aerobic mechanism requires a reductant, usually NADPH or NADH, an electron carrier, usually ferredoxin in plants and cytochrome b_5 in animal and yeasts, and a desaturase which presumably couples the reductant to molecular oxygen to form a species of oxygen which in turn extracts the H_D atoms at C_9-C_{10} to form a *cis* double bond system. At present, there is no evidence supporting the anaerobic mechanism in plants, whereas all evidence points to the aerobic mechanism as the principal, if not the only, mechanism for the synthesis of unsaturated fatty acids.

Nagai and Bloch first demonstrated (see Gurr, 1974) in *Chlorella* and in spinach chloroplasts a stearoly-ACP desaturase; more recently these observations have been extended to include a wide variety of plant tissues. In essence, the stearoyl-ACP desaturase in all plants examined is a soluble protein found either in the proplastid of the seed cell or in the stroma phase of chloroplasts; however, in yeasts and animal tissues the substrate is stearoyl-CoA and the desaturase is membrane-bound (Gurr, 1974). An input of two electrons from NADPH is required, and the intermediate electron-carrier protein between the electron pair and molecular oxygen in plants is ferredoxin. In fact, spinach ferredoxin has been employed in most studies because of its stability, availability and reactivity. Whether the actual endogenous electron carrier is indeed ferredoxin, or any of a number of non-heme iron proteins, remains to be determined. A number of possible heme and non-heme proteins were tested with the safflower system and spinach ferredoxin seems to be the most effective electron carrier.

McKeon and Stumpf (1982) purified the safflower stearoyl-ACP desaturase approximately 200-fold by DEAE and affinity chromatography. The protein exists in the native state as a dimer with a mol. wt. of 68,000.

Stearoyl-ACP desaturase is essentially specific for stearoyl-ACP. The desaturase is only 5% as active with stearoyl-CoA and 1% as active with palmitoyl-ACP. The K_ms for the two acyl-ACPs are similar (i.e. palmitoyl-ACP, 0.51 μM; stearoyl-ACP, 0.38 μM), yet the V_{max} for stearoyl-ACP is 100 times greater than that for palmitoyl-ACP. This is in sharp contrast to the acyl-CoA desaturase in mammalian systems where the K_ms and V_{max}s for stearoyl-CoA and palmitoyl-CoA are quite similar. Thus, the plant desaturase virtually requires an 18-carbon chain length for activity. This specificity seems to involve more than mere recognition of chain length, since the K_ms of the acyl-ACPs are similar although the stearoyl-ACP allows the formation of a more reactive Michaelis complex.

The specificity of the desaturase toward stearoyl-ACP relative to stearoyl-CoA is of further interest. The specificity is derived from the binding of the thioester to the enzyme since the K_ms differ by 20-fold (stearoyl-ACP, 0.38 μM; stearoyl-CoA, 8.3 μM). Since the V_{max} for stearoyl-CoA is the same (within experimental error) as that for stearoyl-ACP, the substrate concentration plays a critical role. Indeed, the difference in K_m indicates the importance of ACP for substrate recognition.

The spectrum of stearoyl-ACP desaturase reveals no obvious absorption peaks from 325 to 800 nm. However, because the desaturase could not be concentrated without a great loss in activity, the spectra obtained for active enzyme would require a molar absorptivity of greater than 3000 to detect a peak. While this is below the ε_{max} for most protein pigments, the possibility of a low absorbance cofactor or a quenched redox pigment cannot be eliminated. The nature of the activation of oxygen by the desaturase therefore remains unresolved. Although cyanide, at a final concentration of 1 mM, inhibited desaturation, the effect may be on the transport of electrons from NADPH to molecular oxygen via

NADPH ferredoxin reductase and ferredoxin, rather than directly on the desaturase.

Since lipids of some plants (though not safflower) are more highly unsaturated when the plants are grown at low temperature(Gurr, 1974), this phenomenon has been explained as being related to the decreasing solubility of oxygen with increasing temperature and the requirement of oxygen for desaturation. Thus, oxygen has been considered the rate-limiting factor in fatty acid desaturation in non-photosynthetic tissue.

The desaturase shows an oxygen dependency; the oxygen concentration necessary for half-maximal activity was 56 μM, approximately one-fifth the concentration of oxygen in air-saturated water. On the other hand, the reaction requires 400 μM oxygen for saturation. Since only a 2-fold increase in activity would result from a 7-fold increase in oxygen (going from half-maximal to maximal) and assuming similarity to stearoyl-ACP desaturases from other oil seeds, it would seem unlikely that oxygen could be a major controlling factor in the biosynthesis of oleic acid.

All proplastids or chloroplasts synthesize oleic acid as their main unsaturated fatty acid from [^{14}C]acetate. Since Ohlrogge et al. (1979) have shown that all the ACP of a leaf cell is localized in the chloroplast, it follows that the only site of stearoyl-ACP desaturase must be the chloroplast. The product of the stearoyl-ACP desaturase in crude extracts is always free oleic acid whereas with highly purified desaturase, oleoyl-ACP accumulates. A highly specific acyl-ACP thioesterase occurs in both chloroplasts and proplastids which has a marked preference for oleoyl-ACP, converting this product to free oleic acid and ACP. This reaction is significant because it releases ACP for recycling into the FAS system and it forms free oleic acid that can readily move to other compartments for further modifications.

The thioesterase has a strong preference for oleoyl-ACP and is essentially inactive with oleoyl-CoA. With acyl-ACPs as substrates, specificity is a function of reaction rate and not binding selectivity. The K_ms for the acyl-ACPs are quite similar, ranging from 0.25 to 0.50 μM. This similarity points to ACP as the principal determinant of binding. The V_{max}s for palmitoyl-ACP, stearoyl-ACP, oleoyl-ACP, stearoyl-CoA and oleoyl-CoA are 140, 296, 1650, 0 and 0 nmoles/min/mg protein, respectively. The difference in V_{max}s, therefore, implies a specific recognition of the acyl chain bound to the enzyme. It also seems that the double bond of oleate is a more important recognition site than chain length, since the thioesterase has a 12-fold preference for the unsaturated and only a 2-fold preference for the longer of the saturated fatty acyl moieties.

In summary, three different enzymes interrelate to guarantee the formation of oleic aicd, namely the β-ketoacyl-ACP synthetase II, stearoyl-ACP desaturase, and the acyl-ACP thioesterase. Because of the high specificity of these enzymes, the only product is free oleic acid.

Biosynthesis of Linoleic and α-Linolenic Acids

The introduction of the first double-bond system into a hydrocarbon chain is now quite well understood. The substrate is defined, and the characteristics of the enzyme system reasonably well described.

However, a remarkable change occurs in the systems involved in the introduction of the second and third double bonds into the hydrocarbon chain. The substrates are not clearly defined, and the enzyme systems appear to be membrane-bound. In addition, while the major site of linoleic and α–linolenic acids in leaf cells are the chloroplast lamellar membrane lipids, numerous workers have demonstrated that intact chloroplasts only synthesize oleic acid, although small amounts of linoleic and α–linolenic synthesis have been noted. One is forced to conclue that (1) chloroplasts and proplastids can only synthesize oleic acid or (2) in the isolation of these organelles, a soluble effector is lost which under in vivo conditions modulates rigidly the oleic → linoleic → linolenic reactions or activities of an enzyme (acyl-ACP hydrolase?) which channels the appropriate substrate away from further desaturation or (3) linoleic acid is synthesized in a cytosolic compartment and then transported back to the chloroplast for desaturation to α–linolenic acid. Superimposed on this problem is the very good possibility that the expression of activity of the two enzymes, namely, oleoyl desaturase and linoleoyl desaturase, is related to the type of tissue examined and the previous history of the tissue, i.e. the age of the tissue, the temperature at which the tissue was grown, and the light regime the tissue was exposed to. For example, some etiolated tissues such as maize leaves possess a high capacity for the conversion of oleate to linoleic acid and linolenate, whereas etiolated germinating cucumber cotyledons are essentially totally devoid of such activities until exposed to a light regime. Non-photosynthetic tissues such as developing safflower seeds possess a high capacity for conversion of oleate to linoleic acid, and potato tubers on aging in the dark show a remarkable induction of capacity to convert oleate to linoleate. Evidently, there appears to be a wide variation among different plant tissues to form linoleic and α–linolenic acids. Unfortunately, there does not appear to be a consistent pattern. Moreover, all attempts to obtain systems which can be purified and thereby fully characterized have met with failure.

The problem of elucidating the biosynthesis of these two important polyunsaturated fatty acids is therefore complex. While early results suggested oleoyl-CoA as the primary substrate for the Δ^{12} desaturase , the work of Gurr, Kates, and Slack and Roughan provided evidence that the actual substrate was 2-oleoyl phosphatidylcholine. Later work from other laboratories expanded the substrate to include 2-oleoyl phosphatidylethanolamine. The insertion of oleoyl-CoA into the 2-position of PC is very rapid although the mechanism of insertion is not too well defined. One possible route is the initial formation of a 2-lyso-PC and then a rapid acylation by oleoyl-CoA. This conclusion is supported by the observation that the addition of 2-lyso-PC to a microsomal preparation and then the addition of oleoyl-CoA greatly increase the conversion of oleate to linoleate. The other possibility is a direct transacylation from oleoyl-CoA to PC to form oleoyl-PC and acyl-CoA. Some evidence for this mechanism has also been presented. Regardless of what mechanism is employed, Figure 3.3 appears to fit the present available data.

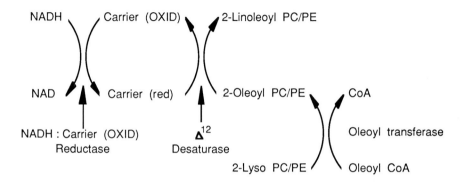

Fig. 3.3 A probable mechanism for the desaturation of oleic acid in the Δ^{12} position.

In summary, the site of oleate desaturation is most likely the endoplasmic reticulum. This organelle contains, in addition, all the enzymes involved in phospholipid and triacylglycerol biosynthesis. Whether or not a specific polar lipid or an acyl-CoA or an acyl-ACP is directly or indirectly involved for linoleic synthesis remains for further investigations to clarify. There is indirect evidence suggesting that the monogalactosyldiglyceride in the outer envelope of the chloroplast may be involved in the conversion of linoleic acid to linolenic acid. Once linoleic acid and linolenate are formed, these acyl moieties must be transported to their specific sites. In the leaf cell, the principal site of these acids is the chloroplast lamellar membrane. At present, there is no direct evidence for the occurrence of polyunsaturation in these specific membranes or even in chloroplasts themselves. Thus, these acyl moieties must be presumably transferred directly or indirectly to their final site from their synthesizing site.

Obviously, much more research with in vitro systems must be carried out before a final definition of these desaturation systems can be made.

BIOSYNTHESIS OF FATTY ACIDS OTHER THAN THE $C_{16}C_{18}$ GROUP

Synthesis of Very Long Chain Fatty Acids

Although much is now known about the synthesis of the C_{16} and C_{18} fatty acids, only in recent years has progress been made in understanding the synthesis of the very long chain fatty acids defined as those in the range C_{20} to C_{30} chain length. The investigations of Kolattukudy and Cassagne and Lessire laid down the basic ideas that C_{16} and C_{18} fatty acids when introduced into leaf slices or epidermal cells were elongated stepwise through C_{20}, C_{22}, etc. to the final product usually C_{30} or C_{33} fatty acids. Elongation systems are membrane-bound enzymes that utilize acyl-CoAs as their initial substrate with the C_2 unit being malonyl-CoA. For example, erucic acid is synthesized by the following sequence (Agrawal and Stumpf, 1985):

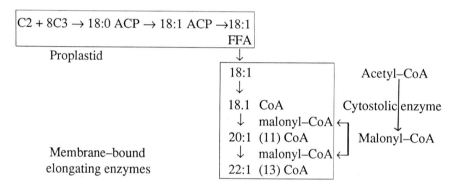

The elongating enzymes in the case of mustard or rapeseed can utilize both oleoyl-CoA and stearoyl-CoA as substrates. Palmitoyl-CoA is inactive. At first glance, these results would be in conflict with the fact that the major fatty acid is erucic acid and not behenic acid. A closer examination of the scheme presented suggests a logical explanation for the data and argues strongly for the compartmental localization of sets of enzymes. Because erucic acid is the principal fatty acid formed, saturated acyl-CoAs must be excluded in the cell from the elongating system. We can suggest that although stearoyl-ACP is rapidly formed as outlined above, because of the high activity of both the stearoyl-ACP desaturase and the oleoyl-ACP hydrolase, only free oleic acid is synthesized; stearoyl-CoA never is formed. Moreover, any palmitic acid that may be channelled away from the C_2 and C_3 de novo system is not elongated to $C_{18} \rightarrow C_{20} \rightarrow C_{22}$ because it is inactive as substrate. In this manner, the *Brassica* cell guarantees the synthesis of 20:1(11) and 22:1(13) fatty acids. Moreover, the elongation systems that convert 18:1(9) to 20:1(11) differs from the 20:1(11) $\rightarrow$ 22:1(13) systems in that the former has no marked preferences for NADPH or NADH whereas the latter exhibits a pronounced preference for NADH. Thus, there may be two different reductases involved although all the other enzymes required for the elongation process may be the same (Agrawal and Stumpf, 1985).

In contrast, the leek epidermis is the site for the synthesis of the normal, saturated cuticular hydrocarbons (C_{29}, C_{31}). Cassagne and Lessire have analyzed this system in some detail. With recent work, a fairly detailed picture emerges.

Microsomes prepared from leek epidermal tissue readily elongate stearoyl-CoA to very long chain fatty acid with malonyl-CoA as the C_2 unit. Palmitoyl, stearoyl, and higher saturated acyl-CoAs are readily elongated by the microsomal system but oleoyl-CoA is ineffective; however, the higher monounsaturated acyl-CoAs can be elongated. Since the very long chain fatty acids of the leek epidermis are all saturated, it would appear that the reaction controlling the nature of the final acyl product is the inactivity of oleoyl-CoA as a substrate. There is no evidence that acyl carrier protein participates in the elongation reactions. Evidence also suggests that (a) there may be two elongation systems, one responsible for the conversion of stearoyl-CoA to arachidoyl-CoA and the second involved in the conversion of arachidoyl-CoA to very long chain fatty acids, and that (b) the elongation activities may be associated with a large polypeptide.

In summary, two elongating systems have been examined, one in the cotyledonous cell of the developing *Brassica* seed, the other in the epidermal cells of the leek leaves. Both are membranous systems; both employ acyl-CoAs as the acceptor unit and malonyl-CoA as the donating C_2 unit and both control the final product by the specificity of the elongating enzymes. With the *Brassica* system, the acceptor molecule is oleoyl-CoA and with the leek, it is palmitoyl or stearoyl-CoA.

Synthesis of Medium Chain Fatty Acids -

A Problem of Termination

The oleochemical industry has a large requirement for the medium chain fatty acid, lauric. This acid is an important starting material in the manufacture of detergents.

Two sources of lauric acid are from coconut oil and palm kernel oil, both of which have about 45% of their fatty acids as lauric acid. A dramatic new source of medium chain fatty acids is from the *Cuphea* species, an annual that can be grown in temperate zone climates. The seed lipids contain unusually high amounts of medium chain fatty acids, depending on the species of the plant. Lauric acid predominates in 43% of the species composing of from 50 to 75% of the total fatty acids and decanoic acid dominates in 32% of the species studied composing as much as 87% of the total fatty acid content.

Although much is now known about the factors that control the synthesis of C_{16}, C_{18} fatty acids as well as their high homologues, very little is known about the biosynthesis of the medium chain fatty acids.

In animal systems, there is now good information about the synthesis of short chain fatty acids in mammary tissues. A specific thioesterase clips the lengthening fatty acid chain at appropriate lengths leading to the accumulation of C_4, C_6, and C_8 fatty acids. In plants, however, the mechanism for the termination of fatty acid synthesis is not well defined.

The following mechanisms have been proposed but no evidence has as yet been presented to support any of these; (a) a specific thioesterase that hydrolyzes lauroyl-ACP/CoA to form lauric acid, (b) a specific acyl-transacylase that transfers lauroyl-ACP to a suitable acceptor leading ultimately to a triacylglycerol rich in lauric acid, (c) controlled β-oxidation leading to a stepwise breakdown of palmitic to myristic to lauric acid, and (d) separate compartmental synthetases one of which is limited to the synthesis of medium chain fatty acids.

There are, however, two mechanisms which do introduce perturbations of fatty acid synthesis leading to the formation of medium chain fatty acids. One is the observation that if acetyl-CoA:ACP transacetylase activity is increased from its normal low rate-limiting level to high levels in reconstituted fatty acid synthetase systems, then the medium chain fatty acids accumulate in rather significant levels. The other mechanism involves the increase of malonyl-CoA levels. When these are raised to high levels, a dramatic shift from shorter chain fatty acids to longer chain fatty acids occurs. These results are of a kinetic nature.

Whatever the nature of the mechanisms involved, once the precise mechanism is determined, plant molecular biologists will be able to reconstruct plant fatty acid synthetase systems to the needs of industry.

Synthesis of Unique Fatty Acids

Nature produces a large number of rather exotic lipids, the physiological function of which is not at all known. Examples are ricinoleic acid, and a combination of fatty acids and alcohols in the jojoba lipids. Many other acids can be cited but limitation of space permits only a brief reference to these examples.

Ricinoleic acid is the predominant acid in the castor bean lipid. Its synthesis involves a proplastid to generate oleic acid and a membrane-bound hydroxylase which inserts a hydroxyl function in the 12th carbon of oleic acid. One can then demonstrate the synthesis of this interesting acid by employing an extract rich in proplastids and microsomes and radioactive acetate with suitable cofactors.

The jojoba wax esters are unique in the plant world. The desert shrub, *Simmondsia chinensis*, is the source of the bean which has as its sole storage lipid 40 to 44 carbon wax esters; no trace of triacyl glycerols can be detected. The mechanism for the synthesis of these wax esters have been elucidated in recent years. There is good evidence that the sucrose synthesized in the leaf cell is transported to the developing seed there to be converted to pyruvic acid which then enters the proplastid to undergo changes in the exact manner described for seed proplastids (Pollard et al. 1979).

The principal product of the jojoba proplastid of the developing seed is free oleic acid. The pathway of synthesis is as described above. This acid is then translocated to the cytosolic compartment there to be converted to oleoyl-CoA:

$$\text{Oleic acid} + \text{ATP} + \text{CoA} \xleftrightarrow{\text{Acyl-CoA synthetase}} \text{Oleoyl-CoA} + \text{AMP} + \text{PP}$$

18:1(9) CoA is now elongated with malonyl-CoA as the elongating unit to form 20:1(11) CoA and 22:1(13) CoA by a specific elongating system.

Now each of these elongation products is reduced:

$$20:1(11) \text{ CoA} + 2\text{NADPH} \xleftrightarrow{\text{reductase}} 20:1(11) \text{ alcohol}$$

$$22:1(13) \text{ CoA} + 2\text{NADPH} \xleftrightarrow{\text{reductase}} 22:1(13) \text{ alcohol}$$

The alcohols and the acyl-CoAs now combine in the presence of a membrane-condensing enzyme to form C_{40} to C_{44} wax esters.

A GENERAL THEME

By now the reader should have noticed a common theme that repeats itself. In Figure 3.4, this theme is further clarified. We have two compartments called the synthesizing compartment and the modifying compartment. Each compartment has its battery of enzymes. The synthesizing compartment can be either a chloroplast, the site of C_{16} and C_{18} fatty acid synthesis in the leaf cell or a proplastid, the site of synthesis in developing seeds and mesocarp tissue. Both compartments have essentially identical sets of fatty acid synthase enzymes (see Table 3.2) and both synthesize oleic acid as their main fatty acid. They differ in that with chloroplast, the source of ATP, O_2 and NADPH is generated via the non-cyclic photophosphorylation system whereas in proplastids, these important components are generated by a combination of the glycolytic and pentose phosphate pathways. It is assumed that O_2 diffuses in from the exterior. Once oleic acid is formed, it is then transported to the modifying compartment at which site the plant has its unique modifying reactions. Thus, in the case of the castor bean seed, the proplastid generates oleic acid which is then modified to form ricinoleic acid. The modifying reaction is a hydroxylation. In the case of the synthesis of eicosenoic acid or erucic acid, once again the proplastid of the seed forms oleic acid which is transported into the modifying compartment for elongation to the appropriate chain length. The modifying reaction involves the elongating enzymes. With the jojoba seed, once again oleic acid is exported to the cytosol where three modifying reactions occur, namely, elongation to 20:1(11) and 22:1

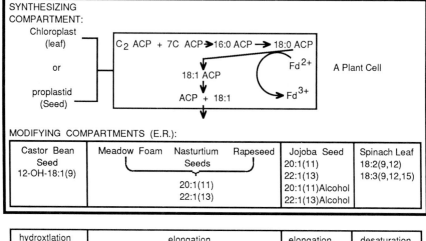

Fig. 3.4   A general scheme that illustrates the central role of oleic acid in the synthesis of a number of important fatty acids.

(13), reduction to the corresponding primary alcohols and condensation to form the wax esters. Finally in the leaf cell, the only modification that oleic acid requires is a Δ^{12} and a Δ^{15} desaturation which presumably occurs in the cytosolic compartment in association with the endoplasmic reticulum.

Triglycerides are the end products of commercial interest. Their synthesis is catalyzed by membrane-bound acyl transferases and associated with the endoplasmic reticulum.

Some years ago, it was shown that in avocado mesocarp the so-called Kennedy pathway (animal systems) is responsible for the synthesis of triglycerides:

$$\text{Glycerol-3-phosphate} + 2\ \text{Acyl-CoA} \xrightarrow{\text{acyl transferase}} \text{Phosphatidic acid}$$

$$\text{Phosphatidic acid} + H_2O \xrightarrow{\text{phosphatase}} \text{Diacylglycerols} + PO_4$$

$$\text{Diacylglycerol} + \text{Acyl-CoA} \longrightarrow \text{Triacylglycerol} + \text{CoA}$$

Superimposed on this system is an additional step that has been demonstrated in safflower seeds in which an apparent acyl exchange occurs:

$$\text{1-acyl, 2-acyl phosphatidyl choline} + \text{acyl*CoA} \longleftrightarrow$$
$$\text{1-acyl, 2-acyl* phosphatidyl choline} + \text{acyl CoA}$$

In this manner, the diacylglycerol pool is enriched with polyunsaturated acyl components. Probably a combination of the two systems participates in the formation of triacylglycerols in high oil seeds and in mesocarp tissue.

Thus, we can now essentially predict the mechanisms involved in synthesizing and modifying C_{16} and C_{22} fatty acids. As with all generalizations, however, there are always exceptions to the rule. With the framework established in Figures 3.2, 3.3, and 3.4, the next generation of biochemists can fill in, modify and alter this framework so that eventually the molecular biologist and the breeder can make rational rather than random modifications of oil crop plants.

REFERENCES

Agrawal, V.P., and Stumpf, P.K. 1985. Elongation systems involved in the biosynthesis of erucic acid from oleic acid in developing *Brassica juncea* seeds. Lipids 20: 331-397.

Cseke, C., Balogh, A., Wong, J.H., Buchanan, B.B., Stitt, M., Herzog, B., and Heldt, H.W. 1984. Fructose 2,6 bisphospahte: A regulator of carbon processing in leaves. Trends Biochem. Sci. 9: 533-535.

Dennis, D.T., and Miernyk, J.A. 1982. Compartmentation of non-photosynthetic carbohydrate metabolism, pp. 27-50. *In* W.R. Briggs (ed.), Annu. Rev. of Plant Physiol. 33: 27-50. Annual Reviews Inc., Palo Alto, Calif.

Eastwell, K.C., and Stumpf, P.K. 1983. Regulation of plant acetyl-CoA carboxylase by adenylate nucleotides. Plant Physiol. 72: 50-55.

Egin-Buhler, B., Loyal, R., and Ebel, J. 1980. Comparison of acetyl-CoA carboxylase from parsley cell cultures and wheat germ. Arch. Biochem. Biophys. 203: 90-100.

Finlayson, S., and Dennis, D.T. 1984. Personal Communication.

Gurr, M.I. 1974. The biosynthesis of unsaturated fatty acids, pp. 181-235. *In* T.W. Goodwin (ed.), Biochemistry of Lipids 4: 181-235. Butterworths, London.

Matsumura, S., and Stumpf, P.K. 1968. Partial primary structure of spinach acyl carrier protein. Arch. Biochem. Biophys. 125: 932-941.

McKeon, T.A., and Stumpf, P.K. 1982. Purification and characterization of stearoyl-acyl carrier protein desaturase and the acyl-acyl carrier protein thioesterase from maturing seed of safflower. J. Biol. Chem. 257: 12141-12147.

Newcomb, E.H., and Stumpf, P.K. 1953. Fat metabolism in higher plants. I. Biogenesis of higher fatty acids by slices of peanut cotyledons in vitro. J. Biol. Chem. 200: 233-239.

Ohlrogge, J.B., Pollard, M.R., and Stumpf, P.K. 1978. Studies on the biosynthesis of waxes by developing jojoba seed tissue. Lipids 13: 203-210.

——, Kuhn, D.N., and Stumpf, P.K. 1979. Subcellular localization of acyl carrier protein in leaf protoplasts of *Spinacia oleracea*. Proc. Natl. Acad. Sci. (USA) 76: 1194-1198.

Overath, P., and Stumpf, P.K. 1964. Properties of a soluble fatty acid synthetase from avocado mesocarp. J. Biol. Chem. 239: 4103-4110.

Pollard, M.R., McKeon, T.A., Gupta, L.M., and Stumpf, P.K. 1979. Studies in the biosynthesis of waxes by develping jojoba seeds. II. The demonstration of wax biosynthesis by cell-free homogenates. Lipids 14: 651-662.

Roughan, P.G., and Slack, C.R. 1982. Cellular organization of glycerolipid metabolism. Annu. Rev. Plant Phyisiol. 33: 97-132.

Shimakata, T., and Stumpf, P.K. 1982. The procaryotic nature of the fatty acid synthetase of developing *Carthamus tinctorius* L. (safflower) seed. Arch. Biochem. Biophys. 217: 144-154.

———. 1983. The purification and function of acetyl-CoA: Acyl carrier protein transacylase. J. Biol. Chem. 258: 3592-3598.

Simcox, P.D., Reid, E.E., Canvin, D.T., and Dennis, D.T. 1977. Enzymes of the glycolytic and pnetose phosphate pathway in proplastids from the developing endosperm of *Ricinus communis* L. Plant Physiol. 59: 1128-1132.

Simoni, R.D., Criddle, R.S., and Stumpf, P.K. 1967. Purification and properties of plant and bacterial acyl carrier proteins. J. Biol. Chem. 242: 573-581.

Stumpf, P.K. 1984. Fatty Acid Biosynthesis in Higher Plants in Fatty Acid Metabolism and Its Regulation, pp. 155-180. S. Numa (ed.), Chapter 6. Elsevier, Amsterdam.

Wakil, S.J., Stoops, J.K., and Joshi, V.C. 1983. Fatty acid synthesis and its regulation. Annu. Rev. of Biochem. 52: 537-579.

Weaire, P.J., and Kekwick, R.G.O. 1975. The synthesis of fatty acids in avocado mesocarp and cauliflower bud tissue. Biochem. J. 146: 425-437.

Yamada, M., and Stumpf, P.K. 1964. Enzymic synthesis of ricinoleic acid by extracts of developing *Ricinus communis* seeds. Biochem. Biophys. Res. Commun. 14: 165-171.

Zilkey, B.F., and Canvin, D.T. 1969. Subcellular localization of oleic acid biosynthesis enzymes in the developing castor bean endosperm. Biochem. Biophys. Res. Commun. 34: 646-653.

Chapter 4

Nutritional Characteristics and Food Uses of Vegetable Oils

R.O. Vles and J. J. Gottenbos

INTRODUCTION

There is a growing awareness of the importance of oils and fats in human nutrition. The period during which dietary lipids were considered only as a means for making food tastier, as a source of energy and a vehicle for fat soluble vitamins, has come to an end. Vegetable oils can make an important contribution to the balanced fatty acid composition of the total fat consumed. Research findings during the last decades have revealed the involvement of some important vegetable oil constituents in the structure of cells and tissue and in the metabolic regulation of vital processes.

Vegetable oil sources account for about 70% of the world's edible fat production, the rest coming from animal fats (ca. 30%) and marine oils (ca. 2%). Trends in production of edible oils have shown a steady increase over the last decades. The available quantities are still insufficient to adequately feed the world's present population. Man's need for more food and more adequate food has actively and successfully stimulated the development of new plant breeding techniques and has led to many improvements in fat processing. These achievements have contributed to an increase in the availability of these relatively cheap food items and to an improvement in their quality in the sense of taste, physical properties and aspects related to health and prevention of diseases.

FUNCTIONS OF DIETARY FATS

Humans derive their energy from the three major nutrients, protein, fat and carbohydrate. Of these energy sources, fat has the highest available energy density, 9 kcal (38 kJ)/g as compared with 4 kcal (17 kJ)/g for protein and carbohydrate. The diets of most countries provide an average of about 11% of calories from protein. For most parts of the world, the non-protein dietary energy is about 90% of the total and comes from fat and carbohydrate. In most developed countries, average energy intakes from dietary fat currently range from 35 to 45 energy percent (en%). In many developing countries, intakes of 10 to 20 en% of fat or less are common. Thus on a global basis, there could be an approximately six-fold difference in the fraction of energy that is derived from fat by various populations.

In developing countries with dietary fat comprising about 10 en%, there is evidence that an increase to 15 to 20 en% of fat would have beneficial effects. Such an increase will raise the energy density of the diet and help to satisfy the energy needs. Until a decade ago, it was widely believed that malnutrition, especially childhood malnutrition, was due primarily to insufficiency of protein in the diet. There is now adequate evidence to show that the most limiting factor is not protein, but energy. Especially as young children cannot cope with the bulk of unrefined carbohydrate-rich food products in order to have an adequate energy intake, a higher fat concentration can solve that problem. If of the right composition, this also will improve their borderline intake of essential fatty acids, which will improve their resistance to infectious diseases.

Dietary fats also make meals tastier and add satiety value, they act as carriers for, and facilitate the absorption of vitamins A, D, E and K. They have to provide the organisms with sufficient essential fatty acids which form indispensable elements in all cell membranes and from which metabolic regulators, the eicosanoids (prostaglandins, leukotrienes and other hydroxy fatty acids) are made. By choosing wisely from the available dietary fat which differ widely in fatty acid composition, a balanced fatty acid composition of the total diet can be achieved.

COMPOSITION OF OILS AND FATS

Structure of Fatty Acids

Dietary fats are mainly (98 to 99%) triacylglycerols (triglycerides), the most important of the remaining components being sterols, flavouring substances, and vitamins A, D and E. The triacylglycerols are made up of one glycerol molecule and three fatty acid molecules (Fig. 4.1).

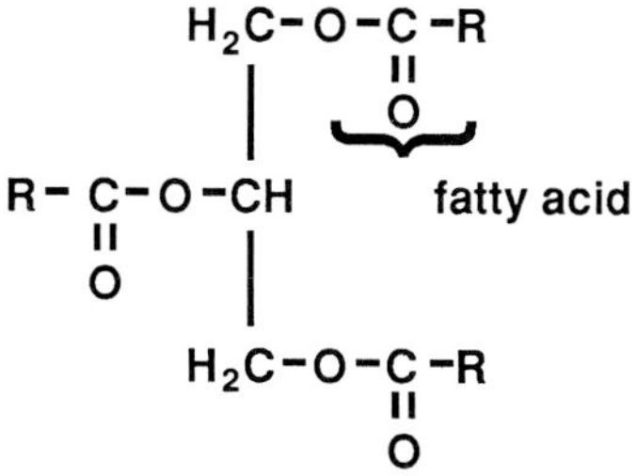

$$H_2C-O-C-R$$
$$O$$

$$R-C-O-CH \quad \text{fatty acid}$$
$$O$$

$$H_2C-O-C-R$$
$$O$$

triacylglycerol

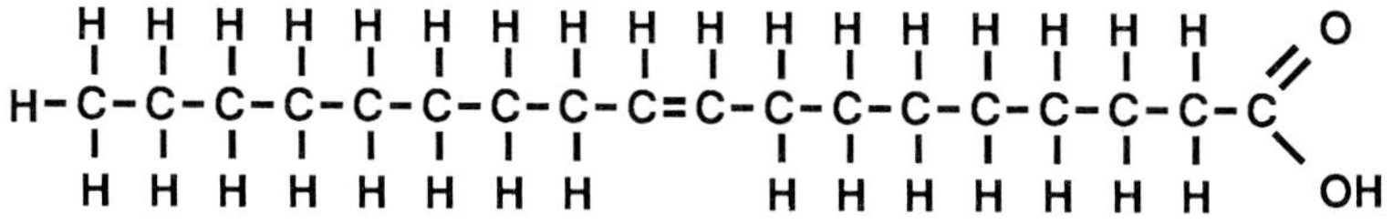

oleic acid

Fig. 4.1 Structural formula of triacylglycerol and, as an example of a fatty acid, that of oleic acid.

The fatty acids differ in number of carbon atoms and/or number of double bonds in the chain (Fig. 4.2). They are divided into saturated fatty acids, without double bonds, monounsaturated fatty acids and polyunsaturated fatty acids. The position of the double bonds in the carbon chain of the unsaturated fatty acids is important for their physiological action. There are three common families of unsaturated fatty acids, the n-3, n-6 and n-9.

In linoleic and arachidonic acid the first double bond is between the 6th and 7th carbon atom counting from the terminal CH_3-group (indicated as n-6). The other double bonds in linoleic- and arachidonic acid are always three carbon atoms further, so in linoleic acid at position 9 and in arachidonic acid at positions 9, 12 and 15. Linoleic acid with eighteen carbon atoms and two double bonds is therefore represented as C18:2(n-6, 9) and arachidonic acid with twenty carbon atoms and four double bonds as C20:4(n-6,9,12,15); these fatty acids belong to the so-called n-6 family of the polyunsaturated fatty acids. In linolenic acid, eicosapentaenoic acid and docosahexeanoic acid the first double bond is between the 3rd and 4th carbon atom (n-3). The other double bonds are likewise three carbon atoms further. So linolenic is designated as C18:3(n-3,6,9), eicosapentaenoic acid as C20:5(n-3,6,9,12,15) and docosahexaenoic acid as C22:6(n-3,6,9,12,15,18); they belong to the n-3 family.

In oleic and erucic acid the double bond is between the 9th and 10th carbon atom (n-9). From oleic acid the organism can synthesize a non-essential

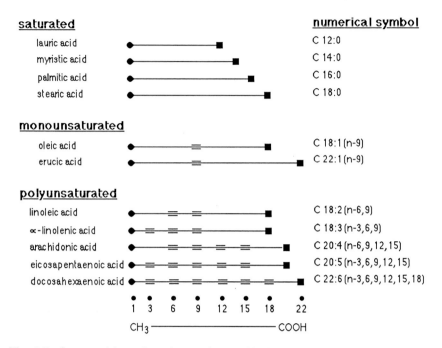

Fig. 4.2 Structural formulae of some fatty acids. The numerical symbol after the 'C' indicates the number of carbon atoms and the number of double bonds; the position of the double bond is given between brackets. The carbon atoms are numbered from the terminal CH₃ - group. This numbering clearly indicates the various "families" of unsaturated fatty acids (similar position of the double bond with respect to the terminal CH₃ - group). According to the IUPAC rules which are used in the chemical literature, the carbon atoms are numbered from the COOH - group.

polyunsaturated fatty acid with twenty carbon atoms and three double bonds at positions 9,12,15 (C20:3, n-9,12,15; see section Essential Fatty Acids and Eicosanoids).

The unsaturated fatty acids oleic, linoleic and linolenic acid are elongated and desaturated in the organism by the same enzyme systems. These have the highest affinity for the n-3 family.

Fatty Acid Composition of Oils and Fats

The majority of vegetable oils contain large amounts of unsaturated fatty acids with eighteen carbon atoms e.g. olive oil about 75% oleic acid and 10% linoleic acid, peanut oil about 50% oleic acid and 30% linoleic acid, corn oil about 55% linoleic and 30% oleic acid, and sunflower seed oil about 65% linoleic acid and 20% oleic acid. In most vegetable oils, the monounsaturated fatty acids consist almost entirely of oleic acid. An exception is the traditional rapeseed oil variety which in addition to the 15% oleic acid contains 30 to 50% of erucic acid, a C22:1 fatty acid. In the new low erucic acid rapeseed oils, the contents of saturated fatty acids are even lower than those of soybean and peanut oils, oleic acid is as high as in olive oil, linolenic acid is as high as in soybean oil; the levels of linoleic acid are intermediate compared to other oils.

The polyunsaturated fatty acids in the vegetable oils usually consist almost entirely of linoleic acid, the most important essential fatty acid; the main exceptions are soybean oil with about 55% linoleic acid and 7% linolenic acid, rapeseed oil with about 20% linoleic acid and 10% linolenic acid, and particularly linseed oil with about 15% linoleic acid and 55% linolenic acid.

A few vegetable fats, namely coconut, palm-kernel and palm oil, contain large amounts of saturated fatty acids: coconut and palm-kernel oil about 15% short- and medium-chain fatty acids with 4 to 10 carbon atoms, 50% lauric acid and 15% myristic acid. Palm oil contains about 50% palmitic acid.

The animal fats (except the marine oils) contain large amounts of saturated fatty acids: beef tallow about 55% (of which 30% palmitic and 20% stearic acid), butterfat more than 60% (of which 25% palmitic, 10% stearic and 12% myristic acid and also 10% short- and medium-chain fatty acids). Marine oils contain, apart from 10 to 30% palmitic acid , 20 to 50% fatty acids with a long-chain and many double bonds, such as fatty acids with twenty carbon atoms and 4 or 5 double bonds and fatty acids with twenty-two carbon atoms with 5 or 6 double bonds which belong to the n-3 family of the polyunsaturated fatty acids. Linoleic acid is found only in very small quantities in fish.

It should be realized that the fatty acid composition of given oils and fats is variable and depends on the strain and climate, e.g. the linoleic acid content of corn oil ranges from 35 to 60% and of peanut oil from 20 to over 40%. The main composition of the oils and fats is given in Table 4.1.

In practice, dependent on type of fatty acid predominating in a fat, people talk of saturated, monounsaturated and polyunsaturated fats; however, as discussed above, a fat never consists of only saturated or monounsaturated or polyunsaturated fatty acids, but is characterized by the various contents of these fatty acids (Table 4.1).

Food Uses of Vegetable Oils

Edible oils are used for different purposes. In warmer climates they are largely used as such for cooking. In the more temperate Western world, they are consumed for a considerable part in spreadable form, their main use being in the form of margarine. Vegetable oils are also used in the manufacture of cooking fats and oils, salad dressings, confectionery fats and ice cream.

The fatty acid composition of margarines differs widely; the content of polyunsaturated fatty acids for instance, varies between 5 and 65%, depending on the oils and fats used and on their technological processing.

Table 4.1 Fatty Acid Composition (%) of Some Important Dietary Fats

Fat type and source	Saturated	Mono-unsaturated	Polyunsaturated total	Polyunsaturated linoleic
"Saturated" fats				
butter	63	33	4	1
beef	55	41	4	2
lard	43	47	10	9
coconut oil	90	8	2	2
palm oil	50	39	11	10
"Monounsaturated" fats				
olive oil	17	73	10	10
groundnut	18	52	30	30
rapeseed oil	6	67	27	17
"Polyunsaturated" fats				
maize oil	15	30	55	55
soybean oil	16	24	60	53
sunflowerseed oil	12	21	67	67
safflower oil	10	15	75	75
fish oils*	20-35	20-55	20-50	1
e.g. herring oil	20	55	25	1

*Fish oils differ considerably depending on the type of fish

    To obtain a spreadable product, liquid oils are mixed with higher melting fats; these can also be obtained from liquid oils by means of the so-called hardening process. During this process part of the unsaturated fatty acids are changed into saturated fatty acids, and some double bonds in the unsaturated fatty acids change their position and/or stereochemical configuration from the *cis* to the *trans* form. *Trans* fatty acids are also found in nature either as short-lived intermediates in biochemical pathways or in some seed oils and in fats from ruminants (e.g. cows, sheep, goats) where they are produced by bacterial hydrogenation of dietary unsaturated fatty acids in the rumen (Sommerfeld, 1983).

    By reducing the degree of unsaturation, the hardening process raises the melting point of the oil and decreases its susceptibility to oxidative deterioration. The *trans* fatty acids produced do not differ from those produced by the microflora of ruminants.

    Interesterification in addition to blending, fractionation (including winterization) and hardening, has also contributed to the widening range of uses of vegetable oils and fats and to making the various oils more interchangeable in their application. During interesterification, the fatty acids, which together with glycerol make up the molecules of fats, interchange position. In this way it is possible to modify the melting characteristics of fats or mixtures of fats without changing the fatty acid composition of the blend, thereby enabling a more efficient use of practically every commercial oil.

THE DAILY INTAKE OF FAT AND FATTY ACIDS

In the prosperous countries, the average daily fat intake is about 100 to 300 g per person; this is more than 40% of the total amount of calories (over 40 en%). Half or less of this total fat intake consists of the so-called visible fat (butter, margarine, edible oil, cooking fat) and the remaining part is defined as invisible fat. The majority of invisible fat comes from dairy and other animal fats such as milk, meat, meat products and cheese, and the rest mainly from pastry, snacks, bread and nuts. Although some fish is rich in fat, the total contribution to the average diet is small. Figure 4.3 gives, as an example, the average fat and fatty acid intake in Western Germany.

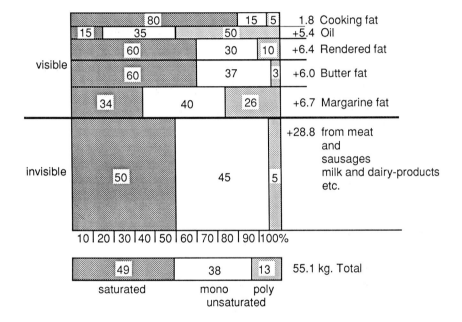

Fig. 4.3 Fat consumption (1982) in Western Germany (kg per person per year) and fatty acid composition of the consumed fats. 55.1 kg/year = 151.0 g/day = 39 en%. Note the high proportion of invisible fats.

The usual fatty acid composition of the total dietary fat is over 50% saturated fatty acids, 40% monounsaturated fatty acids and less than 10% polyunsaturated fatty acids. These are average values; individual values will diverge considerably, dependent on the ratio visible/invisible fat and the choice and availability of the foods, especially of the visible fat type (Table 4.1). The composition of the invisible fats from dairy products, meat and meat products is fairly constant; the amount, however, may vary strongly (compare high-fat and low-fat products).

All dairy and meat products contain about 50% saturated fatty acids and only small amounts of linoleic acid, viz. in products of bovine origin less than 2% and in those from the pig about 10%, dependent on the pig's diet. The fatty acid composition of fish varies widely, dependent on the type of fish (Table 4.1). The amount of fat in fish likewise varies considerably; in the case of fish like plaice, sole and trout (low-fat content), the nature of the fat in which the fish is fried is more important than that of the fish as such. The fatty acid composition of the fat from snacks, pastry and such foods similarly depends on the type of fat which has been used for their preparation.

NUTRITIVE VALUE OF OILS AND FATS

The nutritional effects of edible oils with respect to absorption, growth and food efficiency and their safety in use received the early attention of many investigators.

Digestibility

Within the digestive tract, long-chain triacylglycerols (14 to 18 carbon atoms) are split by pancreatic lipase into 2-monoacylglycerol and free fatty acids. These fatty particles are emulsified by bile salts to form micelles that are absorbed by the gut wall. After resynthesis to triacylglycerols within the intestinal cells, the fat passes to the lymphatic system in the form of globules known an chylomicrons. From the lymphatic system the chylomicrons pass into the bloodstream to be transported to the various tissues to provide energy by oxidative combustion. Surplus fat is deposited in the adipose tissue. Short- and medium-chain triacylglycerols (ten carbon atoms and shorter) have a greater water solubility. They are absorbed largely as free fatty acids which leave the intestinal cells and, via the portal vein, reach the liver without necessitating the formation of chylomicrons. The particular physical and physiological properties of medium-chain triacylglycerols make them of interest in the nutritional and therapeutic treatment of patients with fat maldigestion and malabsorption (Sickinger, 1975). Short- and medium-chain fatty acids are rapidly absorbed.

The most important physical parameter of a fat that influences its digestibility under physiological conditions is its melting point. All usual vegetable oils and hardened and/or interesterified blends with a melting point below 50° are virtually completely digested by humans. Although chain length, degree of saturation, and the position of the fatty acid on the glycerol molecule have effects on its digestibility, these effects are of no practical significance in daily nutrition. In a usual diet, it is the melting characteristic of the mixture of all fats present that determines the digestibility, the low melting fat improving the digestibility of the high melting fat.

Effects on Growth and Food Efficiency; Safety in Use

Many animal experiments have been conducted on the comparative nutritive value of oils and fats. Considerable effort has been spent in testing vegetable oils for their effects on growth, food efficiency, and for their safety (Mattson, 1983; Gottenbos and Visek, 1983). These studies disclosed no major differences in the nutritive value of the common vegetable oils. The same applies to processed oils. Specific physiological effects for *trans* fatty acids formed during the hardening process of edible oils, relative to saturated and *cis*-monounsaturated fatty acids, have not been demonstrated as discussed in three recent reviews (Beare-Rogers, 1983; Emken, 1983; Gottenbos, 1983).

Likewise, the other processing steps in use (refining, fractionation, interesterification) have not been shown to affect the wholesomeness of vegetable oils. In fact, proper processing may improve the safety in use of unrefined oils by removing natural or human-made toxicants, e.g. aflatoxin, cyclopropenoid fatty acids, pesticides or other environmental hazards (Mattson, 1973, 1983).

High erucic acid rapeseed oil constitutes an exception to the concept of equal nutritive value for all vegetable oil products. When fed in large amounts to experimental animals, this oil was shown to retard growth and to induce changes in various organs. These detrimental effects were attributed to erucic acid and stimulated plant breeders to search for genetic variation in this component. Rapeseed cultivars that are practically devoid of erucic acid have been successfully developed. Although high erucic acid rapeseed oil has never been shown to be a hazard to human health, it was felt prudent to effect a changeover to new, low erucic acid varieties. Most animal species fed the low erucic acid rapeseed oils performed as well as control animals fed other oils (Kramer and Sauer, 1983). Today, practically all edible rapeseed is of the low erucic type and it ranks fourth in the world production of edible vegetable oils providing 8% of total oil production (Downey, 1983).

As will be discussed in sections on diet and atherosclerosis and cardiovascular diseases, diets with reduced levels of saturated fatty acids and increased levels of linoleic acid are recommended for the prevention of coronary heart disease. However, some reservations have been expressed about the safety of these diets. Generally speaking, polyunsaturated fatty acids are susceptible to oxidation resulting in the formation of lipid peroxides. Peroxides can be formed in fats and oils during storage at room temperature. Peroxides formed in the fat before it is eaten are poorly absorbed by the intestinal tract. But peroxides could also be formed in biological tissues. It has been suggested that lipid peroxidation in vivo is related to free radical initiation and carcinogenesis. It should be stressed that polyunsaturated fatty acids are essential components of cell membranes. In the absence of dietary polyunsaturated fatty acids, non-essential polyunsaturated fatty acids are synthesized and incorporated into cell membranes. Therefore, membranes always contain polyunsaturated fatty acids. Uncontrolled peroxidation and free radical initiation do not normally occur in vivo since living tissues are amply supplied with protective mechanisms and structure which prevent the formation of excessive peroxides (Dormandy, 1983). One of these devices is the natural antioxidant α-tocopherol or Vitamin E. High intakes of polyunsaturated fatty acids increase the vitamin E requirements. Fortunately, the linoleic acid-rich oils are the richest natural dietary sources of vitamin E and this advantage is retained after proper processing (McLaughlin and Weirauch, 1979). So, diets containing the recommended levels of linoleic acid supply a more than adequate amount of vitamin E (Mattson, 1973; Bieri and Poukka Evarts, 1975). Heating oils and fats, e.g. deep-frying, also leads to the formation of oxidized compounds. Abusively heated fats may contain compounds which are toxic when fed at high levels. However, under these extreme conditions, the oils are organoleptically unacceptable. In normal household or commercial practice the amounts formed of these compounds do not reach levels that cause concern (Sinkeldam et al. 1983). The polyunsaturated fatty acids from fish oils (linolenic- or n-3 family), however, are more unsaturated than linoleic acid and more prone to oxidation both in vitro and in vivo. Furthermore, they are not naturally accompanied by high levels of vitamin E. Therefore, diets rich in this type of polyunsaturated fatty acids increase the risk of unwanted oxidative changes (Hornstra et al. 1983; Bijster and Vles, 1984). In man, no evidence has been found of an association between cancer mortality and intake of unsaturated fat (Carroll and Khor, 1975; Lewis, 1983).

Animals fed a high-saturated fat diet containing 3% linoleic acid developed as many chemically induced tumors as those fed a diet containing 20% sunflower-seed oil, with 13% linoleic acid. This illustrates that once the diet covers a basic requirement of essential fatty acids for tissue growth, no further promotion of chemically induced tumors occurs with higher linoleic acid intakes (Hopkins et al. 1981).

The amount of dietary fat has also been suggested as a factor promoting carcinogenesis (Carroll and Khor, 1975). However, it remains unclear whether the enhancing effects of high amounts of fats on chemically induced cancer in rats is due to an increased caloric availability or the consequence of a specific fat effect (Pariza, 1984).

ESSENTIAL FATTY ACIDS AND EICOSANOIDS

The classical experiments by Burr and Burr demonstrated the great importance of a specific group of polyunsaturated fatty acids, the essential fatty acids (EFA). The animal organism is able to synthesize many fatty acids but not the EFA, which have to be obtained from the diet. Young rats fed a diet without EFA develop a great many symptoms ranging from the classical signs of reduced growth rate and skin lesions to more recently recognized symptoms of decreased prostaglandin synthesis and abnormal thrombocyte aggregation (Vergroesen, 1976). All these symptoms disappear, or can be prevented, by feeding relatively small amounts of EFA. Only the polyunsaturated fatty acids of the n-6 family, namely linoleic acid and the fatty acids derived from it (e.g. arachidonic acid), can cure or prevent all symptoms. EFA have been shown to be indispensable for many other species including man.

The FAO/WHO recommendations (FAO/WHO, 1977) state that the minimum intake of linoleic acid required to prevent the EFA deficiency syndrome is 3 en%. Since the requirements for linoleic acid are higher in pregnancy and lactation, this value is raised to 4.5 en% in pregnancy and 5 to 7 en% in lactation. The diversity of the symptoms of the essential fatty acid deficiency syndrome suggests a very important role of linoleic acid in most cells and organs. It is therefore regrettable that until a relatively short time ago no attention was paid to the equally important aspect of the optimum amounts of linoleic acid in the diet.

In the body, particularly in the liver, the linoleic acid taken up with the diet is partly converted to arachidonic acid. This bioconversion proceeds via γ-linolenic acid (C18:3, n-6,9,12) and dihomo-γ-linolenic acid (C20:3, n-6,9,12). Linoleic acid and particularly arachidonic acid (the intermediary fatty acids occur only in small amount in the body) have a structural function as integral parts of the phospholipids which occur in all cell membranes. A sub-optimum amount of essential fatty acids in these membranes leads to a decreased integrity and fluidity of the membrane and consequently to decreased functioning of the cells. If the diet does not contain sufficient linoleic acid, the organism uses oleic acid to synthesize a polyunsaturated fatty acid with twenty carbon atoms and three double bonds at positions 9,12,15 or C20:3 n-9,12,15. This fatty acid is incorporated into the phospholipids of the membranes in an effort to retain the membrane integrity as much as possible.

The essential fatty acids not only have structural but also dynamic functions in serving as precursors of metabolic regulators, the eicosanoids.

The eicosanoids are formed from the C20 fatty acids synthesized from linoleic acid and incorporated into the membrane phospholipids: mainly arachidonic acid and to a much lesser extent dihomo-γ-linolenic acid (Figs. 4.4 and 4.5). The prostaglandins D, E, F, thromboxanes (TXA) and prostacyclin (PGI) are formed via the cyclo-oxygenase pathway (Fig. 4.4). The end product is dependent on the type of cell and organ, e.g. in the kidney mainly PGE_2 and $PGF_{2\alpha}$, in blood platelets mainly thromboxane A_2, TXA_2 and in the vessel wall prostacyclin I_2, PGI_2. Via the lipoxygenase pathways a series of leukotrienes and other hydroxy fatty acids are produced (Fig. 4.5).

In addition to the linoleic acid family or n-6 family of polyunsaturated fatty acids, there is also a linolenic acid or n-3 family. It is present as α-linolenic acid (C18:3, n-3,6,9) in some vegetable oils, in particular in linseed oil (55%) and to a smaller extent in soybean oil (7%), and as timnodonic or eicosapentaenoic acid (EPA: C20:5, n-3,6,9,12,15) in some fish oils at a level of about 10%. EPA from dietary sources or formed in the body from α-linolenic acid, is preferentially incorporated into the phospholipids at the expense of arachidonic acid. From this fatty acid, prostaglandins of the 3-series can be formed in vitro, e.g.

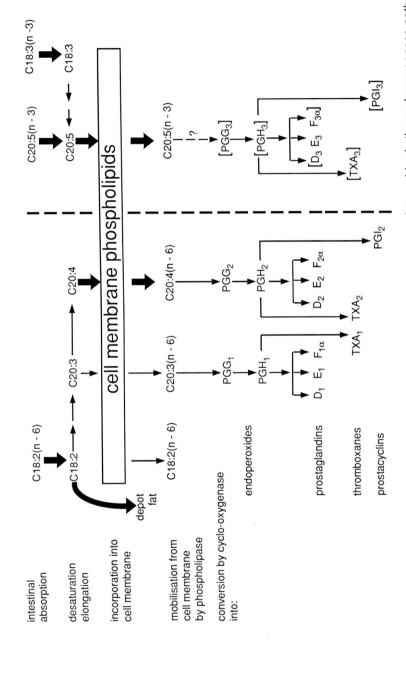

Fig. 4.4 Biosynthesis of prostaglandins and thromboxanes from dietary precursor fatty acids via the cyclo-oxygenase pathway.

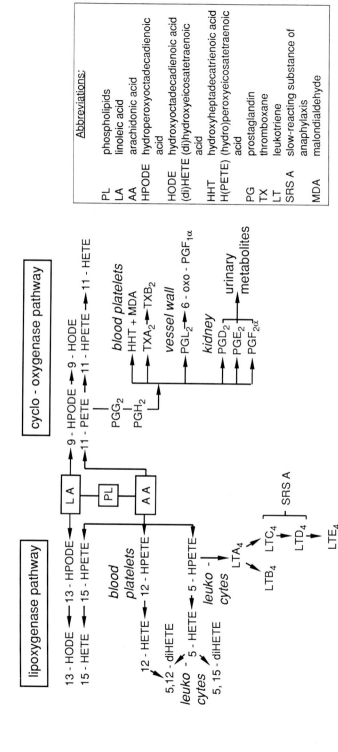

Fig. 4.5 Conversion of arachidonic acid into prostaglandins, thromboxanes, leukotrienes and hydroxy fatty acids and of linoleic acid into hydroxy fatty acids.

thromboxane A_3, TXA_3, and prostacyclin I_3, PGI_3. However, EPA is a much poorer substrate for the cyclo-oxygenase enzyme than arachidonic acid. The result of feeding rats substantial amounts of n-3 polyunsaturated fatty acids is a decreased availability of dihomo-γ-linolenic acid and arachidonic acid in the membrane phospholipids and, therefore, a greatly decreased production of prostaglandins of the 1- and 2-series whereas the generation of prostaglandins of the 3-series in vivo is negligible (Ten Hoor et al. 1980).

The different prostaglandins display a divergent degree of activity and often cause opposite effects. They influence the function of the central nervous system, the contractions of smooth muscles of intestines, lungs, blood vessels and reproductive organs. They also inhibit the mobilization of fatty acids from adipose tissue, influence blood pressure, the aggregation of blood platelets and cardiac function.

Leucocytes, lymphocytes, and platelets have different lipoxygenases, which produce various leukotrienes and other hydroxy fatty acids from arachidonic acid and EPA (which is a good substrate for lipoxygenase). These metabolites fulfil important roles in hypersensitivity reactions and inflammation and probably play a role in thrombosis (Dutilh et al. 1981). Claeys et al. (1982), reported that linoleic acid can also be converted via the lipoxygenase pathway to 13-HODE (hydroxyoctadecadienoic acid) and via the cyclo-oxygenase pathway to 9-HODE.

In summary, the n-3 and n-6 polyunsaturated fatty acids serve as substrates for the biosynthesis of a variety of different prostaglandins, hydroxy fatty acids and leukotrienes. Which types and how much of these compounds are produced depend in part on the composition of dietary fat. Many other factors also play a role in the synthesis of the eicosanoic precursors from the dietary fatty acids, their incorporation into cell membranes, their release from the membrane phospholipids and the conversion to eicosanoids.

The overall physiological effects of various dietary fatty acid compositions cannot be predicted from the results of studies on the metabolism and formation of eicosanoids in isolated cells, tissues and organs. From a nutritionist's point of view, a much more rewarding approach is to study the effects of various levels of saturated and polyunsaturated fatty acids on important degenerative conditions, e.g. atherosclerosis and its complications.

ATHEROSCLEROSIS AND ITS COMPLICATIONS

Atherosclerosis, a very common chronic degenerative disease of the arteries, is the underlying cause of most heart attacks and strokes (cardiovascular diseases). It is characterized by deposits of predominantly fatty substances, mainly cholesterol esters, in the innermost layer of the arterial wall (the intima). The gradually extending atherosclerotic lesions thicken the arterial wall, reducing the diameter of the lumen, thus hindering the flow of blood. This can even result in complete blockage of the artery. Total blockage, however, is usually due to blood clotting on the affected narrowed arterial wall. This phenomenon, known as thrombosis, starts with blood platelets adhesion and aggregation. Platelets are minute cells circulating in the blood stream. They have the ability to adhere to the walls of blood vessels and to each other. A thrombus is chiefly a solid mass of adhering platelets. This can be a very necessary process for it is one of the ways in which bleeding is stopped after an injury. But if it occurs on the atherosclerotic vessel wall, it can be harmful. Intra-arterial thrombosis is not only frequently responsible for the total blockage of the atherosclerotic arteries in heart, brain or kidneys, it might also be a primary factor in the early development of the atherosclerotic lesions.

This latter aspect has been strongly emphasized by Ross and Glomset (1976), who developed the best available picture of the origin of atherosclerosis. They envisage the following train of events. When the inner lining of the artery is injured in any way, platelets adhere to the damaged patch, forming a small thrombus. The platelets release a factor which stimulate proliferation of certain cells in the arterial wall, causing thickening of the wall. At the same time these changes facilitate the penetration of cholesterol esters from the blood into the arterial wall. Given sufficient time, this lesion can be repaired. However, if there are too many damaging factors (such as toxins from bacterial and viral infections, products of tobacco smoke or other chemicals, high blood pressure or a high content of blood cholesterol) or the frequency of the damaging factors is too high, the healing process is interrupted by the next injury. The cholesterol esters which are accumulated in the intima mainly come from the lipoproteins circulating in the blood, notably the so-called low-density lipoproteins (LDL).

Blood cholesterol and fat come partly from the diet, and are partly produced by the body. They do not dissolve in water. For this reason cholesterol and fat in the blood have to be transported in the form of minute particles, consisting of cholesterol esters, free cholesterol, triacylglycerols, phospholipids and a number of highly specific proteins. The proteins and phospholipids form, as it were, the boats in which the triacylglycerols and cholesterol travel.

These fat/protein particles are called lipoproteins and are divided on the basis of their density into four main classes; a) the chylomicrons, b) very low-density lipoproteins (VLDL), c) low-density lipoproteins (LDL), and d) high-density lipoproteins (HDL). The HDL and particularly the LDL are the principal cholesterol carriers in the blood.

All tissues in the body require some cholesterol. Most tissues, other than the liver, obtain their cholesterol supply chiefly by taking up LDL from the blood. The greater the LDL level in the blood the more of this cholesterol-rich substance enters the wall of the artery. Thus the LDL are the lipoproteins which transport the cholesterol into the arterial walls and hence the popular designation: "the bad cholesterol" for the LDL cholesterol.

The main function of the HDL is probably the transport of the excess cholesterol from the cells (arterial wall), the so-called garbage truck function, to the liver, where the cholesterol will be uncoupled and excreted via the bile, and to other organs such as adrenals, testes and ovaries for the production of adrenal and sex hormones. For these reasons HDL cholesterol is sometimes called "the good cholesterol." It has to be realized that in cases of elevated LDL levels in the blood, the HDL is no longer able to remove all the excess cholesterol. An elevated cholesterol concentration in the arterial wall ultimately leads to the atherosclerotic changes described.

According to the "filtration theory," lipoproteins (LDL) diffusing from the blood into the vessel wall can to a degree be trapped in the intima to a degree, depending on the concentration of the blood lipids, the arterial blood pressure and the permeability of the vessel wall. There are a number of other important risk factors associated with increased risk of developing the disease in subsequent years. Such factors include the time of exposure to the risk factors, genetic factors, excessive smoking, diabetes, overweight, stress and lack of physical exercise. These risk factors should be classified into three types according to whether they influence the LDL cholesterol content, the arterial wall or the thrombotic process. Moreover, the mechanism of action of these factors should be elucidated. In the case of smoking it is assumed that through carbon monoxide and nicotine the permeability of the vessel wall and the tendency to develop thrombosis are increased. Although the risk factor of genetic predisposition can not be influenced, other risk factors can be modified by changing the life style (change diet, stop smoking, more exercise) and/or by drugs (e.g. treatment of hypertension).

RELATION BETWEEN DIET AND CARDIOVASCULAR DISEASES

Lipoprotein Metabolism

Clinical, epidemiological and biochemical research has shown that an increased blood (LDL) cholesterol content is the main risk factor for cardiovascular disease caused by atherosclerosis and its complications. Epidemiological investigations have also shown that the frequency of coronary heart disease (CHD) and the blood cholesterol level are related to eating habits. For example, population groups with high coronary death rate invariably consume high-caloric diets characterized by a high level of saturated fats and cholesterol.

Moreover, about thirty years ago the type of diet, particularly the nature of the dietary fat, was found to raise or lower the blood cholesterol content in man and experimental animals. Since then numerous investigations have been carried out to ascertain the effect of different fatty acid compositions. In general, saturated fatty acids, especially lauric acid, myristic acid and palmitic acid, raise the blood cholesterol level. Linoleic acid has a reducing effect, whereas the monounsaturated fatty acids occupy a middle position (McGandy and Hegsted, 1975). After much confusion it has now been clearly demonstrated that the cholesterol in the human diet also raises the blood cholesterol content, although the degree may differ considerably between individuals depending on their genetic susceptibility.

Recently, it has been established in man that blood cholesterol-lowering reduces the incidence of coronary heart disease (Lipid Research Clinics Program, 1984). The results of numerous investigations have led a large number of advisory committees to include changes in eating habits with respect to dietary fats in their recommendations for the prevention of CHD (FAO/WHO, 1977; AHA, 1982; Truswell, 1983). The recommendations differ in detail but the common theme concerns a reduction of the total amount of fat and a change in its fatty acid composition. The amount of fat consumed in most Western countries should be reduced from the present level of over 40 en% to about 35 en%. The fatty acid composition of the total dietary fat should be changed from the present one of about 50% saturated fatty acids, 40% monounsaturated fatty acids and 10% polyunsaturated fatty acids (in practice linoleic acid) to equal parts of these three fatty acids classes. This means a polyunsaturated/saturated fatty acid ratio of 1 (P/S ratio 1) in the total dietary fat or a recommended intake of linoleic acid of about 10 en% instead of the current level of about 2 to 4 en%.

Most invisible fats (e.g. dairy and meat products) are rich in saturated fatty acids and contain only small amounts of linoleic acid. It is clear that a higher P/S ratio can only be realized by moderating the consumption of foods rich in saturated fatty acids (or by switching to low-fat products) combined with the use of visible fats with a high content of linoleic acid and a low content of saturated fatty acids. These visible fat products are, in fact, the only rich source of linoleic acid available. They compensate for the highly unbalanced fatty acid composition of the invisible fats and help achieve a more balanced composition of the total dietary fat.

The recommended changes in the amount and composition of the fat intake are intended to lower plasma cholesterol levels or prevent an increase of these levels. The diet-induced changes in plasma total cholesterol are mainly changes in the level of low-density lipoprotein cholesterol. The ratio of high-density lipoprotein cholesterol to low-density lipoprotein cholesterol is increased, which is regarded as a lowering of the risk of CHD.

In more recent recommendations (WHO, 1982; AHA, 1983), the emphasis is on a reduction of the fat intake (especially of saturated fatty acids) to 30 en% or less. This advice is given without providing any data showing that such diets are the most effective to prevent or cure high plasma LDL cholesterol levels.

Most human studies on the effects of dietary fats have been performed using diets containing 40 en% of fat with different P/S ratios. There are hardly any data from experiments in which different levels of dietary fat and various P/S ratios were studied. The results of only two such studies using practical diets are available (Brussaard et al. 1980; Lewis et al. 1981). These studies showed that diets containing 27 to 30 en% fat with a P/S ratio of 1 are no better in controlling LDL cholesterol levels than those containing 40 en% fat with a P/S ratio of 1.

Brussaard et al. (1980) also reported that the 30 en% fat diet (P/S=1) is more effective than a low-fat diet (22 en%) with a P/S ratio of 0.4. The 40 en% fat diet has the advantage that it also lowers very low density lipoprotein triglyceride levels in comparison to the 22 or 30 en% fat diets. The results of these studies using different levels of dietary fat indicate that a P/S ratio of about one is necessary for an optimal control of blood lipid levels.

In practice, a drastic reduction in the total fat intake is difficult to realize and generally poorly accepted for taste reasons. If achieved, it usually leads to a reduction of visible fats and not of the invisible fat sources. This makes it more difficult to attain a desirable P/S ratio.

An important question is to what extent other physiological functions, apart from the regulations of lipoprotein metabolism, will be influenced by the recommended dietary changes. During the last fifteen years, a number of investigators have systematically studied whether dietary fats have physiological effects on organs and organ systems, the dysfunction of which is related to the development of CHD. The effects of dietary fat containing different amounts of saturated fatty acids and linoleic acid, can also have a bearing on arterial thrombosis, blood pressure and diabetes mellitus will be discussed.

Arterial Thrombosis

Basically, thrombosis starts with blood platelet adhesion and aggregation. Intra-arterial thrombosis is not only frequently responsible for the total blockage of atherosclerotic arteries in the heart, brain or kidneys, but it might also be a primary factor in the early development of atherosclerotic lesions. PG's and related substances are involved in these complicated processes, e.g. aggregating platelets rapidly convert arachidonic acid to TXA_2, a potent stimulator of platelet aggregation and a vasoconstricting substance. On the other hand, the major PG released by the blood vessel wall is PGI_2, which is not only a powerful vasodilating agent but also a potent inhibitor of platelet aggregation. For these reasons, the influence of various dietary fats on arterial thrombosis tendency has been studied in animals and man.

Hornstra (1982) reviewed the numerous studies showing the relationship between type of dietary fat and the risk of arterial thrombosis. It has been clearly demonstrated that in animals saturated fatty acids with more than twelve carbon atoms enhance and linoleic acid inhibits arterial thrombus formation in a dose-dependent manner, whereas the monounsaturated fatty acids (e.g. oleic acid) are neutral in this respect and have an anti-thrombotic effect only if they replace dietary saturated fatty acids. These dietary effects have also been observed in several clinical studies.

Much research is being conducted to unravel the mechanisms of these effects. The fatty acid composition of adipose tissue, plasma-free fatty acids and the platelet membrane may play a role. The balance between TXA_2 and PGI_2 has been suggested as a determining factor in arterial thrombosis.

The dietary significance of α-linolenic acid and in particular of EPA, the precursor for eicosanoids of the 3-series, is now under discussion. TXA_3, derived in vitro from EPA was originally reported to be less aggregating than TXA_2, whereas PGI_3 derived in vitro from EPA is as antiaggregating as PGI_2. These findings together with the fact that in Greenland Eskimos, eating an - EPA containing - marine diet, plasma and platelet arachidonic acid is largely replaced by EPA (Dyerberg and Bang, 1979), led to the speculation that the observed lower mortality from acute myocardial infarction of these Eskimos can be explained by a higher production in the body of prostaglandins of the 3-series, resulting in a favorable shift in the TXA/PGI balance. Feeding large amounts of EPA indeed leads to a lower thrombosis tendency, but it also results in a prolonged bleeding time (Ten Hoor et al. 1980). If the production of both PGI_2 and TXA_2 is impaired; the decreased production of TXA_2 could well explain the prolonged bleeding time. The depression of the prostaglandins of the 2-series resembles the effects of linoleic acid deficiency and cyclo-oxygenase inhibitors, e.g. aspirin. As already stated, PGI_3 and TXA_3 were produced only in trace quantities despite the large amounts of EPA available in the cell membranes.

In many experimental studies of the effects of n-3 polyunsaturated fatty acids, extreme dietary compositions (e.g. amount of fat, unrealistic dominance of one type of fatty acid) have been used and frequently only very limited criteria (e.g. blood platelet composition and function) have been studied. In view of the competition between n-6 and n-3 polyunsaturated fatty acids in metabolic processes, it is necessary for a nutritional evaluation to have more data on the effects of various realistic ratios of these polyunsaturated fatty acids at different P/S ratios (e.g. at the current ratio of about 0.3 and the recommended value of about 1). There is evidence indicating that excessive intake of linolenic acid and/or fats with low ratios of n-6/n-3 fatty acid may not be advantageous (Hornstra et al. 1983; Bijster and Vles, 1984; Scherhag et al. 1982). Metabolites of linolenic acid are found as components of brain and retinal phospholipids. Their precise functional role in these highly differentiated tissues is difficult to define (Sanders et al. 1984). An optimum ratio of linoleic to linolenic acid has still to be defined.

Blood Pressure

Hypertension is an important and frequently found risk factor for cardiovascular disease. The kidneys play a pivotal role in regulating blood pressure. They are also very rich in PG's, i.e. PGE_2, $PGF_{2\alpha}$, PGD_2, PGI_2. It seems very probable that renal prostaglandins are a vital part of the integrated control systems determining blood pressure (Weber et al. 1981). They exert their control via their actions as vasodilators, vasoconstrictors, natriuretic substances and as activators or inhibitors of the renin-angiotensin system.

It has generally been accepted that a sustained high sodium intake contributes to the induction of hypertension, especially in genetically predisposed individuals. This focuses attention on the relationship between prostaglandins and sodium. Prostaglandins have been found to influence renal sodium and water excretion. Exposing rats to a high sodium intake reduces urinary PG excretion and intrarenal PGE_2 concentration. Diminished urinary PGE_2 levels, which points to impaired renal production in patients with essential hypertension, have also been reported. These data suggest that (sodium-induced) hypertension might be caused by a changed prostaglandin biosynthesis and metabolism. Dietary linoleic acid is the ultimate precursor of endogenous prostaglandin biosynthesis and might influence blood pressure via this metabolic pathway. Therefore, several studies of the effects of dietary linoleic acid on hypertension have been carried out. Increasing the amount of dietary linoleic acid normalized the blood pressure and the $PGE_2/PGF_{2\alpha}$ ratio of renal PG synthesis in rats exposed to a high sodium intake.

Similarly blood pressure lowering effects of dietary linoleic acid were reported in man. Iacono et al. (1975) showed that an increase in dietary linoleic acid from 4 to 8 en% reduced systolic and diastolic blood pressure. In later studies (Iacono et al. 1981), this group compared the effects of diets containing 25 or 43 en% fat, both with P/S ratios of 0.3 and 1. Again, a rise in linoleic acid consumption at the expense of saturated fatty acids and independent of the amount of fat in the diet lowered the blood pressure. Maximum reduction was observed in the subjects with the highest initial blood pressure. Furthermore, both a 25 en% fat, P/S=1 and a 35 en% fat, P/S=1 diet induced the same blood pressure lowering effect in comparison to the average US diet (P/S 0.22). Many other studies supporting these findings have been reported (Puska et al. 1983). All these findings suggest that linoleic acid enriched diets help normalize moderate hypertension in populations having a "normal" salt intake of 10 g or more per day.

Adult-Onset Diabetes

Many obese people have hypertension and hyperinsulinemia and develop adult-onset diabetes later in life. This increases the risk of developing coronary heart disease and micro-angiopathy, the typical microvascular changes leading to diabetic retinopathy, nephropathy and peripheral vascular disease.

After observing that blood lipid lowering therapies could diminish the severity of retinal exudates in many patients, Houtsmuller et al. (1980), investigated the influence of a linoleic acid enriched diet on the progression of diabetic retinopathy. Two groups of patients with recently discovered adult-onset, insulin-independent diabetes mellitus participated in the study. All participants were free from any clinical sign of cardiovascular disease at the start. Half of the patients were prescribed a linoleic acid enriched diet (P/S ratio of 1). The other half of the patients continued with their normal diabetic diet (P/S ratio 0.3).

After a dietary intervention of six years, highly significant differences in severity and incidence of retinopathy were observed. Half the patients on the saturated fat rich diet had a doubling of both the severity and incidence of retinopathy whereas only 15% of the patients on the linoleic acid enriched diet showed a minor progression of retinopathy. Also with respect to coronary heart disease, the dietary differences were impressive: electrocardiographic signs of cardiac ischemia were three times more frequent in the low P/S group than in the high P/S group. Especially the difference in clinically manifest myocardial infarctions was highly significant.

Furthermore, Houtsmuller et al. (1980) found a strong inverse correlation between both progression of retinopathy and coronary heart disease on the one hand and serum cholesteryllinoleate concentration on the other. The data suggest that a serum cholesteryllinoleate concentration of over 55% indicates a very low risk of micro- and macro-angiopathy, whereas patients with a cholesteryllinoleate concentration of under 45% are at much greater risk.

In conclusion, the changes in dietary fats recommended for the prevention of coronary heart disease by many advisory committees, namely, a lower intake of saturated fat and a higher intake of linoleic acid, so that the P/S ratio of the total dietary fat intake becomes one, not only reduce plasma cholesterol levels (especially LDL) but also exert favorable effects on arterial thrombosis tendency, blood pressure and adult-onset diabetes, which are important factors in cardiovascular diseases. This means that the optimal linoleic acid requirement for the human diet (about 10 en%) is considerably higher than the minimal requirement of about 3 en%.

CONCLUDING REMARKS

Many types of dietary fats with widely divergent fatty acid compositions are available for human consumption as such or hidden in a variety of food products. In order to attain a balanced fatty acid composition of total dietary fat intake, attention has to be paid primarily to the amounts of saturated and polyunsaturated fatty acids present in the foods. Saturated fats are inevitably present in relatively high amounts in the Western diet and these have to be balanced by approximately equal amounts of polyunsaturated fatty acids. The polyunsaturated fatty acids should consist mainly of linoleic acid which is abundant in most vegetable oils. Thus edible fat products made from vegetable oils can make an important contribution to the right fatty acid balance of the daily diet and hence to health and well-being.

REFERENCES

AHA. 1982. Rationale of the diet-heart statement of the American Heart Association. Circulation 65, 839A-854A.
——. 1983. Diet in the healthy child. American Heart Association committee report. Circulation 67, 1411A-1414A.

Beare-Rogers, J.L. 1983. Trans- and Positional Isomers of Common Fatty Acids, pp. 171-200. *In* H.H. Draper (ed.), *Advances in Nutritional Research* . Vol. 5. Plenum Publishing Corp., New York.

Bieri, J.G., and Poukka Evarts, R. 1975. Vitamin E adequacy of vegetable oils. J. Amer. Diet. Assoc. 66: 134-139.

Bijster, G.M., and Vles, R.O. 1984. Ernahrungsphysiologische Wirkung unterschiedlicher Gemische von 01-, Linol- und Linolensaure bei wachsenden Schweinen. 6. Histomorphometrische Untersuchung von Herz, Leber, Nieren und Fettgewebe. Fette Seifen Anstrichm. 86: 93-98.

Brussaard, J.H., Dallinga-Thie, G., Groot, P.H.E., and Katan, M.G. 1980. Effects of amount and type of dietary fat on serum lipids, lipoproteins and apolipoproteins in man. Atherosclerosis 36: 515-527.

Burr, C.O., and Burr, M.M. 1929. On the nature and role of the fatty acids essential in nutrition. J. Biol. Chem. 82: 345-367.

Carroll, K.K., and Khor, H.T. 1975. Dietary fat in relation to tumorigenesis. Prog. Biochem. Pharmacol. 10: 308-353.

Claeys, M., Coene, M.C., Herman, A.G., Jouvenaz, G.H., and Nugteren, D.H. 1982. Characterization of monohydroxylated lipoxygenase metabolites of arachidonic and linoleic acid in rabbit peritoneal tissue. Biochem. Biophys. Acta 713: 160-169.

Dutilh, C.E., Haddeman, E., Don, J.A., and Ten Hoor, F. 1981. The role of arachidonate lipoxygenase and fatty acids during irreversible blood platelet aggregation in vitro. Prostaglandins and Medicine 6: 111-126.

Dormandy, T.L. 1983. An approach to free radicals. Lancet 2 (8357): 1010-1014.

Downey, R.K. 1983. The Origin and Description of the Brassica Oilseed Crops, pp. 1-20. *In* J.K.G. Kramer, F.D. Sauer and W.J. Pigden (eds.), *High and Low Erucic Acid Rapeseed Oils* . Academic Press, Toronto.

Dyerberg, J., and Bang, H.O. 1979. Haemostatic function and platelet polyunsaturated fatty acids in Eskimos. Lancet 2 (8140): 433-435.

Emken, E.A. 1983. Biochemistry of unsaturated fatty acids isomers, J. Am. Oil Chem. Soc. 60: 995-1004.

FAO/WHO. 1977. Dietary Fats and Oils in Human Nutrition. FAO Food and Nutrition Paper No. 3. FAO, Rome.

Gottenbos, J.J. 1983. Biological Effects of *trans* Fatty Acids, pp. 375-390. *In* E.G. Perkins and W.J. Vles (eds.), *Dietary Fats and Health* . Am. Oil Chem. Soc. Monograph 10. Champaign, Ill.

——, and Visek, R.O. 1983. The Nutritive Value of Palm Oil, pp. 5-11. *In* K.G. Berger (ed.), *Nutrition* . PORIM Occasional Paper, No. 8. PORIM, Kuala Lumpur.

Hopkins, G.J., Kennedy, T.G., and Carroll, K.K. 1981. Polyunsaturated fatty acids as promoters of mammary carcinogenesis induced in Sprague-Dawley rats by 7,12-Dimethylbenz[*a*]anthracene. J. Natl. Cancer Inst. 66: 517-522.

Hornstra, G. 1982. Dietary Fats, Prostanoids and Arterial Thrombosis. *In Developments in Hematology and Immunology* . Vol. 4. Martinus Nijhof, The Hague.

——, Haddeman, E., Kloeze, J., and Verschuren, P.M. 1983. Dietary-Fat-Induced Changes in the Formation of Prostanoids of the 2 and 3-Series in Relation to Arterial Thrombosis (Rat) and Atherosclerosis (Rabbit), pp. 193-202. *In* B. Samuelsson, R. Paoletti and P. Ramwell (eds.), *Advances in Prostaglandin and Leukotriene Research* . Vol. 12. Raven Press, New York.

Houtsmuller, A.J., Van Hal-Ferweda, J., Zahn, K.J., and Henkes, H.E. 1980. Favourable influences of linoleic acid on the progression of diabetic micro-and macro-angiopathy. Nutr. Metab. 24: 105-118.

Iacono, J.M., Marshall, M.W., Dougherty, R.M., Wheeler, M.A., Mackin, J.F., and Canary, J.J. 1975. Reduction of blood pressure associated with high polyunsaturated fat diets that reduce blood cholesterol in man. Prev. Med. 4: 426-443.

——, Judd, J.T., Marshall, M.W., Canary, J.J., Dougherty, R.M., Mackin, J.F., and Weinland, B.T. 1981. The Role of Dietary Essential Fatty Acids and Prostaglandins in Reducing Blood Pressure, pp. 349-364. *In* R.T. Holman (ed.), *Progress in Lipid Research.* . Vol. 20. Pergamon Press, Oxford.

Kramer, J.K.G., and Sauer, F.D. 1983. Results Obtained With Feeding Low Erucic Acid Rapeseed Oils and Other Species, pp. 413-474. *In* J.K.G. Kramer, F.D. Sauer and W.J. Pigden (eds.), *High and Low Erucic Acid Rapeseed Oils* . Academic Press, Toronto.

Lewis, B., Katan, M., Merkx, I., Miller, N.E., Hammett, F., Kay, R.M., Nobels, A., and Swan, A.V. 1981. Towards an improved lipid-lowering diet: additive effects of changes in nutrient intake. Lancet 2 (8259): pp. 1310-1313.

——. 1983. Dietary recommendations for coronary heart disease prevention: implications for non-cardiovascular diseases. Z. Ernährungswiss. 22: 147-156.

Lipid Research Clinics Program. 1984. The Lipid Research Clinics Coronary Primary Prevention Trial Results. 1. Reduction in Incidence of Coronary Heart Disease. J. Am. Med. Assoc. 251(3): 351-364.

——. 1984. 2. The Relationship of Reduction in Incidence of Coronary Heart Disease to Cholesterol Lowering. J. Am. Med. Assoc. 251(3): 365-374.

Mattson, F.H. 1973. Potential Toxicity of Food Lipids, pp. 189-209. *In Toxicants Occurring Naturally in Foods* . NAS, Washington, D.C.

——. 1983. Implications of the Nutritional and Physiological Roles of Fat, pp. 241-246. *In* E.G. Perkins and W.J. Visek (eds.), *Dietary Fats and Health* . Am. Oil Chem. Soc. Monograph 10. Champaign,Ill.

McGandy, R.B., and Hegsted, D.M. 1975. Quantitative Effects of Dietary Fat and Cholesterol on Serum Cholesterol in Man, pp. 211-230. *In* A.J. Vergroesen (ed.), *The Role of Fats in Human Nutrition* . Academic Press, London.

McLaughlin, P.J., and Weirauch, J.L. 1979. Vitamin E content of foods. J. Amer. Diet. Assoc. 75: 647-665.

Pariza, M.W. 1984. A perspective on diet, nutrition, and cancer. J. Am. Med. Assoc. 251: 1455-1458.

Puska, P., Iacono, J.M., Nissinen, A., Korhonen, J. H., Vartiainen, E., Pietinen, P., Dougherty, R., Leino, U., Mutanen, M., Moisio, S., and Huttunen, J. 1983. Controlled, randomised trial of the effect of dietary fat on blood pressure, Lancet 1 (8314-8315): 1-5.

Ross, R., and Glosmet, J.A. 1976. The pathogenesis of atherosclerosis. New England Journal of Medicine 295: 369-377, 420-425.

Sanders, T.A.B., Mistry, M., and Naismith, D.J. 1984. The influence of a maternal diet rich in linoleic acid on brain and retinal docosahexaenoic acid in the rat. Brit. J. of Nutr. 51: 57-66.

Scherhag, R., Kramer, H.J., and Dusing, R. 1982. Dietary administration of eicosapentaenoic acid and linolenic acid increases arterial blood pressure and suppresses prostacyclin synthesis in the rat. Prostaglandins 23: 369-383.

Sickinger, K. 1975. Clinical Aspects and Therapy of Fat Malassimilation With Particular Reference to the Use of Medium-Chain Triglycerides, pp. 115-209. *In* A.J. Vergroesen (ed.), *The Role of Fats in Human Nutrition* . Academic Press, London.

Sinkeldam, E.J., Wysman, J.A., Roverts, W.G., and Woutersen, R.A. 1983. pp. 1690-1699. In: *Proc. 6th Intern. Rapeseed Conf.* CETIOM, Paris.

Sommerfeld, M. 1983. *Trans* unsaturated fatty acids in natural products and processed foods. Prog. Lipid Res. 22: 221-233.

Ten Hoor, F., De Deckere, E.A.M., Haddeman, E., Hornstra, G., and Quadt, J.F.A. 1980. Dietary Manipulation of Prostaglandin and Thromboxane Synthesis in Heart, Aorta and Blood Platelets of the Rat, pp. 1771-1781. *In* B. Samuelsson, P.W. Ramwell and R. Paoletti (eds.), *Advances in Prostaglandin and Thromboxane Research* . Vol. 8. Raven Press, New York.

Truswell, A.S. 1983. The development of dietary guidelines. Food Technology in Australia 35: 498-502.

Vergroesen, A.J. 1976. Early signs of polyunsaturated fatty acid deficiency. Biblthca. Nutr. Dieta 23: 19-26.

Weber, P.C., Siess, W., Lorenz, R., and Scherer, B. 1981. The role of prostaglandins in essential hypertension. Intern. J. of Obesity 5 (Suppl. I): 125-130.

WHO. 1982. Prevention of coronary heart disease. WHO Technical Report Series No. 678. WHO, Geneva.

Chapter 5

Industrial and Nonfood Uses of Vegetable Oils

E. H. Pryde and J. A. Rothfus

INTRODUCTION

For a world confronted by the certainty of change, plants and molecular tools for manipulating them are powerful implements with which to meet oncoming challenges. Industrial change to eliminate energy-intense processes, reduce dependence on fossil resources, protect the environment and move toward stable commodity markets enhances the appeal of global chemurgy in general and the liberal utilization of vegetable oils in particular. Commercial fats and oils and a variety of unexploited lipids in plants (Smith, 1979) constitute raw materials for this change. Combinations of botany, chemistry, molecular biology and biotechnology provide necessary tools. Together they promise new access to botanical resources and a greater diversity of agricultural feedstocks for chemical manufacture. To realize such long-range benefits requires perceptions of utility in specific botanicals and visions of economically viable mechanisms for exploiting them. It is to these crucial insights that we devote much of this chapter.

INDUSTRIAL OILS FROM PLANTS

Among approximately 300,000 known plant species, only about 3000 have been tried as sources of useful materials, and less than 300 are exploited in organized agriculture. Fewer than twenty provide the principal vegetable oils of international commerce. These account for 65 to 70% of approximately 60 million tonnes of fats and oils consumed annually world-wide in food and industrial products. In the USA; plant oils, including tall oil, constitute about 75% of all fats and oils consumed and 40% of those entering non-food use (Table 5.1).

Table 5.1   Major Plant Oils Consumed in the United States

Source	Oil consumption	
	Total	Nonfood
	----------1000 tonnes----------	
Soybean	4312.3	93.1
Sunflower	34.1	0.7
Palm	139.1	15.3
Rapeseed	15.3	6.3
Cottonseed	289.9	1.7
Coconut	363.7	209.5
Groundnut	80.1	1.0
Olive	29.2	-
Palm Kernel	69.5	6.1
Linseed	44.4	44.4
Corn	290.5	1.0
Sesame	2.7	-
Safflower	8.4	1.0
Vegetable Oil Foods	30.5	30.5
Castor	32.7	32.7
Tung	5.6	5.6
Tall Oil	523.3	523.3
TOTAL	6271.3	972.2

About 2.5 million tonnes of fats and oils are consumed annually in the USA in various industrial products (Table 5.2).

Animal fats and vegetable oil soapstocks are principal contributors to the major markets in fatty acids and feeds. Surprisingly, agricultural fats and oils account for substantial portions of some markets commonly thought to have petrochemical origins (Table 5.3).

The five plant oils most widely used industrially are coconut, soybean, linseed, castor and tall oil. Use of coconut oil fluctuates around half edible and half inedible depending on market conditions with about 60% currently going into industrial products. The value of coconut oil derives from a high concentration of lauric acid (45 to 50%), which is consumed in soaps and lauryl alcohol-based surfactants. However, less than 20% of the medium-chain fatty alcohols required

Table 5.2 Percentage of Fats and Oils Consumed by Product Classes in the United States

Product class	Use (%)
Fatty acids	36
Feeds	29
Soap	15
Paint or varnish	3
Resins and plastics	2
Lubricants	2
Other	13
TOTAL	100

Table 5.3 Estimated Vegetable Oil Contributions to Chemical Markets in the United States

Market Segment	Percent from Vegetable Oils
Adhesives	1
Agrichemicals	10
Coatings	40
Engineering thermoplastics	2
Fabric softeners	90
Plastics additives	15
Surfactants	35
Synthetic lubricants	20

for detergents come from vegetable oils; most come from petroleum or natural gas feedstocks.

Relatively low cost and dependable supply make soybean oil one of the most important sources of industrial products. At one time annual consumption in the USA drying oil industry alone amounted to 80,000 tonnes, primarily in alkyd paints. This use, the most important for soybean oil, has been reduced 20 to 30% by trends toward solventless paints and polymeric coatings. Epoxidized soybean oil, however, finds good use (ca 40,000 tonnes per year) as a plasticizer/stabilizer for vinyl plastics. There are numerous major applications as well (Table 5.4). Other diverse examples of soybean oil products and their uses include: maleinized oils for resins, modified fatty amines for anticorrosion agents, sulfurized oil factices as rubber extenders, the oil itself as a binding agent for sand cores in metal casting and brominated oil in fruit-based soft drinks to improve cloud stability and reduce ring deposits. In animal feeds, soybean soapstock provides dust control in addition to dietary calories.

Table 5.4 Industrial Applications for Soybean Oil and Oil Products

Oil	Mono-/Diglycerides
Epoxidized oil plasticizers	Detergents
Acrylated epoxidized oil	Oil recovery agents
Other coatings	
Methyl esters	
Grain dust control	
Pesticide dispersion	

Fatty acids	Soapstock fatty acids
Alkyd resins	Animal feed products
Dimer acids	Medium-grade soap products
Coatings	Low-cost oleochemicals for
Toilet soap	petroleum and rubber industries
Surfactants	
Fatty amines/amides	
Nylon-9	
Stearate oleochemicals	
Vegetable oleic acid	
Acylated polylactate resins	

Linseed oil from flaxseed contains about 57% linolenic acid, which reacts rapidly with atmospheric oxygen to form insoluble, tough and adherent films. Use of this drying oil and pigment binder appears to have plateaued in the USA at about 70,000 tonnes per year during the late 1970s. Nevertheless, many latex paints contain linseed oil because the natural product imparts superior adhesion to substrate surfaces. Epoxidized linseed oil (ca 3000 tonnes) is also used commercially to achieve high oxirane concentrations in plasticizer/stabilizers for vinyl plastics.

With castor oil, exceptionally high concentrations of ricinoleic acid (86%) and hydroxy functionality allow for chemical modifications not achieved easily with other commercial oils. Accordingly there are important applications for several different types of castor-based products in lubricants, plasticizers, coatings, surfactants and pharmaceuticals. Ricinoleic acid derivatives are also consumed in polyester, polyamide and urethane polymers, cosmetics, flavorings, fungistats and greases (Naughton et al. 1979).

Tall oil is a byproduct of pine tree pulping in Kraft paper mills. Although not a vegetable oil in the same sense as those from seed, tall oil is nevertheless a dominant source of industrial fatty acids. In the USA, industrial coatings account for about 25% of tall oil fatty acid usage. Adhesives, cosmetics, soaps and detergents as well as dimer acid products account for the remainder. Declining use of pine in United States paperboard could create demand for vegetable oil products in markets currently supplied by tall oil.

OLEOCHEMISTRY AND OLEOCHEMICALS

During more than 40 years, 1935-1977, the ratio of food to nonfood use for fats and oils in the USA remained near 2:1. More recently, food use has increased, and per capita consumption in industrial products has declined about 2% per year. In 1983, food preparation consumed 73% of all fats and oils, and the food to nonfood ratio expanded to nearly 3:1. Throughout the same period, the per capita consumption of synthetic organic chemicals rose dramatically, and it continues to increase. Nutritional practice will ultimately limit per capita use of vegetable oils in food, but static or declining industrial use, even during chemical market expansion, suggests that a new utility and cost/benefit advantages for natural fats and oils needs to be established.

Oleochemistry emphasizes alkene, ester, hydroxy and carboxy reactivities. Thus the industrial value of a vegetable oil generally depends on its content of a specific fatty acid and the ease with which that acid can be modified or combined with other chemicals. Major commercial acids from plant oils range from C:12 to C:22 inclusive and, with the notable exception of ricinoleic acid from castor oil, all are saturated or mono-, di- or triunsaturated acids with double bonds at mid-chain and distal to the carboxyl. Common industrial transformations of these acids are summarized in Figure 5.1. The glycerol portion of vegetable oils remains sufficiently valuable to justify its preservation in modified glycerides or its recovery intact when oils are converted to acids. Such transformations deliver an impressive array of useful chemicals, but the variety of compounds offered at low cost from vegetable oils is limited compared to that offered from petrochemicals. The 2.5 million tonnes of fats and oils consumed industrially per year in the USA represent less than 2% of the 170 million tonnes of organic chemicals marketed there each year.

One route to a larger market share for vegetable oils depends clearly on innovations that economically impart novel chemical functionality to lipids. In addition, nature provides oleochemicals in much greater variety than is currently exploited. Such novel botanochemicals produced in quantity via agriculture might compete effectively with petrochemicals. In at least a few instances, the switch from petrochemicals to alternative crops is proving feasible. Several prospective oil crops that appear promising in terms of overall feasibility are identified in Chapter 30.

Unusual natural fatty acids have generally been found in seed, but the occurrence of 3-trans-hexadecenoic acid in photosynthetic tissue, the presence of long-chain hydroxy, epoxy and keto acids in cutin and suberin (Kollattukudy, 1981), and high levels of "polyphenols" and other valuable chemicals in plant extracts (Balandrin et al. 1985) demonstrate that the vegetative portions of plants likewise contain potentially useful structures. Seed components are emphasized only because seed provides a convenient container for oil storage and transport. Considering that accomplishments in molecular biology already allow magnification of selected plant constituents, it may no longer be appropriate to

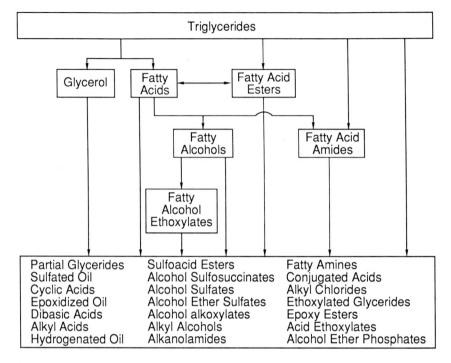

Fig. 5.1   Industrial transformations of vegetable oils.

distinguish between major and minor or unusual fatty acids or to segregate them in terms of where they occur in each plant. It is appropriate, however, to focus on the potential utility of plant constituents. If applications for a botanical feedstock can be identified, decisions to develop it by chemically modifying an existing oil or by genetically manipulating "parent" and "host" plants can be left to economic and other considerations.

The 250 to 300 different acids already identified in seed can provide chain lengths C:8 through C:30. Fatty acids with eighteen carbons constitute the largest class known to contain multiple or mixed types of chemical functional groups in the same acid (see Chapter 2). The chemistry by which vegetable oils are already transformed could easily produce a much broader selection of oleochemicals from such multifunctional acids.

Hydrolysis/Alcoholysis/Aminolysis

The conversion of about one million tonnes of fats and oils to fatty acids annually in the USA alone makes simple hydrolysis by steam splitting, saponification or enzyme action the single most important commercial modification of fats and oils.

Mono- and diglycerides, from partial hydrolysis of triglycerides or from transesterification to added glycerol, are excellent emulsifiers and are indispensable in most processed or manufactured foods containing fats and oils. Sulfation or mono- and diglycerides further improves their surfactant properties and makes them useful household detergents. Analogous compounds that are likewise excellent surfactants also occur naturally. Certain grasses, particularly *Briza humilus* Bieb. contain exceptionally high concentrations of glycolipids that are common to Poaceae (Gramineae). Nearly 80% of the oil from *Briza* seed is mono- and digalactosyl glycerides, which are effective food emulsifiers and bread volume expanders.

Acyl transfer reactions, alcoholysis or aminolysis, offer limitless possibilities for direct preparation of valuable multifunctional fatty acid derivatives. The USA thus produces more than 100,000 tonnes of neutral fatty acid surfactants each year. Fatty amides and amines derived in turn from such amides are used widely as antistatics or antiblock and mold-release agents. Quality antiblock performances, for example, allows erucamide derived from the high-erucic oils of crambe and rapeseed to command premium prices relative to those paid for shorter chain amides. Behenyl amine, the corresponding antistatic agent from erucic acid, also finds good commercial use.

Acyl transfer products can, in addition, serve as intermediates in other syntheses especially polymerization. Thus, allyl fatty esters from the alcoholysis of glycerides in allyl alcohol can be polymerized (Fig. 5.2A) to poly (acyloxypropylene) counterparts of commercial alkyl acrylate polymers (Chang, 1979).

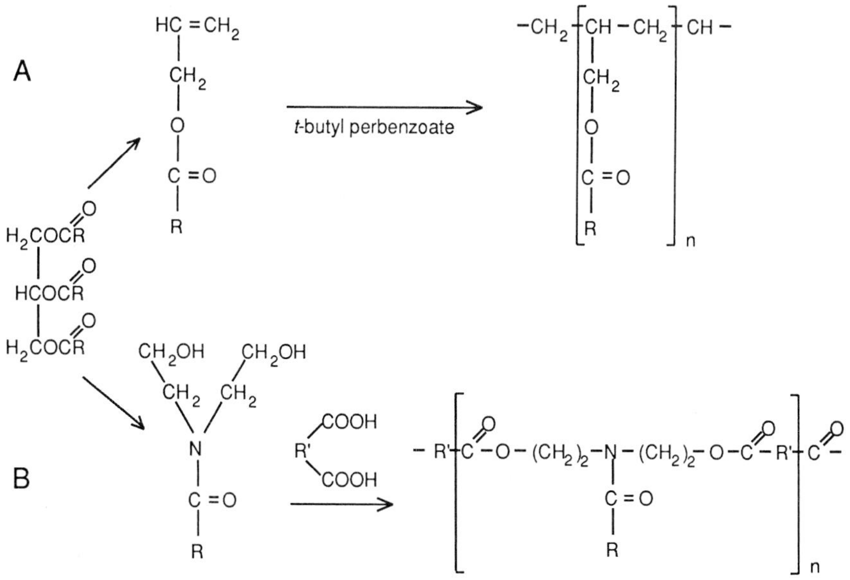

Fig. 5.2 Monomers and polymers from triglyceride alcoholysis products: (A) free radicle polymerization, (B) condensation polymerization.

In analogous fashion, (Fig. 5.2B) linseed oil can be converted to intermediates suitable for condensation polymerization with dibasic acids or diisocyanates to produce polyesteramides that are excellent binders for air-dried and baked coatings (Schneider and Gast, 1979).

Reduction/Hydrogenation

Hydrogenation in the presence of metal catalysts; e.g. nickel, platinum or palladium, is the traditional way to "harden" oils and change the physical properties of solid fats. When conducted at higher temperatures and pressures in the presence of zinc chromite or copper-cadmium catalysts, hydrogenation also causes hydrogenolysis and is the method of choice for converting fats to glycerol and long chain alcohols that are used extensively in detergents, plasticizers and cosmetics. Such alcohols can, of course, be reesterified to fatty acids to produce linear wax esters analogous to those found naturally in jojoba oil (Chapter 25).

Fatty alcohols can also be reacted with vinyl acetate or acetylene under pressure to produce vinyl ethers (Fig. 5.3), which are readily polymerized by strong acid to products useful as adhesives, surface coating materials and waterproofing agents or, depending on the type of alcohol, possibly polymeric plasticizers (Teeter, 1963).

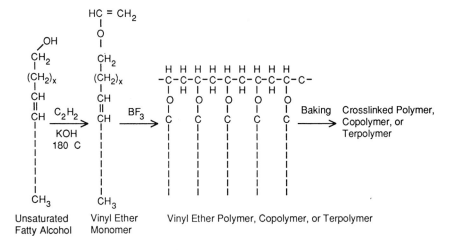

Fig. 5.3 Vinyl ether polymers from fatty alcohols.

Hydrogenation, when applied to *Sterculia* oil, is a quick route to methyl-substituted branched-chain esters that have exceptionally low freezing and pour points (Kai, 1982). Such properties are desired in plasticizers and lubricants.

Addition/Substitution

Among many addition and substitution reactions theoretically possible with alkenes, only a few are applied extensively in vegetable oil commerce. Reactions known to yield useful products include:

Sulfurization..................................	Factice, lubricants
Sulfurchlorination..........................	Metal-working fluids
Sulfation/sulfonation.....................	Surfactants
Alkoxylation..................................	Detergents, plasticizers
Hydroformylation..........................	Urethane resins, plasticizers

Addition/substitution reactions provide convenient means to modify the hydrocarbon properties of vegetable oils and fatty acids. With hydroformylation, which adds aldehyde (oxo) functionality, the degree and location of the substitution can be controlled through the choice of catalyst and the reaction conditions (Pryde, 1984). Additional treatments of the products lead to an assortment of useful chemicals (Fig. 5.4).

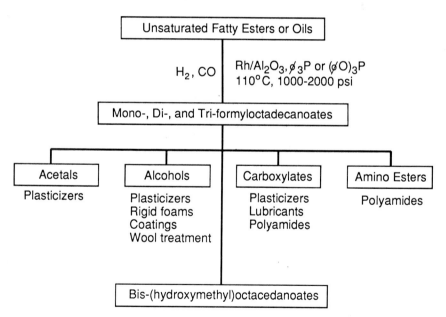

Fig. 5.4 Transformation of fatty esters and vegetable oils by hydroformylation.

Acids with oxo groups introduced by hydroformylation or acids that naturally contain groups readily converted to oxo functions should easily yield amino acids and thence unusual engineering nylons. For example, linear polyamides can be made from omega-hydroxy acids common in plant waxes; e.g. carnauba wax from *Copernicia cerifera* Mart., or branched polyamides from keto or unsaturated acids such as alpha-licanic acid or cis-vaccenic acid. Alternatively, the oxo function can be reduced to obtain hydroxy acids useful in polyester resins and urethane plastics.

In terms of oxidized products, hydrocarboxylation typically produces 34% monocarboxy, 24% dicarboxy and 33% tricarboxy acids with quantitative conversion and no isomerization of double bonds. Such unfractionated mixtures should yield effective plasticizers and polyester resins when further derivatized.

Selective functional group location in fatty acids allows subtle balance between hydrophobic and hydrophilic substructure. It is thus possible to tailor physical properties of products to meet specific requirements. For example, lithium 12-hydroxystearate from the ricinoleic acid of castor oil, a performance standard among grease thickening agents, forms a hydrogen-bonded salt-bridged network with sufficient hydrophobic character to entrap simple hydrocarbons. Greases thickened with lithium 12-hydroxystearate are nevertheless inadequate beyond specific temperature ranges. Acids as long as C:30 and as short as C:10 with hydroxyl groups near mid-chain might easily extend the the performance limits of lithium 12-hydroxystearate. *Lesquerella* spp. provide 14-hydroxy-11-eicosenoic acid, a likely candidate for this purpose.

Cyclization

Structures that impart aromatic properties and allow competition with benzenoid petrochemicals are rare in vegetable oils, but they can be achieved via Diels-Alder type condensations or internal cyclizations of polyenoic fatty acids (Fig. 5.5A and B).

Acids of the C:21 dibasic form, made by the addition of acrylic acid to conjugated tall oil fatty acids, have become useful in heavy-duty industrial detergents. Cyclic C:18 fatty acids, made by alkaline cyclization of linolenic acid, or C:20 cyclic fatty acids, from addition of ethylene to soybean soapstock, yield esters that have low pour points, which makes them attractive as lubricants. Alternatively, they can be converted to amides that are good antiblock agents for polyethylene film.

Dimer and trimer acids, formed by clay-catalyzed condensations of tall oil and soy fatty acids (Fig. 5.5C), already find extensive use in hot-melt adhesives, surface coatings and reactive resins.

The general commercial importance of aromatic chemicals and commercial interest in cyclic fatty acids, dimer acids and Diels-Alder adducts of fatty acids, justify simple speculation about other cyclic and heterocyclic materials from vegetable oils. The 2,4-decadienoic acid present at low levels in *Sapium sebiferum* (L.) Roxb. (Chinese tallow tree--stillingia oil) and the 2,4 dodecadienoic acid from *Sebastiana lingustrina* (Muell.) Arg. are especially interesting because they could theoretically yield dimers that aromatize to substituted m-phthalic acids (Fig. 5.6A). Enormous quantities of phthalate esters are used worldwide as plasticizers.

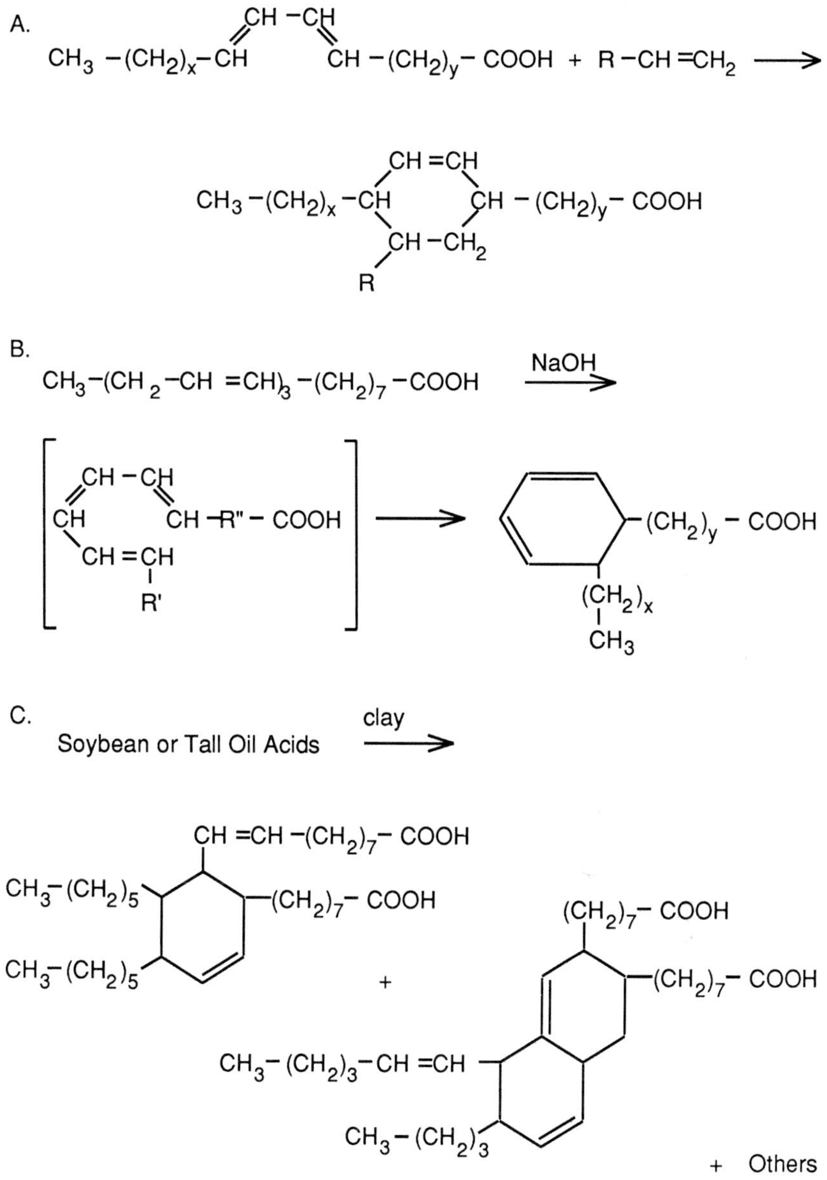

A.

$$CH_3-(CH_2)_x-CH \underset{}{\overset{CH=CH}{\diagup}} CH-(CH_2)_y-COOH + R-CH=CH_2 \longrightarrow$$

$$CH_3-(CH_2)_x-CH \underset{\underset{R}{CH-CH_2}}{\overset{CH=CH}{\diagup}} CH-(CH_2)_y-COOH$$

B.

$$CH_3-(CH_2-CH=CH)_3-(CH_2)_7-COOH \xrightarrow{NaOH}$$

$$\left[CH \underset{CH=CH}{\overset{CH-CH}{\diagup}} CH-R''-COOH \right] \longrightarrow$$

with R' substituent

$$\text{(ring)}-(CH_2)_y-COOH$$
$$\underset{CH_3}{\overset{(CH_2)_x}{|}}$$

C.

Soybean or Tall Oil Acids $\xrightarrow{\text{clay}}$

$$CH=CH-(CH_2)_7-COOH$$
$$CH_3-(CH_2)_5 \quad -(CH_2)_7-COOH$$
$$CH_3-(CH_2)_5$$

+

$$(CH_2)_7-COOH$$
$$-(CH_2)_7-COOH$$

$$CH_3-(CH_2)_3-CH=CH$$
$$CH_3-(CH_2)_3$$

+ Others

Fig. 5.5 Commercial cyclic products from unsaturated fatty acids: (A) Diels-Alder type addition to alkali-isomerized linoleic acid, (B) internal cylization of linolenic acid, (C) dimer and trimer acid products from soybean and tall oil fatty acids.

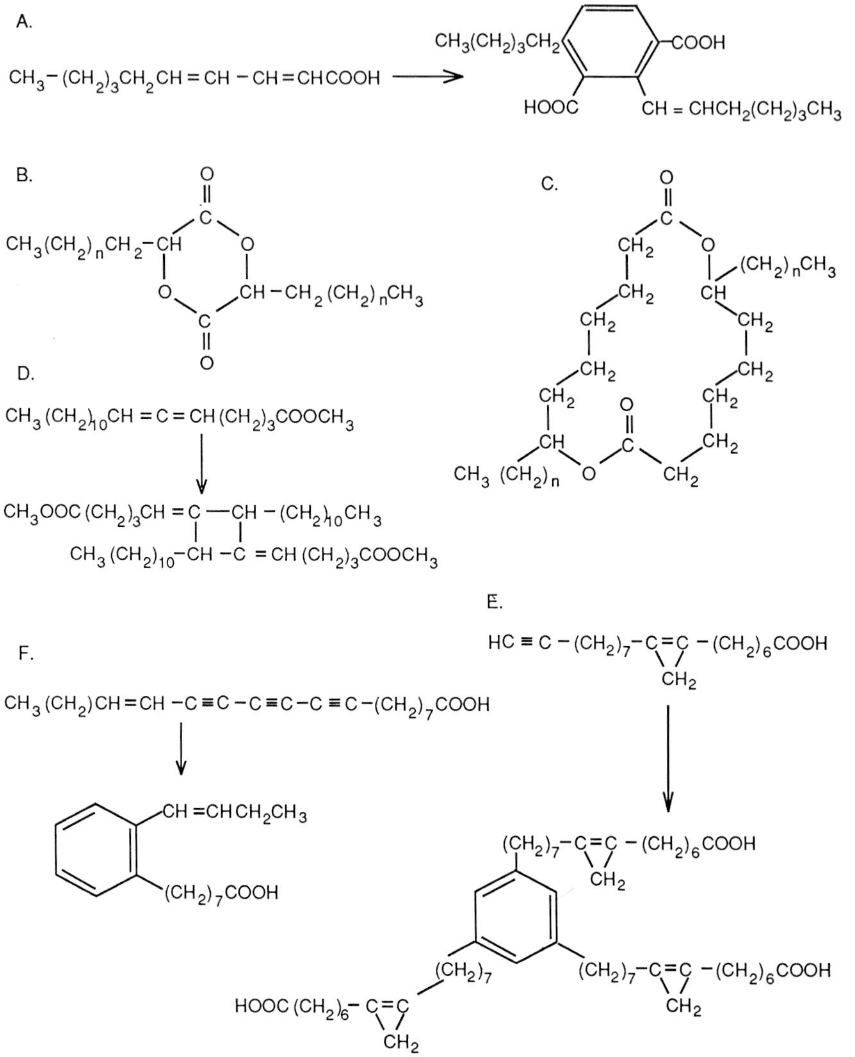

Fig. 5.6 Potential cyclic products from unusual vegetable oils: (A) substituted m-phthalic acid from Diels-Alder type dimerization, (B and C) cyclic esters of hydroxy fatty acids, (D) cyclobutane from an allenic fatty acid, (E) trimerization of sterculynic acid, (F) intramolecular cyclization of a conjugated triynoic acid.

In addition to Diels-Alder dimerization, cyclizations typical of linolenic acid; i.e. those involving double bond isomerization and conjugation, could conceivably convert triene, tetraene and pentaene structures from the seed of other plants into alkylbenzenes and polynuclear aromatics.

Similarly, various hydroxy acids available in nature could yield a family of substituted cyclic esters (Fig. 5.6B), possible good lubricants and plasticizers. Combinations of unsaturation within hydroxy acids might further allow terpene-like ring closures to also give 5- and 6-membered rings. Certain prospective cyclic esters from plant hydroxy acids (Fig. 5.6C) are reminiscent of macrolide antibiotics even though the unmodified esters would lack substituent groups necessary for biological activity.

If proper conditions were known, allenic acids, as found in seed oils of Labiatae, could cyclodimerize to yield unusual substituted cyclobutanes (Fig. 5.6D). Certain alkyl cyclobutane derivatives form liquid crystal mixtures useful in electrooptical display devices. Numerous other cyclobutane derivatives are valuable because they attract insects or have novel pharmacological or pesticidal properties.

Acetylenic oils, such as isano oil from *Onguekoa gore* Engler or others from members of the Santalaceae, Olacaceae, Compositae and Simarubaceae, are also appealing candidates for cyclization. Apparently their chemistries are not well-studied, perhaps because acetylenic oils often undergo violent polymerizations when heated. Considering the greater reactivity of 1-alkynes in intermolecular cyclizations, sterculynic acid from *Sterculia alata* Roxb. might cyclotrimerize to an interesting aromatic structure (Fig. 5.6E) provided its cyclopropene structure would not interfere. The intramolecular cyclization of conjugated triynoic acids from *Santalum acuminatum* DC. also seems feasible (Fig. 5.6F).

The chemistry of crepenynic acid, which accounts for about 60% of the seed oil in *Crepis foetida* L., illustrates how acetylenic acids can provide a variety of compounds (Fig. 5.7).

Realistically, cyclic compounds envisioned from vegetable oils are not all easily associated with needs that compel their commercial development. As with petrochemicals, best applications may be identified well after the compounds are first prepared. The purpose of open speculation about such syntheses is to demonstrate that oleochemistry has a versatility not unlike the versatility prized so highly in petrochemistry or coal tar chemistry.

Special plant groups that deserve mention in any account of cyclic and aromatic botanochemicals include members of the Anacardiaceae, Gingkoaceae and Myristicaceae that contain phenolic fatty acids. Anacardic acids from cashew nut shell oil have long been valued constituents of brake linings and thermoset adhesives. They also kill mosquito larvae and aquatic snails (Kubo et al. 1986).

Polymerization/Condensation

Cyclic and polymeric structures of various types are also achieved in whole vegetable oils by thermally-induced condensations, by free radical crosslinking concurrent with oxidation, and by metathetical rearrangements in the presence of suitable promoters (vanDam et al. 1974). Though industrially significant from antiquity, most of these transformations of whole oils are poorly understood

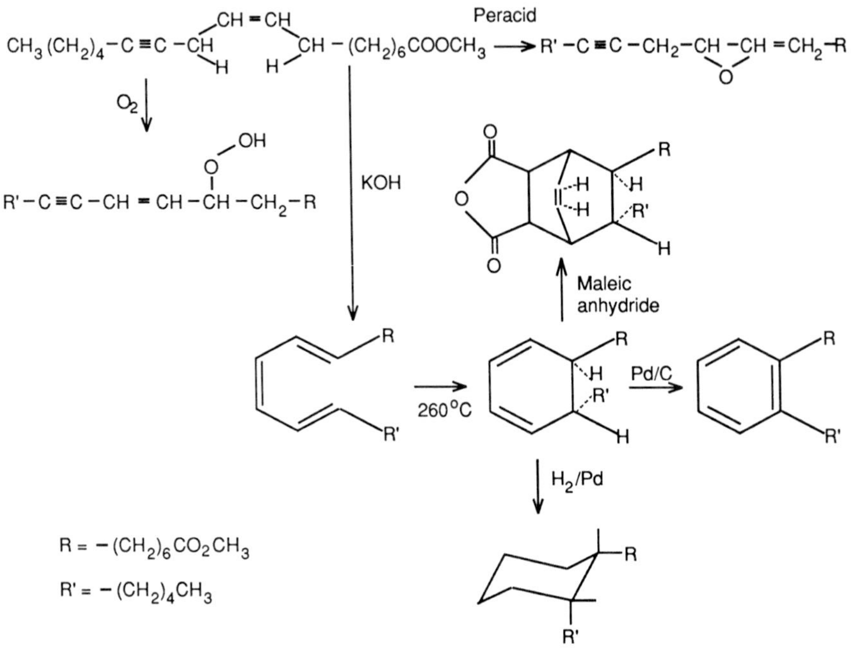

$CH_3(CH_2)_4-C\equiv C-CH$ $CH=CH$ $CH-(CH_2)_6COOCH_3$ Peracid $\longrightarrow R'-C\equiv C-CH_2-CH-CH=CH_2-R$

$R'-C\equiv C-CH=CH-CH-CH_2-R$ KOH

Maleic anhydride

$\xrightarrow{260°C}$ Pd/C

H_2/Pd

$R = -(CH_2)_6CO_2CH_3$

$R' = -(CH_2)_4CH_3$

Fig. 5.7 Chemical transformations of crepenynic acid methyl ester.

chemically and thus remain underexploited routes to specific molecular species. Economics and chemical simplicity instead favor modification of isolated fatty acids to achieve desired products. Versatile alpha-alkyl, beta-keto acids; for example, are prepared easier by alkaline condensation of simple fatty acid esters (Krause, 1984) than by isolating them from base-treated oil. Similarly, dimeric acids are obtained in dependably higher proportions by decomposing known fatty acid hydroperoxides (Gardner et al. 1974) than by isolating them from oxidized whole oils.

Oxidation

Apart from non-specific atmospheric oxidation, which is critical in air-dried coatings, the industrial chemistry of vegetable oils contains only two other prominent oxidation processes; namely, ozonolysis (Pryde and Cowan, 1970) and epoxidation (Carlson and Chang, 1985) (Fig. 5.8). Both processes are applied commercially on a large scale in the manufacture of intermediates that lead to nylons, polyesters, adhesives and plastics additives.

Ozonolysis and/or oxidation of known unsaturated and hydroxy acids can provide dibasic acids with chain lengths up to C:21 including adipic (C:6), azelaic (C:9) and sebacic (C:10) acids, which are established ingredients of polymers,

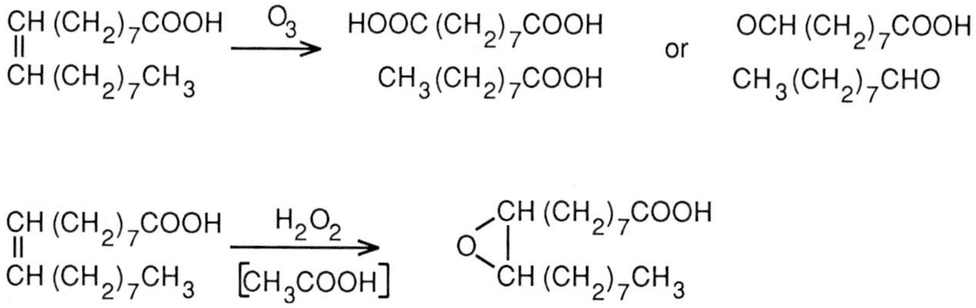

$$\underset{\underset{\displaystyle CH(CH_2)_7CH_3}{\|}}{CH(CH_2)_7COOH} \xrightarrow{O_3} \underset{CH_3(CH_2)_7COOH}{HOOC(CH_2)_7COOH} \quad or \quad \underset{CH_3(CH_2)_7CHO}{OCH(CH_2)_7COOH}$$

$$\underset{\underset{\displaystyle CH(CH_2)_7CH_3}{\|}}{CH(CH_2)_7COOH} \xrightarrow[{[CH_3COOH]}]{H_2O_2} \underset{\overset{\displaystyle CH(CH_2)_7COOH}{O}}{\overset{\diagdown}{\underset{\diagup}{}}}\underset{CH(CH_2)_7CH_3}{}$$

Fig. 5.8 Oxidation reactions of unsaturated fatty acids: (A) ozonolysis, (B) epoxidation.

lubricants and plasticizers. Interesting unexploited sources of such dibasic acids include petroselinic acid, perhaps from *Foeniculum vulgare* Mill., vaccenic acid from *Asclepias syriacas* L., 11-eicosenoic acid from *Marshallia caespitosa* Nutt. and erucic acid from *Crambe abyssinica* Hochst.. By ozonolysis, petroselinic yields adipic acid, which is used in making nylon-66, and lauric acid, a valued ingredient of detergents. Vaccenic or 11-eicosenoic acid and erucic cleave by the same process to C:11 or C:13 dibasic acids for engineering nylons 1111 or 1313 (Nieschlag et al. 1977) and to heptanoic or pelargonic acids, which are used extensively in jet aircraft lubricants. Similarly, unsaturated hydroxy acids, as found in *Lesquerella* spp., can be cleaved to hydroxylated mono- and dicarboxylic acids, which find applications in alkyd and urethane resins.

Air oxidation, by hydroperoxidation or singlet oxygen addition, is potentially one of the most direct means by which reactive polar groups can be introduced into vegetable oils or fatty acids. Recent developments in knowledge of autoxidation mechanisms (Frankel, 1985) make direct commercial-scale hydroxylations and other specific oxidative syntheses more feasible. Certainly, simplified processing of vegetable oils is needed to render prospective botanochemicals attractive economically.

Especially appealing prospects for controlling oxidation with a high degree of specificity are offered by plant enzymes normally responsible for the degradation of fatty acids. Polyunsaturated fatty acids freed by the action of lipolytic enzymes on vegetable oils are converted by a group of isoenzymes, lipoxygenases, into either 9-hydroperoxides, 13-hydroperoxides or mixtures of both (Gardner, 1987). These hydroperoxides, in turn, are converted by other plant enzymes into aldehydes, ketols, epoxyols or cyclic fatty acids and then to complex hydroxy compounds, some of which possess biological activity. In mammals, analogous enzymatic oxidations of arachidonic acid lead to valuable pharmacological agents including prostaglandins, thromboxanes, prostacyclin and leukotrienes.

Chemical epoxidation converts unsaturated vegetable oils to useful plasticizer/stabilizers for poly (vinyl chloride) plastics. It also offers routes, through epoxy ring opening, to substituted hydroxy and keto acids or to furano and pyrano structures. Unexploited plant oils that have much higher levels of unsaturation are capable of delivering higher epoxy (oxirane) concentrations than currently available. Seed oil from *Lithospermum tenuiflorum* L., for example, contains enough octadecatrienoic and octadecatetraenoic acids to carry 12% oxirane oxygen, which is less than the 18% theoretical limit for oil containing only octadecatetraenoic acid but still much higher than the 7 to 8% common to present commercial epoxidized vegetable oils or the approximate 4% that occur naturally in various unusual seed oils (Chapter 30).

Caustic Fusion/Pyrolysis

Castor oil, due to its high content of ricinoleic acid, undergoes two unusual cleavage reactions in addition to the other types of modifications typical of vegetable oils (Fig. 5.9). Caustic fusion of ricinoleic acid generates 2-octanol, a common ingredient of perfumes and soaps, and sebacic acid, which is converted industrially to diester polymers, plasticizers and lubricants. The USA produces some 3000 tonnes of simple sebacic acid esters annually. About half of this production is the traditional industrial standard plasticizer-lubricant, di (2-ethylhexyl) sebacate. Pyrolysis of ricinoleic acid produces undecylenic acid, which is a well-known fungistat and intermediate in the synthesis of a major engineering polymer, nylon-11.

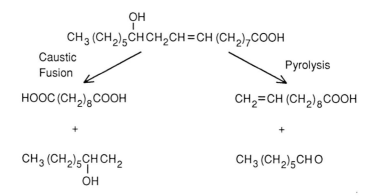

Fig. 5.9 Cleavage reactions of ricinoleic acid which result in industrial chemicals.

The necessary chemistry that can provide useful products from fats and oils is firmly in hand. To summarize, vegetable oil products that could be applied more broadly or anew to form the basis for new technologies include:

> *Vinyl ethers.* Fatty vinyl ethers of long-chain alcohols can be either polymerized alone to adherent chemical-resistant coatings or copolymerized with styrene to make coatings of various degrees of flexibility (Brand et al. 1964).

Cyclic fatty acids. Alkali treatment of polyunsaturated vegetable oils causes cyclization of linolenic acid. The resulting cyclic acids are potentially useful as lubricants (Friedrich et al. 1965) or in alkyd resins (Miller et al. 1962). Other types of cyclic acids can also be made from polyunsaturated acids or soybean soap stock.

Fatty aldehydes. Omega-oxo compounds can be made by reductive ozonolysis of unsaturated acids (Pryde and Cowan, 1970); branched fatty aldehydes by addition of carbon monoxide and hydrogen to unsaturated acids by the hydroformylation (oxo) reaction (Pryde, 1984). The aldehyde group can be converted easily to acetals, alcohols, carboxylic acids and amines, which have potential value in polymers, plastics and plastics additives.

Keto esters. Branched beta-keto esters obtained by alkaline condensation offer routes to interesting heterocyclic compounds, secondary amines and hydroxy acids (Krause, 1984).

Wax esters. Jojoba,*Simmondsia chinensis* (Link) Schneid. the sole member of the Simmondsiaceae, produces seed containing 50% oil composed entirely of liquid wax esters (Chapter 25). This oil, a promising sperm whale oil replacement, is finding use in cosmetics, skin conditioners and lubricants. Jojoba oil is also an excellent botanical source of *cis* - unsaturated long chain alcohols, which are valued ingredients of fine soaps and toiletries.

Acetals. Spiro-acetals made by condensation of pentaerythritol with aldehyde esters have potential value as plasticizers whether from C:9 or C:19 aldehyde esters (Awl et al. 1972). They can also be converted to poly (ester-acetals) and poly (amide-acetals) that have special uses in coatings and plastics (Awl et al. 1976).

Amino acids. Reductive amination of aldehyde esters leads to linear or branched amino acids that can be polymerized to engineering thermoplastics (Perkins et al. 1975) or polyamide resin adhesives and printing inks.

Polyols. Compounds potentially useful in urethane coatings, lubricants and plasticizers are attainable from fats and oils by a variety of proven methods including the reaction of formaldehyde with C:9 aldehydes or C:19 aldehydic acids (Miller et al. 1978).

Polycarboxylic acids. Products from catalytic hydroformylation and hydrocarboxylation of unsaturated fatty compounds are possible coatings, lubricants, plasticizers and resin constituents (Kohlhase et al. 1977).

APPLICATIONS

Commercialization of vegetable oil products requires more than proof of chemical feasibility. Technical, economic, social and political factors all interact in complex ways to determine the ultimate fate of chemically feasible products. Under even the best circumstances, opportunities other than those associated with traditional applications of vegetable oils tend to be obscured by the petrochemical orientation of chemical markets. New applications for vegetable oils must thus be found by assessing market needs for petrochemicals and systematically adapting botanical constituents to specific applications. Applications that can arise from the novel features of oleochemicals must also be pursued through basic research.

Annual production of organic chemicals in the USA stands near 150 million tonnes. In addition, nearly 20 million tonnes are imported in excess of exports. Approximately one-third of the total represents primary petroleum and gas products intended for fuel or further unspecified chemical conversion. About 100 million tonnes of synthetic organic chemicals can thus be identified as intermediates or end products associated with specific applications (Table 5.5). Several in a group composed primarily of surfactants, plasticizers and nylons 6 and 66 can, in theory, be related to plants even though they are not currently obtained entirely from botanical sources. Derivation of these chemicals entirely from plants rather than petroleum would double the current nonfood use of natural fats and oils.

Table 5.5 Synthetic Organic Chemical Production in the United States

Category	Production (1000 tonnes)
Misc. cyclic and acyclics	42,431
Plastics and resins	20,128
Cyclic intermediates	19,691
Misc. end-use chemicals	9,613
Surface-active agents	2,304
Elastomers	1,824
Plasticizers	777
Pesticides	462
Rubber-processing chemicals	133
Dyes	111
Medicinals	106
Flavor and perfume materials	79
Organic pigments	36
TOTAL	97,695

Botanicals can benefit from the proven performance of recognized compounds. Growth of established markets and displacement of the corresponding petrochemicals for cost, performance, or supply reasons ensure expanded use of vegetable oils. Several areas of the specialty chemicals market already identified for positive growth throughout the remainder of this century are listed in Table 5.6 (Lurie, 1985). Those that will see exceptional change should be targeted for new products. In the more stable markets, research should seek cheaper ways to deliver product performance.

Table 5.6   United States Specialty Chemicals Markets and Expected Growth (Lurie, 1985)

Market segment	1983 Market growth (%)	Average annual ($ millions)
Agriculture	5,500	3
Oil production	4,200	4
Industrial coatings	4,000	3
Specialty lubricants	3,300	2
Industrial cleaners	2,900	3
Electronics	2,500	13
Specialty polymers	1,800	9
Adhesives & sealants	1,600	7
Plastics additives	1,600	5
Lubricant additives	1,500	3
Diagnostic chemicals	1,500	10
Food additives	1,200	4
Catalysts	1,200	5
Photographics	1,000	7
Water management	950	5
Textiles	780	4
Metal finishing	570	3
Biocides	520	4
Cosmetics	520	3
Rubber	470	4
Specialty surfactants	420	6
Explosives	410	3
Paints and coatings additives	380	3
Reagents	370	5
Paper	340	4
Mining	340	3
Refinery chemicals	260	5
Fuel additives	210	4
Printing inks	170	3
Foundary chemicals	130	3
TOTAL	40,640 AVE.	5

Adhesives

Consumption of adhesives and sealants within the USA is expected to approach 7 million tonnes by 1995. Specialty adhesives, which currently account for 1.6 million tonnes annually, constitute the fastest growing component of this market. These are acrylics, anaerobics, cyanoacrylates, epoxies, polyamides, polyesters, polyethylenes, silicones, urethanes and vinyl acetate copolymers as opposed to natural products such as starches and dextrin or high-volume commodity adhesives such as urea-formaldehyde. Hot-melt adhesives, which are used largely in packaging (100,000 tonnes) and to a lesser extent in automobiles, textiles, electrical equipment and furniture (total ca. 200,000 tonnes), already provide a substantial demand for dimer acids from fats and oils. Interest in waterborn systems promises to create additional demand for emulsifiers and dispersing agents tailored to adhesive applications.

Agrichemicals

Home use of pesticides continues to grow, but agriculture still accounts for about 70% of the pesticides consumed annually in the USA. The most widely used pesticides are 2,4-dichlorophenylacetic acid, malathion and diazinon but research promises great change in this industry. Concern over environmental impact and desire for narrowly-targeted agents are expected to lead to hormone-like nonpersistent chemicals. Fatty acids can serve as starting materials for insect attractants such as gossyplure and muscalure or growth regulators such as triacontanol (Sonnet, 1984). Long-chain compounds including fatty amines, alcohols and esters, can be antimicrobials, pesticides, chemical processing agents and sucker inhibitors. Emulsifiers and surfactants from fats and oils are already used in formulating pesticides. Additional fatty materials may find use in controlled-release formulations for delivering bioactive agents under specific environmental conditions or during critical periods in insect or crop development.

Coatings

Annual paint production in the USA is about 3.5 million tonnes. Europe and Japan produce an additional 6.1 million tonnes. Systematic efforts to reduce volatile organic compounds in coatings are causing change in this industry. Currently, waterborn coatings account for nearly 75% of architectural coatings and about 25% of original equipment coatings, and the proportion will continue to increase. Due to environmental and health concerns, the paint industry is abandoning solvent glycol ethers and acetates. An increasing use of high-solids (powder) coatings and base-coat clear-coat technologies is also expanding markets for different oxygenated solvents, including longer-chain glycol ethers. Nonpolluting water-dispersed resins and high-solids baked coatings are both feasible from vegetable oils (Schneider and Gast, 1979). In addition, a definite trend toward urethane finishes for automobiles promises further change in coatings formulations. Some 60,000 tonnes of urethane resins are already used annually for coatings in the USA. Components for the formulation of polyester-polyurethane and polyester-triglycidyl isocyanurate powder coatings are now common. Epoxies are likely to be the resins of choice for electrodeposition primers and undercoats for these finishes. Whether or not a natural epoxy oil; e.g. *Vernonia* oil (Carlson et al. 1981), will be suitable for such applications remains to be seen. Latex paints, based on polyvinyl acetate and acrylics, and alkyds, composed of phthalic anhydride and polyols or vegetable oils, nevertheless, remain mainstays of the coatings industry. Vegetable oils continue to hold a substantial portion of the paint binder market.

Vegetable oil applications in the less traditional but potentially important areas of crop spray formulations, dust suppressants and sealers or curing agents for concrete should be pursued. Printing inks and photocopy toners also represent billion dollar markets in which vegetable oil derivatives have yet to be exploited, although jojoba oil might easily replace the sperm whale oil products that were once components of printing inks.

Cosmetics

Inherent profitability and product trends emphasizing natural constituents make cosmetics and toiletries appealing outlets for vegetable oil products even though the markets are tightly population-linked and subject to surges in consumer preferences. The USA beauty care industry consumes nearly one million tonnes of raw materials, worth about $1.2 billion, to manufacture items that sell for more than $11 billion. Expenditures worldwide for beauty care are estimated at $33 billion. Fragrance compounds and surfactants account for roughly half the cost for raw materials. The remainder is attributed to: organic commodities such as ethanol, glycerin, and sorbitol; organic specialties such as cellulose derivatives, sunscreen agents and proteins; inorganic chemicals, including antiperspirant salts, fatty chemicals and fatty acid derivatives; biocides; mineral oil and petrolatum.

Beauty care products sustain a fledgling jojoba industry, which provides natural liquid wax esters that serve as skin and hair conditioners. A rising popularity of thickened shampoos and lathers is further expected to provide new opportunities for emulsifiers and foaming agents from natural oils. Hair care products also emphasize quick-setting gels to achieve good hold and combability. Foams that dry as powders are expected to find further commercial acceptance especially in infant care products and foamed-on medicinals and protectants.

Flavors and Fragrances

Chemicals that impart esthetic qualities and account for much of the value of cosmetics and toiletries deserve mention more because of historical association with essential oils from plants than because this market offers any real opportunities for expanded vegetable oil useage. Synthetic compounds now account for 91% of the volume and 77% of the value of chemicals marketed by the industry. Of the 3000 or so aroma chemicals used in compounding flavors and fragrances only about twenty are used in quantities greater than 1000 tonnes per year worldwide. Nevertheless, world sales amount to $4.6 billion annually. Profitable products can thus be derived from vegetable oils; such as ethylene brassylate from rapeseed or crambe oil, but their use will hardly sustain a major crop.

Fuels and Fuel Additives

When fossil fuels are relatively scarce and expensive, attention focuses on vegetable oils as alternative fuels, particularly for generating steam and/or electricity (Chapter 6).

Under favorable economic conditions, vegetable oils can also be converted with zeolite catalysts to gasoline and other high-grade fuels (Weisz et al 1979).

Fuels for internal-combustion engines are generally augmented with additives to improve performance. The introduction of standard-equipment fuel-injection engines in automobiles and higher olefin levels in gasolines have compelled changes in fuel additives to reduce fuel injector fouling. Two types of additives solve this problem: conventional amine detergents with chain lengths from C:12 to C:22 and proprietary ashless polymeric dispersants that contain nitrogen, alkenyl succinimides and polyether polyamines. About 25,000 tonnes of such additives, in addition to other additives, would be required each year to treat all gasoline consumed in the USA.

Lubricants

The USA uses about 9 million tonnes of petroleum-based lubricating oils annually. In addition, an estimated 30,000 tonnes of synthetic fluids perform a variety of lubricating, hydraulic and heat-transfer functions. The best known synthetics that can be made from vegetable oils are dioctyl (2-ethylhexyl) esters of adipic, azelaic, and sebacic acids, which are proven low-temperature hydraulic fluids and engine lubricants for jet aircraft. Others include fatty acid esters of glycols and polyols, organic phosphates, polyalphaolefins and silicones.

Motor oils account for nearly half of the petroleum-based lubricants. These highly-formulated fluids generally contain 7 to 12% by volume viscosity index improvers and 6 to 8% proprietary mixtures of detergents, anticorrosion agents, friction modifiers, antifoaming agents, antioxidants and dispersants. Certain of these, especially anticorrosion and antiwear agents, can be obtained from plant oils. For example, fatty amines, C-21 dibasic acids and dimer/trimer acids are used as rust inhibitors, and sulfurized jojoba oil or similar sulfurized wax esters made from vegetable oils are effective replacements for sulfurized sperm whale oil, a traditional extreme-pressure lubricant (Miwa et al. 1979). Cosulfurization of *Limnanthes* triglycerides with methyl lardate also produces an effective lubricant (Kammann and Phillips, 1985). Expected changes in engine lubricants to improve fuel economy and to avoid deactivation of emission catalysts and degradation of oxygen sensors should increase additive use and possibly create new specialty chemical opportunities for vegetable oils. Jojoba oil is already used in a patented crankcase additive.

Greases are lubricants gelled by thickening agents; notably lithium 12-hydroxystearate. Not all of the 250,000 tonnes of lubricating greases consumed in the USA are thickened with lithium soaps, but this application accounts annually for several 1000 tonnes of castor oil.

Plastics

USA production of all polymers including plastics, synthetic fibers and synthetic rubber, reached 22 million tonnes in 1985. Packaging, which constitutes the largest single use, consumed about 30% of production. Ten chemical groups account for more than 90% of the total production, which is approximately three-quarters thermoplastic resins such as polyolefins, polystyrene and poly (vinyl-chloride), and one-quarter thermosetting resins; e.g. phenolics, polyesters, epoxies and urea/melamines. One small but rapidly-growing group of polymers, engineering plastics, is especially interesting (Table 5.7), from the standpoint of vegetable oil use because nylons analogous to those that can be obtained from vegetable oils are expected to find new uses and grow at rates well above the average for polymers. Major changes in plastics use will come, particularly as applications of engineering polymers and/or their composites and alloys grow with electrical and electronics industries. In addition, such plastics are expected to continue replacing metals in automobiles and/or other materials in building construction. Fabrication conveniences allowed by plastics are sufficient to propel manufacturers toward engineering resins; product performance advantages are incidental benefits.

In the electronics industry, which spends an estimated $7 billion per year worldwide for specialty chemicals to make semiconductors, integrated circuits and printed circuit boards, a trend to injection-molded circuit boards and away from copper-clad epoxy-glass laminates will soon require some 7000 tonnes of thermoplastic resins, probably polyesters, polyethersulfones, polyetherimides, and polyakylsulfones.

In some automobiles in the USA, engineering polymers already account for as much as 7% of the body weight. On average, though, the industry uses about 25 kg per car, up sharply from 8 kg, which was the average during the 1970s. Use of plastic in auto bodies is expected to reach one million tonnes in the USA by the end of the century as car makers seek reduced fabrication costs and are compelled by legislation to improve fuel economy and by consumer demand to produce automobiles that neither rust nor dent. At least one automobile already has body panels made of nylon. Polyamides also find use in electrical harness

Table 5.7 Engineering Plastics - Production Levels and Applications in the United States

Plastic Resin	Production (1000 tonnes)	Applications
Acrylonitrile-buta-diene-styrene	580	Telephone and business machine housings, cassette cases, portable tools, auto grilles, trim parts and instrument panels
Thermoplastic polyester	420	Electrical bobbins, TV tuners, fuse cases, bearings, cams, auto-ignition coil caps, speedometer frames, pump impellers, housings
Nylon	180	Gears, bushings, films, wire cable jacketing, auto body panels, fuel system/emission control units, electronic parts, switches, relays, cable straps, connectors, fishing line, rope
Polycarbonate	140	Helmets, power-tool housings, battery cases, safety glass, auto lenses, 5-gal. bottles
Polyphenylene oxide	80	Auto dashboards, shower heads, plated auto grilles & trim, appliance housings, wiring splice devices, protective shields
Acetals	60	Sinks, faucets, electrical switches, gears, aerosol bottles, meat hooks, lawn sprinklers, ballcocks, shaver cartridges, zippers, telephone pushbuttons
Polysulfone and Polyphenylene sulfide	10	Electrical connectors, meter housings, coffeemakers, camera bodies, auto switch and relay bases, light fixture sockets, fuel cell components, battery cases
Other	150	
TOTAL	1620	

and emission control elements. These applications are mostly based on nylons 6 and 66. Other nylons, which have been made from vegetable oil-based monomers, need to be examined for automotive use. Nylon 11 is available commercially from castor oil. Nylons 9 and 1313 have been produced in pilot scale from soybean (Perkins et al. 1975) and crambe oils (Nieschlag et al. 1977), respectively. Several others; notably nylons 13 and 613 have been made in the laboratory (Perkins et al. 1969). Generally these polymers exhibit low moisture absorption, excellent dimensional stability in humid environments and good electrical properties.

As the plastics industry grows so also will demand for processing aids and modifiers, many of which are either currently or potentially derived from fatty acids. Table 5.8 lists established plasticizers that are easily related to plant oils. Plants thus provide about 15% of the plasticizers used in the USA. In addition, plastics contain other additives derived from fatty acids or vegetable oils. Stabilizers, processing aids and flame retardants each account for fractions of the additives market that are roughly ten times smaller than that held by plasticizers. Several metallic stearates are processing aids, for example, zinc stearate for crystalline polystyrene, sodium stearate for modified polystyrene, calcium stearate for polypropylene and magnesium stearate for acrylonitrile-butadiene-styrene polymers. Erucamide (from rapeseed or crambe oil) and other fatty amides are valuable antiblocking agents, and the corresponding alkyl amines are effective antistatic additives. Epoxidized soybean oil and mercaptoethyl oleate are proven plasticizer/stabilizers for poly (vinyl chloride). Azelate and sebacate esters contribute to low temperature flexibility and permanency. Plasticizers derived from seed oils are also prominent among a group of compounds approved for food packaging and medical uses.

Table 5.8 Plasticizer Production in the United States Including Plasticizers Related to Plant Oils

Category	Production ('000 tonnes)
All plasticizers	777
Epoxidized linseed oil	3
Epoxidized soybean oil	50
Other epoxidized esters	7
Isopropylmyristate	2
Oleic acid esters	6
Palmitic acid esters	3
Sebacic acid esters	3
Stearic acid esters	4
Other acyclic ester plasticizers	37

Surfactants

Though not as vast as the plastics industry, commerce in soaps and detergents is every bit as specialized. With increasing frequency, products are specially formulated to meet needs of specific tasks, to reduce pollution, to accommodate preferences of demographic groups, to cope with mineral environments and/or to reduce production costs. In this changing industry, surfactants from natural fats and oils account for near one-third of a market estimated to be 26 million tonnes worldwide. Surfactant volume is linked closely to population and economic conditions. In household and personal care markets, gains made by a single type of surfactant are often at the expense of other types. Declining soap use, for example, correlates with a rising popularity of liquid heavy-duty detergents that contain nonionic surfactants derived, for the most part, from petroleum and natural gas. Real growth for surfactants based on vegetable oils, therefore, will most likely come from other sources; e.g. from developing markets and from industries where technology demands new products. For example, the introduction of fuel-injection engines in automobiles produced double-digit increases in the use of fuel detergents.

In the USA, institutional and industrial markets account for 51% of the 2.4 million tonnes of surfactants consumed annually. Such markets are expected to grow about three times faster than household and personal care uses. Table 5.9 lists major industrial surfactant types and use-distribution in the USA (Dean and Bradley, 1984).

With formulated detergents commonly compounded to include performance enhancers in addition to major surfactants, there are numerous product combinations in which new chemicals might find use. Interest in replacing phosphate builders, which commonly represent 20 to 40% of formulated detergents, is expected to increase demand for polycarboxylic acids or multifunctional sequestering agents.

New opportunities for natural fats and oils also seem likely to arise from uses for nonionic and cationic/amphoteric surfactants because fats and oils currently provide a comparatively small proportion of nonionics and because commercial chemical routes from fatty acids to esters, amides and amines are well established, and intermediates along these routes and the amine end-products find uses outside the soap and detergent industry. For example, some 12,000 tonnes of N,N'-ethylene-bis-stearamide, the nitrogen analogue of ethylene glycol distearate, a nonionic surfactant, are used annually in the USA as a detackifier and mold release agent in manufacturing rubber products.

FUTURE

For hundreds of years, oilseed crops and animal fats have supplied societal needs for both calories and chemicals. They will continue to do so for hundreds

Table 5.9   Industrial Surfactant Types and United States Market Distribution

Surfactant type	
Lignosulfonates	Alkyl naphthalene sulfonates
Formaldehyde naphthalene sulfonates	Branched alkylbenzene sulfonates
Linear alkylbenzene sulfonates	Alkylphenol ethoxylates
Ethylene/propylene oxide copolymers	Polyethylene glycol esters
Sulfates	Phosphates
Carboxylic acid esters	Fatty acid alkanolamides
Amines	Betaines and imidazolines

Surfactant market distribution

Use	Market %
Petroleum additives	30
Oil and gas production	17
Emulsion polymerizaton	12
Textile processing	10
Pesticides	5
Concrete additives	3
Metal working and cleaning	3
Water treatment	2
Gypsum wallboard	2
Mining	2
Paint production	2
Leather tanning	1
Papermaking	1
Other	10
TOTAL	100

more with, perhaps, even greater intensity as civilization exits the minerals age and moves further toward a world fueled by solar energy and tuned to recycling atmospheric and edaphic resources. Consistent with this evolution, petrochemistry, which exploits the residue of primeval plants, is a logical progenitor of botanochemistry.

In industrial markets to which fats and oils contribute, trends point to increased demand for organic chemicals. Large-scale uses of high-performance polymers and polymer composites lie ahead in autos, aircraft, recreational equipment, heavy machinery, robotics and construction. Likewise, thermoplastic polymers with good moisture stability and electrical properties will find increased use in the electronics industry. Volume growth in all plastics will, in turn, generate need for additives; notably, plasticizers and stabilizers, that logically can be derived from plant oils. High solids adhesives and coatings that can reduce fabrication and maintenance cost will also be in demand, as will liquid surfactants designed to fulfill precise requirements of specialized tasks; e.g. emulsion polymerization and textile processing.

Within agriculture, more pesticides could be formulated with surfactants made from vegetable oils. Botanochemical seed coatings or soil amendments might conserve water, reduce tillage, control pests and lower production costs. Applications for fats and oils in specialty plastics or chemicals designed for agricultural purposes remain relatively unexplored, but starch derivatives and other polymers are proving effective. Coatings to protect commodities during storage and handling also are undeveloped.

Certain unusual fatty chemicals from plants should find novel application in the manufacture of biocides or pest control pheromones. Frequently, unsaturated long-chain aliphatic structures are found to be effective insect attractants or behavior-control agents. Similar opportunities exist in the plant growth regulator field. Pharmaceuticals also offer highly profitable applications for specialty chemicals from plant oils. Links between gamma-linolenic acid, arachidonic acid and prostaglandins continue to generate interest in plant sources; notably, the seed oil of *Oenothera biennis* L., evening primrose.

Finally, lubricants and fuels represent the largest potential market for vegetable oils if not the most attractive from a value-added standpoint. Plant-derived lubricants can command premium prices in specialty formulations; e.g. viscosity index improvers for low-temperature operation, leather conditioners, video tape lubricants, retail crankcase additives, etc. Jojoba oil and other ester lubricants derivable from vegetable oils can satisfy performance requirements of a variety of lubrication tasks. The hydrocarbon-like structure of jojoba oil also makes it a logical diesel fuel extender even though triglyceride oils are currently more economical for this purpose.

Major new products and technologies must come from material science and processing research. Tough plastics based on interpenetrating polymer networks of different type polymers; e.g. polyesters and polyolefins, have already been made from oils of flaxseed, castor, *Lesquerella* , *Lunaria* and *Vernonia* (Fernandez et al. 1985). Other types of polymeric alloys and organic-inorganic polymer composites should be explored. Organosulfur research offers prospects of improved extreme-pressure lubricant additives (Schwab et al. 1980), and organosilicon polymers that contain relatively long aliphatic chains are feasible (Saghian and Gertner, 1975). Simultaneously, production costs must be reduced by improving existing technologies; e.g. catalytic transformations, or by developing relatively new ones; perhaps organic electrosynthesis.

Prospects for wholly new technologies to transform vegetable oils efficiently focus on microbiological or enzymological processes (Ng et al. 1983). Carbohydrate-transforming and detergent enzymes, which have achieved commodity status, are prototypes for enzymes in the fats and oils industry. Lipases and lipoxygenases are well known to oleochemistry, and the oxidative conversion by natural catalysts of arachidonic acid to prostaglandins and other physiologically-active compounds is a classic example of transformations that may someday be standard commercial practice in oleochemistry (Ahern, 1984). Microbial transformations of lipids, other than those that occur in cheese making and leather processing, are still in their infancy, but appear equally promising. *Acinetobacter* spp., for example, are known to convert hydrocarbons to wax esters although conversion efficiency is quite low.

Alternative to cheaper chemical transformations of fats and oils, the future may see plants modified to provide improved and therefore more economical feedstocks or specialty chemicals (Rattray, 1984). Plant breeding accomplishments with oilseeds already allows selection of oil versus protein and regulation of specific fatty acids levels (Röbbelen, 1984). Ultimately, securing lauric acid in one or two simple processing steps from *Cuphea* seed should be more economical than synthesizing it from fossil fuels or by chemically degrading longer acids. The ability to willfully specify unusual structures as required by industry; such as dibasic or cyclic acids, at precise concentration in seed oil is promised by molecular biology, but, realistically, this technology lies somewhat more remotely in the future because lipid constituents, unlike proteins, are linked indirectly to nucleic acid sequences that determine their nature and concentration. It might be easier to eliminate deleterious constituents from oilseeds and thereby simplify processing to allow new economy in the vegetable oils industry.

There is little doubt from a theoretical standpoint that renewable botanochemicals can replace chemicals derived from fossil resources. Pertinent questions are to what extent and when? Plant oil production can be expanded at will by use of high-oil varieties, but with the bulk of arable land devoted to food production traditional vegetable oils cannot be the sole replacements for petrochemicals until breakthroughs uncouple them from food/feed and reduce energy inputs to their production and processing. Where fats and oils find commercial use currently, they compete effectively on a cost to performance basis because they are food coproducts or because they benefit from constraints; natural, political or cultural, that preclude alternatives. Realistically, oleochemicals remain relatively expensive for what they deliver in terms of advantages over petrochemicals. Their immediate future is thus to complement and augment petrochemicals and to supplant them wherever possible. As long as organic chemicals are derived from feedstocks like ethylene, propylene, benzene, toluene and xylene there will be synthesis expenses that can accrue to the benefit of oleochemicals if they achieve desired performance via more economical means.

REFERENCES

Ahern, T.J. 1984. Plant-derived catalysts and precursors for use in prostaglandin synthesis. J. Am. Oil Chem. Soc. 61: 1754-1757.

Awl, R.A., Frankel, E.N., Pryde, E.H., and Cowan, J.C. 1972. Acetal derivatives of methyl 9(10)-formylstearate: plasticizers for PVC. J. Am. Oil Chem. Soc. 49: 222-228.

——, Neff, W.E., Weisleder, D., and Pryde, E.H. 1975. Poly(amide-acetals) and poly (ester-acetals) from polyol acetals of methyl 9(10)-formylstearate: preparation and physical characterization. J. Am. Oil Chem. Soc. 53: 20-26.

Balandrin, M.F., Klocke, J.A., Wurtele, E.S., and Bollinger, W.H. 1985. Natural plant chemicals: sources of industrial and medicinal materials. Science 228: 1154-1160.

Brand, B.G., Schoen, H.O., Gast, L.E., and Cowan, J.C. 1964. Evaluation of fatty vinyl ether polymers and styrenated polymers for metal coatings. J. Am. Oil Chem. Soc. 41: 597-599.

Carlson, K.D., and Chang, S.P. 1985. Chemical epoxidation of a natural unsaturated epoxy seed oil from *Vernonia galamensis* and a look at epoxy oil markets. J. Am. Oil Chem. Soc. 62: 934-939.

——, Schneider, W.J., Chang, S.P., and Princen, L.H. 1981. *Vernonia galamensis* Seed Oil: A New Source for Epoxy Coatings, pp. 297-318. *In* E. H. Pryde, L. H. Princen and K. D. Mukerjee (eds.), *New Sources of Fats and Oils* . AOCS Monograph No. 9, Am. Oil Chem. Soc., Champaign, Ill.

Chang, S.P., and Miwa, T.K. 1979. Allyl esters of crambe-derived long-chain fatty acids and their polymers. J. Appl. Polym. Sci. 24: 441-454.

Dean, J.C., and Bradley, R. 1984. Industrial surfactants. Chem. Week 135 (24): SAS3-34.

Fernandez, A.M., Manson, J.A., and Sperling, L.H. 1985. Simultaneous interpenetrating networks based on vernonia oil polyesters and polystyrene. II. A comparison of the reactivities of vernonia oil and castor oil toward the formation of polyesters. Polym. Mater. Sci. Eng. 52: 169-176.

Frankel, E.N. 1985. Chemistry of free radical and singlet oxidation of lipids. Prog. Lipid Res. 23: 197-221.

Friedrich, J.P., Bell, E.W., and Gast, L.E. 1965. Potential synthetic lubricants: esters of C:18 saturated cyclic acids. J. Am. Oil Chem. Soc. 42: 643-645.

Gardner, H.W. 1988. Lipoxygenase Pathway in Cereals, pp. 161-215. *In* Y. Pomeranz (ed.), *Advances in Cereal Science and Technology* . Vol. 9. Am. Assoc. Cereal Chem., St. Paul, Minn.

——. 1974. Homolytic decomposition of linoleic acid hydroperoxide: identification of fatty acid products. Lipids 9: 696-706.

Kai, Y. 1982. Production of branched-chain fatty acids from sterculia oil. J. Am. Oil Chem. Soc. 59: 300-305.

Kammann, K.P., and Phillips, A.I. 1985. Sulfurized vegetable oil products as lubricant additives. J. Am. Oil Chem. Soc. 62: 917-923.

Kohlhase, W.L., Frankel, E.N., and Pryde, E.H. 1977. Polyamides from carboxystearic acid. J. Am. Oil Chem. Soc. 54: 506-510.

Kollattukudy, P.E. 1981. Structure, biosynthesis and biodegradation of cutin and suberin. Annu. Rev. Plant Physiol. 32: 539-567.

Krause, H.J. 1984. Neue fettderivate aus der esterkondensation von fettsäuremethylestern. Fette Seifen Anstrichm. 86: 293-297.

Kubo, I., Komatsu, S., and Ochi, M. 1986. Molluscicides from the cashew *Anacardium occidentale* and their large-scale isolation. J. Agric. Food Chem. 34: 970-973.

Lurie, M. 1985. Specialty chemicals *are* special. Chem. Week 136(5): SAS3-32.

Miller, W.R., Pryde, E.H., and Riser, G.R. 1978. 9,9(10,10)-Bis(acetoxy methyl) octadecanoate esters as plasticizers for poly (vinyl chloride). J. Am. Oil Chem. Soc. 55: 469-470.

——, Teeter, H.M., Schwab, A.W., and Cowan, J.C. 1962. Alkyd resins modified with cyclic fatty acids. A preliminary evaluation. J. Am. Oil Chem. Soc. 39: 173-176.

Miwa, T.K., Rothfus, J.A., and Dimitroff, E. 1979. Extreme-pressure lubricant tests on jojoba and sperm whale oils. J. Am. Oil Chem. Soc. 56: 765-770.

Naughton, F.C., Duneczky, F., Swenson, C.R., Kroplinski, T., and Cooperman, M.C. 1979. Castor Oil, pp. 1-15. *In* M. Grayson and D. Eckroth (eds.), *Kirk-Othmer Encyclopedia of Chemical Technology* . 3rd Ed., Vol. 5. Wiley, New York.

Ng, T.K., Busche, R.M., McDonald, C.C., and Hardy, R.W.F. 1983. Production of feedstock chemicals. Science 219: 733-740.

Nieschlag, H.J., Rothfus, J.A., Sohns, V.E., and Perkins, R.B. 1977. Nylon 1313 from brassylic acid. Ind. Eng. Chem. Prod. Res. Dev. 16(1): 101-107.

Perkins, R.B., Roden, J.J., and Pryde, E.H. 1975. Nylon 9 from unsaturated fatty derivatives: preparation and characterization. J. Am. Oil Chem. Soc. 52: 473-477.

——,——, Tanquary, A.C., and Wolff, I.A. 1969. Nylons from vegetable oils: 13, 1313, and 613. Mod. Plast. 46: 136-142.

Pryde, E.H. 1984. Hydroformylation of unsaturated fatty acids. J. Am. Oil Chem. Soc. 47: 47-55.

——, and Cowan, J.C. 1970. Ozonolysis, pp. 1-98. *In* F. D. Gunstone (ed.), *Topics in Lipid Chemistry* . Vol. 2. Wiley, New York.

Rattray, J.B.M. 1984. Biotechnology and the fats and oils industry - an overview. J. Am. Oil Chem. Soc. 61: 1701-1712.

Röbbelen, G. 1984. Biogenese und verfügbarkeit pflanzlicher fettrohstoffe. Fette Seifen Anstrichm. 86: 373-379.

Saghian, N., and Gertner, D. 1975. Polymerization of 1,3,5-tri (1,3,5,7-tetra)-methyl-1,3,5-tri(1,3,5,7-tetra)-10-carbomethoxy-decylcyclotri(tetra)-siloxane. J. Macromol. Sci. Chem. A 9: 597-605.

Schneider, W.J., and Gast, L.E. 1979. Poly (ester-amide-urethane) water dispersible and emulsifiable resins. J. Coat. Technol. 51(654): 53-57.

Schwab, A.W., Gast, L.E., and Kenney, H.E. 1980. Tetrasulfide extreme pressure lubricant additives. U.S. Patent 4,218,332.

Smith, C.R. 1979. Unusual Seed Oils and Their Fatty Acids, pp. 29-47. *In* E. H. Pryde (ed.), *Fatty Acids* . Am. Oil Chem. Soc., Champaign, Ill.

Sonnet, P.E. 1984. Tabulations of selected methods of syntheses that are frequently employed for insect sex pheromones, emphasizing the literature of 1977-1982, pp. 371-403. *In* H. E. Hummel and T. A. Miller (eds.), *Techniques in Pheromone Research* . Springer, New York.

Teeter, H. M. 1963. Vinyl monomers derived from fats and oils. J. Am. Oil Chem. Soc. 40: 143-156.

vanDam, P.B., Mittelmeijer, M.C., and Boelhouwer, C. 1974. Homogeneous catalytic metathesis of unsaturated fatty esters: New synthetic method for preparation of unsaturated mono- and dicarboxylic acids. J. Am. Oil Chem. Soc. 51: 389-392.

Weisz, P.B., Haag, W.O., and Rodewald, P.G. 1979. Catalytic production of high-grade fuel (gasoline) from biomass compounds by shape-selective catalysis. Science 206: 57-58.

Chapter 6

Oilseeds as Energy Crops

G. R. Quick

INTRODUCTION

Vegetable oils have been considered as fuels for diesel engines since the earliest days of the compression-ignition engine. In 1912 Rudolf Diesel wrote, "The use of vegetable oils for engine fuels may seem insignificant today. But such oils may become in the course of time as important as petroleum and the coal tar products of the present time." The French Otto Company demonstrated a diesel-cycle engine running on peanut oil at the Paris Exposition in 1900 (Nitske and Wilson, 1965). The largest experiment using this type of fuel took place during the closing months of World War II when the Japanese navy, desperate for fuel, bunkered soybean oil to fire the boilers of the 65,000 tonne Yamoto, the most powerful battleship of its time.

In the Western world practically all tractors and self-propelled farm machines sold nowadays are diesel-powered. Diesel engines have the performance characteristics that more favorably suit farming tasks, and they are more reliable than spark-ignited engines. The fuel is also safer to store than gasoline. Therefore, any factor which threatens the supply, price and quality of diesel fuel is of immediate concern to the rural community (Quick, 1980).

Whenever alternatives to fossil-derived fuels are considered, fuel alcohols are the popular choice, but these are not readily suited to diesel engines. For agriculture, vegetable oils and their derivatives would be the most attractive candidates as substitutes or extenders for diesel fuel. The potential range, from seeds, nuts or even directly from sapwood or algae, is vast. One thing these "bio-oils" have in common is that virtually none are suited to spark-ignited engines. In an emergency, such oils have the potential to keep the wheels of mechanized agriculture turning. But the constraint on adoption has been and still is cost.

THE PRINCIPLES OF THE DIESEL ENGINE

Diesel-cycle engines operate on the ignition of a compressed air/fuel mixture. To achieve combustion of the fuel, the induced air is compressed in the engine cylinder to around thirty atmospheres pressure. This is two to three times as high as the compression pressure in a spark-ignited engine, which has a compression ratio of 8:1, compared with 18 to 24:1 in a diesel engine.

The fuel is injected as a fine spray into the cylinder near the end of the compression stroke and injection continues for a precisely metered period. The injection system required to inject the fuel under high pressure (250 atmospheres for example) calls for extreme precision in manufacture and cleanliness during fuel handling.

There are two principal classes of diesel engines on the market: direct-injected (DI) and indirect-injected (IDI), (Figures 6.1 and 6.2). In the DI engine the fuel is injected directly into the combustion space, whereas with the IDI engine, combustion begins in an ante-chamber or pre-combustion cell. The larger tractors tend to be direct-injected. These engines are easier to start, simpler and slightly cheaper to produce than the more elaborate but quieter IDI engine. As far as the fuel burning capability of these engines is concerned, however, there are significant differences. These differences are of great interest to anyone considering the use of vegetable oils as fuels as will be explained later in this chapter.

RENEWED INTEREST IN OILSEED FUELS

The "energy crisis," which began in 1973, revived interest in fuels of non-fossil origin. Fuel alcohols and vegetable oils were the main candidates. The rural community was particularly attracted by the possibilities of making their farms or co-operatives self-sufficient in liquid fuels. Under modern cropping practices, farmers could theoretically have provided the equivalent of all their diesel fuel needs by setting aside as little as one-tenth of their cropping area to oilseeds. Some also saw "fuel crops" as a potential means of increasing

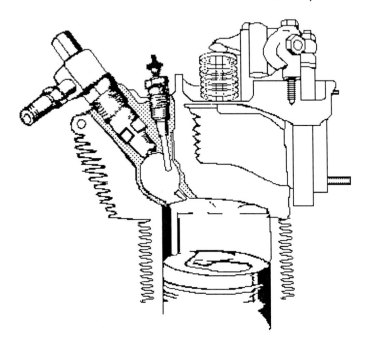

Fig. 6.1 A direct-injection (DI) diesel engine cylinder head in cross-section.

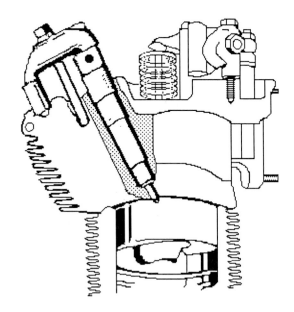

Fig. 6.2 An indirect-injection (IDI) diesel engine combustion chamber. (Deutz, air-cooled).

the demand for farm commodities. Indeed, a rapid rise in the demand in the USA for fuel-grade ethanol, used as an octane enhancer and extender for gasoline, has slightly increased the price of the corn used as feedstock in the USA Midwest during the early 1980s. But fuel-alcohols are unsuitable as direct substitute fuels in diesel engines. Major modifications or complex fuel additives are needed to exploit alcohol fuels in diesel engines.

Vegetable oil extraction, as distinct from fuel ethanol production, does not require a distiller's licence, requires far less water and energy, and produces a dry, high-protein meal by-product which, if correctly processed, is a most valuable stock feed. Oilseed fuels have a low sulfur content, are safe to store (e.g. sunflower oil's flashpoint is 215°C, compared with 77°C for diesel), and there have been no reports of the skin ailments suffered by some diesel fuel handlers.

SHORT-TERM TESTING IN DI AND IDI ENGINES

Compression-ignition engines have been operated on over forty different vegetable oils since those first tests in 1900. Initially, engine performance has been encouraging with most of these candidate diesel fuel alternatives. Short-term tests on both DI and IDI engines show that power output, torque and brake thermal efficiency on oilseed fuels were similar to those when the same engine was used on diesel fuel. Fuel consumption is usually somewhat higher due to the lower heat energy of the oil. A range of the more important fuel-related properties is listed in Table 6.1, comparing sunflower oil with Australian distillate. Figures 6.3 shows performance envelopes for a light tractor engine operating in short-term tests on crude and degummed sunflower oil as well as diesel fuel.

Table 6.1 Comparison of Certain Fuel Characteristics of Commercial Crude

Fuel Properties	Diesel Fuel[1]	Sunflower Oil
Gross heat value MJ/kg	45.93	39.38
Specific gravity	0.835	0.925
Viscosity @ 37.8°C,mm^2/5	3.90	34.7
Cetane number (Typ.)	47-48	28-37
Flash point °C	55-77	215.5
Cloud point °C	-0.6	-6.6
Carbon residue %	0.15	0.42
Ash weight %	0.01	0.04
Distillation 90% point °C	335.0	355.0
Sulfur %	0.25-0.29	0.12
Copper strip corrosion	No. 1	No. 1B

[1] Australian automotive diesel distillate

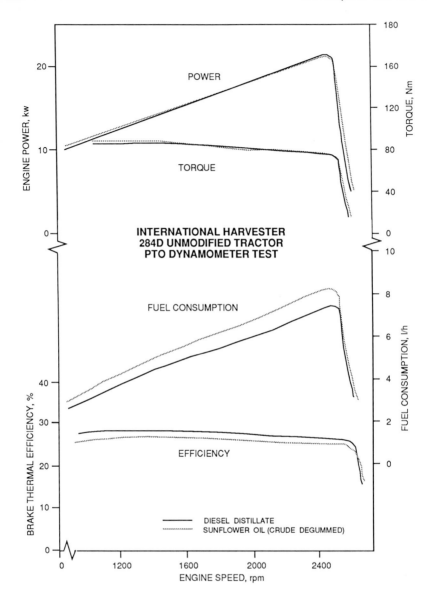

Fig. 6.3 Performance envelopes of an International Harvester 284D three cylinder indirect injection naturally aspirated diesel tractor engine, tested on a power take-off dynamometer, operating in short-term tests on crude degummed sunflower oil and on distillate.

The results of a range of short-term direct-injected engine tests show that, in general, maximum power is lowered by 3 to 4%, fuel consumption is increased by 5 to 10% and brake thermal efficiency is reduced by 1 to 4%. Unexpectedly, results vary between makes and models of DI engines, with some engine models performing more efficiently in the short-term on vegetable oils than on diesel fuel. After a certain number of hours of sustained operation in the unmodified DI engine, however, the injector tips become fouled and performance deteriorates (Humke and Barsic, 1981; Pestes and Stanislao, 1984).

Other problems specific to oilseed fuels, used as substitutes for diesel distillate, are fuel filter plugging and cold starting. Crude degummed vegetable oils must be prefiltered to diesel fuel specification, i.e. 4 micron or better, otherwise expensive fuel filters may be plugged in as little as three hours. The refining of vegetable oils to edible standards would help, but it is expensive, reduces storage life and is unnecessary for fuel purposes.

Engine start-up problems have been reported by most researchers, particularly in cooler weather. Starting aids such as glowplugs, thermo-start or heating the fuel lines, as used with normal diesel fuel, will generally overcome starting problems. The lower cetane numbers of vegetable oils may have an effect on starting ability, but cetane improvers are commercially available.

LONGER TERM TESTING IN DI ENGINES

The amount of time before power loss and engine deterioration becomes obvious varies with engine type, loading and condition, and the type of vegetable oil. It may be as brief as ten hours for linseed oil or 100 to 600 hours for sunflower oil. By comparison, DI tractor engines operated on conventional diesel fuel have a typical "life" of between 3000 and 10,000 hours before their first out-of-frame engine and injection system overhaul.

Problems with buildup of deposits around injector tips are caused, in part, by the much higher viscosity of the oilseed fuels. For example, sunflower oil is typically nine times as viscous as diesel fuel at 37.8°C. Higher viscosity means that fuel line flow and the spray pattern from regular injector nozzles are significantly altered from standard, and this affects fuel combustion. Carbon buildup around the injector holes interferes with and can eventually prevent injection. Furthermore, the greatly reduced injector bypass flow due to the higher viscosity oil (reduced to one half to one tenth, depending on class and condition of injection system) could reduce nozzle cooling and lubrication. The use of fuels of elevated viscosity without suitable injector modification interferes with needle seating and possibly aggravates post-injection dribble from the nozzles.

Coking, from whatever cause, leads to a decline in engine power, an increase in exhaust smoke and misfiring in multi-cylinder engines. Unburnt fuel washes down cylinder walls leading to ring gumming and lubricating oil contamination and subsequent polymerization of the vegetable oil in the sump. The result could be piston ring seizure and lubricant deterioration leading to a major engine breakdown. However, frequent maintenance of injectors can enable a direct-injected engine to be operated over extended periods. For example, a test on a 90KW, 600 rpm DI diesel generator in Western Australia, fueled with spoiled and discolored rapeseed oil, was continued successfully for 2000 hours of operation by; a) adding a commercial combustion-improver additive to overcome cold-starting difficulties, and b) installing a clean set of injectors at each routine oil change interval, i.e. between 150 and 300 engine hours. (State Energy Commission, Western Australia, 1981, personal communications).

With the exception of castor oil, the viscosity range of the more common oilseed fuel candidates is small (Fig. 6.4). Thus any viscosity-related problem with vegetable oils should be common to all of them. Blending with mineral distillates markedly lowers viscosity and postpones coking problems, although not indefinitely(German et al. 1985). Heating the oils also lowers their viscosity, and fuel heaters, using engine coolant as the heating medium, are commercially available.

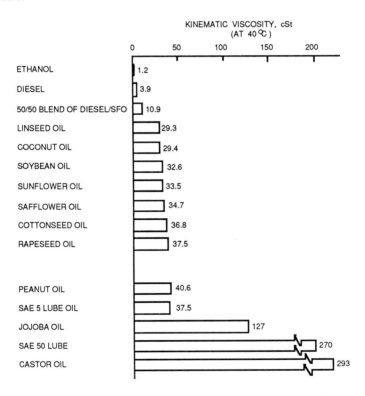

Fig. 6.4 Kinematic viscocity ranking of a range of oilseed fuel candidates at 37°C. Data for diesel fuel, ethanol, a diesel/SFO blend, safflower methyl esters, and certain lubricating oils (representative values) presented for comparison.

Experimental work has shown that blending and fuel heating does not eliminate injector coking problems in DI engines. To suggest that viscosity is the sole cause of injector fouling is therefore an oversimplification. If high viscosity was the principal cause of coking, then most vegetable oils should foul injectors at similar rates, but they do not. Linseed oil has been used at the Agricultural Engineering Center, Glenfield, Australia, to demonstrate that this oil is the most conducive to injector fouling of the common vegetable oils. A distinguishing characteristic of linseed oil is its very high degree of unsaturation. The degree of unsaturation of an oil can be measured by its Iodine number; the higher the number, the higher the oxidative instability (Fig. 6.5). The fact that in the same engine, linseed oil was used for only ten hours before performance declined, compared with 100 hours for both sunflower and rapeseed oils, points towards chemical reactivity as the primary cause of the injector-fouling propensity in the DI engine.

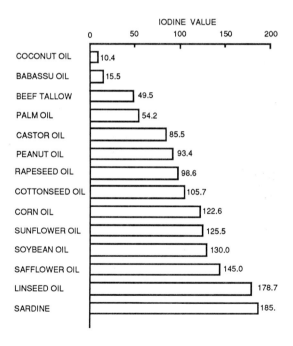

Fig. 6.5 Iodine number ranking for a range of bio-oils. Iodine number relates to the tendency of a thin film of the oil to form a skin.

LONG-TERM TESTING OF IDI ENGINES

The work of South African agricultural engineers has shown that IDI engines could operate satisfactorily long-term, at least on sunflower oil. South African tests on unmodified Deutz tractors (equipped with IDI engines) were successfully carried through to 3000 hours, with only fuel filtration needing attention. Similar results were achieved with Caterpillar pre-chamber engines running on soybean oil in Brazil. Both Caterpillar and Deutz have accordingly announced qualified warranty extension in those countries on their IDI engines if operated on the respective oils. The warranties DO NOT extend to DI engines in those companies' product line.

Work at the New South Wales Department of Agriculture's Engineering Center, Glenfield, Australia, using linseed oil, confirmed that even on linseed oil the operation of an IDI engine was apparently unaffected. At 200 hours the engine was found to show no abnormal component wear.

CHEMICAL MODIFICATION OF VEGETABLE OILS

As early as 1938 a need for chemical modification was anticipated by Walton (1938), who noted that "...to get the utmost value from vegetable oils as fuels it is academically necessary to split off the glycerides and to run on the residual fatty acid" because "...the glycerides are likely to cause an excess of carbon in comparison." During World War II, Chinese scientists hastily developed a batch-cracking procedure for refining "veg-gasoline" and "veg-diesel" from vegetable oil feedstocks, using tung and rapeseed oils in particular (Chang and Wan, 1947). Some military equipment was kept moving this way.

Esterification is a potentially less-expensive way of transforming the molecular structure to prevent the formation of the large three-dimensional networks which result from polymerization of bio-oils. The esterification process involves the transformation of the large, branched, triglyceride molecules of bio-oils and fats into smaller, straight-chain molecules, similar in size to components of diesel fuel as follows:

$$\text{Triglyceride} + \text{Alcohol} \xrightarrow{\text{catalyst}} \text{Ester} + \text{Glycerol} + \text{Alcohol}$$

The esterification process was extensively patented in the 1940s as widening industrial uses were found for esters. The first documentation of engine tests on esters appears to be that of Mensier (1952) in which a team from the Division of Agricultural Engineering in South Africa conducted exhaustive studies of vegetable oil-derived fuels and small-scale esterification from 1978 onwards. Their aim was to establish whether localized processing of sunflower oil could alleviate South Africa's farm diesel fuel supply problems. They demonstrated, and others have since verified that;

a) the ester phase of vegetable oils has a high potential and is well suited as an extender or replacement for diesel fuel.

b) Methyl and ethyl esters are effective in eliminating injector-fouling problems in DI engines. Indeed, Hawkins (1982) was enthusiastic enough to conclude that "the combustion characteristics of those fuels are actually better than those of the diesel fuel with which they are being compared...brake thermal efficiency is consistently better than for diesel while power outputs are comparable." Esters can also be used as an agent for mixing diesel fuel with alcohol.

c) Esters can be produced on a small-scale in an unsophisticated plant, although the chemical reactions must be understood and carefully controlled for maximum ester yield and to avoid catalyst corrosion of engine components. Injector needle sticking, pump failures, and storage drum and engine corrosion deposits have been cited as problems elsewhere, most likely due to catalyst in the ester.

d) The viscosities of methyl, ethyl and butyl esters are similar to diesel fuel, or significantly lower than the vegetable oils from which they were derived. Methyl esters are more stable than ethyl esters and require less steps in production(DuPlessis and DeVilliers, 1983; Quick and Woodmore, 1984). The important fuel characteristics of esters are summarized in Table 6.2.

Table 6.2 Fuel Properties of Sunflower and Linseed Methyl Esters in Comparison with their Respective Oils and Australian Diesel Fuel

Fuel property	Aust. diesel (typ.)	Crude degummed sunfl. Oil	Sunfl. methyl esther	Raw linseed oil	Linseed oil methyl esther
Specific Gravity	0.835	0.924	0.880	0.9315	0.8962
Cloud Point °C	- 0.6 to + 4.0	- 6.6	0 to +1		
Pour Point °C	- 6.6 to - 3.0	- 6.6	- 4.0	- 9	- 6
Flash Point °C	67	215	183		
Heat of Combustion:					
-Gross MJ/L	38.35	36.50	35.34	36.89	35.60
-Nett MJ/L	35.40	34.14	33.04		
Viscosity mm^2/S					
@ 40°C	2.63	34.9	4.22		
@ 20°C				50.5	8.4
Cetane Number	46	33	47-51		
Carbon Residue %	0.15	0.42	0.05		0.22
Sulphur %	0.29	0.01	0.01	0.35	0.24

Unfortunately, esters do not have an entirely clear "bill of health." Brazilian and West German researchers have cautioned of serious lubricating oil deterioration when using ester fuels, principally methyl esters of soybean oil (Pischinger et al. 1983; Blackburn et al. 1983). The establishment and maintenance of standard ester fuel specifications is a major challenge, and would be essential before widespread use could be contemplated. Contamination resulting from failure to remove catalyst was reported to be a problem, as were fuel stability, corrosion of ester storage vessels, and degradation of certain engine components. Esters are organic solvents and can have harmful effects on certain painted surfaces and plastic materials.

Crystal formation in cooler weather was cited as problematic with esters in North America (Kaufman and Ziejewski, 1983). Esters made by some Australian researchers have not been as "cold-resistant" as local diesel fuel, so fuel filter blockages must be anticipated in winter. Fuel chemists could likely produce suitable additives to cope with this particular ester problem.

Thus, not all the engine issues have been resolved. Only one manufacturer has made concessions on diesel engine warranty, allowing possible operation on ester fuels. Atlantis Diesel Engines of South Africa have indicated they will warrant their DI engines operating on ethyl esters of sunflower oil in South Africa, once this fuel becomes commercially available.

ECONOMIC CONSIDERATIONS

In some circumstances, vegetable oils can be in surplus and may be cheap in a given region. The Philippines Government, for example, is allowing surplus coconut oil to be added to commercial diesel fuel at 5% concentration. On the world market, vegetable oil prices fluctuate widely (Fig. 6.6). In any fuel costing exercise, factors such as by-product credits on oilseed meal can be used to manipulate the local value of an oilseed fuel candidate. But the inescapable feature of all costing exercises is that the opportunity cost of oilseed production must be considered for the seed alone. That is, if the seed was marketed, it would be worth the going rate on a fuel-equivalent basis, without the producer having to go to the bother of developing and operating a fuel production facility (Stewart et al. 1981; Swanson et al. 1983).

As for the oilseed meal by-product, it could be valuable, depending on the degree of sophistication of the oil extraction plant, meal quality control, keeping qualities in storage, and proximity of the market. Oilseed cake from single stage expellers, or "squeezings" as it is called in North Dakota, typically contains 18% oil from sunflower seed (a recovery rate of 67% from seed with 40% oil), but we have measured fat levels as high as 37.6% (only 10% recovery) from a screw expeller. Oil recovery from simple screw expellers is very low from such oilseeds as soybeans, without seed pretreatment. Since ruminant animals should

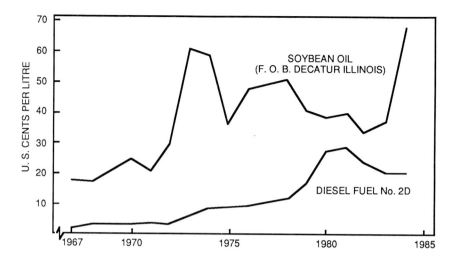

Fig. 6.6 Price relativity of U.S. diesel fuel and soybean oil 1967-1985.

not be fed diets higher than 10% oil in the squeezings; this by-product could at best form only a component of feed ration (Dinusson et al. 1982).

The keeping quality of squeezings is variable, with loss of nutritive qualities and rancidity occurring in as short a period as a week in some conditions. For these reasons, in North Dakota consideration was given to the use of sunflower squeezings as a fertilizer source (Deibert and Lizotte, 1982). Assigning the going market value to such oilseed "meals" is therefore unrealistic.

The cost of esterification may add up to 50% to the cost of the oil, depending on the size of the processing operation and the value and marketability of the glycerol by-product. There is an Australian manufacturer of a small-scale esterification process plant. This company, Bio-Energy Australia Pty. Ltd., of Kirrawee, NSW, produces "Bio-Diesel" fuel (a vegetable oil ester) and "Bio-Protein" concentrate, direct from a range of oilseeds. The raw oil component is converted into the fuel by the addition of their proprietary catalyst-alcohol mixture. The catalyst is neutralized and later removed to avoid possible corrosion of engine components. An expeller module and esterification unit, which combine to make up the Bio-Diesel plant is claimed to have a capacity of 1000 litres of fuel per day. The combined equipment was expected to sell for $42,200 Aust. as of January 1985 and units are said to be in operation in Fiji and the People's Republic of China.

CONCLUSIONS

Significant advances in knowledge have occurred since vegetable oils and their derivatives were revived as promising candidates for diesel fuel substitution after the 1973 oil embargoes. In an emergency, certain vegetable oils could be used as a fuel for short-term operation of direct-injected diesel engines. There are currently no engine warranties offered for direct-injected engines operated on straight vegetable oils.

IDI engines, on the other hand, have multi-fuel capability and run very well on vegetable oils, apparently without long-term problems. They have even been operated with success on filtered linseed oil, a very unlikely fuel candidate. In Brazil and South Africa certain manufacturers have offered an engine warranty for operation of their indirect-injected engines on particular vegetable oils.

Esters of vegetable oils are very promising candidates for both indirect and direct-injected engines, though at greater cost than straight vegetable oils.

From 1979 to 1983 there were indications that differences between the prices of diesel fuel and vegetable oils were narrowing (Fig. 6.6). Following a stabilization of world crude oil prices, vegetable oil price relatives have returned to virtually the same position as before 1979, or about twice the price of diesel fuel, with its tax included. Thus, price is still the major constraint and agricultural production will continue to rely on diesel engines and conventional diesel fuel for the foreseeable future.

REFERENCES

Backer, L.F., Kaufman, K.R., Pratt, G.L., and Quick, G.R. (eds.). 1982. American Society of Agricultural Engineer's Monograph "Vegetable Oils Fuels." Proc. Intern. Conf. on Plant and Vegetable Oils as Fuels. Fargo, N. Dak. August 1982. Am. Soc. Agric. Eng. (ASAE) Publ. 4-82. St. Joseph, Mich.

Blackburn, J.H., Pinchin, R., Nobre, J.I.T., Crichton, B.A.L., and Cruse, H.W. 1983. Performance of lubricating oils in vegetable oil/ester fuelled diesel engines. Proc. Vegetable Oil as Diesel Fuel (VODF) III: 169. Peoria, Ill. October 1983.

Chang, C., and Wan, S. 1947. China's motor fuels from Tung oil. Ind. and Eng. Chem. 3(12): 1534-1548.

Deibert, E.J., and Lizotte, D. 1982. Soil applications of sunflower meal as potential fertilizer sources. N. Dak. Farm Res. 39(6): 15, 16.

Dinusson, W.E., Johnson, L.J., and Danielson, R.B. 1982. "Squeezings" - sun oil meal for cattle. N. Dak. Farm Res. 39(6): 25,26.

Duplessis, L.M., and DeVilliers, J.B.M. 1983. Stability studies on methyl and ethyl fatty esters of sunflower seed oil. Proc. Vegetable Oil as Diesel Fuel (VODF) III: 57. Peoria, Ill. October 1983.

German, T.J., Kaufman, K.R., Pratt, G.L., and Derry, J. 1985. Field Endurance Test of Diesel Engines Fueled with Sunflower Oil/Diesel Fuel Blends. Soc. Autom. Eng. (SAE) Tech. Paper 850239.

Hawkins, C.S. 1982. Alcohol/Sunflower Oil Esters: Fuel performance tests in compression ignition engines. Proc. Fifth Intern. Alcohol Fuel Technology Symp., 2-285-292. Auckland, N.Z.

Humke, A.L., and Barsic. 1981. Performance and Emission Characteristics of a Naturally Aspirated Diesel Engine with Vegetable Oil Fuels (Part 2). Soc. Autom. Eng. (SAE) Paper 810955. Milwaukee, Wis. September 1981.

Kaufman, K.R., and Ziejewski, M. 1983. Laboratory Endurance Test of Sunflower Methyl Esters for Direct Injected Diesel Engine Fuel. Paper 83-3557. Proc. Am. Soc. Agric. Eng. (ASAE) Winter Meeting. Chicago, Ill. December 1983.

Mensier, 1952. Oleagineux 7(2): 69-74.

Nitske, W.R., and Wilson, C.M. 1965. Rudolf Diesel, Pioneer of the Age of Power. Univ. of Oklahoma Press. Norman, Okla.

Pestes, M.N., and Stanislao, J. 1984. Piston ring deposits when using vegetable oil as a fuel. J. of Testing and Evaluation (JTEVA) 12(2): 61-68.

Pischinger, G.H., Falcon, A.M., and Siekmann, R.W. 1983. Soybean ester as alternative diesel fuel tested in DI engine-powered Volkswagon trucks. Proc. Vegetable Oil as Diesel Fuel (VODF) III: 145. Peoria, Ill. October 1983.

Quick, G.R. 1980. Developments in use of vegetable oils as fuel for diesel engines. Paper 80-1525. Proc. Am. Soc. Agric. Eng. (ASAE) Winter Meeting. Chicago, Ill. December 1980.

———, and Woodmore, P.J. 1984. Vegetable oil ester fuels for diesel engines. Proc. Conf. Agric. Eng. Bundaberg, Qnsld. Aust. August 1984.

Stewart, G.A., Rawlins, W.H.M., Quick, G.R., Begg, J.E., and Peacock, W.J. 1981. Oilseeds as a renewable source of diesel fuel. CSIRO Search 12(5): 107-115.

Swanson, A.L., Johnson, R.G., Helgeson, D.L., and Kaufman, K.R. 1983. Economics of Producing Sunflower for Fuel on Diverted Acres. Agr. Econ. Rep. 176, Dept. of Agric. Econ. N. Dak. State University. Fargo, N. Dak.

Walton, J. 1938. The fuel possibilities of vegetable oils. Gas and Oil Power 33: 167, 168.

Chapter 7

Analytical Methods for the Selection of Oil Content and Fatty Acid Composition

W. Thies and D. I. McGregor

INTRODUCTION

Measurement of the quantity and quality of seed oil is essential to the establishment of the value of oilseed crops. To establish oil content and quality, analyses of many samples are required, both in the development of new superior varieties and in quality control associated with transportation, processing and marketing of vegetable oils. In addition to accuracy and precision, speed and simplicity are particularly important attributes of the analytical methods. Sensitivity may be important, for example, in the analysis of fatty acid composition where inheritance is embryonically controlled making it advantageous to carry out the analysis on a portion of a single seed. Retaining viability can also be an asset for plant breeding because it permits selections to be planted and grown to produce subsequent generations. Ideally, an analytical method should contain all of the above attributes, but this is rarely the case. To obtain the economical benefits of speed and simplicity it is often necessary to sacrifice some accuracy, precision and/or other attributes. Alternatively, multiple-step selection techniques have been developed. Simple tests are applied to screen large numbers of samples, then sophisticated and time-consuming, but more accurate and precise methods, are used to determine the content or composition of a limited number of selections.

DETERMINATION OF OIL CONTENT

A variety of analytical procedures have been developed to determine the oil content of oilseeds, including gravimetry, specific gravity, nuclear magnetic resonance spectroscopy and near-infrared reflectance spectroscopy.

Historically methods for determining oil content have shown a progression from the more time-consuming traditional gravimetric methods, which require oil extraction and the resulting destruction of the seed, to newer, faster, non-destructive, physical methods where oil extraction is not necessary.

Gravimetry

Gravimetric methods for determination of the oil content in seeds are based on extraction of the oil with petroleum ether and weighing the oil after evaporation of the solvent. The existence of several official and approved methods (Table 7.1) reflects the existence of numerous factors which may influence the analytical results i.e. the kind of seeds (plant species), the water content, the grinding technique, the type of extraction apparatus (Soxhlet for cold extraction; Butt/Twisselmann/Goldfish for hot extraction), the polarity of the extraction solvent, the solvent evaporation conditions, and several others. As a general rule, the seed material to be analyzed should be, a) as dry as possible, b) ground twice (the second time after the main portion of the oil has been extracted) and, c) extracted with petroleum ether b.p. 40-60 °C for a period of at least 16 hours (Hughes, 1969a). Modern extraction devices such as the SOXTEC system 81 (Tecator AB, S-26301 Hogenas, Sweden) or the 810/428 system (Büchi GMBH, D-7332 Eislingen, Germany) not only allow the simultaneous analysis of up to six samples, but also permit shorter analysis times (three hours) giving excellent precision (rel. ± 1%).

For the analysis of large numbers of samples, methods which allow simultaneous extraction of several samples have been proposed. Hughes (1969b) extracted up to 20 samples at the same time in stapled filter paper sachet with a 600 ml Soxhlet extractor, subsequently weighing the dried contents of the sachets to calculate their initial oil content. Another very successful method, the so-called Swedish tube method, was developed by Tröeng (1955a, b). He achieved the disintegration of the seeds and simultaneous extraction of the oil by shaking 5 g of seed together with four steel balls and 40 ml petroleum ether (b.p. 96-100 °C) in 70 ml steel centrifugation tubes for one hour. This combined method compared favourably with the conventional Soxhlet and Butt/Twisselmann/Goldfish

Table 7.1   Approved Methods for Oil and Moisture Determination in Oil Seeds

Organization	Oil	Moisture
British Standards Institution. Methods for the analysis of oil seeds. London 1968	BS 4289 I-V	4289 I-V
International Seed Testing Association, Proceedings 1966	ISTA 31(1)	31 (1)
Deutsche Gesellschaft fur Fett- wissenschaft. Einheitsmethoden1982	DGF B-14 (57)	B-I 5a (59)
European Community Regulations	EC 1470/68 II	1470/68
International Organization for Standardization	ISO 665	659
American Oil Chemists Society. Technical Committee	AOCS Aa 4-38	Ba 3-38

techniques, which need relatively long extraction times (4 to 6 and 2 to 4 hours, respectively) as well as drying and grinding of the seed material with sand between the two extraction steps. Appelqvist (1967) summarized the advantages of the Swedish tube technique which has been applied worldwide to a variety of oilseeds including rapeseed, flax, groundnut, sunflower, safflower and poppy. Recently Raney et al. (1987) developed an apparatus for the rapid preparation of large numbers of oil and oil-extracted meal samples from *Brassica* seed based on the Swedish tube method. Batches of sixty 0.2 g to 2.0 g seed samples can be simultaneously ground, solvent extracted, filtered and the meal solvent washed for gravimetric oil determination.

Specific Gravity

Specific gravity, the first of the methods not requiring oil extraction, functions on the principle of a negative correlation between oil content in the seed and its specific gravity. Zimmermann (1962) screened and selected lines of flax for high oil content by calculating the exact weight, and volume (specific weight) of 5 to 35 g seed samples using a the Beckman model 930 air comparison pycnometer. A similar method was applied by Pawlowski (1963) who used mercury instead of water for the displacement of the air between the seeds. He obtained highly significant positive correlations between seed specific gravity and oil content in flax seeds, r= -0.90; rapeseed, r= -0.84 and dehulled sunflower seeds, r= -0.90.

Pawlowski (1963) proposed the use of specific gravity to select individual seeds of different oil content. The method has the advantage that individual seeds of high oil content can be selected from a low oil content seed sample. Fractions with high (floating seeds) and low (descending seeds) oil contents are selected by immersing the seed sample in different mixtures of kerosene (d=0.8) and bromobenzene (d=1.5). Riemann and Krüger (1967) used solutions of saccharose in water for the selection of rapeseed genotypes with high oil contents. In order to remove interfering air bubbles adhering to the seed coats, seed was soaked for 24 hours in an aqueous detergent solution. The correlation between specific gravity and oil content of the seeds, determined by a refractometric method, was relatively good (r= -0.94; N=33). Fehr and Weber (1968) selected soybean seeds with high protein/low oil and high oil/low protein contents in a similar way using a solution of glycerol in water (d=1.224).

Nuclear Magnetic Resonance

Nuclear magnetic resonance (NMR) operates on the principle that when oil, or seeds containing liquid oil, are placed in a strong permanent magnetic field the nuclei of the hydrogen atoms of the oil molecules behave like tiny rod magnets and align themselves parallel to the field. By applying a second magnetic field in the form of electromagnetic radiation with a specified frequency (resonance conditions) the orientation of the nuclei is changed with the absorption of a finite amount of energy per hydrogen nucleus. The corresponding loss of energy of the radio frequency sender is used to measure the amount of hydrogen atoms and thus the amount of oil present in the sample holder. In order to improve the precision of the measurements resonance can be suspended and restored after some microseconds. By this means a thousand or more single NMR-signals may be summed and averaged. For the interruption of the resonance two techniques have been developed, continuous wave (CW) and pulsed NMR. In the CW version a relatively weak radio frequency (rf) field is continuously applied and the permanent magnetic field is periodically intensified and reduced by two "sweep" coils which are connected with a sweep generator. Conversely, in the pulsed NMR very short and strong rf pulses are applied to the sample.

For oil determinations on the above mentioned principles only relatively small permanent magnets are necessary (magnetic inductions of 0.06 to 0.5 Tesla with corresponding radio frequencies between 3 and 20 MHz). This distinguishes instruments for "low resolution NMR" (formerly "wide line NMR") from instruments for "high resolution NMR" used for elucidation of chemical configurations (1.4 to 2.4 Tesla and 60 to 100 MHz resp.).

For the practical application of low resolution NMR to oil determinations it is important to know whether the sample contains water and/or partially crystallized fat since the hydrogen nuclei of the former contribute to NMR signals, the latter do not. In both cases pulsed NMR has advantages compared with CW-NMR. If the sample contains oil and water, a two pulse ("spin echo") sequence is applied which allows the measurement of the oil content, and the oil plus water content by using the signal after the first pulse. For the determination of the content of solid fat, normal pulse sequences are used, but the signal amplitudes are measured at 11 microseconds (solid plus liquid fat) and 70 microseconds (liquid fat) after onset of the pulses. Using CW-NMR instruments oil and water determinations are possible by two successive measurements at different rf-levels (Conway, 1971), otherwise the samples have to be dried before measurement. Hougen et al. (1983) indicated that unless care is taken in establishing the conditions of drying the analytical result may be affected. If seed containing some solid fat is to be analyzed, measurements must be done at temperatures above the melting point of the fat, e.g. at 50 °C for cocoa beans and 35 °C for palm kernels and copra. Special temperature controllers must be used for this purpose.

As early as 1963, Conway and Earle proposed the use of NMR as an excellent method for the determination of oil content in seeds. In the same year Baumann et al. (1963) demonstrated that even single maize kernels could be used as examination material. Selections for high oil content on single seed basis were feasible in this case because the oil content in maize kernels is predominantly under embryonic control. Later Singh and Hadley (1968) and Brown and Aryeetey (1973) found that this does not apply to soybean or oat seed in which the oil accumulation is largely determined by the genotype of the maternal plant. At a symposium especially devoted to the wide line NMR all experiences to date concerning the CW-NMR technique were presented (Bosin, 1971). After 1971 the more advanced pulse NMR technique became popular (e.g. Van Putte and Van den Enden, 1974; Tiwari et al. 1974; Gambhir and Agarwala, 1985). Today "application notes" published by the instrument companies producing low resolution NMR's are excellent information sources for those who wish to make use of this elegant analytical tool. Since 1984 the determination of oil in oilseeds by the NMR technique has obtained the status of an official method of the European Economic Community (EEC regulation 3519/84).

Not only hydrogen but ^{13}C nuclei can be used for NMR oil analysis. Schaefer and Stejskal (1974a) obtained ^{13}C-NMR spectra from intact seeds at 22.6 MHz which displayed characteristic maxima for oil, starch and protein. They claimed that at least semiquantitative determinations of these compounds ($\pm$ 10%) should be possible. Later the same authors used the high resolution Fourier transform ^{13}C-NMR technique for the determination of individual fatty acids in intact soybeans (Schaefer and Stejskal, 1974b,1975). Apparently, the ^{13}C-NMR techniques have not been continued perhaps due to the progress in the field of near-infrared reflectance spectroscopy (see the following section) and the fact that the analysis of fatty acids by gas chromatography is relatively uncomplicated.

Near-Infrared Reflectance Spectroscopy

The potential of near-infrared reflectance (NIR) spectroscopy for quantitative analysis was realized in the 1960's when near-infrared spectroscopy was combined with reflectance spectroscopy and correlation transform spectroscopy (Norris and Hart, 1965). Reflectance spectroscopy permitted rapid measurement with minimal sample preparation. Correlation transform spectroscopy permitted accurate quantitative analysis of complex mixtures, typified by agricultural commodities and products. To date the potential of NIR analysis to determine oil content has been examined for corn, oat, soybean, rapeseed and sunflower seed (Hymowitz et al. 1974; Williams, 1975; Shenk et al. 1981; Kaffka et al. 1982; Robertson and Barton, 1984).

A particular advantage of NIR analysis is its rapid nature. A sample can be measured and final results produced in only seconds. Speed is further enhanced by the fact that several constituents may be analyzed simultaneously. Simplicity of sample preparation is also an asset. Seed samples in some instances may be analyzed as is (Tkachuk, 1981; Starr et al. 1985) or simply ground. Nonconsumption of the sample allows the material to be reanalyzed, analyzed by another procedure or, in the case of plant breeding, grown to produce subsequent generations.

Disadvantages of the NIR technique include the need for a high-precision spectrophotometer. In addition, the technique is heavily dependent on computers and specialized computer software. This is necessitated because small changes in reflectance at specific wavelengths must be measured. Calibration is required for each constituent and, in general, a calibration is valid only for the same type of sample. Because different instrument manufactures use different data treatment procedures, and various proponents of the NIR technique do not agree on the optimum data treatment, it is left up to the analyst to develop calibration and operation procedures suitable for the commodities and constituents of interest.

An additional problem is that NIR is a secondary analytical method. As currently used it does not analyze for the constituent of interest directly. The technique requires a subset of samples, called the learning subset, for which the values of the constituent of interest are known. Of utmost importance is the choice of the learning subset. These samples must be comprehensive, representing such variables as the expected range of oil content and the intercorrelations with, and variability of, other constituents (Hirschfeld and Stark, 1984).

Sample preparation (milling and mixing) may also influence results particularly if seeds have a high oil content, as oil separation may occur. For the grinding of sunflower seeds equal weights of Hyflo Super Cel has been used to adsorb and evenly disperse the oil throughout the ground sample (Robertson and Barton, 1984). Williams (1986) tested 21 burr, hammer, cyclone, impeller, cutter and centrifugal mills and concluded that the Culatti DMF 48 and the Krups-75 mills are best suited for the grinding of oilseeds. For the oil determination in rapeseeds Starr et al. (1985) compared various preparation treatments and concluded that drying the seed resulting in easier milling and better overall accuracy of prediction.

The task of calibrating NIR equipment involves selection of a minimum set of analytical wavelengths and determining corresponding regression coefficients by multiple linear regression mathematics. Wavelength selection and regression is typically performed for several possible wavelength combinations. Starr et al. (1985) compared addition of wavelengths by forward stepwise regression (FSR), best combination two wavelengths (the best pair method) (BPM), and best combination three wavelengths (the best triplet method) (BTM) and found that results obtained by the BTM method were slightly better than results obtained by FSR and BPM methods. Working with sunflower seeds Kaffka et al. (1982) used a single term equation, but second derivatives of the log (1/R) spectra at two characteristic wavelengths. Applying this method they obtained better accuracy compared to results obtained by the usually applied multi-term calibration equations.

Near-Infrared Transmittance Spectroscopy

The recently developed near infrared transmission (NIT) technique is a non-destructive method per se and would therefore be ideal for plant breeding purposes. In contrast to the NIR technique, the spectral region between 800 and 1100 nm is used. In this region cereal seeds are sufficiently translucent and can be analyzed for their protein, starch and water content (Williams and Panford, 1981; Williams et al. 1985; Glattes et al. 1985). As yet, no report on oil determinations with the NIT technique has been published, probably because of the lack of usable absorption peaks characteristic for oil in the operational spectral region.

DETERMINATION OF FATTY ACID COMPOSITION

Various forms of chromatography, paper, thin-layer, gas-liquid and high performance liquid, have been applied to fatty acid analysis. Newer chromatographic methods have improved speed, simplicity, accuracy and precision but often at high capital cost because of the sophisticated equipment required. Analysis cost have been reduced by employing the multiple-step approach. Rapid screening methods have also been developed which employ, solubility, ultra-violet photometry or visible colour complexing. To retain viability, techniques have been developed for extracting only a portion of the seed oil, or extracting only a portion of the seed.

Paper Chromatography

First attempts to separate fatty acids (FAs) by paper chromatography (PC) were initiated by Kaufmann et al. (1950a, b, 1951). Initial methods employed various mixtures of methanol in water (10 to 99%) as the mobile phase. Water formed the stationary phase since it adhered to the cellulose fibers. Later Spiteri (1954) replaced the water with paraffin oil as the stationary phase. This technique of "reversed phase" chromatography resulted in improved separations and became the standard for FA analysis. Mangold et al. (1955, 1958) and Kaufmann

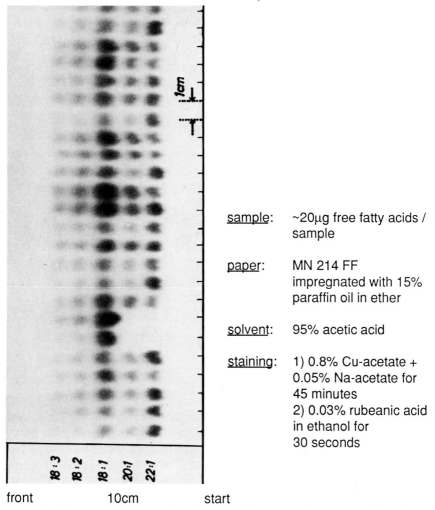

sample: ~20µg free fatty acids / sample

paper: MN 214 FF impregnated with 15% paraffin oil in ether

solvent: 95% acetic acid

staining: 1) 0.8% Cu-acetate + 0.05% Na-acetate for 45 minutes 2) 0.03% rubeanic acid in ethanol for 30 seconds

front   10cm   start

Fig. 7.1. Paper chromatography of FFAs with acetone/water as mobile phase. Migration velocity (R_f value) depends on the water content in the acetone/water mixture (Thies, unpublished).

and Mohr (1958) showed that undecane and silicone oil could be used as alternative nonpolar stationary phases. Glacial acetic acid or acetone/water mixtures became the most popular mobile phases. In accordance with the theory of the partition chromatography fatty acids could be separated by reversed phase PC according to their polarity, i.e. their chain lengths and number of double bonds. With water/acetone mixtures as the mobile phase increasing the proportion of water reduces the mobility of all FAs. Skipski et al. (1959) used a 65% acetic acid in water mixture to achieve a separation of 2-hydroxy-myristic, -palmitic, -stearic and -lignoceric acid from saturated and unsaturated C16 and C18 FAs.

In extensive investigations to find suitable detection reagents for FAs Kaufmann (1950a) tested salts of 16 heavy metals as well as osmium tetroxide and potassium permanganate. Later Kaufmann and Khoe (1962) proposed a copper/rubeanic acid reagent which is possibly the best detection agent for most applications. Using this reagent Seher (1956, 1959) and Krzymanski (1965) developed a densitometric method for quantitative determinations of FAs.

Even though the separation efficiencies which can be achieved by PC are not as good as those which can be obtained by thin layer (see below), PC is still important for special fields of applications, such as the rapid screening of erucic acid. Thies (1971 and 1974) developed a technique for the rapid homogenization, extraction and saponification of 400 to 600 single seeds or cotyledons of rapeseeds and the subsequent simultaneous paper chromatography of the free fatty acids (FFAs) of these samples. The developed and stained chromatograms allowed clear recognitions of "zero erucic" samples (Fig. 7.1). This method was later modified by Holmes et al. (1975) who smeared cotyledons onto the paper at the origin, added two drops of a lipase solution and hydrolyzed the oil traces over night at 37 °C. It was observed by these authors that in contrast to rice bran or oat lipases, which are specific for hydrolyzing FA ester bonds at the 1,3-position of the triglycerides, some commercial lipase preparations did not cause hydrolysis of rape oil.

Thin-layer Chromatography

Thin layer chromatography (TLC) came into its own in the 1960's. Methods are many and varied (Table 7.2). Reverse phase PC gave rise to reverse phase TLC. In addition to impregnating plates with undecane (Kaufmann and Makus, 1960), silicone (Subbaram et al. 1960; Paulose, 1966) or paraffin oil (Hammonds and Shone, 1964), two new hydrophobation techniques, siliconization (impregnating with silicone fluid and heating) (Malins and Mangold, 1960; Paulose, 1966) and silanization (treatment with vapours of trimethylchlorosilane or hexamethyldisilazane) (Heusser, 1968; Ord and Bamford, 1966; Douglas and Powell, 1969), have been developed to separate saturated and unsaturated FAs as their methyl esters. Argentation chromatography (impregnation with silver nitrate) has been applied to the separation of unsaturated fatty acid methyl esters and the efficient separation of their cis/trans isomers (Morris and Nicols, 1970; Chen et al. 1976). A combination reverse phase two dimensional TLC and argentation chromatography has been recently used for separation of FAs (Svetasher and Zhnkova, 1985).

A number of techniques have been developed to achieve otherwise difficult separations. Formation of mercury adducts (Thompson and Hedin, 1966) and oxygenation with peracetic acid (Malins and Mangold, 1960) has been used to separate saturated and unsaturated fatty acids. Bromination (Kaufmann and Khoe, 1962; Gosselin and De Graeve, 1975) and hydrogenation (Kaufmann and Khoe, 1962) techniques have been used for the separation of "critical pair."

Branch chain and straight chain fatty acid methyl esters have been separated using urea adduct inclusion compounds (Hradec and Mensik, 1968). Complexing with borate (Morris, 1962) and arsenite (Morris, 1963) have been the basis for the separation of threo- and erythreo-di-hydroxy fatty acid methyl esters and trihydroxy fatty acid methyl esters, respectively. Derivatization to form dinitrobenzyl bromide esters has been used for the separation of the short and medium chain fatty acids (Churacek and Pechova, 1970).

A number of detection reagents have been employed for visualizing FAs and fatty acid methyl esters (FAMEs) (Table 7.3). Reaction of unsaturated FAs and FAMEs with iodine vapour is particularly useful for semipreparative isolations intended for further characterization and identification as it is non-destructive (Barret, 1962 1974). Charring with chromosulfuric acid can be applied to unimpregnated layers, siliconized layers or layers containing silver nitrate (Dudley and Anderson, 1975). A more sophisticated charring technique involving the application of dry SO_3 vapour is especially well suited to quantitative analysis by densitometry (Martin and Allen, 1971). Reaction with rhodamine B renders FAs and FAMEs fluorescent under ultra violet light (Kaufmann and Budwig, 1951). Reaction with phosphomolybdic acid renders FFAs and FAMEs as blue spots (Ord and Bamford, 1966). Reaction with 2',7'-dichlorofluoresceine yields pink-violet spots for saturated and unsaturated FAs on a pale-yellow background (Dudzinski, 1967). Ferric chloride/sodium molybdate (Hammonds and Shone, 1964) or bromothymol blue (Ruseva-Atanasova and Janák, 1966) can be used to differentiate between saturated and unsaturated FAMEs. Copper acetate/rubeanic acid has the advantage that the reaction proceeds at room temperature and that the spots are very stable (some years) and therefore suitable for quantitative determinations by densitometry (Kaufmann and Khoe, 1962).

Derivatization of FAs prior to their separation has been used to enhance the sensitivity of quantitative determination. Ultraviolet absorbing phenacylesters were prepared by Heilweil and Beesley (1981), and fluorescent coumarin derivatives by Dünges (1977). Smith (1973) prepared fluorescent chromophores by reaction with t-butyl hypochlorite. Similar techniques are the basis of more recent high performance liquid chromatographic (HPLC) methods for the separation and detection of FAs.

A further development of TLC is the "Iatroscan TLC/FID" technique in which silica gel coated quartz rods are used instead of plates. This method permits the quantitative determination of the separated components by the aid of a flame ionization detector (FID). Using this technique Sebedio et al. (1985) separated the six Z/E-isomers of 18:1n6, 18:1n9 and 18:1n11 FAs on silver impregnated "Chromarods-S" rods.

Although newer forms of chromatography, gas-liquid and high performance liquid chromatography, have in many instances supplanted TLC, it is still an important technique particularly for fast screening analyses, and as a pilot technique for transferring retention data to HPLC (Jost et al. 1984).

Table 7.2   Special Techniques which have been Applied in Order to Improve the Separation of Individual Species or Groups of Free Fatty Acids (FFAs) and FAMEs (Fatty Acid Methyl Esters) by TLC

1) Reverse-phase chromatography

- Impregnation of the sorption layers with undecane [1,2] (Kaufmann and Makus, 1960, silicone oil [3] (Subbaram et al., 1966, Paulose, 1966) or paraffine oil [6] (Hammonds and Shone, 1964) dissolved in organic solvents

- Siliconization of the sorption layers: impregnation e.g. with 5% Dow Corning silicone fluid 200 and heating the plates at 105°C for 15 minutes [1] (Malins and Mangold 1960, Paulose 1966)

    Separation of saturated and unsaturated FAMEs except "critical pairs" e.g. erucate/palmitate (Paulose, 1966)

-Silanization of the sorption layers: Exposing the plates 1 to 16 hours to vapors of trimethylchlorosilane or hexa-methyldisilazane [5] (Heusser 1968, Ord and Bamford 1966, Douglas and Powell 1969)

2) Argentation chromatography

-Impregnation of the sorption layers with silver nitrate e.g. spraying with 20% AgNO$_3$ [8] (Ruseva-Atanasova and Janak 1966)

    Separation of FAMEs with 0 to 6 double bonds and separation of cis/trans isomers

-Separation of silanized silica gel layers with methanol/water 9:1 saturated with silver nitrate (Ord and Bamford 1967, Dudley and Anderson, 1975)

3) Other complex formations

-Formation of the mercury adducts of unsaturated FAs in a mixture with unsaturated FAs and chromatography on silica gel plates [12] (Thompson Hedin, 1966)

    Separation of unsaturated FAs (remaining at the starting point) from saturated FAs

-Impregnation of the sorption layers with boric acid or sodium borate or boric acid plus silver nitrate [9] (Morris 1962)

    Separation of threo- and erythreo-dihydroxy FAMEs

-Impregnation of the sorption layers with sodium arsenite [9] (Morris 1963)

    Separation of trihydroxy FAMEs

4) Formation of inclusion compounds

-Impregnation of Celite 545 with urea-saturated methanol [10](Hradec and Mensik,1968)

Separation of branched chain FAMEs (Rf 0.4-0.5) from straight chain FAMEs (solvent front

5) Bromination

-Development of FFAs with solvent mixtures containing 0.5% bromine [2] (Kaufmann and Khoe 1962)

Separation of "critical pairs" such as lauric/linolenic, palmitic/oleic etc.

-Bromination of FFAs in chloroform containing 4% bromine before their separation (Gosselin and Graeve 1975)

6) Hydrogenation

-Spraying of the plates with 2% colloidal palladium solution and placing the plates in a H₂-atmosphere for 1 hour [2] (Kaufmann and Khoe 1962)

Separation of "critical pairs" (alternative to the bromination technique)

7) Oxidation

-Development of siliconized silica gel plates with peracetic acid/acetic acid/water 2:13:3 (Malins and Mangold 1960)

Separation of all unsaturated FAs (travelling as oxygenated derivatives with the solvent front) from saturated FAs

8) Formation of aromatic esters

-Reaction of neutralized FFAs with 2,4-dinitrobenzylbromide and separation of the esters on unimpregnated silica gel plates or layers impregnated with dimethylformamide [11] (Churacek and Pechova 1970)

Separation of short and medium chain FAs (C₁ to C₁₂)

Solvent systems

[1] acetic acid/water 24:1 to 6:1
[2] acetic acid/acetonitrile 1:1 to 1:2.3
[3] acetic acid/acetonitrile/water 7:1:2, 1:7:2.5
[4] dioxane/water/formic acid 12:7:1
[5] methylcyanide/acetic acid/water 7:1:2.5
[6] nitromethane/acetonitrile/acetic acid 15:2:2
[7] acetone/methanol/water 7:5:3.5
[8] petroleumether/diethylether 7:3
[9] methanol/chloroform 1:9 to 1:99
[10] petroleumether
[11] cyclohexane or cyclohexane/benzene 12:1
[12] chloroform/ethylether 8:2

143

Table 7.3   Thin Layer Chromatography (TLC) Reagents for the Visualization of Free Fatty Acids (FFAs) and Fatty Acid Methyl Acids (FAMEs) After their Separation on TLC Plates

Unspecific reagents

1) Charring with chromosulfuric acid (Dudley and Anderson, 1975). Spray the plate with a solution of 0.6% $Na_2Cr_2O_7$ in 55% H_2SO_4 and heat at 150°C for 20 min. Most organic substances appear as brown spots. Can be applied for unimpregnated layers, siliconized layers or layers containing silver nitrate. A more sophisticated charring technique applicating dry SO_3 vapor especially suited for quantitative analyses by densitometry has been described by Martin and Allen (1971).

2) Iodine (Barret, 1962) Place the plate for some minutes in a vessel containing some iodine granules or spray with 0.5% iodine in chloroform. Unsaturated FFAs and FAMEs appear as brown spots on a white background.

3) Rhodamine B (Kaufmann and Budwig, 1951) Spray the plate with 0.03 to 0.3% Rhodamine B in ethanol. FFAs and FAMEs appear as bright fluorescent spots under ultra violtet light (366nm).

Reagents not distinguishing between saturated and unsaturated FAs

4) Cuprice acetate/dithioxamide (Kaufmann and Khoe, 1962) Immerse the plate in water and after that for 10 min in a solution of 20 ml saturated cupric acetate in 1000 ml water. Remove the excess of copper by washing the plate for 30 min in running water and rinse with distilled water. Immerse the plate for 10 min in 0.1% dithioxamide in ethanol. Saturated and unsaturated FFAs appear as green spots on a white background.

5) Phosphomolybdic acid (Ord and Bamford, 1966) 10% Phosphomolybdic acid in ethanol. Heating at 140°C for 2 min. Saturated and unsaturated FFAs and FAMEs appear as blue spots.

6) 2' , 7'-Dichlorofluoresceine/$ALCL_3FeCL_2$ (Dudzinski, 1964)
   Solution a)   0.05% 2' , 7'-dichlorofluoresceine in 95% ethanol
   "   b)   1% $AlCl_3$ in ethanol
   "   c)   1% $FeCL_3 \cdot 6 H_2O$ in water
   Spray successively with solutions a) to c), heat the plate after each spraying some minutes at 160°C. Pink-violet spots of saturated and unsaturated FAs appear on a pale-yellow background.

Reagents which allow the distinction between saturated and unsaturated FAs

7)   Ferric chloride/sodium molybdate (Hammonds and Shone, 1964)
   Solution a) saturated solution of ferric chloride. Solution b) 0.1 mol sodium molybdate/l water (immediately sprayed after application of solution a).
   Orange spots of saturated FAMEs and blue-purple spots of unsaturated FAMEs appear on a brown background.

8) Bromothymol blue (Rusewa-Atanasova and Janak, 1966)
   40 mg bromothymol blue in 100 ml 0.01 mol NaOH/l water. Heat the plate for 10-15 min at 70-80°C. Yellow spots of saturated FAMEs appear on a blue background. For the detection of unsaturated FAMEs, separated by argentation chromatography, the NaOH solution has to be replaced by 20% NH_4OH. They appear as quickly fading light or dark blue spots on a grey background.

Gas-Liquid Chromatography

Currently gas liquid chromatography has to be considered as the most elegant, reliable and precise method for the quantitative determination of FAs. The high precision requires a comparable precision in the preparative steps, extraction and derivatization.

The extraction of lipids is relatively simple if, for example, seed samples with a high content of triglycerides have to be analyzed. These compounds are readily soluble in petroleum ether, and need not be extracted quantitatively because the analytical results are usually calculated by the "100%-method" (percentage of an individual FA of the sum of all measured FAs.) Also the homogenization technique (particle size of the milled seeds) usually has little effect on the analytical results, provided the sample size is adequate. For the homogenization of one half of a single seed to 25 seeds of rapeseed, Appelqvist (1968) used 5 ml Potter-Elvehjem glass homogenizers. Half-seeds or single seeds of rapeseed have been crushed by Thies (1974) in round bottomed microliter trays with a steel rod. To homogenize 200 mg seed samples of rapeseed Thies (1982) used a through-running grist mill and for 5 to 10 g samples a "Krups 75" high speed mill (Thies, 1985).

The extraction of lipids is much more difficult if, for example, young ripening seeds or leaf material has to be analyzed which contains only few percentages of mainly polar lipids and FFAs. In these cases the two-step procedure of Folch (1957) or the four-step procedure of Bligh and Dyer (1959) have usually been applied. With both methods chloroform/methanol mixtures (2:1 and 3:2 v/v, respectively) are used in conjunction with water or salt solutions (0.04 to 0.9% Na, K, Ca or Mg chlorides) for the extraction of the lipids and FFAs. These extraction procedures have been re-examined by Schmid and coworkers among others in view of the relatively instability of chloroform (Schmid and Hunter, 1971; Schmid, 1973; Schmid et al. 1973). But after extensive studies they concluded that "chloroform is probably the best solvent for complete extraction of lipids at present." However, care has to be taken if lipids which have been extracted with chloroform are subsequently transmethylated. Ethanol which is usually used as chloroform stabilizer may form FA ethyl ester artifacts resulting in extraneous peaks in GLC chromatograms (Johnson et al. 1976).

Fatty acids can be separated by GLC as free acids. Metcalfe (1960) used polyester phase treated with phosphoric acid and Emery and Koerner (1962) used Tween 80-phosphoric acid to suppress the dissociation. However, despite these and other precautions peak tailing and ghost peaks, i.e. peaks due to the appearance of substances belonging to previous analyses, could not be fully eliminated. Thus the analysis of FAs as their methyl esters, already proposed by Quinn and Hobbs (1958), is today common practice. Methyl esters have been prepared by either methylation of FFAs following saponification of lipids or direct transmethylation of lipid esters.

Saponification is typically performed by hydrolyzing the lipid in potassium hydroxide at elevated temperature, followed by acidifying and extracting the liberated FFAs with organic solvents (Appelqvist, 1968). An interesting saponification method using the exothermal reaction with a solution of one part chloroform two parts saturated methanolic potassium hydroxide for the fast and complete hydrolysis of triglycerides, phospholipids and cholesterol esters has also been described by Husek et al. (1973).

Originally methylation of the liberated FFAs (Table 7.4) was performed in methanol using acid as a catalyst (i.e. Stoffel et al. 1959). In 1961 Metcalfe and Schmitz proposed the use of a Lewis acid, boron trifluoride, as an effective methylation catalyst. In a comprehensive study, Kleiman et al. (1969) pointed to the usefulness of boron trifluoride as catalyst for the methylation of FAs containing conjugated double bonds, hydroxy and epoxy groups and the cyclopropene ring in addition to common FAs. However, care has to be taken if boron trifluoride is used as transmethylation reagent. Solomon et al. (1974) demonstrated the strong influence of the sample size/amount of reagent ratio on the analytical results. Supina (1964) suggested the use of boron trichloride noting that boron trichloride is more stable, can be stored at room temperature and, because of its lower vapor pressure, reactions can be carried out at higher temperatures, which is desirable e.g. if very long chain FFAs have to be methylated. Employing boron trichloride as catalyst Barnes and Holaday (1972) demonstrated the feasibility of the methylation of FAs of peanut oil directly in ground peanuts without oil extraction. Data collected using this technique showed a mean standard deviation of 0.19% compared to a mean standard deviation of 0.31% for a conventional technique.

Transmethylation is the preferred method if samples contain mainly triglycerides. The method of Luddy et al. (1960) for the transmethylation of cholesterol esters undoubtedly has some advantages over other transmethylation procedures. The reagent, sodium methylate in methanol, is very stable, no other hazardous chemicals are necessary and the reaction proceeds relatively fast at room temperature for triglycerides, or at slightly elevated temperatures for polar lipids, steroid esters and waxes. Various modifications of transmethylation with sodium methylate have been applied by numerous authors (Appelqvist, 1968; Oette, 1968; Oette et al. 1970). A micromethod for the transmethylation of phosphatidyl choline on potassium methoxide impregnated Celite microcolumns has been described by Marmer (1978). In order to determine FFAs methanolysis using 0.2 N-methanolic (m-trifluoromethylphenyl) trimethylammonium hydroxide may be applied (McCreary et al. 1978). This strongly basic compound catalyses the transmethylation of ester bonded lipids with the same efficiency as sodium methylate but has the advantage that FFAs are converted to the salts which thermally decompose to form the corresponding FAMEs when injected into the GLC. Similar "on column" pyrolysis techniques have been applied by Gerhardt and Gehrke (1977) using trimethyl-(α,α,α-trifluoro-m-tolyl) ammonium hydroxide and by Metcalfe and Wang (1981) using tetramethyl ammonium hydroxide.

Table 7.4   Most Widely Used Techniques for the Methylation and Silyation of Fatty Acids before their Analysis by GLC

A) Transmethylation of lipids

1) Weak base catalyzed, sodium methoxide method (Luddy,1960)
Heating of fats and oils (glycerides, phosphoglycerides, waxes, cholesterol and cerebroside esters) in 0.1 to 0.5 mol sodium methoxide/l dry methanol for 5 min at 65°C, acidification with 50% $NaHSO_4$ and extraction of the FAMEs into a hexane phase.

2) Strong base catalyzed, TFMP-TMH method (McCreary et al. 1978)
Reaction of the lipids in benzene and 0.2 N methanolic (m-tri-fluoromethylphenyl) trimethylammonium hydroxide at room temperature for 30 min. Direct injection of an aliquot of the crude reaction mixture into the gas chromatograph.

3) Acid catalyzed, DMP method (Mason and Waller, 1964)
Reaction of fats and oils in a mixture of dry benzene and dry methanolic HCl containing DMP (2,2-dimethoxypropane) for at least six hours at room temperature. After neutralization with a mixture of $NaHCO_3$, and Na_2SO_4 the solution is ready for GLC analysis. The addition of DMP elimiinates the need for elevated temperatures because it drives the reaction to completion (formation of isopropylidene glycerol which does not disturb the following GLC analysis).

4) Acid catalyzed, acetyl chloride method (Downey and Craig, 1964)
Refluxing of oils or oil bearing seed tissues in a mixture of methanol, benzene and acetyl chloride (20:4:1, v.v.v) for 30 to 60 minutes followed by evaporation of the reagent mixture on a rotary evaporator.

B) Methylation of free fatty acids

1) BF_3 catalyzed method (Metcalfe and Schmitz, 1961)
FFAs are heated a few mintues at 100°C with 12 to 14% BF_3 in dry methanol. After addition of water the FAMEs are extracted with hexane.

2) Cu^{++} catalyzed method (Hoshi et al. 1973)
FFAs are dissolved in a mixture of chloroform-methanolic HCl-cupric acetate and kept at room temperature for 30 minutes. After addition of water the FAMEs are extracted with hexane.

C) Silyation of free acids including their hydroxy and keto derivatives (Donike, 1969)
Dissolution and heating of the FAs in N-methyl-N-trimethylsilyltrifluoroacetamide (MSTFA) at 70°C for 20 minutes

Medium polar stationary phases, such as ethylene glycol adipate (EGA), diethylene glycol adipate (DEGA), ethylene glycol phthalate (EGP), butanediol succinate (BDS), ethylene glycol succinate (EGS), diethylene glycol succinate (DEGS) and Reoplex 400, which allow the separation according chain length and degree of unsaturation have been used for the analysis of FAMEs on packed columns. Hofstetter et al. (1965) has separated 79 individual FAMEs on four different stationary phases. A mixed cyano silicone phase, especially useful for rapeseed FAMEs, has been developed by Supelco Inc., Bellefonte, USA. But this stationary phase can also be used for the separation of medium chain FAs. The same company offers FAME mixtures according to the recommendations of the American Oil Chemist's Society and the National Institute of Health for identification and calibration purposes. The GLC of FAMEs is usually straight forward. But variation of the sample size may have a considerable influence on the analytical values (Seher and Josephs, 1969; Seino et al. 1973). The presence of "critical pairs," FAMEs that are not fully separated on packed columns, can contribute to intra- and interlaboratory variability. However, this problem can be resolved by employing the high resolution of fused silica capillary columns. The chromatogram shown in Fig. 7.2 has been obtained with helium as carrier gas. Hydrogen, which has been used in one of the authors' (Thies) laboratories for 15 years without incident, further improves separation.

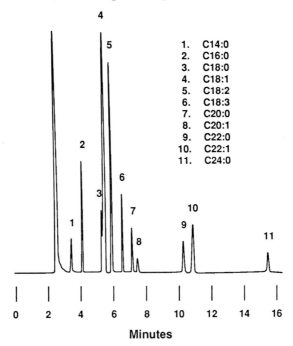

Fig. 7.2 Capillary gas chromatogram of rapeseed FAMEs. *Column*: Supelcowax 10 fused silica capillary column, 30m x 0.25 mm i. d., 0.25 μm d$_f$, 240 °C. *Carrier gas*: He, 20 cm/sec., split ratio 100:1. *Sample*: 5 μg each component on column.

All FAs which are not straight chain saturated, cis monounsaturated or poly-unsaturated FAs with all-cis homoallylic double bonds, are termed "unusual fatty acids." Such FAs may possess double bonds with a trans configuration, double bonds at an uncommon position within the chain, triple bonds, conjugated double bonds, oxygen containing functional groups, branch chains, ring structures and others (Smith, 1970). Some unusual FAs have been widely used for technical purposes, for example, licanic acid [4-oxo-18:3 (9, 11, 13)] which is an important constituent of the oiticica oil, and the unsaturated C12-hydroxy-FAs of the carnauba wax (Godin and Spensley, 1967). Others are of pharmaceutical interest, for example, hydnocarpic acid [11-(cyclopent-2-enyl)-11:0] which has been used as a drug against leprosy (Abdel-Moety, 1981). Since the early 1960's when a research group of the USDA in Peoria (USA) started their extensive program "Search for New Industrial Oils" (Miller et al. 1965) interest in new natural sources of unusual FAs for industrial utilization has increased considerably. Prerequisites were suitable identification and quantification techniques.

Comprehensive reviews on identification methods for unusual FAs have been compiled by Gunstone (1975) and Smith (1976). Ultraviolet spectra may be used for the identification of conjugated dienes, trienes and FAs containing a keto group. FAs with trans-trans configurations, cyclopropene or OH-groups may be identified on the basis of the characteristic absorption maxima in the infrared region. To date, the most powerful method for the determination of the structure of FAs has been capillary gas liquid chromatography/mass spectrometry (GC/MS).

Gas liquid chromatography has also proved to be very useful for quantitative determinations. Positional and stereo isomers can be separated on high polar, wall coated open tubular (WCOT) fused silica capillaries (anonymous, 1983; anonymous, 1984; Beaumelle and Vial, 1986), cyclopentenyl FAs on glass capillaries coated with "Free Fatty Acid Phase" (FFAP) (Spener and Tober, 1981) and cyclopropenoic FAs on glass capillaries coated with Carbowax 20 M (Gaydou and Ramanoelina, 1984).

High Performance Liquid Chromatography

Application of high performance liquid chromatography (HPLC) is relatively new to fatty acid analysis. It has been particularly useful for separating species of FFAs, FAMEs and FA derivatives which can not be separated by GLC. This includes FAs with hydroxy groups near the middle of the chain, and oxidation products of FAs and FAMEs which have relatively long retention times or cannot be eluted from GLC columns at all. Almost without exception, reverse phase columns have been used for HPLC separation (Table 7.5 and references therein). The notable exception was the use of Porasil by Netting and Duffield (1984). The chromatogram depicted in Fig. 7.3 illustrates the resolution that can be achieved between oxidized FAs which in turn have been well separated from normal FAs.

Table 7.5 Analytical Conditions which have been Used for the Separation by HPLC of FFAs, FAMES, or FA Esters with UV Absorbing or Fluorescent Chromophores

Separation as:	Fatty acid species and number	Detection	Type of column	Mobile phase	Reference
FFAs	16:0 to 22:6 (16 FAs in 100 min)	192 nm[a] 205 nm[b]	Zorbax-ODS,5-6μ 150/250 x 4.6 mm	(1)	Aveldano et al. 1983
FFAs	14:0 to 18:3 (8 FAs in 50 min)	RI, 8x	LiChrosorb-8,10μ 250 x 4.6 mm	(2)	Bailie et al. 1982
FFAs	16:0 to 18:3 (9 FAs in 13 min)	215 nm	Supelcosil LC-8,5μ 250 x 4.6 mm	(3)	N.N. 1984
FAMEs	16:0 to 18:3 (5 FAs in 17 mm)	RI, 4x	Supelcosil LC-18,5μ 250 x 4.6 mm	(4)	N.N. 1984
FAMEs	16:0 to 18:3	RI	μ Bondapak C18 300 x 4 mm	(5)	Manku, 1983
FAMEs	4:0 to 18:1	RI	LiChrosorb-10 RP18 250 x 5 mm	(6)	Christie et al. 1984
FAMEs	14:0 to 30:0	210 nm	Separon SI CL	(10)	Rezanka and Podojil, 1985
FAMEs	14:0 to 18:3 (7 FAs in 20 min)	195- 215 nm	LiChrosorb RP 8 LiChrosorb RP 18 250 x 4.6 mm	(6)	Bianchini et al., 1982
phenacyl-ester,	12:0 to 24:0 (15 FAs)	254 nm	μ Bondapak C18	(6)	Borch, 1975

Derivative	Range (FAs)	Detection	Column	Mobile phase	Reference
p-bromo-phenacyl, p-chloro-phenacyl, 2-naphthacyl-ester	2:0 to 22:6 (42 FAs)	254 nm	µ Bondapak C18	(6)	Jordi, 1978
p-phenylazo-phenacyl ester	C1-C20	330 nm	Bio-Sil ODS, 5µm 250 x 4 mm	(6)	Vioque et al. 1985
pentafluoro-benzyl ester	saturated FAs unsaturated FAs	254 nm	µ Bondapak C18 µ Porasil, 10µ 300 x 7.8 mm	(7) (8)	Netting & Duffield, 1984
4-bromo-methyl-7-acetoxycoumarin derivative	6:0 to 20:4 (18 FAs in 70 min)	ex: 365 nm em: 460 nm	LiChrosorb RP-18,5µm 250 x 4.0	(9)	Tsuchiya, 1984
9-anthryldiazo methane	18:0 to 20:5	ex: 345 nm em: 416 nm	Zorbax-C8 150 x 4.6 mm	(5)	Ichinose and Nakamura, 1984

Mobile phases:

(1) acetonitrile/8-30 mmol H_3PO_4 per liter (different proportions)

(2) acetonitrile/tetrahydrofurane/water, 67:3:30 with 0.1% acetic acid

(3) acetonitrile/tetrahydrofurane/0.1% H_3PO_4, 50.4:21.6:28.0

(4) acetonitrile/tetrahydrofurane/acetone, 42:7.6:50

(5) methanol/water 90:10

(6) acetonitrile/water

(7) methanol/water, 19:1

(8) dichloromethane/hexane, 3:17 half saturated with water

(9) gradient elution: Solvent a): methanol/acetonitrile/water, 35:35:30 solvent b): methanol/water, 90:10

(10) methanol/water, 50:50 to 100% methanol

Abbreviations: RI = refractive index detector, ex: exitation, em: emission a) wavelength used for unsaturated FAs b) wavelength used for saturated FAs

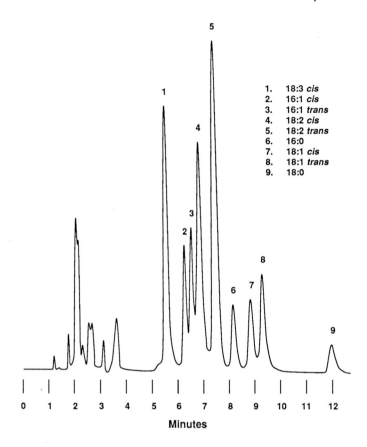

Fig. 7.3 HPLC chromatogram of FFAs and FFA oxidation products. *Column:* Supelcosil LC-8 (RP), 25 cm x 4.6 mm, 5 μm packing. Supelcosil guard column LC-8, 2 cm x 4.6 mm, 5 μm. *Mobile phase:* acetonitrile: tetrahydrofuran: 0.1% H_3PO_4 (50.4:21.6:28), 1.6 ml/min., 1332 psig. *Detector:* 215 nm UV, 0.05 AUFS. *Sample:* 10μl.

Suitable systems for the detection and quantitation of FAs include refractive index, ultra violet and fluorescence photometry. Each has advantages and drawbacks. Refractive index detectors have the advantage that their response is similar for saturated and unsaturated FAs. In order to compensate for the low sensitivity, relatively high amounts of sample have to be analyzed. This presupposes mobile phases with high proportions of organic solvents for proper dissolution, but this impedes satisfactory separations. Ultraviolet detectors are more sensitive, at least at very short wave lengths (195-215 nm), but the response to FAs depends on the number and configuration of their double bonds. These drawbacks may be the reason that HPLC analyses of FAs as derivatives containing ultraviolet absorbing or fluorescent chromophores has become popular despite

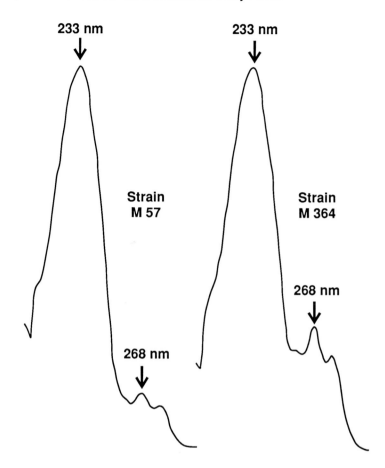

Fig. 7.4 UV spectra of seed oils from two rape mutants after transmethylation of the triglycerides and alkali isomerization of the polyenioc FAs. The linoleic and linolenic acid content was 18.1 and 4.1% in mutant M57 and 22.0 and 16.6% in mutant M364, respectively.

additional sample preparation steps. For example, ultraviolet detection of phenacyl esters allows detection down to the nanogram level and this sensitivity may even be further improved down to picogram quantities by labelling the FAs with fluorescent chromophores. In addition to examples cited in Table 7.5, the following publication dealing with similar labelling techniques have appeared: ultraviolet absorbing chromophores (Politzer et al. 1973; Cooper and Anders, 1974; Durst et al. 1975; Hoffmann and Liao, 1976; Pei et al. 1976; Miller et al. 1978; Miwa et al. 1986) and fluorescent chromophores (Dünges and Seiler, 1978; Lam and Grushka, 1978; Lloyd, 1979, 1980; Barker et al. 1980; Yamaguchi et al. 1985; Ito et al. 1985).

Rapid Screening Methods

Several methods of fatty acid analysis have been developed to facilitate handling of large numbers of samples either for plant breeding purposes, or for quality control in the transportation and marketing of oilseeds. These include measurement of linoleic and linolenic acid by photometry, measurement of linolenic acid with thiobarbituric acid, and determination of erucic acid content by solubility (Crismer value).

Extraction of a portion of the seed oil, or a portion of the seed without destroying the viability of the seed can also facilitate plant breeding.

a) Photometry:

Fatty acids with methylene interrupted double bonds, such as linoleic and linolenic acid, can be measured photometrically by reacting them with tert-potassium butylate and ethylene glycol dimethyl ether dissolved in tert-butanol to convert them to their corresponding isomers with conjugated double bonds. These isomers, e.g. the conjugated dienes from 18:2 with double bonds distributed between C5 and C16 and predominantly with *cis, trans* configuration, possess characteristic absorption maxima in the ultraviolet spectral region (233 nm for linoleic and 268 nm for linolenic) which can be used for quantitative determinations (Fig. 7.4). On the basis of this principle Rakow and Thies (1972) screened 13,000 cotyledons of rapeseed within the framework of a mutation experiment and selected single plants with seeds containing relatively high contents of linoleic acid (35 to 40%) or low concentrations of linolenic acid (4 to 6%).

b) Thiobarbituric Acid Test:

After oxidation with the aid of ultraviolet light linolenic and higher unsaturated FAs yield malonaldehyde which reacts with thiobarbituric acid (TBA) resulting in a red coloured complex (Holman and Rahm, 1966). Since linolenic acid containing oilseeds like rapeseed, flax and soybean do not contain FAs with more than three double bonds this reaction can be used for the selection of plant genotypes with reduced or increased linolenic acid levels. For the visual differentiation between rapeseeds containing low and high concentrations of linolenic acid McGregor (1974) proposed a spot test technique. This method was used by Green (1985) for the selection of flax genotypes with reduced contents of linolenic acid (from 34 to less than 3%). A more sophisticated procedure has been proposed by Thies (1974). A 1 cm wide paper strip was impregnated with a solution containing TBA, benzophenone (as photosensitizer), Fe^{+++} (as oxidation catalyst) and glycerol (for higher reaction speed). The paper strip was used for continuous running of an "analysis street" permitting automatic densitometry of the formed spots.

c)   Crismer Values:
      For the rapid and simple estimation of the erucic acid content, such as
      commercial lots of rapeseeds, McGregor (1977) developed a method
      based on the Crismer value, the miscibility of glycerides in alcohol sol-
      vent mixtures at given temperatures. A measured amount of oil, extract-
      ed by pressing, was solubilized in a methanol/propanol mixture by heat-
      ing to 70 °C and the time required for the mixture to cloud at ambient
      temperature noted. When unknown samples were compared to samples
      of known erucic acid content, erucic acid could be determined with a
      reliability of ±2 % at the 5 % erucic acid level. Ribailler and Riout
      (1978) improved the oil extraction procedure using the chlorofluorocar-
      bon "Flugene 113" (trichloro-112, trifluoro-122 ethane) as extraction
      solution. Sahasarbude (1977) using the official method of the AOCS
      (method Cb 4-35) found that oil samples containing up to 5.1% erucic
      acid gave an average "Crismer" value of 68.45 ± 0.92 and oils with 20-
      45% erucic acid values between 76 and 82. Shpota and Podkolzina
      (1982a and 1982b) determined erucic acid contents of rapeseed oils
      working at much lower temperatures (-30°C).

d)   Half-seed Technique:
      The "half-seed technique" provides a means of optimizing selection
      work within plant breeding programs. It can be applied if a desired or
      unwanted quality characteristic is determined by the genetic constitu-
      tion of the embryo developing in seeds of a F_1 plant, and if the storage
      materials are mainly deposited in the cotyledons. One cotyledon, or a
      portion of both, can be used for the chemical analysis and the remainder
      can be saved for growing into a plant. Downey and Harvey (1963) de-
      veloped the technique and used it for selection of zero-erucic rapeseed
      cultivars (Downey and Craig, 1964). It has been subsequently used to
      select Spanish-type peanuts with a high oleic/linoleic fatty acid ratio
      (<25% linoleic acid) (Young and Waller, 1972), to follow the oil com-
      position of sunflower inbred lines (Putt et al. 1969), and to study the in-
      heritance of oleic acid in sunflower seeds (Urie, 1985) . Advantages of
      the half-seed technique over the sampling of seeds from F_2 plants are, a)
      its ability to allow genetic analysis one generation earlier, b) to reduce
      growing space as it is required for only a few F_1 plants and, c) to avoid
      misclassification of plants, due to inadequate sampling or random devi-
      ation within the sample of seed from F_2 plants (Downey and Harvey,
      1963). For highly self-incompatible species, such as *Brassica campes-
      tris* turnip rape, it avoids any difficulty in obtaining an adequate sample
      of selfed-seed to characterize the plant, and avoids the considerable
      work required to obtain selfed seed by bud pollination (Downey and
      Harvey, 1963).

REFERENCES

Abdel-Moety, E.M. 1981. Cyclopentenfettsauren als Ausgangsmaterial zur Gewinnung neuer Wirkstoffe. Fette Seifen Anstrichm. 83: 65-70.

Anonymous 1983. Supelco, Inc., Bellefonte, Pennsylvania, USA, Catalog 21, 1983, pp. 18-19.

Anonymous 1984. Analyze free fatty acids and fatty acid methyl esters by HPLC. The Supelco Reporter 3: No. 3., pp. 6-7.

Appelqvist, L.-A. 1968. Rapid methods of lipid extraction and fatty acid methyl ester preparation for seed and leaf tissue with special remarks on preventing the accumulation of lipid contaminants. Arkiv for Kemi 28(36): 551-570.

Aveldano, M.I., Van Rollins, M., and Horrocks, L.A. 1983. Separation and quantitation of free fatty acids and fatty acid methyl esters by reverse phase high pressure liquid chromatography. J. Lipid Res. 24: 83-93.

Bailie, A.G., Wilson, T.D., O Brien, R.K., Beebe, J.M., Stuart, J.D., McCosh-Lilie, E.J., and Hill, D.W. 1982. HPLC analysis of underivatized fatty acids in margarines. J. Chromatogr. Sci. 20: 466-470.

Barett, G.C. 1962. Iodine as a "non-destructive" colour reagent in paper- and thin-layer chromatography. Nature 194: 1171-1172.

——. 1974. Non-destructive Detection Methods in Paper and Thin Layer Chromatography, pp. 145-179. *In* J. C. Giddings and R. A. Keller (eds.), *Advances in Chromatography* . Vol. 11. Marcel Dekker, N.Y.

Barker, S.A., Monti, J.A., Christian, S.T., Benington, F., and Morrin, R.D. 1980. 9-diazomethyl anthracene as a new fluorescence and ultraviolet label for the spectrophotometric detection of picomole quantities of fatty acids by high-pressure liquid chromatography. Anal. Biochem. 107: 116-123.

Barnes, P.C., Jr., and Holaday, C.E. 1972. Rapid preparation of fatty acid esters directly from ground peanuts. J. Chromatogr. Sci. 10: 181-183.

Baumann, L.F., Conway, T.F., and Watson, S.A. 1963. Heritability of variation in oil content of individual corn kernels. Science 139: 498-499.

Beaumelle, B.D., and Vial, H.J. 1986. Model for the structure-retention relationship for positional isomers of unsaturated fatty acid methyl esters on polar capillary columns. J. Chromatogr. 356: 409-412.

Bianchini, J.P., Ralaimanarivo A., and Gaydou, E.M. 1982. Reversed-phase high performance liquid chromatography of fatty acid methyl esters with particular reference to cyclopropenoic and cyclopropanoic acids. J. High Resolut. Chromatogr. and Chromatogr. Commun. 5: 199-204.

Bligh, E.G., and Dyer, W.J. 1959. A rapid method of total lipid extraction and purification. Can. J. Biochem. Physiol. 37: 911-917.

Borch, R.F. 1975. Separation of long chain fatty acids as phenacyl esters by high pressure liquid chromatography. Anal. Chem. 47: 2437-2439.

Bosin, W.A. (Chairman) 1971. Symposium: Wide-line nuclear magnetic resonance (NMR). J. Am. Oil Chem. Soc. 48: 1-17 and 47-69.

Brown, C.M., and Aryeetey, A.N. 1973. Maternal control of oil content in oats (*Avena sativa* L.) Crop Sci. 13: 120-121.

Chen, S.L., Stein, R.A., and Mead, J.F. 1976. Epoxidation of unsaturated fatty esters in argentation chromatography. Chem. Phys. Lipids 16: 161-166.

Christie, W.W., Connor, K., and Noble, R.C. 1984. Preparative separation of milk fatty acid derivatives by high-performance liquid chromatography. J. Chromatogr. 298: 513-515.

Churacek, J., and Pechova, H. 1970. Dunnschichtchromatographie von Fettsauren als 2,4-Dinitrobenzylester und N,N-Dimethyl-p-Amino-Benzolazophenacylester. J. Chromatogr. 48: 250-258.

Conway, T.F. 1971. A wide-line NMR R-F saturation method to measure fat in moist samples of defatted corn germ. J. Am. Oil Chem. Soc. 48: 54-58.

——, and Earle, F.R. 1963. Nuclear magnetic resonance for determining oil content of seeds. J. Am. Oil Chem. Soc. 40: 265-268.

Cooper, M.J., and Anders, M.W. 1974. Determination of long chain fatty acids as 2-naphtacyl esters by high pressure liquid chromatography and mass spectrometry. Anal. Chem. 46: 1849-1852.

Donike, M., Hollman, W. and Stratmann, D. 1969. Quantitative gaschromatographische Bestimmung von gesättigten und ungesättigten Fettsäuren als Trimethylsilylester. J. Chromatogr. 43:490-492.

Douglas, A.G., and Powell, T.G. 1969. The rapid separation of fatty acids from fossil lipids by impregnated adsorbent thin layer chromatography. J. Chromatogr. 43: 241-246.

Downey, R.K., and Harvey, B.L. 1963. Methods of breeding for oil quality in rape. Can. J. Plant Sci. 43: 271-275.

——, and Craig, B.M. 1964. Genetic control of fatty acid biosynthesis in rapeseed (*Brassica napus* L.). J. Am. Oil Chem. Soc. 41: 475-478.

Dudley, P.A., and Anderson, R.E. 1975. Separation of polyunsaturated fatty acids by argentation thin layer chromatography. Lipids 10: 113-115.

Dudzinski, A.E. 1967. A spray sequence specific for the detection of free fatty acids. J. Chromatogr. 31: 560.

Dünges, W. 1977. 4-Bromomethyl-7-methoxycoumarin as a new fluorescence label for fatty acids. Anal. Chem. 49: 442-445.

——, and Seiler, N. 1978. High-performance liquid chromatographic separation of esters of 4-hydroxymethyl-7-methoxy-coumarin. J. Chromatogr. 145: 483-488.

Durst, H.D., Milano, M., Kitka, E.J., Conelly, S.A., and Gruska, E. 1975. Phenacyl esters of fatty acids via crown ether catalyst for enhanced ultraviolet detection in liquid chromatography. Anal. Chem. 47: 1797-1801.

Emery, E.M., and Koerner, W.E. 1962. Double column programmed temperature gas chromatography. Anal. Chem. 34: 1196-1198.

Fehr, W.R., and Weber, C.R. 1968. Mass selection by seed size and specific gravity in soybean populations. Crop Sci. 8: 551-554.

Folch, J., Lees, M., and Sloane-Stanley, G.H. 1957. A simple method for the isolation and purification of total lipids from animal tissues. J. Biol. Chem. 226: 497-509.

Gambhir, P.N., and Agarwala, A.K. 1985. Simultaneous determination of moisture and oil content in oilseeds by pulsed nuclear magnetic resonance. J. Am. Oil Chem. Soc. 62: 103-108.

Gaydou, E.M., and Ramanoelina, A.R.P. 1984. Cyclopropenoic fatty acids of malvaceae seed oils by gas-liquid chromatography. Fette Seifen Anstrichm. 86: 82-84.

Gerhardt, K.O., and Gehrke, C.W. 1977. Rapid microdetermination of fatty acids in biological materials by gas-liquid chromatography. J. Chromatogr. 143: 335-344.

Glattes, H., Schoggl, G., and Haschke, H. 1985. NIT (near-infrared transmission), Grundlagen und erste praktische Erfahrungen bei der Getreideuntersuchung Getreide, Mehl Brot 39: 99-102.

Godin, V.J., and Spensley, P.C. 1967. Crop and Products Digest. No. 1 - Oils and Oilseeds, Tropical Products Institute, London.

Gosselin, L., and De Graeve, J. 1975. Preparation and thin-layer chromatography of bromo derivatives of unsaturated fatty acid esters. J. Chromatogr. 110: 117-124.

Green, A.G. 1985. Genetic Modification of Seed Fatty Acid Composition in *Linum usitatissimum* L. Thesis, School of Botany, Australian National University, Canberra, Australia.

Gunstone, F.D. 1975. Determination of the Structure of Fatty Acids, pp. 21-42. *In* T. Galliard and E. I. Mercer (eds.), *Recent Advances in the Chemistry and Biochemistry of Plant Lipids* . Academic Press, London.

Hammonds, T.W., and Shone, G. 1964. The separation of fatty acid methyl esters (including "critical pairs") by thin-layer chromatography. J. Chromatogr. 15: 200-203.

Heilweil, E., and Beesley, T.E. 1981. Densitometric determination of C-18 fatty acids as phenacyl esters following reversed-phase thin layer chromatrography. J. Liq. Chromatogr. 4: 2193-2203.

Heusser, D. 1968. Dunnschichtchromatographie von Fettsauren auf silanisiertem Kieselgel. J. Chromatogr. 33: 62-69.

Hirschfeld, T. and Stark, E.W. 1984. Near-infrared reflectance analysis of foodstuffs, pp. 505-551. *In* G. Charalambous (ed.), *Analysis of Foods and Beverages: Modern Techniques*. Academic Press, London.

Hoffmann, N.E., and Liao, J.C. 1976. High performance liquid chromatography of p-methoxyanilides of fatty acids. Anal. Chem. 48: 1104-1106.

Hofstetter, H.H., Sen, N., and Holman, R.T. 1965. Characterization of unsaturated fatty acids by gas-liquid chromatography. J. Am. Oil Chem. Soc. 42: 537-540.

Holman, R.T., and Rahm, J.J. 1966. Thiobarbituric Acid Reaction, pp. 18-20. *In* R. T. Holman (ed.), *Progress in the Chemistry of Fats and other Lipids*. Vol. 9. Pergamon Press, Oxford.

Holmes, M.G., Blankeney, A., and Wratten, N. 1975. Screening for fatty acids in oilseed breeding programmes using lipase and paper chromatography. J. Chromatogr. 115: 652-654.

Hoshi, M., Williams, M. and Kishimoto, Y. 1973. Esterification of fatty acids at room temperture by choroform-methanolic HCl-cupric acetate. J. Lipid Res. 14:599-601.

Hougen, F.W., Blank, M.J.T., Simpson, W.R. 1983. Sources of error in the determination of oil content of rapeseed by nuclear magnetic resonance (NMR), pp. 1321-1325. Proc. Intern. Rapeseed Conf.

Hradec, J., and Mensik, P. 1968. Purification of fatty acid present in carcinolipin. J. Chromatogr. 32: 502-510.

Hughes, M. 1969a. Determination of moisture and oil in the seed of winter rape (*Brassica napus*). I. Comparison of oven methods for the determination of moisture. J. Sci. Food Agric. 20: 741-744.

——. 1969b. Determination of moisture and oil in the seed of winter rape (*Brassica napus*). II. Comparison of extraction methods for the estimation of oil. J. Sci. Food Agric. 20: 745-747.

Husek, P., Kralikova, M., and Felt, V. 1973. Minutenschnelle Verseifung von Lipiden bei Raumtemperatur. Z. Klin. Chem. Klin. Biochem. 11: 509-512.

Hymowitz, T., Dudley, J.W., Collins, F.I., and Brown, C.M. 1974. Estimations of protein and oil concentration in corn, soybean, and oat seed by near-infrared light refectance. Crop Sci. 14: 713-715.

Ichinose, N., and Nakamura, K. 1984. High-performance liquid chromatography of 5,8,11,14,17-eicosapentaenoic acid in fatty acid (C18 and C20) by labelling with 9-anthryldiazomethane as a fluorescent agent. J. Chromatogr. 295: 463-469.

Ito, S., Hayashi, K., and Saitoh, M. 1985. Microdetermination of fatty acids high-performance liquid chromatography with fluorescence prelabeling. Seikagaku 57: 1290-1291.

Johnson, A.R., Fogerty, A.C., Hood, R.L., Kozuharov, S., and Ford, G.L. 1976. Gas-liquid chromatography of ethyl ester artifacts formed during the preparation of fatty acid methyl esters. J. Lipid Res. 17: 431-432.

Jordi, H.C. 1978. Separation of long and short chain fatty acids as naphtacyl and substituted phenacyl esters by high performance liquid chromatography. J. Liq. Chromatogr. 1: 215-230.

Jost, W., Hauck, H.E., and ˋEisenbeiß, F. 1984. Thin-layer chromatography as a pilot technique for transferring retention data to HPLC. Kontakte (E. Merck, Darmstadt, Germany) 3: 45-51.

Kaffka, K.J., Norris, K.H., Peredi, J., and Balogh, A. 1982. Attempts to determine oil, protein, water and fiber content in sunflower seeds by the nir technique. Acta Alimentaria 11: 253-269.

Kaufmann, H.P. 1950a. Neue Wege der Fettanalyse. Fette Seifen Anstrichm. 52: 713-721.

——. 1950b. Adsorptionstrennungen auf dem Fettgebiet VI: Papierchromatographie. Fette Seifen Anstrichm. 52: 331-342.

——, and Budwig, J. 1951. Die papierchromatographie auf dem Fettgebiet VII: Nachweiss und Trennung von Fettsauren. Fette Seifen Anstrichm. 53: 390-399.

——, and Mohr, E. 1958. Die Papier-Chromatographie auf dem Fettgebiet XXIV: Weitere Untersuchungen uber die Papier-Chromatographie der Fettsauren. Fette Seifen Anstrichm. 60: 165-177.

——, and Makus, Z. 1960. Die Dunnschicht-Chromatographie auf dem Fettgebeit I: Trennung von Modell-Mischungen. Fette Seifen Anstrichm. 62: 1014-1020.

——, and Khoe, T.H. 1962. Die Dunnschicht-Chromatographie auf dem Fettgebiet VII: Trennung von Fettsauren und Triglyceriden auf Gips-Schichten. Fette Seifen Anstrichm. 64: 81-85.

Kleiman, R., Spencer, G.F., and Earle, F.R. 1969. Boron trifluoride as catalyst to prepare methyl esters from oils. Lipids 4: 118-122.

Krzymanski, J. 1965. Modifications of the quantitative method for determination of fatty acids in vegetable oil by paper chromatography. Hodowla Rosl. aklim. Nasienn. 9: 423-429.

Lam, S., and Grushka, E. 1978. Labeling of fatty acids with 4-bromomethyl-7-methoxycoumarin via crown ether catalyst for fluorimetric detection in high-performance liquid chromatography. J. Chromatogr. 158: 207-214.

Lloyd, J.B.F. 1979. Fatty acid esters of 4-hydroxymethyl-7-methoxy coumarin: Fluorescence characteristics and their variation in high-performance liquid chromatographic solvents. J. Chromatogr. 178: 249-258.

——. 1980. Phenanthrimidazoles as fluorescent derivatives in the analysis of fatty acids by high-performance liquid chromatography. J. Chromatogr. 189: 359-373.

Luddy, F.E., Barford, R.A., and Riemenschneider, R.W. 1960. Direct conversion of lipid components to their fatty acid methyl esters. J. Am. Oil Chem. Soc. 37: 447-451.

Malins, D.C., and Mangold, H.K. 1960. Analysis of complex lipids mixtures by thin-layer chromatography and complementary methods. J. Am. Oil Chem. Soc. 37: 576-578.

Mangold, H.K., Lamp, B.G., and Schlenk, H. 1955. Indicators for the paper chromatography of lipids. J. Am. Oil Chem. Soc. 77: 6070-6073.

——, Gellerman, J.L., and Schlenk, H. 1958. Paper chromatography of lipids. Federation Proc. 17: 268.

Manku, M.S. 1983. A comparison of GLC and HPLC methods for determining fatty acid composition of evening primrose and soybean oil. J. Chromatogr. Sci. 21: 367-369.

Marmer, W.N. 1978. Rapid transmethylation of microgram amounts of phosphatidylcholine on potassium methoxide/celite columns. Lipids 13: 835-839.

Martin, T.T., and Allen, M.C. 1971. Charring with sulfur trioxide for the improved visualization and quantitation of thin layer chromatograms. J. Am. Oil Chem. Soc. 48: 752-757.

Mason, M.E. and Waller, G.R. 1964. Dimethoxypropane induced transferesterification of fats and oils in preparation of methyl esters for gas chromatographic analysis. Anal. Chem. 36:583-586.

McCreary, D.K., Kossa, W.C., Ramachandran, S., and Kurtz, R.R. 1978. A novel and rapid method for the preparation of methyl esters for gas chromatography: application to the determination of fatty acids of edible fats and oils. J. Chromatogr. Sci. 16: 329-331.

McGregor, D.I. 1974. A rapid and sensitive spot test for linolenic acid levels in rapeseed. Can. J. Plant Sci. 54: 211-213.

——. 1977. A rapid and simple method for determining the erucic acid content of rapeseed and mustard. Can. J. Plant Sci. 57: 133-142.

Metcalfe, L.D. 1960. Gas chromatography of unesterified fatty acids using polyester columns treated with phosphoric acid. Nature 188: 142-143.

——, and Schmitz, A.A. 1961. The rapid preparation of fatty acid esters for gas chromatographic analysis. Anal. Chem. 33: 363-364.

——, and Wang, C.N. 1981. Rapid preparation of fatty acid methyl esters using organic base-catalyzed transesterification. J. Chromatogr. Sci. 19: 530-535.

Miller, R.A., Bussel, N.E., and Ricketts, C. 1978. Quantitation of long chain fatty acids as the methoxyphenacyl esters. J. Liq. Chromatogr. 1: 291-304.

——, Earle, F. R. and Wolfe, I. A. 1965. Search for new industrial oils. XIII. Oils from 102 species of cruciferae. J. Am. Oil Chem. Soc. 42: 817-821.

Miwa, H., Yamoto, M. and Nishida, T. 1986. Assay of free and total fatty acids (as 2-nitrophenylhydrazides) by high performeance liquid chromatography. Clin. Chim. Acta 155: 95-102.

Morris, L.J. 1962. Separation of higher fatty acid isomers and vinylogues by thin-layer chromatography. Chem. Ind. (Lond.) 1962: 1238-1240.

——. 1963. Separation of isomeric long-chain polyhydroxy acids by thin-layer chromatography. J. Chromatogr. 12: 321-328.

——, and Nichols, B.W. 1970. Argentation Thin Layer Chromatography of Lipids, pp. 75-93. *In* A. Niederwieser and G. Pataki (eds.), *Progress in Thin-Layer Chromatography and Related Methods* . Vol. I.

Netting, A.G., and Duffield, A.M. 1984. High-performance liquid chromatographic separation of fatty acids as pentafluorobenzyl esters. J. Chromatogr. 336: 115-123.

Norris, K. and Hart, J.R. 1965. Direct spectroscopic determination of moisture content of grain and seeds, pp 19-25. *In* P. N. Win (ed.), *Humidity and Moisture* . Van Nostrand-Reinhold, Princeton, New Jersey.

Oette, K., and Doss, M. 1968. Mikromethode zur schnellen Umesterung von Lipoiden auf Dunnschichtplatten mit Natriummethylat fur die gas-chromatographische Analyse der Fettsuremethylester. J. Chromatogr. 32: 439-450.

——, ——, and Winterfeld, M. 1970. Umesterung und Veresterung von lang- und kurz-kettigen Fettsauren in Kapillaren fur die Gaschromatographie. Z. Klin. Chem. Klin. Biochem. 8: 525-528.

Ord, W.O., and Bamford, P.C. 1966. Reversed-phase thin-layer chromatography of fatty acids and fatty acid methyl esters on sinalized Kieselgel G. Chem. Ind. 1966: 1681-1682.

——,——. 1967. The thin-layer chromatographic separation of fatty acid methyl esters and glycerides according to chain length and unsaturation. Chem. Ind. (Lond.) 1967:277-278.

Paulose, M.M. 1966. The thin-layer chromatographic separation of fatty acid methyl esters accoring to both chain length and unsaturation. J. Chromatogr. 21: 324-326.

Pawlowski, S.H. 1963. Method for rapid determination of specific gravity of single seeds and seed samples and the correlation of specific gravity with oil content. Can. J. Plant Sci. 43: 151-156.

Pei, P.-T.S., Kossa, W.C., Ramachandran, S., and Henley, R.H. 1976. High pressure reverse phase liquid chromatography of fatty acid p-bromophenacyl esters. Lipids 11: 814-816.

Politzer, I.R., Griffin, G.W., Dowty, B.J., and Laseter, J.L. 1973. Enhancement of ultraviolet detectability of fatty acids for purposes of liquid chromatography-mass spectrometric analyses. Anal. Lett. 6(6): 539-546.

Putt, E.D., Craig, B.M., and Carson, R.B. 1969. Variation in composition of sunflower oil from composite samples and single seeds of varieties and inbred lines. J. Am. Oil Chem. Soc. 46: 126-129.

Quinn, L.D., and Hobbs, M.E. 1958. Analysis of the non volatile acids in cigarette smoke by gas chromatography of their methyl esters. Anal. Chem. 30: 1400-1405.

Rakow, G., and Thies, W. 1972. Schnelle und einfache Analysen der Fettsaeurezusammensetzung in einzelnen Rapskotyledonen. II. Photometrie der Polyenfettsaeuren. Z. Pflanzenzuechtg. 67: 257-266.

Raney, J.P., Love H., Rakow G. and Downey, R.K. 1987. An apparatus for the rapid preparation of oil and oil-free meal from Brassica seed. Fette Seifen Anstrichmittel (in press).

Rezanka, T., and Podojil, M. 1985. Gradient separation of fatty acids (C14-C30) by reversed-phase high performance liquid chromatography. J. Chromatogr. 346: 453-455.

Ribailler, D., and Riout, M. 1978. Methode simple d'estimation de la teneur en acide erucique des graines de colza, pp. 35-37. Vol. 2. Proc. 5th Intern. Rapeseed Conf., Malmo, Sweden.

Riemann, K.-H., and Krüger, H. 1967. Untersuchungen uber Moglichkeiten zur Fruhselektion auf hohen Fettgehalt bei Winterraps. Zuchter 37: 226-231.

Robertson, J.A., and Barton, F.E. 1984. Oil and water analysis of sunflower seed by near-infrared reflectance spectroscopy. J. Am. Oil Chem. Soc. 61: 543-547.

Ruseva-Atanasova, N., and Janák, J. 1966. Multi-dimensional chromatography using different developing methods. IV. Rational identification of fatty acid esters by means of programmed distribution of fractions in two-dimensional (GC-TLC) chromatograms. J. Chromatogr. 21: 207-212.

Sahasrabudhe, M.R. 1977. Crismer values and erucic acid contents of rapeseed oils. J. Am. Oil Chem. Soc. 54: 323-324.

Schaefer, J., and Stejskal, E.O. 1974a. Determination of oil, starch, and protein content of viable intact seeds by carbon-13 nuclear magnetic resonance. J. Am. Oil Chem. Soc. 51: 562-563.

———,———. 1947b. Carbon-13 nuclear magnetic resonance measurement of oil composition in single viable soybeans. J. Am. Oil Chem. Soc. 51: 210-213.

———,———. 1975. Carbon-13 nuclear magnetic resonance analysis of intact oil seeds. J. Am. Oil Chem. Soc. 52: 366-369.

Schmid, P. 1973. Extraction and purification of lipids: II. Why is chloroform-methanol such a good lipid solvent. Physiol. Chem. Phys. 5: 141-150.

———, and Hunter, E. 1971. Extraction and purification of lipids: I. Solubility of lipids in biologically important solvents. Physiol. Chem. Phys. 3: 98-102.

Schmid, P., Hunter, E., and Calvert, J. 1973. Extraction and purification of lipids: III. Serious limitations of chloroform and chloroform-methanol in lipid investigations. Physiol. Chem. Phys. 5: 151-155.

Sebedio, J.L., Farquharson, T.E., and Ackman, R.G. 1985. Quantitative analysis of methylesters of fatty acid geometrical isomers, and of triglycerides differing in unsaturation, by the iatroscan TLC/FID technique using AgNO3 impregnated rods. Lipids 20: 555-560.

Seher, A. 1956. Quantitative Bestimmung päpierchromatographicsch getrennter langkettiger Carbonsauren auf photometrischem Wege. Fette Seifen Anstrichm. 58: 498-504.

———. 1959. Quantitative Papier-Chromatographie der Fettsauren II. Das photometrische Verfahren. Fette Seifen Anstrichm. 61: 855-859.

———, and Josephs, P. 1969. Quantitative evaluation of gas chromatograms. Reaction of methyl oleate with the stationary phase. Fette Seifen Anstrichm. 71: 1007-1014.

Seino, H., Watanabe, S., Nihongi, T., and Nagai, T. 1973. Influences of operating conditions on determination of fatty acid methyl esters by gas chromatography. J. Am. Oil Chem. Soc. 50: 335-339.

Shenk, J.S., Landa, I., Hoover, M.R., and Westerhaus, M.O. 1981. Description and evaluation of a near infrared reflectance spectro-computer for forage and grain analysis. Crop Sci. 21: 355-358.

Shpota, V.I., and Podkolzina, V.E. 1982a. Cryoscopic method for the rapid determination of erucic acid content in the oil of cruciferae. Fiziol. Biokhim. Kul't. Rast. 14: 387-392.

———,———. 1982b. Rapid method of evaluating breeding material in the cruciferae. Sel. Semonovod. (Mosc) 6: 22-23.

Singh, B.B., and Hadley, H.H. 1968. Maternal control of oil synthesis in soybeans, *Glycine max* (L.) Merr.. Crop Sci. 60: 622-625.

Skipski, V.P., Arfin, S.M., and Rapport, M.M. 1959. Identification of 2-hydroxystearic acid in spinal cord phrenosine by chromatographic separation of hydroxy fatty acids. Arch. Biochem. Biophys. 82: 487-488.

Smith, C.R. 1970. Occurence of Unusual Fatty Acids in Plants, pp. 139-177. *In* R. T. Holman (ed.), *Progress in the Chemistry of Fats and other Lipids* . Vol. 11.

Smith, B.G. 1973. A new procedure for inducing fluorescence in quantitative thin-layer chromatography for organic compounds. J. Chromatogr. 82: 95-100.

Smith, C.R., Jr. 1976. Chromatographic methods in the determination of absolute and relative configurations of fatty acids. J. Chromatogr. Sci. 14: 36-40.

Solomon, H.L., Hubbard, W.D., Prosser, A.R., and Sheppard, A.J. 1974. Sample size influence on boron trifluoride-methanol procedure for preparing fatty acid methyl esters. J. Am. Oil Chem. Soc. 51: 424-425.

Spener, F., and Tober, I. 1981. Cyclopentenylfettsauren im Brennpunkt. Fette Seifen Anstrichm. 83: 401:402.

Spiteri, J. 1954. Chromatographie de partage des acides gras. Bull. Soc. Chim. Biol. Sci. 36: 1355-1362.

Starr, C., Suttle, J., Morgan, A.G., and Smith, D.B. 1985. A comparison of sample preparation and calibration techniques for the estimation of nitrogen, oil and glucosinolate content of rapeseed by near infrared spectroscopy. J. Agric. Sci., Camb. 104: 317-323.

Stoffel, W., Chu, F., and Ahrens, E.H. 1959. Analysis of long-chain fatty acids by gas-liquid chromatography. Anal. Chem. 31: 307-308.

Subbaram, M.R., Roomi, M.W., and Achaya, K.T. 1966. Separation of epithio and epoxy fatty acids and their derivatives by thin-layer chromatography. J. Chromatogr. 21: 324-326.

Supina, W.R. 1964. Analysis of Fatty Acids and Derivatives by Gas Chromatography, pp. 271-305. *In* H. A. Szymanski (ed.), *Biomedical Applications of Gas Chromatography* . Plemun Press, N.Y.

Svetasher, V.I., and Zhnkova, N.V. 1985. Analysis of labelled fatty acid methyl esters by argentation and reversed-phase two-dimensional thin-layer chromatography. J. Chromatogr. 330: 396-400.

Thies, W. 1971. Schnelle und einfache Analysen der Fettsaeurezusammensetzung in einzelnen Raps-Kotyledonen. I. Gaschromatographische und papierchromatographische Methoden. Z. Pflanzenzuechtg. 65: 181-202.

——. 1974. New methods for the analysis of rapeseed contstituents, pp. 275-281. Proc. 4th Intern. Rapeseed Conf., Giessen, Germany.

——. 1982. Complex-formation between glucosinolates and tetrachloropalladate (II) and its utilization in plant breeding. Fette Seifen Anstrichm. 84: 338-342.

——. 1985. Determination of the glucosinolate content in commercial rapeseed loads with a pocket reflectometer. Fette Seifen Anstrichm. 87: 347-350.

——, and Nitsch, A. 1974. Rapid analyses of the fatty acid composition in single cotyledons of rapeseed. III. A spot test analysis street for the "specific" determination of linolenic acid. Z. Pflanzenzuechtg. 72: 72-83.

Thompson, A.C., and Hedin, P.A. 1966. Separation of organic acids by thin-layer chromatography of their 2,4-dinitrophenylhydrazide derivatives and their analytical determination. J. Chromatogr. 21: 13-18.

Tiwari, P.N., Gambhir, P.N., and Rajan, T.S. 1974. Rapid and nondestructive determination of seed oil by pulsed nuclear magnetic resonance technique. J. Am. Oil Chem. Soc. 51: 104-109.

Tkachuk, R. 1981. Oil and protein analysis of whole rapeseed kernels by near infrared reflectance spectroscopy. J. Am. Oil Chem. Soc. 58: 819-822.

Tröeng, S. 1955a. Bestimmung des Oelgehaltes von Raps II. Fette Seifen Anstrichm. 57: 411-413.

——, 1955b. Oil determination of oilseed. Gravimetric routine method. J. Am. Oil Chem. Soc. 32: 124-126.

Tsuchiya, H. 1984. Simultaneous separation and sensitive determination of free fatty acids in blood plasma by high-performance liquid chromatography. J. Chromatogr. 309: 43-52.

Urie, A.L. 1985. Inheritance of high oleic acid in sunflower. Crop Sci. 25: 986-989.

Van Putte, K., and Van den Enden, J. 1974. Fully automated determination of solid fat content by pulsed NMR. J. Am. Oil Chem. Soc. 51: 316-320.

Vioque, E., Maza, M.P., and Millan, F. 1985. High performance liquid chromatography of fatty acids as their p-phenylazophenacyl esters. J. Chromatogr. 331: 187-192.

Williams, P.C. 1975. Application of near infrared reflectance spectroscopy to analysis of cereal grains and oilseeds. Cereal Chem. 52: 561-576.

——. 1986. A study of grinders used for sample preparation in laboratory analysis of grains. In Focus (Tecator AB) 9: 4-5.

——, Norris, K.H., and Sobering, D.C. 1985. Determination of protein and moisture in wheat and barley by near-infrared transmission. J. Agric. Food Chem. 33: 239.

——, and Panford, J.A. 1981. Determination of protein and moisture in wheat and barley by near-infrared transmission (NIT) instrument. Cereal Foods World 26: 490.

Yamaguchi, M., Hara, S., Matsunaga, R., and Nakamura, M. 1985. 3-bromomethyl-6,7-dimethoxy-1-methyl-2(1H)-quinoxalinone as a new fluorescence derivatization reagent for carboxylic acids in high-performance liquid chromatgraphy. J. Chromatogr. 346: 227-236.

Young, C.T., and Waller, G.R. 1972. Rapid oleic/linoleic microanalytical procedure for peanuts. J. Agric. Food Chem. 20: 1116-1118.

Zimmermann, D.C. 1962. The relationship between seed density and oil content in flax. J. Am. Oil Chem. Soc. 39: 77-78.

Chapter 8

Nature and Biosynthesis of Storage Proteins

G. Norton

INTRODUCTION

Approximately 20-40% of the weight of oilseeds is protein. A large proportion of this protein is storage protein which is specifically produced in the seed to act as a source of amino acids and reduced nitrogen during germination and early seedling growth. Oilseeds along with many other seeds constitute a major source of protein for both animal and human consumption. Because of their economic and nutritional importance the storage proteins of seeds including oilseeds were some of the first proteins to be studied at the turn of the century.

In the interim period, however, characterization of storage proteins has tended to lag behind that of other plant proteins and it is only in the last 10 years or so that there has been a resurgence of research interest in the seed proteins. There are a number of reasons for this. Firstly there is a growing awareness that in the future more reliance will have to be placed on proteins of plant origin (mainly seeds) in order to maintain today's level of protein nutrition in a world of rapid population growth. Secondly, improvements in technology have enabled detailed studies on the characterization and biosynthesis of storage proteins to be undertaken.

In this chapter, the protein content and amino acid composition of oilseeds will be briefly considered, the chemical, biochemical and physical characteristics of the storage proteins from a number of oilseeds will be described and, where information is available, the biosynthesis of specific storage proteins will be discussed.

PROTEIN CONTENT AND AMINO ACID COMPOSITION OF OILSEEDS

Protein Content

Both protein content and amino acid composition have been shown to vary considerably between families, genera, species and cultivars (Mossé and Baudet, 1983). Variations in these parameters often exist between plants, depending on the developmental and growth stage. Microvariations in the protein and amino acid composition of individual seeds of a plant may occur, depending on the position of the seed in the fruiting organ and its location on the plant. Major differences in these values can be attributed to two principal factors, genetics and environment. These factors interact and the ultimate response obtained represents an amalgam of the many individual components concerned.

When comparing analytical data for the protein and amino acid composition, it should always be borne in mind that the values often relate to a single cultivar grown in a particular area in a particular year, and quite often under unique environmental conditions. In addition, different analytical procedures may also have been employed in different laboratories, and frequently the analysis may have been performed as a subsidiary part of the major investigation. It is clear from these considerations that the values for protein and amino acid composition can only provide a relative indication of these components.

Generally the crude protein content of seeds is obtained by determining the nitrogen, normally by Kjeldahl digestion procedure, and multiplying percentage nitrogen values by 6.25. The conversion factor of 6.25 is widely used, because a wide range of proteins of different origin do contain 16% nitrogen. Biological materials, however, contain other nitrogenous compounds apart from protein, and the nitrogen of these will also be included in crude protein estimates by the Kjeldahl procedure. These non-protein nitrogen compounds include soluble amino acids, nucleic acids, purine and pyrimidine bases and their derivatives and nitrogen bases in lipids,which in total may account for 10-15% of the total nitrogen in legume seeds. Generally between 85-90% of the total nitrogen of legume seeds is protein in origin.

Although the conversion factor of 6.25 is routinely used, other more accurate figures have been derived from amino acid analyses. Thus for oilseeds, values of 5.3 for sunflower, 5.46 for peanut, 5.71 for soybean and 5.67 for oilseed rape have been used by some workers (Mossé and Pernollet, 1983). Since the amino acid composition of many seeds will change with the protein content, the necessity of having absolutely accurate conversion factors is academic. Provided the limitations in the use of the classical conversion factors are appreciated, protein content values so obtained are a useful if somewhat variable overestimate of the true protein content.

Values for the protein content of a range of oilseeds vary from 20-40% or higher on a dry matter basis. Soybean (*Glycine max*), lupins (*Lupinus* spp.) and winged bean (*Psophocarpus tetragonolobus*) are rich in protein (35-40%) but contain low amounts of oil (10-20%). Ground nut (*Arachis hypogaea*), however, is rich in oil (45%) but has a lower protein content (25%). Other oilseeds belonging to different botanical families contain between 20-30% protein with oil contents ranging from 20-40%. Important among these are cotton seed (*Gossypium* spp.), rapeseed (*Brassica napus* and *Brassica campestris*) and other cruciferous oilseeds, sunflower (*Helianthus annuus*), sesame (*Sesamum indicum*), safflower (*Carthamus tinctorius*), Linseed (*Linum usitatissimum*) and castor bean (*Ricinus communis*).

Considerable interspecific variation in the protein content of oilseed legumes has been found (Mossé and Pernollet, 1983). For example, in a study involving 14 wild species of *Arachis*, the protein contents were found to vary between 19 and 35%, while for a similar number of species of *Lupinus* the range was 27-50%. Intraspecific variations in protein content are also well known. Intervarietal values for a sample of 21 cultivars, lines and varieties of *A. hypogaea* ranged from 23.5-33.3. Such variability is important in breeding programs aimed at optimizing both crop and protein yield.

Seed Amino Acid Composition

Comparisons between the published values of the amino acid composition of various oilseeds should be made cautiously because of the considerable variability that has been reported in such analyses. Some of this variability may be due to the different analytical procedures employed in the different laboratories, but the amino acid composition will be affected by the same factors that affected the protein content.

Guidelines have been proposed which, if followed, would improve the accuracy and reliability of seed amino acid analysis and enable more valid comparisons to be made between them (Mossé and Pernollet, 1983).

Despite the limitations inherent in the data (see Chapter 9 Table 2), certain broad conclusions are possible. With minor exceptions, the amino acid compositions of the seeds resemble each other, indicating that generally the major proteins (storage globulins) in the seed are similar. These proteins are richer in amides (not indicated in table) and arginine but poorer in sulfur amino acids than the functional proteins. Certain amino acids, including glycine, alanine, valine, leucine, isoleucine, serine, threonine, cystine, histidine, aspartic acid-asparagine, glutamic acid-glutamine, occur in seed proteins within narrow limits, whereas

tyrosine, phenylalanine, proline, methionine, lysine, and arginine exhibit a much
wider variation in content. Particularly noteworthy are the extremely low values
for lysine in *A. hypogaea* and methionine and tryptophan in *Lupinus* spp. Nutritionally, legume seed proteins are regarded as being limiting in the sulfur amino
acids methionine and cysteine while being adequate in the other essential amino
acids (threonine, leucine, isoleucine, valine, lysine, histidine, tryptophan, arginine and tyrosine). Generally the proteins of the non-legume oilseeds are richer
in sulfur amino acids than those of their legume counterparts and may be regarded as being nutritionally adequate in these. Apart from *B. napus* and *B. campestris*, non-legume oilseeds (*Gossypium* spp., *H. annuus, Sesamum indicum* and
L. usitatissimum) have low lysine contents, being similar to those of *A. hypogaea*. Such levels must be regarded as being nutritionally inadequate (Mossé and
Pernollet, 1983). A full discussion of the nutritional value of oilseed meals is
found in Chapter 9.

STORAGE PROTEINS

Definitions

The protein of oilseeds, particularly that of the more economically important
legume oilseeds such as *G. max* and *A. hypogaea*, has been extensively studied.
Clearly much of the discussion that follows is heavily biased to the storage proteins of these seeds because of the wealth of information that is available on
them.

Proteins in the majority of oilseeds consist of the water-soluble albumins and
the salt-soluble water-insoluble globulins (storage proteins). This characterization, based on solubility criteria devised by Osborne (1924), is simple and convenient to use for the isolation of broad categories of proteins. Storage proteins
so obtained, however, were found to be heterogeneous when examined by column chromatography and gel electrophoresis. With the need to obtain homogeneous preparations of storage proteins for detailed characterization, the classical
methods of protein purification (salt fractionation and recrystallization) have
been entirely superseded or supplemented by techniques utilizing direct physical
and chemical properties of proteins, i.e., charge, molecular weight and shape.

The albumins contain the majority of the metabolically active proteins which
are essential in every cell. These proteins are also responsible for the biosynthesis and degradation of the second group of proteins, the globulins, which constitute the bulk of the storage proteins and which serve as nitrogen reserves for the
embryonic axis during germination. Some albumins, however, do occur in ap-
preciable amounts which are not consistent intergenerically or interspecifically,
suggesting alternative roles for these proteins (Müller, 1983). Evidence has been
obtained which indicates that some of these proteins are utilized during germination in much the same way as globulins. Albumins then should be regarded as

being multifunctional proteins with some storage role. It has been suggested that any extractable protein accounting for more than 5% of the total seed protein should be tentatively regarded as a storage protein (Derbyshire et al. 1976). From a nutritional standpoint, the inclusion of certain albumins in the storage protein category is important in breeding strategies because of their superior amino acid composition, especially with regard to the sulfur amino acids. In addition to functional proteins, the albumins also often contain variable but considerable amounts of proteinase inhibitors and lectins.

Storage globulins are sequestered in protein bodies in the storage cells of oilseeds but albumins, with a storage protein role, will be located in the cytosol of the cell.

General Properties of Storage Globulins

The globulins represent the major storage proteins in all oilseeds, accounting for 70% or more of the total seed protein of *G. max, A. hypogaea* and *Lupinus* spp. Like the seeds of many other species of legume, these oilseeds contain two predominant globulins. The major globulin sediments in the ultracentrifuge at approximately 12S (mol. wt. 300,000-350,000) and is classified as being legumin-like, whereas the other has a sedimentation coefficient around 7S (mol. wt. 140,000-250,000) and is regarded as being a classical vicilin-like globulin (Derbyshire et al. 1976). Non-legume oilseeds such as *B. napus* and *B. campestris, Gossypium* spp., *H. annuus, R. communis, S. indicum* also contain the 12S globulin but the 7S protein is less widely distributed having been shown to be present only in *Gossypium* spp., *H. annuus* and *S. indicum*. Both the 12S and 7S globulins appear to be absent from the seeds of *P. tetragonolobus*, but are replaced by many smaller globulins (Gillespie and Blagrove, 1978).

A high degree of similarity exists between the 12S globulins of the various oilseeds with respect to size, shape, charge, solubility and other characteristics. All are hexameric proteins (pI 4.5-7.0), consisting of six acidic (α - or A-) polypeptides (pI 4.75-5.40 mol. wt. ca. 38,000-42,000) and six basic (β - or B-) polypeptides (pI 8.0-8.5 mol. wt. ca. 17,000-20,000) which are usually, but not necessarily, disulfide linked in pairs (αβ or AB) in a non-random manner to form subunits or monomers (mol. wt. ca. 60,000). This structure is reflected in the dissociation characteristics of the 12S molecule. At low ionic strength and pH, the 12S molecule (hexamer) dissociates into two 7S molecules (trimers). In the presence of detergents or dissociating agents (SDS, urea or guanidine HCl) the 7S trimer dissociates into three 3S molecules (monomers). In the presence of reducing agents (2-mercaptoethanol, dithiothreitol) the monomer dissociates into the acidic and basic polypeptides (2S proteins). Both the acidic and basic polypeptides exhibit variation in charge and size which in turn will lead to microheterogeneity in the 12S molecule. Models of the structure of the 12S molecule have been constructed. One model of the 12S globulin from *G. max, B. napus* and *H. annuus* envisages the six monomers or subunits (αβ or AB pairs) as being arranged in the form of a trigonal antiprism (dihedral point group symmetry 32) (Plietz et al. 1983) whereas in an earlier model of the 12S globulin of *G. max* the six monomers or subunits were arranged in the form of a hexagon (Badley et al. 1975). In the latter model, the acidic and basic polypeptides were envisaged as being arranged alternately in identical hexagons placed one on top of the other so that each acidic subunit was opposite three basic subunits and vice versa.

All the 12S globulins have high contents of glutamic and aspartic acids, presumably present in the amidated form which is entirely consistent with a storage role for these proteins. Cysteine and methionine are present in low and rather variable amounts. Much of this variability may be due to problems associated with the estimation of small amounts of these amino acids. Carbohydrate is generally absent from the 12S globulin.

The 7S globulins of oilseeds and pulse legumes are regarded as being more complex than the 12S proteins because of their subunit complexity, association-dissociation characteristics in response to changes in pH and ionic strength, and considerable physical and serological heterogeneity. Despite these difficulties it is generally agreed that the 7S globulin (vicilin type) is a trimer (mol. wt. ca. 100,000-200,000 pI 5.0) consisting of three major polypeptides (mol. wt. ca. 50,000) and often minor and smaller polypeptides. These polypeptides are randomly assembled in the 7S complex without the involvement of covalent linkages. The 7S proteins are glycoproteins which undergo association or dissociation, depending on the pH and ionic strength of the media. Thus at low ionic strength, the 7S trimer associates to form a 9S hexamer. Like other storage proteins, the 7S globulins are rich in aspartic and glutamic acids which in this case are not amidated, arginine and lysine but are poor or entirely lacking in cysteine and methionine. Compared with the 12S globulins, the 7S globulins are relatively poor in sulfur amino acids.

A number of smaller storage proteins have been found in various oilseeds. Collectively these have been referred to as globulins but some of these cannot be globulins in the classical sense. A good example of this is the 1.7S protein fraction of *B. napus* and other *Brassica* spp. which is water soluble. These smaller molecular weight fractions represent a heterogeneous group of 'storage' proteins which have been investigated in a few instances. These proteins along with other globulin types will be considered as appropriate in the detailed consideration of the proteins of individual species.

Characteristics and Properties of the Globulins of Specific Oilseeds
Storage Proteins of *Glycine max*

Considering the commercial importance of this crop, it is hardly surprising that the chemistry and molecular biology of the storage proteins of this seed have been studied more extensively than any other oilseed. In early work, four types of globulin were identified following the analysis of seed protein extracts in the ultracentrifuge (Koshiyama, 1983). These fractions sedimented as 2S (containing α -conglycinins), 7S (β - and γ -conglycinins), 11-12S (glycinin) and 15S at high ionic strength (0.5M). At lower ionic strength (0.1M) the 7S fraction associated to form a 9S component. Irrespective of the method of analysis used (ultracentrifugation, gel filtration or iso-electric focusing) the content of the individual globulin fractions in seed extracts was identical to that of protein bodies isolated from the seed, indicating that these proteins were all sequestered within these organelles. Using ultracentrifugation, the proportions of the various globulins in *G. max* were as follows: 2S, 15.0%, 7S, 34% (γ -conglycinin, 3.1% and β - conglycinin, 30.9%); 11-12S, 41.9%; 15S, 9.1%. Both the 7S and the 11-12S globulins were found to be heterogeneous when examined by gel electrophoresis.

Glycinin (11-12S globulin) with a mol. wt. 309,000-393,000 is the major storage protein of *G. max*, with the classical legumin structure described earlier. This protein has been intensively studied in recent years (Nielsen, 1984). Each glycinin molecule contains six subunits or monomers mol. wt. ca. 60,000 (range 58,000-69,000). Each subunit generally consists of one acidic (A) polypeptide mol. wt. ca. 40,000 (range 37,000-42,000 with a minor component 10,000) and one basic (B) polypeptide mol. wt. ca. 20,000 when examined by SDS-polyacrylamide electrophoresis (SDS-PAGE). The polypeptides are covalently linked in the subunit (termed an AB complex) by a single disulfide bond involving half-cysteine residues located in analogous positions in the respective subunits (Staswick et al. 1984b).

All the acidic and basic polypeptide components of glycinin have been isolated by chromatography of the products of the reductive dissociation of the S-alkylated protein on DEAE- and CM-Sephadex respectively and subsequently characterized (Moreira et al. 1979). In all, six acidic polypeptides (designated A_{1a}, A_{1b}, A_2, A_3, A_4, and A_5) and five basic polypeptides (B_{1a}, B_{1b}, B_2, B_3, and B_4) have been identified and characterized by amino acid analysis, NH_2-terminal sequence analysis, SDS-PAGE and isoelectric focusing (IEF) (Table 8.1).

Apart from polypeptide A_4, there was substantial homology between the acidic polypeptides, and differences in primary structures were internal rather than restricted to the ends. The sequence homologies of the NH_2-terminal ends of the basic polypeptides were more extensive than the acidic ones. To ascertain which acidic and basic polypeptides were associated in the AB complexes, highly purified unreduced S-alkylated and denatured glycinin was chromatographed on DEAE-Sephadex (Staswick et al. 1981). Five subunits (AB complexes) were isolated, and it was found that the association of the acidic polypeptides, apart from A_4, with the basic polypeptides was non-random (Table 8.2).

Specific pairing of the acidic and basic polypeptides occurs in the subunits because each is synthesized as a precursor molecule containing, from the NH_2-terminus, the acidic polypeptide linked by a short peptide to the basic polypeptide. The precursor polypeptides are processed to produce the mature subunits. Three subunits contained appreciably more methionine than the other two. It is pertinent to note that high methionine acidic and basic peptides pair and those

Table 8.1 Amino Acid Composition of the Glycinin Polypeptides (Residues per Polypeptide)

Amino acid	Polypeptide									
	A_{1a}	$A_{1b}{}^a$	A_2	A_3	A_4	$A_5{}^b$	B_{1a}	B_2	$B_3{}^c$	B_4
Aspartic acid[d]	36.8	34.8	42.1	45.5	50.8	9.0	25.5	24.3	19.2	20.7
Threonine	12.0	12.4	12.3	15.5	11.8	3.9	8.1	9.1	6.2	5.4
Serine	18.3	19.0	16.4	27.1	23.5	7.7	13.5	12.4	12.1	12.4
Glutamic acid[e]	85.3	85.3	86.4	91.6	92.6	14.9	22.5	22.7	24.8	21.0
Proline	24.0	25.0	21.3	33.9	27.3	8.1	10.5	10.8	10.2	9.1
Glycine	31.0	27.3	29.9	29.5	22.4	7.9	11.1	10.4	13.4	16.1
Alanine	14.4	15.9	18.1	10.9	6.2	5.0	15.6	14.3	12.4	11.2
Valine	11.9	12.4	15.3	17.4	12.1	3.8	11.4	10.8	17.0	19.2
Methionine	3.6	4.1	5.8	2.4	1.4	1.1	2.3	2.7	0	1.3
Isoleucine	17.6	16.6	15.3	12.2	10.4	5.1	9.2	9.8	7.0	7.3
Leucine	20.1	18.7	20.0	21.8	14.0	10.7	17.9	17.4	18.1	18.1
Tyrosine	7.3	8.7	6.6	5.6	4.4	2.0	2.8	2.5	5.8	8.4
Phenylalanine	12.2	17.9	12.3	12.0	7.7	0.9	8.6	9.1	6.0	5.7
Histidine	6.0	4.8	2.6	14.1	9.5	2.8	2.1	2.7	4.8	4.2
Lysine	21.2	15.9	14.9	14.8	18.8	3.9	5.9	5.9	7.0	6.5
Arginine	18.1	21.2	22.7	22.2	28.4	3.1	8.9	9.9	10.9	12.5
Half cystine	4.5	N.D.	4.3	3.6	0.7	N.D.	1.7	1.5	0.2	1.5

From Moreira et al. 1979.
a,b Original nomenclature F2-(1) and F2-(2) respectively.
c B_{1b} is eluted as a shoulder on the leading edge of B_3 when the basic polypeptides are separated on CM-Sephadex (Nielsen, 1984).
d Includes asparagine.
e Includes glutamine.

low in this amino acid also pair. The sequence homology between the methionine rich subunits was 85-90%, whereas that of the other two subunits was 50%.

Complex $A_5A_4B_3$ appears to be somewhat anomalous and needs further explanation. Polypeptide A_5 (mol. wt. ca. 10,000) is covalently linked via a disulfide bond to B_3 (mol. wt. ca. 20,000) to form a complex A_5B_3 (mol. wt. ca. 30,000). A_4 associates non-covalently with A_5B_3 to form $A_4A_5B_3$ (mol. wt. 69,000). Recently A_5 and A_4 have been identified as being formed from the same acidic polypeptide precursor, which would be part of a single polypeptide precursor incorporating B_3. The acidic polypeptide would be cleaved at residue 100, and polypeptide A_5 represents the NH_2-terminal part of this molecule. This has a high degree of homology with NH_2-terminal sequences of the other acidic polypeptides. Polypeptide A_4, however, as might be expected, possesses considerable homology with acidic polypeptide A_2 post residue 100 but low NH_2-terminal sequence homology with the acidic polypeptides. Complex $A_5A_4B_3$ would have a total molecular mass around 69,000 which is similar to the other subunits.

Table 8.2 Some Properties of the Acidic and Basic Polypeptides of the AB-Complexes of Glycinin

Acidic polypeptide	No. methionine	Molecular mass	Basic polypeptide	No. methionine	Molecular mass	AB-complex	No. methionine	Molecular mass
A_{1a}	4	37000	B_2	3	19000	$A_{1a}B_2$	7	58000
A_{1b}	4	37000	B_{1b}	2	19000	$A_{1b}B_{1b}$	6	58000
A_2	6	37000	B_{1a}	2	19000	A_2B_{1a}	8	58000
A_3	2	42000	B_4	1	19000	A_3B_4	3	62000
(A_5)	1	10000	B_3	0	19000	$A_5A_4B_3$	2	69000
(A_3)	1	37000						

Compiled from Moreira et al. 1979; Staswick et al. 1981; Nielsen, 1984.

All the purified acidic and basic polypeptides exhibited considerable charge heterogeneity when subjected to IEF-PAGE (Moreira et al. 1981). This heterogeneity may be attributed to primary sequence heterogeneity at a number of positions in both polypeptides. Such heterogeneity has been observed in both polypeptides of the A_2B_{1a} complex for which an amino acid sequence has been determined (Staswick et al. 1984a). Such differences have been interpreted as indicating that several coding sequences direct the synthesis of the A_2B_{1a} subunit. The synthesis of the other glycinin subunits may be directed in a similar manner.

The second major group of storage proteins in *G. max* are the 7S globulins consisting of the β - and γ-conglycinins (Koshiyama, 1983). β -Conglycinins are the predominant 7S globulins (vicilins) but these are always less abundant than the glycinins (average ratios glycinin/β -conglycinin = 1.6 with a range 3.0-1.0. β–Conglycinins are glycoproteins consisting of three major acidic subunits designated α, α' and β with mol. wt. 59,000, 57,000 and 42,000 respectively and one minor γ subunit (mol. wt. ca. 42,000) (Thanh and Shibasaki, 1978a). The NH_2-terminal amino acids for the α-, α'- and β -subunits are valine, valine and leucine respectively. In all seven isomers of β -conglycinin (mol. wt. 140,000-175,000) have been identified (Thanh and Shibasaki, 1978a). All are trimers of non-covalently linked subunits associated in a random manner as follows: $β_3$, $α β_2$, α' $β_2$, αα' β, $α_2$ β, $α_2$α' and $α_3$. $β_3$ was the last of these isomers to be isolated and identified with certainty because it co-precipitated with glycinin in crude preparations (Sykes and Gayler, 1981). Complete amino acid compositional data are available for all seven β -glycinins and their constituent subunits (Table 8.3). All the subunits are lacking in half-cysteine and while the α and α' subunits contain small amounts of methionine the β subunit is completely devoid of this amino acid also. Subunits α and α' have almost identical amino acid and carbohydrate composition (5%) while the β subunit, in addition to being a smaller molecule, contains appreciably less Glx and Asx and carbohydrate (2.5%). These compositional differences are reflected in the more basic pI of the β -subunit. In addition, the β–subunit exhibits charge heterogeneity and four components (pI ranging from 5.66 to 6.00) have been identified. In reality the quaternary structure of the β -conglycinins may be more complex than is envisaged at present because of the need to include the different β -subunit isomers as well as the minor γ subunit in the 7S molecule.

A characteristic feature of the β -conglycinins is their ability to undergo reversible association and dissociation at low and high ionic strength (pH range 4.8-11.0) (Thanh and Shibasaki, 1978b). The trimeric forms are stable at high ionic strength (0.5M) while at low ionic strength dimerisation occurs to give 9S forms (hexamers). At extreme pH (2 or 12) the β -conglycinins dissociate into their respective subunits. This process is also reversible but only six (all the naturally occurring trimers excluding $β_3$) have been identified out of a possible 10 molecular species.

As indicated above, β -conglycinins are glycoproteins whose carbohydrate components have been found to consist of N-acetylglucosamine (GlcNAc) and

Table 8.3   Amino Acid Composition of Isolated Subunits of β –Conglycinin

Amino acid	Observed Residue/Subunit		
	α	α'	β
Aspartic acid	55.27	51.70	45.72
Threonine	10.29	10.90	9.44
Serine	31.02	30.55	25.39
Glutamic acid	96.30	100.39	58.92
Proline	33.23	30.55	17.93
Glycine	20.77	23.41	15.53
Alanine	21.48	20.02	18.77
Half-cystine	Trace	0	0
Valine	20.77	22.65	19.02
Methionine	1.97	2.26	0.39
Isoleucine	27.03	22.94	21.87
Leucine	40.80	35.01	36.70
Tyrosine	10.86	10.58	9.08
Phenylalanine	24.49	23.83	22.51
Lysine	29.23	34.36	18.81
Histidine	5.50	17.15	7.11
Arginine	40.89	33.65	24.97
Molecular mass	54000	54000	40500
pI	4.90	5.18	5.66-6.00

Data obtained from Thanh and Shibasaki (1977)

mannose (Man) in the same relative proportions (1:3) irrespective of subunit type. Three L-β -aspartamide carbohydrates have been isolated from pronase degraded β -conglycinin and these identified as Asn-$(GlcNAc)_2$-Man_n where n = 9,8, or 7. Linkage to the polypeptide occurs through the asparagine. It has been suggested that the structure of the oligosaccharide side chains is similar or identical to that of soybean agglutinin.

γ -Conglycinin, the minor 7S globulin is also a glycoprotein (5.5% carbohydrate) consisting of three identical subunits (mol. wt. 50,000).

Storage Proteins of *Arachis hypogaea*

Two major reserve globulins, arachin and conarachin have been isolated from *A. hypogaea* (Mossé and Pernollet, 1983). Crude arachin has been shown to account for about 73% of the salt soluble proteins which in turn amount to 93% of the total seed protein. Arachin exhibits unusual association-dissociation characteristics in respect to the ionic strength of the medium. Two molecular species of arachin (I and II) have been isolated from crude arachin preparations by means of DEAE-Sephadex chromatography (Yamada et al. 1979a & b). Arachin I has a sedimentation coefficient of 9S (mol. wt. 180,000) at low ionic strength (0.01M).

However, it reversibly dimerises at higher ionic strength (0.3M) and constant pH (7.9), or at a lower pH (6.8) and ionic strength 0.03M, to form a 14S molecule (mol. wt. 350,000). Arachin II (sedimentation coefficient 14S mol. wt. 350,000) existed as a dimer at pH 7.9 irrespective of the ionic strength, but partially dissociated at 0.03M pH 6.8 to yield a 9S molecular species (mol. wt. 180,000). This dissociation was reversible in the same manner as Arachin I. Arachin I and II (9S and 14S) have identical amino acid and subunit composition. Six subunits, S_1-S_6, have been isolated by preparative isoelectric focusing in sucrose density gradient of the reduced and dissociated protein, and characterized in terms of pI, amino acid composition, NH_2-terminal amino acids and molecular weight (Table 8.4). Two types of subunit have been identified. S_1, S_2 and S_3 are acidic polypeptides (pI 5.8, 6.0 and 6.3 respectively) while S_4, S_2 and S_6 are basic polypeptides (pI 7.1, 7.4, and 8.3 respectively). S_1, S_2 and S_3 were larger molecules (mol. wt. 25,500, 37,500 and 40,500 respectively) compared with the basic polypeptides, all of which had a mol. wt. 19,500. NH_2-terminal amino acids of S_1, S_2 and S_3 were valine, isoleucine and isoleucine respectively, whereas all the basic polypeptides had the same NH_2-terminal amino acid (glycine). All three basic subunits had a similar amino acid composition but only S_4 contained sulfur amino acids. In contrast to the basic subunits, the acidic subunits were richer in the sulfur amino acids, glutamic acid and arginine but poorer in histidine. Each subunit was present in the same molar ratio in both the 9S and 14S proteins. Thus the 9S

Table 8.4   Amino Acid Composition of Arachin Subunits (Residues/100 Residues)

Amino	Subunit					
acid	S_1	S_2	S_3	S_4	S_5	S_6
Lysine	1.2	0.9	1.1	2.8	3.1	3.2
Histidine	1.6	1.5	1.7	3.0	2.1	2.0
Arginine	10.3	12.3	11.7	5.5	6.3	6.0
Aspartic acid	11.5	12.2	12.4	14.1	14.8	16.1
Glutamic acid	24.6	25.0	24.5	13.4	13.7	12.1
Glycine	7.5	7.9	7.9	5.6	6.2	6.3
Alanine	4.0	5.2	4.9	8.7	8.5	8.7
Valine	4.9	3.5	3.3	7.8	6.4	7.1
Leucine	4.5	5.2	4.9	8.0	8.6	8.6
Isoleucine	3.2	3.1	3.3	4.5	4.5	4.7
Proline	5.4	5.1	5.1	6.3	5.6	6.0
Serine	6.7	5.8	5.9	7.6	7.6	7.7
Threonine	3.3	2.3	2.6	2.5	2.6	2.7
Half-cystine	1.3	0.8	0.7	1.0	0	0
Methionine	0.2	0	0.2	0.9	0	0
Phenylalanine	5.5	5.2	5.3	3.9	5.5	4.0
Tyrosine	3.4	3.2	3.4	3.5	3.6	4.0
Tryptophan	0.9	0.9	1.0	0.8	0.9	0.8

Data obtained from Yamada et al. (1979b).

molecule would contain all six subunits in non-covalent association since dissociation into the subunits occurred in urea in the absence of a reducing agent.
Such a molecule would have a calculated mol. wt. 172,000 which is relatively
close to the experimentally obtained value (180,000), This 9S form will dimerise
to form the 14S molecular species consisting of 12 polypeptides. Apart from the
absence of disulfide bonding, the 14S arachin molecule resembles the classical
legumin structure (12S globulin).

Storage Proteins of *Brassica* and Other Cruciferous Oilseeds

Two of the major storage proteins, 12S and 1.7S globulins, have been shown
to be present in the seeds of important cruciferous oilseeds, including oilseed
rape (*B. napus* and *B. campestris*), yellow mustard (*Sinapis alba*) and black mustard (*B. nigra*) along with other cruciferous seeds such as radish (*Raphanus sativa*) (Bhatty et al. 1968; MacKenzie and Blakely, 1972; Laroche et al. 1984). The
12S globulin (cruciferin) accounts for about 60% of the total seed proteins of *B.
napus* while the 1.7S protein (napin) is approximately 20%.

Early work showed that cruciferin was a neutral molecule with an amino acid
composition resembling that of other 12S globulins (Bhatty et al. 1968) (Table
8.5). Recent more detailed physical and chemical investigations revealed that
this protein (mol. wt. 300,000-350,000 pI 7.25) consisted of six subunits arranged as a trigonal antiprism and had dissociation-association characteristics resembling other 12S globulins (Schwenke et al. 1981; Plietz et al. 1983). Thus
under appropriate conditions of extreme pH and high urea concentrations, the
hexameric molecule dissociated into its constituent subunits or monomers.

Information on the subunit and polypeptide composition of the 12S globulins
of cruciferous seeds is sparse compared with that for glycinin and arachin. Recent work on the 12S globulins of *R. sativa* and *B. napus* has revealed an almost
identical polypeptide composition following analysis of the reduced protein by
one-dimensional SDS-PAGE (Laroche et al. 1984). In both these species the 12S
globulin consisted of two distinct polypeptide types with mol. wt. 29,000, 32,000
and 33,000 and mol. wt. 21,000 to 23,000 respectively. Equivocal evidence was
presented which indicated that each polypeptide in the molecular mass range ca.
30,000 was covalently linked to a polypeptide mol. wt ca. 20,000 by a single disulfide bond to form a subunit (mol. wt. ca. 55,000). Detailed analyses of the subunits and their constituent polypeptides have not been undertaken but two-
dimensional IEF/SDS PAGE of the 12S globulin from *R. sativa* revealed considerable charge and size heterogeneity of the nine major polypeptides (mol. wt.
range 20,000-33,000) identified. Similar analysis of cruciferin revealed an even
more diverse pattern which may be indicative that this protein exhibits a greater
degree of heterogeneity than the corresponding protein from *R. sativa* .

The napin protein group, common to many cruciferous seeds, are highly basic
(pI ca. 11.0), with a mol. wt. of 12,000 to 14,000. Four individual proteins comprising the napins in oilseed rape have been isolated and two of these

**Table 8.5   Amino Acid Composition of the Storage Proteins of *B. napus*
Integer Values**

Amino	Cruciferin	Napin (1.7S protein) subunit [b]		
acid	(12S globulin)[a]	Large	Small	Total
Lysine	81	4	3	7
Histidine	46	2	2	4
Arginine	144	3	3	6
Aspartic acid	270	2	-	2
Threonine	120	4	-	4
Serine	129	4	2	6
Glutamic acid	434	22	10	32
Proline	151	10	3	13
Glycine	257	5	3	8
Alanine	177	3	4	7
Valine	182	6	-	6
Isoleucine	139	3	1	4
Leucine	233	6	2	8
Tyrosine	58	1	-	1
Phenylalanine	121	1	2	3
Half-cystine	31	5	2	7
Methionine	44	1	1	2
Tryptophan	20	-	-	1

Data from: [a] Schwenke et al. (1981)
[b] Lönnerdal and Janson (1972). B_3 Napin only

characterized in terms of amino acid composition and polypeptide content
(Lönnerdal and Janson, 1972). Each napin consists of two polypeptides, mol. wt.
9,000 and 4,000 respectively, which are covalently linked by two disulfide
bonds. Both the napins characterized were found to have identical amino acid
compositions, with approximately 25% of their residues as glutamine and high
amounts of proline and half cystine (Table 8.5).

Storage Proteins of *Gossypium hirsutum*

The storage proteins of cotton seed have not been characterized as thoroughly
as many of the less important oilseeds. Recently the storage proteins of this en-
dospermic seed have been purified and some of the properties of the major polypeptide constituents described (Dure and Chlan, 1981). The properties and subunit composition of the quaternary storage protein have not been described but
presumably are globulins (Derbyshire et al. 1976) because of their solubility in
0.5M NaCl but insolubility in 0.125 M. Two major polypeptide components
(mol. wt. ca. 52,000 and 48,000) were identified in SDS-PAGE. Both had similar isoelectric points (range 6.7-7.0). Each size grouping contained a number of
similar polypeptides which were referred to as protein sets. Although the

polypeptide, mol. wt. 52,000, was a glycoprotein, both types had an identical amino acid composition (similar to other storage protein polypeptides) and antigenic determinants. These properties were assumed to indicate that both polypeptides originated from the same ancestral gene.

Influence of Environment on Storage Protein Composition

The composition of the storage proteins in the seeds of any one species, both in terms of individual protein types and the polypeptides that comprise them, is genetically controlled. These proportions, however, are not rigidly fixed. Considerable variation in the spectrum of storage globulins and their polypeptide components has been recorded. Many of these variations result from genetic changes such as mutations and selection but other factors such as nutrition may modify these genetically determined characteristics. Particularly noteworthy in this respect are the changes induced in the storage protein composition of oilseed legumes (*G. max* and *L. angustifolius*) by sub-optimal levels of sulfur in the growth medium (Blagrove et al. 1976; Spencer, 1984). It has been found that under conditions of limiting sulfur supply, that have no effect on total protein synthesis, the seed levels of the 12S globulins were reduced and the 7S globulins increased i.e., globulins especially low in sulfur amino acids increased while those richer in sulfur decreased. In *G. max* not only did limiting sulfur levels result in an increase in β -conglycinin (7S globulin) production but it also modified the temporal sequence of subunit production of these proteins. Under normal conditions, the α' and α subunits are synthesized much earlier than the β types, but when sulfur was deficient, synthesis of the β subunit, which is particularly low in sulfur amino acids, started shortly after the two α subunits and continued at a much higher rate over a longer period. The net effect was that the β–subunit was the major polypeptide synthesized in the second half of seed development, and this was accommodated in the specific β_3 isomer of β -conglycinin.

The mechanism by which sulfur deficiency mediates the production of the storage globulins has been investigated in *Pisum sativum* (Chandler et al. 1983; Spencer, 1984). Contrary to expectation, the reduction in legumin produced in this species was found to be the result of a reduction in the level of legumin-mRNA and not due to a shortage in the sulfur amino acids available for protein synthesis. The levels of vicilin-mRNA in these seeds increased in proportion to the vicilin synthesized. It is pertinent to note that the sulfur deficiency effects were rapidly reversed with a normal resumption of legumin biosynthesis and levels of m-RNA when the element was returned to the plants.

Potassium deficiency also affects storage protein biosynthesis in *P. sativum*. The proportion of legumin in the seed was elevated due to an earlier onset and prolonged synthesis of this protein. Legumin-mRNA also increased under these conditions. It appears that the developing seed can accommodate nutritional stresses by modifying the normal developmental-regulated pattern of synthesis of specific proteins. The modified pattern of storage protein production does not appear to affect the seed adversely.

BIOSYNTHESIS OF STORAGE PROTEINS

Seed Development

This topic will be discussed in outline only since detailed accounts can be obtained from recent reviews (Dure, 1975; Müntz, 1982; Norton et al. 1978). Seed development in non-endospermic dicotyledonous seeds can be divided into three stages. In stage one, following fertilization of the ovule, rapid development of the seed integuments and endosperm ensues, but the embryo, despite undergoing rapid cell division, remains small. By the end of this phase the embryo has a full complement of cells but its size is insignificant and the seed consists mainly of integuments (testa) and liquid endosperm. In stage two, growth of the cotyledonary cells of the embryo is rapid to accommodate the intracellular deposition of oil and storage protein which commences immediately after cell division ceases. Starch and sucrose also accumulate at the beginning of this stage, these being temporary energy reserves which are used in oil and protein formation. Cotyledonary cells become endopolyploid (16-64C), and RNA (mainly rRNA and tRNA) increases in proportion with the DNA to obtain a maximum before the end of the phase and while storage globulin synthesis is still proceeding. Between 1-2% of the total RNA is mRNA and this turns over rapidly throughout this stage. At the end of this developmental phase the cotyledons are the predominant seed tissues while the embryonic axis is small and consists of a rudimentary plumule and radicle and the endosperm is rudimentary or non-existent. In stage three, the seed desiccates and chlorophyll, if present in the seed, disappears. At maturity the seed consists mainly of oil and storage proteins packaged in oleosomes and protein bodies located in the cotyledonary cells.

Site of Storage Protein Synthesis in the Cell

The rough endoplasmic reticulum (r.e.r.) is recognized as the major site of storage protein synthesis in the cotyledonary cells of most seeds, including oilseeds. Supporting evidence for this has been obtained from autoradiographic studies (Bailey et al. 1970) and experiments on protein synthesis carried out in vitro using microsomes, polysomes or m-RNA (Bollini et al. 1983; Beachy et al. 1978; Higgins and Spencer, 1981).

In all seeds prior to or concomitant with the onset of storage protein deposition, there occurs a rapid proliferation of the r.e.r. which in electron micrographs of thin sections appears as vesicles and cisternae. Recently, studies with thick sections (one µm stained with zinc iodide and osmium tetroxide) in the high voltage electron microscope have revealed that the r.e.r. exists as a continuous system of double membrane sheets or cisternae with attached polysomes interconnected by smooth tubules (Harris, 1979). The vesicular appearance of the r.e.r. in thin sections is now thought to represent an artifact of sectioning. Tubular connections between the r.e.r. and dictyosomes are also visible in thick sections.

Following synthesis on the polysomes bound to the r.e.r. the nascent polypeptides are transported vectorially across the membrane and sequestered within the lumen of the cisternae. Evidence in support of this process has been obtained from ultrastructural studies on seeds of the pulse-legume *Phaseolus vulgaris*. Using ferritin-labelled affinity purified antibodies against phaseolin (the major storage globulin of this species), the presence of antigenic material in the cisternae of the r.e.r. has been shown in addition to that in the vesicles and protein bodies (Baumgartner et al. 1980). Further, by supplying the cotyledons with tracer amino acids, radiolabelled storage protein polypeptides have been found in r.e.r. (Bollini et al. 1982).

Storage proteins are eventually deposited in protein bodies of various sizes within the cytoplasm. These organelles possess a single bounding membrane and are incapable of protein synthesis. Although dictyosomes classically have been implicated in the transport of storage protein from the r.e.r. to the protein bodies, the evidence for this is equivocal. These conclusions have been based on ultrastructural studies which have revealed the presence of proteinaceous material that is pronase digestible and has the same electron density as material in vesicles segregated from dictyosomes and in protein bodies. Unambiguous verification of the role of dictyosomes in storage protein transport by the use of immunocytological procedures is still awaited.

Precursor Molecules with Signal Peptides

As indicated above, the precursors of storage proteins are synthesized on polysomes bound to the r.e.r., transported via membrane bound organelles and eventually deposited in the protein bodies. Precursor molecules therefore, must cross a membrane as the primary step in their sequestration. This process occurs in the r.e.r. and the translocation of the nascent polypeptide across the membrane involves a specific amino acid sequence (signal or leader sequence) at the NH_2-terminus of the molecule. The signal peptide is also primarily involved in binding the ribosome to the membrane. Once inside the lumen of the r.e.r. the signal peptide is removed by a peptidase when the nascent polypeptide is some 80 or so amino acids long. Storage proteins then are formed as precursor molecules each with a signal peptide consisting of approximately 10-20 amino acid residues (molecular mass 1000-2000) attached to the NH_2-terminus. Such molecules, irrespective of their final form, are devoid of carbohydrate.

Supporting evidence in a number of oilseeds has been obtained for the presence of a leader sequence on precursor molecules of the storage proteins (glycinin, conglycinin, cruciferin, napin and cottonseed proteins) (Tumer et al. 1981; Beachy et al. 1978; Nielsen, 1984; Crouch et al. 1983b; Dure and Galau, 1981). This evidence was obtained by comparing the products of translation of poly (A^+)-RNA in vitro with those of immature seeds. For example, the glycinin precursor polypeptides produced in acellular systems (wheat germ or rabbit reticulocyte lysate) and isolated by immuno precipitation procedures were found to be slightly larger than their counterparts produced in vivo either by translation or poly (A^+)-RNA by *Xenopus laevis* oocytes or after short-term amino acid incorporation studies in immature seeds (Tumer et al. 1982; Beachy et al. 1981). Microsequencing of the translational products of the oocyte system revealed that the NH_2-terminal sequences of the glycinin subunit precursor and those of the acidic polypeptide of the mature glycinin subunit were similar, indicating that the nascent polypeptides had been processed by the removal of a small peptide. Pre-glycinin polypeptides from the lysate system, however, had NH_2-terminal amino acid sequences rich in leucine which were different from those of either the acidic or basic subunits of mature glycinin. Recently, nucleotide sequencing of the cloned gene for a specific glycinin subunit (A_2B_{1a}) has revealed the provision for an 18 amino acid signal sequence at the NH_2-terminus of the precursor. This nucleotide sequence was located between the start codon and that for the NH_2-terminal amino acid of the mature acidic polypeptide (Nielsen, 1984). The signal peptide for the A_2B_{1a} gene was predicted to be leucine-rich and the position of these residues agreed well with the microsequencing data for the glycinin precursors produced in vitro.

Subunits (α and α') of the glycoprotein conglycinin are synthesized as precursor molecules in translation systems in vitro. Each precursor polypeptide possessed a signal sequence at the NH_2-terminus and was devoid of carbohydrate (Sengupta et al. 1981; Beachy et al. 1981). Analogous products of protein synthesis in vivo were glycosylated and devoid of the signal polypeptide. Presumably the nascent polypeptide is modified by co-translational removal of the signal peptide and glycosylation in association with the r.e.r.

Both cruciferin, the 12S globulin, and napin, the low molecular mass storage protein, of *B. napus* have been shown to be produced in vitro as a precursor molecule of much larger size than the corresponding mature protein (Crouch et al. 1983a&b). It has been predicted from the nucleotide sequence analysis of cloned cDNA for napin that the precursor molecule possesses a leucine-rich signal peptide sequence of 17 amino acids at the NH_2-terminus. Precursor polypeptides of the cruciferin subunits synthesized in vitro are several thousand daltons larger than those produced in vivo, inferring that the signal polypeptide is removed in the latter case. Similarly the polypeptide components of the storage proteins of cottonseed are produced in translation systems in vitro as precursor polypeptides with signal sequences (Dure and Galau, 1981). In vivo, these precursors undergo considerable processing before appearing as polypeptides characteristic of the mature storage protein.

Nature of the Precursor Polypeptides Synthesized in vitro

In recent years, the majority of studies on the synthesis of storage proteins in vitro have employed poly (A^+)-RNA or other suitable RNA preparations isolated from immature seeds at a stage of rapid storage protein syntheses in acellular protein synthesizing systems. The products of poly (A^+)-RNA translation in wheat germ or reticulocyte lysate systems, isolated by immunoprecipitation techniques, are generally of a different molecular size from the mature polypeptides synthesized in vivo. This in itself indicates that considerable processing of the polypeptides occurs in vivo.

Although the presence of the signal peptide will affect the size of the precursor, this is not the only reason for the difference in molecular mass from the mature polypeptide. In the case of the glycinin subunit precursors it is known that these consist of a family of polypeptides containing at least three different sized components (mol. wt. 58,000 to 63,000 which for convenience will be considered to be mol. wt. ca. 60,000), (Tumer et al. 1981; Barton et al. 1982). Each precursor consists of a single polypeptide which is insensitive to reducing agents. It will be remembered that the specific glycinin subunit (e.g. A_2B_{1a}) consists of an acidic polypeptide (A_2) (mol. wt. 37,000) which is covalently linked by a single disulfide bond to a basic subunit (B_{1a}) (mol. wt. 19,000). Thus the precursor molecule of the glycinin subunit is produced as a single polypeptide which consists, from the NH_2-terminus, of the signal peptide followed by the acidic and basic polypeptides. Amino acid sequence prediction from the nucleotide sequence of the cloned gene for the subunit has verified this finding, but has also revealed that the acidic and basic polypeptides are joined together in the precursor molecule by a linker peptide consisting of four amino acids which is proteolytically cleaved during post-translational processing. In addition, the presence of a pentapeptide on the carboxyl terminus of the basic polypeptide is predicted from the nucleotide sequence and this will be cleaved post-translationally.

From the information available it is evident that the subunit components of the glycoprotein β-conglycinin are also synthesized as precursor molecules. The products of enriched poly (A^+)-RNA fractions translated in vitro and isolated by immunoprecipitation techniques are precursors of the α', α and β subunits with mol. wt. 80,000, 78,000 and 50,000 respectively compared with values of 76,000, 83,000 and 53,000 for the respective mature subunits (Beachy et al. 1981; Sengupta et al. 1981). A careful comparison of these precursor polypeptides with those obtained from pulse labelling in vivo has revealed that α' and α polypeptides were quickly co-translationally cleaved of the signal peptide and glycosylated in the cotyledonary cell.

Napins, the family of small basic storage proteins of *B. napus* consisting of two subunits (mol. wt. 9,000 and 4,000), are synthesized as single polypeptide precursors containing both subunits (Crouch et al. 1983b). In vitro translation products isolated by immunoprecipitation contained 178 amino acid residues (mol. wt. 21,000). Predicted amino acid sequence from the nucleotide sequence of cloned cDNA revealed that the precursor consisted of five regions, arranged as follows from the NH_2-terminus; a signal sequence (21 amino acids), a short acidic peptide (17 amino acids), the glutamine-rich small polypeptide (37 amino acids) found in the mature napin, a short acidic peptide (19 amino acids), and finally the glutamine-rich large polypeptide (80 amino acids) again typical of the mature napin. The amino acid composition of the large and small subunits as predicted from the nucleotide sequence resemble closely that published earlier for the same subunits of mature napin. Clearly this precursor undergoes both co- and post-translational processing to remove the leader sequence and the acidic peptide regions to form the mature napin molecule. Precursor polypeptides of cruciferin (mol. wt. 51,000, 48,000 and 43,000) were isolated from the translation products of total RNA from immature rapeseed embryos in the reticulocyte lysate system and precipitated with antisera against cruciferin (Crouch et al. 1983a). These precursors were insensitive to reducing agents and consisted of a signal polypeptide and the two polypeptides constituting the mature cruciferin subunit in a single polypeptide.

Co- and Post-Translational Modifications
of Protein Synthesis Products

From the foregoing discussion and the properties of the constituent subunits and polypeptides of the mature storage proteins, it is evident that the precursor polypeptides synthesized in the r.e.r. undergo considerable co- and post-translational modification. Co-translational events occurring on the r.e.r. include the removal of the signal peptide and glycosylation of those polypeptides which appear in the mature state as glycoproteins. Post-translational processing of the precursor polypeptides occurs in several locations, including the lumen of the r.e.r., dictyosomes and the protein bodies. Such modifications include oligomer formation, further glycosylation and de-glycosylation and proteolytic processing. Although details of these processes in oilseeds, are incomplete, sufficient information is available which, when supplemented with that obtained with pulse legume seeds, enables a more detailed picture of the overall process to be constructed.

Co-translational modification of the precursor polypeptides of glycinin occurs rapidly during translation. On the other hand the post-translational processing resulting in the formation of the characteristic subunits of mature glycinin, and the assembly of these into the hexameric protein (12S globulin) takes hours or even several weeks to complete (Sengupta et al. 1981; Barton et al. 1982). At some stage either during or shortly after the formation of the precursor polypeptide, a disulfide bond is formed between the acidic and basic components so that these remain covalently linked together when the linker peptide is proteolytically removed during post-translational processing. Since this intermolecular disulfide bond is located at homologous positions in each subunit, it is likely that a specific folding of the precursor polypeptide takes place facilitating the formation of the bond. One of the major products of protein synthesis, following long (two day) incubations with ^{14}C-leucine and isolation on sucrose density gradients, was a 7S oligomer which represented a trimer of precursor peptides (mol. wt. ca. 60,000) (Barton et al. 1982). Although activity was also incorporated into the 12S globulin fractions, unaggregated precursors were relatively weakly labelled. Formation of the half-molecule appeared to precede the proteolytic cleavage of the precursors, which may be obligatory prior to the assembly of the hexamer (12S globulin). In similar but more detailed investigations on the post-translational processing of legumin precursors in *Pisum sativum* the trimer of the precursor polypeptide (mol. wt. ca. 60,000) was located in the r.e.r. and then transported to the protein bodies, where, following proteolytic processing and hexamer formation, the formation of the mature 12S globulin occurred extremely slowly, possibly over several weeks, (Chrispeels et al. 1982a; Chrispeels et al. 1982b).

Co-translational processing of the precursor polypeptides of the α' and α polypeptides of β -conglycinin (mol. wt. 80,000 and 78,000 respectively) involved both the proteolytic cleavage of the signal peptide and core glycosylation (Sengupta et al. 1981; Beachy et al. 1981). Since the molecular masses of the co-translationally processed and unprocessed precursor polypeptides were almost identical, it must be concluded that the cleaved signal peptide and core carbohydrate had similar masses. It was also shown that core glycosylation occurred only after the removal of the signal peptide and when the precursor polypeptide was complete (Sengupta et al. 1981). Proteolytic cleavage of the signal peptide was independent of glycosylation since in the presence of tunicamycin, a specific inhibitor of glycosylation, the major labelled polypeptides synthesized in vivo and isolated by immunoprecipitation using antisera against the 7S α -subunits, were of identical size to the proteolytically cleaved translation products (α' and α polypeptides minus signal peptide only). Additional glycosylation of the co−translationally modified precursors occurred in the lumen of the r.e.r. over a period of 5-90 minutes. This was concluded from the appearance during that time of larger polypeptides corresponding to the α' and α precursors on dissociating gels. Slow post-translational processing involving proteolytic cleavage and de-glycosylation took place outside the r.e.r. over a period ranging from 1.5 to 16 hours to yield mature α' and α polypeptides (mol. wt. ca. 76,000 and 83,000). In general the results of Beachy et al. (1981) confirmed these findings and differed only in detail, particularly with respect to the time required to produce the mature subunits which was stated as being three hours. Also the β -subunit of con-glycinin was found to be weakly labelled in pulse-chase studies and it was shown that the mature form of this subunit has a mol. wt. 53,000 compared with 50,000 for the translation product in vivo. Assuming that the post-translational processing of the 7S globulin precursor is the same in all developing legume seeds whether they be oilseed or not, it is relevant to consider some of the details of vicilin synthesis in *P. sativum*. Following pulse-labelling of developing pea cotyledons with ^{14}C-labelled amino acids, both the r.e.r. and protein bodies were isolated from tissue extracts by fractionation in sucrose density gradients at various times during the chase (Chrispeels et al. 1982a&b). The products of protein synthesis associated with these organelles were examined by means of immunoaffinity gels and sucrose density gradient centrifugation. Precursor polypeptides of vicilin were located primarily in the r.e.r. The average half-life of this material in the r.e.r. was 1.5 hours. Within the r.e.r. the precursor polypeptides were associated into trimers (7-8S proteins) and transported as such to the protein bodies via the dictyosomes. Slow proteolytic processing of the precursor polypeptides still in association occurred over a period of up to 24 hours, until the polypeptides characteristic of mature vicilin predominated. Similar processing of the precursors of β -conglycinin may also occur.

In pulse-chase experiments with cultured immature rapeseed embryos, precursors of napin and cruciferin occurred as polypeptides mol. wt. 18,500 and 43,000-48,000 respectively (Crouch et al. 1983a&b). These polypeptides were slightly smaller than the products of protein synthesis in vitro, indicating that the signal sequence had been removed co-translationally. Within a few hours, both the precursors had been cleaved post-translationally to yield the mature polypeptide components of napin (mol. wt. 9,000 and 4,000) and cruciferin (mol. wt. 20,000 to 22,000 and 26,000 to 29,000). In the case of the napin precursor, extensive regions of the polypeptide were removed during this post-translational processing.

The two major storage protein subunits of cottonseed (mol. wt. 52,000 and 48,000) are synthesized in vitro as precursor polypeptides with respective mol. wts. of 60,000 and 69,000 (Dure and Galau, 1981). In vivo these precursors undergo co-translational processing to form polypeptides having mol. wts. of 70,000 and 67,000 respectively. The processing of the smaller precursor molecule involved proteolytic cleavage of the signal peptide and glycosylation while the larger molecule was cleaved of its signal peptide only. These co-translationally processed polypeptides are abundant in immature seeds but disappear in late embryogenesis. This suggests that post-translational processing of both these polypeptides (mol. wt. 70,000 and 69,000) to produce the respective subunits of the mature storage proteins (mol. wt. 52,000 and 48,000) was extremely slow and occurred in the protein bodies.

Cloning of Storage Protein Genes

The application of recombinant DNA technology has greatly enhanced the study of storage proteins in seeds. In this section the significance of some of the work on cloned complementary DNAs and genomic DNAs pertaining to oilseeds will be considered.

Size fractionation of total poly (A^+) RNA isolated from immature seeds of *G. max* has revealed the presence of two major mRNAs (18S and 20-25S) (Beachy et al. 1981; Tumer et al. 1981; Barton et al. 1982). These enriched fractions of mRNA directed the synthesis of the subunit precursors of glycinin and β -conglycinin respectively in translational systems in vitro. Complementary DNAs (cDNAs) have been produced from the respective glycinin and β - conglycinin-mRNAs and these cloned into bacterial plasmids. Clones which encoded the glycinin and β -conglycinin were identified by heteroduplex-hybridization of translatable messages. Glycinin- and β -conglycinin- precursor mRNAs identified by Northern hybridization had molecular weights of 710,000 and 840,000 or approximately 2050 and 2500 nucleotides respectively. These are of sufficient size to code for their respective proteins. Although the β - conglycinin mRNAs coding for the α, α' and β subunits of that protein were selected by a single cDNA clone, these mRNAs were not identical because of their different thermal elution characteristics (Beachy et al. 1981; Barton et al. 1982).

A cDNA clone encoding the precursor of the A_2B_{1a} subunit of glycinin has been cloned and sequenced (Marco et al. 1984; Nielsen, 1984). The predicted amino acid sequence was in close agreement with that of the isolated subunit determined chemically (Staswick et al, 1984a). Confirmation was obtained that in the precursor molecule (A_2B_{1a} subunit) the acidic and basic polypeptides are joined together by a small linker peptide which is subsequently removed by processing.

Recently several genomic clones with coding sequences corresponding exactly for the primary structure of the A_2B_{1a} subunit of glycinin have been isolated from a genomic library constructed from a partial restriction enzyme digest of leaf DNA (Marco et al. 1984; Nielsen, 1984). Nucleotide sequence data of the genomic clone and an homologous cDNA clone enabled the structure of the complete gene for this subunit to be determined. The complete transcriptional unit of the A_2B_{1a} subunit extended to 2799 base pairs and contained three introns of 238, 292 and 624 base pairs respectively. Two untranslatable sequences of 43 and 226 base pairs were located at the 5' and 3' ends of the unit. The 3' untranslatable unit contained three potential polyadenylation signals in addition to a polyadenylated tail. From the nucleotide sequence it was deduced that the acidic and basic polypeptides were part of the same transcriptional unit. Also predicted were the presence of a signal sequence (18 amino acids), a linker peptide (4 amino acids) and a pentapeptide at the carboxyl terminus in the precursor molecule. All these were co- and post-translationally cleaved. Comparisons between the nucleotide sequence of the basic polypeptide of the A_2B_{1a} subunit gene with that for the analogous polypeptide of pea legumin revealed 70% homology in the coding regions. Such results support the hypothesis that genes coding for the 12S globulins have developed from a common ancestral gene.

Complementary DNA clones have been derived from the total RNA of rapeseed embryos and selected by hybrid release for cruciferin and napin mRNA (Crouch et al. 1983a&b). Nucleotide sequencing of both the cruciferin and napin cDNAs predicted that the large and small polypeptide components of mature cruciferin and napin were present in the respective single polypeptide precursors. Extensive processing of these precursors occurred in vivo to produce the mature cruciferin and napin subunits.

Cloned cDNA, encoding the two major storage protein subunits of cottonseed, have been used to characterize the principal cotton storage protein and gene family (Galau et al. 1983). These proteins were encoded in three sets of mRNA rather than two as expected from electrophoretic and immunoprecipitation characteristics of the proteins. A mRNA subfamily (2260 base pairs) specifically encoding one subunit (mol. wt. 69,000) and two mRNA subfamilies (1960 base pairs) encoding the other subunit (mol. wt. 60,000) were identified by hybrid selection and hybrid-arrested translation. Some homology was detected between the two smaller mRNA subfamilies but not between these and the larger mRNA subfamily. The relationships between these subfamilies may be elucidated following cDNA sequencing.

CONCLUSIONS AND PROSPECTS

The principal storage proteins of oilseeds are the salt soluble globulins and of these the 12S types are almost universally present while the 7S and other globulins appear to be less widely distributed. On the basis of mainly physicochemical criteria, the 12S globulins of different species are broadly similar. This similarity has in a few instances been extended to the level of their primary structures, namely, the NH_2-terminal sequences of the basic polypeptides which show a high level of conservation. Within a given species, the 12S globulins exhibit microheterogeneity and this is also observed in the subunits and polypeptides. Interspecific relationships between the 7S and other globulin types are less well defined owing to the complexity of some of these proteins and paucity of information, particularly with respect to the primary structure of the subunits.

Storage proteins are located in special organelles (protein bodies) in the cell. All storage protein subunits are synthesized in the r.e.r. as precursor molecules with a signal peptide. These undergo considerable processing (co- and post-translational) to produce the subunits of the mature storage proteins. Processing occurs in the r.e.r., dictyosomes and protein bodies and may take up to several days to complete.

Storage proteins are seed specific and are only produced at certain stages of seed development. The means by which gene expression is regulated is unknown but control is probably mediated at the transcriptional level.

Complementary DNAs have been produced from a number of mRNAs coding for precursors of the subunits of a number of oilseed storage proteins and these cloned into bacterial plasmids. A cDNA coding for a specific glycinin subunit has been sequenced and the predicted amino acid sequence of the polypeptide corresponded closely with that determined chemically. Using cDNA as a probe three gene subfamilies have been identified as encoding the two major storage protein subunits in cotton. Complementary DNA probes may also be used to measure mRNA levels and factors regulating mRNA transciption. Gene number and their copy number can be estimated by hybridizing cDNA for specific proteins with restriction enzyme digests of genomic DNA. Complementary DNA can be hybridized in situ to determine the location of storage protein genes. Genomic DNA clones encoding a specific glycinin subunit have been analysed and the structure of the complete gene determined.

Probably the most exciting prospect for the future will be the genetic manipulation of oilseed proteins. Provided a suitable means can be obtained whereby DNA can be introduced, integrated and transcribed in the nucleus, and cloned cDNA or genomic DNA suitably modified, varieties could be developed with modified genes coding for storage proteins of superior quality. Such technologies although not yet available are almost certain to be developed in the future.

REFERENCES

Badley, R.A., Atkinson, D.A., Hajser, H., Oldani, D., Green, J.P., and Stubbs, J.M. 1975. The structure, physical and chemical properties of the soybean protein glycinin. Biochim. Biophys. Acta 412: 214-228.

Bailey, C.J., Cobb, A., and Boulter, D. 1970. A cotyledon slice system for the autoradiographic study of the synthesis and intracellular transport of the seed storage proteins of *Vicia Faba*. Planta (Berl.) 95: 103-118.

Barton, K.A., Thompson, J.F., Madison, J.T., Rosenthal, R., Jarvis, N.P., and Beachy, R.N. 1982. The biosynthesis and processing of high molecular weight precursors of soybean glycinin subunits. J. Biol. Chem. 257: 6089-6095.

Baumgartner, B., Tokuyasu, K.T., and Chrispeels, M.J. 1980. Immunocytochemical localisation of phaseolin in the endoplasmic reticulum of developing bean (*Phaseolus vulgaris*) cotyledons. Planta (Berl.) 150: 419-425.

Beachy, R.N., Thompson, J.R., and Madison, J.T. 1978. Isolation of polyribosomes and messenger RNA active in in vitro synthesis of soybean seed proteins. Plant Physiol. 61: 139-144.

——, Jarvis, N.P., and Barton, K.A. 1981. Biosynthesis of subunits of the soybean 7S storage protein. J. Mol. Appl. Genet. 1: 19-27.

Bhatty, R.S., McKenzie, S.L., and Finlayson, A.J. 1968. The proteins of rapeseed (*Brassica napus* L.) soluble in salt solutions. Can. J. Biochem. 46: 1191-1197.

Blagrove, R.J., Gillespie, J.M., and Randall, P.J. 1976. Effect of sulfur supply on the seed globulin composition of *Lupinus angustifolius*. Aust. J. Plant Physiol. 3: 173-184.

Bollini, R., Van Der Wilden, W., and Chrispeels, M.J. 1982. A precursor of the reserve protein phaseolin is transiently associated with the endoplasmic reticulum of developing *Phaseolus vulgaris* cotyledons. Physiol. Plant. 55: 82-92.

——, Vitale, A., and Chrispeels, M.J. 1983. In vivo and in vitro processing of seed reserve protein in the endoplasmic reticulum: evidence for the glycosylation steps. J. Cell Biol. 96: 999-1007.

Chandler, P.M., Higgins, T.J.V., Randall, P.J., and Spencer, D. 1983. Regulation of legumin levels in developing pea seeds under conditions of sulfur deficiency. Rates of legumin synthesis and levels of mRNA. Plant Physiol. 71: 47-54.

Chrispeels, M.J., Higgins, T.J.V., Craig, S., and Spencer, D. 1982a. Role of the endoplasmic reticulum in the synthesis of reserve proteins and kinetics of their transport to protein bodies in developing pea cotyledons. J. Cell Biol. 93: 5-14.

——, ——, and Spencer, D. 1982b. Assembly of storage protein oligomers in the endoplasmic reticulum and processing of the polypeptides in the protein bodies of developing pea cotyledons. J. Cell Biol. 93: 306-313.

Crouch, M.L., Tenbarge, K.M., and Simon, A.E. 1983a. Molecular cloning of the mRNA sequences of the storage proteins of *Brassica napus*. Proc. 6th Intern. Rapeseed Congress 1: 613-618.

——, ——, ——, and Ferl, R. 1983b. cDNA clones for *Brassica napus* seed storage proteins: evidence from nucleotide sequence analysis that both subunits of napin are cleaved from a precursor polypeptide. J. Mol. Appl. Genet. 2: 273-283.

Derbyshire, E., Wright, D.J., and Boulter, D. 1976. Legumin and vicilin, storage proteins of legume seeds. Phytochemistry (Oxf.) 15: 3-24.

Dure, L.S. 1975. Seed formation. Annu. Rev. Plant Physiol. 26: 259-278.

——, and Chlan, C. 1981. Developmental biochemistry of cottonseed embryogenesis and germination. XII. Purification and properties of principal storage proteins. Plant Physiol. 68: 180-186.

——, and Galau, G.A. 1981. Developmental biochemistry of cottonseed embryogenesis and germination. XIII. Regulation of biosynthesis of principal storage proteins. Plant Phsyiol. 68: 187-194.

Galau, G.A., Chlan, C.A., and Dure, L.S. 1983. Developmental biochemistry of cottonseed embryogenesis and germination. XVI. Analysis of the principal cotton storage protein gene family with cloned cDNA probes. Plant Mol. Biol. 2: 189-198.

Gillespie, J. M., and Blagrove, R. J. 1978. Isolation and composition of the seed globulins of wing bean (*psophocarpus tetragonolobus* L.) D.C., Aust. J. Plant Physiol. 5: 357-369

Harris, N. 1979. Endoplasmic reticulum in developing seeds of *Vicia faba*. Planta (Berl.) 146: 63-69.

Higgins, T.J.V., and Spencer, D. 1981. Precursor forms of pea vicilin subunits. Modification by microsomal membranes during cell-free translation. Plant Physiol. 65: 205-211.

Koshiyama, I. 1983. Storage Proteins of Soybean, pp. 427-450. *In* W. Gottschalk and H. P. Müller (eds.), *Biochemistry, Genetics, Nutritive Value*. Martinus Nijhoff-Junk, Hague, Boston, London.

Laroche, M., Aspart, L., Delseny, M., and Penon, P. 1984. Characterisation of radish (*Raphanus sativus*) storage proteins. Plant Physiol. 74: 487-493.

Lönnerdal, B., and Janson, J-C. 1972. Studies on Brassica seed proteins. 1. The low molecular weight proteins in rapeseed. Isolation and characterisation. Biochim. Biophys. Acta. 278: 175-183.

MacKenzie, S.L., and Blakely, J.A. 1972. Purification and characterisation of seed globulins from *Brassica junea, B. nigra* and *B. hirta*. Can. J. Bot. 50: 1825-1834.

Marco, Y.A., Thanh, V.H., Tumer, N.E., Scallon, B.J., and Nielsen, N.C. 1984. Cloning and structural analysis of DNA encoding an A_2B_{1a} subunit of glycinin. J. Biol. Chem. 259: 13436-13441.

Moreira, M.A., Hermodson, M.A., Larkins, B.A., and Nielsen, N.C. 1979. Partial characterisation of the acidic and basic polypeptides of glycinin. J. Biol. Chem. 254: 9921-9926.

——,——,——, and——. 1981. Comparison of the primary structure of the acidic polypeptides of glycinin. Arch. Biochem. Biophys. 210: 633-642.

Mossé, J., and Baudet, J. 1983. Crude protein content and amino acid composition of seeds; variability and correlations. Qual. Plant. Plant Foods Hum. Nutr. 32: 225-245.

———, and Pernollet, J.C. 1983. Storage Proteins of Legume Seeds, pp. 111-193. *In* S. K. Arora (ed.), *Chemistry and Biochemistry of Legumes*. Edward Arnold, London.

Müller, H.P. 1983. The Genetic Control of Seed Protein Production in Legumes, pp. 309-353. *In* W. Gottschalk and H. P. Muller (eds.), *Seed Proteins. Biochemistry, Genetics, Nutritive Value*. Martinus Nijhoff-Junk, Hague, Boston.

Müntz, K. 1982. Seed Development, pp. 505-558. *In* D. Boulter and B. Parthier (eds.), *Nucleic Acids and Proteins in Plants 1*. Encyclopedia of Plant Physiology, New Series 14A. Springer Verlag, Berlin.

Nielsen, N.C. 1984. The chemistry of legume storage proteins. Philos. Trans. R. Soc. Lond. B. Biol. Sci. 304: 287-296.

Norton, G., Harris, J.F., and Tomlinson, A. 1978. Development and Deposition of Proteins in Oilseeds. *In* G. Norton (ed.), *Plant Proteins*. Butterworths, London, Boston.

Osborne, T.B. 1924. *The Vegetable Proteins*. Longman, Green & Co. Ltd.

Plietz, P., Damaschun, G., Muller, J.J., and Schwenke, K.D. 1983. The structure of 11S globulins from sunflower and rapeseed. A small-angle X-ray scattering study. Eur. J. Biochem. 130: 315-320.

Schwenke, K.D., Raab, B., Linow, K.J., Pähtz, W., and Uhlig, T. 1981. Isolation of the 12S globulin from rapeseed (*Brassica napus* L.) and characterisation as a 'neutral' protein. On seed proteins - Part 13. Nahrung 25: 271-280.

Sengupta, C., Deluca, V., Bailey, D.S., and Verma, D.S. 1981. Post-translational processing of 7S and 11S components of soyabean storage proteins. Plant Mol. Biol. 1: 19-34.

Spencer, D. 1984. The physiological role of storage proteins in seeds. Philos. Trans. R. Soc. Lond. B. Biol. Sci. 304: 275-285.

Staswick, P.E., Hermodson, M.A., and Nielsen, N.C. 1981. Identification of the acidic and basic subunit complexes of glycinin. J. Biol. Chem. 256: 8752-8755.

———, ———, and ———. 1984a. The amino acid sequence of the A_2B_{1a} subunit of glycinin. J. Biol. Chem. 259: 13424-13430.

———, ———, and———. 1984b. Identification of the cystines which link the acidic and basic components of the glycinin subunits. J. Biol. Chem. 259: 13451-13435.

Sykes, G.E., and Gayler, K.R. 1981. Detection and characterisation of a new β -conglycinin from soyabean seeds. Arch. Biochem. Biophys. 210: 525-530.

Thanh, V.H., and Shibasaki, K. 1977. Beta-conglycinin from soyabean proteins. Biochim. Biophys. Acta. 490: 370-384.

———, and ———. 1978a. Major proteins of soyabean seeds. Subunit structure of β -conglycinins. J. Agric. Food Chem. 26: 492-695.

———, and———. 1978b. Major proteins of soyabean seeds. J. Agric. Food Chem. 26: 695-698.

Tumer, N.E., Thanh, V.H., and Nielsen, N.C. 1981. Purification and characterisation of mRNA from soybean seeds. Identification of glycinin and β -conglycinin precursors. J. Biol. Chem. 256: 8756-8760.

———, Richter, J.D., and Nielsen, N.C. 1982. Structural characterisation of the glycinin precursors. J. Biol. Chem. 257: 4016-4018.

Yamada, T., Aibara, S., and Morita, Y. 1979a. Dissociation-association behaviour of arachin between dimeric and monomeric forms. Agric. Biol. Chem. 43: 2549-2556.

———, ———, and ———. 1979b. Isolation and some properties of arachin subunits. Agric. Biol. Chem. 43: 2563-2568.

Chapter 9

Nutritional Characteristics and Protein Uses of Oilseed Meals

J. M. Bell

INTRODUCTION

Oilseed meals are generally regarded as protein supplements for use in animal feeds but they are also extensively used as fertilizers and soil improvers in areas such as China and Japan. Some oilmeal is further processed for use in human food.

Production and utilization patterns are changing in response to growth in world population as well as to the demand in developing countries for better diets with more animal protein. The growing understanding of the need for balanced diets for animals producing meat, milk and eggs also affects oilmeal use. The recent spectacular increase in palm oil production modifies the traditional balance between oil and meal supply because of the high oil:oilmeal ratio of palm.

A recent review embracing the period 1958 to 2007 (Oil World, 1983) indicates a linear increase in total world oilmeal production. Selecting the 30-year period 1970 to 2000 a 2.8-fold increase from 54 to 150 million tonnes is expected. Over the same period soybean production is expected to increase 3.8-fold from about 26 to 98 million tonnes.

It was also concluded that total world livestock production (in terms of meat, milk, eggs) will increase about 67% from 180 to 300 million tonnes over this period while per capita annual livestock production will increase about 17%, from 43.7 to 51.0 kg. These large increases in production of livestock and poultry were seen to require increasing increments of oilmeal use per unit of animal product as increasing proportions of the producing animals are fed and managed better so as to maximize production and efficiency of feed utilization. However, the trend tends to level off with time. Possible reasons include limitation of supply of oilmeals, decreasing margins for nutritional improvement of animal diets, increasing availability of improved energy feeds such as high lysine corn and barley, and increasing use of non-protein nitrogen for supplementary ruminant diets.

CHARACTERISTICS OF OILMEALS

Oil is removed by hydraulic expeller, screw press, solvent extraction or pre-press solvent extraction methods. The method of extraction may affect the amount of residual oil in the meal which in turn may affect the energy value for feeding. In some cases by-products of edible oil refining (e.g. gums) may be added to the meal. The seed or meal may be subjected to heat if cooked prior to extraction, if expelled by pressure, or if heated to remove solvent or to inactivate antinutritional factors. Such processing variables influence meal composition and nutritional value.

Oilmeals vary widely in chemical composition (Tables 9.1 and 9.2). A few contain less than 20% crude protein (CP) and by some standards would not qualify to be called protein supplements whereas some meals contain over 50% CP (%N x 6.25). The crude fibre content varies from about 3 to 35%, with the higher values often being associated with the presence of hulls which also affects the CP content and nutritional value generally.

The composition data in Tables 9.1 and 9.2 do not fully reflect variations associated with dehulling, processing conditions, cultivar, growing conditions, seed quality or methods of analysis. These variations may affect the metabolizable energy (ME) values as well as the CP level and amino acid availability.

Amino acids are expressed as percentages of air-dry feed (Table 9.2), the method most useful in feed formulation. However, comparisons of protein quality are more meaningful when amino acids are expressed as percentages of the protein in the oilmeal (Table 9.3). For this purpose protein is CP, or %N x 6.25. Only lysine and the sulfur amino acids are presented in Table 9.3 since these are the amino acids most frequently in limited supply in the energy grains used in pig and poultry diets. In these comparisons soybean is the richest in lysine, followed closely by rapeseed, with all other oilmeals well below these two meals. In contrast soybean meal is the lowest in sulfur amino acids with some meals containing twice that of soybean meal. It is emphasized that any procedure that

Table 9.1 Major Nutrient and Metabolizable Energy Composition of Oilseed Meals[a]

Component	Soybean[b]	Cotton-seed	Ground-nut [c]	Sun-flower[b]	Rape-seed	Linseed	Mustard
Moisture, %	10.9	8.6	8.5	7.0	9.0	8.9	8.9
Crude protein, %	48.5	41.6	47.4	46.8	38.5	35.9	41.0
Crude fiber, %	3.0	11.0	13.1	10.8	10.9	8.9	6.9
Ether extract, %	1.0	1.6	1.2	2.9	3.7	5.1	2.0
Ash, %	5.9	6.5	4.5	7.7	6.3	5.6	5.7
Calcium, %	0.30	0.15	0.17	0.53	0.61	0.39	
Phosphorus, %	0.65	1.10	0.55	0.50	1.35	0.87	
Magnesium, %	0.27	0.58	0.04		0.58	0.56	
Manganese, mg/kg	30.0	20.0	29.0	23.0	45.0	32.5	
Metabolizable energy, Mcal/kg							
Cattle	2.65	2.31	2.54	2.19	2.31	2.66	2.44
Swine	2.82	2.60	2.43	2.59	2.77	2.71	
Poultry	2.53	1.82	2.20	2.29	1.92	1.52	

Component	Saf-flower[b]	Sesame	Poppy	Corn Germ	Castor Bean	Palm Kernel	Coconut (Copra)	Jojoba[d]	Niger
Moisture, %	11.5	7.8	10.8	8.3	13.3	9.7	7.3	4.9	10.0
Crude protein, %	40.4	44.3	36.6	21.4	26.0	21.4	20.7	14.0	33.0
Crude fiber, %	8.5	5.4	11.6	15.3	35.5	14.5	11.3	6.1	19.7
Ether extract, %	6.7	8.6	7.9	9.0	1.0	7.3	6.7	51.0	5.6
Ash, %	6.4	10.3	12.4	3.5	7.5	4.6	6.6	1.4	10.8
Calcium, %	0.32	1.99		0.05			0.21		
Phosphorus, %	0.59	1.33		0.57			0.62		
Magnesium, %							0.31		
Manganese, mg/kg		48.0		16.0			65.4		
Metabolizable energy, Mcal/kg									
Cattle	2.51	2.62	2.37	2.65		2.48	2.73		2.25
Swine	2.91	3.07		3.02		2.89	3.53		2.50
Poultry	1.69	1.91	2.76	1.70			1.77		

[a] For additional information on composition see Anon. (1970, 1971), Bell (1983) et al. (1981), Church (1977).
[b] Dehulled.
[c] Partly dehulled.
[d] Composition of unextracted seed.

affects protein digestibility or amino acid availability will affect these comparative evaluations.

The B-vitamins and the essential minerals in oilmeals should not be overlooked. However, space precludes adequate discussion of these nutrients and while they are important in ration balancing they are seldom deciding factors when deciding on kinds or levels of oilmeals to use.

Table 9.2   Essential Amino Acid, Cystine and Tyrosine Composition of Oilseed Meals (% in Air-Dry Meal)

Amino Acid, %	Soybean	Cotton- seed	Ground- nut	Sunflower (dehulled)	Rapeseed	Linseed	Mustard
Arginine	3.8	4.5	5.2	3.7	2.3	3.2	2.1
Cystine	0.8	0.8	0.8	0.7	0.5	0.7	0.8
Histidine	1.2	1.1	1.2	0.9	1.1	0.7	1.0
Isoleucine	2.6	1.6	1.9	1.6	1.5	1.5	1.4
Leucine	3.8	2.5	3.2	2.5	2.6	2.2	2.7
Lysine	3.2	1.7	1.8	1.4	2.2	1.2	2.0
Methionine	0.7	0.6	0.5	0.6	0.7	0.6	0.9
Phenylalanine	2.7	2.2	2.5	2.0	1.5	1.7	1.5
Threonine	2.0	1.4	1.4	1.3	1.7	1.1	1.7
Tryptophan	0.6	0.5	0.5	0.6	0.4	0.6	0.4
Tyrosine	2.0	0.7	1.6	-	0.9	1.0	1.3
Valine	2.7	2.2	2.2	2.2	1.9	1.9	1.8

Amino Acid, %	Safflower (dehulled)	Sesame	Corn Germ	Castor Bean	Palm Kernel	Coconut (Copra)	Niger
Arginine	3.8	4.7	1.1	2.8	2.8	2.7	2.8
Cystine	0.5	0.6	0.5	-	0.4	0.3	0.5
Histidine	1.0	1.1	0.6	0.5	0.4	0.6	0.8
Isoleucine	1.7	2.1	1.1	1.0	1.0	0.7	1.4
Leucine	2.7	3.4	1.7	1.4	1.5	1.5	2.2
Lysine	1.3	1.3	0.9	0.8	1.0	0.6	1.5
Methionine	0.7	1.4	0.3	0.4	0.4	0.3	0.5
Phenylalanine	1.9	2.2	0.8	0.8	1.0	0.9	1.4
Threonine	1.4	1.6	0.9	0.7	0.8	0.6	1.3
Tryptophan	0.6	0.8	0.3	-	0.2	0.2	-
Tyrosine	-	2.0	1.5	0.7	-	0.6	0.6
Valine	2.4	2.4	1.3	1.3	1.2	1.0	1.2

UTILIZATION OF OILSEED MEALS IN ANIMAL FEEDS

The usefulness of an oilmeal is influenced by several factors including palatability, digestibility, the nutritional balance of the absorbed amino acids and the presence of anti-nutritional or toxic factors. Digestibility coefficients vary according to the class and age of animal, the level of meal fed in the diet, the kind of meal and the processing to which the meal was subjected. Energy digestibility coefficients tend to be highest for swine, followed by cattle and then poultry, as indicated by the ME values for soybean, groundnut (peanut), safflower, coconut and rapeseed meals (Table 9.1).

Digestible energy (DE) accounts only for fecal losses of undigested energy whereas ME recognizes fecal, gaseous and urinary energy losses. Metabolizable energy values are typically 90 to 95% of DE values for pigs and about 82% of DE values for ruminants.

Table 9.3 Lysine, Methionine and Cystine Concentrations in the Proteins of Oilmeals

Oilseed Meal	Amino Acid in Protein (N x 6.25), % Lysine	Methionine	Cystine	Relative Concentration Soybean=100 Lysine	Methionine + Cystine
Soybean	6.2	1.4	0.6	100	100
Cottonseed	4.1	1.4	1.9	66	160
Sunflower	3.0	1.4	1.4	48	135
Groundnut	3.8	1.1	1.6	61	129
Rapeseed	6.0	1.8	1.2	96	148
Coconut	4.6	2.0	1.7	74	184
Linseed	3.3	1.8	1.8	54	178
Mustard	4.8	2.2	2.0	77	208
Safflower	3.3	1.8	1.3	53	166
Sesame	2.9	3.1	1.3	46	216
Corn germ	3.5	1.2	1.9	56	150
Palm kernel	4.4	2.0	1.7	71	178
Niger	4.4	1.5	1.7	71	156
Castor bean	3.0	1.4		48	

The protein digestibility coefficient of an oilmeal is influenced by the dietary conditions under which the coefficient is derived as well as by the characteristics of the meal being assayed, and the age and class of animal used. The *apparent* digestibility method, the usual procedure, in effect attributes endogenous or metabolic fecal nitrogen (MFN) to the meal under test and results in a lower digestibility coefficient than if *true* digestibility were determined. The lower the dietary level of CP fed the greater the difference between true and apparent digestibility. In addition, the so-called MFN component increases as the fibre and indigestible carbohydrate fraction of the diet increases, hence the digestibility of protein is a function of the type of diet used as well as of the dietary CP level and the kind of oilmeal. The MFN effects appear to be most pronounced with non-ruminants.

True digestibility of protein is seldom determined because it is a complicated procedure and while this would help to identify differences between meals, such values would be of limited use in practical feed formulation. It is essential to off-set fecal protein losses regardless of their origin (metabolic or undigested) in order to provide the necessary levels of absorbed amino acids to meet the animal's protein requirements. Thus the apparent digestibility coefficients are most useful, although they may over-rate protein digestibility because the coefficients are often derived from diets containing higher dietary CP levels than would be fed in normal production diets. This would apply to amino acid availability as well. Obviously care must be taken in making comparisons between meals not tested within the same experiment and under comparable conditions.

Following digestion the ability of the absorbed amino acids to meet the animals' requirements determines the "quality" or biological value of the digested protein. The amino acids of main interest are arginine, histidine, isoleucine, leucine, lysine, methionine, phenylalanine, threonine, tryptophan and valine. These are the essential or indispensable amino acids. Cysteine, tyrosine and glutamic acid are non-essential amino acids but may satisfy part of the need for essential amino acids.

Protein quality evaluations may be conducted in several ways and there is extensive literature on this subject. Perhaps the simplest method is the Essential Amino Acid Index (EAAI) whereby the amino acids of the protein in the meal are expressed as percentages of the amino acids present in a protein of high nutritional quality such as whole egg protein. The amino acid having the lowest percentage value is regarded as the first limiting amino acid. The second and third limiting amino acids are similarly determined, if desired.

This method is useful but, as with all protein quality methods, it has certain weaknesses or limitations. It ignores digestibility and availability of protein and amino acids. Egg protein also may be a less valid base of comparison than the amino acid requirement levels for the class and age of animal to be fed the meal. In addition the oilmeal would never constitute the sole source of protein in practical diets so the EAAI does not allow for complementarity of amino acids from several sources within the diet. Thus a protein given a low EAAI rating may perform very well in certain dietary situations.

Several protein quality evaluation methods involve feeding trials with weanling rats. Among these is the Protein Efficiency Ratio (PER) method which uses diets containing 9 or 10% CP derived totally from the test and standard protein (casein) sources and compares responses in terms of weight gain per unit of protein consumed. The Net Protein Ratio (NPR) method uses a protein-free control diet and several levels of test protein and casein. The results are derived from a slope-ratio response difference between weight gain of a test group and the weight loss of the group fed the protein-free diet.

These methods are generally superior to those such as the EAAI but retain some of its shortcomings. Protein quality may be under-rated for samples that are unpalatable or that contain anti-nutritive or toxic factors.

Lysine is the essential amino acid most likely to be deficient in diets based on cereal grains fed to pigs and poultry. It is also the amino acid most likely to be most adversely affected by excessive heat during the crushing process, either because of excessive temperatures during cooking prior to extraction or later during hydraulic or screw press expelling or during solvent removal and toasting. The chemical determination of available lysine is often used to monitor such damage and is of value to the feed formulator to help ensure adequacy of available lysine.

Oilmeals contain some non-protein nitrogen (Millar et al. 1962) which rumen microflora may be able to convert to useful protein but which is of little value to pigs or poultry. For this reason, as well as because of the variable amino acid composition of the protein, the %N x 6.25 factor does not accurately reflect the protein contents of oilmeals and to some extent affects biological value or protein quality evaluations. While the 6.25 factor is subject to criticism it is still widely used in nutritional work and a more suitable factor is not available. The ultimate alternative may be to discontinue reliance on % CP as a dietary descriptor and to emphasize amino acid adequacy.

For some purposes the solubility of oilmeal protein in a saline solution resembling saliva is determined. Oilmeals with high proportions of soluble protein are undesirable for ruminant feeding because rumen bacteria tend to degrade the protein too rapidly, leading to loss of ammonia into the blood stream and increased excretion of urea in the urine. Applications of heat during meal manufacture or treatment with a low concentration of formaldehyde are methods designed to decrease solubility. Such treated protein proceeds through the rumen and is digested by intestinal enzymes. As indicated previously, excessive application of heat may reduce protein quality for use with pigs and poultry. Obviously decisions on the matter of modifying protein solubility must take into account the animal species to which the meal will be fed.

Several of the oilmeals are commercially available either with or without hulls or may be partially dehulled. Since hulls are fibrous, low in protein and in other nutrients, and low in digestibility, their removal results in higher contents of DE and digestible CP and generally improved nutritional value. In some cases, such as with sunflower and safflower meal, dehulling is necessary to render the meals generally useful as protein supplements. A decision on whether or not to dehull often depends on finding an appropriate use for the hulls.

HUMAN FOOD USES

Oilseeds may be specially processed or refined for food use. This technology is most advanced with the soybean which has long been used in the human diet in various forms. Some progress has also been made with groundnuts, rapeseed, sunflower, cottonseed and sesame. There appears to be an important future role for new protein foods of this type but more research is needed on processing technology, flavour, color, anti-nutritional properties and functionality (Milner et al. 1978) before the new products will be widely accepted for food use.

The refined plant protein products are generally referred to as flours or concentrates when they are upgraded to contain 50 or 60% CP and as isolates if the final product is nearly pure protein. Some of these products may find use in certain animal feeds such as pet feeds and milk substitutes for calves and piglets.

OILSEEDS AS FEED INGREDIENTS

Unextracted or 'full-fat' oilseeds may sometimes be used in rations to increase their ME content or to reduce dustiness of the feed. Low quality oilseed, perhaps damaged by weather, insects or disease may be appropriately processed and used to advantage as feed ingredients. Grinding or rolling is necessary to ensure high digestibility and cooking may be required to inactivate toxic or anti-nutritional factors.

THE OILSEED MEALS

Soybean Meal

Soybean meal is the most extensively used oilmeal and serves as a protein supplement for all classes of animals. The meal contains from 44 to 50% CP (Table 9.1) and from 2.5 to 2.8 Mcal ME/kg depending on the amount of hull present and the species of animal being fed. Dehulling increases the ME values by about 5% for cattle and 12% or more for pigs and poultry, and increases the CP content. Most soybeans are processed by solvent extraction, which results in very low oil content in the meal.

Soybeans contain several anti-nutritional factors including trypsin inhibitors, a goitrogenic factor and an estrogenic compound (Liener, 1983). The trypsin inhibitor is inactivated by heat in the toasting stage of meal production and under normal conditions of use the other factors do not emerge as problems affecting animal performance. Another anti-nutritional factor that occurs commonly in cereal grains and oilseed meals is phytate, which renders about one-half of the 0.6% phosphorus in soybean meal unavailable to pigs and poultry.

Soybean meal is an excellent protein supplement for lactating dairy cattle as well as as for calves following weaning from milk or milk replacer. It is highly palatable and well digested. Similarly it serves well as the supplemental protein in rations for growing and fattening cattle. However, in cattle feeding where high energy starchy grain is used to promote high growth rates or milk production, soybean meal or other oilmeals often must compete with non-protein ingredients such as urea, because of cost.

Rations for pigs and poultry may contain soybean meal as the only protein supplement. It was formerly necessary to include some animal or marine-origin protein to ensure adequacy of amino acids and vitamin B_{12} but now that lysine, methionine and vitamin B_{12} are commercially available animal protein is an option based mainly on economics.

There is renewed interest in feeding whole or 'full-fat' soybeans. These contain 15 to 22% oil and consequently at least 10% more ME than meal. Their use in rations of high producing dairy cows helps to offset weight loss characteristic of the early post-partum period when cows have difficulty consuming enough energy to meet their requirements. It is essential to heat soybeans before feeding and some small-scale cooking-extruding equipment is available for use on farms. Rumen microflora may be adversely affected if the fat or oil content of the diet becomes too high and also if large amounts of fatty acids enter the blood stream the fatty acid composition of milk fat may be altered.

Full-fat, cooked soybeans may be fed at dietary levels up to 10% to market pigs but beyond this level their use may result in 'soft pork'. This condition simply reflects increased direct deposition of absorbed fatty acids when more soybean oil is being digested than can be modified into typical porcine fat. Soft pork has lower eye appeal to the consumer but its nutritional value is not adversely affected and may be improved if the fat contains a larger proportion of polyunsaturated fatty acids.

The use of full-fat soybeans in animal feeding depends largely on the cost of alternative sources of energy and protein, plus whatever advantages are perceived for the incorporation of oil on characteristics of feed or product.

Cottonseed Meal

Cottonseed meal ranks second to soybean meal in amount produced. The cake or meal was originally used as fertilizer but for the past half-century or more it has been used widely as a protein supplement. Over 95% of the U.S. production is now used in feeds.

The meal in the U.S.A. is standardized at about 41% CP by adjusting the hull content to achieve a uniform product. Otherwise quality and composition variations would be relatively large. The crude fibre content is about twice that of soybean meal (Table 9.1) and the ME values are lower. Cottonseed meal protein is also relatively low in lysine compared with soybean meal but superior in methionine and cysteine (Table 9.3).

Cottonseed meal contains gossypol, a yellow pigment, the major compound among eight or more present in the pigment glands of cottonseed (Liener, 1980). It is a highly reactive, toxic compound, existing in three tautomeric forms and occurs either bound to amino groups in the seed protein or in free form which is regarded as the toxic form. The mechanism of gossypol toxicity remains largely unknown (Liener, 1980). General symptoms include depressed appetite and weight loss. Antemortem and postmortem findings indicate widespread effects in the body and on its functions. There appear to be important differences in susceptibility among animal species.

Research on the gossypol problem has followed several lines. Removal of gossypol or chemically modified gossypol by solvent extraction has been found technically feasible but has not been commercially adopted for meal improvement. Gossypol reacts with ferrous iron forming an insoluble complex which is not absorbed in the gastrointestinal tract. Various other mineral elements interact with gossypol, including calcium, sodium and potassium and these aspects are taken into account when formulating rations, especially for poultry.

Another avenue for gossypol reduction is the development of glandless strains of cottonseed. This results in superior meal but problems in agronomic performance require resolving before such genetic strains are widely grown.

Low gossypol meal is defined in the U.S.A. as containing not more than 0.04% of free gossypol. Meal produced by screw press and hydraulic processes may have free gossypol contents of 0.04 to 0.10 and 0.02 to 0.05%, respectively, but solvent processed meal contains 0.1 to 0.5% (Liener, 1980). Obviously the processing method used affects free gossypol content and there are also cultivar and regional differences in free gossypol content of the seed.

Cottonseed is processed by hydraulic, screw press, prepress solvent or direct solvent extraction. In the U.S.A. screw pressing is most common but prepress and solvent methods each account for 20 to 25% of the crush. One of the objectives during prepressing is to cause binding of the free gossypol to hold it in the meal and to render it inactive. In some crushing plants the seed is flaked and cooked at 93 to 135°C while in others no cooking of seed is involved. Screw press pressures up to 20,000 psi (138 Mpa) may be applied, with associated elevated temperature, whereas much less rigorous conditions prevail in direct solvent operations.

Cottonseed meal has long been used successfully for feeding to cattle, sheep, goats, horses and mules, where it is regarded as being nearly equivalent to soybean meal. Feeding recommendations have been developed taking into account the type and quality of meal available and the nature of the other ingredients in the ration.

In pig feeding the gossypol level, the DE level and protein quality affect the amount that can be used. Even the glandless type meals have not proven very suitable for young pigs. When the meal is used for pigs as the sole source of supplemental protein it is recommended that not more than 0.01% free gossypol occur in the meal and that iron sulfate be included in the ration on a 1:1 basis relative to gossypol content, weight basis.

Cottonseed meal is used extensively in broiler chicken rations but only to a limited extent in layer rations. Gossypol and a cyclopropenoid fatty acid (sterulic acid) cause discoloration in the yolks and whites of eggs. Procedures have been developed for testing and predicting egg discoloration properties of meal so it is now possible to feed 'egg tested' meal to laying birds. The inclusion of a supplement of ferrous iron salts is recommended in all poultry rations.

Sunflower Meal

The world output of sunflower meal ranks third after soybean meal and cottonseed meal. This meal has been used effectively in feeds for cattle and pigs. It is palatable and evidently free of significant amounts of toxic or anti-nutritive components (Coune, 1979). Meal containing the hull fraction has about 24% crude fibre and 32% CP, but without hull the corresponding values are about 11 and 47%, respectively.

Dehulled meal is relatively rich in sulfur amino acids (methionine and cyst eine) but rather low in lysine (Table 9.3). It therefore appears that dehulled sunflower meal should be widely useful in animal rations when formulated with appropriate attention to essential amino acids, especially lysine.

Up to one-half of the soybean meal used in broiler and layer rations has been replaced by dehulled sunflower meal without significantly affecting performance. Higher levels of substitution may be effective with such meal when lysine adequacy is assured by appropriate supplementation.

Pigs utilize sunflower meal well if it is dehulled and if dietary lysine levels meet requirements.

Groundnut (Peanut) Meal

Groundnut meal ranks about fourth in world tonnage among oilmeals. Its CP content varies from about 45 to 55% depending on the amount of hulls remaining in the meal. This meal has CP that is lower in lysine than soybean meal CP but higher than soybean meal in sulfur amino acids (Table 9.3). Protein digestibility tends to be low, possibly because of the tannins present in the skins. Depressed protein digestibility may reduce the availability of lysine. Energy digestibility is high when the meal is well dehulled.

Groundnuts contain protease inhibitors that can be totally inactivated by moist heat at 100°C for 15 min. This oilseed may be contaminated occasionally by mold that produces aflatoxin which is toxic to animals and man, and is carcinogenic. Groundnuts also contain some heat stable allergens (Liener, 1980) but these do not appear to cause problems when feeding the meal to animals.

Rapeseed Meal

During most of the long history of this crop the cake or meal was used as a fertilizer or soil conditioner, a practice which persists today in China and Japan. The first nutritional studies appear to have been those of Kuen and co-workers in Germany about 1872 (Schneider, 1947).

Early experience with the meal was not encouraging. It would have been unpalatable, high in goitrogen content and the processing conditions probably did not enhance its feeding value. Both the crop and processing technology have changed markedly in recent decades (Bell, 1983).

Rapeseed meal contains 36 to 38% CP and a favourable assortment of essential amino acids in its protein (Table 9.1, 9.2 and 9.3). It contains more fibre (about 12%) than soybean meal and has lower ME values. The crude fibre is largely in the hull fraction which comprises about 16% of the seed and 25 to 30% of meal. Hulls are poorly digested, especially by non-ruminants and are largely responsible for the relatively low ME values.

Dehulling improves the ME value of the meal but the practice has not been adopted by the industry, largely because of the problem of utilizing hulls. In France, however, promising results have been obtained from using hulls in rabbit rations.

Another approach to increasing the digestible energy value of the meal is the development of cultivars with thinner seed coats. Such strains contain less hull on the seed, the hull contains less fibre and is more digestible (Stringam et al. 1974; Bell and Shires, 1982). Meal derived from such seed contains more CP and DE.

Rapeseed contains glucosinolates which, upon enzymatic hydrolysis, yield goitrogenic factors known as oxazolidinethione, isothiocyanates and thiocyanates, depending on the parent compound, and which interfere with iodine uptake and thyroxine synthesis by the thyroid gland. Under certain conditions nitriles may be produced which are also toxic but not especially goitrogenic. The seed contains myrosinase, the enzyme responsible for glucosinolate hydrolysis. Hydrolysis may also occur in the gastrointestinal tract in the absence of rapeseed myrosinase by means of bacterial enzymes but this does not appear to be highly effective. The feeding of glucosinolates in the absence of myrosinase appears to have relatively little effect on thyroid enlargement.

Improved processing technology has been aimed at inactivation of myrosinase without allowing glucosinolate hydrolysis. Moist cooking for 20 to 30 min after the seed is flaked in rollers inactivates myrosinase. Some crushing plants employ less rigorous cooking and depend on very low seed moisture content to minimize enzyme activity and the residual enzyme activity is destroyed in the toasting stage. This final heating may also reduce the glucosinolate content to some extent but care must be taken to avoid excessive heat damage to protein, especially lysine availability.

The successful reduction of glucosinolates in rapeseed by plant breeders was a notable breakthrough. Unfortunately some countries have been less successful to date than others in achieving this goal. This appears related to differences in the species and types of rapeseed that perform best agronomically in different areas. In Canada the rapeseed industry has converted completely to low glucosinolate cultivars of both *B. napus* and *B. campestris*, summer types, and the name 'canola' now applies within the trade to designate the superior meal resulting from this change. Low glucosinolate meal contains about 10% of the original complement of the major kinds of glucosinolates. This enables such meal to find its role in animal feeds on the basis of its nutrient content in most instances without concern about goitrogenicity.

The successful feeding of rapeseed meal requires knowledge of the kind of meal and the age and class of animal involved. Winter types of rapeseed contain more glucosinolates than summer types. *B. napus* cultivars contain more glucosinolates than *B. campestris* cultivars. Low glucosinolate meal is becoming increasingly available. It is important that the glucosinolate status of the meal be known.

Rapeseed meal is suitable as the sole protein supplement in the rations of calves, growing heifers and bulls, lactating dairy cows and beef cattle. Milk from cows fed rapeseed meal contains less iodine but milk is not usually regarded as a significant source of iodine in the human diet.

High glucosinolate rapeseed meal is not advised as the major supplementary protein in pig feeding, particularly for young pigs and breeding females. Low glucosinolate meal has been successfully fed as the only supplement in both growing and breeding pig rations at levels up to 15% in barley type rations. Supplemental lysine is sometimes beneficial, especially with young pigs. There is a minor problem of palatability with young pigs, consequently it is common to use more soybean meal during the early feeding stage. The efficiency of feed conversion is lower with rapeseed meal than with soybean because of the differences in DE and ME contents.

Poultry derive less ME from rapeseed meal than do cattle or swine but when the meal is fed in diets that meet energy requirements excellent performance is obtained. With the advent of low glucosinolate meal much higher dietary levels can be used and such meal is extensively used especially in the broiler industry.

In the case of laying hens low glucosinolate meal may be used as the major protein supplement but two problems deserve mention. The compound sinapine, present in the meal, has been implicated in the production of eggs with 'fishy taint'. This condition is associated with a minority of birds within certain strains of brown-egg laying birds. Sinapine is hydrolyzed in the digestive tract to release relatively large amounts of choline which is converted into trimethylamine, the agent responsible for the odour or flavour. Selecting layer strains not having this genetic anomaly has been suggested as a potential solution to this problem where rapeseed meal is available and where brown-shelled eggs are preferred by the consumer.

The incidence of mortality from hemorrhagic liver syndrome (HLS) in layers fed high levels of high glucosinolate meal has been found to increase, especially in layer strains predisposed to this condition. Low glucosinolate meal has little or no effect on HLS incidence when fed at recommended levels.

As with soybeans there is some interest in feeding full-fat rapeseed to poultry, pigs and lactating cows. It is high in energy since the seed contains about 40% oil. It should be ground or rolled for pigs and cattle to ensure high digestibility. Excellent results have been obtained by feeding low glucosinolate seed that was severely frozen before harvesting and included in pig rations at levels up to 30%.

Linseed Meal

Linseed meal has been a popular protein supplement for use in rations for dairy and beef cattle as well as for sheep and horses. It was especially valued for fitting animals for shows as it was said to promote 'bloom' and mellowness of hide. These properties may have been due to residual oil in expeller cake and to the laxative nature of the meal arising from its content of pentosans and mucilaginous matter.

Linseed meal contains about 36% CP (Table 9.1) and is similar to soybean meal in ME for swine and cattle but not for poultry. Its protein quality is relatively low for non-ruminants, mainly because of a low lysine level. Satisfactory performance will not occur without blending with other protein supplements or use of supplementary amino acids to improve protein quality.

The presence of an antipyridoxine factor, linatine, renders linseed meal toxic to chickens unless the diet is adequately supplemented with pyridoxine. The high mucilage content causes problems of beak necrosis with poultry and the laxative nature of the meal limits its use as well. Flax also contains a cyanogenetic glucoside, linamarin, which appears to fluctuate under various growing conditions and consequently requires monitoring in the meal to prevent toxic levels of hydrocyanic acid being included in feeds.

Linseed meal is useful in swine rations and is palatable. It should be used with due regard to its lysine content and its anti-nutritive properties. Therefore it appears to function best when used in conjunction with other protein sources and appropriate amino acid supplements.

Coconut Oilmeal (Copra Meal)

Coconut oilmeal is relatively low in CP (21%) and its successful use in pig and poultry diets requires inclusion of supplementary lysine or a protein source such as fish meal. It is relatively high in ME for cattle and pigs but low for poultry. Some results indicate a maximum of 20% in poultry diets but others have shown good results with 40% when energy and amino acids were adequate. No toxic factors have been found in coconut meal but mold contamination may occur on copra during storage. This apparently can be prevented by spraying fresh copra with an alcoholic solution of sodium propionate.

The Minor Oilmeals

Limitation of space and of scientific knowledge preclude detailed descriptions of the composition and feeding value of the other oilmeals mentioned in Tables 9.1 and 9.2.

Mustard meal (*B. hirta* and *B. juncea*) resembles rapeseed meal. It may contain slightly more protein but has less lysine and is rich in sulfur amino acids. It contains more glucosinolates than rapeseed although of a different kind. No low glucosinolate cultivars have been developed since the glucosinolates are important when mustard is used as a food condiment. Several methods for detoxifying have been developed, including alkali salts and ammoniation.

Safflower meal is high in fibre, unless well dehulled, and its protein is low in lysine. It is most useful in ruminant rations.

Sesame meal can be used in limited quantities in feed if due attention is given to offsetting compounds that affect zinc utilization and to its low lysine level. The meal is relatively rich in methionine and tryptophan.

Among the remainder of the oilmeals corn germ meal is relatively low in CP and ranks more as a milling by-product than as a protein supplement, although it may be a very useful feed ingredient. Germ meals may be more important as B-vitamin sources. Little has been published about the feeding value of poppy, castor bean, palm kernel, jojoba or niger oilmeals. However jojoba contains a toxic factor, simmondsin (Liener, 1980), and its meal was poorly utilized in one feeding trial reported. Palm kernel meal is somewhat low in lysine and the fibre content is relatively high. It may lack palatability but may be used successfully at low levels (Oyenuga, 1959; Owusu-Domfeh et al. 1970).

REFERENCES

Anonymous. 1971. *Atlas of Nutritional Data on United States and Canadian Feeds.* National Academy of Sciences, Washington, D.C.

Anonymous. 1970. *Amino-Acid Content of Foods and Biological Data on Protein. Nutritional Studies No. 24.* Food Policy and Food Service, Nutrition Division, FAO, Rome.

Bell, J.M. 1983. Nutrients and toxicants in rapeseed meal: a review. J. Anim. Sci. 58: 996-1010.

——, and Shires, A. 1982. Composition and digestibility by pigs of hull fractions from rapeseed cultivars with yellow or brown seed coats. Can. J. Anim. Sci. 62: 557-565.

——, ——, Blake, J.A., Campbell, S., and McGregor, D.I. 1981. Effect of alkali treatment and amino acid supplementation on the nutritive value of yellow and Oriental mustard meal for swine. Can. J. Anim. Sci. 61: 783-792.

Church, D.C. 1977. *Livestock Feeds and Feeding.* O & B Books Inc., 1215 NW Kline Place, Corvallis, Ore. 97330.

Coune, F. 1979. Sunflower Meal. Proc. 40th Minnesota Nutrition Conf., pp. 37-43. Minneapolis, Minn.

Liener, I.E. 1980. *Toxic Constituents of Plant Foodstuffs.* Academic Press, New York, N.Y.

Miller, R.W., Van Etten, C.H., McGraw, C., Wolff, I.A., and Jones, Q. 1962. Amino acid composition of seed meals from forty-one species of Cruciferae. Agric. Food Chem. 10: 426-430.

Milner, M., Scrimshaw, N.S., and Wang, D.I.C. 1978. *Protein Resources and Technology: Status and Research Needs.* Avi Publ. Co., Inc., Westport, Conn.

Oil World. 1983. *The Past 25 Years and Prospects for the Next 25.* Publ. ISTA Mielke Gm6H, 2100 Hamburg 90, P.O.B. 900803, W.-Germany.

Owusu-Domfeh, K., Christensen, D.A., and Owen, B.D. 1970. Nutritive value of some Ghanian feedstuffs. Can. J. Anim. Sci. 50: 1-14.

Oyenuga, V.A. 1959. *Nigeria's Feeding-Stuffs.* 2nd ed., Ibadan University Press, Ibadan, Nigeria.

Schneider, B.H. 1947. *Feeds of the World, Their Digestibility and Composition.* Agric. Exp. Sta., West Virginia Univ., Morgantown, W. Va.

Scott, M.L., Nesheim, M.C., and Young, R.J. 1982. *Nutrition of the Chicken*. M.L. Scott and Assoc., Ithaca, N. Y.

Smith, A.K., and Circle, S.J. 1972. *Soybeans: Chemistry and Technology* Vol. 1. *Proteins*. Avi Publ. Co., Inc., Westport, Conn.

Stringam, G.R., McGregor, D.I., and Pawlowski, S.H. 1974. Chemical and morphological characteristics associated with seedcoat color in rapeseed. Proc. 4. *Internationaler Rapskongress*, Giessen, W.-Germany. pp. 99-108.

Chapter 10

Carbohydrate and Fiber Content of Oilseeds and their Nutritional Importance

P. Vohra

INTRODUCTION

Oilseeds differ from cereals in storing most of their energy reserves in the form of fats rather than starch. During the early formation of the seeds, sugars and starch are present, but later, fats and protein start accumulating and residual starch may be present only in trace amounts at the maturation of the seeds. Oilseeds are grown for their oil and not the protein content. Any genetic manipulation to increase the protein level in the seed may have undesirable effects on the fat and the carbohydrate contents which are inversely related to protein content. The fats are mobilized to yield sugars during the germination of the oilseeds.

The energy reserves and protein are enclosed within the cell walls of the seeds when they have a definite structural integrity. The cell walls, which are rich in polysaccharides other than starch, are designated as structural carbohydrates to differentiate them from the energy reserve sugars and starch-like polysaccharides. The structural carbohydrates of oilseeds and cereals are rather similar. The oilseeds may have a thick outer coating or hull. The hull should be removed to obtain a superior quality oilseed meal. The relative proportions of the kernel and the hull and the carbohydrate composition of hulls are highly variable for different oilseeds. Again, the composition of the carbohydrate complex is dependent upon the genetic makeup of the variety of an oilseed and the agronomic conditions for the cultivation of the variety.

CLASSIFICATION AND IMPORTANCE OF CARBOHYDRATES

The carbohydrate complex of oilseeds may be divided into some of its major components (Table 10.1). The carbohydrates are concentrated in the residues (oilseed meals) after removal of oil from the oilseeds, but their relative proportions remain unchanged from that of the starting material. Carbohydrates are also associated with the protein concentrates prepared from oilseeds, but at a much reduced level. They tend to concentrate in the residue of protein extraction and in the supernatant after precipitation of protein.

Table 10.1 Some Components of the Carbohydrate Complex of Oilseeds

CARBOHYDRATES	
SUGARS	NON-SUGARS

MONOSACCHARIDES
 Trioses, Tetroses, Pentoses
 Hexoses, Heptoses, Octoses
 Nonoses, Decoses
	POLYSACCHARIDES
	 HOMOPOLYSACCHARIDES
	 or *HOMOGLYCANS*
	    Pentosans, Hexosans
	    Galacturonans

MONOSACCHARIDE DERIVATIVES
 Deoxysugars, Alditols
 Cyclitols, Aldonic acids
 Aldaric acids, Glycosides
 Glycosans, Nucleosides
 Amino sugars, Phosphate
   esters of sugars
	HETEROPLYSACCHARIDES
	 or *HETEROGLYCANS*
	    Pentosans, Hexosans
	    Glycuronans, Glycoproteins
	    Lipopolysaccharides
	    Mucopolysaccharides

OLIOGOSACCHARIDES Disaccharides Trisaccharides Tetrasaccharides	

A number of carbohydrates are important to the food industry and nutritionists. Many carbohydrates are found in oilseeds. Some of these and their nutritional implications are listed in Table 10.2.

Table 10.2   Some Carbohydrates Used in the Food Industry and their Nutritional Importance

Monosaccharides	Alcohol Derivatives	Polysaccharides
Ribose	Xylitol	*Starch (1)
*Arabinose (2,5)	Mannitol	*Dextrins (1)
*Xylose	Sorbitol (Glucitol)	Glycogen (1)
*Glucose (1)	Maltol (5)	*Cellulose (8)
*Mannose	Ethylmaltol	*Galactomannans (8)
*Fructose (1,7)	*Galactinol	*Arabinans (8)
*Galactose (2,5)	*Inositol	*Xylans (8)
*Fucose		*Galacturonans (8)
*Rhamnose		*Galacturonorhamnan (8)
		Glucogalactans (8)
		*Mannans (8)
		*Galactans (8)
		*Galactarabans (8)

	Oligosaccharides	
Disaccharides	*Trisaccharides*	*Tetrasaccharides*
*Sucrose (1,6,7)	Maltotriose	*Stachyose (4,9)
*Melibiose	Isomaltotriose	*Sesamose
Lactose (3,4,5)	Manninotriose	
Isolactose	*Raffinose (4,9)	*Pentasaccharide*
Maltose (3,4,5)		*Verbascose (9)
Isomaltose (3,4,5)		
Trehalose		
Kojibiose		
Maltulose		
Gentibiose		
*Cellobiose		

*Isolated from oilseeds; (1) nutritionally useful; (2) cataract causing; (3) malabsorption effects; (4) cause flatulence; (5) cause diarrhea; (6) carciogenic; (7) lipogenic; (8) dietary fiber; (9) raffinose group.

Available Carbohydrates

Carbohydrates and fats are the major sources of dietary energy of all animals except carnivores. Monogastric animals have an essential need for glucose, but can utilize efficiently only glucose,fructose(*monosaccharides*), lactose (except avian species), sucrose (*oligosaccharides*), starches, dextrin, and glycogen (*homopolysaccharides*) from the diet. These are grouped as available carbohydrates. Maltose and isomaltose are not generally found in cereals or oilseeds.

Starch exists in two forms: amylose, a linear polymer of alpha-1,4-linked glucose units; and the branched polymer, amylopectin, with alpha-1,4- and alpha-1,6 glucose units. Raw amylopectin is better utilized than amylose, but the differences disappear on heating the starch.

The rest of the members of the carbohydrate complex are grouped as unavailable carbohydrates for monogastric animals.

Unavailable Carbohydrates

The oligosaccharides raffinose and stachyose of the *raffinose* group are considered undesirable or deleterious. This group of food components is often blamed, but not confirmed, for causing the discomfort of excessive gas production or flatulence in humans (Liener, 1980). Their removal from the oilseed protein concentrates is highly desirable.

Polysaccharides, another term for dietary fiber, has been coined to designate the unavailable carbohydrates which cannot be attacked by the enzymes present in the gastrointestinal tracts of animals that have simple digestive systems.

Unavailable carbohydrates or dietary fiber include the following components; cellulose, hemicellulose, pectins, gums, mucilages (mucin in linseed), and lignin-hemicellulose complexes. In oilseeds, most of these carbohydrates are associated with the structural components of the cell walls. The terms such as hemicellulose, pectins and gums are vague. The name hemicellulose was coined by Schulze (1981) for the polysaccharides which were extracted from the plant cell wall by an alkaline solution. The term is loosely applied for the cell wall polysaccharides which are neither cellulose nor pectin. Homoglycans such as xylans, mannans and galactans, and heteroglycans such as glucomannans, galactomannans, arabinogalactans and galactoglucomannans are all grouped as hemicellulose.

Cellulose is a linear polymer of beta-1,4-linked glucose units. All animals lack the enzyme beta-glycosidase capable of hydrolyzing cellulose in their gastrointestinal tract. The microflora resident in the large intestines and ceca of monogastric animals can ferment the unavailable carbohydrates to yield volatile fatty acids (VFA). Ruminants evolved to utilize this symbiosis. VFA's serve as sources of energy for ruminants and cecal fermenters. Ruminants utilize cellulose to meet dietary energy needs more efficiently than monogastric animals.

Hemicellulose has a lower molecular weight than cellulose. Xylans have the basic beta-1,4-xylose linkage with side attachments of single residues of arabinose, glucuronic acid and its 4-0-methylether. Mannans are present in palm seed endosperm. Glucomannans, galactomannan, and galactoglucomannans have been reported in oilseeds. Fucogalactxylglucan has a linear cellulose-like structure with single xylose units and side chains of xylose, galactose, fucose and occasional arabinose. It is found in rapeseed flour. Relatively more hemicellulose than cellulose is digested in the large intestine of monogastric animals. Ruminants have less difficulty in its utilization.

Pectic substances have a backbone of galacturonans, but sometimes rhamnose is also in the linear chain. The side chains may have arabinose, xylose, galactose and fucose. The uronic acid units may be in the form of methyl esters as well as acetylated. Pectic substances form gels when combined with calcium.

A number of glycosides and glycoproteins present in some oilseeds have deleterious effects of the well-being of the animals consuming these oilseeds. The examples are glucosinolates (goitrogens) in rapeseed, linamarin and methyllinamarin (cyanogenic glucosides) in linseed; and lectins (glycoproteins) in soybeans.

METHODS OF ANALYSIS

The methods of analysis of the carbohydrate complex of foods and oilseeds are quite tedious and need further refinement and development.

The proximate analysis system of foods evolved about 1860 from the studies of Henneberg and Stohmann at the Agricultural Experiment Station at Weende near Göttingen in Germany. It is still used today with few modifications. In this system moisture (H_2O), crude protein (CP), ether extract (EE), crude fiber (CF) and ash are the main constituents which are analyzed. The crude fiber is believed to be a measure of the nondigestible (or unavailable carbohydrate). The method of determination of crude fiber is outlined in Figure 10.1. The digestible carbohydrates (or available carbohydrates) are not determined directly, but are estimated inaccurately as nitrogen free extract (NFE) as follows:

$$\% \text{ NFE} = 100 - (\% \text{ } H_2O + \% \text{ CP} + \% \text{ EE} + \% \text{ CF} + \% \text{ ash})$$

From the data presented in Table 10.1, the determined crude fiber and estimated NFE contents of some of the oilseed meals are presented in Table 10.3.

Any errors of determination of the components of proximate analysis are exaggerated in the estimation of NFE. For example, 50 to 90% of lignin, 0 to 50% cellulose and up to 85% of hemicellulose may dissolve in dilute acid and dilute alkali during the crude fiber determination (Van Soest and Robertson, 1980). These components are then estimated as NFE.

The carbohydrate complex of oilseeds is nutritionally as important as the other nutrients determined directly by the system of proximate analysis. Crude fiber is the only member of the carbohydrate complex included in the proximate analysis, but it is an inaccurate measure even of the unavailable carbohydrates. The results of crude fiber determinations for the same sample in different laboratories are not consistent. To improve the precision and reproducibility of analysis, an acid detergent reagent method has been developed (Fig. 10.1) to determine the fiber content of forages, but is also used for other foods. The carbohydrate residue or the acid detergent fiber (ADF) is cellulose.

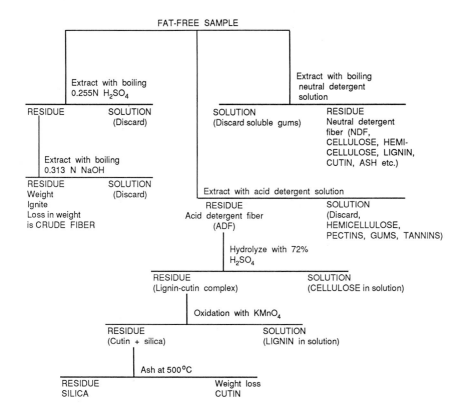

Fig. 10.1   Methods for determination of crude, neutral detergent and acid detergent fiber. The neutral detergent solution contains 3% sodium lauryl sulfate buffered with EDTA, borate, phosphate and ethoxyethanol and the acid detergent solution contains 2 g cetyl trimethylammonium bromide per 100 ml 1 N sulfuric acid (Van Soest and Robertson, 1980).

In oilseeds there is no direct relation between the crude fiber or the ADF content and the digestibility of the nutrients for any animals. The unavailable carbohydrates do tend to be better related to the digestibility of nutrients. The neutral detergent method is an improvement for the determination of the unavailable carbohydrates of the plant cell walls.

The detergent methods (Van Soest and Robertson, 1980) are outlined in Figure 10.1. The information on the NDF content of oilseeds or meals is found in National Research Publications on the Nutrient Requirements for Beef, but not for poultry or swine.

Oil Crops of the World

Table 10.3 Crude Fiber and Calculated NFE Content of Some Oilseed Meals on a Dry Matter Basis

Constituent[1]	Oilseeds						
	Soybean[2]	Cotton	Ground-nut[2]	Sun-flower[2]	Rape-seed	Linseed	Mustard
% CF	3.9	12.1	14.5	11.6	11.0	10.1	18.2
% NFE	34.1/ 41.4	33.3/ 43.4	28.5/ 41.3	26.6/ 47.8	33.9/ 39.2	38.6/ 48.5	45.9
%Avail. carbohyd.	17.5 23.6	9.5	18.5	9.1	15.0	6.0	
% Digest. carbohyd.	24.9	23.6	26.2	10.1		8.2	
% NDF	8.9	28.6	15.5	12.9	26.1	28.1	
ME, kcal/kg							
Poultry	2710	2660	2780	2495	2150	2320	
Swine	3870	2840	3240	2800	2870		

Constituent[1]	Saf-flower[2]	Sesame	Poppy	Corn germ	Castor bean	Palm kernel	Coconut	Jojoba	Niger
% CF	9.2	5.8	19.2	16.7	35.5	37.0	12.0	6.1	18.2
% NFE	28.8/ 40.4	25.3/ 33.8	24.0	46.5/ 63.6	16.7	38.1/ 56.6	48.0/ 56.8	22.6	26.0/ 30.0
% Avail. carbohyd.	- 5.8	3.6		14.1			0.4	0.9	
% Digest. carbohyd.	17.6	15.7		18.7		16.7	15.6		
% NDF	15.2	18.3	ˈ						
ME, kcal/kg									
Poultry	2085	2375		2495		1600	1850		
Swine	2645	2850				2250			

[1] CF=crude fiber; NFE=nitrogen free extract; NDF=natural detergent fiber; ME=metabolizable energy; available carbohydrate=starch + sugars; % digestible carbohydrate=% of crude fiber plus NFE.
[2] dehulled.
Data drawn from the following sources: Bolton, 1967; Lodhi et al., 1969; Keith and Bell, 1983; N.R.C. 1977; Gohl, 1981.

CHARACTERIZATION AND NUTRITIONAL ROLE OF VARIOUS CARBOHYDRATES

The useful methods for characterization are based on selective solubility of the carbohydrates. A general procedure for fractionation of the carbohydrate complex of the oilseeds is outlined in Figure 10.2. The detection and estimation of individual carbohydrates can be done by paper chromatography, column chromatography, high performance liquid chromatography (HPLC), and specific

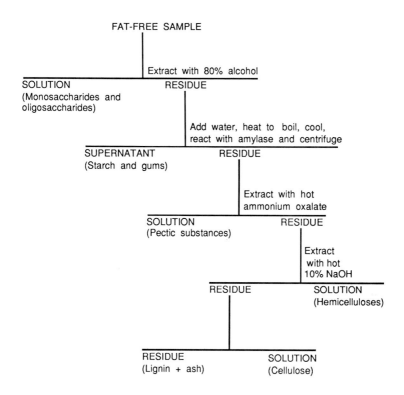

Fig. 10.2 Method for separation of various carbohydrate fractions.

chemical tests. Hydrolysis of polysaccharides and derivatization of various sugars is conducted before chromatographic procedures can be used.

Most of the free sugars are soluble in 80% methanol or ethanol, and starch can be extracted with hot water. The alcohol- and water-soluble fractions are analyzed as available carbohydrates. The methods for these determinations have been summarized by Southgate (1976).

Information on the available carbohydrates of oilseeds or oilseed meals is sparse. Some information on the available carbohydrates and digestibility of the carbohydrate fraction has been developed by Bolton (1967), Table 10.3.

The diet of the people of Europe and the Americas is low in unavailable carbohydrates, and has been blamed for the high incidence of cardiovascular and diverticular diseases and colonic cancer in these populations. Thus nutritionists are now extolling the virtue of dietary fiber in the diet (Burkitt and Trowell, 1975).

Oilseeds are used in animal feeds for their protein and not their oil or available carbohydrate content. The usage is influenced by the quality of protein as discussed in Chapter 9.

Monogastric meat animals are fed diets low in unavailable carbohydrates. The metabolizable energy (ME) and the digestibility of other nutrients is inversely related to the level of the unavailable carbohydrates in the diet. As the levels of the unavailable carbohydrates increase in an oilseed meal, the digestibility of its protein, carbohydrates and fat decreases. Isolated polysaccharides such as galactomannans and pectins depress the growth of chicken, Japanese quail and Tribolium (an insect pest of seeds) if present in the diet at a level of 2% or more (Vohra et al. 1979). It may be inferred that high levels of galactomannans, pectins, polygalacturonic acid, xylans and other hemicelluloses in the oilseeds may protect them against insect infestation. However, their presence at high levels in the diets of monogastric meat animals is not desirable.

Ruminants, on the other hand, require some unavailable carbohydrates for normal function of the rumen microflora and production of milk fat. The oilseed hulls are fed to ruminants for this purpose. The composition of hulls of almonds, cottonseed, peanuts, and soybeans is, respectively, as follows: % CF 15.0, 47.8, 62.9 and 40.1; %NDF 32, 90, 74 and 67; %ADF 28, 64, 65 and 50.

To reduce the deleterious effects of unavailable carbohydrates in oilseeds, the plant breeder could develop seeds with a thinner hull and reduced levels of structural carbohydrates, but not at the expense of the total yield per hectare. Growers, for economic reasons, have resisted planting oilseeds of superior nutritional value that yield less dry matter and/or oil in preference to high yielding strains of inferior nutritional quality. If better quality seeds are not to be used, processors could develop methods of separating hulls from seeds, and could reduce the fibrous material further by screening through proper sieves.

SOME IMPORTANT OILSEEDS AND MEALS

Soybean Seeds and Meal

For centuries soybeans have provided the people of China and Japan with much of their needed protein. Soybeans are processed to obtain soy milk which is further converted into a cheese-like product called tofu. Since World War II, soybean meal has become a major protein source for the world's animal feeds.

The NFE as well as total sugars and reducing sugars decrease as soybean seeds mature. The NFE content of soybeans varies from 17.9 to 30.2%. The carbohydrate composition of soybeans and of dehulled, defatted flour is given in Table 10.4. One sample of soybean analyzed contained 13.2% available and 17.6% unavailable carbohydrates (Vohra, 1986). Soybeans also contain pinitol (1D-3-0-methyl-chiro-inositol).

The hulls comprise from 7 to 13% of the seed and contain about 40% CF, 67% NDF, and 50% ADF. Whistler and Saarnio, (1957), reported the presence in the hull of about 64% alpha cellulose, and 16% hemicellulose, of which 2% is

Table 10.4 Percent Carbohydrate Composition of Full-Fat Soybeans, Defatted Seed Components and Defatted Flour on a % Dry Matter Basis

Component	Seed range	Seed av.	Defatted Cotyledon	Defatted Hypocotyl	Flour	Hull
Weight		100.0	90.3	2.4	N/A	7.3
Carbohydrate						
Total	31.1/ 43.9	35.4	27.4	42.7	16.3	86.2
Sugars	7.6/ 10.4	9.4				
Pentosans	3.4/ 3.8	3.6				
Galactans	2.0/ 2.7	2.3				
Sucrose	4.5/ 5.7	5.1	6.2/ 7.4	6.0/ 9.6	7.2/ 7.8	0.58/ 0.64
Raffinose	1.1	1.1	1.4	1.7/ 2.1	1.0/ 1.2	0.11/ 0.16
Stachyose	3.7/ 4.1	3.9	5.2	6.7/ 8.4	4.8/ 6.3	0.39/ 0.45
Arabinose	0.001/ 0.002					0.015/ 0.023
Glucose	0.005/ 0.007				tr	0.04/ 0.06

Data drawn from Kawamura, 1967; Smith and Circle, 1971; Cegla and Bell, 1977.

galactomannan and 8% lignin. A desirable meal should have a low concentration of hulls.

Soybeans are rich in lectins (glycoproteins) which cause hemagglutination in monogastric animals. Heat-treatment inactivates these lectins and also reduces deleterious effects of galactomannans.

Groundnuts (Peanuts) and Meal

About 20 to 30% of the groundnut pod consists of shell which is of no nutritional value for monogastric animals, but is sometimes mixed with molasses and minerals to be used as roughage for ruminants. The shells contain about 60.8-62.9% CF, 74% NDF, 65% ADF, 6.7% CP, 4.2% ash and 19.6% NFE. They are sometimes used as litter in poultry houses.

Total carbohydrates (NFE) in different varieties of groundnuts vary from 16-19% (Tharanathan et al. 1979). The main sugar is sucrose. The level of raffinose is negligible in the white skin variety (Conkerton and Ory, 1976). Information on the carbohydrate complex of groundnuts is given in Table 10.5.

Table 10.5 Groundnut - Carbohydrates of Kernels and Flour

Component	% in air dried kernels		% in dry defatted flour
	Range	Mean	
Moisture	3.9-13.2	5.0	
NFE			22.4
Total carbohydrates			17.4-39.0
Crude fiber	1.2-4.3	2.8	4.5
Reducing sugars	0.1-0.3	0.2	
Mono-and oligosaccharides			3.2-18
Glucose			0.8-2.1
Fructose			0.4
Sucrose	1.9-5.2	4.5	7.7-13.9
Raffinose			tr.-0.89
Stachyose			1.56
Verbascose			0.4
Starch	1.0-5.3	4.0	13.0-18.2
Pentosans	2.2-2.7	2.5	
Hemicellulose A			
(Glucoaraboxylan)			0.5
Hemicellulose B			3.5
Arabin			0.15
Glucomannan			0.15
Xylan			0.25
Acid polysaccharide			
complex			1.80

Data drawn from Tharanathan et al., 1979; Freeman et al., 1954; Cegla and Bell, 1977.

Groundnut meal was widely used in Britain and India in the diets of mono-gastric animals before the discovery of aflatoxins. The meal has a relatively high level of available carbohydrates if the shell is removed before fat extraction. However, in some locals the shell is not removed to facilitate fat extraction. The resulting meal is used as a fertilizer, although it could be fed to ruminants.

Full-fat groundnuts, generally roasted, are used throughout the world as snacks for humans.

Sesame Seeds and Meal

Full-fat sesame seeds are eaten by humans in a number of specialty foods. The carbohydrates in the defatted sesame meal present no special problems and can be safely fed to animals.

Sesame seed is of some importance in India from where data on the carbohydrate composition of some defatted sesame meals (Wankhede and Tharanathan, 1976) have been obtained (Table 10.6). The seeds may be dehulled by a one minute hot alkali treatment, but normally the whole seed is used.

Table 10.6   Sesame - Carbohydrate Composition of Defatted Flours Without Removal of Hulls (% of Dry Matter)

Component	Fraction		Hemicellulose	
	Soluble in 70% alcohol	Insoluble in alcohol	A	B
Yield	10.30-11.10	88.9-89.7	0.6-2.3	2.0-2.6
Total sugar	95.70-96.10	22.0-23.0	71.0-75.2	56.2-89.8
Pentose			11.3-11.6	52.7-53.8
Uronic acid			2.7-3.7	10.7-11.6
Galacturonic acid		1.8-1.9	5.1-6.4*	6.2-7.6*
Glucose	3.60-3.63	10.1-10.6	65.8-69.1*	27.2-28.8*
Arabinose		8.1-8.6		25.2-29.3*
Xylose		1.4-1.6		24.2-24.9*
Galactose	0.36-0.44			
Fructose	3.38-3.49			
Sucrose	0.14-0.20			
Raffinose	0.54-0.65			
Stachyose	0.34-0.43			
Planteose	0.19-0.27			
Sesamose	0.13-0.15			
Pentasaccharide	0.12			
Hexasaccharide	0.04-0.05			

* Sugars detected
Data drawn from Wankhede and Tharanathan, 1976

Safflower Seeds and Meal

Safflower seeds consist of 33 to 45% hull and 55 to 67% kernel. The hull contains 70% cellulose, 21% lignin and 1% ash. The carbohydrate composition of the oil-free safflower meal as determined by Kohler et al. (1966) and Saunders (1970) is given in Table 10.7.

The excessive hull content of safflower meal reduces its nutritive value. The meal is screened to obtain two fractions, a low-fiber and a high-fiber meal for feeding monogastric animals and ruminants, respectively. The low fiber meal contains about 42% CP and 16% CF. The high fiber meal contains 20% CP and 38% CF.

Table 10.7 Safflower Seed-Carbohydrate Composition (%) on a Moisture and Fat Free Basis

Component	Kernels	Hulls
Crude fiber	5.7	49.1
Lignin	3.2	24.0
Pentosans	4.9	21.5
Cellulose	2.3	35.0
Soluble carbohydrates & organic acids	19.9	4.6
Uronic sugar glycosides	0.43	0.37
Raffinose	1.08	0.06
Sucrose	1.42	0.21
Galactinol	0.09	0.025
D-Glucose		0.14
D-Fructose		0.13
Arabinose	tr	
Glucuronic acid	tr	

Data drawn from Kohler et al. 1966; Saunders, 1970.

Safflower meal is mildly cathartic and is bitter to the taste. The cathartic properties are due to the presence of 2-hydroxyarctiin-beta-glucoside, and the bitterness is caused by matairesinol-beta-glucoside. Both of these can be extracted from the safflower meal with water to obtain a desirable product (Lyon et al. 1979).

Analysis of whole safflower seeds, hulls and kernels indicated the level of available carbohydrates to be 4.5%, 3.0% and 2.8% while the unavailable carbohydrates measured 34.8%, 88.3% and 11.2% (Vohra, 1986).

Brassica Seeds and Meals

The genus *Brassica* contains a number of oilseeds such as rapeseed (*B. napus*), turnip rapeseed (*B. campestris*), brown mustard (*B. juncea*) and white mustard (*Sinapis alba*). The hulls may form 12 to 20% of the seeds. Siddiqui and Woods (1977) have reviewed the topic of carbohydrates in rapeseed. Oil-free, dehulled meal contained about 48% carbohydrate comprising 5% bound lipids. The fraction soluble in 80% alcohol, made up 14% of the meal, and contained 5% low molecular weight sugars with a 29% residual fraction. Kanya and Urs (1983) analyzed the carbohydrate composition of dehulled and defatted mustard. Their data may be compared with that of turnip rapeseed in Table 10.8.

Hulls from *B. napus* cultivars of canola meal contained 51.9 to 57.3% ADF and 26.6 to 28.9% acid detergent lignin on a dry matter basis (Mitaru et al. 1983). Analysis of a dehulled rapeseed sample indicated that 5.1% of the carbohydrates were available and 25.8% were unavailable (Vohra, 1986). Reduction of hull content of rapeseed meal by screening to remove unavailable

Table 10.8 Mustard and Turnip Rapeseed Meal - Carbohydrate Content (% on Dry Matter Basis)

Component	B. juncea[1]	B. napus[2]	B. campestris[3]
Total carbohydrate	36.7		39-48
Free sugars	12.6		5-10
Hot water soluble polysaccharides	2.2		4.5
Pectic substances	6.5		14.5
Hemicelluose	8.1		
Arabinogalactan			1
Arabinan			2
Fucoamyloid			4.5
Cellulose	2.8		7.0
Lignin	tr		tr
	% of Sugars + oligosaccharides		
Stachyose	2.1	1.43-3.04	1.52-2.43
Raffinose	1.2	0.29-0.33	0.31-0.34
Melibiose	0.68	ND	ND
Sucrose	1.68	6.51-8.26	2.26-7.49
Galactose	1.80	ND	ND
Glucose	0.96	0.10-0.24	0.28-0.40
Fructose	2.10	0.10-0.27	0.15-0.51
Unidentified	2.01	ND	ND

[4] not determined

Data drawn from: [1]Kanya and Urs, 1983; [2] Theander and Aman, 1976; [3] Siddiqui and Wood, 1977.
ND - not deternined.

carbohydrates improved its utilization by poultry (Shires et al. 1983). Low hull meal is also more digestible by swine.

Sunflower Seeds and Meal

Sunflower seeds contain about 42% hulls (Sabir et al. 1975). After removal of seeds, the head is a rich source of pectins. Flour from dehulled and defatted sunflower seed contains about 18.5% total carbohydrates. About 10.5% of these are mono- and oligosaccharides, and the rest are polysaccharides. About 6.3% of the carbohydrates are insoluble in water or dilute NaOH. The carbohydrate composition is given in Table 10.9.

About 34% of the seedless sunflower head consists of carbohydrates that are soluble in 80% alcohol, with a composition of 11.4% arabinose, 16.4% galactose, and 6.2% sucrose. The main water soluble polysaccharide is galacturonic acid (about 11%), and the main hemicellulose is xylan (about 3%).

Table 10.9 Sunflower - Carbohydrate Composition of Dehulled, Defatted Flour (% Dry Matter Basis)

		Polysaccharides	
Component	Total sugars	Arabinogalactan	Hemicellulose[1]
Arabinose	0.3	0.3	9.3
Fructose	0.2		
Glucose	0.2-0.6	0.5	
Galactose		0.6	1.1
Sucrose	2.3-4.4		
Rhamnose		tr	
Galacturonic acid		tr	
Maltose	0.9		
Melibiose	2.0		
Raffinose	2.5-3.2		
Trehalose	0.8		
Total	8.3-10.5	1.4	10.4

[1] Hemicellulose also contained some glucose, galacturonic acid and mannose.
Data drawn from Sabir et al., 1975; Cegla and Bell, 1977.

Analysis of a sample of whole sunflowers, hulls and kernels indicated respectively that 1.7%, 0.8% and 1.8% of the carbohydrates were available and 44.1%, 88.3% and 15.8% were unavailable (Vohra, 1986).

Dehulled, defatted sunflower meal is widely used in Eastern Europe for feeding poultry and swine. Sunflower seeds are also popular as snacks for humans.

OTHER OILSEEDS AND MEALS

Cottonseed and Meal

Cottonseed kernels contain about 14% carbohydrate on a dry matter basis. These include mono- and oligosaccharides, 7.5%; dextrins and soluble pectins, 0.53%; hemicellulose and pectin-like substances, 3.33%; and cellulose, 2.16%. Starch was not found, but raffinose was present (Dollear and Markley, 1948). The carbohydrate composition of defatted, dehulled flour is given in Table 10.10.

Linseed Meal

Linseed has a high level of mucin and a cyanogenic glycoside. Its use in the diet of monogastric animals is very limited.

Table 10.10 Carbohydrate Composition of some Defatted Oilseed Flours (% Dry Matter Basis)

Component	Cottonseed Deglanded	Glandless	Coconut	Linseed
Total carbohydrate	9.2	16.1		
Fructose			1.2	
Glucose	tr	tr	1.2	
Sucrose	2.4	2.6	14.3	
Raffinose	7.9	11.9		
Stachyose	0.9	0.7		
Starch			0.9	
Pentosans			2.2	
Hemicellulose				5.2
Cellulose			15.4	1.8

Data drawn from Cegla and Bell, 1977; Hardings et al., 1965.

Coconut Meal

Coconut meal has more than 45% NFE with a digestion coefficient of about 94% for pigs, and about 10% CF (Creswell and Brooks, 1971). It is used along with dried fish powder for pigs and poultry in tropical countries.

Palm Kernels

Dry palm kernels contain 52% oil, 8.8% protein, 5.2% cellulose, 2.0% ash and 23.6% NFE. The starch, sucrose and reducing sugars in dry kernels were reported as 0.55 to 2.21%, 0.77 to 1.46% and 0.17 to 0.41%, respectively (Cornelius, 1966).

Information on CF and NFE contents of many other oilseeds is available but is of limited usefulness for diet formulations for monogastric animals.

CONCLUSION

More data are needed on the available and unavailable carbohydrates in oilseeds and meals rather than crude fiber and NFE. The latter value is of very little nutritional significance. Although the characterization of the carbohydrate complex is tedious, it is useful in evaluating the nutritional value of oilseeds.

REFERENCES

Bolton, W. 1967. Poultry Nutrition. Ministry of Agric. Fisheries and Food, Bull. No. 174. HMSO, London.

Burkitt, D.P., and Trowell, H.C. 1975. *Refined Carbohydrate Foods and Disease. Some Implications of Dietary Fiber.* Academic Press, London.

Cegla, G.F., and Bell, K.R. 1977. High pressure liquid chromatography for the analysis of soluble carbohydrates in defatted oilseed flours. J. Am. Oil Chem. Soc. 54: 150-152.

Conkerton, E.J., and Ory, R.L. 1976. Peanut proteins as food supplements: A compositional study of selected Virginia and Spanish peanuts. J. Am. Oil Chem. Soc. 53: 754-756.

Cornelius, J.A. 1966. Some technical aspects influencing the quality of palm kernels. J. Sci. Food Agric. 17: 57-61.

Creswell, D.D., and Brooks, C.C. 1971. Composition, apparent digestibility and energy evaluation of coconut oil and coconut meal. J. Anim. Sci. 33: 366-369.

Dollear, F.G., and Markley, K.S. 1948. Miscellaneous Constituents, pp. 466-493. *In* A. E. Bailey (ed.), *Cottonseed and Cottonseed Products, Their Chemistry and Chemical Technology..* Interscience. New York.

Freeman, A.F., Morris, J.J., and Willich, R.K. 1954. Peanut Butter. U.S. Dept. Agric. AIC-370.

Gohl, B. 1981. *Tropical Feeds, Feed Information Summaries and Nutritive Values.* FAO Animal Production and Health Series. No. 12. FAO of the United Nations, Rome.

Hardinge, M.G., Swarner, J.B., and Crooks, H. 1965. Carbohydrates in foods. J. Am. Dietetic Assoc. 46: 197-204.

Kanya, T.C.S., and Urs, M.K. 1983. Carbohydrate composition of mustard (*Brassica juncea*) seed meal. J. Food Sci. Tech. 20: 125-126.

Kawamura, S. 1967. Quantitative Paper Chromatography of Sugars of the Cotyledon, Hull and Hypocotyl of Soybeans of Selected Varieties. Kagawa Univ. Fac. Tech. Bull. 15: 117-131.

Keith, M.O., and Bell, J. 1983. Effect of ammonia and steam treatments on the composition and nutritional value of canola (low glucosinolate rapeseed) screenings in diets for growing pigs. Can. J. Anim. Sci. 63: 429-441.

Kohler, G.O., Kuzmicky, D.D., Palter, R., Guggolz, J., and Herring, V.V. 1966. Safflower meal. J. Am. Oil Chem. Soc. 43: 413-415.

Liener, I.E. 1980. Miscellaneous toxic factors, pp. 455-457. *In* I.E. Liener (ed.), *Constituents of Plant Foodstuffs.* Academic Press, New York.

Lodhi, G.N., Renner, R., and Clandinin, D.R. 1969. Available carbohydrate in rapeseed meal and soybean meal as determined by a chemical method and a chick bioassay. J. Nutr. 99: 413-418.

Lyon, C.K., Gumbmann, M.R., Betschart, A.A., Robbins, D.J., and Saunders, R.M. 1979. Removal of deleterious glucosides from safflower meal. J. Am. Oil Chem. Soc. 56: 560-564.

Mitaru, B.N., Blair, R., Bell, J.M., and Reichert, R. 1983. Effect of canola hulls on growth, feed efficiency, protein and energy utilization in broiler chickens. Can. J. Anim. Sci. 63: 655-662.

National Research Council. 1984. *Nutrient Requirements of Beef.* National Academy Press, Washington, D.C.

Sabir, M.A., Sosulski, F.W., and Hamon, N.W. 1975. Sunflower carbohydrates. J. Agric. Food Chem. 23: 16-19.

Saunders, R.M. 1970. The sugars of safflower. J. Am. Oil Chem. Soc. 47: 254-255.

Schulze, E. 1891. Zur Kenntnis der Chemischen Zusammensetzung der pflanzlichen Zellmembranen. Ber. d.d. Chem. Ges. 24: 2277-2287.

Shires, A., Bell, J.M., Laverty, W.H., Fedec, P., Blake, J.A., and McGregor, D.I. 1983. Effect of desolventization conditions and removal of fibrous material by screening on the nutritional value of canola rapeseed meal for broiler chickens. Poultry Sci. 62: 2234-2244.

Siddiqui, I.R., and Wood, P.J. 1977. Carbohydrates of rapeseed: a review. J. Sci. Food Agric. 28: 530-538.

Smith, A.K., and Circle, S.J. 1978. Chemical composition of the seed, pp. 61-92. In A.K. Smith and S.J. Circle (eds.), Chemistry and Technology. Vol. 1. Proteins. Avi Publishing Co., Westport.

Southgate, D.T.A. 1976. Determination of Food Carbohydrates. Applied Science Publishers, London.

Tharanathan, R.N. Wankhede, D.B., and Rao, M.R.R. 1979. Groundnut carbohydrates—a review. J. Sci. Food Agric. 30: 1077-1084.

Theander, O., and Aman, P. 1976. Low-molecular weight carbohydrates in rapeseed and turnip rapeseed meals. Swed. J. Agric. Res. 6: 81-85.

Van Soest, P.J., and Robertson, J.B. 1980. Systems of Analysis for Evaluating Fibrous Feeds, pp. 49-60. In W.J. Pigden, C.C. Balch, and M. Graham (eds.), Standardization of Analytical Methodology for Feeds. International Development Research Center (IDRC) 134 E, Ottawa, Canada.

Vohra, P. 1986. Personal Communication. Department of Avian Sciences, Univ. of California, Davis, Calif.

——, P., Shariff, G., and Kratzer, F.H. 1979. Growth inhibitory effect of some gums and pectin for Tribolium castaneum larvae, chickens and Japanese quail. Nutr. Reports Intern. 19: 463-469.

Wankhede, D.B., and Tharanathan, R.N. 1976. Sesame (Sesamum indicum) carbohydrates. J. Agric. Food. Chem. 24: 655-659.

Whistler, R.L., and Saarnio, J. 1957. Galactomannan from soybean hulls. J. Am. Chem. Soc. 79: 6055-6057.

Chapter 11

Processing of Oilseed Crops

R. Carr

INTRODUCTION

The utilization of edible oil-bearing materials has been a challenge and benefit for mankind since the beginning of history. Both rudimentary and sophisticated systems have been developed to separate seeds, nuts and fruits into liquid and solid components for both food and non-food uses.

As a food, they can be eaten raw or cooked. They produce a useful ingredient in baking, provide a heat transfer medium in frying and oil fractions are a source of calories and of fat soluble vitamins. In addition, the oil fractions have a number of non-food uses. They can be boiled with alkali to manufacture soaps, serve as an ingredient in cosmetics, perform as lubricants and act as a drying base for paints.

Because of a wide range in physical characteristics of these materials and their components, various techniques have been developed to extract the oils and process them to finished products. The common objective of all these processes is to,

a) maximize the yield of fat or oil from the oil-bearing material
b) minimize the damage to the fat or oil and solid fraction
c) produce components as free as possible from undesirable impurities
d) produce a residual oil cake of the greatest possible value

Commercial processing systems and conditions used to achieve these objectives will be reviewed for the major sources of edible vegetable oils.

OVERVIEW OF THE TRADITIONAL PROCESSING SYSTEM

The first step in the total operation is to "crush" the oilseeds and separate the cooked flakes by extraction into its crude oil and meal components. Crude oil may then have the hydratable gums removed by either a water-degumming process, or have most of the gums taken out by an acid-degumming operation. Crude or degummed crude oils may then be conditioned with phosphoric acid and treated with sodium hydroxide in a continuous centrifugal alkali-refining operation. The refined oil is bleached with activated clay to remove color pigments. Hydrogenation is an optional process, which is used to adjust the consistency of fats and oils according to the physical properties required by the final products. Bleached oil, hydrogenated oil or various combinations of these oils are then deodorized to produce finished products such as salad and cooking oils, shortenings, margarine oils and specialty products, e.g. frying fats.

CRUSHING

Materials

The type of extraction system used to separate the oils from the solid fraction of an oilseed, depends primarily on the oil content of the raw material. Mechanical pressing is generally used for materials exceeding 20% oil content. Solvent extraction may then be used to extract oil from raw materials such as soybeans, or press cakes with oil contents less than 20%.

Oilseeds and nuts with relatively high oil contents are usually processed first by mechanical presses (Table 11.1).

Oil Crops of the World

Table 11.1 Example of Oil Crops Normally Processed by Mechanical
Pressing, Together with their Oil Content and End Uses

Seed	Oil Content %	Use
Almond	50	food, salad oil, soap
Castor	50	medicine, lubricant
Cottonseed	30	food, paint, resin
Hemp seed	35	paint, varnish, soap
Linseed	40	paint, soap, varnish
Olive	40	salad oil, cooking oil
Peanut (ground nuts)	50	salad oil, cooking oil
Perilla seed	50	drying oil/paint, resin
Poppy seed	50	salad oil, cooking oil
Rapeseed/Canola	40	salad oil, cooking oil
Sesame seed	50	salad oil, cooking oil
Sunflower seed	35	salad oil, cooking oil, soap
Tung nuts	20	paint

In addition to the oil content of the source material, the fatty acid composition is also important for establishing processing conditions. Vegetable *oils* remain liquid at room temperature, because of the degree of unsaturation and the number of carbons in the fatty acid radicals of the triglyceride. Vegetable *fats* (Table 11.2) are semi-solid at room temperature, because their more saturated fatty acid composition results in a higher melting point than that for vegetable oils. Source materials from vegetable fats are heated before pressing.

Table 11.2 Some Common Vegetable Fat Sources, Average Oil Yield and
End Uses

Source	Oil Content %	Use
Cocoa butter	40	chocolate, food
Coconut oil (copra)	50	food, chemicals, soap
Hahua butter (illipe)	60	food, candles, soap
Japan wax	30	lubricant, leather dressing
Palm kernel oil (nut)	50	food, chemicals, soap
Shea butter	55	food, candles, soap

Origins

Over the years, humans have found that fats and oils can be extracted from nuts and seeds by heat, solvents or pressure. Experience has taught us that extraction by excessive heat is not recommended for the production of vegetable oils.

Our ancestors determined that pressure extraction can separate the oil from the solid particles by simply squeezing oil out of the crushed mass of oilseeds. An early method was to fill a cloth bag with ground seed pulp and hang the bag so that it could drain. Some of the oil, called "free run oil," could flow out through the bag. Additional oil could be obtained by pressing the bag. The simplest methods were to apply pressure by hands and feet, or by placing heavy rocks on top of the materials. An improved method was to place one bag above another in a box or cylinder and apply great pressure at the top of the pile, on the whole mass. A lever and weight system could exert up to 689.5 kPa pressure on the oilseed mass. In later days, the lever was often replaced by heavy and strong mechanical jacks such as a screw jack, ratchet jack or hydraulic jack. Oil recovery was improved because a 20 tonne jack can exert 6895 kPa pressure on a small cylinder of seeds.

Presses

Batch presses were developed to process one batch of seeds at a time. They ranged from small, rudimentary hand driven presses, up to power driven commercial presses capable of processing many tonnes of seed a day. Small batch presses are simple and do function, but they are very inefficient. However, they can be used in remote areas and can help determine whether or not there is a market for the locally produced oil. Few resources, such as wood fires for heating and hand labour for pressing, are required for an operation of this type.

Advantages of small batch presses include; local materials will suffice; produce a good quality product; easy to repair; purchase and operating costs are low; do not require trained operators. The disadvantages are that they are labour intensive and the oil yield is low.

In many parts of the world, commercial hydraulic presses are the most practical and economical way to extract oil from seeds. They may be powered either by hand or by electricity. Ground seed material or wet plant tissue is placed in the press in layers, with each layer separated from the next by a press cloth. Pressure is applied, slowly at first and then increased, as the oil content in the tissue decreases. Maximum total pressure is 13,970 kPa for one inch layers. Total time to load, apply pressure and remove cake is approximately one hour. Drainage of the oil while under pressure may require 30-45 minutes.

The advantages of the commercial size batch press are that they can be driven by hand or electricity; are simple and economical to operate and maintain; require minimum operator training and provide an excellent oil recovery.

Disadvantages include; the substantial cost of the machinery; long delivery times; difficult to obtain spare parts in remote areas; and the necessity of electric power to operate larger models.

Expellers

Continuous screw presses, or expellers, are used in higher technology areas throughout the world for the expulsion of oil from copra, palm kernels, peanuts, cottonseed, flax seed, and other varieties of seed where there is sufficient seed supply to justify a continuous operation. Sufficient pressure is achieved by means of an auger that turns inside a barrel. The barrel is closed, except for small openings through which the oil drains and a choked outlet for departing pressed cake.

Expellers exert much greater pressure on seed cake than that produced by a hydraulic batch press. This increased pressure results in a greater recovery of the oil content in the feedstock. Expellers can vary in size from units that process 40 kgs of conditioned seed per hour, to machines that process 200 tonnes of seed per hour. Expellers are an essential part of most modern oilseed extraction plants that employ a prepress step in the oil extraction process.

Expellers have a higher plant capacity and a higher rate of oil recovery with a lower labour requirement than the press system. Disadvantage of the expeller system include the requirement for electric power, continuous operation and availability of skilled mechanics. Equipment and maintenance costs are also high. The oil produced contains more impurities and must be heated and filtered for edible use.

COMMERCIAL EXTRACTIONS

The modern processing of oil bearing materials to separate oil from meal evolved from the development and utilization of continuous expellers. Currently, three types of commercial processing systems are employed for oilseeds and nuts in the higher technology sectors of the world.

a) Expeller pressing - Oil is mechanically squeezed from the seed.
b) Prepressing solvent extraction - A portion of the oil is removed by expellers and the remainder is then extracted with an organic solvent.
c) Direct solvent extraction - Removes the oil directly from the conditioned seed with an organic solvent.

Regardless of the method used, caution must be exercised to maintain the quality of the protein in the meal, as its end use is as a food or feed supplement. During processing, a significant amount of protein denaturation can take place. For feeding purposes, this denaturing is generally considered desirable, because of the resultant improvement in digestibility. However, excessive heat during processing can result in extensive loss of certain amino acids, particularly the essential amino acid, lysine. The extent of such damage will depend on the processing time and temperature, moisture, and reducing sugar content of the feedstock as well as other variable constituents and foreign materials in the starting material.

When some crops are crushed, for example rapeseed/canola, enzymes such as myrosinase are brought into contact with undesirable materials, such as glucosinolates. This action can develop and release toxic compounds. However, careful control of moisture and temperatures during processing has made it possible to inactivate the enzymes without lowering the lysine content of the meal. Therefore, the development of improved processing techniques has improved the quality of not only the meal, but also the oil.

The crusher's task is to remove from each microscopic oil cell within each tiny seed, the maximum quantity of oil present without chemically altering the oil or protein quality. During extraction, the various processing steps can never improve the quality of an oil, but only minimize the damage done to the oil.

The following steps are essential for the extraction operation.
a) rupture the cell wall
b) obtain diffusion and agglomeration of the oil
c) make a final and complete separation of liquid and solids

Oil bearing materials contain significant quantities of solid material, in addition to the oil. Therefore, careful size reduction of the source material, followed by controlled heat treatment is necessary for optimum separation of these components. This "conditioned" material then requires the application of heavy pressure to obtain satisfactory separation of the oil from the solid fraction. The sequence of operations for processing oil bearing materials is outlined in Figure 11.1 and described in the following text.

Seed Cleaning

The first step in the commercial processing of oilseeds is "cleaning." Its function is to remove foreign materials, such as sticks, stems, leaves, other seeds, sand and dirt. High capacity dry screeners, such as a Burnaby cleaner, are used to remove all materials that are over or under size, by utilizing a combination of screens and aspiration. Permanent or electromagnets are also used for the removal of tramp iron objects. The cleaning is done carefully, so that the resultant oil is not contaminated with foreign materials.

Seed cleaning is an important operation in the preparation of oil bearing materials for extraction. Proper seed cleaning will increase capacity and reduce maintenance as well as improve oil and meal quality. Final cleaning of the seed can be carried out prior to processing. It is essential that oil-bearing materials, destined for the manufacture of products for human consumption, be well-ripened, sound and clean before processing.

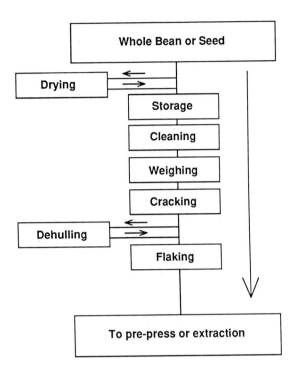

Fig. 11.1   Basic unit operations for processing oil bearing materials prior to the extraction operation.

Storage

After cleaning, the seeds, nuts, or plant tissue containing the oil must be properly stored and prepared for extraction, to maintain high quality in the final product. During receipt, raw materials should be carefully inspected for content and quality.

If the oil-bearing material is dry, it must be stored so that it remains dry, for optimum extraction and quality of oil. If the oil-bearing material is wet plant tissue, it should be processed as soon as possible after harvest so that storage time is kept to a minimum. Oils in the presence of water deteriorate rapidly, forming free fatty acids and rancid "off-flavours."

Dehulling

After raw material has been cleaned, it may be necessary to remove its outer seed coat. There are several reasons for doing this. The seed coat contains little or no oil, hence its inclusion would make extraction less efficient. Also, the next processing step is grinding to reduce particle size, and any tough seed coats would interfere with this process. If the hulls are not removed prior to extraction, they will reduce the total yield of oil by absorbing and retaining oil in the press cake. In addition, their inclusion will reduce the capacity of the extraction plant.

Some seeds, such as peanuts, can be shelled by hand. Some others, such as sunflower seeds and soybeans, are usually machine hulled. Still others, like rapeseed/canola and safflower, are usually processed whole not dehulled. If the seed hull is a minor portion of the whole seed and presents no problem in grinding the seed, it may be left on. Because rapeseed/canola seeds are small in size and high in oil content, they are difficult to dehull efficiently and economically in commercial scale plants.

The hulling machines used for the decortication of medium-sized oilseeds with a flexible seed coat, such as cottonseed, peanuts and sunflower seeds, are of two principal types, bar or disc hullers. Different seeds vary considerably in the readiness with which they fall out of the split hulls. The separation systems used for cottonseed, peanuts, etc., consist of various combinations of vibrating screens and pneumatic lifts.

In the past, soybeans were seldom decorticated before processing for oil, except in cases where the meal was destined for human consumption. This was due to mechanical difficulties and because the hull constitutes only a small part of the seed and is relatively nonabsorbent. Today, however, dehulling is common. It is usually accomplished by first cracking the beans on cracking rolls and then separating the hulls from the kernels in two stages.

Grinding, Rolling or Flaking

Raw oil-bearing materials are usually not pressed whole, because oil extraction is much more efficient if the starting material is in small particles. Grinding the oilseed is one effective way to reduce the particle size. For example, a hand-operated mortar, millstone grinder, or even a kitchen meat grinder can be used to convert the seeds to a coarse meal. Small hammer mills, motor or hand-powered, can also be used for grinding.

Another way to reduce particle size is to roll the oilseeds to produce flakes for extraction. Most commercial extraction plants find this to be most effective approach. With large oilseeds it may be necessary to rough grind the seed first, and then put the pieces through flaking rollers.

Either process makes the actual pressing more efficient. The final particle size that leads to most efficient extraction can best be determined by experiment, as the size will vary depending on the type of seed and the method of pressing operation. Generally, smaller-sized pieces are better for oil removal, but if the pieces are too small, they may contaminate the oil and be difficult to remove during the subsequent filtration step.

Obviously, rolling seed or seed particles into thin flakes will facilitate solvent extraction both from the disruptive effect of rolling and by reducing the distances that solvent and oil must diffuse in and out of the seed during the extraction process. Early work indicated that the rate controlling factor in the solvent extraction of seed flakes was probably the internal resistance of the flakes to the molecular diffusion of solvent and oil. The thickness of these flakes is very important. For example, rapeseed/canola flakes thinner than 0.2 mm are very fragile, where flakes thicker than 0.3 mm process less satisfactorily. Therefore, the general practice has been to flake the seed to a thickness within these limits.

When the seed is flaked in this manner, the seed coat is fractured and many oil cells are ruptured, thereby increasing enormously the overall surface/volume ratio. Flakes should be rolled as thin as possible without undue "oiling out" on rolls and/or requiring undue amounts of power. The importance of good "flakes" cannot be over-stressed. Flake quality is essential to achieving success during all the succeeding extraction processing steps.

Cooking

The final step in raw materials preparation prior to extraction, is heating the ground or flaked oilseed to increase oil yields. Heating is also necessary to combat enzymes in the plant tissues which would have a detrimental effect on the oil quality. If the oilseed cake, i.e. the residue remaining after oil removal by pressing, is to be used for feed or food, controlled heating may be useful in increasing protein availability in the resultant meal fraction.

Cooking oil-bearing materials prior to expelling tends to:
a) thermally rupture cells which have integrally survived the flaking process
b) reduce oil viscosity and promote coalescing of minute droplets of oil
c) increase the diffusion rate
d) denature hydrolytic enzymes
e) permit moisture control of the expeller feedstock to an optimum 4 to 6%. Inadequate moisture levels during pressing results in a "granular" discharge from the press or expeller, while excessive moisture results in a "sloppy" product. Either type of expeller cake will cause problems in the solvent extraction process.

Drum and stack-type cookers can both be used satisfactorily for the cooking of oilseeds. The drum cooker may offer higher heat transfer rates, but at the expense of the integrity of the fragile flakes. Stack cookers consist of a series of four to eight vertical, closed, cylindrical steel kettles, with each kettle usually 30 to 50 cm in diameter and 50 to 70 cm high. Product cascades from kettle to kettle, by the mixing and pushing action of sweeps in each kettle. The peripheral velocity, shape and clearances of these sweeps, plus the depth of process products, will influence the cooking process. Bed depth and sweep blade clearance, have a profound effect on heat transfer and thus cooking capacity.

Oilseeds are usually moistened before cooking, or during the early stages of cooking, unless they are initially high in moisture content. Moisture content of the material is then reduced during cooking. An initial moisture content of 9 to 14% is commonly used in the top kettle of a cooker. During cooking, careful moisture control is important, because moisture content affects the affinity between the seed and the oil.

Cooking temperatures within the cookers can vary with the type of seed source and may range from 80°C to 105°C. Proper cooking results in:

a)   the complete breakdown of oil cells
b)   coagulation of the proteins to facilitate the oil and meal separation
c)   insolubilization of the phospholipids
d)   increased fluidity of the oil at higher temperature
e)   destruction of molds and bacteria
f)   inactivation of enzymes
g)   drying to a suitable moisture content

For low erucic varieties of rapeseed, such as canola, cooking is generally carried out for ca. 30 minutes above 80°C, the lowest temperature for myrosinase inactivation. Marked thermal decomposition of glucosinolates occur if cooking is done above 100°C for an extended time period. Therefore, it is desirable that optimum cooking be performed at ca 100 to 105°C for 15 to 20 minutes. This amount of time is necessary for good oil release. Further extensions of cooking time can promote protein degradation.

The nutritive value of soybean meal is markedly improved by moderate cooking. This is due to the coincident inactivation of specific undesirable heat-labile factors, e.g. trypsin inhibitor, hemagglutinin, saponin, goitrogenic factor, anticoagulant factor, diuretic principle, and lipoxidase. One of the prime purposes of cooking cottonseed is to bring about the destruction or deactivating of a complex polyphenolic compound called gossypol, which is toxic to certain animals, particularly swine and poultry.

Pressing

In recent years, increased mechanization and higher labour costs have made hydraulic pressing of oilseeds uneconomical for modern commercial operations. Continuous expellers or screw presses are now used for the mechanical extraction of soybeans, rapeseed/canola, cottonseed, flaxseed, and peanuts in most countries. They are also used extensively throughout the world for the expression of copra, palm kernels, peanuts, cottonseed, flaxseed and most other varieties of oilseeds.

There is general agreement throughout the industry that prepressing followed by solvent extraction in medium to large scale plants give better overall economy when high oil content seeds are processed. This holds true, despite the higher power requirements and mechanical maintenance costs required of the prepress operation.

Cooked flakes, of crops such as rapeseed/canola, containing ca 4% moisture and 44% oil, are fed to a series of screw presses or expellers, to receive a mild pressing operation. This removes most of the oil while avoiding excessive pressure, power consumption and temperature. These expellers will reduce oil content of well flaked and cooked rapeseed from 42% to ca 15%, with a power consumption of ca 125 to 300 H.P., at a throughput of up to 250 tonnes per day, per unit.

On a continuous basis, each screw press gradually increases the pressure on the incoming material as it progresses through the interior of a closed barrel. There are provisions for the oil to drain out through small gaps between carefully positioned, hardened steel bars in the barrel cage. A column or plug of compressed meal is formed by a choke device at the discharge end of the barrel. This acts as a continuous hydraulic presshead with "new cake" being formed at the choke, as the "old cake" is continuously discharged from the expeller, past the choke device. Good quality cake is considered to be spongy and permeable and resists disintegration during conveying to the solvent extractor.

Pressing also consolidates the tiny flakes into larger units of cake fragments. Cake fragments substantially larger than the original flakes are essential in the subsequent extraction operation to obtain satisfactory rates of solvent gravity percolation through the cake bed. Some compromise must be accepted between percolation rate, which is a function of size and thickness of the cake fragment reaching the extractor, and the mean diffusion dimension, cake thickness. Fortunately, cake thickness is the one and only dimension that can be directly controlled at the press and it also remains the most durable physical parameter throughout the conveying and extraction operations.

The coordination of the flaking, cooking and press operations, is still considered to be more of an art rather than an exact science. Good cake is characterized as having a dry texture, with a preferred moisture level of 4 to 5% (6% maximum) and an oil content of 15 to 18%. The cake should be between 1/8 to 3/16 of an inch thick with good physical integrity and durability.

Cold Pressing

In some cases, oil-bearing materials are pressed without the cooking step. Oil extracted in this manner is called "cold press" oil. In some cases, cold pressed oil from fresh and good quality seeds need not require a subsequent refining step typically used in the industry to remove undesirable cloudiness, color or flavour.

A German company, Krupp, has introduced a new VPEX screwpress design which combines the functions of flaking, cooking and pressing. This machine alternately crushes, shears, compresses, and then relaxes the flow of seed. It is claimed that adequate heat for good processing is provided by the mechanical energy output. This design is only for prepressing.

Oil Settling and Filtering

All expelled press oils contain some entrained solid matter and should be gravity settled in a screening tank. The settlings may be continuously dredged off, drained and recycled back through the cooker for repressing. They can also be repressed in a separate "foots" screw press, a specialized version of the previously described expeller. The re-pressed cake is then sent to the solvent extraction operation, along with the main cake stream. Expelled oil from a foots press is recycled back to the screenings tank for resettlement of the suspended fines. The dredges may be sent directly to solvent extraction along with the main cake stream, provided their inclusion does not adversely affect the overall efficiency of the solvent extraction operation.

Settled oil is continuously drawn off from the screenings tank and the remaining suspended fines in the oil can be removed by either filtration or centrifugation. A totally enclosed multiple screen type filter is commonly used. The enclosed filtering plates consist of double sided stainless steel screens, precoated with the fines themselves. Many units are powered to open and close for cleaning and some are fully automated.

SOLVENT EXTRACTION

When dealing with relatively low oil content materials, extraction with a solvent, normally hexane, is the most efficient technique for oil recovery (Fig. 11.2). Oil produced by this method is of high quality, because very little heat treatment is required. In addition, the resultant meal fraction contains protein which has encountered a minimum amount of deterioration from heat damage.

There are, however, several disadvantages related to the solvent extraction process including:

a)   more expensive equipment compared to other extraction systems
b)   the danger of fire and explosion unless non-flammable solvents can be used
c)   the direct extraction of raw unheated flakes may contain material that is toxic to nonruminants. Therefore, products of direct solvent extraction such as cottonseed flakes, require additional treatment to ensure adequate inactivation of such contaminants.

Although elevated temperatures reduce oil viscosity and enhance diffusion, the hexane vapour pressure limits the practical operating temperature of the extractor and its contents to ca 50 to 55°C. Higher temperature and the resulting higher vapour pressure unduly increases the quantity of solvent vapour which the recovery systems must capture and recycle. Furthermore, if the cake temperature is at or near the boiling temperature of the solvent, a vapour phase may occur at the interface between the cake fragments and the solvent, effectively blocking liquid diffusion.

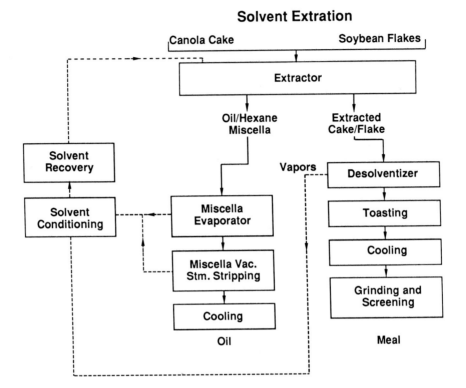

Fig. 11.2 Basic unit operations for extracting oil from cake produced from the preparation operation.

Except on start-up, the solvent does not normally require heating, because the hot cake from the prepress process often provides more than sufficient heat to maintain the required extraction temperature. In some plants it has been found necessary to utilize air cooling to lower the cake temperature during transit from the preparation process to the solvent extraction plant.

When satisfactory cake is obtained from the expellers, it is conveyed to a solvent extractor for treatment with commercial normal hexane. The objective in solvent extraction is to remove as much oil as possible from the meal with a minimum amount of solvent. Since the oil is usually the most valuable part of the seed, it is desirable to recover as much oil as possible from the cake by the solvent extraction method. The recovery of an extra 0.5% of oil will make a substantial contribution to operating profits.

The majority of extractors are designed to operate countercurrently and continuously. In such extractors, the solid oil bearing material is conveyed in the opposite direction to that of the solvent flow. The extracted meal leaves at one end, and the miscella, a mixture of oil and solvent, at the other end.

A number of different mechanical designs for solvent extractors are used to move the ground cake and miscella in opposite directions with good intermixing and to effect final separation of miscella from the solvent saturated meal. A basket type extractor, such as the Rotocell, is widely used, as well as a shallow bed loop extractor, such as the Crown Iron Works unit (Fig. 11.3).

The conveyor for transporting the cake from the prepress plant must be well insulated, resistant to corrosion by organic acids and moisture and must convey the cake gently with minimum damage to cake integrity. An inclined drag conveyor equipped with heavy wooden casing is quite suitable for this operation.

The cake is introduced into the extractor at 50 to 55 °C through a vapour seal unit. It is deposited into a cell or basket, which is then flooded with a solvent or miscella in five to eight stages. A series of pumps spray the miscella over the baskets, with each stage using a successively "leaner" miscella, thereby containing a higher ratio of solvent in proportion to the oil. In addition to temperature, the extraction operator can, within limits, control bed depth, solvent feed and solvent/miscella distribution within the extractor.

The solvent percolates by gravity down through the cake bed, diffusing into and saturating the cake fragments. Oil diffuses into a miscella solution, with a viscosity much lower than that of the oil alone. Oil and/or oil solution diffuses to the surface of the cake particle where it is continuously washed away by the vigorously percolating flow of miscella. The particles are progressively washed by fresh "leaner" miscella, which is continuously supplied to the top of the cake bed. The oil enriched solvent flows out through the screen at the bottom of each basket, which supports the entire cake bed. This miscella is then pumped to the next successive basket of "oil-richer" cake. Each basket is given a final wash with pure solvent before it is emptied.

Regardless of the type of extractor, the end result is the same. The meal discharged from the unit is saturated with solvent and contains ca 1.5% residual lipid. The extracted meal is drained in the extractor for several minutes; however, after discharge it still contains 30 to 35% by weight of solvent.

This wet meal is stripped of solvent in units called desolventizers, or DT's (Fig. 11.4), which are similar in design to the stacked cookers previously described for the cooking process. They are cylindrical vessels with heated trays and equipped for direct steam injection. The meal drops by gravity through the unit from tray to tray as the solvent is gradually volatilized and recovered for reuse. If required, the meal can be further heated to assist in the desolventization. By passing over the successive trays, the meal can be heated to 100 to 103 °C, for drying and crisping the meal. After this treatment, the meal is finally discharged at approximately 100°C, with 10 to 12% moisture content.

Rapeseed/canola meal need not be toasted under the more severe conditions required for soybean meal to destroy trypsin inhibitors. Under such temperature/moisture conditions, protein solubility will be reduced and some loss of amino acids, such as lysine, will result. Two types of heat damage appear to take place. In one case, the amino acids are bound in such a form that they are not liberated

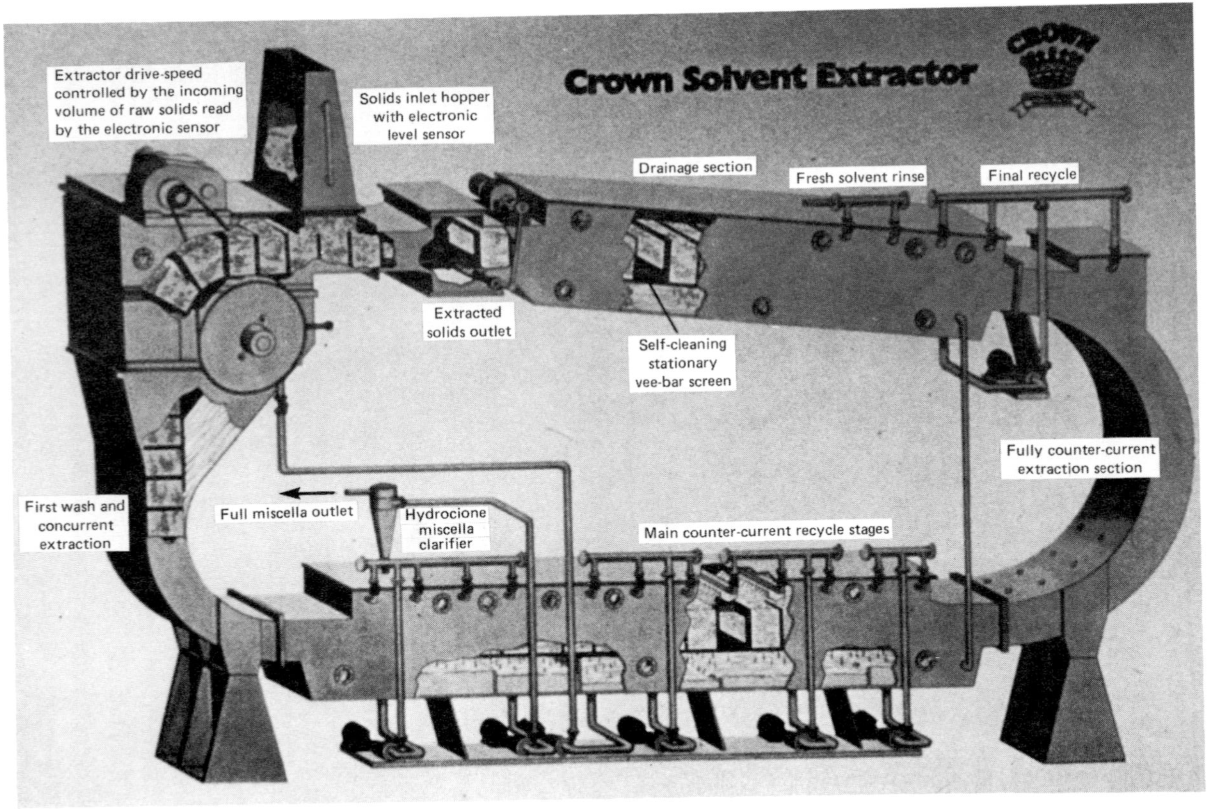

Crown Solvent Extractor

Extractor drive-speed controlled by the incoming volume of raw solids read by the electronic sensor

Solids inlet hopper with electronic level sensor

Drainage section

Fresh solvent rinse

Final recycle

Fully counter-current extraction section

Self-cleaning stationary vee-bar screen

Extracted solids outlet

Main counter-current recycle stages

Hydrocione miscella clarifier

Full miscella outlet

First wash and concurrent extraction

Fig. 11.3 A shallow bed loop extractor manufactured by Crown Iron Works.

Fig. 11. 4 A Desolventizer toaster used for stripping solvent from wet meal discharged from the extrctor.

by acid hydrolysis. In the second type, the amino acids appear to be irreversibly lost and are not recovered by acid hydrolysis.

Separation of the oil and solvent is accomplished by conventional distillation methods. Most of the solvent is recovered for repeated use. Distillation and recovery of the solvent requires energy, thus, the operating objective is to concentrate as much oil as possible in the least practical amount of solvent.

The full miscella leaving the extractor is usually directed to a surge tank, from which it is pumped at a steady rate to the distillation equipment. Solvent evaporation is normally effected in three stages.

Solvent Recovery

The solvent from the desolventizer is condensed, so that the heat of condensation can be applied to the distilling of the solvent from the miscella. The oil is freed from the miscella, by using a series of stills, stripping columns and associated condensers. The hexane-free oil is cooled and filtered before leaving the solvent extraction plant for storage or further treatment.

The air and vapours from the solvent condensers and other parts of the extraction plant must be essentially solvent free before being discharged to the atmosphere. This is frequently achieved by "scrubbing" the vapours in a column with mineral oil. An efficient scrubbing system is essential for reasons of economy and safety. All the recovered solvent is separated from water in a gravity separation tank and used over and over in the solvent extraction operation.

High Pressure Extraction

A new experimental method for extracting fats and oils from oilseed crops utilizes carbon dioxide, heated and compressed above its critical temperature and pressure to alter its properties. Such supercritical carbon dioxide is an ideal solvent because it is nontoxic, nonexplosive, cheap, readily available, and easily removed from the extracted products. It is as efficient as hexane at removing triglycerides while yielding a high quality, gum-free, light-colored crude oil with low iron content. However, additional development work is required to overcome the high pressure engineering problems related to an economical high volume continuous process.

OIL PROCESSING

Crude Oils

Most crude edible oils, obtained from oil-bearing materials consist primarily of triglycerides (Triacyl glycerols), which are esters resulting from the union of one unit of glycerine with three units of fatty acids. The triglycerides, which make up approximately 95% of the crude oil, are the constituents we wish to recover and use as neutral oil in the manufacture of finished products. The remaining non-triglyceride portion contains variable amounts of impurities, such as free fatty acids (FFA) non-fatty materials, generally classified as "gums," phospholipids (phosphatides), tocopherols, color pigments, sterols, meal, oxidized materials, waxes, moisture and dirt. Most of these impurities are detrimental to finished product color, flavour, foaming and smoking stability; and thus must be separated from the neutral oil by a purification process. Of these impurities, the primary concern is with the adequate removal of the FFA and phosphatides.

FFA is the amount of fatty acid, occurring naturally or produced during storage or processing, which exists in edible oils, as a distinct chemical unit in an uncombined state. The quantity of FFA present is a good measure of the quality of the crude oil. Crude oils, such as soybean and rapeseed/canola, contain approximately 0.5% FFA. Other oils, such as palm oil, can contain up to 2 to 3% FFA.

Phosphatides consist of polyhydric alcohols combined with fatty acids, phosphoric acid, and a nitrogen-containing compound. Their primary classifications are phosphoglycerides, phosphoinositides, and phytosphinogosines. Lecithin and cephalin are common phosphatides found in edible oils. Soybean, rapeseed/canola, corn and cottonseed are the major oils which contain significant quantities of phosphatides. Alkalide treatment used for FFA reduction is also capable of removing most of the phosphatides from these crude oils.

On the other hand, tocopherols are important minor constituents of vegetable oils. They perform the important function of performing as natural antioxidant protectors of oil-keeping qualities by retarding the development of rancidity. Proper processing allows most of the tocopherols to remain in the finished oils. Thus, the objective of the following purification steps is to remove the objectionable impurities, with the least possible damage to the neutral oil and tocopherols, and minimum loss of oil during such processing.

Purification of Crude Oils

Processors have the option of approaching this purification step in three ways. First of all, crude oil may be water-degummed before refining by water treatment followed by centrifugation to remove the phosphatides as hydrated gums. Secondly, some oils can be acid-degummed, bleached and satisfactorily physically refined to finished products. Thirdly, either the water-degummed oil or crude oil can be treated with caustic soda to saponify impurities, which are subsequently removed as soapstock by a primary refining centrifuge.

Degumming

Some solvent extracted crude oils, including soybean or rapeseed/canola, contain ca 2 to 3% gums, which are mainly phosphatides. If left in the oil, gums will cause problems through higher than necessary refining losses, or by settling out in storage tanks.

The degumming operation exploits the affinity of most phosphatides for water, which converts them to hydrated gums, that are insoluble in oil and readily separated by centrifugal action. The principal phosphatides lecithin and cephalin are triglyceride compounds with one fatty acid radical replaced by phosphoric acid. Some phosphatides, called "Alpha-Lipoids" are hydratable and may be removed by water degumming prior to caustic refining. The "Beta-Lipoids" are not hydratable and cannot be removed during conventional water degumming operation.

Water Degumming

Gum containing crude oil is treated with a small quantity (2 to 4%) of water or steam, in order to precipitate the hydratable gums. Precipitated gums and the water are separated from the oil in continuous centrifuges, similar to those used in continuous refining. Hermetic centrifuges are recommended to minimize contact with air while the oil is hot (80°C). Usually, the extracted gums are blended back into the meal by adding them to the top tray of the DT (desolventizer-toaster) in the solvent extraction plant. Such addition makes the meal powder agglomerate more readily. Degummed oil from the centrifuge, still containing approximately 0.5% phosphatides, is vacuum dried, cooled, and stored prior to being further processed or sold as crude degummed oil. Removal of gums prior to alkalide refining often improves the overall yield, because phosphatides act as emulsifiers in a caustic solution and increase the quantity of neutral oil entrained in the soapstock.

Physical Refining

When dealing with high free fatty acid and low phosphatide content crude oil, such as palm oil, physical refining or steam refining can provide a major economic advantage over caustic refining. Oil with a low phosphatide content is pumped through a deaerator to a deodorizer-deacidifier with a dwell time of approximately one hour at 260°C and 1 mm mercury vacuum. Injection of steam volatilizes most of the free fatty acids. The desired steam-distilled oil passes through a filter into a storage tank.

Physical refining can reduce the loss of neutral oil in byproducts, reduce the number of unit operations in the purification process, and eliminate the acidulation problems associated with the soapstock byproduct produced by alkali refining. The removal of pro-oxidants and phosphatides is crucial to preparing quality oils by physical refining.

Although there has been considerable controversy over the possibility of achieving satisfactory results from soybean oil processed by physical refining, it has been verified in Canada that excellent quality can be consistently achieved with canola oil processed by acid-degumming followed by physical refining. The basic requirements to prepare high phosphatide content oils for successful physical refining are as follows:

a)   thoroughly acid degum to less than 30 ppm phosphorus
b)   bleach to less than 2 ppm phosphorus
c)   remove thoroughly all traces of iron and copper

Acid-degumming of crude oil can successfully produce super-degummed oils with ca 30 ppm phosphorus content. When followed by thorough bleaching, successful physical refining results have been consistently achieved. Finished oil from proper acid-degummed crude canola oil has been judged equal in quality to finished oil produced by the conventional alkali-refining process.

Continuous Caustic Refining

Of all the unit operations to which vegetable oils are subjected during conversion to finished products, the refining process has the most impact on quality and economic performance. If oils are not adequately refined, subsequent operations such as bleaching, hydrogenation, deodorization, etc., will be troublesome, and finished products will fail quality standards for fresh and aged performance (Fig. 11.5). Inefficient refining will also reduce the yield of finished product and adversely affect manufacturing profits.

Despite the development of other techniques, such as "miscella" and "steam refining" systems, most refiners currently use the conventional caustic soda refining method to purify crude vegetable oils, including canola oil. The basis of this process is the addition of a solution of sodium hydroxide to crude oil, followed by a separation through centrifugal force in a continuous process.

In the basic process (Fig. 11.6), oil, either crude or degummed, is transferred from a storage tank to a "day tank" in preparation for refining. It is treated with a solution of phosphoric acid, then continuously mixed with a proportioned stream of dilute caustic soda solution and heated to obtain a break in the emulsion. Soapstock is continually separated from the neutral oil by centrifugal action. The resultant refined oil is mixed with hot, soft water and again centrifugally separated to remove small amounts of residual soap. This water-washed refined oil, containing traces of moisture, is then passed through a continuous vacuum-drying stage and on to the refined oil storage tank.

Key factors in determining the success of any edible fat and oil refining operation are:

a)   uniform feedstock
b)   proper quantity of refining agents

c)   proper mixing of the oil and refining agent
d)   proper control of residual contact time and temperature
e)   efficient centrifugation.

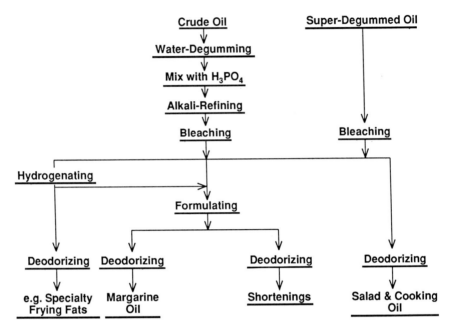

Fig. 11.5   Basic unit operations for the production of finished products from crude oil.

Pre-Treatment

Vegetable oil from the crushing plant is pumped to the refinery day tanks which are equipped with slow speed, side-entering agitators. Agitation is particularly important for phosphatide-containing source oils, such as non-degummed soybean or rapeseed/canola oil. Tanks should be sized to provide homogeneous batches of crude oil, sufficient for twenty-four hour minimum continuous refining runs. Smaller batches increase refining losses due to frequent start-ups and shutdowns. Several day tanks may be necessary to provide sufficient time to prepare the crude oil batch, test the oil, and select the appropriate refining conditions.

Prior to the refining start-up, the crude oil in the day tank should be bleach tested on cup refined oil and evaluated for FFA and neutral oil or cup loss. Oils with significant quantities of phosphatides are usually treated with 100 to 500 ppm of food-grade 75% phosphoric acid, prior to the caustic addition step.

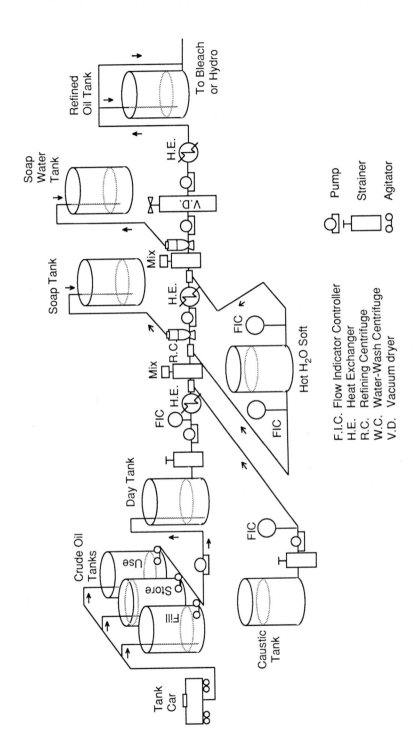

Fig. 11.6 Flowchart of the processing steps for the continuous caustic soda refining process.

F.I.C. Flow Indicator Controller
H.E.   Heat Exchanger
R.C.   Refining Centrifuge
W.C.   Water-Wash Centrifuge
V.D.   Vacuum dryer

Pump   Strainer   Agitator

The phosphoric acid tends to denature the phosphatides to improve the efficiency of their removal during the caustic refining step. In addition, the phosphoric acid acts as a sequestering agent by combining with metal ions in the oil, retarding their catalytic potential for oxidizing the neutral oil and facilitating their removal during subsequent processing. The acid also reacts with the magnesium in chlorophylls, to decrease the green color content of the refined oil.

Caustic Storage and Preparation

Refiners usually receive concentrated caustic soda at 50°Bé in tank cars or tank wagons and unload the contents to the caustic storage tank. Prior to the refining run, concentrated caustic is transferred to the caustic dilution tank and blended with water to obtain the desired concentration. After thorough mixing, the operator checks the strength with a hydrometer. When within tolerances, a sample is submitted to the laboratory for percent NaOH and °Bé, prior to startup. Some installations utilize a caustic-water proportionating system, such as the Bran & Lubbe metering unit, to replace the caustic dilution tank. Diluted caustic of the desired concentration is pumped through a strainer and if necessary, a heat exchanger to the flow indicator/controller and on to the caustic-oil mixing "T."

Key control points for caustic preparation are concentration, flowrate or "treat," and temperature. The control levels are determined by the type of crude oil to be refined, the results of laboratory tests, past refining experience with similar oils, and the refining equipment available. In general, the smallest amount of the weakest strength caustic, necessary to achieve the desired endpoint control, is used to minimize saponification of the neutral oil and prevent "three-phasing" or emulsions during separation.

Caustic strengths of 15 to 18°Bé are usually prescribed for oils other than palm, palm kernel and coconut. The latter require weaker caustic of approximately 12°Bé to optimize centrifugal separation, reduce saponification of neutral oil and minimize emulsions.

The treat selected for the crude oil to be refined will vary with the FFA content of the oil and the level of caustic "excess" over "theoretical," determined for each oil type from previous experience. The theoretical quantity of caustic is based on the ratio of molecular weights of sodium hydroxide to oleic acid. Most oils are refined with 0.1 to 0.2% excess, but there are important exceptions. Lauric and palm oils require a minimal excess of approximately 0.02%, because they are refined for FFA reduction purposes only.

A smooth, reproducible flow of caustic to the mixing T is of prime importance to efficient refining. Pulsating delivery will carry through the mixers and produce varying mixture densities in the separators. Refiners now utilize ration units with proportional band, reset, and rate action to achieve a non-pulsating reagent delivery of the crude oil. This ratio controller permits only the specified quantity of caustic to enter the crude oil stream, even if there are fluctuations in the crude oil flow. In addition, rotometers are installed in the reagent line for visual observation and emergency manual control. Prompt accurate readings of oil and caustic flow rates are essential for the refining operator to control the refining efficiency.

Caustic-Oil Mixing

After the caustic reagent has been proportioned into the 30°C crude oil at the mixing T, it must be sufficiently blended to ensure adequate contact with the free fatty acids, phosphatides and color pigments. Caustic reacts with the free fatty acids to form soapstock, while hydrolyzing phosphatides and removing unsaponifiable matter from the crude oil. After mixing, the soap-oil blend is heated to approximately 85°C for optimum separation in the refining centrifuges.

The usual mixing system includes a high-speed, inline mixer for all oils, plus an optional bank of dwell mixers for soft oils, such as soybean. High-speed mixing by the inline mixer is used to obtain intimate contact between the caustic and oil. The gums are hydrolyzed by water in the caustic solution and become insoluble in the oil. Inline mixing is followed by a delay period. In a number of dwell mixers, the delay may be varied to achieve the refined oil endpoint control. Gum containing oils usually require three dwell mixers to provide approximately six minutes contact time for adequate phosphatide removal.

Once the mixing operation has been completed, the soap-oil mixture should be delivered to the separators at a temperature suitable for optimum separation. Soap-oil mixtures are usually heated to 85°C to provide the thermal shock necessary to "break" the emulsion of the oil-caustic-soap mass. Too high an oil temperature during the addition of caustic can increase the saponification rate of neutral oil and reduce the yield of refined oil. The degree of refining is controlled by the caustic treat, plus the caustic-oil mixing temperature and time.

Soap-Oil Separation

All of the previous operations are in preparation for the primary separation step, the key to efficient refinery yield. From the caustic-oil mixer, the resultant soap-in-oil suspension is fed to high-speed centrifuges for separation into light and heavy density phases. These separators are designed to divide suspensions of insoluble liquids and solids in suspension with different specific gravities. The light phase discharge is comprised of refined oil containing traces of moisture and soap, while the heavy phase is primarily insoluble soap, meal, free caustic, phosphatides and small quantities of neutral oil.

Centrifugal separation is several thousands times faster than the gravity separation method used in batch refining. Separation efficiency within a centrifuge can be controlled primarily by the temperature of the oil-caustic feed.

A centrifuge contains a bowl or hollow cylinder turning on its axis. As the flow of material to be treated by centrifugal force enters this rotating bowl, it is forced outwards into a separation area called the disc stack. The flow then separates and the soap, having a heavier specific gravity, is thrown out to the bowl periphery. The lighter specific gravity phase, which is the desired neutral oil, is displaced to the center of the bowl and eventually discharges from the neck of the top disc. In the meantime, the soap phase flows over the top disc and out the soapstock discharge port.

In either a top-feed or bottom-feed centrifuge, the composition of the phases can be adjusted by changing the position of the neutral zone in the centrifuge. In the old atmospheric centrifuges, zone changes were obtained by modifying the diameter of the heavy phase discharge port and using various ring dam sizes. Most centrifuges are now of the pressure or hermetic type, in which zone changes can be readily achieved by adjusting the back pressure applied to the light phase discharge. Regardless of the system employed, complete separation of the two phases is never achieved.

For satisfactory operation, the interface should be near the midpoint between the center and periphery of the bowl. Its position within the bowl depends upon the refined oil discharge back pressure. Increasing this back pressure reduces the soap content in the oil phase, but increases the neutral oil lost in the soapstock. Conversely, reducing the back pressure decreases the neutral oil loss in the soap phase, but increases the soap in refined oil to a level which is beyond the capacity of the subsequent water-washing step.

Key factors in improving the completeness of separation are:
a)   maximize the differences in specific gravity of the phases
b)   reduce viscosities
c)   increase temperature
d)   minimize the travel distance for the heavy particles
e)   maximize the centrifugal force
f)   increase the centrifuge dwell time

For centrifuge start-up conditions, most refiners use refined oil back pressure guidelines such as 45 psig, selected from previous refining experience. Once the process starts to line out, refined oil back pressure is carefully adjusted until the refined oil, as viewed through a lighted sight glass, becomes slightly turbid from the presence of soap particles. A high-speed test tube centrifuge may then be used to determine the quantity of heavy phase left in the refined oil. The spin test provides a rapid guide to separation efficiency and back pressure adjustment. Spin test evaluations and back pressure adjustments are continued until the soap content in the refined oil is compatible with water-washing capability, usually 300 ppm maximum.

Once steady-state is achieved, key control features such as flow rates, temperatures and pressures should be frequently monitored and adjusted as necessary. Permanent log sheets for processing data and equipment maintenance are very important for long term satisfactory performance. The refined oil phase, containing minute quantities of soap, is pumped continuously from this primary refining step to the secondary refining stage, called water-washing.

Soapstock or "foots," formed during the alkali neutralization of free fatty acids and removed during this primary centrifugation, can be sold to soapmakers for further processing, or can be split by sulphuric acid to form a mixture of crude free fatty acids, phospholipids, proteins and other impurities. This mixture can be sold to animal feed manufacturers as "acidulated soapstock" or used as a raw material for the production of purified products, such as fatty acids.

Water-Washing, Vacuum Drying and Storage

Refined oil from the primary centrifuge is reheated as necessary to 85°C. Hot softened water, or recovered steam condensate, is proportioned into the refined oil at a rate of 10 to 20% by weight of the oil flow. This water-oil combination passes through a high-speed inline mixer to obtain intimate contact for maximum soap transfer from the oil to the water phase. The soapy water-oil mixture continues through secondary separators, such as DeLaval B-214-C centrifuge. Similar to the action of the refining centrifuge, water-washed oil is discharged as the light phase and the soapy water solution is the heavy phase. The water-washing operation removes approximately 90% of the soap content in the refined oil and a single washing pass is usually sufficient. Wash water temperature is important to efficient separation in the centrifuge, while the water-wash flow rate controls soap removal and oil losses in the wash water.

The control of the water-washing separator is easier than the refining centrifuge. The critical factors are the selection of the correct discharge ring and the relationship of the water temperatures. Wash water must be as hot as, or preferably 5° to 8°C hotter than the oil to prevent emulsions. Problems, such as emulsion or very high soap content in the washed oil, are typically caused by improper separation at the refining centrifuge.

Washed oil at approximately 85°C is passed through nozzles into the evacuated section of a continuous vacuum dryer, which controls the moisture content of the washed oil to below 0.1%. A typical dryer operates at 70 cm Hg and is equipped with high-level alarm and automatic shutdown capability. Before entering the refined oil storage tank, the dried oil is continuously cooled to approximately 49°C. If extended storage is necessary, a nitrogen blanket may be applied to the surface of the oil to minimize oxidation.

REFINING EQUIPMENT

The overall refining equipment package should be designed and selected for its capability of producing a high yield of quality product, with operating flexibility to handle all types of edible fats and oils. For most refining installations, hermetic centrifuges are the cornerstone of the equipment presently utilized to achieve these requirements. In addition to their efficiency and flexibility, hermetic centrifuges provide a closed, air-free system which eliminates the risk of oxidizing the oil during refining. For example, peroxide values of all-hermetic refined oils are approximately 0.2 meq (milli equivalents) vs 2 to 4 meq values for batch refined oils.

Typical hermetic centrifuges are the DeLaval VO, SRG and PX series. VO hermetic machines, such as the VO 194 with a capacity of 2250 kg/hour, are widely used by vegetable oil processors for lower volume applications. SRG-214 hermetic machines, with approximately four times the capacity of the VO 194, can be used in higher volume vegetable oil refining operations. The B-124 is used for water-washing refined oils, with a capacity of approximately 18,000 kg/hour.

REFINING PERFORMANCE

Refinery performance control systems are designed to monitor the refining yield efficiency of the system, evaluate the quality level of the refined oil, and initiate prompt adjustment of processing conditions for out-of-control incidents.

Yield

Refining efficiency is generally considered to be the yield of dry neutral refined oil as a percentage of the available neutral triglyceride content of the crude oil. The former is either measured volumetrically and adjusted as necessary for temperature by specific gravity tables, or by scale tank weights. Crude oil quantity is determined in a similar manner and then adjusted to available neutral triglyceride by a laboratory loss evaluation. The laboratory loss method, and hence the efficiency terminology, varies with the oil type. Gum-containing crude oils, such as soybean and rapeseed/canola, are usually evaluated by the chromatographic method for lab loss and the refining efficiency is expressed as the ratio of neutral oil produced over the calculated neutral oil in the crude oil. The lab loss basis for cottonseed and corn oils is the AOCS cup loss method (American Oil Chemists' Society, Official Method Ca 9a-52) and refining efficiency is expressed as "savings over cup." Palm and lauric oils' refining efficiency is controlled by the refining factor, a ratio of plant loss to FFA content of the crude oil. Canola refining losses will vary from 1.2 to 3.5%, but are usually well below 2% for degummed oil.

Quality

Refined oil quality standards are established to be compatible with the finished product quality objectives of the individual company. Final refined oil control samples are generally taken downstream from the vacuum dryer. At this point in the process, moisture content of the oil should not exceed 0.1%. In most cases, 0.05% FFA and 50 ppm soap content maximums are the primary endpoint limits for refined oils. Phosphatide-containing crude oils, such as canola and soybean, are also controlled by the residual gum level. These gums precipitate when the refined oil sample is treated with acetone. The quantity of precipitate can then be measured by visual comparison with a standard tube or by nephelo-metric equipment, to determine whether or not the oil is fully refined. In the case of dark colored oils, completeness of refining can also be controlled by comparing laboratory bleach test colors of plant refined oil, vs. a similar test on the laboratory refined crude oil samples.

BLEACHING

Water washed, vacuum dried oil from the refinery must then be bleached to reduce the color pigments to an acceptable level. A properly refined, water wash and vacuum dried oil may still contain small quantities of soap (10-100 ppm), which must be removed by the bleaching step to ensure proper hydrogenation. Poorly refined oil, with high soap content exceeding 100 ppm, will inhibit the bleaching activity of the clay and hence decrease the de-colorizing effect.

Continuous bleaching is usually employed because it protects the oil from oxidation during periods of elevated bleaching temperatures. The dried oil is heated to approximately 100°C as it enters the bleacher, where it comes in contact with a continuous addition of deaerated bleaching earth. The quantity of bleaching earth and the oil flow are ratio controlled, to ensure that a constant percentage of bleaching earth of approximately 0.5 to 1.5% activated clay is in contact with the oil. The flow rates are adjusted to provide a contact time of 15 to 45 minutes, depending upon the type of equipment and bleaching clay used. The bleached oil is continuously pumped from the bottom of the bleacher into a filter to separate the spent clay from the oil. In some cases, open filter presses, which are manually emptied and cleaned, are still used for the filtration operation. However, new types of automatic or mechanical discharge presses are now being used to protect the oil from exposure to air at the high filtration temperatures.

A typical refined, bleached soybean oil might have the following analytical characteristics:

a) FFA   -0.04% (as oleic)
b) Color   -2.5 red, 25 yellow (5 1/4 inch Lovibond tube)
c) Peroxide Value   -1 meq (milli equivalents)
d) Acetone Insoluble -0.02%

HYDROGENATION

Usually, at least some of the refined, bleached liquid oil must be converted to semi-solid, plastic fats suitable for shortening or margarine manufacture.

A hydrogenation process is used to provide the direct addition of hydrogen into the unsaturated double bonds of the fatty acid chains within the neutral oil. In addition to increasing the solids content and melting point of the oil, it also enhances the stability and color of the final product. For the hydrogenation reaction to take place, gaseous hydrogen, liquid oil and a nickel catalyst are combined by mechanical agitation, at a specific temperature and pressure in a closed reaction vessel. The rate at which the hydrogenation reaction proceeds, the final solids curve and melting characteristics of the fat, all depend upon the temperature, the nature of the oil being hydrogenated, the activity and concentration of the catalyst, and the rate at which hydrogen and unsaturated oil molecules are combined at the active points of the catalyst surface.

In practice, batch dead-end hydrogenators, or convertors, are held under vacuum until approximately 4,500 to 18,000 kg of liquid oil are loaded and the catalyst in oil suspension is charged to the vessel. During a heat-up period, the vacuum deaerates and dries the oil before it reaches the elevated reaction temperature. When the required hydrogenation temperature is reached, the vacuum line is closed, and hydrogen is metered into the vessel until the pressure builds to the desired level. Each company may use different hydrogenation techniques, but typical conditions would be:

a) Catalyst concentration - 0.03% to 0.1% Nickel
b) Reaction temperature - 150 to 185°C
c) Hydrogen pressure - 3 to 5 atmospheres
d) Agitation speed - approximately 150 rpm
e) Reaction time - 10 to 60 minutes

The reaction end point is controlled in the hydrogenation department by determining the refractive index, which relates relatively closely to the iodine value. The solids content and melting point evaluations are later performed in the laboratory (Fig. 11.7). At the end of the reaction, hydrogen flow is stopped and the hydrogen in the head space, with accumulated impurities, is blown off to the atmosphere. Vacuum is again applied to the vessel and the hydrogenated oil is cooled to approximately 80 to 85°C before being discharged from the vessel. The cooled, hydrogenated oil is then sent through a catalyst filtration unit and a post bleaching operation before being sent to tank storage.

DEODORIZATION

Depending upon the characteristics desired in the finished product, liquid oil, hydrogenated oil, or various blends of the two are prepared and evaluated prior to a steam distillation, or deodorization operation. The large difference in volatility between the low volatile triglycerides and their natural flavour and odour components makes steam deodorization feasible for stripping these relatively volatile substances. In addition, the process destroys peroxides in the oil, removes aldehydes and ketones, or other volatile products resulting from atmospheric oxidation and reduces the oil color by the destruction of unstable carotenoid pigments.

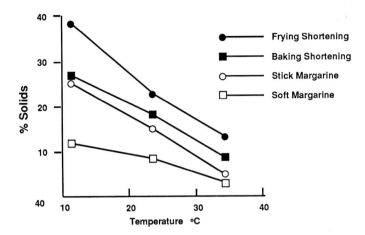

Fig. 11.7 Examples of solid content evaluations for different product categories.

In most cases, the deodorization operation is carried out in "continuous" or "semi-continuous" vertical stainless steel deodorizers fitted with approximately five to seven shallow trays (Fig. 11.8). The oil is deaerated under vacuum and then charged to the top steam heating tray from where it falls to the second, or Dowtherm heating tray, in which it is heated to approximately 250°C. The oil then proceeds through two deodorization trays, counter current to the stripping steam flow. A three-stage steam ejector system maintains a pressure of approximately 6 mm mercury to enhance volatilization of the impurities and to protect the quality of the neutral oil. Dwell time in each of the trays is approximately 20 minutes. Under normal operating conditions, the stripping steam requirements are approximately 4.5 kg per 45 kg of oil. The deodorized oil then exits the second deodorizer tray and is cooled in a water chilled cooling tray, before being filtered and transferred to a deodorized oil storage tank. Typical deodorized oil characteristics would be:

a) Color   -0.4 red, 4 yellow (5 1/4" tube)
b) FFA   -0.02%
c) PV   -0.0 meq
d) Tocopherols   -15 mg/100 ml

PRODUCTS

Bland, deodorized fats and oils from the deodorized oil storage tanks are now ready for finishing as packaged cooking oils, salad oils, shortenings, salad dressings and margarines.

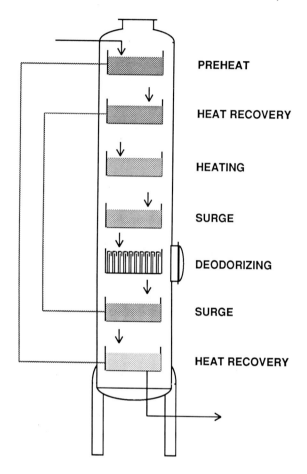

Fig. 11.8 A vertical semi-continuous deodorizer manufactured by the Cambrian Engineering Group Ltd.

Shortenings

One category "shortening and shortening oils" includes the partially hydrogenated plastic fats used in baking as well as the more heavily hydrogenated products designed for heavy-duty frying. For baking breads, cakes and pastries, most institutions, as well as homemakers, use a plastic fat prepared from blended, hydrogenated vegetable oils. Blending is done to assure the stability of the fine crystal structure that is necessary for plasticity. Traditionally, fat plasticity has been considered the key to its successful performance in cake baking. However, recent baking research suggests that liquid oil may be preferred as the form of fat for cakes of the future. Liquid oils provides the double nutritional reward of reducing the fat content of baked products and reducing the need for hydrogenation of the fat used in them.

A good frying fat must be bland in flavour and heat stable; that is, it should resist breakdown under the stress of temperatures of 175° to 190°C. Frying stability is assessed by measuring how much certain properties change during extended use, such as: increase in free fatty acids, increase in viscosity, and the drop in smoke point.

Institutions and food processors can vary in their choice of solid or liquid fat for frying. Because of their increased level of hydrogenation, solid fats exhibit more stability. However, liquid oils are easier to handle and approximately 5 to 10% less fat is absorbed by the food, because the oil drains more readily when the food is removed from frying. Most consumers pan-fry more frequently than they deep-fry. When they fry, they use more liquid oil than solid fat or table spreads.

Margarines

Table spreads are enjoyed because of their flavour and mouth feel and consumers have shown growing preference for the ones that spread easily at refrigerator temperatures, where they keep best. From the nutritional standpoint, there is also an increasing interest in low-calorie products which contain only 40% fat, rather than 80% fat common to both butter and conventional margarine.

A margarine's structure is a network of small fat crystals trapping oil and water globules. Its degree of spreadability depends a good deal on the proportions of the liquid oil and crystalline fat. For example, soft margarines are spreadable at refrigerator temperatures because most of them contain up to 70% liquid oil in the margarine oil formula. Butter and the stick margarines are brittle when cold and only become spreadable as they warm up to room temperature, when some of the solid crystals begin to melt. These differing consistencies are achieved by the combination of the hydrogenation process, plus the blending of varying oil types and solid contents.

Margarine consumers fall into two main groups, i.e. the homemakers (for table use, baking and frying) and the professional baker. For the table, the homemaker demands a margarine with a pleasant flavour, which is released fully and quickly. It must spread easily over a wide range of room temperatures and melt rapidly in the mouth, leaving no sensation of fattiness, yet it must not be too soft. For baking, the chief qualities required by the homemaker are plasticity and creamability (the ability to take up air when beaten). For frying, the fat must remain stable at high temperatures and must not contain excessive free fatty acids or the problem of smoking will arise.

For the professional baker, taste is slightly less crucial and plasticity and creamability become considerations. To meet these requirements, margarine manufacturers combine the properly designed margarine oil with an aqueous phase, so that the water globules are finely dispersed but combine loosely enough for the emulsion to break easily on melting. The aqueous phase in margarines, generally consists of reconstituted milk powder, brine and water. Milk is pasteurized by rapidly heating it to 75°C and holding it at that temperature for 30 minutes. It is cooled rapidly to 5°C and held at that temperature until required. Salt, at approximately 2%, is added to the milk to discourage the growth of micro-organisms and also accentuate the flavour. Vitamins, coloring and flavouring agents are included, and emulsifiers, such as monoglycerides and lecithin, are added to the oil phase.

The liquid fat phase and the aqueous milk phase are brought together in a premix tank, where mixing is sufficient to keep the milk from settling out. The margarine mixture enters the "A" unit at 38°C and is chilled to 10°C in approximately 16 seconds. At that stage, the mixture is quite fluid, since it is in a super-cooled condition. A typical "A" unit would contain three chilling cylinders with a total heat transfer area of approximately one square meter and a rating capacity of 2,025 kg/hour. These cylinders are constructed of chrome plated commercially pure nickel. Stainless steel is used in all other components and interconnecting pipe lines are of sanitary design. This system provides for continuous flow of the material from the emulsion premix tank. It is totally enclosed, and the product is not exposed to atmosphere until it reaches the print-forming equipment.

The super-cooled emulsion from the "A" unit then passes through a "B" unit. The margarine "B" unit differs radically in design from the one used for working shortenings in that no provision is made for mechanical agitation. The margarine "B" unit is a good deal smaller in diameter and considerably longer. Solidification of this super-cooled margarine emulsion, therefore, takes place under almost static conditions. The purpose of limiting the amount of work given to the product in the "B" unit is three-fold. First, to ensure the product produced is not too soft to be handled in automatic print-forming and wrapping equipment. Second, to prevent the aqueous phase from being dispersed in an extremely fine state of subdivision. Third, to induce growth of larger crystals from the super-cooled mass. If the same amount of mechanical work applied to shortening were used in margarine, the aqueous phase would be dispersed in very small droplets, the solid portion of the fat would be crystallized in minute particles, and a long resting period would be required for the product to become firm enough for packaging.

CONCLUSIONS

Research activities continue on an on-going basis to develop new raw materials, produce new products, improve the quality and yield for existing processes and develop new manufacturing equipment. The pace of these developments is increasing due to the application of new scientific practices, such as biotechnology. For each step forward, efficient manufacturing procedures will need optimization for the efficient production of quality products from oil bearing materials.

REFERENCES

Carr, R.A. 1976. Degumming and refining practices in the U.S. World Conference on Oilseed and Vegetable Oil Processing Technology. June, 1976. J. Am. Oil Chem. Soc. 53: 347-352. Amsterdam.

——. 1986. Oilseeds, fats and oils. Presentation for National Research Council Training Seminar, Chatham, Ont. (Personal Communication).

——. 1987. La Semilla Oleaginosa De Canola Y El Procesamiento Del Aciete Una Panoramica. Technology Transfer Program. Curso De Canola Mexico-Canada. POS Pilot Plant Corp., Saskatoon, Sask.

Casten, J.W., and Snyder, H.E. 1985. Understanding pressure extraction of vegetable oils. Volunteers in Technical Assistance, Arlington, Va.

Hamilton, H., and Bhati, A. 1980. *Fats and Oils Chemistry and Technology.* Applied Science Publishers, London.

Schafer, H.W. 1986. Oilseed crushing and processing. Presentation for the Technical Mission in India and Pakistan. CSP Foods Ltd., Saskatoon, Sask.

Swern, D. 1082. *Baileys Industrial Oil and Fat Products.* Vol. 2, 4th Ed. John Wiley & Sons, New York.

Chapter 12

Genetics and Breeding of Oil Crops

P. F. Knowles

INTRODUCTION

Breeding and genetics have played major roles in the establishment and improvement of oil crops, and undoubtedly will continue to play major roles in the domestication of promising wild species, in adapting crops to new areas, and in the improvement of the yield and quality of long established crops. In the present chapter only annual oil crops are considered, details on the genetics and breeding of perennial tree crops are discussed in appropriate chapters. In addition, discussions of genetics and breeding, supplemental to those given here, will be found in each crop chapter. Röbbelen (1982) and Knowles (1983) have reviewed the roles of genetics and breeding in the improvement of oil crops.

At one time in the USA oil crop breeding was in the domain of public agencies, the United States Department of Agriculture and the state experiment stations. Now most of the breeding in both the USA and Europe is being done in the private sector by seed companies or companies involved directly or indirectly in processing oilseeds. In most other countries breeding is conducted by government agencies.

Plant breeding has three principal components; a) increasing variability, or expanding the reservoir of alleles of genes within a species, b) constructing from components of the reservoir a genotype or assembly of genotypes to serve as a potential cultivar, and c) evaluation of potential cultivars. Before dealing with these components, the oldest form of plant breeding, domestication, will be considered.

DOMESTICATION

For some crops domestication began at least 10,000 years ago. The process involved hundreds, even thousands of years, and was done by primitive societies. Most of the major accomplishments were achieved more than 2,000 or 3,000 years ago. Success was related in part to the fact that primitive peoples were close to their plants, where they could identify those with desirable traits when they appeared. Such plants were used as a source of seed for subsequent generations. Continuous selection, by man and nature, molded potential crop species into their present forms.

Primitive societies gave major attention to the cereal crops, wheat, rice, maize and barley because of their importance as food. On the time scale of domestication, oil crops came much later, some of them being domesticated first for other purposes. For example, sesame, sunflower and peanut were chosen for their edible seeds; cotton and flax for their fiber; and safflower for its flowers and the dye they contain. In early times oil was squeezed from the seed for lamp oil and may have been used as a substitute for animal fats in cooking. Large-scale use of vegetable oils for edible and industrial purposes began some two hundred years ago. Because of this short time-period the full potential of the plant kingdom as a source of different kinds of oil has not been fully realized. Only in the last fifty years have several wild species been identified as having unique oils showing qualities of interest for industrial purposes. Thus domestication will continue to play an important role in the improvement of vegetable oils.

Traits Affected by Domestication

Some traits have received major attention during domestication of both oil-seed and other grain crops. Resistance to seed shattering was selected to a level best suited to the prevailing cultural practices. This characteristic is still receiving attention in sesame and rapeseed. Resistance has been increased by selection for several genes with small effects, as evidenced in the soybean crop during this century. On the other hand, the difference between levels of seed shattering in domesticated safflower and a closely related wild species appeared to be due to a change in one gene (Imrie and Knowles, 1970).

Seed dormancy was reduced, such that germination would not occur prior to and during harvest operations, but would disappear in all seeds prior to the next planting. Plant architecture was changed toward an upright growth habit. A unique feature of domestication in sunflower was the elimination of branches and the consolidation of all flowers into a single head.

Self-incompatibility systems have sometimes been eliminated, as in safflower (Imrie and Knowles, 1971), where it was determined by alleles at one locus. In sunflower self-incompatibility was maintained until the development of hybrid cultivars, while in some *Brassica* species hybrids may be based on incompatibility alleles.

NEW CROP DEVELOPMENT

New oil crops may be developed from local wild species, from domesticated crops introduced from other regions, or by genetically modifying the oil composition to meet a market need. With mounting surpluses and declining exports of long-established crops there has been much interest in the potential of new crops (CAST, 1984). Important candidates are species producing oil (Pryde et al. 1981); among them are okra, buffalo gourd, lupine, crambe, jojoba, meadowfoam, Stokes aster, *Vernonia* species, wild cucurbit, *Brassica* species and several forest species. Additional species are listed by Princen (1983). Stein (1982) stressed the need for research and development on annual species bearing fatty acids that are; a) saturated and have chain lengths of C12 or shorter, b) unsaturated with chain lengths other than C18, and c) that have higher levels of linoleic acid. With the exception of flax, peanuts and cotton, all oil-bearing crops in North America, including soybean, oilseed sunflower, safflower, sesame, and now rapeseed and mustard, have been new crops at some time during the last seventy-five years. Even corn is now a significant source of edible oil.

The theoretical time frame for the development of a new crop from a wild species is outlined in Table 12.1. It will be obvious that it involves not only domestication but chemical and utilization studies, and initiation of crop production, processing and marketing of the oil. More likely than not it will require a longer period than shown in Table 12.1. Even with adaptation of a domesticated species from another region, or development of an established species with a genetically modified oil, commercialization normally requires production and processing research and market development (see Chapter 30).

INCREASING AND PRESERVING VARIABILITY

The maximum level of variation in both commercially produced and wild oil-bearing species is resident in plant populations grown where the crop species was indigenous or domesticated. Increasingly, efforts have been made to collect and preserve the naturally occurring variability. Periodically breeders draw on these germplasm (gene) banks, usually to search for specific traits. Of particular

Table 12.1 A Timetable for Domestication of a Wild Species with Potential Value as an Oil Crop (adapted from CAST, 1984)

Domestication stages	Years of development							
	1-3	4-6	7-9	10-12	13-15	16-18	19-21	22-24
Germplasm collection	x							
Germplasm evaluation	x——x							
Chemical and utilization studies		x———————————————————x						
Agronomic evaluation		x—————————————————x						
Breeding program		x————————————————						
Production and processing scale-up						x——x		
Commercialization							x——	

interest will be genes for increased oil content, changed or improved oil quality, and resistance to some feature of the environment such as a disease or insect, salinity, and high or low temperatures.

The United Nations Food and Agriculture Organization (FAO) and the International Board for Plant Genetic Resources (IBPGR) have provided leadership and initiative for germplasm conservation programs, and several countries and international research institutes have established and maintained collections of oil crops and their relatives. In most instances these collections have been made available to oil crop researchers worldwide.

Longevity of seed viability can be extended by storage at low temperatures and low levels of moisture. Temperatures should be below +5°C, and preferably below freezing. Low levels of moisture, below 6% in oilseeds, can be achieved by drying the seed and using containers sealed against entry of moisture, or using refrigeration equipment designed to maintain low water vapor pressures. Viability of seed should be maintained above 90%, otherwise the seed samples may become less representative. At progressively lower viabilities, seeds may accumulate both chromosome damage and gene mutations. Details of optimum seed storage are provided by Roberts (1975).

An alternative is to grow germplasm collections at regular intervals when seed viability begins to fall below 90%. Except for highly self-pollinated species this is a laborious task, requiring that many plants from each collection be selfed, or in the case of self-incompatible species that measures be taken to provide cross-pollination within each collection.

Often the breeder may not find the desired plant type in germplasm banks. In that case the breeder may resort to; a) crossing different genotypes to obtain the desired recombination of genes, b) inducing mutations, or c) transferring genes through special plant breeding techniques, using DNA segments.

Recombination of Genes

Most breeding programs involve crossing of selected genotypes (single-plant selections, cultivars, or related species). The purpose is to permit new combinations of characteristics. Usually two genotypes are crossed, but some breeders use composite crosses which are bulks of crosses of several genotypes in all combinations, the purpose being to develop populations with a vast array of variability. Difficult crosses, perhaps those of a cultivar to a different and wild species, may be facilitated by embryo rescue techniques, which entail the removal of the developing embryo at an early stage and culturing it under suitable in vitro conditions until fully developed.

Somatic hybridization has been achieved by fusion of protoplasts of different genotypes, even those derived from different species, genera or families. Protoplasts are cells whose walls have been removed by enzymes. They thus can be used to merge both nuclear and cytoplasmic germplasm not possible using sexual hybridization. In contrast to sexual hybridization, where the cells of the resulting embryo have cytoplasm from the female parent only, somatic hybridization merges the cytoplasms of both parents, which could extend the range of variability. Frequently chromosomes are lost in mitoses following fusion. Cybrid is a term used to denote cells, or plants, which have nuclear material from one or both parents and cytoplasm from both.

Mutagenesis

If a characteristic is not available within a species, the variation may be induced by mutation breeding. Mutagens that are used to produce changes in genes include ionizing or ultraviolet (UV) radiation and chemicals. Ionizing radiation used in plant breeding includes X-rays, gamma rays and sometimes neutrons and radioisotopes, all of them hazardous in application unless special precautions are taken. In addition to genetic changes ionizing mutagens may cause physiological changes and abnormal growth. UV radiation has limited application in plant breeding since it has low penetrating power. Its use is limited almost entirely to pollen grains, but it does produce more gene changes relative to chromosome aberrations than ionizing radiation. Several chemicals have been used, the most common being ethyl methane sulfonate (EMS), which appears to produce gene changes with less damage to chromosomes than does ionizing radiation. Chemical mutagens are hazardous to handle, and great care should be exercised to avoid personal contact with them.

Except for UV radiation most mutagens are applied to seed. The progeny from such treated seed, the M_1 generation, rarely shows the effects of gene changes because these are mostly recessive. In M_2 and later generations the effects of recessive genes are manifested.

In Vitro Single-Cell or Tissue Culture Techniques

Another means of obtaining newly induced mutants is by in vitro selection. Callus or single-cell cultures may be developed from vegetative plant tissue, including developing embryos, meristems, stems, hypocotyls and leaves. Callus tissue is a disorganized mass of cells, but by using an appropriate growth medium and environment, cells may be induced to form stems and/or roots. The derived plants, called regenerates, are often variable, and have been the source of useful genotypes. The variation observed in such cultures is called somaclonal variation. To the plant breeder the interesting feature of this technique is that thousands, even millions of individual cells can be screened for useful traits. For example, screening may be done with a toxin produced by a pathogen, enabling the very rare resistant cells to be identified. These can then be used to develop resistant regenerates. Similarly by growing flax callus cultures in a saline medium, salt-resistant regenerates were developed (McHughen and Swartz, 1984). But such screening is limited to cases where the desired trait is expressed at the cell level. An obvious extension of cell and callus cultures is to expose them to mutagens which will induce additional variability.

Gene Transfer

Geneticists are showing increased interest in gene manipulation which involves; a) the identification of a specific and defined small piece of DNA - a gene or including a gene, and b) the transfer of that piece of DNA into a different host organism where it is integrated into the host genome. When this results in the phenotypic expression of the gene, the host organism is said to be transformed. DNA segments of the donor organism are produced by appropriate treatment with a restriction endonuclease enzyme. Transfer of the DNA requires a vector, which may be a plasmid of a bacterium or a virus into which the DNA is incorporated. Old and Primrose (1985) list some characteristics that may be transferred to crop plants including; a) enzymes of bacterial origin, b) herbicide detoxification from soil bacteria, c) improvement in the quality of seed proteins, and d) commercially valuable or therapeutic proteins in large amounts. Improved or unusual oil characteristics in established oil crops would be another possibility (Knauf, 1987).

PLANT BREEDING METHODS

Plant breeding, originally an art, has become more scientific with the passage of time. Methods vary with the type of reproduction, whether it is sexual or asexual, and whether self-pollination or cross-pollination prevails in the species.

Sexual Versus Asexual Reproduction

Most oil crops reproduce sexually through production of seeds. The embryos in the seeds are the source of oil in many oil crops such as soybean, sunflower, peanut and rapeseed. In most oil crops the endosperm is reduced to a thin layer or a few cells, and provides little or no oil. Exceptions are in castor where the bulk of the seed is endosperm which surrounds a small embryo and flax where about 15 to 20% of the oil comes from the endosperm. In a few crops such as olive and oil palm, oil is produced in the mesocarp layers of the fruit.

Perennial oil crops may reproduce sexually or asexually. Asexual reproduction is achieved in most cases by vegetative propagation, where a plant part is removed and induced to produce roots. Through in vitro culture techniques vegetative propagation has been made easier and cheaper. The advantage of asexual reproduction is that selected productive plants can serve as the initial stock, their progeny being equally productive and very uniform. Breeding by asexual reproduction will be discussed in chapters dealing with such crops.

Self- Versus Cross-Pollination

The level of self-pollination can range from zero to complete, although most crop species fall into two groups: those that are nearly always self-pollinated; and those that are frequently or always cross-pollinated. The two groups require different breeding methods.

Near-obligate or obligate cross-pollination may be imposed by separation of the sexes through either monoecy or dioecy. In monoecy the pollen and functional ovaries are produced by different flowers on the same plant, as in castor and corn. With plants showing dioecy as in jojoba, the male and female flowers are on different individuals. Obligate cross-pollination may also be imposed by systems of self-incompatibility where all flowers of a plant are perfect, but self-pollination will not occur due to inhibition of pollen produced by the maternal plant. Examples are turnip rape and sunflower.

Self-pollinated species have high levels of homozygosity, so single-plant progenies will breed true or almost true to type. Furthermore, they do not manifest inbreeding depression. As a consequence breeding programs focus on the identification of a superior plant that will give rise to a pure, or a near-pure line which on further propagation may become a commercially grown cultivar.

Cross-pollinated species have high levels of heterozygosity, so single-plant progenies will not breed true. The imposition of some form of self-pollination will usually lead to inbreeding depression, where plants may lack vigor, fail to produce seed, and/or show abnormalities. Breeding techniques are designed to produce populations that are agronomically superior, uniform and stable for use as commercial cultivars.

Breeding Self-Pollinated Crops

Where a variable population is available, single superior plants are selected and selfed, or if the level of outcrossing is very low, open-pollinated seed may be harvested. Progenies from such plants are grown in plots, with check cultivar plots at regular intervals. Those that are uniform and superior to the check cultivar are harvested and the seed evaluated in a laboratory for appearance, oil content and oil quality. Superior phenotypes, perhaps 5% of those grown in the field, are advanced to yield trials the following year. Such yield trials are planted according to a statistically sound experimental design and will have row and plant spacings similar to those used commercially. Candidate cultivars are compared with the standard check. Three years of yield trials at different locations will usually give reliable estimates of field performance for all important characteristics. From such trials, one selection may be chosen for release or for further evaluation in strip tests in commercial fields for comparison to the commonly grown cultivar. If in the latter case it continues to show superiority it will be advanced to cultivar status. The format of this selection program is very similar to that followed in Figure 12.1 from F_5 to F_{11} or F_{12}.

Early in a breeding program it will be apparent that cultivars may be improved by combining the good features of two genotypes, perhaps two cultivars. The two genotypes are crossed to give F_1 and F_2 plants. The latter will be the first segregating generation in which the plants will express various combinations of the characteristics of the parents. Most of the plants will be highly heterozygous.

In generations from F_3 to F_6 homozygosity of the populations will increase rapidly in a highly self-pollinated species, so that most F_5 or F_6 plants will breed true. For this reason some breeders elect to carry populations as bulks through to F_5 or F_6 before making single-plant selections. This is known as the *bulk method* of breeding (Fig. 12.1). A refinement of this system is to harvest one seed from each plant in the F_2 to F_5 or F_6 bulk population, thus insuring that there are descendants from all F_2 plants in the F_5 or F_6 field population. This breeding system is called the *single-seed descent* method. Selections in F_5 or F_6 are evaluated and carried forward to cultivar status in the same manner as described above (Fig. 12.1). The advantages of bulk methods are that labor and record keeping are kept to a minimum, and that nonadapted genotypes in the bulk populations may be eliminated by natural selection.

In the *pedigree method* of breeding, superior single-plant selections are made among F_2 plants, and seed from each evaluated for appearance, oil content and oil quality. Those superior in at least some categories are grown as F_3 lines in single rows with appropriate check cultivars at regular intervals. From the best rows, two or three plants are selected for laboratory evaluation of the seed. As with the F_2, the best F_3 plants are identified and their progenies grown out as F_4. The process continues through to F_5 (or F_6) when most progenies will appear as pure lines (Fig. 12.2). Plants from these are selected and handled in the same manner as those selected in F_5 or F_6 in the bulk method. The pedigree method

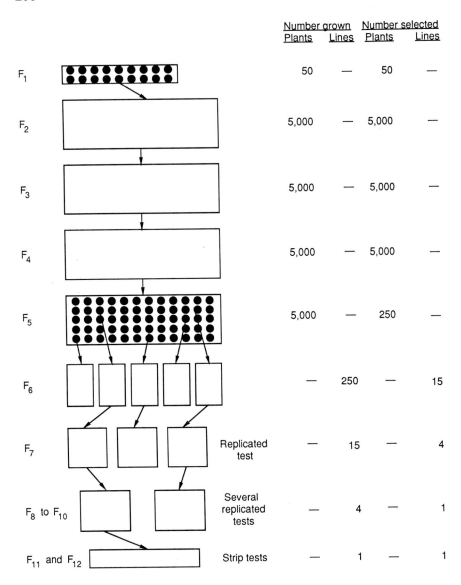

Fig. 12.1 Diagram of the bulk method of handling populations after crossing. Dots indicate populations grown and examined as single plants; rectangles show populations grown as bulk populations, up to F_5 as mixtures, and thereafter as pure lines; and arrows indicate the route of materials from one year to the next (Briggs and Knowles, 1967).

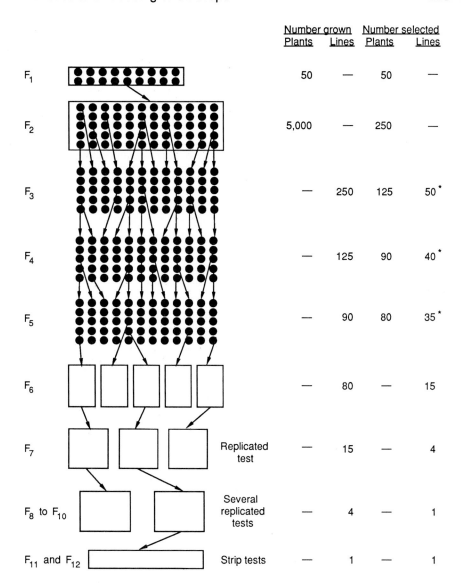

	Number grown		Number selected	
	Plants	Lines	Plants	Lines
F_1	50	—	50	—
F_2	5,000	—	250	—
F_3	—	250	125	50[*]
F_4	—	125	90	40[*]
F_5	—	90	80	35[*]
F_6	—	80	—	15
F_7	Replicated test	—	15	—	4
F_8 to F_{10}	Several replicated tests	—	4	—	1
F_{11} and F_{12}	Strip tests	—	1	—	1

Fig. 12.2 Diagram of the pedigree method of handling a cross progeny. Dots indicate populations grown as single plants; dots in vertical lines in F_2 to F_5, represent families or lines examined as single plants; rectangles are selections grown in bulk; arrows show the route of materials from one year to the next; and asterisks are the number of lines or families giving selected plants (Briggs and

requires much more work than the bulk method, but allows for continuous evaluation of progenies, and continuous elimination of inferior material over a period of several years. Where speed is essential in the pedigree system, progenies may be yield tested in F_3 or F_4, and final selections made then instead of in F_5 or F_6.

There are many variations for each method or combinations of them. Selfing of selected single plants will be necessary where the level of outcrossing is 10% or higher, and in critical materials even though the degree of outcrossing is considerably lower.

The time required to achieve homozygosity in breeding populations can be abbreviated by the use of *doubled haploids*. Haploids are produced spontaneously in some breeding populations, but are induced in large amounts by culturing anthers or microspores on appropriate nutrient media to produce plantlets. In many cases the chromosomes of such seedlings double spontaneously, and in other cases they are induced to double after colchicine treatments. If anthers or microspores are taken from an F_1 hybrid plant, the doubled progeny will be completely homozygous F_2 plants and give true breeding F_3 lines. The F_2 population, however, will be heterogeneous. Thus, 3 to 4 generations (F_3 to F_5 or F_6) are eliminated from conventional breeding programs. This technique has been adopted by breeders of *Brassica* species (Chuong and Beversdorf, 1985). It can also be used to produce inbred lines in cross-pollinated species.

The *backcross method* is used where a superior cultivar needs improvement in one or two simply inherited traits, e.g., disease resistance or oil quality. The superior cultivar (the recurrent parent) is crossed to the genotype (the donor parent) carrying the desirable trait. In the progeny a few plants with the desirable trait are backcrossed to the recurrent parent. The process may be carried forward for 4 to 6 backcrosses, enough to recover the genotype of the superior recurrent parent. At the same time the desirable allele or trait from the donor parent is retained by selection. Advantages of the backcross method are; a) it provides a method of stepwise improvement of a well known superior cultivar, b) populations may be very small, c) the breeding can be accelerated by growing offspring in the greenhouse or out of the adapted area, and d) the improved cultivar needs little or no field testing because it is already in widespread use. Its main shortcomings are that it is limited to traits that are simply inherited, and the ceiling on cultivar improvement, except for the trait under selection, is the recurrent parent.

Breeding Cross-Pollinated Crops

The emphasis in improvement of cross-pollinated crops is on populations or gene pools. Each cultivar growing in a field is a mixture of largely heterozygous plants which are reasonably uniform in appearance and performance. Theoretically at flowering time there is random cross-pollination of all plants, or a thorough mixing of the gene pool, so that succeeding generations of the cultivar are similar. Breeding methods may be complicated in some species because they suffer severe inbreeding depression or, if obligately cross-pollinated, inbreeding is difficult to accomplish.

The simplest method of breeding is *mass selection* where several similar and superior single plants are selected, the seed evaluated in the laboratory, and those superior in the characteristics of interest are composited. A refinement is to progeny test the single-plant selections, and to composite reserve seed of only those plants with superior progenies. The process may be continued over two or three generations in which case it is called *recurrent selection.* An example of such recurrent selection is that used by Pustavoit (1967) to improve populations of sunflower for agonomic performance, quality, and resistance to broom-rape and downy mildew.

A further refinement, particularly where inbred lines or clones are available, is to measure combining ability of each potential component of a cultivar. This can be done in several ways, one being to cross each line or clone to each other in a *polycross*, another being to cross them to a single superior cultivar in a *top cross*. In both methods the bulked crossed seeds of each component are used to plant progeny yield tests. Such trials are usually replicated and may be repeated in different locations. Superior entries are identified and the seed sources (lines or clones) are considered to be good combiners. The latter are composited by bulking and growing out selfed seed of inbred lines, or by growing out clones, in both cases using an arrangement to maximize cross-pollination and isolating the increase plot to avoid cross-pollination with other materials. The seed from the increase plot is used in yield tests in comparisons with other composites and established cultivars. If superior it is given cultivar status. Where components of a cultivar are identified by measuring their combining ability, and where the components are preserved for future syntheses of the cultivar, the result is called a *synthetic cultivar.* However, many breeders extend the term to include all composites, even those in self-pollinated species. The isolated population of composited inbred lines or clones is termed syn-0, which produces syn-1 seed, which in turn gives syn-1 plants. The succeeding generations are syn-2, syn-3 and so on.

Breeding Hybrid Cultivars

Hybrid cultivars have had their greatest utilization in cross-pollinated crops, among them corn, and sunflower. However, in recent years hybrid cultivars are also being developed in self-pollinated crops, including wheat, safflower and rapeseed. It is likely that their use will spread to all crops.

Usually two inbred lines are used to produce hybrid cultivars. The female parent is male-sterile, achieved most effectively if it is due to components of the cytoplasm interacting with genes in the nucleus. Such sterility is termed cytoplasmic male sterility (CMS). The male-sterile line, often referred to as an *A-line*, is maintained by crossing it to a genetically identical male-fertile line which has "fertile" cytoplasm. Such a line is referred to as a *maintainer* or *B-line*. In sunflower, crossing is done in an isolated crossing block where 4 to 8 rows of the

A–line alternate with two rows of the B-line, the level of crossing in such insect-pollinated species being greatly increased by using 2 to 4 bee hives per hectare. Plants grown from the crossed seed will again be male-sterile because their cytoplasm comes from the female parent.

To produce hybrid seed, the A-line and a third inbred line are grown together in an isolated crossing block like that described above for A- and B-lines. The third inbred line must combine well with the A-line, thus giving a high yielding cultivar, and carry nuclear genes that will restore fertility in the hybrid cultivar (hence the term *R-line* but also known as *C-line*). The seed harvested from the A-line is grown commercially as a hybrid cultivar. The R-line is discarded after flowering is complete and well before the harvest of the A-line.

Where two inbred lines, an A- and an R-line, are used to produce a hybrid cultivar, it is called a *single-cross hybrid*. Because all plants have the same genotype the hybrid cultivar will be very uniform, an important advantage, particularly at harvest time or where pesticides must be applied at a particular stage of plant development.

In sunflower and corn a *three-way cross* is sometimes used. To produce such a hybrid a single-cross is made between an A-line and a related B-line. The relationship should be close enough to give a male-sterile hybrid that is largely homozygous, yet different enough to give a hybrid that is more vigorous than the A-line. The male-sterile hybrid is then used as the female parent in a crossing block with an unrelated male R-line. The advantage over the single-cross hybrid is that the male-sterile hybrid female parent in the three-way cross is much higher yielding than an inbred A-line, thus providing seed that is lower in price than that of the single-cross hybrid. Since the male-sterile hybrid female parent is heterozygous in part, there will be more variability in the three-way cross than in the single-cross.

Field Techniques

Field technique and equipment for most oil crops are similar to those used for other grain crops. In some cases modifications or adjustments may be necessary to handle fragile or small seeds. Where yields are being compared it is important that plant spacings be both similar to those used commercially and uniform from one entry to another.

Where plants are large or spiny as in safflower, segregating rows are often sown in pairs, with wide row spacings between pairs. This permits access to the plants for evaluation and selfing.

There should be an evaluation of field nurseries in terms of the uniformity of the test area and the reliability of the separate tests. Field records for all genotypes may include; a) time from seeding to emergence, b) uniformity of stand and, for some crops, plant populations, c) date of flowering (often first, full and last), d) flower color, e) height, f) branching habit, g) degree of lodging of plants, h) date mature, i) date harvested, j) an estimate of the amount of seed lost before harvest, and k) degree of damage from diseases, insects, birds and rodents.

Laboratory Techniques

For evaluations of oilseeds for oil content and quality, it is extremely important that fully mature, undamaged seeds be used. Where seeds fail to develop fully because of lack of moisture, disease, or premature harvest, seed weight will be reduced, mostly because of reduced production of oil and meal. Fatty acid (FA) composition may be affected also, inasmuch as their formation may vary with stages of development.

Details of measurements of oil content and quality are given in Chapter 7. Advances in instrumentation and technology have made possible very rapid analyses, often without destruction of the seed, and often using samples consisting of a single seed or a part of a seed. The advantage of the half-seed technique results from the fact that in most oil crops the FA composition of the oil is determined by the genotype of the embryo, and not by the genotype of the plant bearing the seed. Thus F_2 seeds developing on an F_1 plant can be analyzed and those seeds with the desired oil composition identified. The remaining half from seeds of the desired type can be germinated and grown in a greenhouse or nursery. Not only does this advance the breeding program more rapidly, it permits analyses of the mode of inheritance of fatty acid composition in F_2. Further analyses of the F_3 seeds (or half-seeds) of F_2 plants grown from half-seeds may be made to identify the exact genotype of the F_2 plants and to confirm the mode of inheritance.

Where the oil of a species varies in two fatty acids of different saturation, a measure of fatty acid composition may be obtained by measuring the refractive index of the oil, which varies with the level of unsaturation. This has been the case in sunflower and safflower oils which usually vary only in levels of oleic (C18:1) and linoleic (C18:2) acids. Hand refractometers sufficiently accurate for breeding material and calibrated to give a reading of iodine value may be used. Enough oil may be squeezed from a half-seed of safflower or sunflower for a measurement. The test may be done in a few minutes.

Fatty acid compositions may vary with the environment, in particular the temperature. For example, in sunflower oil linoleic acid is higher, and oleic acid lower, with lower temperatures, and the reverse with high temperatures. It is obvious, when breeding for a high level of a particular fatty acid, that breeding material should be tested over a range of environments.

In oil crop breeding programs laboratory analyses will be required for other characters such as protein content, amino acid profiles, and toxic components. Many of these analyses have been adapted for use in breeding programs dealing with large numbers of small samples.

Cultivar Approval, Preservation and Protection

An important phase of breeding programs of all crops comes after development of a new cultivar, and involves; a) approval of the cultivar for commercial production, b) preservation of the purity or identity of the cultivar, and c) protection of ownership. In general, methods are similar in different countries, though details may not be the same. That used in the United States will be considered here.

Approval of a cultivar for commercial production will require tests in comparison with established cultivars for at least a three-year period over the area where the cultivar will be grown. The tests should measure yield, oil content of the seed and quality characteristics of the oil, in addition to several other characteristics such as earliness, height, stem strength, protein levels, and reaction to pests. Tests should be designed to permit statistical analyses which measure significance of differences. In summary, accurate data should be obtained to verify the claims made for the cultivar. Only after approval by the appropriate agency may certified seed be sold.

The public agency or private company developing a new cultivar has an obligation to maintain seed stocks that will give plants that match the description of the cultivar. The original seed stock of the cultivar is known as *breeder seed*, and may consist of a few pounds or several sacks of seed. Depending on its breeding behavior purity may be maintained as follows:

a) If self-pollinated, single plants are harvested from an isolated increase plot grown from breeder seed (often a field growing foundation seed). Progenies of these plants are grown under isolation and all deviating progenies discarded, if possible before flowering. The balance are harvested in bulk to provide a new supply of breeder seed.

b) If cross-pollinated, breeder seed is grown under isolation and all off-types removed, again before flowering if this is possible. The balance of the field is harvested in bulk to provide breeder seed.

c) If a synthetic cultivar, the components are propagated either as inbred lines as in a) above, or if clones, by preserving and growing them together as described in the section on breeding cross-pollinated crops. The harvested seed from this planting is breeder seed, or more often is called syn-1 seed.

d) If a hybrid cultivar, the inbred lines are maintained in a manner similar to a) above, with careful examination of A-lines to insure that male sterility is maintained, and B- and R-lines to insure that they do not deviate from original stocks.

Except for hybrid cultivars, the first grow-out of breeder seed is called *foundation seed*. The appropriate isolation must be maintained, and off-types must not exceed a specified number. Depending on the crop, foundation seed may produce seed eligible for foundation or registered or certified status.

Registered seed, the progeny of foundation seed, is usually grown by farmers, sometimes under contract to the company owning the cultivar. *Certified seed* is the propagation of either foundation or registered seed, and is also grown by farmers. Both are grown under prescribed conditions of culture and isolation, and both are officially field-inspected to insure that the standards of purity are maintained. The harvested seed is also inspected to make sure that it conforms to the cultivar description and maintains standards of freedom from impurities and standards of germination. If standards are met the seed may be labeled as registered or certified seed.

Certification standards are set by the International Crop Improvement Association, with offices in most states of the USA as well as in Canada. The certifying agency usually includes personnel from state crop improvement associations, state departments of agriculture, state agricultural experiment stations, and cooperative extension.

Cultivar protection is provided in many countries through plant breeder's rights legislation which restricts the sale of a protected cultivar to the owner or an agency or company on licence to the owner. This is particularly essential for the private sector which must recover the costs of cultivar development to stay in business. Asexually propagated cultivars of crops, mostly ornamentals, may be protected by plant patents in some countries. New cultivars proposed for a plant breeder's right must meet the requirements of novelty, uniformity and stability. Certification provides a means to verify identity of cultivars because it requires evidence of sources of all seed sown by registered or certified seed growers. The most effective protection of hybrid cultivars is biological, through control of both the inbred lines and the production of planting seed for commercial production.

BREEDING OBJECTIVES

In many respects breeding objectives for oil crops are similar to those for other crops. Objectives for individual oil crops will be discussed in the following crop specific chapters. However, some general objectives specifically related to oil crops are considered here.

Adaptation to Stress and Environment

Adaptation of a species to an area is in some respects a continuation of the process of domestication. It requires changes in both production practices and genotype, a change in one usually requiring a change in the other. If all components of the environment are considered, including features of the climate, nutrient availability, and plant pests, it is a never ending challenge. Very often the most difficult task for the breeder is to decide on the priorities of change needed.

Some examples of characters receiving serious attention in adaptation are discussed below.

Day-length insensitivity will do much to expand the geographic range of a cultivar. In sunflower most commercial types appear day-length insensitive, but a widely used inbred line, HA-89, has proved to be a long-day type which has complicated, even prohibited, its use in crossing blocks under short-day conditions. Day-length insensitivity would be a major improvement in soybean where it would eliminate the need to change cultivars over short distances in latitude.

Early maturity has been a breeding objective for many crops, in particular where a) the frost-free season is short, b) winter-grown crops must mature before the hot, dry spring period, or where 2 or 3 crops are grown each year, and c) where escape from regularly occuring diseases is required. However, there is usually a positive correlation between time to mature and yield. Time to mature in most instances is a quantitative character, though there are examples, as in the Mexican Dwarf cultivar of safflower, where a single gene when homozygous will reduce the time to mature by 2 to 3 weeks.

Adaptation of crop plants to a mechanized agriculture usually requires a reduction in plant height. Single genes often have major effects on plant height, usually expressed as a reduction in internode length, with no reduction in number of nodes and leaves, diameter of stem and time to mature. Plant height may also be shortened by reducing all dimensions of the plant, including stem diameter, node number and leaves, internode length, and size of the inflorescence. Very often such changes may include earlier maturity. The problem is to identify the ideal type of short plant, divorced if possible from reductions in root length and adverse effects on yield.

In many instances it has been pests that have governed the geographic range of an oil crop. Safflower, extremely susceptible to foliar diseases under humid conditions, has never been successful outside of areas with dry atmospheres during and after flowering. A major block to soybean production in Mediterranean climates has been mites (*Tetranychus* spp.) favored by very dry conditions. Genetic resistance to mites would do much to expand areas of production.

The genetic strategy to achieve and maintain resistance to pests is the same as for other crops. Usually resistance to specific diseases has been found in world collections of oil crops, as was achieved for Fusarium wilt (Knowles et al. 1968) and Verticillium wilt (Urie and Knowles, 1972) of safflower. Also in safflower a related wild species, *Carthamus oxyacantha*, provided a very high level of resistance to rust (Zimmer and Urie, 1968). Complete resistance to blackleg caused by *Leptosphaeria maculans* was transferred from Indian mustard to rapeseed by Roy (1984). The backcross method has been widely used to add one or two genes for pest resistance to an established cultivar.

Resistance provided by a single gene or a few genes with major effects has been called vertical resistance and that by many genes, each with a small effect, has been termed horizontal resistance. Vertical resistance is easier to manage in breeding programs, but it is usually race-specific, and when it breaks down due to the development of a new race of the pathogen, the plant is totally susceptible. Horizontal resistance, on the other hand, is usually expressed against a number of races, so it is more durable though often not as strongly expressed as vertical resistance. An important step in understanding the genetics of virulence and non-virulence in a pathogen and resistance and susceptibility in the host was the gene-for-gene hypothesis advanced by Flor (1971), which was developed from his studies of the inheritance of resistance of flax to rust. A review of breeding strategies used in the development of disease resistant cultivars is provided by Parlevliet (1981).

The genetics of, and breeding for resistance to insects are similar to those for disease, but generally more complicated because of difficulties in managing the insect. Often a breeding progam is one component of an integrated pest management (IPM) program. Breeding programs for insect resistance are reviewed by Jenkins (1981).

Increased Oil Yield

Increased oil yield is achieved by increasing seed or fruit yield and/or increasing the percentage of the harvest that is oil. For most oilseed crops there has been a continuing increase in yield, achieved without a decrease in oil content. A part of the increase has been achieved through improved production practices, but much can be attributed to the use of better cultivars. The genetic basis for increased yields of soybean, peanut and flax lies in the selection of better combinations of genes, each with a small effect. There have been no sudden breakthroughs. On the other hand, the rapid increase in yield of sunflower in the early 1960s was due to the introduction of hybrid cultivars to commercial production, augmented by continuous selection for genes having small effects.

Partitioning of increased amounts of substrate into the embryo, i.e., into oil and meal, and decreased amounts into hull or seed coat should increase oil content of the seed and possibly oil yield per unit area. A partial illustration of this was provided by safflower where a recessive gene, *th*, when homozygous, reduced hull content to 20%, compared to 40% in a cultivar with normal hulls (Rubis, 1967). At the same time oil content was raised to 46%, and protein content of the meal to 34%, compared respectively with 39% and 20% in the cultivar with normal hulls. Unfortunately the *thth* genotype had not only reduced levels of secondary thickening of walls of sclerenchyma cells in the hull, but also reduced secondary thickening of walls of sclerenchyma cells in the stem, thus reducing stem strength, and absence of secondary walls and rib formations in the connective regions and endothecial cells of the anther, thus reducing seed set because pollen was retained entirely or in part within the anther sacs. More recently hull contents have been reduced by a gene which, when homozygous, reduced hull such that oil content was raised to 48 or 50% without adversely affecting stem strength and pollen release (Urie, 1986).

In *Brassica* species and in flax, yellow-seeded cultivars have thinner seed coats and higher oil contents than cultivars with darker seed colors. In flax, but not in rapeseed, yellow-seeded cultivars are not favored because the seed coat is easily broken, leading to reduced germination, greater incidence of damage from soil-borne organisms and lower yields. In India, cultivars of soybean from the USA have done well in experimental trials, but not in commerical production because the thin seed coats proved to be easily injured during harvest, leading to reduced levels of germination and poor yields. When indigenous types with smaller seeds and thicker seed coats, and particularly when similar types derived from crosses of indigenous and exotic types were used, soybean became a successful crop over large areas. Oil contents and protein contents were reduced only slightly.

There is little information on the limits to which the oil content of the embryos of oil crops may be increased. At one end of the spectrum among commercially grown oil crops would be soybean with a range of 15 to 20% oil, and at the other end sunflower where oil cultivars range from 57 to 67% (Fick, 1978).

The relationship between oil content and protein content has been studied intensively in soybean (Johnson and Bernard, 1963), where it was found that the correlation was negative. In studies in other crops, where oil content was raised by reducing hull and/or seed coat contents, protein content was also increased, or the correlation was positive.

Oil Quality

Improvement or change in oil quality is largely a matter of changing fatty acid composition, which in turn is a matter of manipulation of the biosynthetic pathways of fatty acids (Fig. 12.3). Major changes, which have been amenable to genetic change, have involved length of the carbon chain and degree of unsaturation. Such changes have resulted from genetic blocks, probably by control of specific enzymes, at particular steps in the biosynthetic pathway.

Changes in single genes have been found to have profound effects on fatty acid composition. In most cases such changes have occurred naturally, but in recent years important changes in genes affecting quality have been induced by mutagens. Genetic engineering technology with or without mutagens will also contribute to changes in fatty acid composition.

What this means is that vegetable oils of the future can be developed, probably in a number of species, to more closely meet the needs of the user. The same species may produce both edible and industrial oils. One desirable development will be oils essentially pure for a desirable fatty acid, or completely free from one that is undesirable.

Of less concern now, but undoubtedly important in the future, will be positions of fatty acids on the triglyceride molecule. Oils of similar fatty acid composition but different triglyceride configurations may prove to have different values for specific uses. In many, if not all cruciferous species only the outer sites of the

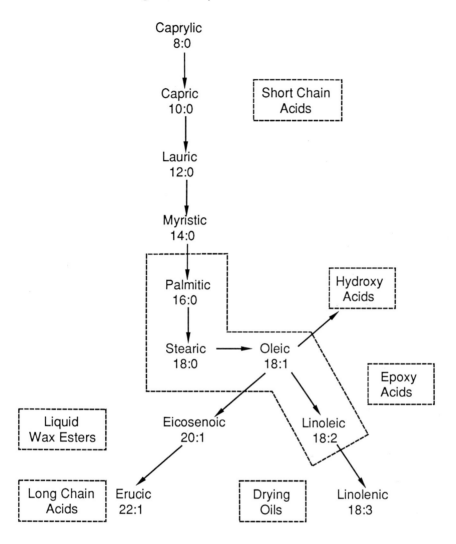

Fig. 12.3 Steps in the biosynthesis of fatty acids where genes have been shown in some cases to govern equilibria (D. L. Auld, Univ. of Idaho)

glycerol molecule will attach erucic acid. The carbon in the center position appears to be reserved for other fatty acids. This puts the upper limit of erucic acid at 66%, two thirds of the total. A mutation allowing attachment of erucic acid at all three positions would permit the production of rapeseed oil very high in erucic acid.

The classic example of genetic change in carbon chain length is provided by rapeseed and turnip rapeseed (Chapter 16). Changes in one gene in turnip rapeseed, a diploid, and two genes in rapeseed, an alloploid, blocked the carbon chain elongation of oleic acid (C18:1) to eicosenoic acid (C20:1) and erucic acid (C22:1), thus making the oils similar to soybean oil in fatty acid composition. Changes in unsaturation, in levels of oleic, linoleic and linolenic acids, are underway.

Improvement in Meal Quality

A review of the role of genetics in improving meal quality in oilseed crops was provided by Beard and Knowles (1976). It was noted that most oilseed meals contain products that are toxic or undesirable. Among these are: trypsin inhibitors in soybeans; aflatoxins in peanuts; chlorogenic acid in sunflower; gossypol in cottonseed; matairesinal monoglucoside and lignan glucoside in safflower; oxalates in the seed coats of sesame; ricin in castor bean; and glucosinolates in cruciferous species. A classic example of the removal of toxic compounds is provided by both rapeseed and turnip rapeseed, where the glucosinolates were reduced to a low level genetically, thus greatly improving the quality of the meal as feed for livestock and poultry (Chapter 16). Gossypol has been genetically removed from cotton seeds, and cultivars of peanuts have been identified that are resistant to aflatoxin development for a short period after harvest.

The proteins of most oilseed meals are valued because of their high quality. Minor improvements in amino acid composition may be desirable for methionine in soybean, methionine and lysine in peanut, and lysine in sunflower, safflower and sesame.

CONCLUSIONS

Oil crops have had an exciting history during the last sixty years. In large measure the plant breeder has shaped that history. Cultivars have been developed that are: higher in yield, higher in levels of oil and/or protein, more widely adapted geographically, better adapted to mechanized production, and more resistant to diseases and insects. Hybrid cultivars of sunflower are now widely used commercially, and have recently been developed for safflower and rapeseed. Rapeseed, because of genetic changes in oil and meal quality, and safflower and sunflower, because of a change in oil quality, have provided essentially new crops. Genetic engineering technology has been introduced to many breeding programs. In countries where vegetable oils are in short supply breeding programs have been initiated or augmented.

The next sixty years will be even more exciting, in part because of a continuation of the developments of the past. Compositions of the oil and protein of existing oil crops will be changed genetically with the needs of society, and will be improved for specific purposes. Indeed, changes in compositions of oils may lead to new market developments. Perhaps most interesting is the possible domestication of some members of a vast array of wild species, in particular those that possess unique oils of potential value to industry.

REFERENCES

Beard, B.H., and Knowles, P.F. 1976. Improving Protein Supplies from Oilseed Crops and Large-Seeded Legumes, pp. 159-174. *In* B. H. Beard and M. D. Miller (eds.), *Opportunities to Improve Protein Quality and Quantity for Human Food*. Univ. California Special Publ. 3058.

Briggs, F.N., and Knowles, P.F. 1967. *Introduction to Plant Breeding*. Reinhold, New York.

CAST. 1984. Development of New Crops: Needs, Procedures, Strategies and Options. Task Force Rep. No. 102, Council for Agricultural Science and Technology, Ames, Ia.

Chuong, P.V., and Beversdorf, W.D. 1985. High frequency embryogenesis through isolated microspore culture in *Brassica napus* L. and *B. carinata* Braun. Plant Sci. 39: 219-226.

Fick, G.N. 1978. Breeding and Genetics, pp. 279-338. *In* J. F. Carter (ed.), *Sunflower Science and Technology*. Monograph No. 19. Am. Soc. Agron., Madison, Wis.

Flor, H.H. 1971. Current status of the gene-for-gene concept. Annu. Rev. Phytopathol. 9: 275-296.

Imrie, B.C., and Knowles, P.F. 1970. Inheritance studies in interspecific hybrids between *Carthamus flavescens* and *C. tinctorius*. Crop Sci. 10: 349-352.

————, and Knowles, P.F. 1971. Genetic studies of self-incompatibility in *Carthamus flavescens* Spreng. Crop Sci. 11: 6-9.

Jenkins, J.N. 1981. Breeding for Insect Resistance, pp. 291-308. *In* K. J. Frey (ed.), *Plant Breeding II*. Iowa State University Press, Ames, Ia.

Johnson, H.W., and Bernard, R.L. 1963. Soybean Genetics and Breeding, pp. 1-73. *In* A. G. Norman (ed.), *The Soybean*. Academic Press, New York.

Knauf, V.C. 1987. The application of genetic engineering to oilseed crops. Trends in Biotechnol. 5: 40-47.

Knowles, P.F. 1983. Genetics and breeding of oilseed crops. Econ. Bot. 37: 423-433.

————, Klisiewicz, J.M., and Hill, A.B. 1968. Safflower introductions resistant to Fusarium wilt. Crop Sci. 8: 636-637.

McHughen, A., and Swartz, M. 1984. A tissue-culture derived salt-tolerant line of flax (*Linum usitatissimum*). J. Plant Physiol. 117: 109-117.

Old, R.W., and Primrose, S.B. 1985. *Principles of Gene Manipulation*. Blackwell Scientific Publications, Oxford.

Parlevliet, J.E. 1981. Disease Resistance in Plants and its Consequence for Plant Breeding, pp. 309-364. *In* K. J. Frey (ed.), *Plant Breeding II*. Iowa State University Press, Ames, Ia.

Princen, L.H. 1983. New oilseed crops on the horizon. Econ. Bot. 37: 478-492.

Pryde, E.H., Princen, L.H., and Mukherjee, K.D. 1981. *New Sources of Fats and Oils*. Am. Oil Chem. Soc., Champaign, Ill.

Pustavoit, V.S. 1967. *Handbook of Selection and Seed Growing of Oil Plants.* English translation from National Technical Information Service. United States Department Commerce, Springfield, Va.

Röbbelen, G. 1982. Plant Breeding and Management - Their Role in Modifying the Availability and Composition of Certain Vegetable Fats and Oils, pp. 17-61. *In: Improvement of Oil-Seed and Industrial Crops by Induced Mutations* (Proc. Advisory Group Meeting). Intern. Atomic Energy Agency (IAEA), Vienna.

Roberts, E.H. 1975. Problems of Long-Term Storage of Seed and Pollen for Genetic Resources Conservation, pp. 269-295. *In* O. H. Frankel and J. G. Hawkes (eds.), *Crop Genetic Resources for Today and Tomorrow.* Cambridge University Press, Cambridge.

Roy, N.N. 1984. Interspecific transfer of *Brassica juncea*-type high blackleg resistance to *Brassica napus.* Euphytica 33: 295-303.

Rubis, D.D. 1967. Genetics of Safflower Seed Characters Related to Utilization, pp. 23-28. Safflower Utilization Conference. USDA Agric. Res. Service Publ. 74-73. Albany, Calif.

Stein, W. 1982. Improvement of Oil-Seeds from an Industrial Point of View, pp. 233-242. *In : Improvement of Oil-Seed and Industrial Crops by Induced Mutations* (Proc. Advisory Group Meeting). Intern. Atomic Energy Agency (IAEA), Vienna.

Urie, A.L. 1986. Inheritance of partial hull in safflower. Crop Sci. 26: 493-498.

Urie, A.L., and Knowles, P.F. 1972. Safflower introductions resistant to Verticillium wilt. Crop Sci. 12: 545-546.

Zimmer, D.E., and Urie, A.L. 1968. Inheritance of rust resistance in crosses between cultivated safflower, *Carthamus tinctorius*, and wild safflower, *C. oxyacantha*. Phytopathology 58: 1340-1342.

Chapter 13

Soybean

W. R. Fehr

IMPORTANCE AND DISTRIBUTION

The soybean [*Glycine max* (L.) Merrill] (Fig. 13.1) accounts for approximately 50% of the total production of oilseed crops in the world. Its seed, which contains about 40% protein and 20% oil, provides approximately 60% of the world supply of vegetable protein and 30% of the oil (Foreign Agricultural Service, 1985).

The soybean is grown as a commercial crop in over 35 countries; however, about 90% of the current world production occurs in the United States, Brazil, the People's Republic of China, and Argentina (Table 13.1). In 1985, the United States had 56% of the world production, Brazil 18%, the People's Republic of China 10%, and Argentina 6%. Soybean production has increased in virtually every country during the past 15 years, with more than 10-fold increases in several countries.

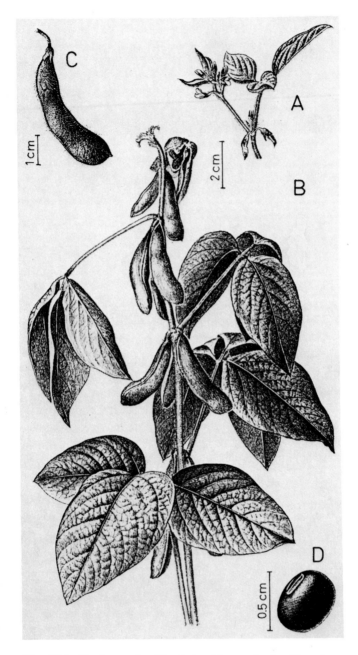

Fig. 13.1   Soybean. A – Short shoot from a leaf axil bearing a raceme of several flowers. B – Branch of a plant with determinate growth bearing fruits up to the top. Note the dense hairiness of all plant organs. C – Ripening fruit with three seed loculi. D – Seed with hilum.
Reproduced from Severa (1983).

Table 13.1 World Soybean Production by Region and Major Producing Countries

Region or Country	Production area ('000 ha)			Seed yield (kg/ha)			Seed production ('000 tonnes)		
	1969-71	1979-81	1985	1969-71	1979-81	1985	1969-71	1979-81	1985
World	**32346**	**50577**	**52368**	**1386**	**1701**	**1925**	**44820**	**86016**	**100833**
Africa	**193**	**346**	**403**	**413**	**963**	**906**	**80**	**333**	**365**
Nigeria	162	195	200	376	385	300	61	75	60
N. & C. America	**17308**	**28145**	**25835**	**1831**	**1993**	**2286**	**31684**	**56095**	**59099**
Canada	138	279	425	1860	2338	2501	257	651	1063
Mexico	134	304	500	1860	2338	2501	257	651	1063
U.S.A.	17036	27561	24922	1830	1991	2292	31174	54861	57114
S. America	**1433**	**10936**	**14007**	**1222**	**1644**	**1838**	**1751**	**17976**	**25746**
Argentina	30	1837	3269	1299	1991	1988	39	3657	6500
Brazil	1314	8510	10153	1178	1583	1800	1547	13468	18278
Paraguay	27	419	420	1690	1391	1667	45	582	700
Asia	**12438**	**9758**	**10675**	**857**	**1067**	**1315**	**10662**	**10409**	**14033**
China	10976	7506	7376	862	1101	1426	9646	8266	10519
India	4	558	1250	545	757	880	2	422	1100
Indonesia	643	775	900	728	875	917	468	679	825
Japan	100	140	134	1280	1370	1783	128	192	238
Korea D.P.R.	278	300	330	918	1133	1288	255	340	425
Korea Rep.	292	214	156	780	1192	1500	228	255	234
Thailand	53	110	198	965	1009	1492	51	111	296
Europe	**108**	**491**	**600**	**1082**	**1270**	**1549**	**117**	**624**	**929**
Bulgaria	9	95	64	876	1299	1328	8	123	929
Italy			92			3063			283
Romania	93	325	285	1095	1127	982	102	366	280
Yugoslavia	4	32	101	1129	2014	1722	5	64	174
Oceania	**5**	**50**	**64**	**1111**	**1696**	**1764**	**5**	**85**	**111**
U.S.S.R.	**860**	**852**	**766**	**606**	**580**	**718**	**521**	**494**	**550**

Source: FAO Production Yearbooks 1980 (vol. 34) and 1985 (vol. 39).

ORIGIN AND SYSTEMATICS

The cultivated soybean originated in China. Current evidence indicates that it probably evolved from the wild annual species *Glycine soja* Sieb. & Zucc. Extensive genetic variation in natural populations of the wild species occurs in Asia (Table 13.2). Variation within the cultivated species occurs among native cultivars, particularly in China; however, the degree of the variation has been reduced in recent years by the introduction of cultivars developed by plant breeding.

The gene pool considered for genetic improvement of the cultivated species is the genus *Glycine* (Table 13.2). The genus has two subgenera, *Soja* (Moenck) F. J. Herm. and *Glycine* Willd. *Soja* includes the cultivated species *G. max* and its wild progenitor *G. soja*. Both are annual diploid species with a somatic chromosome number of 2n=40. Hybrid seed can be obtained readily from *G. max* x *G. soja* crosses, and no major barriers to gene transfer between the species by conventional breeding procedures have been identified.

The subgenus *Glycine* currently includes nine perennial species (Table 13.2). It is not currently possible to transfer genes from the perennial to the cultivated species, although a limited number of hybrid plants have been obtained in crosses between the species by use of in vitro culture to rescue hybrid embryos (Brown et al. 1985). Fertile progeny from the interspecific hybrids have not yet been obtained.

MODE OF REPRODUCTION

The soybean is a self-pollinated species propagated commercially by seed. It has a complete flower consisting of a calyx, corolla, pistil, and stamens. A fully developed flower measures only 7 mm at its greatest dimension. The calyx is made up of five sepals that enclose the corolla and reproductive organs until a day before anthesis (Fig. 13.2A). As anthesis approaches, the corolla emerges from the calyx. The corolla consists of a standard, two wing petals, and two keel petals (Fig. 13.2D).

The pistil has a single ovary with one to five ovules, a style, and a club-shaped stigma (Fig. 13.2C). The 10 stamens are in a ring around the pistil. At anthesis, the filaments elongate and lift the anthers around the stigma. Pollen is shed from the anthers, and the sperm and egg cells unite in the ovary to produce self-pollinated seed.

Hybrid seed for breeding purposes is produced manually and by the use of genetic male sterility (Fehr, 1980). Genetic male sterility is controlled by one of several recessive alleles that have been identified as spontaneous mutations. Its use for breeding is limited to population improvement by recurrent selection.

Artificial hybridization is employed to develop the populations commonly used for cultivar development. The stigma is receptive to pollen about one day

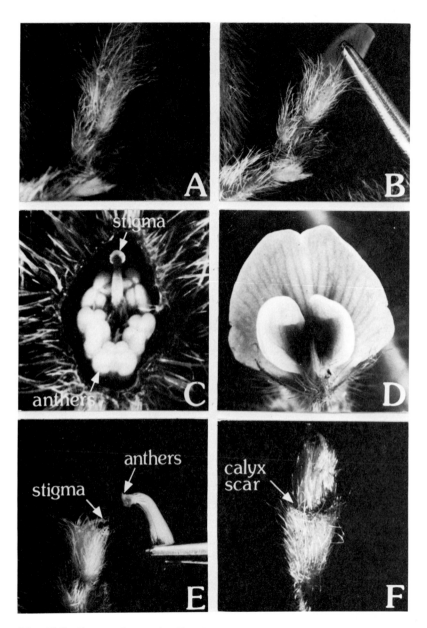

Fig. 13.2 Preparation and pollination of a soybean flower. A – Flower at stage for preparation and pollination. B – Removal of the corolla from the female flower after tha calyx has been removed. C – Ring of 10 anthers and the stigma. D – Flower with pollen available. E – Pollination of the stigma. F – A pod 7 days after pollination with the calyx scar differentiating it from self-pollinated pods. Photographs A,B,D,E and F by C.J. Deutsch and P. Krumhardt; photograph C by G.I. Berkey. Reproduced from Fehr (1980).

Table 13.2. Taxonomy of the genus *Glycine* Willd.[1]

Species	Chromosome number (2n)	Distribution
Subgenus *Glycine* Willd.		
G. *argyrea* Tind.	40	Australia
G. *canescens* F. J. Herm.	40	Australia
G. *clandestina* Wendl.	40	Australia
G. *cyrtoloba* Tind.	40	Australia
G. *falcata* Benth.	40	Australia
G. *latifolia* (Benth.) Newell & Hymowitz	40	Australia
G. *latrobena* (Meissen.) Benth.	40	Australia
G. *tabicina* (Labill.) Benth.	40,80	Australia, south China, south Pacific Islands, Ryukyu Islands, Taiwan
G. *tomentella* Hayata	38,40 78,80	Australia, south China, Papua New Guinea, Taiwan, Philippines
Subgenus *Soja* (Moenck) F. J. Herm.		
G. *max* (L.) Merr.	40	Cultigen (world wide)
G. *soja* (L.) Sieb. & Zucc.	40	China, Japan, Korea, Taiwan, Soviet Union

[1] from Hymowitz and Newell (1981) and Brown et al. (1985).

before pollen is shed from anthers of the same flower, which permits foreign pollen to effect fertilization before self-pollen is available. Artificial hybridization begins with forcep removal of the portion of the sepals surrounding the corolla of an immature flower (Fig. 13.2A). The exposed corolla is removed to expose the pistil and stamens (Fig. 13.2B and 13.2C). Pollen from the male parent is available from flowers that are fully open (Fig. 13.2D). The reproductive organs are removed from the male parent and the anthers are brushed against the stigma of the female parent (Fig. 13.2E). If hybridization is successful, a pod will be visible about seven days after pollination (Fig 13.2F). From one to three hybrid seeds can be obtained from a successful pollination. The percentage of successful pollinations varies widely among persons and environments, ranging from near zero to over 90%.

There are three types of stem termination in soybean: indeterminate, semideterminate, and determinate. The determinacy of a cultivar is closely associated with the relationship between vegetative and reproductive development, and has a major influence on the environments in which a soybean cultivar will be grown commercially. The difference between the three determinacy types is controlled by major genes at two loci (Bernard, 1973).

Indeterminate cultivars begin to flower relatively early in vegetative development when the main stem is less than half of its mature length. Vegetative and reproductive development occur simultaneously until the mature plant height is attained. Pod and seed development begins at the lower nodes of the plant and progresses upward as new nodes are produced. Although there is a difference in the timing of seed development throughout the length of the plant, all of the seeds reach maturity at the same time and can be harvested together. The terminal node of the main stem of indeterminate cultivars has from zero to a few pods.

Semideterminate cultivars resemble indeterminate types in that they flower when the plant is relatively small and undergo simultaneous vegetative and reproductive development. Pod and seed development in the lower portion of the plant is more advanced than in the upper portion, yet all of the seeds mature at the same time. Semideterminate types reach their mature height earlier, have fewer nodes on the main stem, and more pods at the terminal node of the main stem than indeterminate types of comparable maturity.

The main stem of a determinate cultivar is at or near its full length when flowering begins. Reproductive development occurs simultaneously throughout the length of the plant. Determinate cultivars have fewer nodes on the main stem and more pods at the terminal node of the main stem than indeterminate or semideterminate cultivars of the same maturity.

Indeterminate cultivars are grown commercially at latitudes of 40 degrees or higher and determinate cultivars are produced at latitudes lower than 40 degrees. At the lower latitudes, determinate growth is an effective means of controlling height and lodging of plants. Determinate cultivars are used to a limited extent to control plant height and lodging in highly productive environments at latitudes of 40 degrees or higher. Indeterminate cultivars have been developed for use at lower latitudes with late-season plantings as a means of enhancing plant height and seed yield. Only a few semideterminate cultivars have been developed and grown in the United States; however, they are more widely used in Asia. The shorter plant height of semideterminate cultivars results in a slight reduction in lodging compared with indeterminate cultivars.

BREEDING PROCEDURES

Pure-line cultivars or planned seed mixtures of pure lines are used for commercial production of the soybean. The breeding procedures for development of improved pure lines can be divided into four steps: development of segregating populations, pure line formation, evaluation and selection of superior pure lines, and seed increase of new pure lines for commercial use.

Development of Segregating Populations

The majority of soybean cultivars are selected from single-cross populations formed by artificial hybridization between high-yielding cultivars or pure lines. Because increased seed yield is the character of primary importance in cultivar development, parents that have the highest yield are chosen. Additional characteristics that are considered in parent selection depend on the objectives of the breeding program.

Three-parent crosses and backcross populations are used when a desired characteristic is available in a parent that lacks a high level of agronomic performance. This is particularly true for characteristics that are quantitatively inherited or for which difficulties in evaluation and selection limit the use of extensive backcrossing. The three-parent and backcross populations have been particularly effective for selection of improved cultivars for such characteristics as resistance to the soybean cyst nematode (*Heterodera glycines* Ichinohe).

Populations with multiple parents that are improved by recurrent selection are a potential source of genetic variability for cultivar development. Although recurrent selection has been effective for improvement of populations for characteristics such as protein percentage and iron efficiency of soybeans grown on calcareous soils, only a limited number of cultivars have been selected for commercial use from populations developed by this method.

Artificial mutagenesis has not been used by North American breeders for the development of segregating populations, except when a particular characteristic is not available in existing germplasm.

Pure Line Formation

The inbreeding necessary for the development of pure lines is a natural process in the self-pollinated soybean. Segregating populations are generally inbred to the F_3 to F_6 generations before lines are derived for evaluation as potential cultivars.

The most popular breeding method for the development of pure lines is single seed descent. A bulk sample of F_2 seeds of the population is planted, one or a few seeds is harvested from each plant, and the harvested sample is planted for the next generation of inbreeding. The popularity of the method is due to its suitability for use in winter nurseries and greenhouses where plant productivity is not typical of that observed in the field during the summer. Soybean breeders in North America routinely grow two generations each winter in a tropical environment, such as Belize, Hawaii, or Puerto Rico. The soybean is a short-day plant, and the 12-hour day length in such environments causes rapid flowering and seed development, reduced plant growth, and reduced seed production per plant. Because only one or a few seeds are needed for single seed descent; the limited seed production is not a disadvantage.

Other methods of inbreeding available for pure line formation, including the bulk, pedigree, and early-generation testing, are used to a limited extent by soybean breeders. Their lack of widespread adoption relates in part to the disadvantage of each for use in a winter nursery environment. With the bulk method, undesirable natural selection could occur in a winter nursery environment, reducing the frequency of genotypes that would be superior in the normal summer habitat. In a winter nursery it is not possible to visually select for the pedigree method or conduct replicated trials for early-generation testing for yield, maturity, standability, and other important agronomic traits since genetic differences are not adequately expressed. The inability to take advantage of multiple generations each year for inbreeding increases the length of time for cultivar development compared with the single seed descent method (Fehr, 1978).

Backcrossing has been used extensively for development of pure lines with improved pest resistance that are released as cultivars. The method has been used most extensively for the incorporation of major genes for resistance to phytophthora rot, caused by *Phytophthora megasperma* (Drechs.) var. *sojae* A. A. Hildebrand. The tradition of soybean breeders in the United States has been to name backcross-derived cultivars with the name of the recurrent parent and the year of release of the improved version. Hawkeye 63, Amsoy 71, and Williams 82 are examples of backcross-derived cultivars that differ from their recurrent parent by an allele for resistance to phytophthora rot.

Evaluation and Selection of Superior Pure Lines

Evaluation of genotypes can be based on single plants, single plots, or replicated plots. The selection unit depends on the extent to which the environment can influence expression of the trait and the relative differences among genotypes. Selection for traits controlled by a major gene can be based on single plants. Phytophthora rot is an example of an important pathogen that is controlled by major genes. The evaluation for presence of the major gene is usually carried out in the greenhouse. The most common procedure is to infect individual seedlings by making a small slit in the hypocotyl and inserting a piece of agar containing the fungus. Susceptible plants die after about one week.

Selection on a single-plant basis is commonly practiced for quantitative traits whose expression is not strongly influenced by environmental variation. Time of maturity, plant height, seed size, protein and oil percentage of the seed, and resistance to iron-deficiency chlorosis are examples of traits that can be selected on the basis of single plant performance. Selection is carried out during inbreeding whenever the plants are grown in an environment where differences among genotypes are expressed effectively. Cultivars that are known to differ genetically for the trait are grown as standards and the segregants in the population are compared to them. As an example, segregants in a population are commonly classified for maturity before tests are conducted for seed yield. Cultivars are used as standards that define the appropriate maturity classes.

The evaluation of genotypes for quantitative traits in unreplicated plots commonly precedes more extensive testing in replicated trials. Visual selection for standability, time of maturity, plant height, and pest resistance can eliminate lines that are not adequately uniform or that have an unacceptable level of the trait compared with standard cultivars. Visual selection for seed yield can be effective for eliminating lines that are markedly inferior in productivity, but cannot be relied on for detecting small genetic differences in yield potential. The unreplicated plot also serves to provide a seed increase for subsequent replicated tests.

Replicated tests in different locations and years are required for evaluation of seed yield. The initial evaluation is carried out in a total of two to four replications. The replications may be at a single location or divided among locations. With each subsequent year of evaluation, the number of locations increases to provide an assessment of the ability of a line to perform well under a range of environmental conditions. The plot size also may increase in subsequent years of yield evaluation. The number of lines included in the different stages of testing progressively decreases until one or a few lines are identified that have adequate genetic superiority over existing cultivars to merit release for commercial production.

Seed Increase of New Cultivars for Commercial Use

The production of seed of a new cultivar includes consideration of the timing of the increase relative to evaluation of experimental lines, the amount of seed required, and its genetic purity. It is most desirable to have adequate quantities of breeder seed available when the decision to release a new cultivar is made. This necessitates the purification and increase of lines early in the evaluation process, even though most will be discarded eventually.

The procedures for obtaining genetic purity include selection among individual seeds and plants, progeny evaluation, or both. The most common procedure is to select individual seeds and plants with similar characteristics in one season, and evaluate their progeny for uniformity in the following season. Seed of progeny with similar characteristics for visual traits are bulked to form the breeder seed.

Seed characteristics that are considered for genetic purity are hilum color and seed coat luster. Hilum color is controlled by the interaction of several major genes, which results in several different patterns including yellow, light brown, dark brown, light gray, and black (Fehr, 1978). Seed coat color also can differ; however, all of the cultivars of commercial importance have a yellow seed coat. Seeds with colored seed coats occur as a result of spontaneous mutation and are considered an off-type. There is no preference for hilum color of soybeans that are processed for their protein and oil. Preference for yellow hilum sometimes exists for soybeans that are consumed as human food. Seed coat luster is classified as shiny or dull.

Qualitative plant characteristics of importance for genetic purity are flower, pubescence, and pod color. Flower color is purple or white, pubescence color is brown or gray, and pod color is brown or tan. Quantitative characters that are considered in genetic purity include time of maturity and plant height. In addition, unique characteristics of a cultivar for pest resistance, seed size, or other characters also can be evaluated for achieving genetic purity.

Pure-Line Blends

There is some commercial use of planned seed mixtures, also referred to as blends or multilines. In the United States, blends have been used to obtain a unique product for merchandising and to minimize the risk of growing a pure stand of a cultivar that is susceptible to a production problem.

The merchandising aspect of blends in the United States is based on the desire of seed producers to market a seed product that is different from that of other companies. Under federal law, it is legal to mix seed of two or more cultivars and sell the seed under a brand name assigned by the seed producer. The identification tag for the seed provides the brand name and the statement "Variety not stated". Presumably, two or more seed producers could merchandise the same seed mixture under different brand designations.

The second use of blends relates to the lack of resistance of some high-yielding cultivars to pests or other production hazards that occur sporadically. Seed of the high-yielding susceptible cultivar is mixed with a lower-yielding resistant cultivar. In absence of the production hazard, the blend will yield more than a pure stand of the resistant component, but less than a pure stand of the susceptible cultivar. When plants of the susceptible cultivar are killed or severely damaged, the resistant component will ensure that some yield is realized from the field. Blends currently are marketed to provide protection against phytophthora rot, soybean cyst nematode, and iron-deficiency chlorosis on calcareous soils.

No special breeding procedures have been developed for the development of pure lines for use in a blend. Mixtures of pure lines yield about the same as the average yield of their components. In selecting cultivars for a blend, high yield is a primary consideration. In a blend of high-yielding susceptible and lower-yielding resistant cultivars, the frequency of the high-yielding cultivar is kept at the highest level possible without sacrificing the protection provided by the resistant component.

BREEDING OBJECTIVES

Seed Yield

The character of primary importance in soybean cultivar development is seed yield. The two approaches used to enhance productivity are to develop cultivars with a greater genetic potential for yield *per se* and to develop cultivars that have genetic resistance against production hazards that can prevent a cultivar from expressing its yield potential. In some breeding programs, the two approaches are considered simultaneously during population development and inbred line evaluation, while in other programs they are considered somewhat independently. The approach that is used depends to some extent on the relative importance of production hazards in the area for which the new cultivar is being developed. As an example, some of the major soybean cultivars in the northern United States are not resistant to phytophthora rot or soybean cyst nematode because the pests do not cause economic loss in all areas of the region. In some areas of the southern United States where the two pests consistently cause serious yield loss, cultivars without resistance to these two pests are not released for commercial use.

When genetic potential for yield is considered independent of the resistance to production hazards, parent selection is based primarily on the yield potential of available germplasm. Selection of superior segregants within the population is based primarily on seed yield in replicated tests. Pure lines with superior yield potential are released for commercial use. In these same breeding programs, genes for resistance to production hazards are incorporated in high-yielding pure lines by some form of backcrossing. The resistant lines are released for commercial use in areas where the susceptible version cannot be produced reliably.

Simultaneous selection for yield and resistance to production hazards requires that at least one parent of a population has the necessary genes for resistance. Segregating populations are exposed to the production hazard during pure line formation and only resistant lines are chosen for evaluation in replicated yield tests.

Time of Maturity

Soybean cultivars are classified into maturity groups from 000 to X that relate to the latitude at which they are adapted for commercial production (Fig. 13.3). Standard cultivars are used in determining the maturity group of genotypes developed in a breeding program. Classification of genotypes for maturity is necessary to ensure that they are evaluated for yield in the area to which they are best adapted.

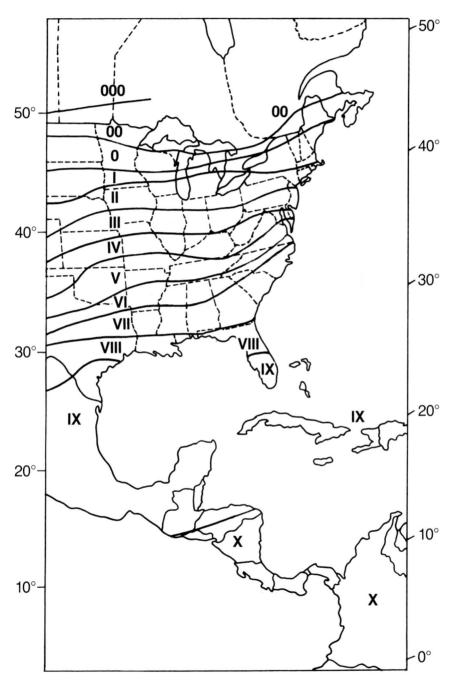

Fig. 13.3 Maturity classification of soybean cultivars relative to the area in which they are grown commercially.

Lodging Resistance

Excessive lodging of soybeans can reduce seed yield and make mechanical harvest difficult. Selection for adequate lodging resistance is an important criterion in soybean breeding; however, there is no uniform standard for determining how much lodging can be tolerated in a cultivar. In rating the lodging of soybean genotypes, a score of one represents all genotypes perfectly upright and three indicates that the main stems of the plants are leaning at a 45 degree angle. Most breeders do not insist that a cultivar have a rating of one in all environments, but likely would reject a genotype that consistently rates higher than a three.

Breeding for lodging resistance generally involves selection among plants with indeterminate stem termination in maturity groups IV and earlier, and among determinate types in maturity groups V and later. The exception would be the development of determinate types of maturity groups IV and earlier for use in high-yielding environments where lodging is a consistent problem.

Shattering Resistance

The ability of soybeans to retain their seeds after maturity is an essential characteristic. Cultivars commonly used as parents for population development have a high level of shattering resistance; therefore, the majority of their progeny are acceptable for the trait. When plant introductions are used as parents, however, selection for shattering resistance can be an important consideration.

Mineral Deficiencies and Toxicities

There is extensive variation among soybean cultivars for the ability to effectively utilize iron when grown on certain calcareous soils (Fehr, 1984). Selection for improved levels of resistance to iron-deficiency chlorosis has resulted in the development of lines that serve as useful parents in cultivar development programs. Breeding for iron efficiency and high yield is practiced in areas where calcareous soils are prevalent.

Mineral toxicity can reduce yields on highly acid soils. There is genetic variation for the trait; however, resistance to mineral toxicity generally is not an objective in cultivar development. This may be due in part to the production practice of liming acid soils to raise the pH, which eliminates or reduces mineral toxicity in soybean.

Disease, Nematode and Insect Resistance

Pest resistance is an objective of virtually every cultivar development program in soybeans. The pests of major importance vary among locations; therefore, breeding programs differ in the pests that are considered and the amount of resources devoted to selection for genetic resistance (Sinclair, 1984). In Florida, the root knot nematode, caused by *Meloidogyne* spp., can cause major economic losses. Genetic resistance to the pest is an important objective for developing new cultivars to be grown in that area. In most of the other soybean-producing areas of the United States, the root knot nematode is not of economic importance and genetic resistance to the pest is not considered in cultivar development.

Specific resistance, general resistance, and tolerance are considered in developing cultivars that will not sustain economic injury from a pest. Specific resistance controlled by one or a few major genes has been an important means of control for many pests, including phytophthora rot and downy mildew, caused by *Peronspora manshurica* (Naum.) Syd. ex Gaum. General resistance is important in providing protection against severe loss to a number of pests, including brown stem rot, caused by *Phialophora gregata* (Allington and Chamberl.) W. Gams. and phytophthora rot. The usefulness of tolerance in minimizing loss from pests is currently under investigation for control of the soybean cyst nematode and the root knot nematode.

Seed Composition and Size

The soybean is a major crop because of the protein and oil content of its seed. Nevertheless, the composition of the seed is not considered when the crop is marketed by the farmer. As a result of the lack of any economic incentive for producing seed with a particular protein and oil composition, the farmer does not consider the character when selecting a cultivar. Likewise, the breeder does not select for protein and oil composition when developing cultivars for general commercial use.

High protein percentage is preferred for soybeans that are used for the production of tofu, a soft curd made from soymilk. Despite the preference for high protein, the majority of the product is made from seed of conventional commercial cultivars. There is a small demand for high-protein seed for which the purchaser is willing to pay a premium. This market is satisfied with cultivars that have above-average protein, but lower yield than conventional cultivars.

Soybean seeds of current cultivars contain enzymes that reduce the digestion and utilization of the protein. Research is underway to reduce or eliminate the anti-nutritional factors; thereby, reducing or eliminating the need for heat treatment of seeds before they are consumed. A major gene has been identified that eliminates one of the anti-nutritional factors, the Kunitz trypsin inhibitor (Orf and Hymowitz, 1979). The commercial usefulness of seeds lacking the Kunitz trypsin inhibitor is under investigation.

Genetic modification of the fatty acid composition of soybean oil has been achieved (Hammond and Fehr, 1984). Oil from lines with lower levels of linolenic acid may reduce or eliminate the need for chemical hydrogenation of oil to obtain products with acceptable flavour. Lines with oil containing high stearic acid may be useful in the development of unique products. Research is underway to determine the economic value of the oils with unique fatty acid composition. The seed size of conventional cultivars is between 12 and 20 g/ 100 seeds. The character is not given special attention in developing cultivars for general commercial use. There is a limited market for a seed size of less than 10 g/ 100 seeds for the use in soy sprouts and for a fermented Japanese product called natto. There also is a small market for a seed size of greater than 20 g/ 100 seeds when soybeans are consumed as a green vegetable, as a confectionery product, and as a fermented Japanese product called miso.

HISTORY OF CULTIVAR DEVELOPMENT

Cultivar development began in Asia with selection for preferred plant and seed characteristics by the persons who first understood its value as a food source. Differences in preference among the early cultivators of the soybean led to a wide range of native cultivars. Cultivar development was based on selection within heterogeneous natural populations of *G. max*. As seeds of the soybean were taken from their place of origin to other countries of the world, selection was practiced among and within the native cultivars for those best suited to the new environment and which had the characteristics desired by the producer.

The importance of selection among plant introductions as a means of cultivar development can be illustrated with the development of the crop in the United States, Brazil, and Argentina. The first soybean cultivars grown extensively in the United States during the early 1900s were native cultivars from Asia (Hartwig, 1973). The plant introductions brought to the United States were named and released for commercial use. Selection also was practiced within heterogeneous plant introductions to develop pure-line cultivars.

Cultivars developed by hybridization were first grown commercially in the United States during the 1940s. Plant introductions that were successful as cultivars were used as parents to develop segregating populations. Superior pure lines selected from the populations were released as cultivars and were used as parents for the second cycle of hybridization conducted during the 1940s and 1950s. Cultivars selected from the second cycle were in turn used as parents for the third cycle of hybridization during the 1960s and 1970s. Most of the cultivars of commercial importance today are from the third and fourth cycle of hybridization and selection.

The rapid expansion of soybean production in Brazil during the past two decades was based initially on the use of cultivars introduced from the United States. Those cultivars and plant introductions from other countries were used as parents to initiate hybridization and selection. Cultivars selected from the initial hybridization programs are widely used for commercial production in Brazil.

Extensive soybean production in Argentina began during the 1970s. At present, the most widely grown cultivars for commercial production were introduced from Brazil and the United States. Breeding programs have been initiated in Argentina to develop cultivars that are well suited to its climatic conditions.

UTILIZATION OF PRODUCTS

The soybean is utilized primarily as a source of protein and oil. The crop was used as forage in the past, but it is no longer important for that purpose.

Soybean seed is an important food in the diets of millions of people in the world. The immature seeds are eaten as a green vegetable. Mature seeds are roasted for consumption as a confectionery product. Soymilk is produced by grinding seeds that have been soaked in water (Orthoefer, 1978). The liquid is consumed directly or can be flavoured artificially. Soymilk is the base for production of tofu, one of the principal ways in which the soybean is consumed in Asia. A coagulant is added to the soymilk to obtain a soft curd (Cowan, 1973). Tofu is consumed fresh, frozen, or dried. It is fried or prepared in a variety of other manners according to the custom of the consumer.

Some soybean products for human consumption are prepared by fermentation (Cowan, 1973). Soy sauce is probably the best known of the fermented products. Miso is a fermented paste to which water is added to obtain a clear soup. Temph is a solid product obtained by fermenting soybean seed with a fungus.

In the major soybean producing countries of Argentina, Brazil, and the United States, the majority of the seed is processed within the country or is exported. The initial products from processing are defatted protein meal or flakes and crude oil. Over 90% of the protein obtained from processing is used as livestock feed. Soybean seed is not consumed directly as a protein feed because it contains enzymes that prevent proper digestion of protein. A heat treatment is required to inactivate the enzyme.

Defatted protein meal is processed into a number of products that vary in protein percentage (Orthoefer, 1978). Flour and grits containing 49% protein are used in bakery and other food products. Concentrates with 70% protein and isolates with 90% protein are used to replace nonfat milk solids in meat products, in bakery products, and for the manufacture of textured protein with meat-like qualities. The textured protein is used as replacement for meat in pet foods, as a gound meat extender, and as simulated edible meats. Soybean protein also has industrial use in adhesives and coatings.

Crude soybean oil is refined into a number of useful products. The majority of soybean oil is consumed as salad oil, shortening and margarine. The oil usually is hydrogenated chemically to reduce the content of linolenic acid from about 8% to 3% or less, which results in a longer shelf life. Specialty oils are used for preparation of frozen desserts, cookie shortenings, confections, icings, ice cream coating, whipped toppings, and coffee whiteners. Industrial uses of soybean oil include soap, paints, resins, and drying oil.

REFERENCES

Bernard, R.L. 1973. Qualitative genetics, pp. 117-154. *In* B.E. Caldwell (ed.), *Soybeans: Improvement, Production, and Uses.* Am. Soc. Agron., Madison, Wis.

Brown, A.H.D., Grant, J.E., Burdon J.J., Grace J.P., and Pullen, R. 1985. Collection and utilization of wild perennial *Glycine*, pp. 345-352. *In* R. Shibles (ed.), Proc. World Soybean Research Conference III, Westview Press, Boulder, Colo.

Cowan, J.C. 1973. Processing and Products, pp. 619-664. *In* B.E. Caldwell (ed.), *Soybeans: Improvement, Production and Uses.* Am. Soc. Agron., Madison, Wis.

Fehr, W.R. 1978. Breeding, pp. 119-155. *In* A.G. Norman (ed.), *Soybean Physiology, Agronomy, and Utilization.* Academic Press, New York.

——. 1980. Soybean, pp. 589-599. *In* W.R. Fehr and H.H. Hadley (eds.), *Hybridization of Crop Plants.* Am. Soc. Agron., Madison, Wis.

——. 1984. Current practices for correcting iron deficiency in plants with emphasis on genetics. J. Plant Nutr. 7: 347-354.

Hammond, E.G., and Fehr, W.R. 1984. Improving the fatty acid composition of soybean oil. J. Am. Oil Chem. Soc. 61: 1713-1716.

Hartwig, E.E. 1973. Varietal development, pp. 187-210. *In* B.E. Caldwell (ed.), *Soybeans: Improvement, Production, and Uses.* Am. Soc. Agron., Madison, Wis.

Hymowitz, T., and Newell, C.A. 1981. Taxonomy of the genus *Glycine*, domestication and uses of soybeans. Econ. Bot. 35: 272-288.

Orf, J.H., and Hymowitz, T. 1979. Inheritance of the absence of the Kunitz trypsin inhibitor in seed protein of soybeans. Crop Sci. 19: 107-109.

Orthoefer, F.T. 1978. Processing and utilization, pp. 219-246. *In* A.G. Norman (ed.), *Soybean Physiology, Agronomy, and Utilization.* Academic Press, New York.

Severa, F. 1983. Schester Bernadines große Naturapotheke, p. 154. Mosaik Verlag, Munchen.

Sinclair, J.B. (ed.). 1984. Compendium of Soybean Diseases, 2nd ed. Am. Phytopathol. Soc., St. Paul, Minn.

Whigham, D.K., and Minor, H.C. 1978. Agronomic characteristics and environmental stress, pp. 77-118. *In* A.G. Norman (ed.), *Soybean Physiology, Agronomy, and Utilization.* Academic Press, New York.

Chapter 14

Sunflower

G. N. Fick

IMPORTANCE AND DISTRIBUTION

Sunflower ranks second to soybean among annual field crops grown in the world for production of edible oil. Total production of sunflower oil in 1984-1985 was estimated at about 6.1 million metric tonnes as compared to about 14.0 million metric tonnes for soybean (Mielke, 1985-1986). The quantity of sunflower oil represents about 14% of the total world production of the nine major vegetable oils.

Sunflower (Fig. 14.1) performs well in most temperate zone regions of the world, with significant production occurring in each of the six crop-producing continents. Europe is the leading producer of sunflower seed, accounting for about 60% of the world's total production of over 19 million metric tonnes. Among individual countries the USSR is the largest producer with over four million hectares grown annually and total seed production in excess of five million metric tonnes (Table 14.1). Argentina is the second leading producer with an estimated 2.3 million hectares for the 1984-85 season and 3.4 million metric tonnes of production. Other leading producers are China, the USA, Spain, France, Romania, Turkey, Hungary, Bulgaria, India, Australia, South Africa and Yugoslavia.

Fig.14.1 – A. Sunflower plant in early flowering stage.
B. Typical plants in North Dakota sunflower field.
C. Seeds of oilseed sunflower.

Table 14.1 World Sunflower Seed Production by Region and Major Producing Countries.

Region or Country	Production area ('000 ha)			Seed yield (kg/ha)			Seed production ('000 tonnes)		
	1969-71	1979-81	1985	1969-71	1979-81	1985	1969-71	1979-81	1985
World	**8413**	**12252**	**14589**	**1173**	**1175**	**1308**	**9872**	**14396**	**19078**
Africa	**230**	**558**	**608**	**680**	**969**	**736**	**156**	**541**	**447**
South Africa	140	326	320	757	1195	822	106	389	263
N. and C. America	**175**	**1883**	**1239**	**965**	**1347**	**1236**	**169**	**2536**	**1532**
Canada	48	138	71	809	1328	1153	39	183	82
U.S.A.	110	1741	1151	1101	1349	1242	121	2347	1430
S. America	**1398**	**1694**	**2445**	**736**	**913**	**1438**	**1209**	**3087**	**4910**
Argentina	1283	1546	2350	739	925	1460	949	1447	3430
Asia	**515**	**1448**	**2668**	**985**	**1123**	**1194**	**507**	**1626**	**3186**
Burma	1	40	131	326	374	469	-	15	65
China	81	750	1190	873	1147	1597	71	860	1901
India	-	100	689	-	655	530	-	66	365
Turkey	347	507	600	1104	1260	1333	383	638	800
Europe	**1347**	**2134**	**3207**	**1404**	**1446**	**1531**	**1930**	**3087**	**4910**
Bulgaria	277	246	260	1697	1713	1654	471	421	430
France	31	117	635	1768	2393	2378	55	280	2378
Hungary	98	268	343	1243	1870	1960	122	500	672
Romania	562	511	480	1370	4641	1500	769	838	720
Spain	179	677	1125	803	760	813	146	515	915
Yugoslavia	199	211	112	1679	1823	2088	334	385	233
Oceania	**38**	**226**	**338**	**680**	**687**	**760**	**26**	**156**	**257**
Australia	38	226	338	680	687	760	26	156	257
U.S.S.R.	**4682**	**4307**	**4085**	**1293**	**1138**	**1280**	**6055**	**4903**	**5230**

Source: FAO Production Yearbooks 1980 (vol. 34) and 1985 (vol. 39).

Sunflower derives most of its economic value from the oil extracted from the seed, the remaining value from the meal. The oil is considered of very high quality and generally sells for a premium in world markets over soybean, palm (*Elaeis guineensis* Jacq.) and rapeseed (*Brassica* spp.) oils. The sunflower meal, obtained after the oil is extracted from the seed, has a high protein percentage and is used primarily in food rations for livestock and poultry. It traditionally sells at prices competitive to cottonseed meal (*Gossypium hirsutum* L.)

Although sunflower is grown primarily for its oil, there is limited production of certain cultivars grown for nonoilseed or confection purposes, especially in the USA. The edible kernel is the main marketable product of the nonoilseed production. Total nonoilseed production in the USA for 1985 was estimated at 120,000 metric tonnes from about 100,000 hectares. Significant nonoilseed production is grown also in Spain, China, Turkey, the USSR, Canada and other countries, but accurate production figures are not generally available.

ORIGIN AND SYSTEMATICS

The cultivated sunflower (*Helianthus annuus* L.) is a member of the family Compositae (*Asteraceae*). The closest relatives appear to be *Viguiera, Tithonia* and *Phoebanthus* (Heiser et al. 1969).

The genus name for sunflower is derived from the Greek *helios*, meaning "sun," and *anthos*, meaning "flower." The Spanish name for sunflower, *girasol*, and the French name, *tournesol*, mean literally "turn with the sun," a trait exhibited by sunflower until anthesis after which the heads face east.

According to Heiser et al. (1969), the most widely recognized publication on *Helianthus* taxonomy, the genus is comprised of sixty-seven species, all native to the Americas. The genus is divided into four sections: I. Annui--thirteen species, mostly annuals, of North America; II. Ciliares--six perennial species of western North America; III. Divaricati--thirty perennial species mostly of eastern North America, which are placed in five series; and IV. Fruticosi--South American shrubby species, which appear to have an origin separate from that of the North American species, and recently have been transferred to the new genus *Helianthopus* by Robinson (1979).

The genus *Helianthus* has a basic chromosome number of n=17, and diploid, tetraploid and hexaploid species occur. Information on interspecific hybridization among the species was summarized by Whelan (1978) and by Chandler and Beard (1983). The use of wild species in breeding programs to develop improved cultivars has proven extremely useful in recent years, especially for disease and insect resistance.

While the common sunflower *H. annuus* L. is by far the most important species of sunflowers grown commercially, several additional species are also cultivated. These include *H. tuberosus* L. which is grown for production of edible tubers, and several species which are grown as ornamentals, the principal ones being wild *H. annuus, H. argophyllus* T. & G., *H. debilis* Nutt., *H. decapetalus* L., *H. X laetiflorus* Pers., *H. maximiliani* Schrad., *H. X multiflorus* L., and *H. salicifolius* A. Dietr.

Heiser (1978) suggests that the most plausible hypothesis on the origin of cultivated sunflower is that the wild sunflower (*H. annuus*) of the western USA became a camp-following weed of the North American Indians. With time it was introduced into the central part of the country where it was domesticated for use primarily as food. Archaeological evidence indicates the occurrence of heads and achenes of domesticated types of sunflower as early as the first millenium B.C., and at least one reference suggests cultivation began as early as 3000 B.C. (Semelczi-Kovacs, 1975). During the early 16th century European visitors to America introduced the sunflower to Europe, principally to Spain from where it spread throughout the continent. It was grown initially as an ornamental and later for food and medicinal purposes.

Sunflower was developed as an important source of oil during the early 1800s in Russia. The success of the Soviet breeders in improving the oil content of seeds from less than 30% to over 50% was a major factor in the development of sunflower as a major world oilseed crop.

MODE OF REPRODUCTION

Sunflower is distinguished from other cultivated crops by its single stem and conspicuous, large inflorescence (Fig. 14.1A and B). Knowles (1978) provides detailed information on morphological and anatomical characteristics of the stems, leaves, roots, inflorescence and achenes (commonly called seeds). Of major interest to the plant breeder is the inflorescence because it determines in part the appropriate breeding procedures and crossing techniques.

The inflorescence or head of the sunflower consists of an outer whorl of showy and generally yellow ray flowers, and from 700 to 3000 or more individual disk flowers arranged in arcs radiating from the center of the head (Fig. 14.2). The ray flowers are normally sterile having vestigial styles and stigmas but no anthers. The disk florets, which produce the seeds, are perfect flowers, each with a tubular corolla and anther column. The flowering process and the development of individual disk flowers has been described in detail by Putt (1940) and Knowles (1978).

For self pollination or controlled crosses the heads must be covered with bags or otherwise isolated prior to flowering to prevent natural cross-pollination. Artificial hybrids are produced by emasculation of the female parent. This involves removing the anthers of the disk flowers with forceps early in the morning before the anthers have dehisced, and before the stigmas have extended far enough into the anther tubes to be damaged by removal of the anthers. The stigmas remain receptive for up to 4 or 5 days, but normally pollen is best applied the day after emasculation when the stigmatic lobes have separated and the receptive

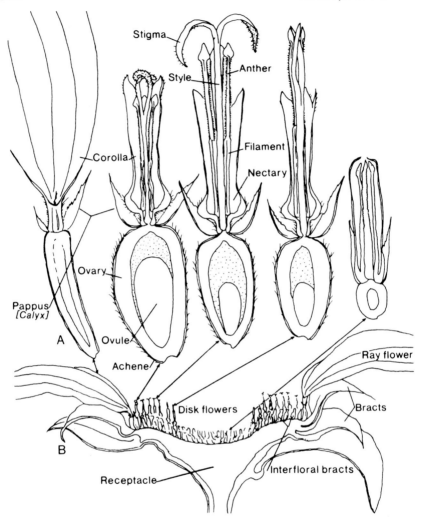

Fig. 14.2 Longitudinal section of a sunflower head with individual flowers. A. Left, single ray flower: right, four disk flowers in different stages of development, X3.5. Head, X0.35. Reproduced from Sunflower Science and Technology, Agronomy Monograph No. 19:70, 1978 by permission of the American Society of Agronomy, Inc.

surfaces are exposed. Pollen for crossing may be collected from heads, isolated with bags prior to flowering, and applied with a small piece of cotton, a brush, a section of leaf, or other suitable applicator. Heads of genetic, cytoplasmic or gibberellic acid-induced male sterile plants are pollinated without emasculation, often simply by bumping heads with a designated male parent planted in an adjacent row of a breeding nursery. Additional details on sunflower pollination and crossing techniques are given by Fick (1978) and Dedio and Putt (1980).

BREEDING PROCEDURES

Sunflower is a highly cross-pollinated crop, with pollination occurring primarily by insects and only to a limited degree by wind. A system of genetic self-incompatibility exists in certain lines, but generally a wide range of self-fertility occurs among individual plants in breeding populations. Most breeding procedures utilized in maize (*Zea mays* L.) and other cross-pollinated crops are suitable for sunflower, with certain modifications required due to floral morphology. Development of hybrids is the primary objective of most breeding programs, although improved open-pollinated varieties and synthetic cultivars may also have value, especially in countries where hybrid seed production is not feasible for technical or economic reasons.

Breeding procedures for sunflower were reviewed by Fick (1978). Mass selection was commonly used during the early stages of cultivar improvement, especially in the USSR and also in Argentina. The procedure was effective in developing cultivars with earlier maturity, resistance to broomrape (*Orobanche cumana* Wallr.), seeds possessing the armor layer, disease resistance and higher oil percentage.

The "method of reserves" developed by Pustovoit in the USSR for improving cultivars was widely used and highly successful in improving oil content and certain other traits of sunflower. The method is a form of recurrent selection that includes progeny evaluation and subsequent cross pollination among superior progenies (Fig. 14.3).

According to Pustovoit (1967) from 10,000 to 15,000 plants are selected from a heterogeneous population, and their seed analyzed for hull and oil percentage. Based on these analyses the progeny from 1000 to 1200 heads are evaluated for agronomic, disease and seed quality traits in single row plots with two replications. A check, consisting of the best cultivar most similar to the lines being evaluated, is included in every third plot as a control. On the basis of the first year observations, 15 to 20% of the best plants are evaluated for a second year using reserve seed from the reserve plants, and similar testing procedures. After the second year the original seed of the best remaining 20 to 50 plants is planted in a replicated isolation nursery for cross-pollination. Undesirable plants are removed during the season, seeds from individual heads are again analyzed for hull and oil percentage, and the seed from the best plants is mixed for use in the next cycle of selection, for cultivar testing and for seed production.

Inbreeding as a method of improving sunflower was used as early as the 1920s. The most common procedure is to self-pollinate phenotypically desirable plants within existing cultivars, populations, or segregating generations of planned crosses. Selection is practiced at harvest for agronomic type, disease resistance or other desired traits. After threshing, seeds are further evaluated in laboratory or greenhouse tests for seed and kernel characteristics and seedlings for disease reaction. Progenies from the best plants are planted the next season in

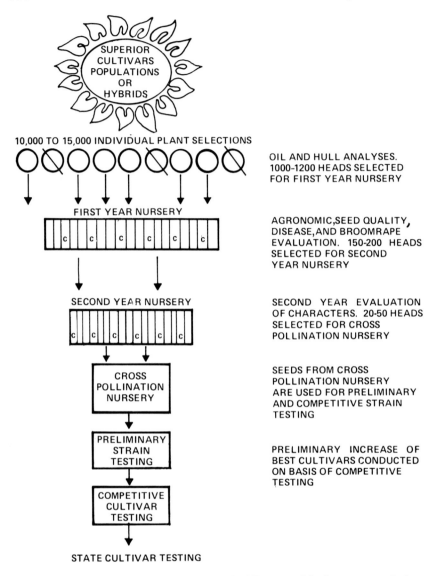

Fig. 14.3 Diagram of Pustovoit "Method of Reserves" for improvement of sunflower cultivars. Reproduced from Sunflower Science and Technology, Agronomy Monograph No. 19:282, by permission of the American Society of Agronomy, Inc.

head rows where selection is continued among and within progeny rows. The process of inbreeding and selection may continue for 2 to 5 generations before the lines are tested for combining ability. Inbreeding may decrease yield from 30 to 60%, with most of the reduction occurring during the first 3 or 4 generations.

The final merit of an inbred line for use in a hybrid or a synthetic cultivar can be determined only by its performance in hybrid combinations. Testing for general or specific combining ability involves production of hybrid seed using an appropriate tester line which is usually a genetic, cytoplasmic, or gibberellic acid-induced male sterile. Normally the test crosses are made by hand or in isolated crossing blocks. Subsequent evaluation of the hybrids is then conducted in the areas of potential use, often for a 2 or 3 year period. Methods for field evaluation of lines and hybrids for agronomic, disease and seed quality characteristics have been described by Fick (1978).

Inbred lines are used primarily in the production of single crosses or three way hybrids using the cytoplasmic male sterility and fertility restorer system. The backcross method is used to develop and maintain cytoplasmic male sterile lines for use in seed production. Fertility restoring lines can also be developed by backcrossing, but an easier procedure is to cross plants with restorer genes to a cytoplasmic male sterile line and select male fertile plants in subsequent generations.

Utilization of inbred lines to produce synthetic cultivars, while not used extensively, may have value in certain areas of the world where hybrid seed production is not practical. Synthetics with significantly higher yields than open-pollinated check cultivars have been produced from relatively few inbred lines. In order to maximize heterosis in a synthetic, the lines utilized must not only have good combining ability but also be relatively self-incompatible with a strong tendency to cross-pollinate. The latter trait is necessary in order to minimize inbreeding during seed multiplication and subsequent loss in seed yield and oil content.

Recurrent selection has been used as a method for improving source populations and thus increasing the chances of success in isolating superior inbred lines. The procedure has been successful in increasing seed yield, oil percentage and certain other traits. Miller and Hammond (1985) reported on a reciprocal full-sib sunflower selection scheme in which, after three cycles of selection, the yield of hybrids derived from the source populations increased an average of 70 kg/ha or 6.3% per cycle. In addition to improving the breeding populations, the scheme was also effective in identifying lines with good general combining ability.

During the last decade molecular biology and genetic engineering have received a great deal of attention as basic techniques for improving plants. Regeneration of plants from cell culture is being used to create new sources of genetic variability in a wide range of crop species including sunflower, and transfer of genes for pest resistance, stress tolerance or other traits from one species to another is likely. An example in sunflower is the transfer and subsequent expression of the bean (*Phaseolus vulgaris* L.) seed protein phaseolin in sunflower cells grown in tissue culture (Murai et al. 1983). Other biotechnology procedures that may be useful to breeders include the production of doubled haploids by anther or microspore culture procedures and transfer of cytoplasmic male sterility by micro injection techniques. Although it is too early to determine the full impact that genetic engineering will have on sunflower improvement, it seems likely to become an important supplement to conventional sunflower breeding.

BREEDING OBJECTIVES

Objectives in sunflower breeding vary with specific programs and with production areas but generally emphasize high seed yield and high oil percentage. High seed yield depends on many factors including suitable agronomic type, tolerance to stress environments, and resistance to diseases, insects and other pests. Generally, characteristics that contribute to good vegetative plant growth are associated with high yield. These include days from sowing to maturity, plant height, head diameter, stem diameter, leaf area per plant, seed weight and disease resistance. A high degree of self-fertility is also considered important for high yield in many areas, especially where insect-pollinator populations are limiting. Where stalk breakage caused by strong winds and storms during the growing season is a problem, dwarf sunflower hybrids that grow only about one meter tall have shown yield advantages (Fick et al. 1985).

The oil percentage of the achenes is determined primarily by their hull content and by oil percentage of the kernel. The heritability of oil percentage is relatively high and good progress has been made in increasing oil content from approximately 30% in the 1920s to over 50% among current cultivars. Evaluation and selection for high oil has been greatly facilitated in recent years by development of wide line nuclear magnetic resonance (NMR) spectroscopy. The NMR analysis of whole seed samples is rapid, accurate and non-destructive.

Wide genetic variation, which serves as the basis for developing improved cultivars, occurs in sunflower for agronomic and morphological traits, seed and kernel characteristics, and resistance to pests (Fick, 1978). Examples of the type of variation that exist include wide ranges in the vegetation period (65 to 165 days), plant height (50 to 400 cm), number of disk flowers per head (100 to 8000) and oil percentage of the kernel (26 to 72%). Resistance or tolerance to most of the important diseases has also been identified, especially among the wild species of sunflower. Sunflower disease symptoms are color illustrated by Zimmer and Hoes (1978) and the American Phytopathological Society "Diseases of Sunflowers" 35mm. slide set No. 41.

Because of the importance of diseases, breeding for resistance is a major objective of most sunflower improvement programs. Rust (*Puccinia helianthi* Schw.), downy mildew (*Plasmopara halstedi* (Farl.) Berl & de Toni), Verticillium wilt (*Verticillium dahliae* Klebahn), Sclerotinia stalk and head rot (*Sclerotinia sclerotiorum* (Lib.) de Bary and Phoma black stem (*Phoma macdonaldii* Boerma) are considered major diseases in the USA and Canada.

Resistance to rust was identified among crosses of wild annual sunflower in early studies by Putt and Sackston (1957). Two dominant genes, R1 from the accession 953 – 102 and R2 from 953 – 88, have been used extensively by breeders throughout the world to develop resistant cultivars. Studies on wild sunflower suggest that many different races of rust and many different genes for resistance occur. In the absence of specific genes for resistance the "slow rusting" or field resistance exhibited by many of the Soviet cultivars has been adequate to prevent serious losses in most environments.

Resistance to downy mildew is controlled by single dominant genes, all of which trace to the wild species. Resistant cultivars are available in the major production areas of Europe where the disease is a major problem, and until recently in the USA and Canada. During the early 1980s new races of downy mildew were identified in the USA to which all cultivars grown at the time were susceptible. New resistance genes have been identified and are being incorporated into commercial cultivars (Fick and Auwarter, 1982).

Resistance to Verticillium wilt occurs among both cultivated and wild sunflower species. The inbred line HA 89, with a single dominant gene for resistance, has been used extensively in breeding programs to produce resistant hybrids.

Significant differences exist among sunflower genotypes for resistance to Sclerotinia stalk and head rot, but generally the level of tolerance is not considered adequate for control. Recent studies suggest that lines with the best resistance have less than one-half of the infection percentage of highly susceptible lines (Fick et al. 1983), and that lines or hybrids can be developed that have better resistance than those currently available.

Resistance or differences in susceptibility among genotypes have been reported for Phoma blackstem, Alternaria leaf and stem spot (*Alternaria* spp.), Septoria leaf spot (*Septoria helianthi* Ell & Kell.), charcoal stem rot [*Macrophomina phaseoli* (Tassi) Goid], powdery mildew (*Erysiphe cichoracearium* DC), Phomopsis stem canker (*Diaporthe helianthi* Munt.-Cvet. et al.) and other diseases, but generally genetic information is lacking. Breeding for resistance to most of these diseases appears feasible.

Unlike diseases, resistance to the major insect pests of sunflower is generally not available although a few examples have been reported. Resistance to the sunflower moth (*Homoeosoma nebulella* Hb.), which occurs in eastern Europe, is determined by the presence of a dark colored "armor" layer in the seed coat. The armor layer is also at least partially effective in reducing damage from the sunflower moth (*H. electellum* Hulst) which attacks the North American crop. Resistance to the sunflower midge (*Contarinia schulzi* Gagne) and to the sunflower beetle (*Zygogramma exclamationis* Fab.) has also been suggested (Fick, 1978; Fick and Auwarter, 1981). At least some resistance to several additional insect pests of cultivated sunflower has been reported among the wild species of *Helianthus* (Gershenzon et al. 1985).

Breeding to improve seed and oil quality characteristics has generally not been an important objective in developing improved cultivars, although significant genetic variation exists for the protein and lipid fractions of seeds.

Protein percentage of seeds has been reported to vary from 9 to 24 and of kernels from 24 to 40 (Fick, 1978). Significant differences in amino acids composition of the protein have also been reported.

The fatty acid composition of sunflower oil varies with the environment, but in the northern production area of the USA the fatty acid composition has been approximately 6% palmitic, 5% stearic, 19% oleic and 68% linoleic. However, some sunflower lines have been identified recently that produce up to 90% oleic acid regardless of the environment under which they are grown(Fick, 1984). Hybrids from these lines were grown on about 20,000 hectares in the USA in 1985. It is expected that these high oleic types will create new markets for sunflower oil, especially in the areas of deep fat frying and where greater oxidative stability of sunflower oil is required.

While most breeding efforts have been centered on the improvement of oilseed cultivars, significant research also has been conducted on nonoilseed or confection types. Important objectives in breeding nonoilseed types include large seed size, a high kernel-to-hull ratio, and uniformity in seed size, shape and color.

HISTORY OF CULTIVAR DEVELOPMENT

Aside from the local strains of sunflower grown by the North American Indians, the first cultivars grown for significant commercial production were developed in the USSR. According to Pustovoit (1967), large numbers of local peasant cultivars were available by the 1880s, some of which had higher yield, greater uniformity in plant and seed type, and improved resistance to broomrape (*Orobanche cumana* Wallr.) and the sunflower moth, compared to unimproved strains. The largest group of local cultivars was known as Zelenka, with Chernyanka, Fuksinka and Puzanok also comprising large groups of widely grown types.

The first cultivars developed at experiment stations in the USSR were introduced during the first part of the 20th century. Resistance to broomrape and the sunflower moth were the main improvements over previously grown types. Saratov 169, Kruglik A-41 and Zhdanovsky 8281 were several of the more popular cultivars grown. Kruglik A-41, introduced in 1927, was among the first cultivars to be developed with significantly higher oil percentage, confirming that sunflower could in fact be improved for this trait.

Seed oil percentages among Soviet cultivars increased from less than 30 in the early 1900s to over 40 during the 1930s and to over 50 by the early 1960s. Peredovik and Armavirsky 3497 were two of the most widely grown cultivars in the USSR during the last twenty years, each accounting for about 1.2 million hectares of production in 1966. Peredovik, which was introduced in 1960, also was grown extensively in the USA, Canada, Europe and other parts of the world prior to the introduction of hybrids. Peredovik is a very widely adapted cultivar, high in oil percentage, of medium height and maturity, moderately resistant to the diseases rust and Verticillium wilt, and resistant to broomrape and the sunflower moth. Cultivars developed relatively recently in the USSR include Sputnik, Voshod and Mayak with very high oil percentage; Progress and Novinka with disease resistance transferred from *H. tuberosus*; and Pervenets with high oleic acid oil.

The first hybrid sunflower cultivars were introduced for commercial production in Canada in 1946 (Putt, 1962). Advance, and later Advent and Admiral, were grown for most of the oilseed production in that country during the 1950s. These hybrids were produced by natural crossing in seed production fields, with the two parents planted in alternating groups of rows. Because self and sib pollination occurred on the female parent in addition to the desired cross pollination, hybridization percentages were often less than 50 and the full yield potential of the hybrids was not realized.

Genic male sterility was used to produce hybrid seed in France and Romania during the early 1970s. A close linkage between genes for male sterility and anthocyanin pigment in the seedling leaves allowed easy identification and removal of the male fertile plants prior to flowering, thus allowing nearly 100% hybridization. Some of the best hybrids produced by the genic male sterile system yielded up to 24% more than open-pollinated check cultivars. INRA 6501 in France and Romsun 52 and Romsun 53 in Romania were some of the more common hybrids grown.

The first hybrids produced by the cytoplasmic male sterile and nuclear fertility restorer system (Fig. 14.4) were introduced in the USA in 1972, and within five years were grown on about 90% of the production area. The best hybrids yielded over 20% more than the open-pollinated cultivars available at that time. The hybrids were also highly self-compatible, resistant to rust, downy mildew and Verticillium wilt, and more uniform than the former cultivars in height, flowering and maturity. Hybrid 894 was one of the most popular hybrids. It is estimated that at one time it or closely related types were grown on as much as 80% of the production area in the USA, and also on large areas throughout Europe, South America, and other regions of the world.

Improved cultivars for nonoilseed production also trace their origin to the USSR. Nonoilseed types known as Giant or Mammoth Russian were introduced into North America during the 19th century, and were grown in gardens for food by the early Russian immigrants to the USA and Canada. These types served as the basis for the development of improved cultivars for commercial production. Mennonite, Mingren, Commander, and Sundak, all of which had relatively good seed size, shape and color suitable for the nonoilseed markets, were the principal cultivars grown during the 1950s through the late 1970s period. Nonoilseed hybrids were introduced in the USA in 1974 and currently account for all of the production.

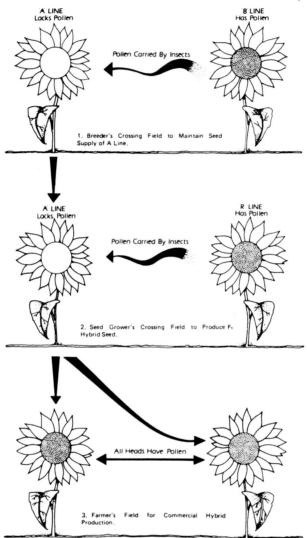

Fig. 14.4 Cytoplasmic male sterile and fertility restorer method of hybrid sunflower seed production. From Cobia and Zimmer (1978).

UTILIZATION OF PRODUCTS

The oil extracted from the seed contributes about 80% of the total value of the crop. This is in contrast to soybean which derives the majority of its value from the meal, and to corn and cotton from which the oil is a by-product of the starch and fiber industries, respectively.

Sunflower oil is generally considered a premium oil compared to most other vegetable oils because of its light color, bland flavor, high smoke point, high level of linoleic acid and absence of linolenic acid. Typically the unsaturated fatty acids oleic and linoleic comprise about 90% of the total, the remainder consisting primarily of the saturated fats palmitic and stearic. The ratio of oleic to linoleic acid varies with temperature during seed maturation, the cooler temperatures producing higher linoleic percentages which typically range from 60 to 75 for much of the production in the USA and Canada.

The high level of unsaturated fats in sunflower oil is of special interest from a nutritional standpoint. Generally it is accepted that increasing the proportion of unsaturated to saturated fatty acids in a diet will reduce the level of blood cholesterol, a factor which is believed to be related to the incidence of coronary heart disease. Of further nutritional interest is the high level of linoleic acid, an essential fatty acid which must be supplied by diet, and the high level of alpha tocopherol, a form of vitamin E.

The primary use of sunflower oil is as a salad and cooking oil, and as a major ingredient in some margarine and shortening products. In the USA sunflower oil accounts for about 8% of the salad and cooking oil market (Campbell, 1983), and a lesser percentage of the margarine market. This is in contrast with consumption trends in most other major sunflower–producing countries where sunflower generally is the preferred and most commonly used vegetable oil for these markets.

High oleic sunflower oil, consisting of more than 80% oleic acid, was available in commercial quantities in the USA for the first time in 1985. Because it has greater oxidative stability than conventional sunflower oil, high oleic oil is expected to significantly expand food and industrial use of sunflower oil in the USA. Initial interest in food use of the high oleic oil is primarily in frying of snack foods to enhance shelf life of retail products, and as an ingredient in infant food formulas requiring stability, bland flavor and specific fatty acid composition.

In some countries sunflower oil is used directly following oil extraction, but the more common procedure is to further process the oil to modify the color, odor, flavor and physical properties to meet consumer demands. Most processing plants extract sunflower oil by prepressing the seeds in an expeller (or screwpress) followed by hexane extraction (Campbell, 1983). Thereafter, processing follows similar steps used in production of other vegetable oils, and may involve several or all of the following procedures: degumming, bleaching, refining, hydrogenation, deodorizing, and dewaxing. Specific characteristics of refined, bleached and deodorized sunflower oil, typical of seeds from northern grown production in the USA, are shown elsewhere in this book.

Sunflower oil is not commonly used for industrial purposes because of generally higher prices in relation to soybean and other alternative fats and oils. However, it is used to some extent in certain paints, varnishes and plastics because of good semidrying properties without the yellowing problems associated with oils high in linolenic acid. Sunflower oil is also used in the manufacture of soaps and detergents, especially in the USSR and some Eastern bloc countries. Along with other vegetable oils it has potential value for use in the production of adhesives, agrichemicals, surfactants, additional plastics and plastic additives, fabric softeners, synthetic lubricants, coatings and other products, but actual use will depend primarily on the relative price of petroleum and petro-based chemicals.

High oleic sunflower oil, from which a relatively pure oleic acid can be derived quite economically compared to alternative sources, has potential value in industrial products where oleic acid and related chemicals are currently utilized. The high level of oleic acid and corresponding high degree of oxidative stability in a natural-occurring oil is also of value for use in the manufacture of certain cosmetics and pharmaceuticals.

Considerable research has been conducted on the use of sunflower oil as an alternative fuel source in diesel engines. It is reported that sunflower oil has an octane rating of 37 and produces 130,000 BTU/gal., or about 93% of the energy in US number 2 diesel fuel. Blends of sunflower oil and diesel fuel are expected to have the most potential for long term usage.

Sunflower meal is used primarily as an animal food protein concentrate. Protein percentage varies with the hull content of the meal, ranging from about 28 for meal from hulled seeds to as high as 42 for meal from completely dehulled seeds. Fiber percentages range from 28 to 14. Color of the meal varies from gray to black depending on the percentage of hulls and the heat treatment during oil extraction.

Non dehulled or partially dehulled sunflower meal can usually be substituted successfully for soybean meal of equal protein percentage in feeding ruminant animals. Partially or completely dehulled sunflower meal is desired for feeding swine and poultry. Compared to soybean meal, high fiber sunflower meal has a lower energy value, and is substantially lower in lysine content, although higher in methionine. Lysine supplementation or feeding of sunflower and soybean meal mixtures may be necessary in rations for swine and poultry.

Nonoilseed sunflower is used primarily as a snack food, an ingredient in baked foods, salads and candies, and for feeding birds and small animal pets. During processing the seed is generally divided into three sizes; 1) large for roasting in shell, 2) medium for dehulling, and 3) small for birdseed. Nonoilseed sunflower has enjoyed a consistent market growth during the last decade, particularly the use of dehulled and roasted or unroasted kernels for human consumption.

Sunflower protein ingredients derived from dehulled kernels have been evaluated extensively for use in human foods both in Europe and in the USA (Lusas, 1982). Sunflower flour and protein concentrates and isolates show promise or are being used to a limited extent in bakery products, infant formulae, and as meat and milk extenders.

Sunflower hulls are used primarily in animal feeds as a source of roughage, as a fuel to generate steam or electricity, and in production of furfural and ethyl alcohol. Other possible uses include building or insulation board, fireplace logs, and litter for livestock or poultry.

REFERENCES

Campbell, E.J. 1983. Sunflower oil. J. Am. Oil Chem. Soc. 60: 387-392.

Chandler, J.M., and Beard, B.H. 1983. Embryo culture of *Helianthus* hybrids. Crop Sci. 23: 1004-1007.

Cobia, D.W., and Zimmer, D.E. 1978. Sunflower Production and Marketing. N. Dak. State Univ., Fargo. Extension Bull. 25 (revised).

Dedio, W., and Putt, E.D. 1980. Sunflower, pp. 631-644. *In* W.R. Fehr and H.H. Hadley (eds.), *Hybridization of Crop Plants*. Am. Soc. Agron. Crop Sci. Soc. Am., Madison, Wis.

Fick, G.N. 1978. Breeding and Genetics, pp. 279-338. *In* J.F. Carter (ed.), *Sunflower Science and Technology*. Agronomy Monograph No. 19: Am. Soc. Agron., Madison, Wis.

———. 1984. Inheritance of high oleic acid in the seed oil of sunflower, p.9. Proc. Sunflower Research Workshop. Bismarck, N. Dak.

——— and Auwarter, G.E. 1981. Resistance to the sunflower midge, p. 18. Proc. Sunflower Forum and Research Workshop. Fargo, N. Dak.

———. 1982. Resistance to a new race of sunflower downy mildew, pp. 175-177. Proc. Tenth Intern. Sunflower Conf. Surfers Paradise, Australia.

———, Caroline, J.J., Auwarter, G.E., and Duhigg, P.M. 1985. Agronomic characteristics and field performance of dwarf sunflower hybrids, pp. 739-742. Proc. Eleventh Intern. Sunflower Conf. Mar del Plata, Argentina.

———, Gulya, T.J., and Auwarter, G.E. 1983. Inheritance of Sclerotinia wilt resistance in sunflower, pp. 21-22. Proc. Sunflower Research Workshop. Minot, N. Dak.

Gershenzon, J., Rossiter, M., Mabry, T.J., Roger, C.E., Blust, M.H., and Hopkins, T.L. 1985. Insect antifeedant terpenoids in wild sunflower: A possible source of resistance to the sunflower moth, pp. 433-446. *In* P.A. Hedlin (ed.), ACS Symposium Series No. 276 *Bioregulators for Pest Control*. Am. Chem. Soc.

Heiser, C.B., Jr. 1978. Taxonomy of *Helianthus* and Origin of Domesticated Sunflower, pp. 31-53. *In* J.F. Carter (ed.), *Sunflower Science and Technology*. Agronomy Monograph No. 19: Am. Soc. Agron., Madison, Wis.

———, Smith, D.M., Clevenger, S.B., and Martin, W.C. 1969. The North American Sunflowers *(Helianthus)*. Mem. Torrey Bot. Club. 22(3): 1-218.

Knowles, P.F. 1978. Morphology and Anatomy, pp. 55-87. *In* J.F. Carter (ed.), *Sunflower Science and Technology*. Agronomy Monograph No. 19: Am. Soc. Agron., Madison, Wis.

Lusas, E.W. 1982. Sunflower Meals and Food Proteins, pp. 25-36. *In* J. Adams (ed.), *Sunflower*. Natl. Sunflower Assoc., Bismarck, N. Dak.

Mielke, S. (ed.). 1985-1986. *Oil World Statistics Update*. ISTA Mielke GmbH, 2100 Hamburg 90, POB 900803, W. Germany.

Miller, J.F., and Hammond, J.J. 1985. Improvment of yield in sunflower utilizing reciprocal full-sib selection, pp. 715-717. Proc. Eleventh Intern. Sunflower Conf. Mar del Plata, Argentina.

Murai, N., Sutton, D.W., Murray, M.G., Slightom, J.L., Merlo, D.J., Reichert, N.A., Sengupta-Gopalan, C., Stock, C.A., Barker, R.F., Kemp, J.D., and Hall, T.C. 1983. Phaseolin gene from bean is expressed after transfer to sunflower via tumor - inducing plasmid vectors. Science 222: 476-482.

Pustovoit, V.S. (ed.). 1967. *Handbook of Selection and Seed Growing of Oil Plants.* Izdatel'stvo "Kolos," Moscow. (Transl. Israel Program for Scientific Translations, Jerusalem. 1973).

Putt, E.D. 1940. Observations on morphological characters and flowering processes in the sunflower (*Helianthus annuus* L.). Sci. Agric. 21: 167-169.

——. 1962. The value of hybrids and synthetics in sunflower seed production. Can. J. Plant Sci. 42: 488-500.

——, and Sackston, W.E. 1957. Studies on sunflower rust. I. Some sources of rust resistance. Can. J. Plant Sci. 37: 43-54.

Robinson, H. 1979. Studies in the Heliantheae (Asteraceae). XVIII. A new genus *Helianthopsis.* Phytologia 44: 257-259.

Semelczi-Kovacs, A. 1975. Acclimatization and dissemination of the sunflower in Europe. (German). Acta Ethnogr. Acad. Sci. Hung. 24: 47-88.

Whelan, E.D.P. 1978. Cytology and Interspecific Hybridization, pp. 339-369. *In* J.F. Carter (ed.), *Sunflower Science and Technology.* Agronomy Monograph No. 19: 339-369. Am. Soc. Agron., Madison, Wis.

Zimmer, D.E., and Hoes, J.A. 1978. Diseases, pp. 225-262. *In* J.F. Carter (ed.), *Sunflower Science and Technology.* Agronomy Monograph No. 19: Am. Soc. Agron., Madison, Wis.

Chapter 15

Peanut

T. A. Coffelt

IMPORTANCE AND DISTRIBUTION

Peanut or groundnut (Fig. 15.1A) is one of the most widespread and potentially most important food legumes in the world (Norden et al. 1982). The crop is grown on over 18 million hectares in the tropical and subtropical areas of over one hundred countries on six continents (Table 15.1). The peanut has been identified as one of the leguminous species with the greatest potential for both food and industrial purposes in the tropical regions of Africa, specifically for lowland, semi-arid savannah regions (Milner, 1973). As an edible oil crop, the peanut competes with sesame, sunflower, and soybean (Hammons and Caldwell, 1974). However, each has somewhat different ecological adaptations.

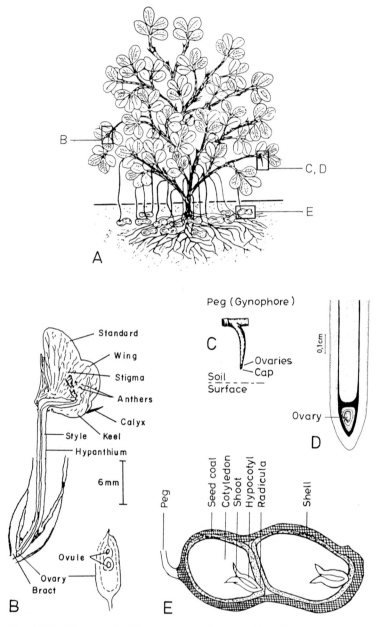

Fig. 15 1 Peanut. A - Plant, ready to harvest. B - Flower, fully developed. Note the long hypanthium formed by fusion of the basal part of corolla lobes.
C - Gynophore (Peg) about to enter the soil; formed after fertilization by meristematic tissue below the ovary. D - Cross section through the gynophore carrying the ovary at its tip. E - Pod, with two mature seeds.

The three leading peanut producers for over twenty-five years have been India, China, and the USA. Yields have remained stable in most developing countries for about three decades. Yields in developed countries have steadily increased. This is evident when the production in India and the USA is compared. India has about 40% of the world production area, but produces only about 31% of the world production; whereas the USA has only about 3% of the world production area, but produces 8% of the world production. The yield plateau in developing countries is partly due to the lack of effective peanut breeding programs. However, the low yields are largely due to damage by disease and insect pests, poor stands from low seed viability and inferior planting equipment, production expansion to less productive areas, and poor environmental conditions, such as frequent drought. These problems call for a thorough and revised approach to breeding programs in many countries in which other disciplines (plant pathology, entomology, physiology) will have to associate actively to develop desirable plant types to suit specific situations.

ORIGIN AND SYSTEMATICS

An extensive review of the origin and early history of the peanut (*Arachis hypogaea* L.) was made by Hammons (1982). The peanut plant is a self-pollinating, indeterminate, annual, herbaceous legume. It is indigenous in South America to the area east of the Andes and lying between the Amazon River and the Rio de La Plata (Fig. 15.2). Peanut remnants dating from about 1500 to 1200 B.C., very similar to the peanut types found there today, have been recovered from archaeological sites on the northern coast of Peru. The cultivated peanut was likely first domesticated in the valleys of the Paraguay and Parana rivers in the Chaco region of South America. The peanut was extensively cultivated throughout South America by the Indians prior to the Spanish conquest, some of which were even grown under irrigation. From South America, Portuguese explorers and traders are thought to have carried the peanut to Europe, Asia, both coasts of Africa, and the Pacific Islands. Much later, the peanut was introduced into the USA from Africa, the Caribbean Islands, and Spain.

The genus *Arachis* is in the family Leguminosae, sub-family Papilionaceae, tribe Aeschynomeneae, sub-tribe Stylosanthinae (Smartt and Stalker, 1982). Some of the closest relatives are in the genera *Stylosanthes, Chapmannia, Arthrocarpum,* and *Pachecoa. Arachis* is separated from these genera on the basis of geocarpy and the formation of the peg. Agents capable of physically moving soil plus pods, such as water, are the most likely means of effectively distributing *Arachis* over wide areas. This is supported by the distribution of taxa which are closely associated with specific drainage basins of both recent and ancient times (Fig. 15.2). Thus, the geocarpic habit of peanut imposes considerable restrictions on distribution, but is advantageous from the standpoint of survival in harsh environments. The cultivated species (*A. hypogaea*) has not been found in

Table 15.1 World Peanut (in Shell) Production by Region and Major Producing Countries

Region or Country	Production area ('000 ha)			Seed yield (kg/ha)			Seed production ('000 tonnes)		
	1969-71	1979-81	1985	1969-71	1979-81	1985	1969-71	1979-81	1985
World	**19834**	**18573**	**18955**	**925**	**1003**	**1122**	**18347**	**18636**	**21260**
Africa	**7179**	**6196**	**5284**	**789**	**748**	**757**	**5664**	**4637**	**4001**
Burkina Faso	-	126	200	-	540	385	-	70	77
Cameroon	244	337	320	845	405	438	206	137	140
Central African Rep.	106	125	139	647	983	1007	68	123	140
Chad	143	167	170	668	588	471	129	98	80
Gambia	87	73	100	1485	1083	1200	129	79	120
Ghana	90	98	117	978	1273	1097	88	125	128
Guinea	115	127	130	644	651	577	74	83	75
Malawi	233	250	260	781	703	692	182	176	180
Mozambique	220	173	150	636	481	400	140	83	60
Niger	357	184	100	623	602	400	223	111	40
Nigeria	1846	600	600	900	954	1000	1660	573	600
Senegal	1006	1073	605	789	683	970	794	733	587
South Africa	370	245	250	984	1211	744	364	297	186
Sudan	490	960	476	756	792	723	370	760	344
Tanzania	49	91	98	662	591	602	32	54	59
Uganda	263	111	120	786	678	833	207	75	100
Upper Volta	140	-	-	487	-	-	68	-	-
Zaire	377	474	530	703	702	717	265	332	380
Zimbabwe	170	183	100	673	567	500	114	104	50

N. and C. America	**740**	**768**	**751**	**1982**	**2263**	**2740**	**1466**	**1738**	**2058**
U.S.A.	591	595	592	2182	2607	3175	1289	1550	1879
S. America	**979**	**643**	**415**	**1230**	**1507**	**1571**	**1204**	**969**	**651**
Argentina	255	289	145	1099	1558	1579	280	451	229
Brazil	670	282	193	1307	1535	1759	876	433	339
Asia	**10887**	**10914**	**12452**	**915**	**1027**	**1162**	**9960**	**11210**	**14471**
Burma	655	489	620	751	797	1075	492	390	667
China	2165	2346	3553	1216	1492	1902	2634	3501	6757
India	7287	7132	7200	797	841	778	5807	5999	5600
Indonesia	376	496	530	1230	1534	1509	462	761	800
Thailand	97	103	132	1317	1245	1261	462	128	166
Viet Nam	78	105	160	1007	847	750	78	89	120
Europe	**10**	**11**	**11**	**1890**	**2234**	**2493**	**19**	**24**	**27**
Oceania	**39**	**40**	**41**	**851**	**1401**	**1181**	**33**	**56**	**49**
U.S.S.R.	**1**	**1**	**1**	**428**	**1600**	**2500**	**2**	**2**	**3**

Source: FAO Production Yearbooks 1980 (vol. 34) and 1985 (vol. 39).

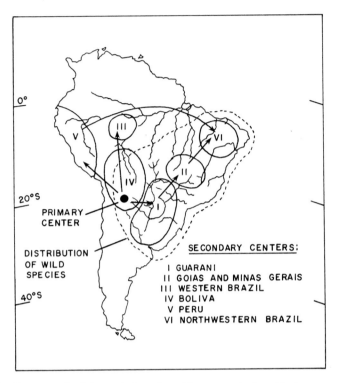

Fig. 15.2 Centers of origin and diversity of the peanut, *Arachis hypogea*.
From Gregory and Gregory, 1976.

the wild, but is found cultivated throughout the tropical and temperate regions of the world. The wild species (over twenty described and forty undescribed) of *Arachis* are found only in South America from latitudes 0° to 35°S, and longitudes 35° to 66°W, south of the Amazon and from the eastern base of the Andes to the Atlantic (Hammons, 1982). Gibbons et al. (1972) have proposed that Africa is an important secondary center of variation for *A. hypogaea* .

Krapovickas (1973) and Gregory et al. (1973) have divided the genus *Arachis* into seven sections (*Arachis, Erectoides, Caulorhizae, Rhizomatosae, Extranervosae, Ambinervosae,* and *Triseminalae.* Each section has been further divided into series and species. This classification has not yet been validly published according to the International Code of Botanical Nomenclature; therefore, all subgeneric epithets are *nomina nuda* (Smartt and Stalker, 1982). This system is generally accepted as correct, is workable, and is of considerable practical value. Interspecific hybridization, chromosome morphology, and chemotaxonomy (utilizing seed proteins, nucleic acids, and flavonoids) have supported the classification system. Since plant, pod, and seed morphology exhibit a wide range of variation, gene introgression and recombinant types have occurred.

A cultivated peanut plant can be erect or prostrate (15 to 60 cm tall or taller), is sparsely hairy, and has a well-developed taproot with many lateral roots and nodules in the root axes (Fig. 15.1A). Roots are usually devoid of hairs and a distinct epidermis, with absorption taking place 8 to 10 cm behind the root cap. A unique characteristic of the peanut plant is the nyctinastic movements of the leaflets (Umen, 1933). The leaf blade consists of four oval or obvate leaflets attached to the midrib by small articulations which allow for movement. During dark periods (night or very cloudy days) or on very hot sunny days, the paired leaflets are close together in a vertical position, while on a normal day without stress the leaflets are separated from each other and almost horizontal. The petiole of the leaf also responds in a similar manner in its relationship to the branch.

All sections have species with 2n=2x=20 chromosomes, while the sections *Arachis* and *Rhizomatosae* also have species with 2n=4x=40 (Smartt and Stalker, 1982). Thus, polyploidy has apparently arisen independently at least twice in the genus. Aneuploids have been reported, but are usually associated with interspecific hybrids or ionizing radiation. *Arachis hypogaea* is in the section *Arachis*, series *Amphiploides* Krap. et Greg. *nom. nud.* The major distinction of this species from other species in the section is chromosome number (2n=4x=40 vs 2n=2x=20). *Arachis monticola* also has forty chromosomes, but is differentiated from *A. hypogaea* on the basis of other traits. Some workers have suggested that *A. monticola* may be more accurately classed as a subspecies of *A. hypogaea*. However, currently *A. hypogaea* is divided into two subspecies which are each subdivided into two botanical varieties. The subspecies *hypogaea* has alternate branching, a spreading or erect growth habit, a longer maturation period, and fresh seed dormancy. The two botanical varieties within spp. *hypogaea* are *hypogaea* (USA market types Virginia and Runner) and *hirsuta* (not grown commercially in the USA, but also known as Peruvian humpback or Chinese dragon type). The subspecies *fastigiata* has sequential branching and an erect growth habit, earlier maturity, and little or no fresh seed dormancy. The two botanical varieties within ssp. *fastigiata* are *fastigiata* (USA market type Valencia) and *vulgaris* (USA market type Spanish).

The chromosomes of *Arachis* are small, 1 to 4 μm, and generally have median centromeres, making them difficult to karyotype (Smartt and Stalker, 1982). The cultivated peanut is a diploidized tetraploid. Husted identified two distinctive chromosome pairs in *A. hypogaea* which he termed the "A" and "B" (Smartt and Stalker, 1982). The "A" chromosome pair is distinctly smaller and the "B" chromosome pair has a secondary constriction. Most diploid species in section *Arachis* have the "A" chromosome pair, *A. batizocoi* being an exception. Since *A. batizocoi* readily crosses with other species of the section, it has been suggested that *A. batizocoi* and another member of the section, possibly *A. cardenasii*, are the progenitors of *A. hypogaea*. Other as yet uncollected or recently collected taxa could also be the true genome donors of *A. hypogaea* (Smartt and Stalker, 1982).

Within the section *Arachis*, most of the genetic resources are accessible to peanut breeders (Smartt and Stalker, 1982). More remote genetic resources might be utilized, but these will be more difficult to work with and results less certain. The most extensive collections of peanut germplasm are maintained by the International Crops Research Institute for the Semi-Arid Tropics (ICRISAT) at Hyderabad, India, with over 10,000 accessions, and the United States Department of Agriculture at Experiment, Georgia.

MODE OF REPRODUCTION

Flowers are born on inflorescences resembling spikes and located in the axils of the leaves (Gregory et al. 1973; Norden, 1980) (Fig. 15.1B). Flowers are never at the same node as vegetative branches, although very short internodes on some plants may make it appear that they are. Environmental conditions may cause the transformation of reproductive axes into vegetative axes, but not the reverse. From one to many flowers may be present at a node and are usually more abundant at the lower nodes. The first flowers appear from 4 to 6 weeks after planting with maximum flower production occurring 6 to 10 weeks after planting. Peanut flowers are sensitive to light, temperature, and moisture (relative humidity). High temperatures and low levels of relative humidity reduce flowering, while temperatures between 22° and 33°C and soil moisture of about 40% are ideal. A light intensity, greater than 45% full sunlight, is necessary for optimum flower development. The white and blue wavelengths are especially important. Flowers are stimulated by light received three days prior to opening. The peanut is usually self-pollinated, but natural hybridization has been reported throughout the world with rates from less than 1% to greater than 6%. Outcrossing is usually associated with atypical flowers and bees. The peanut flower is odorless, which contributes to self-pollination by attracting fewer insects (Umen, 1933).

Flower size, normally 4 to 5 cm, varies with the environment and genotype. The flowers and pods of other species deviate considerably in size, color, orientation, and markings from *A. hypogaea* (Gregory et al. 1973). The basic morphology of all species is essentially the same. Each flower is subtended by two bracts; the lower, on an axis of the inflorescence and the upper, in the axil of the lower bract. The flowers consist of petals, stamens, and a pistil (Fig. 15.1A).

The flower contains five petals: a yellow to orange standard, two yellow to orange wings, and two petals fused to form a paler yellow keel. The standard can be from 10 to 21 mm wide and 8 to 14 mm high. The wings are each about one fourth the width of the standard and equal in height. The keel is even narrower than the wings. There are two calyx lobes, an awnlike one opposite the keel and a broad, four-notched one opposite the back of the standard.

The flower has ten monodelphous stamens, two of which are usually not fully developed. The stamens are fused together from one half to two thirds of their length. The eight fertile, normally developed anthers consist of four globose, dorsifixed, uniloculate anthers alternating with four adnate, introrse, oblong anthers. Of the latter, three are biloculate and the one opposite the standard is uniloculate. The globose anthers are attached to shorter filaments than the oblong anthers. Pollen grains from both types of anthers are fertile, smooth, and spherical in shape.

The pistil consists of an ovary, style, and stigma. The ovary is superior, small (1.5 mm long and 0.5 mm in diameter), and conical with a beak-shaped point at the tip. The ovary contains a single sessile carpel with 1 to 6 ovules. The style is glabrous throughout its length and covered with bristles near the club-shaped stigma. The very thin and tender style is enclosed in a filiform hypanthium (4 to 5 cm long). Compared to other members of the leguminous family, the peanut has an extraordinarily long hypanthium and style.

Before anthesis, the flower bud is 6 to 10 mm long; the day before anthesis, 10 to 20 mm; and at anthesis, 50 to 70 mm long. The stigma becomes receptive to pollen twenty-four hours before to twelve hours after the flower opens, while the pollen is shed 1 to 8 hours before the flower opens. Anthesis and pollination usually occur at sunrise with self-pollination taking place within the closed keel of the flower. About 40% of the flowers fail to begin peg development and another 40% abort before pod development.

The flower withers 5 to 7 hours after opening, depending upon environmental conditions. Cool, cloudy, moist conditions delay flower opening and withering. The hypanthium may be shed following withering, leaving only the fertilized ovary, or it may remain attached for several days. Within about one week after fertilization, a pointed needlelike structure, commonly called the peg or gynophore, develops and elongates quickly (Fig. 15.1C). The ovary (future pod) and fertilized ovules are located behind the tip of the peg (Fig. 15.1D). The cells at the tip of the ovary become lignified, serving as a protective cap as the peg enters the soil. The peg, positively geotropic but not negatively phototropic, grows into the soil to a depth of 2 to 7 cm, where it loses its geotropism. The tip orients itself horizontally away from the tap root, the ovary enlarges rapidly, and pod growth begins.

The mature pod is an indehiscent legume (1-8 x 0.5-2 cm) that is oblong and contains one to five seeds (Fig. 15.1E). The dry pericarp of the mature pod is reticulate, with 11 to 15 longitudinal ridges. The endocarp consists of parenchymatous tissue surrounding the developing seed. The endocarp recedes in front of the advancing growth of the seeds and disappears almost completely when the seeds have matured, forming a thin, papery lining. This lining becomes progressively darker brown; a trait which is associated with increasing tannin content, and by full maturity may appear almost black. This change in color, though easily seen, is difficult to measure, but to the trained eye is one of the most reliable estimates of the degree of maturity (Gregory et al. 1973). Of the pod weight, 20% to 30% is shell or pericarp.

Mature seeds are cylindric or ovoid (1-3.5 x 0.5-1.5 cm). The testae vary among cultivars in size, shape, and color (white, pink, red, purple, shades of brown, or variegated). The seeds, weighing 0.2 to 2 g., do not contain an endosperm but have two large cotyledons, an epicotyl with three meristems, a hypocotyl, and a primary root.

BREEDING PROCEDURES

The breeding procedures currently used for peanut are the same as those used for other self-pollinated crops and are discussed in several plant breeding texts (Norden, 1973; Wynne and Gregory, 1981; and Norden et al. 1982). New breeding programs can often fulfill their early objectives through either mass or pure line selection from, or direct use of, cultivars from the local region or other countries (Wynne and Gregory, 1981). There is a continuing opportunity to select improved strains from these sources (Hammons and Caldwell, 1974). The mass selection method is of more value when the introduction is primarily variable for simply inherited traits which are highly heritable (Norden, 1973). For less heritable traits, such as yield and quality, the pure line method is more effective. In mass selection, several elite plants are composited for comparison with a local cultivar or the original introduction, while in the pure line selection method, the elite plants are maintained separately for comparison. These methods may be practiced singly, alternately, or simultaneously. Each use of the pure line selection method adds 1 to 2 years to the development of a cultivar. The fastest progress is obtained with this system if the introduced germplasm is from regions or countries with similar environmental conditions, the field trials are conducted under conditions favorable to high yields, and all germplasm is given equal treatment (Hammons and Caldwell, 1974). While these methods have been very successful in the development of new cultivars in the past and may still be very useful in some developing countries, many breeders feel they are inadequate to fulfill their present objectives (Norden, 1973). Thus the major current use of mass selection is for seed increase and maintenance of cultivar purity during seed increases (Norden et al. 1982).

Norden et al. (1982) have stated that the primary means of future cultivar improvement will be by hybridization, both among and within species of *Arachis*. Breeders seeking improvement through inter-subspecific hybrids will encounter several deleterious characters (i.e. albinos, brachytics, dwarfs, and sterility) in segregating generations. Although heterosis has been exploited in some self-pollinated crops by use of hybrids, it is probably not feasible in peanut due to its flower morphology and the low amount of pollen produced on any given day. Since crosses are difficult to make and subsequent evaluations time consuming, the breeder should utilize all available information in selecting potential parents. The better choices will result in many superior lines from which to make selections. In selecting parents, the breeder should choose parents which complement each other. The parents, when combined, should have all of the desired traits needed in a new cultivar.

The actual method of crossing the peanut has been described in detail (Umen, 1933; Norden, 1980), so will only be briefly outlined in this chapter. Although each breeder has slight modifications and preferences in the manner some steps are done, the basic procedure is the same. Crossing the peanut can be divided into three stages—emasculation, pollination, and care of the pollinated flower. Inflorescences located low on the plant are usually the most suitable for crossing. Artificial hybridization can be done successfully in either the field or greenhouse. Most breeders prefer the greenhouse because of the ease in which the female parents can be handled. The maintenance of high humidity following crossing is important for success, as is good insect control. Forceps, a sharp knife or razor blade, and a 2x to 3x magnifier are the only equipment needed.

Emasculations should be performed the afternoon or evening prior to flower opening. First, the young flower bud is held with the thumb and index finger of one hand, while forceps are used to remove the calyx lobe in front of the keel and fold down the calyx lobe behind the standard; second, the standard is opened with the forceps and the wing petals pulled out and down or removed; third, the forceps are used to break open the keel and separate it from the anthers and stigma so that the anthers and their filaments can be removed; and fourth, after removal of the anthers, the standard is allowed to return to its original position around the stigma.

Pollination is done the morning after emasculation when the flower opens. First, pollen is collected from the male parent and applied to the tip of the stigma on the emasculated flower by using forceps, a camel hair brush, or the keel full of pollen from the male parent; second, plants and flowers should be handled carefully, since the pollen can easily be dislodged; and third, forceps, brush, and fingers should be dipped in alcohol when changing pollen sources.

Colored strings, thread, wire, and aluminum foil have all been used successfully to tag emasculated and pollinated flowers. Unused flowers should be removed after pollination. Unused inflorescences in the axil of the emasculated flower should be removed prior to pollination to make it easier to keep track of the flowers used in crossing. If fertilization was successful, a peg should be visible 7 to 10 days after pollination and often the withered flower with the marker will remain attached to the peg until it enters the soil. If a peg has not appeared twenty days after pollination, the cross was probably not successful. Pods from crosses can be harvested approximately sixty days after the peg enters the soil.

Following hybridization the F_1 seed should be planted 45 to 90 cm apart in rows 90 to 180 cm apart to produce maximum quantities of seed (Norden et al. 1982). Spacings 30 to 45 cm apart in rows 91 cm apart are recommended for segregating populations to permit each plant to express its potential, visual evaluation by the breeder, and easy manual harvesting. Environment is more important in selecting high-yielding lines than either spacing or branching pattern. Hybridization followed by selection among and within the offspring is currently the most common method used for improving peanut. The most common methods used in selection are pedigree and bulk. The major limiting factor to the use of hybridization in peanut breeding is the time (ten or more years) required for cultivar development.

The single-seed descent method has been used successfully in peanut to save 2 to 3 years in development time (Wynne and Gregory,1981). This method can be used alone or in addition to the traditional pedigree method. The main advantages of the single-seed descent method are genetic variance for characters with low heritability can be easily maintained, less space is utilized, and more than one generation per year can be obtained. The disadvantages of the single-seed descent method are longer retention of inferior lines, selection of traits expressed only at normal planting density is delayed, identity of superior F_2 plants is not maintained, selection for characters with low heritability is ineffective, and genetic variability can be lost. Early generation testing has also been proposed as a method to reduce cultivar development time. This method appears to be most promising for intra-subspecific crosses.

Another limitation to the traditional pedigree method is the restriction on the amount of recombination among linked genes. A modified recurrent selection method has been used in North Carolina to overcome this limitation as well as shorten the cultivar development time (Wynne and Gregory, 1981). With this method, five generations can be grown in twenty-four months. The diallel selective mating system can also be used to increase recombination. The major disadvantage of this system, and to an extent the recurrent selection system, is the mass crossing required for each cycle.

Backcrossing is now being used in several breeding programs. This procedure will probably be used more frequently in the future with increased emphasis on breeding for pest resistance. In backcrossing the objective is generally the transfer of a simply inherited characteristic to an otherwise desirable cultivar (Norden, 1973). Only in simple cases (one or two dominant genes) is it advisable to do all of the backcrossing onto F_1 plants. As a general rule, progeny should be grown to the F_3 after alternate backcrosses. The major limitation of this method with peanut is that most characters are not simply inherited, especially pest resistance. Backcrossing is probably most effective when combined with other methods.

Blending of peanut cultivars to meet specific requirements or increase environmental stability has met with limited success. However, the bulking of phenotypically similar, but genotypically dissimilar, sister lines from a cultivar has proved very successful. The sister lines are maintained individually, then bulked prior to each increase of foundation seed. This method has been used extensively to produce most of the cultivars developed in Florida (Norden, 1973). This method allows the breeder to improve the cultivar after release by adding or dropping component lines. The main advantages are that a breeder can produce a cultivar with wide genotypic variability and stability, yet with a restricted phenotype to satisfy market and grower requirements. The main disadvantages are that the cultivar may be less uniform, seed stocks are more difficult to maintain, and generally the multiline is lower yielding than its best single line.

Mutation breeding in peanut has not produced any more variability than hybridization (Norden, 1973). However, it may be effective in breaking specific linkages, providing variation for specific characters, and/or use in conjunction with other breeding methods. Several types of mutagenic agents (X-rays, gamma-rays, and various chemicals) have been used with some success in peanut.

Several crossing schemes have been proposed to make use of the wild species. These schemes have been used with limited success as have some newer methods such as tissue culture. Unfortunately, the utilization of wild species to improve the cultivated forms, has been hampered by sterility and cross incompatibility (Wynne and Gregory, 1981). After thirty years of research, limited amounts of germplasm which have one or more wild species in their background are becoming available for use in breeding programs. Tissue culture and genetic engineering are not realistic methods for general use in peanut breeding programs at present. Much research remains to be done to adapt these methods for use with peanut.

BREEDING OBJECTIVES

The aim of peanut breeding programs is to develop the potential of peanut by creating new cultivars that meet the needs of the grower, processor, and consumer (Norden et al. 1982). Several objectives, including broadening the germplasm base, must be met to fulfill this aim. Peanut breeding programs have traditionally placed major emphasis on increasing yields. This is still a viable objective of most peanut breeding programs, especially in the developing countries where yields are about one third of the yields in developed countries (Table 15.1). Although development of new peanut cultivars has more than doubled the yielding potential over the last forty years, yield increases are not as great now as they were in the past. This increase has been due to efficient exploitation of existing fruiting sites and increasing site numbers (Seaton, 1986). If this is true, then breeders may do well to alter the structure of the plant to obtain future yield increases.

Increased yields usually have the added benefit of reducing production costs. This is important for all peanut producers. Higher yielding cultivars should also be developed with the goal that their yield potential is stable over varying environments. Environment is known to make it possible for ordinary landraces to equal or surpass the best cultivars from modern breeding programs as well as the reverse (Wynne and Gregory, 1981). The environmental factors are under very limited control. Therefore, the genome must be changed to respond favorably to existing environmental conditions.

Some of the reasons yield increases have not been as dramatic in recent years are increased disease and insect damage and adverse environmental stresses such as drought. In order to increase yields in the future, peanut breeding programs in both developed and developing countries will need to have as part of their objectives the development of cultivars resistant to local disease and insect pests as well as environmental conditions. This includes the development of cultivars with multiple resistance to many factors. Breeding for insect resistance has not received as much attention as disease resistance, since insects tend to be a localized problem (Wynne and Gregory, 1981). Several reviews (Wynne and Gregory, 1981; Norden et al. 1982; Wynne and Coffelt, 1982; Norden, 1973) are available on breeding for resistance to various disease and insect problems.

The two most important peanut diseases world-wide are leafspots, caused by *Cercospora arachidicola* Hori and *Cercosporidium personatum* (Berk. & Curt.) Deighton, and rust, caused by *Puccinia arachidis* Speg. As a result, most breeding programs throughout the world have as an objective the development of cultivars resistant to one or both of these diseases. The identification of usable sources of resistance makes developing resistant cultivars a realistic objective for most peanut breeding programs.

Aflatoxin is another major problem receiving attention world-wide. Sources of resistance have been found, but the resistance does not appear to hold up under all conditions in the field, during harvesting, and/or processing. The sources of resistance appear to differ in their mechanism of resistance. Factors, such as wax, cell structure, testa color, tannins, flavonoids, and amino acids have been linked with resistance. Thus, a realistic objective may be to incorporate several of these mechanisms of resistance into one cultivar that will be resistant under all conditions.

The most successful disease-resistant breeding programs have been the development of rosette virus resistant cultivars in Senegal, Nigeria, and Malawi. These have been the only programs in peanut where the sources of resistance were identified, the genetic models of inheritance determined, and resistant cultivars developed as a result. A cultivar resistant to Cylindrocladium black rot (*Cylindrocladium crotalariae* [Loos] Bell & Sobers), a cultivar resistant to Sclerotinia blight (*Sclerotinia minor* Jagger), and a cultivar resistant to pod rot (*Pythium* spp., *Rhizoctonia solani* Kuhn, and *Fusarium* spp.), have been released in the USA. Resistance to other diseases in addition to those above is included in the objectives of many current breeding programs. Some of these are Southern stem rot (white mold) (*Sclerotium rolfsii* Sacc.), Verticillium wilt (*Verticillium dahliae* Kleb.), web blotch (*Phoma arachidicola* Marasas, Pauer, & Boerema), collar rot (*Diplodia gossypina* [Cke.] McGuire & Cooper), blackhull (*Thielaviopsis basicola* [Berk. & Br.] Ferr.), and peanut stunt virus. Some of the insect pests for which breeding programs are developing resistant cultivars are Southern corn rootworm (*Diabrotica undecimpunctata howardi* Barber), lesser cornstalk borer (*Elasmopalpus lignosellus* Zeller), mites (*Tetranychus urticae* Koch), thrips (*Frankliniella fusca* Hinds), leafhoppers (*Empoasca* spp.) and fall army worms (*Spodoptera frugiperda* J. E. Sm.). These programs vary in their present objectives from searching for sources of resistance to development of models of inheritance and definition of the mechanism of resistance, to the development of resistant cultivars. Nematode resistance is also an objective of several breeding programs. However, a level of resistance great enough to be useful in a breeding program has yet to be identified.

Tolerance or resistance to environmentally induced stresses is an objective of many peanut breeding programs. Development of cultivars that are resistant to drought is becoming increasingly important as water supplies become limited for irrigation. Drought resistance or tolerance is important where production costs are high and short periods of drought can greatly reduce yields and/or quality. Another major environmental stress factor is frost. Frost tolerant or earlier maturing cultivars are means of overcoming this stress factor. Early maturing cultivars have the added advantages of reducing the amount of drought stress, reducing damage by specific (late season) diseases or insects, spreading harvest risks, and being used in multiple cropping systems.

An important objective in most breeding programs is increased oil quantity and quality and/or protein quantity and quality. Improving these characteristics is especially important in developing countries where peanut oil and protein are used as a major part of the diet. Studies have shown that oil content ranges from 46% to 63% for the wild species and 43% to 56% for the cultivated species, indicating the opportunity for dramatic increase in oil content (Wynne and Gregory, 1981). Variation also exists for improving oil quality which includes increasing shelf life, decreasing undesirable odors and flavors, and developing a better fatty acid balance. For example, iodine values of the oil, which are an indication of shelf life, range from 80 to over 105. Such factors are highly heritable, with only a few additive genes apparently involved in their inheritance, making them a reasonable objective for a breeding project.

Similar quality enhancement could be made by increasing protein content and improving protein quality. Peanut seed usually contain about 26% protein and peanut meal about 50% protein. The major quality deficit in peanut protein is its low content of the sulfur-containing amino acids, especially methionine. Oil and protein quality and quantity are greatly influenced by environment, genotype, and methods of curing and processing. These factors must be considered in selecting superior cultivars.

In a breeding program for improving Spanish and Valencia type peanut, an important objective should be the incorporation of fresh seed dormancy. Adverse harvesting conditions can result in significant yield losses of Spanish and Valencia type peanut due to sprouting of the seeds in the soil prior to harvest. Dormancy could reduce these losses and provide for a longer optimum harvest period.

In the USA and other developed countries an important objective for peanut breeding programs is the development of cultivars suitable for mechanization. Cultivars should have uniform maturity, pods, and seed; stronger peg attachments; break resistant pods; tougher seed testae; a nonprotruding radicle; and less erect plants with pods near the tap root. All breeding programs should also include some of the characteristics desired by processors and consumers in their objectives. These include higher shelling and blanching percentages; improved texture, color, flavor, and aroma of the seed and end use products; better roasting characteristics; and improved milling quality or the resistance to splitting and loss of the testa during shelling and processing (Norden et al. 1982). These objectives demonstrate the dilemma with which peanut breeders are continuously faced—the widely differing and sometimes contrasting needs of the various segments of industry (Norden et al. 1982). For example, seedsmen and millers want the testa to remain firmly on the seed, while many processors want the testa to be easily removed during blanching prior to processing.

HISTORY OF CULTIVAR DEVELOPMENT

The difficult process of adapting the peanut to new environments has been in progress since the natives of South America collected the ancestors of modern peanut from the wild (Wynne and Gregory, 1981). Some adjustments of the environment to peanut production have been and will continue to be made, such as the use of fertilizers and irrigation, but the great adaptive contingency lies with plant modification. In the USA and other countries, peanut breeding has been hampered by several factors including the late initiation of breeding programs; the regional importance of the crop; the relatively few breeders involved; lack of funding; and the difficulty associated with breeding an indeterminate crop whose fruit are formed underground (Wynne and Gregory, 1981). As a consequence, peanut breeders are now investigating the somewhat dated estimates of quantitative genetics and methods of field testing, while simultaneously trying to investigate novel approaches to interspecific hybridization and gene transfer.

On a world-wide basis, international breeding efforts were enhanced with the adoption of the peanut as a target crop by the International Crops Research Institute for the Semi-Arid Tropics (Wynne and Gregory, 1981). Recognition of the importance of the peanut, particularly in developing countries, has given impetus to programs of breeding for disease and insect resistance, incorporation of diverse germplasm into breeding populations, and population improvement. During the last two decades much emphasis has been placed on the collection of wild species and exotic cultivars. As this emphasis is changed from collection to evaluation and exploitation of these genetic resources, progress in improving the productivity, pest resistance, and adaptability of the peanut can be expected.

The first, as well as recent, cultivars in the USA and many other countries were developed as either pure-line or mass selections from introductions and lots of producer's peanuts. The importance of this method of breeding is evident by the ability of many of these cultivars to compete satisfactorily. This method may be especially important in developing countries. For example, three of four currently recommended cultivars in Malawi, and three recently released cultivars in Argentina, were derived by mass selection from introductions (Norden et al. 1982).

The earliest recorded peanut breeding program was in Java in the early 1900s, where natural hybridization was used to develop new cultivars. Artificial hybridization and pedigree selection were first used in the USA in Florida in 1928. Almost all of the cultivars released by Florida have been the result of controlled crossing and selection (Norden, 1973). Early peanut breeding programs were started in Georgia in the 1930s and in North Carolina and Texas in the 1940s. In addition, breeding programs in the USA now exist in Virginia, Oklahoma, and New Mexico.

Backcrossing was first used in Malawi to incorporate peanut rosette virus resistance from low-yielding cultivars from the Upper Volta and Ivory Coast area of West Africa into the rosette-susceptible, but high-yielding cultivar, Makulu Red. The rosette virus resistant cultivar RG-1 was released as a result of this program (Norden et al. 1982).

To satisfy preferential demands on the international market for larger peanut seed, TG-1 was released in India as Vikram in 1973 (Norden et al. 1982). It was developed after treating seed of the Spanish Improved cultivar with 75Kr of X-rays and by repeated selection for increased seed weight. Similarly, the Virginia-type peanut cultivar NC 4x was developed from the cultivar NC 4 in North Carolina following irradiation and selection.

Few of the varieties of twenty-five years ago are still acceptable or in wide use today (Norden, 1973). In the last few years, especially in the USA, producers have come to rely on increasingly fewer cultivars. Norden (1973) reported that in recent years over 80% of the USA peanut production came from three cultivars; Florigiant, Florunner, and Starr. This value has changed since his report. Several new cultivars have reduced the dominance of these three cultivars. The complex genetic background and multiline nature of Florunner and Florigiant have contributed to their ability to dominate for so long. However, a narrow genetic base predisposes the peanut crop to major damage from diseases and insects for which resistance is lacking and burdens the producer with the use of increasingly expensive chemicals. In many peanut-production areas of the world, this protection is not economically feasible. Thus, future cultivars will need to have resistance to problem diseases and insects. In addition, estimates of genetic variance are needed to provide information on the inheritance of quantitative characters. These include not only the genetic variance for crosses among cultivars, but also the type and magnitude of genetic variance for important characteristics of both adapted and exotic inter-subspecific crosses (Wynne and Gregory, 1981).

UTILIZATION OF PRODUCTS

All parts of the peanut plant can be easily utilized. The vines with leaves make an excellent high protein hay for horses and ruminant livestock. The shells or pods can be used as feed for livestock, burned for fuel, made into particle board, and many other uses. The first uses of the peanut in the USA were for fattening farm animals such as hogs, turkeys, and chickens (Mottern, 1973). However, the peanut is now grown mainly for human consumption of the seed. The seed can be used directly for food or crushing to produce oil and a high protein meal. The peanut can be processed with primitive home facilities or advanced technology. Used directly for food, the peanut is a major crop for subsistence (Hammons and Caldwell, 1974). Peanut oil can be used in cooking, lighting, fuel, and as a food constituent. Peanut meal is an excellent source of protein to balance diets high in cereals and starchy foods, and to supplement animal proteins. The multiple uses of the peanut make it an excellent cash crop for domestic markets as well as foreign trade. The crop can be marketed as shelled or unshelled nuts, oil, or meal. The principal importers are Western Europe, Canada, Japan, Hong Kong, Singapore, Malaysia, Venezuela, and Algeria.

In the USA and some other countries, such as those of Western Europe, the peanut is utilized primarily as whole seeds (Norden, 1980). The most common method of preparation for human consumption of whole seeds is dry roasting the seed until they are light brown. The whole seeds may also be boiled, broiled, fried, salted, used in candies, or eaten raw. The peanut can also be roasted with or without salt in the shell. Peanut products enjoy widespread popularity because of their unique roasted peanut flavor (McWatters and Cherry, 1982). Peanut is a well-established snack food in many forms and can be utilized in several ways to expand this market. The whole peanut is rich in protein (26%), minerals (2.7%), and vitamins, and has about 43% oil and 24% carbohydrates (Hammons and Caldwell, 1974). The major minerals are calcium, phosphorus, and iron, and the vitamins are thiamine, riboflavin, and niacin. Peanut is deficient in the sulfur-containing amino acids and ascorbic acid (vitamin A). Peanut is an excellent source of food energy, 100 g of peanut seed contain 585 calories (Ahmed and Young, 1982).

In the USA, the major use of peanut is for grinding into peanut butter (Mottern, 1973). The peanut butter can be consumed directly or used in making cookies and other snack foods. Powdered peanut butter has been combined with different flavorings and other components to make an ice-cream-like product (McWatters and Cherry, 1982). Peanut butter is used as a base for one of the foods eaten by astronauts on space flights.

The peanut contains 42% to 52% oil and most of the world production is crushed for that oil. Peanut oil has a high flash point and does not retain flavors during cooking, making it a favored cooking oil. Peanut oil is a desirable cooking and salad oil because of its high quality, containing about 80% unsaturated fatty acids such as oleic and linoleic acids (Ahmed and Young, 1982). Peanut oil has a better keeping quality than soybean, corn, and safflower oils and is a good source of vitamin E. As an energy source, peanut oil makes an excellent substitute for diesel fuel. The peanut is a net energy producer, accumulating 3.26 times the energy required to grow the crop. In Virginia, this energy can be produced on 25 to 30% of the area required to produce the equivalent amount of energy in a soybean crop.

Peanut meal is more concentrated than whole peanuts in protein, minerals, and vitamins (Hammons and Caldwell, 1974). Peanut meal is available as flakes, grits, or flour and can be processed into high protein concentrates or isolates (McWatters and Cherry, 1982). Present economic conditions do not favor the use of peanut meal instead of soybean meal as a meat substitute or extender. However, peanut flakes, grits, and flour have been used successfully as extenders or substitutes for ground beef patties, meat loaf, boneless chicken and turkey rolls, frankfurters, and meat analogs. Peanut flour has been used to replace part or all of wheat flour or corn meal in making various types of breads and other bakery products. This is of particular importance in developing countries, since the protein quality of native cereal-based breads such as the chapati in India could be improved. In addition, peanut flour can be used to fortify various breakfast cereals and gruels, or as part of a dry mix that, with the addition of water, can be used as a soup, beverage, or gravy. Peanut protein isolate can be combined with milk to extend the milk for drinking alone, as cream in coffee or tea, or for production of curds and yogurt (McWatters and Cherry, 1982). Miltone, marketed in India, is an example of a peanut protein product. It supplies 30 to 50% of the protein and about 50% of the vitamins to school age children. Peanut flour can be used in similar ways to make peanut milk products. Peanut protein isolate and peanut oil have been used to make cheese analogs for the production of cream cheese and cheese spread products. The various products from peanut meal can be used to alleviate hunger and malnutrition in many developing countries.

ACKNOWLEDGMENTS

The author expresses sincere appreciation to Drs. R.W. Gibbons, R.O. Hammons, A.J. Norden, and C.E. Simpson for their helpful suggestions in preparing this manuscript.

REFERENCES

Ahmed, E.M., and Young, C.T. 1982. Composition, Quality, and Flavor of Peanuts, pp. 655-688. *In* H. E. Pattee and C. T. Young (eds.), *Peanut Science and Technology.* American Peanut Research and Education Society, Inc., Yoakum, Tex.

Gibbons, R.W., Bunting, A.H., and Smartt, J. 1972. The classification of varieties of groundnut. Euphytica 21: 78-85.

Gregory, W.C., and Gregory, M.P. 1976. Groundnut *Arachis hypogaea* (Leguminosae-papilionatae), pp. 151-154. *In* N. W. Simmonds (ed.), *Evolution of Crop Plants.* Longmans, Green, New York.

——, ——, Krapovickas, A., Smith, B.W., and Yarbrough, J.A. 1973. Structures and Genetic Resources of Peanuts, pp. 47-133. *In* C. T. Wilson (ed.), *Peanuts - Culture and Uses.* American Peanut Research and Education Association, Inc., Stillwater, Okla.

Hammons, R.O. 1982. Origin and Early History of the Peanut, pp. 1-20. *In* H. E. Pattee and C. T. Young (eds.), *Peanut Science and Technology.* American Peanut Research and Education Society, Inc., Yoakum, Tex.

——, and Caldwell, B.E. 1974. Groundnuts (*Arachis hypogaea*), pp. 170-178. *In* S. C. Litzenberger (ed.), *Guide for Field Crops in the Topics and the Subtropics.* Technical Assistance Bureau, Agency for International Development, Washington, DC.

Krapovickas, A. 1973. Evolution of the Genus *Arachis*, pp. 135-151. *In* R. Moav (ed.), *Agricultural Genetics, Selected Topics.* National Council for Research and Development, Jerusalem.

McWatters, K.H., and Cherry, J.P. 1982. Potential Food Uses of Peanut Seed Proteins, pp. 689-736. *In* H. E. Pattee and C. T. Young (eds.), *Peanut Science and Technology.* American Peanut Research and Education Society, Inc., Yoakum, Tex.

Milner, M. (ed.) 1973. *Nutritional Improvement of Food Legumes by Breeding.* Protein Advisory Group of the United Nations System, United Nations, New York.

Mottern, H.H. 1973. Peanuts and Human Nutrition, pp. 593-602. *In* C. T. Wilson (ed.), *Peanuts - Culture and Uses.* American Peanut Research and Education Association, Inc., Stillwater, Okla.

Norden, A.J. 1973. Breeding of the Cultivated Peanut, pp. 175-208. *In* C. T. Wilson (ed.), *Peanuts - Culture and Uses.* American Peanut Research and Education Association, Inc., Stillwater, Okla.

——. 1980. Peanut, pp. 443-456. *In* W. R. Fehr and H. H. Hadley (eds.), *Hybridization of Crop Plants.* Am. Soc. of Agron. and Crop Sci. Soc. of America, Madison, Wis.

——, Smith, O.D., and Gorbet, D.W. 1982. Breeding of the Cultivated Peanut, pp. 95-122. *In* H. E. Pattee and C. T. Young (eds.), *Peanut Science and Technology.* American Peanut Research and Education Society, Inc., Yoakum, Tex.

Seaton, M.L. 1986. A Comparative Analysis of the Reproductive Efficiency of 14 Virginia Market Type Peanut Cultivars (*Arachis hypogaea L* .). M.S. Thesis. Virginia Polytechnic Institute and State University, Blacksburg, Va. 77 pages.

Smartt, J., and Stalker, H.T. 1982. Speciation and Cytogenetics in *Arachis*, pp. 21-49. *In* H. E. Pattee and C. T. Young (eds.), *Peanut Science and Technology.* American Peanut Research and Education Society, Inc., Yoakum, Tex.

Smith, B.W. 1950. *Arachis hypogaea*, aerial flower and subterranean fruit. Am. J. Bot. 37: 802-815.

Umen, D.P. 1933. *Biology of Peanut Flowering*, scientific-practical issue no. 6, All-Union Scientific Research Institute of Oil-Seed Crops (VNIIMK), Krasnodar.

Wynne, J.C., and Coffelt, T.A. 1982. Genetics of *Arachis hypogaea* L., pp. 50-94. *In* H. E. Pattee and C. T. Young (eds.), *Peanut Science and Technology.* American Peanut Research and Education Society, Inc., Yoakum, Tex.

——, and Gregory, W.C. 1981. Peanut breeding. Adv. Agron. 34: 39-72.

Chapter 16

Brassica Species

R. K. Downey and G. Röbbelen

IMPORTANCE AND DISTRIBUTION

Over 13.2% of the world's edible oil supply now comes from the oilseed Brassicas, rapeseed and mustard. Indeed, production and usage of *Brassica* seed oils has grown faster in the period 1975-1985 than any other crop, except the oil palm, making it the third most important edible oil source after soybean and palm.

Due to their ability to germinate and grow at low temperatures, the oilseed Brassicas (Fig. 16.1) are one of the few edible oil crops that can be cultivated in the cooler agricultural regions and at higher elevations, as well as winter crops in the more temperate zones. Major producing regions include China, the Indian subcontinent, Canada and Northern Europe (Table 16.1). In the future, as the required disease resistance and quality characteristics are incorporated into adapted varieties, Australia, the United States, and perhaps South America could become major producers.

The small, round *Brassica* oilseeds normally yield on extraction over 40% oil on a dry weight basis, and a meal containing 38 to 44% high quality protein. In many Asian countries the meal is used as an organic fertilizer for field crops but in the western world it is utilized exclusively as a high protein feed for livestock and poultry.

Fig. 16.1 Brassica. A – Seedling cotyledons. B – Cotyledons and first true leaf of a 14 day old plant. C – Fully developed stand of winter rapeseed at the end of the fall growing season. D – Flower with its 4 yellow petals. E – Inflorescence. F – Mature plant of *Brassica napus*. G – Pod of *B. campestris* showing an intact (left) and opened pod (right) with central lamellae.

Table 16.1 World Oilseed *Brassica* Production by Region and Major Producing Countries

Region or Country	Production area ('000 ha)			Seed yield (kg/ha)			Seed production ('000 tonnes)		
	1969-71	1979-81	1985	1969-71	1979-81	1985	1969-71	1979-81	1985
World	**8487**	**11488**	**14968**	**780**	**972**	**1262**	**6617**	**11165**	**18887**
Africa	**51**	**48**	**46**	**401**	**400**	**496**	**20**	**19**	**23**
N. and C. America	**1540**	**2299**	**2805**	**989**	**1124**	**1235**	**1523**	**2584**	**3465**
Canada	1533	2296	2803	989	1124	1235	1517	2581	3463
S. America	**53**	**71**	**33**	**1400**	**1064**	**1324**	**74**	**76**	**44**
Asia	**5772**	**7496**	**7487**	**533**	**699**	**952**	**3076**	**5242**	**9032**
Bangladesh	219	203	198	604	620	631	132	126	125
China	1902	3134	4494	524	942	1243	996	2952	5587
India	3122	3709	4404	522	503	688	1629	1864	3030
Pakistan	476	420	383	523	594	725	249	249	277
Europe	**1023**	**1516**	**2391**	**1847**	**2112**	**2580**	**1889**	**3203**	**6169**
Czechoslovakia	40	79	116	1852	2079	2455	70	165	285
Denmark	17	98	190	1783	2074	3016	30	204	573
France	326	366	468	1849	2382	2991	603	871	1400
Germany D.R.	102	121	123	1760	2194	2764	180	264	340
Germany F.R.	85	140	266	2252	2531	3024	190	354	803
Poland	269	259	467	1691	1675	2296	455	434	1072
Sweden	105	165	172	2068	1903	2133	218	313	366
U. K.	6	97	296	1842	2829	2770	10	274	820
Oceania	**45**	**27**	**83**	**703**	**905**	**965**	**31**	**25**	**80**
Australia	44	27	83	698	902	964	31	24	80
U.S.S.R.	**4**	**30**	**123**	**977**	**554**	**610**	**4**	**17**	**75**

Source: FAO Production Yearbooks 1980 (vol. 34) and 1985 (vol. 39).

ORIGIN AND SYSTEMATICS

The Cruciferae family, to which the genus *Brassica* belongs, contains many important crop plants and weeds. In domesticating the Brassicas, man has modified almost every plant part, including the root, stem, leaf, terminal and axillary buds, and seeds. The oilseed Brassicas are closely related to the cole vegetables; the condiment mustards and root crops, turnip, rutabaga and radish; as well as weeds, such as black and wild mustard.

Domestication probably occurred at many different times and locations as the economic value of the locally adapted weed was recognized. The Brassicas may well have been among the earliest of the domesticated plants since some of the vegetable forms were in common use in the Neolithic age, and the Indian Sanskrit writing of 1500 to 2000 BC directly refer to oilseed rape and mustard. Greek, Roman and Chinese writings of 200 to 500 BC also specifically mention these crops and also describe their medicinal value. In Europe, domestication is believed to have occurred in the early middle ages. Commercial plantings of rapeseed were recorded in the Netherlands as early as the 16th century. At that time rapeseed oil was used primarily as a lamp oil and later as a lubricant for steam engines. Despite its wide acceptance for edible purposes in Asia it is only through improved processing techniques after World War II and the breeding for superior quality that the oil and meal has gained a major market share in Western nations.

The occurrence of similar plant forms in more than one *Brassica* species resulted in considerable confusion and misclassification by early botanists. However, in the early 1930s cytogenetic studies by Morinaga and his students clarified the relationships among the oilseed Brassicas and their close relatives (Prakash and Hinata, 1980). Cytological analysis of chromosome pairing in the progeny of interspecific crosses clearly demonstrated that the three species with the higher chromosome numbers, *Brassica napus* L., *B. juncea* (L.) Czern. & Coss., and *B. carinata* A. Braun, are amphidiploids, derived from the monogenomic or diploid species *B. nigra* (L.) Koch, *B. campestris* L. and *B. oleracea* L. (Fig. 16.2). The accuracy of this scheme was later corroborated by artificially synthesizihg the amphidiploid species from their diploid parents. Furthermore, chromosome analysis of the monogenomic species revealed that only six chromosomes were distinctly different, the remaining being homologous with one or another of the basic six (Röbbelen, 1960). This evidence suggested an early evolution from a common progenitor species with a basic chromosome number of x=6 and that the diploid *Brassica* species with n=8, 9 and 10 chromosomes resulted from secondary balanced polyploidy. If closely related Cruciferae species are grouped with the diploid Brassicas a continuous series of haploid chromosome numbers from n=7 to n=12 is evident (Fig. 16.2). Crosses among these species have occasionally been successful, thus permitting the breeder to effect interspecific gene transfer.

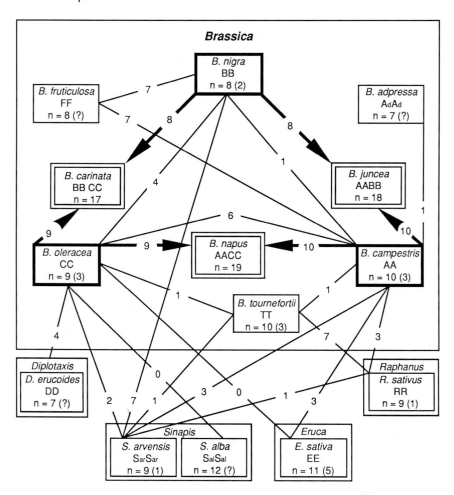

Fig. 16.2 Genome relationship of *Brassica* species and allied genera (from Mizushima, 1980). A, B, C....are the genome symbols . The number in brackets following the haploid chromosome number (n) indicates the maximum possible number of autosyndetic chromosome pairs. The numbers within the lines connecting two genomes give the maximum allosyndesis, i.e. the number of bivalents possible between the respective interspecific hybrids.

Since the original progenitor species is now extinct, it is important to be aware of the centers of origin for the remaining oilseed Brassicas. *B. campestris* appears to have had the widest distribution of the *Brassica* oilseeds. At least 2000 years ago it was distributed from the Atlantic islands in the west to the eastern shores of China and Korea, and from northern Norway south to the

Sahara and northern India, with a primary center near the Himalayan region (Hedge, 1976). Secondary centers of origin are located in the European-Mediterranean area and in Asia. The Asian oleiferous types, known as brown and yellow sarson and toria, differ from European turnip rape in plant morphology and tend to have distinct patterns of fatty acid and glucosinolate composition. Protein and other chemotaxonomic analysis also support separated European and Asian centers of origin, although the Indian forms are conspecific with European turnip rape as well as tame and wild turnips (Denford, 1975; Vaughan et al. 1976).

Wild forms of the amphidiploid rape *B. napus* have not been documented. Since *B. napus* must have originated from an interspecific cross of *B. campestris* x *B. oleracea*, and *B. oleracea* was originally confined to the Mediterranean region, it is generally agreed that *B. napus* originated in southern Europe. *B. napus* was introduced to Asia in the early 1900s where it was found to be more productive in some regions than the indigenous oilseed form of *B. campestris*. Most of the *B. napus* cultivars in China, Korea and Japan have been developed from crosses between European *B. napus* and the indigenous *B. campestris* varieties (Shiga, 1970). However, on the Indian subcontinent both *B. campestris* and *B. juncea* normally outyield *B. napus* .

There is some uncertainty as to the probable center of origin of *B. juncea*. Prakash and Hinata (1980) concluded the species originated in the Middle East where the putative parental species *B. campestris* and *B. nigra* (black mustard) might have first come into contact. However, since black mustard was an important spice of early times, it spread rapidly over Europe, Africa, Asia, India and the Far East. Thus, *B. juncea* has probably arisen by hybridization between different *B. campestris* and *B. nigra* genotypes at several different times and localities, resulting in secondary centers of origin in China, northeastern India, and the Caucasus (Hemingway, 1976).

B. carinata, or Abyssinian mustard, almost certainly originated in northeast Africa where the parental species *B. nigra* and *B. oleracea* were sympatric. Due to its limited distribution to Ethiopia and neighboring countries this fourth *Brassica* oilseed species has had little exposure to modern plant improvement, although its vigor, drought, insect and disease tolerance has recently gained recognition.

Within the two rapeseed species, *B. napus* and *B. campestris*, both spring and winter annual forms occur. The winter forms are more productive than the spring forms but are less winter hardy than winter cereals. The winter form of *B. napus* predominates in northern Europe and central and southern China, whereas under the severe winter conditions in the western regions of Canada and China as well as northern Sweden, the spring forms of *B. napus* and *B. campestris* must be grown. Apparently winter forms did not evolve in *B. juncea* and *B. carinata* .

MODE OF REPRODUCTION

The generally yellow, radial *Brassica* flower has a typical Cruciferae formula of K2+2, C4, A2+4, G(2). The inflorescence is racemose and flowering is indeterminate beginning at the lowest bud on the main raceme. Several new flowers open each day and the total flowering period may last for 2 to 3 weeks. The stigma is normally receptive three days prior to three days after the opening of the flower. Self-pollination occurs in the amphidiploid species and a good seed set can be obtained by enclosing inflorescences in a glassine bag. Under open field conditions an average of 30% outcrossing may result from pollination by wind and insects. In contrast the diploid *B. campestris* is normally self-incompatible. The self-incompatibility is under sporophytic control through a series of S alleles. Numerous techniques have been used to circumvent this natural barrier to self-fertilization (Roggen, 1974). Bud pollination or the use of high atmospheric CO_2 levels following pollination are among the most successful procedures. Some self-compatible strains, such as yellow sarson, occur within the *B. campestris* species, while self-incompatible lines of *B. napus* and *B. juncea* have been isolated from breeding populations. Controlled self- and cross-pollinations are easily carried out on buds which are about to open the same or the following day. If necessary the pollen can be stored in moist petrie plates at 4°C for up to 50 days without loss of viability (Chiang, 1974). For special crossing techniques, see Downey et al. (1980).

Fertilization is normally effected within 24 hours of pollination. The syncarpous ovary develops into a pod (silique) with two carpels separated by a false septum (Fig. 16.1). Strains with three or four carpels have also been found. Each fertilized flower can generate 25 or more seeds per pod. Since each plant produces many pods, the multiplication rate per generation may exceed 1000 to 1, effectively speeding up the breeding, testing and release of improved cultivars.

BREEDING PROCEDURES

The effectiveness of a breeding scheme depends on the breeder's ability to choose suitable parents and evaluate the progeny in the most appropriate sequence using techniques that are both efficient and accurate. An illustration of the classical pedigree breeding system, as applied to winter *B. napus* improvement in Europe, is given in Figure 16.3. The initial variation is obtained by crossing parent lines selected according to the given breeding goals, in this case a zero erucic acid, low glucosinolate winter rapeseed cultivar with high yield and the required disease resistance. In order to save time the F_1 plants are grown in the greenhouse and vernalized artificially. The F_2 generation may be similarly grown and vernalized with the F_2 plants transplanted from the greenhouse to the field the following spring or be field sown in the fall. Seeds of vigorous F_2 plants are analyzed in the laboratory for their glucosinolate content. Seeds of selected

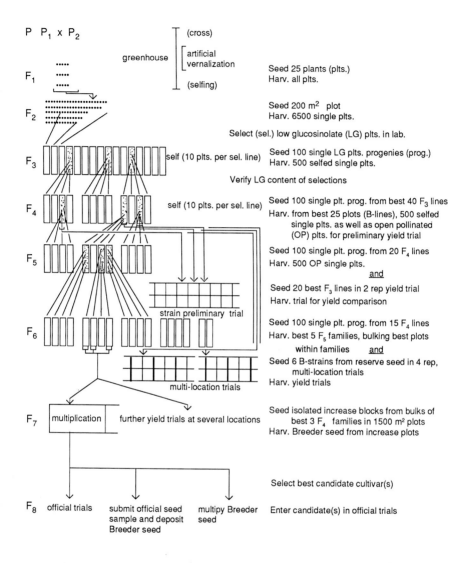

Fig. 16.3 Breeding scheme for a high yielding, low erucic, low glucosinolate, winter hardy *B. napus* cultivar. Both parents (P_1 and P_2) are low in erucic acid, P_2 is also low in glucosinolate.

low glucosinolate single plants are sown in the field as F_3 plots. Within F_3 plots that are rated visually superior prior to flowering, healthy plants are selfed and their seeds checked for glucosinolate content. This ensures that all F_4 plants will contain the desired low glucosinolate and erucic acid levels now defined as "double low" or canola quality. Open pollinated single plants are harvested from each selected F_4 plot, as identified by repeated observations of the nursery throughout the growing season. Seed of these elite plants is used to sow F_5 progeny plots for evaluation the following year. The "plant to plot" selection procedure is continued in the F_5. Plots of F_6 progeny are grown from single open pollinated plants harvested from selected F_5 plots.

In the F_4, the plants in each plot, remaining after single plant selection, are harvested in bulk and used to sow a three replicate yield trial in at least three locations. The best performing lines are retested the following year at as many locations as possible, using reserve seed from the original F_4 seed bulk. Seed harvested from the most uniform and desirable F_6 plots, tracing back to the best F_3 plant, is bulked to form the basic seed for a new candidate cultivar. Seed of this line is further increased under isolation, of which part is used for official trials and part is submitted as the official standard sample for that potential cultivar. The remaining seed is held in reserve for future cultivar maintenance and multiplication.

Backcrossing, combined with pedigree selection, is frequently used in the largely self-pollinating *B. napus* and *B. juncea* species. For example, the incorporation of resistance to blackleg disease (*Leptosphaeria maculans* (Desm) Ces. and deNot.) into Canadian spring *B. napus* cultivars was undertaken by crossing adapted, but susceptible, Canadian cultivars with resistant lines from Australia and Europe. The F_1 were backcrossed to Canadian parents and resistant BC_1F_2 plants identified in artificial epidemic nurseries. Pedigree selection for blackleg resistance and agronomic performance for three generations produced adapted lines with good blackleg resistance but not the combination of superior oil and seed yield desired. Thus an additional backcross to the superior oil and seed yielding Canadian cultivar, Westar, was undertaken and pedigree selection again applied to recover all the characteristics required in an improved cultivar. In this example, only one backcross was made before reselection for blackleg resistance, since no information was available on the inheritance of the disease, and recovery of blackleg resistance after each backcross was therefore essential.

In the self-incompatible, cross fertile *B. campestris* species backcrossing has also been effectively used to incorporate specific traits into adapted cultivars. However, because of the significant loss of vigor and fertility that occurs when this naturally outcrossing species is self-pollinated, the pedigree breeding system is not appropriate and recurrent selection is a more effective approach. Recurrent selection begins with growing in isolation one or more populations segregating for the characteristics of interest. Single open pollinated plants are harvested from within this first composite population and seed of the remaining plants are harvested in bulk. A portion of the seed from each of the harvested single plants is sown in a progeny row, with the check cultivar(s) at regular intervals, or in a two or three replicate single row test arranged in a two restrictional lattice or other appropriate design. The remaining seed from each plant is held in reserve. Equal quantities of the reserve seed from each of the single plants, whose progeny were judged visually superior or were higher yielding in the field and whose seed contained the desired quantity and quality of oil and meal, are composited and sown to initiate a second cycle of recurrent selection. The bulk seed sample harvested from the remaining plants in each cycle's composite block is used to sow replicated yield trials in future years to determine the response to selection in each recurrent selection cycle. With spring *B. campestris*, a full recurrent selection cycle can be completed each year, if the composite crossing blocks are grown in the opposite hemisphere or in regions with mild winters and the progeny evaluated under the local environmental conditions.

High levels of heterosis have been obtained in F_1 hybrids of both spring and winter forms of *B. napus* (Sernyk and Stefansson, 1983; Grant and Beversdorf, 1985; Lefort-Buson and Dattee, 1982). On average seed yields were reported to be about 20% above the better parent, and for the best parental combinations yield heterosis was 40% for the spring and 60 to 70% for the winter form. In spring *B. campestris* hybrids, from Canadian x Indian cultivar crosses, yields up to 40% more than the best parent have also been reported (Hutcheson et al. 1981). Thus considerable effort is devoted to developing economical systems and techniques which will capture as much as possible of the heterosis in hybrid cultivars.

By mixing seed of different *B. napus* lines or cultivars with good combining ability, synthetic cultivars can be produced which will utilize some of the seed yield heterosis expected from F_1 hybrids (Schuster, 1982). However, as the synthetic cultivar is multiplied through the Syn-1,-2, and -3 generations, to produce sufficient seed for commercial sale, the level of heterozygosity changes. The low level of outcrossing (20% to 30%) between individual plants (Rakow and Woods, 1987) limits the degree of heterosis that can be utilized in synthetic cultivars. The proportion of hybrids in the synthetic could be increased by producing multiline synthetics, by selecting lines with a high level of self-sterility or by initiating the synthetic with hand crossed F_1 seed.

The production of hybrids using the sporophytic self-incompatibility to ensure a high level of outcrossing, has also been proposed. Such a system is now used for the production of hybrid radish, cabbage and some other *B. oleracea* vegetables. However, the application of similar techniques to the oilseed form of self-incompatible *B. campestris* has proven impractical. Inbred plants obtained through continuous bud pollination or doubled haploid derived inbreds from anther culture, exhibit high levels of inbreeding depression and are very difficult to maintain by continuous selfing. Thus the difficulties and costs associated with the production of parental seed stocks would severely limit the potential of this system for hybrid oilseed *B. campestris* even if various double, triple and three way cross schemes discussed by Thompson (1983) were employed.

In the amphidiploid *B. napus* species, where inbreeding depression is moderate, the S allele system may be commercially practical. Self-incompatible strains have been developed in this species both by selection within populations and through crosses with *B. campestris* carrying strong S alleles. However, a laborious series of test crosses and the maintenance of the self-incompatible parent lines by bud pollination or their exposure to high atmospheric CO_2 concentration during flowering is involved. To avoid the potential problem of poor seed set in commercial hybrid fields, due to poor pollen dispersal among the self-incompatible plants, Thompson (1983) proposed the use of a three-way hybrid using a dominant self-compatible line as the third parent.

Finally, it has been suggested that a self-incompatible line A, which would also contain the cytoplasmically inherited tolerance to triazine herbicides, be mixed and sown in the hybrid seed production plot with the dominant self-compatible triazine susceptible line C. The farmer would sow the AC mixture at a high rate and obtain a pure hybrid stand by eliminating the self-compatible C line with a triazine spray. Beversdorf et al. (1984) have patented a similar system using a cytoplasmic male sterile, triazine tolerant female and a triazine susceptible male carrying a gene(s) for fertility restoration.

The production of hybrid cultivars is also possible using a genic male sterile system, provided ample cheap labor is available to rouge out the male fertile plants in the seed production fields before they flower. Such a system has been used in China (Lee and Zhang, 1983) but would not be feasible in Western nations because of the high labor costs.

In all the above hybrid production systems, there is either a significant cost associated with producing seed of parental lines or some sacrifice in the level of heterosis that can be utilized in the commercial hybrid. These disadvantages could be overcome through the development of an effective cytoplasmic male sterile (CMS) genic restorer system. Such a system permits the full exploitation of heterosis in F_1 hybrids and a relatively inexpensive means of producing seed of A, B and R lines and the F_1 hybrid cultivar (Shiga, 1980). Several cytoplasms have been reported that induce male sterility in *B. napus* .

a) *nap* cytoplasm or the Shiga-Thompson system

Cytoplasmic male sterile *B. napus* plants were first found in progeny of crosses between several winter and spring cultivars with the Polish spring cultivar Bronowski as the pollen parent (Shiga et al. 1983). Bronowski carried the recessive *rf* allele for male sterility but a male fertility conditioning (F) cytoplasm. All female genotypes carried the dominant restorer allele *Rf* and a sterility inducing (S) cytoplasm.

Unfortunately the male-sterility of the (S) *rfrf* genotype tends to be unstable, particularly at high temperatures. The usefulness of the system is further limited since three to five genes may be involved in fertility restoration.

b) *ogu* cytoplasm or the *Raphanus* system.

Ogura (1968) discovered a male sterility inducing cytoplasm in radish (*Raphanus sativus* L.) and Bennerot et al. (1977) transferred the nucleus of *B. napus* into the male sterile radish (ogu) cytoplasm through intergeneric crossing followed by backcrossing to *B. napus*. The resulting *B. napus* plants had good male sterility under a wide range of environments and the female fertility appeared adequate. However, it was found that leaves developing on the CMS plants under low temperatures (<12°C) were chlorotic. Since the chlorosis problem was located in the chloroplast DNA and the inhibition of pollen production was known to be coded in the mitochondrial DNA, fusions between protoplasts from CMS and normal plants were attempted. Among the fused products CMS, normal green plants were recovered (Pelletier et al. 1983). Unfortunately all *B. napus* genotypes so far tested lack the necessary restorer alleles and attempts are being made to introgress such genes from *R. sativus* or *Raphanobrassica* into *B. napus* .

c) *pol* cytoplasm or the Polima system.

Fu (1981) found CMS plants in the Chinese *B. napus* cultivar Polima which gave stable male sterility under varying environments. At least one dominant allele for fertility restoration is available in *B. napus*. Fan et al. (1986) have developed a *B. napus* restorer line for the *pol* cytoplasm from interspecific crosses to a zero erucic acid mustard (ZEM) *B. juncea* line. The first *B. napus* hybrids, based on the Polima system, were entered in Canadian official spring rapeseed trials in 1986.

d) Korean-CMS.

A fourth CMS system has been described by Lee et al. (1976). Restorer genes have been reported but the system has not been extensively investigated.

e) *Diplotaxis* cytoplasm.

CMS *B. campestris* plants were isolated from the interspecific cross *Diplotaxis muralis* x *B. campestris* [5] cv. Yukina (Hinata and Konno, 1979). Restorer genes for this CMS were found in *B. campestris*. All Canadian spring *B. campestris* cultivars restore male fertility induced by the cytoplasm of *D. muralis*. The transfer of maintainer genes from the Yukina cultivar into adapted Canadian spring oilseed *B. campestris* parents is required before *B. campestris* hybrids can be produced. Attempts to utilize the male sterility inducing effect of the *D. muralis* cytoplasm as a source for CMS in *B. napus*, were complicated by the fact that nearly all Canadian spring *B. napus* cultivars restored male fertility when placed into the *D. muralis* cytoplasm. The identification of maintainer genes in *B. napus* or the transfer of the maintainer characteristic from the *B. campestris* cultivar Yukina into *B. napus* are essential for the development of a *D. muralis* based CMS-system in *B. napus*.

f) *Brassica juncea* CMS.

Reliable expression of CMS has also been found in *B. juncea* (Rawat and Anand, 1979). However, fertility restoration, with restorer genes isolated from *B. campestris* and *B. nigra*, appears to be incomplete. New developments in the area of chemical gametocides may be used for future hybrid seed production however, it is questionable whether they would be as cost effective or reliable as a good CMS-restorer system. For a successful commercial F_1 hybrid program the agronomic advantage of the hybrid over the best conventional cultivar must be more than adequate to cover the additional costs of hybrid seed.

The application of in vitro cell and tissue culture techniques to *Brassica* breeding has shown considerable potential in recent years. The production of doubled haploids and thus completely homozygous plants, from the culture of anthers or microspores of *B. napus* is becoming widely used, although the embryogenesis response varies with the donor parent (Keller and Armstrong, 1983). Theoretically such a system could greatly reduce the size of segregating populations which must be produced as well as cut in half the time required to develop, evaluate and release a new improved cultivar. Similarly, successful culture protocols are being developed for *B. juncea* and *B. carinata* in various laboratories (Chuong and Beversdorf, 1985). Although the diploid *B. campestris* species also responds to anther culture, the resulting homozygous doubled haploids lack vigor and fertility due to extreme inbreeding depression (Sequin-Swartz et al. 1983).

Protoplast fusion has been successfully applied in *B. napus* by combining in a single plant the two desirable cytoplasmic traits of male sterility and tolerance to the triazine herbicides (Pelletier et al. 1983). Similar techniques should also permit the fusion of a nucleus from a desirable female with a CMS inducing cytoplasm to produce instant CMS female inbreds (Aviv et al. 1984). Selection within cell suspensions cultivars, exposed to ever greater concentrations of salt, disease toxins, or certain herbicides, followed by regeneration of surviving cells into mature plants, has become a realistic prospect in the *Brassica* crops. Gene vectoring for tolerance to universal herbicides such as glyphosate (Roundup) and chlorsulfuron (Glean) may well be the first of many such innovations. However, to obtain the advantages of such biotechnologies, integration of these techniques into conventional breeding programs will be essential.

BREEDING OBJECTIVES

Seed Yield

The most important goal in oilseed *Brassica* improvement is increased seed yield (Andersson and Olsson, 1961; Brouwer and Schuster, 1976). Unfortunately yield is also one of the most difficult and expensive characteristics to measure.

Yield determining components include number of pods per unit area (number of pods per plant and number of plants per unit area), the number of seeds per pod and seed weight. Interaction among these yield components and the environment is much more pronounced in the *Brassica* oilseed crops than in cereals, making it difficult to effect yield improvements if selection is centered on just one or two components.

Swedish rapeseed breeders selected their winter *B. napus* material for number of seeds per pod since this character was reasonably well correlated with seed yield (Thompson, 1983). On the other hand, the high yield of the Polish winter rape cultivar Gorczanski resulted from a high 1000 seed weight even though the number of seeds per pod was low. French workers concluded that seed weight per pod was an effective selective criteria for seed yield. Number of pods on the main raceme has been used as an indication for high seed yield. In regions which frequently suffer drought or high temperature stresses at various times during the growing season any one of the individual yield components may be the main determinant for yield. Thus, not only can the measurement of yield components be time consuming but relying on them as estimators for seed yield may be ineffective. In the final analysis replicated yield trials are still required to clearly identify superior material. In these tests, optimal plant stand and growth are prerequisites for an effective selection for seed yield. However, in many producing regions the lack of adequate moisture or other environmental stresses rarely permit such uniform conditions.

In all species and forms there are numerous other plant characteristics indicative of high yield potential including fast and vigorous seedling emergence, rapid and strong rosette formation, deep root penetration, resistance to lodging and shattering and limited secondary branching. In winter forms, a high vernalization requirement ensures the formation of a strong shoot before spring growth begins. Many other plant characteristics such as time and duration of flowering, stem thickness, retention of leaves, as well as pod size and shape may also contribute to yield but their relative importance and desirability will vary with the local environment. Many such plant characteristics have a higher heritability than seed yield per se. To effectively utilize these components it has been suggested that each factor be allotted an optimum weight in suitable selection indices (Thurling, 1974). However, to attempt to record and correctly weight all the yield contributing factors requires a substantial investment in time and resources. Thus, experienced breeders tend to have an ideotype in their mind against which the breeding material is continuously compared.

Winter Hardiness and Frost Resistance

The degree of hardiness required in the winter forms will vary with the producing region. In northern Europe, high yields are possible only with strong winter hardiness. In general, a cultivar should have a survival rate, over several years and locations, of at least 95%. Although a reliable frost resistance rating can be obtained from chemical analysis of cold hardened plants or through direct selection of cold hardened plants in freezing chambers, the cost and labor required to handle the necessary plant populations is prohibitive (Andersson and Olsson, 1961).

In general, cultivars which regularly produce vigorous plants before winter normally give superior survival. Where late spring frosts occur, cultivars should retain their cold hardened condition and not react rapidly to high temperatures early in the season. Winter forms of *B. campestris*, which carry the terminal growing point almost below ground, have the best winter survival.

Young plants of spring *B. campestris* are also better able to survive late spring frosts than plants of spring *B. napus* or *B. juncea*, again due to the lower growing point characteristic of *B. campestris* .

Disease and Insect Resistance

One of the most important diseases which attack *B. napus* and *B. campestris* world-wide is the fungus *Leptosphaeria maculans* (Desm) Ces. and de Not., also known as *Phoma lingam* in its imperfect state. Blackleg infections can occur from both pycnospores and ascospores. The resulting mycelia grow into and can completely girdle the stem, killing the plant. Chemical control is not economic in winter forms, because of the long exposure period to infection, but may be effective in spring crops where the infection period is short. However, the development of resistant cultivars through selection in naturally- or artificially-infected field nurseries offers the best solution. Tests for resistance of seedlings and adult plants under artificial greenhouse inoculation have not always correlated well with resistance ratings in the field. Good sources of resistance in *B. napus* have been identified (Kolte, 1985). In *B. juncea* most cultivars are resistant in both the seedling and mature plant stages. Roy (1984) in Australia successfully transferred genes for adult plant resistance from *B. juncea* to *B. napus*, while in Germany Sacristan (1982) selected resistant *B. napus* plants from cell cultures which were grown on media containing a toxic filtrate obtained from the cultured fungus. It is important that *L. maculans* isolates from geographically distant sources not be transported from region to region on seed or plant residue since genetic recombination between them can occur, resulting in an increased pool of virulence genes (Petrie and Lewis, 1985).

Sclerotinia sclerotiorum, which causes premature ripening of infected plants, is an equally serious disease, particularly under moist environments. Because of the pathogen's wide host range it is unlikely that resistant cultivars can be developed, although it has been reported that some strains appear to have some tolerance (Kolte, 1985). Apetalous mutants may provide another means of reducing *Sclerotinia* infection because petals, which fall to the leaves after flowering, serve as an ideal medium for germinating spores prior to the penetration of the mycelia into the leaves and stems.

White rust (*Albugo candida*) causes economic losses when it attacks and deforms the floral parts. Most *B. campestris* genotypes are susceptible to Race 7 while Race 2 attacks *B. juncea*. All European and Canadian *B. napus* cultivars are resistant to all known races; however, many Chinese cultivars are susceptible to Race 7 (Fan et al. 1983). The Canadian *B. campestris* cultivar Tobin contains a high proportion of plants resistant to Race 7 while many Oriental (yellow seeded) *B. juncea* cultivars are resistant to Race 2.

Many other diseases cause economic losses in the oilseed Brassicas including soilborne organisms (*Fusarium* spp., *Rhizoctonia solani*), blackspot (*Alternaria* spp.), club root (*Plasmodiophora brassicae*), light leaf spot (*Pyrenopeziza brassicae*), bacterial rot (*Xanthomonas campestris*), aster yellows and phyllody (mycoplasms). The Brassicas are also attacked by the parasite broomrape (*Orobanche*) and several viral diseases. Kolte (1985) has reviewed the literature on these pathogens and indicated possible sources of resistance.

Many insects feed on the lush *Brassica* plants and those insects causing economic losses vary from region to region. Fortunately nearly all can be controlled by insecticides of various kinds without risk of residues in the processed products. Breeding for insect resistance has yielded very few successes although selection for rapid and vigorous seedling development and a shorter flowering period has contributed to reduced insect damage. In the future it may be possible to breed for insect resistance or low insect preference. For example, cultivars of *B. juncea* show less pod midge damage than *B. napus*, some *Raphanus* genotypes are reported to have resistance to sugar beet nematode and *Sinapis alba* seedlings are less attractive to the flea beetle. The transfer of these characteristics into *B. napus* and *B. campestris* may be possible in the future. The possibility also exists of incorporating a gene from *Bacillus thuringiensis* which codes for a glycoprotein toxic to the many *Lepidoptera* pests of the Brassicas (Mantell et al. 1985).

Lodging and Shattering Resistance

Resistance to lodging contributes to yield by maintaining an unrestricted flow of nutrients to the aerial plant parts, permitting light to penetrate to the lower pods, avoiding conditions conducive to fungal infections and facilitating harvesting operations. However, a degree of stem flexibility is desired to permit some leaning of the crop and thus prevent the upper pods from being beaten and shattered by the wind.

Resistance to shattering varies with the species and cultivar. In general, *B. napus* tends to be the most susceptible, with *B. campestris* intermediate and *B. juncea* the most resistant to shattering. However, the yellow sarson form of *B. campestris* and four valved pods in sarson and other species have been reported as the most shatter-resistant forms. The resistance to pod splitting is largely determined by the formation and extent of sclerenchymatous tissue which connects the pod valves to the false septum (Josefsson, 1968). Unfortunately simple, precise and rapid methods for determining susceptibility have not been devised, although twisting the pod around its long axis or rolling pods, when laid length-wise in the hand, have been used successfully.

Oil Quantity and Quality

The oil content of air dry *Brassica* oilseeds range from 38 to 44%. About 80% of the monetary value of the seed is derived from the extracted oil, the residual high protein meal contributing the remainder. Thus increased oil content is a prime breeding objective. Correlations between seed yield and oil content have not been observed and the heritability for oil content is higher than for seed yield. The replacement of the slow Soxlhet analysis method with the fast, accurate, non-destructive wide line NMR or NIR techniques has further improved the speed with which higher oil cultivars can be bred.

The value of the seed oil is determined by its fatty acid composition since the amounts of the various fatty acids present in the oil can affect its nutritional or industrial value. *Brassica* seed oils differed from other vegetable oils in containing a significant proportion of the long chain monoenoic fatty acids, eicosenoic and erucic. In the 1950s and again in the early 1970s feeding experiments with laboratory animals indicated that the nutritional value of rapeseed oil would be substantially improved if the erucic acid content could be reduced to <5% of the total fatty acid content (Kramer et al. 1983). The identification of plants with essentially no erucic acid in their seed oil in *B. napus* (Stefansson et al. 1961) and *B. campestris* (Downey, 1964), resulted in the world-wide development of nutritionally superior low erucic oil bearing cultivars (Table 16.2). The amount of erucic acid present in *Brassica* seed oils is controlled by the genetic make up of the developing embryo, rather than the maternal parent, through a series of alleles exhibiting additive gene action. In *B. napus* (Harvey and Downey, 1964), two loci, each with several alleles, determine the level of erucic acid in the seed oil while in *B. campestris* (Dorrell and Downey, 1964) two alleles at a single locus control erucic acid synthesis. By varying the alleles present, it is possible to fix the erucic acid level of a cultivar at almost any level from essentially zero to over 50%. The isolation of zero erucic acid in *B. juncea* plants (Kirk and Oram, 1981) and the determination of its inheritance (Kirk and Hurlstone, 1983) are the basis for the development of this species as an edible oil crop. The oil from high erucic (>50%) cultivars enters the industrial oil market where erucic acid is valued as a slip agent in plastics manufacturing and for other industrial uses.

A second oil quality breeding objective is to reduce the percentage of linolenic acid from the present 8 to 10% to less than 3% while maintaining or increasing the level of linoleic acid. Lower linolenic acid is desired to improve the storage characteristics of the oil while a higher linoleic acid (vitamin F) content may be nutritionally desirable. Selection within available germplasm has resulted in only minor progress. However, the use of chemical mutagens produced one agronomically weak *B. napus* line with about 5% linolenic and 20% linoleic acid content (Rakow, 1973). Stefansson using this and other mutants with reduced

**Table 16.2   Fatty Acid Composition (in Percent of Total Fatty Acids) of Seed
Oil from Conventional and New Rapeseed Cultivars**

Fatty acid		Conventional cultivars		Zero erucic
Name	Symbol	*B. napus*	*B. campestris*	cultivars
Palmitic	16:0	3.8	3.2	9.2
Oleic	18:0	11.2	26.6	59.8
Linoleic	18:2	13.7	17.5	19.4
Linolenic	18:3	8.1	8.8	10.2
Eicosenoic	20:1	9.6	11.8	0.2
Erucic	22:1	52.3	31.0	0.3

linolenic acid content developed agronomically acceptable summer *B. napus* cultivar Stellar containing less than 3% linolenic acid and over 22% linoleic acid.

Increased content of fatty acids with shorter chain lengths is also of interest. Swedish researchers have selected *B. campestris* lines with 10 to 12% of palmitic plus palmitoleic acids compared with 4 to 5% in the unselected population (Persson, 1985) but the value and acceptability of such an oil composition has yet to be determined.

Quality of the Seed Meal

Rapeseed meal, which remains following seed oil extraction, contains between 36 and 40% protein on a dry matter basis with a well balanced amino acid composition. Although oil and protein content tend to be negatively correlated, both characteristics can be increased by selecting for the sum of the two components (Grami et al. 1977). The development of yellow seeded forms of the oilseed Brassicas has resulted in increased oil and protein content at the expense of unwanted fiber due to a thinner seed coat in yellow seeded vs. brown or black seeded forms (Stringam et al. 1974). Partially yellow seeded *B. campestris* and pure yellow *B. juncea* and *B. carinata* cultivars have been developed. The development of pure yellow seeded *B. napus* cultivars with good agronomic characteristics remains an important breeding objective.

The feeding value of meal from traditional oilseed *Brassica* cultivars has been limited by the presence of sulphur compounds called glucosinolates. Glucosinolates contain a central -S-C=N group with different aliphatic or aromatic side chains. When the glucosinolates are hydrolized by the myrosinase enzyme, present in all *Brassica* vegetative and seed tissues, thiocyanates, isothiocyanates or nitriles are released. Although these compounds are desired for the flavour and odour they give to *Brassica* vegetables, when present in feed concentrates they can reduce palatability and, in non ruminant animals, adversely affect iodine uptake of the thyroid gland resulting in metabolic disorders, poor feed efficiencies and reduced weight gains (Fenwick et al. 1983).

To avoid these problems the myrosinase enzyme is heat inactivated as one of the first steps in the oil extraction process. Since the intact glucosinolates are relatively innocuous such processed meal can be freely fed to ruminant animals and at controlled levels to swine and poultry. However, the ultimate breeding goal has been to develop low glucosinolate cultivars.

In the early 1960s rapid and accurate methods for the determination of glucosinolate content in seed and meals were developed. These methods were used to screen the rapeseed germplasm for glucosinolate content and the Polish spring *B. napus* cultivar Bronowski was identified as having a glucosinolate content of 10 to 12 μmoles of the aliphatic glucosinolates per gram of the oil free, moisture free meal as compared to levels of 110 to 150 μmoles in other cultivars.

Inheritance studies indicated that the recessive alleles of at least three genes condition the low glucosinolate characteristic in *B. napus*. The Bronowski cultivar has been used world-wide in backcross programs to incorporate the low glucosinolate characteristic into adapted cultivars of both *B. napus* and *B. campestris* .

Additional minor improvements in the nutritional value and versatility of the meal would also result if the 1 to 1.5% sinapine and phytic acid presently found in *Brassica* oilseeds could be reduced through plant breeding. Fast, accurate analytical methods to determine the level of these compounds in seed and meal are needed to achieve these objectives.

HISTORY OF CULTIVAR DEVELOPMENT

Systematic breeding programs for winter rapeseed improvement were initiated in Europe some 100 years ago and resulted in three ecotypes or land races, a very cold hardy Eastern European form, a high seed and oil yielding Central European type and a relatively non-hardy, strongly vegetative Western European form. The genetic diversity of these and other land races were effectively used in the intensive breeding programs initiated in the mid 1940s for all *Brassica* oilseed forms and species in both Europe and Canada. In India, formal cultivar improvement programs in *B. campestris* and *B. juncea* were begun in the Punjab as early as 1910 while in Asia breeders were already developing adapted *B. napus* cultivars from crosses between local land races of *B. campestris* and introduced European *B. napus* material by 1916. Such interspecific crosses have also resulted in increased genetic diversity and improved European cultivars. From the cross (*B. campestris* x *B. oleracea*) x *B. napus* cv. Lembke's, German breeders in the 1960s, developed the winter *B. napus* cultivar Rapol which outyielded Lembke's, the best German cultivar of that time.

From the 1960s to the present, rapeseed breeding has been dominated by the need to improve the quality of the oil and meal. With each quality change the initial cultivars were lower in seed and oil yield. However, within a few years the agronomic performance of the old, lower quality cultivars were matched or surpassed (Table 16.3).

**Table 16.3 Yield, Maturity Oil and Protein Content and Seed Quality of
Canadian Rape (*Brassica napus*) and Turnip Rape (*B. campestris*)
Cultivars in Western Canada Cooperative Tests**

Year released	Species & cultivar	Yield[1] relative	Maturity days	Oil[2] %	Protein[3] %	Seed[4] quality
B. napus						
1943	Argentine	100	101	40.5	47.1	HEHG
1954	Golden	101	101	41.1	43.9	HEHG
1963	Tanka	106	101	42.7	46.3	HEHG
1966	Target	109	99	43.9	45.4	HEHG
1970	Turret	111	98	44.5	45.4	HEHG
1968	Oro	107	106	41.7	43.4	LEHG
1973	Midas	118	98	43.8	42.9	LEHG
1974	Tower	112	97	42.6	47.2	LELG
1977	Regent	115	98	43.1	47.0	LELG
1981	Andor	119	95	43.6	45.9	LELG
1982	Westar	127	95	44.3	46.0	LELG
B. campestris						
1943	Polish	100	88	40.5	43.6	HEHG
1964	Echo	112	90	40.8	43.7	HEHG
1969	Polar	109	89	42.3	44.2	HEHG
1971	Span	109	87	39.6	42.8	LEHG
1973	Torch	111	87	40.1	43.2	LEHG
1977	Candle	103	87	42.1	43.2	LELG
1981	Tobin	110	87	42.5	43.2	LELG

[1] Yield expressed as percentage of cv. Argentine and Polish respectively
[2] Oil content expressed as percent of moisture-free seed
[3] Protein content expressed as percent of moisture-free, oil-free meal
[4] H = high, L = Low, E = erucic acid and G = glucosinolate

UTILIZATION OF PRODUCTS

Early Asian and European writings mention the use of seed and oil from rape and mustard oil as medicinal remedies for stomach problems and skin diseases (Prakash, 1980). However, the main utilization has been for industrial and edible purposes. Prior to the availability of petroleum products or electricity, rapeseed oil, which burns with a bright smokeless flame, was a popular lamp oil in both Asia and Europe. The oil was also widely used in soap making. The industrial importance of rapeseed oil was further extended with the advent of the steam engine since it was found that high erucic acid rapeseed oil clings to water- and steam-washed metal surfaces better than petroleum products. Indeed, the urgent need for this lubricating oil by the allied navies of World War II was directly responsible for the introduction and establishment of the crop in Canada.

A limited but significant industrial oil market has developed for very high (>50%) erucic acid rapeseed oil. Although there are many minor applications for this oil, such as a lubricant for the cold rolling of steel and in jet engines, most of the oil is fractionated and the erucic acid converted to erucamide for use in the plastics industry. The erucamide is sprayed on plastic sheeting and mouldings to prevent their sticking together or to the extruding machinery.

In Asian countries, such as India and China, the edible uses of rape and mustard oils in liquid form were established early in time and became one of the most important traditional edible oil sources. In Japan rapeseed oil is still considered a premium oil, particularly for deep fat tempura cooking. In the cooler climate of northern Europe, where dietary use of solid fats are traditional, rapeseed oil did not become a major part of the diet except during times of war and famine. However, following World War II improved extraction and processing techniques allowed rapeseed oil to capture a substantial portion of the margarine and shortening market in both Europe and Canada. More recently, the trend in these countries has been to greater use of liquid oils for cooking and in salad dressings. The modified fatty acid composition in the zero erucic acid cultivars without the long chain fatty acids and with its low content of short chain saturated acids, coupled with good natural keeping qualities, has led to its dominance in the Canadian and some European liquid oil markets.

CONCLUSION

The overall breeding objective has been to make the *Brassica* oilseed crops more productive for the producer and more valuable and useful to the processor and end user. Enormous progress has been made in the last two decades and the next 10 to 15 years promise even greater advances. Indeed the opportunity to make the *Brassica* oilseeds and their products premium commodities is well within the reach of today's breeders.

REFERENCES

Anderson, G., and Olsson, G. 1961. Cruciferen-Ölpflanzen, pp. 1-66. *In* H. Kappert and W. Rudorf (eds.), *Handbuch der Pflanzenzuchtung* 2nd Ed. Vol. 5. Paul Parey, Berlin and Hamburg.

Aviv, D., Arzee-Gonen, P., Bleichman, S., and Galun, E. 1984.Novel alloplasmic *Nicotiana* plants by "donor-recipient" protoplast fusion: cybrids having *N. tabacum* or *N. sylvestris* nuclear genomes and either or both plastomes and chondriomes from alien species. Mol. Gen. Genet. 196: 244-253.

Bannerot, H., Boulidard, L., and Chupeau, Y. 1977. Unexpected difficulties met with the radish cytoplasm in *Brassica oleracea*. Eucarpia Cruciferae Newsl. 2: 16.

Beversdorf, W.D., Grant, I., and Erickson, L.R. 1984. Hybridization process utilizing a combination of cytoplasmic male sterility and herbicide tolerance. UK Patent Application GB2139466A.

Brouwer, W., and Schuster, W. 1976. Raps und Rubsen, pp. 388-495. *In* W. Brouwer (ed.), *Handbuch des Speziellen Pflanzenbaues*. Vol. 2. Paul Parey, Berlin and Hamburg.

Chiang, M.S. 1974. Cabbage pollen germination and longevity. Euphytica 23: 579-584.

Chuong, P.V., and Beversdorf, W.D. 1985. High frequency embryogenesis through isolated microspore culture in *Brassica napus* L. and *B. carinata* Braun. Plant Sci. 39: 219-226.

Denford, K.E. 1975. Isoenzyme studies in members of the genus *Brassica*. Bot. Nat. 128 (4): 455-462.

Dorrell, D.G., and Downey, R.K. 1964. The inheritance of erucic acid content in rapeseed (*Brassica campestris*). Can. J. Plant Sci. 44: 499-504.

Downey, R.K. 1964. A selection of *Brassica campestris* L. containing no erucic acid and in its seed oil. Can. J. Plant Sci. 44: 295.

——, Klassen, A.J., and Stringham, G.R. 1980. Rapeseed and mustard, pp. 495-509. *In* W.R. Fehr and H.H. Hadley (eds.), *Hybridization of Crop Plants*. Am. Soc. Agron. Crop Sci. Soc. Am., Madison, Wis.

Fan, Z., Rimmer, S.R., and Stefansson, B.R. 1983. Inheritance of resistance to *Albugo candida* in rape (*Brassica napus* L.). Can. J. Genet. Cytol. 25: 420-424.

——, Stefansson, B.R., and Sernyk, J.L. 1986. Maintainers and restorers for three male sterility inducing cytoplasms in rape, *Brassica napus* L. Can. J. Plant Sci. 66: 229-234.

Fenwick, G.R., Heaney, R.K., and Mullin, W.J. 1983. Glucosinolates and their breakdown products in food and food plants. CRC Critical Rev. Food and Nutrition. 18: 123-201.

Fu, T.D. 1981. Production and research of rapeseed in the People's Republic of China. Eurcarpia Cruciferae Newsl. 6: 6-7.

Grami, B., Baker, R.K., and Stefansson, B.R. 1977. Genetics of protein and oil content in summer rape. Heritability, number of effective factors and correlations. Can. J. Plant Sci. 57: 937-943.

Grant, I., and Beversdorf, W.D. 1985. Heterosis and combining ability estimates in spring-planted oilseed rape (*Brassica napus* L.). Can. J. Genet. Cytol. 27: 472-478.

Harvey, B.L., and Downey, R.K. 1964. The inheritance of erucic acid content in rapeseed (*Brassica napus*). Can. J. Plant Sci. 44: 104-111.

Hedge, I.C. 1976. A systematic and geographical survey of the old world cruciferae, pp. 1-45. *In* J.G. Vaughan, A.J. MacLeod and B.M.G. Jones (eds.), *The Biology and Chemistry of the Cruciferae*. Academic Press, New York.

Hemingway, J.S. 1976. Mustards: Brassica spp. and *Sinapis alba* (Cruciferae), pp. 56-59. *In* N.W. Simmons (ed.), *Evolution of Crop Plants*. Longman, London.

Hinata, K., and Konno, N. 1979. Studies on a male sterile strain having the *Brassica campestris* nucleus and the *Diplotaxis muralis* cytoplasm. I. On the breeding procedures and some characteristics of the male sterile strain (Japanese with English summary). Jpn. J. Breed. 29: 305-311.

Hutcheson, D.S., Downey, R.K., and Campbell, S.J. 1981. Performance of a naturally occurring subspecies hybrid in *B. campestris* L. var. oleifera Metzg. Can. J. Plant Sci. 61: 895-900.

Josefsson, E. 1968. Investigations on shattering resistance of cruciferous oil crops. Z. Pflanzenzuchtg. 59: 384-396.

Keller, W.A., and Armstrong, K.C. 1983. Production of *Brassica napus* haploids through anther and microspore culture, pp. 239-245. Proc. 6th Intern. Rapeseed Conf., Paris.

Kirk, J.T.O., and Hurlstone, C.J. 1983. Variation and inheritance of erucic acid content in *Brassica juncea*. Z. Pflanzenzuchtg. 90: 331-338.

———, and Oram, R.N. 1981. Isolation of erucic acid-free lines of *Brassica juncea* : Indian mustard now a potential oilseed crop in Australia. J. Aust. Inst. Agric. Sci. 47: 51-52.

Kolte, S.J. 1985. Diseases of Annual Edible Oilseed crops. Rapeseed - Mustard and Sesame Diseases, pp. 9-82. Vol. II, Chapter 2. CRC Press, Inc., Boca Raton, Fla.

Kramer, K.G., Sauer, F.D., and Pigden, W.J. 1983. *High and Low Erucic Acid Rapeseed Oils.* Academic Press, New York.

Lee, J.I., Shiga, T., and Kwon, B.S. 1976. Studies on heterosis breeding in rapeseed using cytoplasmic male sterility. I. Heterosis of agronomic characters and fertility restoration in F_1 hybrids using CMS. Korean J. Breed. 8: 63-70.

Lee, S.L., and Zhang, Y. 1983. The utilization of genetic male sterility in *Brassica napus* in Shanghai, China, pp. 360-364. Proc. 6th Intern. Rapeseed Conf., Paris.

Lefort-Buson, M., and Dattee, Y. 1982. Genetic study of some agronomic characters in winter oilseed rape (*Brassica napus* L.). I. Heterosis II. Genetic parameters. Agronomie 2: 315-332.

Mantell, S.H., Matthews, J.A., and McKee, R.A. 1985. *Principles of Plant Biotechnology.* Blackwell Sci. Publ., Boston.

Mizushima, U. 1980. Genome Analysis in *Brassica* and Allied Genera, pp. 89-108. *In* S. Tsunoda, K. Hinata, and C. Gomez-Campo (eds.), *Brassica Crops and Wild Allies. Biology and Breeding.* Japan Scient. Soc. Press, Tokyo.

Ogura, H. 1968. Studies on the new male sterility in Japanese radish with special reference to the utilization of this sterility towards the practical raising of hybrid seed. Mem. Fac. Agric. Kagoshima Univ. 6: 39-78.

Pelletier, G., Primard, C., Vedel, F., Chetrit, P., Remy, R., Rousselle, P., and Renard, M. 1983. Intergeneric cytoplasmic hybridization in Cruciferae by protoplast fusion. Mol. Gen. Genet. 191: 244-250.

Persson, C. 1985. High palmitic acid content in summer turnip rape (*Brassica campestris* var. annua L.). Eucarpia Cruciferae Newsl. 10: 137.

Petrie, G.A., and Lewis, P.A. 1985. Sexual compatibility of isolates of the rapeseed blackleg fungus *Leptosphaeria maculans* from Canada, Australia and England. Can. J. Plant Pathol. 7: 253-258.

Prakash, S. 1980. Cruciferous oilseeds in India, pp. 151-163. *In* S. Tsunoda, K. Hinata and C. Gomez-Campo (eds.), *Brassica Crops and Wild Allies. Biology and Breeding.* Japan Scient. Soc. Press, Tokyo.

———, and Hinata, K. 1980. Taxonomy, cytogenetics and origin of crop *Brassicas*, a review. Opera Bot. 55: 1-57.

Rakow, G. 1973. Selektion auf Linol- und Linolensauregehalt in Rapssamen nach mutagener Behandlung. Z. Pflanzenzuchtg. 69: 62-82.

———, and Woods, D.L. 1987. Outcrossing in rape and mustard under Saskatchewan prairie conditions. Can. J. Plant Sci. 67: 147-151.

Rawat, D.S., and Anand, I.J. 1979. Male sterility in Indian mustard. Indian J. Genet. Plant Breed. 39: 412-414.

Röbbelen, G. 1960. Beitrage zur Analyse des Brassica-Genoms. Chromasoma 11: 205-228.

Roggen, H.P.J.R. 1974. Pollen Washing Influences (in) Compatibility in *Brassica oleracea* Varieties, pp. 273-278. *In* H.F. Linskens (ed.), *Fertilization in Higher Plants.* North-Holland Publ. Co., Amsterdam.

Roy, N.N. 1984. Interspecific transfer of *Brassica juncea* -type high blackleg resistance to *Brassica napus.* Euphytica 33: 295-303.

Sacristan, M.D. 1982. Resistance responses to *Phoma lingam* of plants regnerated from selected cell and embryogenic cultures of haploid *Brassica napus.* Theor. Appl. Genet. 61: 193-200.

Schuster, W. 1982. Uber die Nutzung von Heterosiseffekten durch synthetische Sorten von *Brassica napus* und *Sinapis alba.* Vortrage Pflanzenzuchtg. 1: 137-156.

Seguin-Swartz, G., Hutcheson D.S., and Downey, R.K. 1983. Anther culture studies in *Brassica campestris*, pp. 246-251. Proc. 6th Intern. Rapeseed Conf., Paris.

Sernyk, J.L., and Stefansson, B.R. 1983. Heterosis in summer rape (*Brassica napus* L.). Can. J. Plant Sci. 63: 407-413.

Shiga, T. 1970. Rape breeding by interspecific crossing between *Brassica napus* and *Brassica campestris* in Japan. Japan Agric. Res. Quarterly 5: 5-10.

———. 1980. Maler sterility and cytoplasmic differentiation, pp. 205-221. *In* S. Tsunoda, K. Hinata and G. Gomez-Campo (eds.), *Brassica Crops and Wild Allies. Biology and Breeding.* Japan Scient. Soc. Press, Tokyo.

———, Ohkawa, Y., and Takayanagi, K. 1983. Cytoplasm types of European rapeseed (*Brassica napus* L.) cultivars and their ability to restore fertility in cytoplasmic male sterile lines. Bull. Natl. Agric. Sci., Ser. D. 35: 103-124.

Stefansson, B.R., Hougen, F.W., and Downey, R.K. 1961. Note on the isolation of rape plants with seed oil free from erucic acid. Can. J. Plant Sci. 41: 218-219.

Stringam, G.R., McGregor, D.I., and Pawlowski, S.H. 1974. Chemical and morphological characteristics associated with seedcoat color in rapeseed, pp. 99-108. Proc. 4th Intern. Rapeseed Congress, Giessen.

Thompson, K.F. 1978. Application of recessive self-incompatibility to production of hybrid rapeseed, pp. 56-59. Proc. 5th Intern. Rapeseed Conf. Vol. 1. Malmo, Sweden.

———. 1983. Breeding winter oilseed rape, *Brassica napus.* Adv. Appl. Biol. 7: 1-104.

Thurling, N. 1974. An evaluation of an index method of selection for high yield in turnip rape, *Brassica campestris* L. ssp. *oleifera* Metzg. Euphytica 23: 321-331.

Vaughan, J.G., Phelan, J.R., and Denford, K.E. 1976. Seed Studies in the Cruciferae, pp. 119-144. *In* J.G. Vaughan, A.J. MacLeod and B.M.G. Jones (eds.), *The Biology and Chemistry of the Cruciferae.* Academic Press, New York.

Chapter 17

Safflower

P. F. Knowles

IMPORTANCE AND DISTRIBUTION

Safflower (*Carthamus tinctorius* L.) was not investigated seriously as an oil-seed crop until the 1930s and 1940s. Details of its development, production and uses are provided by Weiss (1971). Worldwide, safflower (Fig. 17.1A) is a comparatively minor oilseed crop, being limited in its distribution by constraints of the environment and the plant's spiny nature. Originating in the Middle East, it is adapted to areas with winter and spring rainfall, or supplemental irrigation during that period and a dry atmosphere during flowering and maturation. High humidities or frequent rains during and after flowering favor the development of several foliar diseases, the most serious being those caused by *Alternaria carthami* Chowdhury, *Ramularia carthami* Zaprometov, *Fusarium oxysporum* Schlecht. f. *carthami* Klis. & Hous., *Puccinia carthami* Cda., *Pseudomonas syringae* Van Hall, and *Botrytis cinerea* Pers. ex. Fr. Prolonged humid periods at maturity often will cause sprouting of seeds in the heads.

Fig. 17.1 Safflower. A - Branch of a typical spiny plant. B - Head of the spiny plant showing the spiny outer bracts. C - Head of a spineless cultivar. Reproductive structures of safflower: D - Disk, or tubular flower, showing ovary at base, tubular corolla terminating in five lobes, an anther tube with short filaments attached to the top of the corolla tube, and the stigma with attached pollen above the anther tube. E - Anther tube slit on one side and opened up to show the five attached anthers. F - Stigma with attached pollen and upper portion of the style. G - Achene (seed). D-G from Hanelt (1963).

Table 17.1 World Safflower Production by Region and Major Producing Countries.

Region or country	Production area ('000 ha)			Seed yield (kg/ha)			Seed production ('000 tonnes)		
	1969-71	1979-81	1985	1969-71	1979-81	1985	1969-71	1979-81	1985
World	**998**	**1392**	**1313**	**707**	**694**	**640**	**706**	**967**	**840**
Africa	**63**	**65**	**66**	**586**	**474**	**485**	**37**	**31**	**32**
Ethiopia	62	65	66	586	474	485	36	31	32
N. and C. America	**287**	**546**	**295**	**1757**	**1141**	**847**	**504**	**623**	**250**
Mexico	195	445	190	1552	1113	789	303	495	150
U.S.A.	92	101	105	2191	1265	952	202	127	100
S. America	**1**	**1**	**3**	**706**	**841**	**800**	**-**	**1**	**2**
Asia	**584**	**720**	**871**	**226**	**383**	**571**	**132**	**276**	**498**
India	582	719	870	223	382	571	130	275	497
Europe	**26**	**19**	**21**	**664**	**752**	**725**	**16**	**14**	**15**
Oceania	**24**	**35**	**47**	**400**	**548**	**830**	**10**	**19**	**39**
Austrailia	24	35	47	400	548	830	10	19	39
U.S.S.R.	**14**	**6**	**10**	**421**	**474**	**400**	**6**	**3**	**4**

Source: FAO Production Yearbooks 1980 (vol. 34) and 1985 (vol. 39).

Soil moisture availability also determines the area of production. Although safflower is often claimed to be drought-resistant it has in fact a rather high water requirement. However, because the crop is deep rooted, penetrating up to four meters when root growth is not restricted, it can complete its life cycle without supplemental moisture, provided the soil has a good water-holding capacity and is at or near field capacity at the time of planting. On the other hand, excessive water, often caused by poor irrigation management, usually results in Phytophthora root rot damage.

Insect pests have also limited the area suitable for safflower production. In much of the Mediterranean Basin, the Middle East, the Sudan and in late plantings in South Asia, the larvae of the safflower fly, *Acanthiophilus helianthi* Rossi, attack the developing seed to such a degree that production has been discouraged. Several other insect pests also cause damage, many of them using wild species of safflower as alternative hosts.

Fertility is not adversely affected by high temperatures (>40°C) per se. However, a combination of high temperatures and high humidities can severely reduce seed set (Zimmerman, 1972).

The photoperiod responses of safflower have not been well worked out, particularly as they are affected by temperature. If mean temperatures are above 20°C, most cultivars will require a minimum growing period of 120 days, some three weeks longer than for wheat. With cool weather during the early developmental period, as in February plantings in central California, the growing period will be extended to 150 or more days, due primarily to a longer rosette period.

Safflower has shown adaptation to three basic environments (Table 17.1). In south central India (the Deccan) the crop does well when sown in October or November into heavy soils moist from the summer rains. The dry spring which follows is well suited to problem-free flowering and seed set. Mediterranean-like climates, with winter rains or irrigation followed by dry summers, are also suited to safflower production. Such regions include the Middle East, the central valleys of California, northwest Mexico, Spain and Western Australia. Safflower can also be grown in climates similar to that of the drier areas of the northern Great Plains of the United States. In such regions the crop is sown in the spring, sometimes irrigated in the early stages, and matures in the dry fall. Production practices for those areas are described by Weiss (1971).

In the USA, safflower has been grown under contract to companies processing the seed for oil or exporting it to other countries. The contract guarantees the farmer a market and a minimum price for the seed.

ORIGIN AND SYSTEMATICS

A detailed taxonomic treatment of *Carthamus* was provided by Hanelt (1963). Ashri (1973) discussed species relationships, and Knowles (1976) the evolution of cultivated safflower.

Safflower and related species are branched plants, the branches terminating in capitula or heads typical of many members of the Compositae family (Fig. 17.1). Following emergence plants form rosettes of basal leaves and remain in this form until bolting is initiated by temperature and plant genotype. Once initiated, a strong central stem grows rapidly, its height being influenced by the time of planting, genotype and environment. Spines are present on all wild species and most cultivars of *C. tinctorius*, being most abundant and longer on the upper portions of the plant and on the outer involucral bracts (Fig. 17.1B). Peripheral flowers in the heads of most species, including cultivated safflower, usually have rudimentary ovaries. Depending on the cultivar and head position, cultivated safflower produces twenty to over one hundred developed seeds in each head.

The safflower seed is a type of fruit called an achene. The outer layer is a thick, white protective hull which may be either smooth or ridged. Inside the hull and partly adhering to it is a thin seed coat which encloses the embryo. The embryo serves as the storage point for the oil and protein.

Safflower is believed to have originated in the area encompassed by southern USSR, western Iran, Iraq, Syria, southern Turkey, Jordan, and Israel, where closely related n=12 wild species, *C. flavescens* Spreng (=*C. persicus* Willd.), *C. oxyacantha* M. B. (=*C. oxyacanthus* M. B.) and *C. palaestinus* Eig, are found. These species readily cross with *C. tinctorius* to give fertile progeny in the F_1 and F_2. *C. gypsicolus* Ilj. and *C. curdicus* Hanelt, also appear to be members of this group (Hanelt, 1963), although cross compatibilities to *C. tinctorius* have not been studied. The wild species are characterized by having mostly yellow, though occasionally white flowers (corollas) and yellow pollen grains. At an early stage in its evolution, *C. tinctorius* spread to Egypt, Ethiopia, southern Europe, south Asia and the Far East where distinctive types have evolved (Table 17.2).

Table 17.2 Safflower Characteristics of Different Geographical Regions, Listed in Order of Decreasing Frequency

Geographical region	Height[a]	Branch-ing[a]	Spines[a]	Head size[a]	Flower color[a]
Far East	tall	int	sp, spls	int	r
India-Pakistan	sh	many	sp	sm, int	o,w,r
Middle East	tall	few	spls	int, large	r,o,y,w
Egypt	int	few	sp, spls	large, int	o,y,w,r
Sudan	sh, int	int	sp	sm, int	y,o
Ethiopia	tall	many	sp	sm	r
Europe	int	int	sp, spls	int	o,r,y,w

[a] Abbreviations: sh=short; int=intermediate; sp=spiny; spls=spineless; sm=small; r=red; w=white; o=orange; y=yellow

Knowles, 1969

A second group of closely related wild species in the Middle East has a chromosome number of n=10, grayish green foliage, white to purple flowers and white pollen. These species will cross with some difficulty with *C. tinctorius* to give highly sterile F_1 progeny.

C. divaricatus Beg and Vacc., (n=11), which grows in the coastal areas of Libya, is characterized by yellow pollen and a range of flower color from white to yellow to purple. Except for the yellow flowers and yellow pollen it resembles and will cross readily with species having 10 pairs of chromosomes to give partially fertile F_1. It will also cross with *C. tinctorius* to give self sterile hybrids with low levels of female fertility in backcrosses to *C. tinctorius*.

C. lanatus L., (n=22), has mostly yellow and occasionally white flowers and yellow pollen. It may be a polyploid resulting from a cross of species with 10 and 12 pairs of chromosomes followed by chromosome doubling of the F_1. However, such F_1 plants, with or without chromosome doubling, did not resemble *C. lanatus*. *C. lanatus* is distributed over almost the entire range of wild *Carthamus* species in Asia, Europe and Africa. *C. lanatus* will cross with species having 10 and 12 pairs of chromosomes to give sterile hybrids.

Two other polyploid species, *C. turkestanicus* Popov and *C. baeticus* (Boiss. & Reut.) Nym., (n=32), are somewhat similar to *C. lanatus* but have white pollen. They appear to have resulted from crosses of *C. lanatus* to different species with 10 pairs of chromosomes, followed by doubling of the chromosomes in the F_1. *C. turkestanicus* has an eastern distribution beyond the range of *C. lanatus*, and *C. baeticus* a western distribution, often in association with *C. lanatus*.

C. nitidus Boiss., (n=12), is distantly related to other *Carthamus* species. It will cross with *C. tinctorius* to give sterile hybrids.

All wild species are weedy in nature. Field evaluations of them should be done with great care, especially in areas with a Mediterranean climate.

MODE OF REPRODUCTION

Cultivars of safflower are highly self-pollinated, with outcrossing below 10% (Knowles, 1969), though there are reports of some genotypes with much higher levels of cross-pollination. Bees and several other insects are attracted to safflower for both pollen and nectar. Safflower pollen is not transported by wind. Excepting the polyploid species, wild species are partially or completely outcrossed. Where tested, as in *C. flavescens* (Imrie and Knowles, 1971), the incompatibility system has been sporophytic in nature.

BREEDING PROCEDURES

Details of safflower breeding have been described by Knowles (1980). Though highly self-pollinated, plants used as parents in crosses for genetic studies or breeding purposes, as well as F_1 plants and selected F_2 plants, are often selfed using paper or cloth bags. Crowding of heads within selfing bags should be avoided as it will lead to the development of molds and a very low level of seed production.

Plant breeding companies have generally used the pedigree method of handling segregating populations, selecting superior plants in F_2 for evaluation as F_3 lines. Superior and uniform F_3 lines have often been the source of single-plant selections which will provide enough open-pollinated seed for yield tests in F_4 and selfed seed for increase. The latter increase of superior F_4 lines in yield tests may be the source material for future cultivars, with or without further selection. Bulk methods of breeding, based on selection among F_5 or F_6 plants, have not been used in safflower. Normally the high level of outcrossing within the bulked populations prevents the desired level of homozygosity from being achieved. The backcross method has been used to introduce genes for disease resistance from resistant lines to commercial cultivars.

Crosses require a special technique of emasculation which involves the removal of anther tubes along with the upper portions of the corolla tubes and petal lobes when the flowers are in the late bud stage (Fig. 17.1 D,E) (Knowles, 1980). The following day, when the styles have elongated, pollen from a single flower or entire head is applied.

A form of structural male sterility has been proposed for use in producing hybrid cultivars (Rubis, 1967). The male sterility resulted from the failure of the anther sacs to open completely, leading to emergence of styles and stigmas almost totally free of pollen. In a crossing block most of the seed resulted from crosses to the male parent, but when the female parent was grown under isolation in the presence of bees, sufficient pollen was released to produce seed, thus propagating the male-sterile parent. Unfortunately, in crossing blocks a considerable proportion of selfed seed was frequently produced on the female parent, resulting in sufficient low yielding plants in the hybrid cultivar to reduce its yield below that of nonhybrid cultivars (Urie and Zimmer, 1970).

Genic male sterility has been identified (Heaton and Knowles, 1982), and considered for use in producing hybrid cultivars. However, the labor involved in removal of male-fertile types in crossing blocks has prohibited its use in the production of hybrid cultivars, at least in the United States. A. B. Hill of Cargill Incorporated reports (personal communication) the use of cytoplasmic male-sterile types in the production of hybrid cultivars.

BREEDING OBJECTIVES

Disease Resistance

A major breeding objective wherever safflower is grown has been greater resistance to disease. A valuable source of resistance has been the United States Department of Agriculture's world collection of safflower. It has provided resistance to rust, Fusarium wilt (Klisiewicz and Urie, 1982), Verticillium wilt (Urie and Knowles, 1972), Alternaria leaf blight, and Phytophthora root rot (Da Via et al. 1981). Two studies financed in part by the U. S. Department of Agriculture, one in Israel (Ashri, 1973), the other in India (Karve, 1979), identified germplasm with tolerance or resistance to major diseases and insects of both areas. Even with the disease resistances that have been identified and in many cases incorporated into cultivars, safflower is still restricted in its distribution by susceptibility to disease. If cultivars with greater resistance to foliar diseases were available, safflower would be much more competitive with sunflower and soybean. Kolte (1985) describes in detail diseases of safflower.

Insect Resistance

Greater resistance to insects is necessary in areas of the world where safflower and related wild species are indigenous. In other areas where safflower has been recently introduced, insects have been less serious, so breeding for resistance has had a low priority.

Early Maturity

Earlier maturity would make safflower more competitive with small grains. Being about three weeks later than wheat, safflower has not been successful in Canada and other areas where the growing season is less than 120 days. Little or no progress has been made in developing acceptable earlier types over the last thirty years in the USA. The cultivar "Mexican Dwarf" (Obeso-S., 1974) and types derived therefrom have required 100 to 105 days to mature, but have been too short and too low yielding to be acceptable for commercial production.

Spines

At an early date in breeding programs in the USA efforts were made to develop superior spineless cultivars, but without success. Spineless types have been consistently lower in both yield and oil content. As a consequence, the elimination of spines has had a low priority in areas where safflower has been harvested mechanically. In areas where hand harvesting of crops is practiced the spines have been a major deterrent to the acceptance of the safflower crop, with the possible exception of India. In India spines do provide a measure of protection from bird and rodent damage.

The discomfort of hand harvesting can be minimized by taking advantage of the absence of spines on the lower leaves and growing the plants close together so that there are no basal branches and the spiny leaves, bracts and heads are concentrated near the top of the plant.

Increased Yield

Commercial yields of safflower, in the absence of diseases, have not increased appreciably in California over the last twenty years. Likewise in other areas there have been no marked increases in yielding ability of cultivars. Experimental data indicate, however, that hybrid cultivars could move safflower yields to a higher plateau.

Oil Content

A primary objective of breeding programs is the development of cultivars with higher oil contents. Since the introduction of safflower to commercial production in the United States in the 1940s, there has been a continued and marked increase in oil content. Present cultivars have oil contents at or above 42%, whereas in the 1940s, it was about 35%. A reduction in hull content has contributed to the increased oil content as well as to an increase in protein levels. The partial hull genotype identified by Urie (1986) may result in the development of cultivars with oil contents approaching 50%.

Oil Quality

Safflower contains genetic variability for fatty acid composition of the oil (Table 17.3). The genetic manipulation of oil quality in safflower was a model for other crops. However, only the standard (high linoleic) type and the high oleic type are grown commercially. Temperature during oil deposition and maturity has had little effect on the fatty acid composition of the high linoleic and high oleic genotypes, but the genotype with intermediate levels of both fatty acids will produce high levels of linoleic acid at low temperatures and high levels of oleic acid at high temperatures.

Table 17.3 Fatty Acid Composition of the Seed Oil of Different Safflower Materials

| Type of seed oil | Genotype | Fatty acid content, % | | | |
		Pal-mitic	Stear-ic	Oleic	Lino-leic
Very high linoleic[a]	OlOlliliStSt	3-5	1-2	5-7	87-89
High linoleic[b]	OlOlLiLiStSt	6-8	2-3	16-20	71-75
High oleic[c]	ololLiLiStSt	5-6	1-2	75-80	14-18
Intermediate oleic[d]	ol¹ol¹LiLiStSt	5-6	1-2	41-53	39-52
High stearic[e]	OlOlLiLiListst	5-6	4-11	13-15	69-72

[a] Introduction from Portugal. [b] Cultivar Gila. [c] Cultivar UC-1. [d] Introduction from Iran.
[e] Introduction from Israel.
(Futehally, 1982)

HISTORY OF CULTIVAR DEVELOPMENT

The first efforts at commercial development of safflower in the USA in the 1930s failed mainly because the genotypes then available, most of them from India, had oil contents below 30%. The introduction of germplasm from Egypt and the Sudan in the 1940s, with oil contents well over 30%, permitted the development of adapted cultivars with 35% oil or better. Such cultivars provided the basis for commercial production of safflower, first in western Nebraska and eastern Colorado, and then in California and Arizona.

Soon after its commercial establishment, *Puccinia carthami* rust threatened production, but was held in check by a sequence of genes for resistance that were rapidly introduced into cultivars, in some instances by backcrossing. Fusarium wilt posed a threat in northern California but was controlled by genes for resistance. Verticillium wilt attacking cotton proved to be pathogenic on safflower until the resistance from certain introductions was transferred to commercial cultivars. Some tolerance to Alternaria and Pseudomonas leaf blights is now available in cultivars developed in Montana and germplasm tolerant to Phytophthora root rot is available. Breeding for resistance to diseases must continue to have a high priority in breeding programs. Breeding cultivars resistant to *Alternaria carthami* and to *Phytophthora cryptogea* will determine the expansion of safflower production in Australia.

The cultivar "UC-1," released in 1966, permitted the production of a high oleic type. It has been replaced by cultivars of the same type with higher oil contents, higher yields and greater resistance to diseases.

In most countries the public sector has taken the lead in the development of cultivars. In the USA, however, cultivar development has been done by commercial companies. This has permitted the public sector to be mainly involved in germplasm development and research of a basic nature.

UTILIZATION OF PRODUCTS

It would appear that safflower was domesticated for its flowers. Garlands of individual florets sown side by side on long narrow strips of fabric were found wrapped around Egyptian mummies dated about 1600 B.C. At a very early date, carthamin, a red dye, was extracted from the flowers and used primarily to color cloth. Dried red or orange flowers are still sold as a substitute for saffron in bazaars of the Middle East, and are used to color foods and beverages. At one time safflower was grown in many countries and, along with indigo, provided most of the dye of commerce. Both were rapidly replaced in the early 1800s by the cheaper and superior aniline dyes.

Flowers are picked every two or three days from much of the red – or orange – flowered safflowers grown in China. After drying, the flowers are used for medicinal purposes. They are reported to have beneficial effects for problems of the circulatory system, for inflammations, and for muscular fatigue. In China a few factories are extracting a yellow and a red color (carthamin) from the flowers for coloring foods and beverages.

Extraction of the oil by primitive means goes back at least to Roman times. Village-level oil extraction still continues in countries of the Middle East and south Asia (Knowles, 1967), the oil and cake being used locally, the former for cooking and the latter for livestock feed.

With minor modifications modern oilseed crushing equipment may be used for safflower. Usually the hulls are removed prior to crushing, then are ground and incorporated in different amounts with the meal to provide a product with levels of protein varying from 20% to 40%. Crushing with expellers will remove most of the oil, but usually reduced pressures are used such that the residue contains 10 to 12% oil which is then removed by solvents.

In the USA the oil was used at first for industrial purposes, mostly for paints, varnishes and other surface coatings. It was rated as a superior oil for clear varnishes and light colored paints because it would not yellow with age. Currently most of the oil with high levels of the polyunsaturated linoleic acid is used in edible products such as salad oils and soft margarines. As a frying oil it polymerizes readily to form a scum on the cooking vessel.

The high oleic oil is a superior cooking oil. It is heat stable and will not form a scum when used as a frying oil. It is used in the preparation of fast foods such as potato chips and french fries. Oils high in oleic acid have increasing uses in industrial products.

The feed value of the oil-free meal is similar to other meals having the same protein content. The hulls, which have essentially no feed value, have been used experimentally, but not commercially, in fiber boards and similar products.

REFERENCES

Ashri, A. 1973. Divergence and evolution in the safflower genus, *Carthamus*. Final Res. Rep., USDA PL480 Project No. A10-CR-18, Hebrew University, Rehovot, Israel.

Da Via, D.J., Knowles, P.F., and Klisiewicz, J.M. 1981. Evaluation of the safflower world collection for resistance to Phytophthora. Crop Sci. 21: 226-229.

Futehally, S. 1982. Inheritance of Very High Levels of Linoleic Acid in the Seed Oil of Safflower (*Carthamus tinctorius* L.), M.S. thesis, Univ. California, Davis.

Hanelt, P. 1963. Monographische Übersicht der Gattung *Carthamus* L. (Compositae). Zeit. Feddes Repert. 67: 41-180.

Heaton, T.C., and Knowles, P.F. 1982. Inheritance of male sterility in safflower. Crop Sci. 22: 520-522.

Imrie, B.C., and Knowles, P.F. 1971. Genetic studies of self-incompatibility in *Carthamus flavescens* Spreng. Crop Sci. 11: 6-9.

Karve, A.D. 1979. Resistance of safflower (*Carthamus tinctorius* L.) to insects and diseases. Final Technical Rep., USDA PL480 Project No. A7-CR-423. Nimbkar Agric. Res. Inst., Phaltan, India.

Klisiewicz, J.M., and Urie, A.L. 1982. Registration of Fusarium resistant safflower (*Carthamus tinctorius*) germplasm. Crop Sci. 22: 165.

Knowles, P.F. 1967. Processing seeds for oil in towns of Turkey, India and Egypt. Econ. Bot. 21: 156-162.

——, 1969. Centers of plant diversity and conservation of crop germplasm: Safflower. Econ. Bot. 23: 324-329.

——, 1976. Safflower, pp. 31-33. *In* N.W. Simmons (ed.), *Evolution of Crop Plants*. Longman, Inc., New York.

——, 1980. Safflower, pp. 535-547. *In* W.R. Fehr and H.H. Hadley (eds.), *Hybridization of Crop Plants*. Am. Soc. Agron., Madison, Wis.

Kolte, S.J. 1985. *Diseases of Annual Edible Oilseed Crops*. III. *Sunflower, Safflower and Nigerseed Diseases*. CRC Press, Boca Raton, Fla.

Obeso-S., E. 1974. Nuevas lineas de cartamo con los caracteristicas enanismo y precocidad. Agricultura Tecnica en Mexico. 3: 376-379.

Rubis, D.D. 1967. Genetics of Safflower Seed Characters Related to Utilization, pp. 23-28. Safflower Utilization Conf., USDA Agric. Res. Service Publ. 74-93, Albany, Calif.

Urie, A.L. 1986. Inheritance of partial hull in safflower. Crop Sci. 26: 493-498.

——, and Knowles, P.F. 1972. Safflower introductions resistant to Verticillium wilt. Crop Sci. 12: 545-546.

——, and Zimmer, D.E. 1970. Yield reduction in safflower hybrids caused by female selfs. Crop Sci. 10: 419-422.

Weiss, E.A. 1971. *Castor, Sesame and Safflower*. Barnes & Noble, Inc., New York.

Zimmerman, L.H. 1972. Effect of temperature and humidity stress during flowering of safflower (*Carthamus tinctorius* L.). Crop Sci. 12: 637-640.

Chapter 18

Sesame

A. Ashri

IMPORTANCE AND DISTRIBUTION

Sesame is an important annual oilseed crop (Fig. 18.1). It is cultivated for its seeds which contain ca. 50% oil of very high quality and 25% protein. Sesame is grown in the tropical to the temperate zones, from about 40° N latitude to 40° S latitude. India is the major producer with ca. 35% of the world's sesame area and 25% of the production (Table 18.1). China, Burma and Sudan account for a further 40% of the world's area. In some growing areas, e.g. Burma, sesame is a major source of edible oil for local consumption. The crop has many agricultural advantages: it sets seeds and yields relatively well under high temperatures, it can be grown on stored moisture without rainfall or irrigation, it grows well in pure or mixed stands, its roots penetrate the soil and improve water percolation and it is considered a good crop in the rotation.

The major obstacles to sesame's expansion are its low yields (Table 18.1), and the absence of non-shattering cultivars suitable for machine harvest. Consequently, it requires much manual labor at the harvest season, which is often scarce even in its traditional growing areas. Thus, sesame is a typical small-holders' crop.

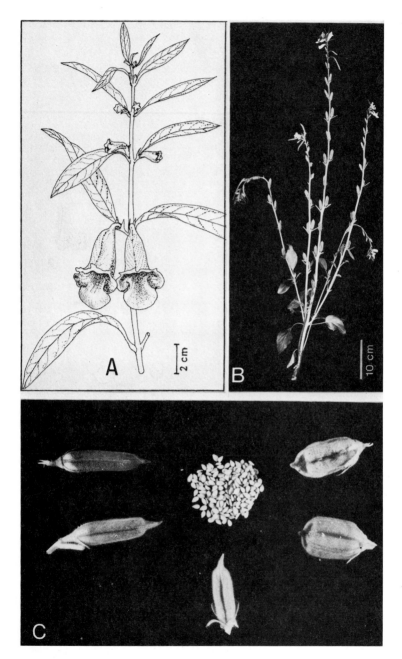

Fig. 18.1   Sesame. A - Upper tip of inflorescence. B - Plant of the Israeli variety "No. 45," with most leaves removed to show the capsules and flowers. C - Seeds and different capsules, bi-carpellate (left) and quadricarpellate (right).
A from Rehm and Espig (1984).

Table 18.1 World Sesame Production by Region and Major Producing Countries

Region or Country	Production area ('000 ha)			Seed yield (kg/ha)			Seed production ('000 tonnes)		
	1969-71	1979-81	1985	1969-71	1979-81	1985	1969-71	1979-81	1985
World	**6249**	**6486**	**6670**	**322**	**304**	**353**	**2014**	**1970**	**2353**
Africa	**1415**	**1586**	**1922**	**361**	**305**	**273**	**511**	**483**	**524**
Ethiopia	153	64	63	533	581	571	81	37	36
Nigeria	205	235	250	290	311	300	59	73	75
Sudan	720	836	1103	355	268	207	256	224	228
Uganda	84	65	80	252	313	475	21	20	38
N. and C. America	**297**	**308**	**246**	**657**	**596**	**557**	**195**	**184**	**137**
Mexico	273	247	189	653	588	528	178	145	100
Venezuela	167	74	93	603	660	484	101	49	45
S. America	**206**	**104**	**125**	**617**	**635**	**503**	**127**	**66**	**64**
Asia	**4310**	**4483**	**4375**	**272**	**275**	**372**	**1174**	**1235**	**1626**
Burma	707	767	800	164	207	290	116	159	232
China	894	814	901	412	487	768	368	396	692
India	2378	2481	2200	205	186	205	487	461	450
Turkey	64	43	68	622	592	603	40	26	41
Europe	**20**	**4**	**2**	**346**	**399**	**552**	**7**	**2**	**1**
Oceania	-	-	-	-	-	-	-	-	-
U.S.S.R.	-	-	-	-	-	-	-	-	-

Source: FAO Production Yearbooks 1980 (vol. 34) and 1985 (vol. 39).

Many factors contribute to the low yield of sesame. It is considered to be a high risk crop therefore inputs of labor and fertilizer are minimal. The high risk is associated with the production environment, erratic rainfall; indeterminate growth and uneven ripening of the capsules; seed shattering due to capsule opening; as well as diseases and pests. In many trials the yield response of the accepted varieties to improved growing conditions and higher inputs has been disappointing. Therefore, the improvement of sesame yields, which is a pre-condition to its acceptance and expansion, will require major efforts.

ORIGIN AND SYSTEMATICS

Sesame *Sesamum indicum* L. (sometimes also called *S. orientale* L.) is one of the oldest cultivated plants and perhaps the oldest oil crop. Its center of origin is not certain. Many authors (Bedigian and Harlan, 1986; Brar and Ahuja, 1979; Joshi, 1961; Mazzani, 1983; Nayar and Mehra, 1970) described archaeological evidence that sesame was a highly prized oil crop in Babylon and Assyria (present day Iraq and Syria) 4000 years ago or even earlier. Charred sesame seeds were found in Harappa (Pakistan) dating back to the same era. Thus, the primary center of origin could be placed in the Fertile Crescent, or the Indian sub-continent or in the Iran-Afghanistan area. Since most of the wild species in the genus are located in Africa, while only a few grow in India, it has been suggested that Ethiopia is the center of origin from whence it spread eastward along the ancient trade routes. The absence of wild species related to the cultivated sesame complicates matters further. A wild form of *S. indicum*, spp. *malabaricum* Nar., is known only in the Malabar Coast of India and is cross-fertile with the cultivated materials. Also, India is very rich in genetic variability in the cultivated species. Recently, Bedigian (1984) reviewed all the various types of evidence and concluded that sesame originated in India.

The genus *Sesamum,* with about thirty-five species, belongs to the Pedaliaceae family (Joshi, 1961; Mazzani, 1983; Nayar and Mehra, 1970; Weiss, 1971). The cytogenetic knowledge of the genus is very limited, thus the chromosome numbers are known only for about one third of the species. The cultivated species and *S. alatum* Thonn., *S. capense* Burm., *S. schenckii* Aschers. (=*S. grandiflorum* Schinz.) and ssp. *malabaricum,* all have 2n=26 chromosomes. Other chromosome numbers known in the genus are 2n=32 and 64. *S. radiatum* Schum. & Thonn. (2n=64) and *S. angustifolium* (Olive) Engl. (chromosome number unknown) are cultivated in some parts of Africa. Crosses of *S. indicum* with *S. capense* and *S. schenckii* give sterile hybrids except for occasional end of season fertility. Findings in other interspecific crosses are summarized by Mazzani (1983) and Nayar and Mehra (1970). Some of the wild species are known to have resistance to diseases, pests and drought but hybridization barriers have prevented gene transfer.

MODE OF REPRODUCTION

The floral morphology and the mode of reproduction of sesame were re-viewed and described in detail by Ashri (1985a), Joshi (1961), Yermanos (1980) and Weiss (1971). Sesame is indeterminate with acropetal flowering; plants con-tinuing to produce leaves, flowers and capsules as long as the weather and soil moisture permit. A determinate mutant, which was recently induced by Ashri (1985b), is discussed below. The flowers are borne on short pedicels in the leaf axil. Generally, there can be plants with one flower and two nectaries per leaf axil or three flowers and no nectaries. These differences are controlled by a sin-gle gene, the dominant allele (*T*) giving the one flower and two nectaries condi-tion. Where there are three flowers per leaf axil, the central bud blooms first and the two side buds open several days later. Cases with more than three flower buds per axil have been reported. Also, in some *tt* plants, the early and the latest nodes sometimes do not produce all three flowers and capsules.

Sesame flowers (Fig. 18.1) vary in color and size. The calyx is usually green (sometimes reddish or yellowish), five-parted and 3 to 7 mm long. The corolla is tubular, five-lobed and 15 to 35 mm long. The corolla tube is usually bent slight-ly downwards and is open at the distal end. In some varieties the distal end is partly closed preventing the entrance of cross-pollinating insects. Sesame corol-las are characterized by a three-parted lower lip, in which the middle part juts out. The corollas vary in color from white to pale rose to dark purple and occa-sionally also reddish-brown. Varieties vary also in the markings and color pat-terns of their corollas.

Each flower has four stamens, or at times five, with four functional, and one sterile, which are inserted at the corolla base. The mature anthers are 1 to 2 mm long, white to yellow or purplish in color, with yellowish pollen grains. The ovaries are superior and can be bicarpellate or tetracarpellate, the difference is controlled monogenically. In bicarpellate genotypes (*Tc-*) the stigma is bifid while in tetracarpellate ones (*tctc*) the stigma is four-parted.

The fruit is a capsule which dehisces along its sutures when mature, shatter-ing the seeds to the ground. A recessive indehiscent mutant (*idid*) was discovered in 1943 by Langham in Venezuela. A capsule may contain 50 to 100 or more seeds depending on genotype and environmental conditions. The capsules (Fig. 18.1) vary in length and in color from green to dark purple. The seeds are flat, round to oval, with a smooth or rough seed coat and they vary in color from white to gray, amber, brown, reddish and nearly black. The more mature seeds are usually darker in color. Seed weight is ca. 3 g per 1000, with slightly lower or higher values for different varieties. The seeds mature 4 to 6 weeks after fertilization.

Sesame is considered a self-pollinated crop, giving full seed set under isola-tion. However, the flowers attract insects and their activity can lead to different rates of cross-pollination from a commonly reported few percent to as high as 65% (Yermanos, 1980). For this reason bagging or isolation (200 to 360 m) are required to assure self-pollination.

According to Joshi (1961), Yermanos (1980) and Weiss (1971) anthesis in the field occurs at dawn (ca. 5 am) on bright sunny days, and lasts for about two hours. Cool, overcast and humid conditions may delay anthesis up to one or two hours. When anthesis occurs, the anthers are about level with the stigmas which unfold and capture the pollen grains. The stigmas may be covered with self-pollen 1 to 2 hours before the flowers open. They are usually receptive from 24 hours before to 24 hours after flower opening, although shorter receptivity periods have been noted (Yermanos, 1980). Within 4 to 6 hours after pollination the pollen tubes reach most if not all of the ovules. Most reports indicated that pollen grains stored at room temperature (20° to 25°) remain viable up to twenty-four hours after flower opening (Yermanos, 1980; Weiss, 1971).

Several cases of male sterility, sometimes accompanied by female sterility have been described in the literature (Brar and Ahuja, 1979; Mazzani, 1983; Osman and Yermanos, 1982; Weiss, 1971). Osman and Yermanos (1982) studied a recessive male sterility allele which originated from Venezuela. The *msms* plants have poorly developed anthers and pollen grains. The sterility is stable over a wide range of environmental conditions and the female fertility is complete. Osman and Yermanos (1982) suggested that until suitable CMS and restorer lines are available, this genic sterility could be used in the production of hybrid varieties.

BREEDING PROCEDURES

Sesame is now at an early stage in its improvement, where rapid advances can be expected from the application of proven plant breeding principles and procedures. The potential of sesame breeding is amply demonstrated by the achievements in tropical Venezuela (Mazzani, 1983) and temperate Korea (Lee and Choi, 1985b).

Sesame is rich in genetic variability. There are still many landraces in the growing areas which often are mixtures. Bedigian (1984) studied the genetic variability and identified eight major groups of landraces within the species, while the germplasm variability for oil was examined by Yermanos et al. (1972). Two FAO Expert Consultations (Anon., 1981b and Anon., 1985) recommended that sesame germplasm collection, evaluation and exchange will be enhanced. A sesame descriptor list published by the IBPGR (Anon., 1981a) will aid in this effort.

Introduction, sometimes accompanied by mass- or single-plant selection, has proved a successful approach and should continue to be so.

Selection, conscious or unconscious, within local germplasm pools has been traditionally practiced by the villagers who maintained, and still maintain, their own seeds. Mass selection can be very useful in many regions since the local landraces are often very heterogeneous, containing productive as well as unproductive genotypes, e.g. in Burma, India and Sudan. Single plant selection has also produced successful varieties. There is much scope for this approach in varietal improvement especially if new variability is created by controlled crosses. The FAO Expert Consultations (Anon.,1981b and Anon., 1985) recommended that selection be utilized wherever possible.

It has been suggested by several authors (e.g. Ashri, 1985b; Kinman and Martin, 1954; Rajan, 1981) that since selection within local materials has been ongoing for a long time, often in low input conditions, the genetic variability for yield has been exhausted and breakthroughs in productivity will have to come from controlled crosses designed to create new and increased variability. Pedigree breeding and selection, composite crosses with bulk populations and selection, population improvement, with or without male sterility and high rates of outcrossing, have been recommended and used successfully (Ashri, 1985b; Kinman and Martin, 1954; Lee and Choi, 1985b; Mazzani, 1983; Rajan, 1981; Weiss, 1971; Anon., 1981b; Anon., 1985).

The backcross method to date has had a more limited impact. It has been used to transfer desirable traits such as indehiscence into adapted varieties. Its use will no doubt expand as better and more productive varieties are developed and additional specific and useful loci are identified.

F_1 hybrid cultivars could potentially be used in sesame. Some of the necessary conditions have been met. High levels of heterosis have been demonstrated in various hybrid combinations (Brar and Ahuja, 1979; Mazzani, 1983; Osman, 1985). In recent studies in Venezuela various hybrid combinations were produced through natural crosses with a male sterile line and significant yield increments were obtained (Mazzani, 1985). With the discovery of a stable source of male sterility by Osman and Yermanos (1982) the research in this area has intensified. Cross pollination using insects presents no problem, and each female plant can produce thousands of seeds. Still, it is the author's opinion that F_1 hybrid cultivars will not come into widespread use for some time for several reasons. In most of the major traditional growing areas production, certification and distribution systems of pedigree seed are limited or nonexistent. Further, it has not been clearly demonstrated that hybrid varieties under low input situations will do sufficiently better than conventional cultivars to justify the higher cost of hybrid seed. On the other hand, in the high input areas a genic-cytoplasmic male sterility system will be needed to eliminate the roguing necessary with an *ms* locus. Even then, in such areas truly non-shattering varieties will be needed to make them economic.

Mutation breeding has been employed successfully in sesame (Ashri, 1982; Ashri, 1985b; Brar and Ahuja, 1979; Kobayashi, 1981; Lee and Choi, 1985b; Weiss, 1971). The FAO Expert Consultations (Anon., 1981b and Anon., 1985) recommended that it should be used to obtain certain desired characters that are not available in the natural germplasm pools. The characters sought should be those that are easily screened from large populations such as non-shattering, modified plant architecture and growing period and resistance to diseases and pests. Sesame seeds are quite resistant to gamma rays and ethyl methane sulfonate, therefore higher dose levels should be utilized (Ashri, 1982).

The wild species in the genus *Sesamum* contain desirable traits such as resistance to pests and diseases and to drought (Brar and Ahuja, 1979; Joshi, 1961; Kolte, 1985; Mazzani, 1983; Uzo and Adedzwa, 1985; Weiss, 1971). However, as noted above, the cytogenetics of the genus and the interspecific relations are little known. The FAO Expert Consultations (Anon., 1981b and Anon., 1985) recommended that the collection and investigation of the wild species be intensified.

Genetic markers are always important in breeding programs. Over the years many markers, most of them monogenic, have been studied. A summary of over fifty markers has been prepared and surprisingly, only two cases of linkage have been identified so far (Brar and Ahuja, 1979).

Crossing in sesame can be easily done. All the steps have been described in detail by Yermanos (1980). The desired flower buds, which will flower the following day, and are identified by their lighter green-cream color are emasculated in the afternoon. The corolla tubes and the stamens attached to them are pulled from the buds and the style covered by a short, folded piece of drinking straw or enclosed in a small paper bag. Stamens for pollination, attached to the corollas, are collected in the same way; or whole buds are gathered and kept overnight at room temperature in Petri-dishes or plastic bags. The addition of one or two leaves to each dish or bag helps maintain an adequate moisture level. Pollination is performed the following morning by rubbing the collected anthers against the stigmas. The flower is recovered and labeled. If on inspection 4 to 6 days later, a growing capsule is evident, the cross has been successful. In the greenhouse emasculation and pollination can be performed throughout the day (Yermanos, 1980).

Sesame seeds can be stored at room temperature for ca. five years and if the humidity and the temperature are lowered, they can be kept viable for ten or more years (van Rheenen - personal communication).

BREEDING OBJECTIVES

As noted earlier, sesame is still at an early stage in its genetic improvement. For that reason, in addition to some of the usual breeding objectives, such as disease resistance, several traits in sesame require special attention.

The development of productive non-shattering cultivars is critical to the successful cultivation of sesame in more advanced, mechanized agriculture. The indehiscent mutant *id/id* discovered by Langham in 1943 (Mazzani, 1983; Weiss, 1971) exhibited many undesirable and probably pleiotropic side effects, including lower seed set and reduced seed quality. Despite continuous breeding efforts it has not yet been possible to separate the indehiscence from the undesirable traits, so that no indehiscent commercial cultivars exist. The best indehiscent *id/id* selections, developed by the late D. M. Yermanos, are now being tested in various countries but generally their yields have been lower than those of shattering varieties. The capsules of the *id/id* plants are so difficult to thresh that yield losses and damaged seeds result.

A second important objective is a short flowering and capsule maturation period. At present, all sesame varieties are indeterminate, producing leaves, flowers and capsules as long as the weather conditions and soil moisture permit. Thus, any harvest date is a compromise and some seeds are lost either to early capsules shattering or the late capsules being immature. Ashri (1982 and 1985b) induced a determinate mutant in the Israeli cultivar No. 45 using gamma radiation. The determinate plants have a totally different plant architecture and mature their capsules within a short period. The mutation, which is monogenic and recessive is now being transferred to many regional cultivars.

Sesame yields are quite low (Table 18.1) and even under very good conditions rarely exceed 1.5 t/ha. In order for sesame to be more competitive its yields must be raised considerably. Some investigators believe that by breeding varieties with three quadricarpellate capsules per axil yields will be increased. However, van Rheenen (1981) showed that within the material available for study this is not so. It is probably a matter of the capacity of the source and not just the sink. Increasing the yield potential of sesame and the harvest index (at present 10 to 30 %) may be difficult since the crop has been grown traditionally under low input conditions where drought tolerance, adjustment to intercropping and low soil fertility have been selected.

Breeding for disease and pest resistance is especially important for sesame because it is usually grown without any applications of pesticides. Several very destructive bacterial, fungi and mycoplasma diseases attack the crop. There are reports of resistance or tolerance to various diseases in the cultivated cultivars, the wild species and stocks derived from interspecific hybridization (Brar and Ahuja, 1979; Kolte, 1985; Lee and Choi, 1985b; Mazzani, 1983; Weiss, 1971). However, closer examination often reveals that the resistance is not clear cut. Thus, breeding for pest resistance is slow and difficult.

Adjustment of the length of the growing period is also an important breeding objective. On the one hand, day length neutral and thermo-insensitive cultivars are desired. On the other hand, in India and Burma two types of varieties are needed; one of long duration, where sesame is the main crop; and one of short duration, where another crop follows sesame during the north-east monsoon.

Since in many parts of the world sesame is a major source of high quality edible oil, the improvement of oil content and modification of its fatty acids' composition are of primary importance. Yermanos et al. (1972) showed that in California oil content ranged from 40.4% to 59.2% and iodine value varied from 106 to 128 among 721 sesame introductions. Similarly, Lee and Choi (1985a) working in Korea, found that oil content ranged from 45.0 to 55.5% in 220 germplasm collections and introductions. There is also variability for the fatty acids composition (Brar and Ahuja, 1979; Lee and Choi, 1985a; Weiss, 1971; Yermanos et al. 1972) and room for further modifications.

In addition to the above objectives, the FAO Expert Consultation (Anon., 1981b) concluded that "a combination of the following characters should be sought, equally applicable to both low- and high-input conditions:"

a) Seed characters: large or medium-large seed, color to satisfy market demand; seed coat rough for easy removal; oil and protein composition and content satisfactory to meet consumer demand; sesamin and sesamolin (anti-oxidants) content high; seed dormancy appropriate for the local cropping system.

b) Seedling characters: fast, vigorous germination; rapid growth and establishment; ability to withstand low temperatures; resistance to soil-borne diseases, waterlogging, drought, salinity and insect damage.

c) Plant characters:

i) Roots: rapid root growth; deep tap root penetration with a well developed secondary root system.

ii) Leaves: medium to broad at the base and narrow-lanceolate towards the apex; short petioles; abscission early and complete at physiological maturity.

iii) Stem: 'Uniculm' if input medium or high, or moderately branched at the lower nodes, if input low; internodes short with corresponding adjustment of capsule angle; medium height.

iv) Flowers: to start 20 to 30 cm from ground level; 1 to 3 flowers and capsules per leaf axil.

v) Capsules: medium-long and bicarpellate; complete seed set without aborted seeds.

vi) General characteristics: rapid natural desiccation at physiological maturity; resistance to lower and higher temperatures; good response to fertilizers and to irrigation without concomitant undesirable effects (e.g. lodging).

HISTORY OF CULTIVAR DEVELOPMENT

In many of the traditional sesame growing areas, local land varieties still occupy much of the acreage. Breeding improved varieties is still in its early phases in many countries. Wherever breeding efforts were initiated they took the usual course of development, starting with mass selection in local landraces, eliminating the obviously undesirable plants. At the same time or somewhat later, single plant selection was used. The first germplasm collection in India was established in 1925 (Brar and Ahuja 1979; Joshi, 1961). Shortly after, a large world collection was assembled in the USSR (Weiss, 1971).

Introduction, sometimes accompanied by mass - or single-plant selection proved successful in various locations. Thus, the improved Venezuelan cultivar "Morada" (Mazzani, 1983) selected from an introduction from Congo (now Zaire) proved very successful in Tanzania. Also the American cultivar "Early

Russian" proved successful in the Republic of Korea and was released to the farmers in 1955 (Lee and Choi, 1985b).

Later, hybridization programs designed to generate new variability and/or to combine specific traits were initiated and followed by mass-or single-plant selection or bulk population procedures. The backcross approach is utilized to transfer specific traits into existing varieties e.g. *id* to produce "Inamar Indehiscente" from "Inamar" in Venezuela.

Mutation breeding has so far produced at least two known commercial varieties: Kalika in India (dwarf, compact, higher yields) by EMS treatment (Micke - personal communication) and Ahnsanggae (disease resistant) by x-rays (Lee and Choi, 1985b). In addition, some promising induced mutants are now utilized in large scale cross breeding programs, e.g. determinate (Ashri, 1985b).

The history of cultivar development can be illustrated by that of the Republic of Korea (Lee and Choi, 1985b). Since 1955, twelve improved cultivars have been released. Of these, four were selections (three from local landraces, and one from an introduction). One was a directly used introduction, six were developed through hybridization and the pedigree method and finally, one was produced by induced mutation in the "Early Russian" cultivar. Twelve improved cultivars have been released in Venezuela since the mid-forties. Five resulted from selection out of introductions originating in China, Congo, Cuba, Dominican Republic and Ethiopia. The pedigree system produced five more, while the backcross method produced the remaining two. Similar development patterns are found in India, Mexico and Sudan.

UTILIZATION OF PRODUCTS

Sesame seeds are used whole, or processed for oil and meal. Whole seeds, often decorticated, are used to prepare sweets (candies and halva) and in baking. The seeds are also eaten whole after they are roasted. In Africa sesame is used to make porridge, soup and confectionery. A sesame paste (tahiny), prepared by grinding sesame seeds, is a favored food in the Middle East.

The main use of sesame is as a source of high quality edible oil. The oil contains about 47% oleic acid and 39% linoleic acid. The oil is very stable and has a long shelf life because it contains an antioxidant called sesamol (a phenolic compound), which is derived from sesamolin. Foods fried in sesame oil, e.g. potato chips, keep much longer than if fried in other oils. The low grade oil obtained at the end of the extraction process is used industrially, e.g. in soap making.

Sesame oil is also used as a solvent or carrier for medicines and cosmetics. Sesamin and sesamolin, which are present in the oil, act as synergists with pyrethrum to effectively control insects. In some countries (e.g. Italy) all margarines and similar products must contain 5% sesame oil to permit detection of adulteration of butter by margarine. Sesame oil was selected because it is the only oil which gives a bright red color in Baudouin's test, due to the sesamol and sesamolin it contains.

The cake or meal obtained after the oil is extracted contains 34 to 50% protein, depending on the efficiency of extraction and the cultivar. The proteins are rich in methionine but low in lysine. Where oil is extracted at the village level, the cake is often fed to animals. However, since the cake contains oil its keeping quality is low. Where the oil is extracted in large mills, the cake is often considered too expensive for animal feed and is processed to obtain a protein-rich flour that can be mixed with other ingredients (e.g. soybean flour, maize flour, chick peas) to produce very nutritious human foods. Research is needed to develop more sesame-based food products.

In the Far East (e.g. China, Korea) sesame cake is sometimes used as manure. Cooked leaves of sesame are sometimes eaten. In the Far East leaves are also used to prepare some folk medicines as are the seeds (preferably black).

REFERENCES

Anonymous. 1981a. *Descriptors for Sesame.* AGP:IBPGR/80/71. Intern. Bd. Plant Genet. Res. Secretariat, Rome.

Anonymous. 1981b. Conclusions and Recommendations, pp. 192-195. *In* A. Ashri (ed.), *Sesame: Status and Improvement.* FAO Plant Production and Protection Paper 29, Rome.

Anonymous. 1985. Conclusions and Recommendations, pp. 218-220. *In* A. Ashri (ed.), *Sesame and Safflower: Status and Potentials.* FAO Plant Production and Protection Paper 66, Rome.

Ashri, A. 1982. Status of Breeding and Prospects for Mutation Breeding in Peanuts, Sesame and Castor Beans, pp. 65-80. *In: Improvement of Oil-seed and Industrial Crops by Induced Mutations.* Intern. Atomic Energy Agency (IAEA), Vienna.

——. 1985a. Sesame (*Sesamum indicum* L.), pp. 309-312. *In* A. H. Halevy (ed.), *Handbook of Flowering.* Vol. 4. CRC Press, Boca Raton, Fla.

——. 1985b. Sesame Improvement by Large Scale Cultivars' Intercrossing and by Crosses with Indehiscent and Determinate Lines, pp. 177-181. *In* A. Ashri (ed.), *Sesame and Safflower: Status and Potentials.* FAO Plant Production and Protection Paper 66, Rome.

Bedigian, D. 1984. *Sesamum indicum* L. : Crop Origin, Diversity, Chemistry and Ethnobotany. Ph.D. Dissert., Univ. of Illinois, Urbana-Champaign, Ill.

——, and Harlan, J.R. 1986. Evidence for cultivation of sesame in the ancient world. Econ. Bot. 40: 137-154.

Brar, G.S., and Ahuja, K.L. 1979. Sesame: its culture, genetics, breeding and biochemistry. Ann. Rev. Pl. Sci. 1: 245-313. Kalyani Publ., New Delhi.

Joshi, A.B. 1961. *Sesamum.* Indian Central Oilseeds Committee. Hyderabad-1, India.

Kinman, M.L., and Martin, A.J. 1954. Present status of sesame breeding in the United States. Agron. J. 46: 24-27.

Kobayashi, R. 1981. Some Useful Sesame Mutants by Induced Mutations, pp. 146-150. *In* A. Ashri (ed.), *Sesame : Status and Improvement.* FAO Plant Production and Protection Paper 29, Rome.

Kolte, S..J. 1985. *Diseases of Annual Edible Oilseed Crops. Vol. II: Rapeseed-Mustard and Sesame Diseases.* CRC Press, Boca Raton, Fla.

Lee, J.I., and Choi, B.H. 1985a. Basic Studies on Sesame Plant Growth in Korea, pp. 131-136. *In* A. Ashri (ed.), *Sesame and Safflower: Status and Potentials*. FAO Plant Production and Protection Paper 66, Rome.

——, and ——. 1985b. Progress and Prospects of Sesame Breeding in Korea, pp. 137-144. *In* A. Ashri (ed.) *Sesame and Safflower: Status and Potentials*. FAO Plant Production and Protection Paper 66, Rome.

Mazzani, B., 1983. Ajonjoli, pp. 169-224. *In* : *Cultivo y Mejoramiento de Plantas Oleaginosas*. FONAIAP and CENIAP. Caracas, Venezuela.

——. 1985. Sesame growing in Venezuela 1980-1984, pp. 86-89. *In* A. Ashri (ed.), *Sesame and Safflower: Status and Potentials*. FAO Plant Production and Protection Paper 66, Rome.

Nayar, N.M., and Mehra, K.L. 1970. Sesame: its uses, botany, cytogenetics and origin. Econ. Bot. 24: 20-31.

Osman, H.E. 1985. Studies in Sesame: II. Heterosis, pp. 157-162. *In* A. Ashri (ed.), *Sesame and Safflower: Status and Potentials*. FAO Plant Production and Protection Paper 66, Rome.

——, and Yermanos, D.M. 1982. Genetic male sterility in sesame: reproductive characteristics and possible use in hybrid seed production. Crop Sci. 22: 492-498.

Rajan, S.S. 1981. Sesame Breeding Material and Methods, pp. 138-140. *In* A. Ashri (ed.), *Sesame : Status and Improvement*. FAO Plant Production and Protection Paper 29, Rome.

Rehm, S., and Espig, G. 1984. *Die Kulturpflanzen der Tropen und Subtropen,* 2nd Ed., p. 102. Eugen Ulmer, Stuttgart.

Rheenen, H.A. van. 1981. The Desirability of Three Versus One Flowers and Capsules Per Leaf Axil in Sesame (*Sesamum indicum* L.), pp. 97-102. *In* A. Ashri (ed.), *Sesame : Status and Improvement*. FAO Plant Production and Protection Paper 29, Rome.

Uzo, J.O., and Adedzwa, D.K. 1985. A Search for Drought Resistance in the Wild Relatives of the Cultivated Sesame (*Sesamum indicum*), pp. 163-165. *In* A. Ashri (ed.), *Sesame and Safflower: Status and Potentials*. FAO Plant Production and Protection Paper 66, Rome.

Weiss, E.A. 1971. *Castor, Sesame and Safflower,* pp. 311-525. Leonard Hill, London.

Yermanos, D.M. 1980. Sesame, pp. 549-563. *In* W. R. Fehr and H. H. Hadley (eds.), *Hybridization of Crop Plants*. Am. Soc. Agron., Crop Sci. Soc. America. Madison, Wis.

——, Hemstreet, S., Saleeb, W., and Huszar, C.K. 1972. Oil content and composition of the seed in the world collection of sesame introductions. J. Am. Oil Chem. Soc. 49: 20-23.

Chapter 19

Poppy

J. Krzymanski and R. Jönsson

IMPORTANCE AND DISTRIBUTION

Poppy has been grown since ancient times for its oil rich seeds and the opium which is exuded from incised seed capsules (Fig. 19.1). In modern agriculture the trend has been to develop cultivars for either their seed oil or opium yield or as an ornamental flower.

The poppy is grown mainly in eastern and southern Asia and southeastern Europe. Since much of this acreage is sown to supply the illicit opium trade, no reliable figures on the area of production are available. However, it is estimated that over half a million hectares of poppies are cultivated for their opium (Lööf, 1966). Little or no data on production and trade of oilseed poppy are available, although it is well-adapted to temperate regions and is grown to a limited extent in several European countries.

Fig. 19.1 Poppy. Poppy field for oilseed production, right, young bud (in inverted position) before pollination, flower (upper middle) and developing capsule in upright position (lower middle).

ORIGIN AND SYSTEMATICS

Poppy, *Papaver somniferum* L., is believed to have originated in the Mediterranean region. The large number of races or subspecies found in Turkey suggests that Anatolia may have been the centre of origin (Küracay, 1946). The fact that poppy seeds have been found in Swiss, Neolithic deposits also indicates its early domestication by man (Gelin and Schwanbom, 1943).

Several *Papaver* species exist but their interrelationship has never been clarified (Danert, 1958; Lörincz and Tetenyi, 1963). *P. somniferum*, with a chromosome number of 2n=22, is the only species that can be regarded as a true crop plant. The progenitor of the cultivated forms is believed to be *P. somniferum* var. *nigrum* which is characterized by violet flowers, black seeds and open, seed-shattering capsules. In contrast, the cultivated varieties normally have white petals with a dark spot at the base, gray, blue or nearly white seeds and nondehiscent capsules. Opium is collected from young capsules only. Some 25 alkaloids occur in mature dry capsules but only morphine, codeine, thebaine and papaverine are of importance today. The morphine practically disappears from the seeds twenty days after the flower opens (Krzymanski and Przyluska, 1967).

MODE OF REPRODUCTION

The poppy plant produces a rosette of oblong, deeply lanceolated leaves above a conical root. A stalk with up to eight branches, each carrying a single flower bud, may arise from the rosette. The stems are normally glabrous and extend 0.5 to 1.5 m above the ground, depending on the cultivar and environment. The bud is retained in an inverted position on the stem until the day prior to blooming when the bent peduncle straightens, carrying the bud to an upright position. Meiosis occurs in the ovules while the bud is in the inverted position. Embryo sacs, with eight nuclei as well as three-celled pollen grains, have been observed at the intermediate bud position (Iljina, 1962). When the peduncle is almost straight, pollination in the bud can occur. The flower has two sepals which fall away, releasing four radially-arranged petals. Numerous anthers surround the single large pistil consisting of several carpels and a radially-branched stigma with 5 to 13 rays. Although poppy flowers possess no nectaries, fields are vigorously worked by bees and other pollen-gathering insects. Since pollination can take place inside the bud, the poppy is considered by some to be autogamous (Iljina, 1962). This conclusion is supported by observations of good seed-setting where plants were bagged or isolated in insect-free greenhouses (Andersson and Lööf, 1966; Martinek, 1962). However, when the crop is grown in the field, a cross-pollination rate of about 30% has been observed (Lööf, 1966).

The multi-carpeled capsule may be spherical, barrel-shaped or oblong. In primitive poppies the capsules open at maturity and the small seeds are dispersed. However, in developed cultivars the capsules remain closed and do not dehisce. Each carpel contains many small seeds with a 1000 seed weight of only 0.4 to 0.5g. The color of the seed coat can range from pure white to yellow, gray, brown, red, lilac, blue or black (Incekara, 1949), with the seed coat surface showing an almost square reticulate pattern (Heeger and Poethke, 1947). The seeds contain 45 to 50% oil. From a nutritional point of view the oil has a desirable fatty acid composition, with 73% linoleic, 10% palmitic and 13% oleic acid (Appelqvist, 1963). Under European conditions, average seed yields of oilseed poppy are 1200 to 1800 kg/ha (Lööf, 1966).

BREEDING PROCEDURES

To improve seed and oil yield as well as other agronomic characteristics, crosses are normally made among adapted cultivars of *P. somniferum* as well as with local, primitive forms of this species. However, to further extend the genetic variation, interspecific crosses with closely related species, such as *P. setigerum, P. bracteatum* and *P. orientale*, have also been used (Lörincz and Tetenyi, 1963). To avoid selfing in crossing programs, the flowers are emasculated when the bud is still in an inverted position and pollinated 1 to 2 days later. In the resulting segregating populations, both pedigree and recurrent selection procedures have been used. Forced inbreeding has resulted in loss of vigor and yield depression. Marked heterosis in hybrid progeny has been observed for seed yield, but the content of oil in the seed and morphine in the mature, dry capsules were reported to be unchanged from parental levels (Miczulska, 1967).

BREEDING OBJECTIVES

As with most oilseed crops, the primary breeding aim in oilseed poppy is to increase seed and oil yield. In addition to developing cultivars with higher seed yields per plant, the aim is to increase resistance to lodging and capsule dehiscence while at the same time improving the plant's ability to compete with weeds. For oilseed production to be permitted, a low alkaloid type is normally required, at least in most western countries. Generally, blue-seeded cultivars are superior in seed yield to white-seeded ones. On the other hand, white seeds have a higher oil content (Lööf, 1966). Where the seeds are to be used in the confectionery trade, white seeds normally command a higher price than those with dark colors.

Resistance to fungal diseases is also an important breeding objective. *Helminthosporium papaveris (Pleospora calvescens)* and *Peronospora arborescens* are the most prevalent and harmful diseases. Sources of resistance to these two diseases occur among present poppy cultivars (Flanderkova, 1979).

HISTORY OF CULTIVAR DEVELOPMENT

Poppy has long been grown in countries where agriculture is not well developed. The possibility of improvement by plant breeding has therefore been examined only on a modest scale. Most attention has been paid to morphological characteristics associated with high seed yield and desired seed color. Many poppy cultivars adapted to local conditions have been produced. Because cytoplasmic male sterility or incompatibility systems have not been found in poppy, no F_1 hybrid cultivars have been developed. In Sweden, where poppy cultivars with high morphine content are prohibited, a low morphine cultivar, "Soma", has been bred (Nyman and Hansson, 1978). Other European varieties include Azur from Czechoslovakia; Pajbjerg, Otofte, Luna and Lori from Denmark; Mahndorfer and Peragis from Germany; Emmabloem, Nobel, Nordster and Marianne from Holland; Niebieski Km, Modry and Bialy Pulawski from Poland; Altai, Barnaul 490, Voronezh 1042, Tatarstan 1, Chishmenskii 171, Novenka 198, Przhevalsk 222, and Tien Shan from Russia, and the Swedish cultivars Flora and Indra.

UTILIZATION OF PRODUCTS

Poppy oil is used as a salad and cooking oil, and as a raw product for margarine manufacture. The oil has also been used in the manufacture of paints and varnishes, as well as in cosmetics and other industrial products.

Poppy seeds are used as a spice on bread and cakes and as a bird feed. The seeds are rich in oil, carbohydrates, calcium and proteins and contain all the essential amino acids except tryptophan (Duke, 1973). Ground seeds are used for porridge or as a filling or glaze for cakes and pastries.

Alkaloids from poppy capsules and straw are widely used in pharmacology (Duke, 1973). Opium is used as a narcotic.

REFERENCES

Andersson, G., and Lööf, B. 1966. Erhöhung des Anbauwertes des Mohns durch Züchtung. Pharmazie 21: 240-245.

Appelqvist, L.-Å. 1963. Quality Problems in Cruciferous Oilcrops, pp. 301-332. *In* E. Åkerberg et al. (eds.), *Rec. Pl. Breed. Res.* Svalöf 1946-1961, Almqvist and Wiksell, Stockholm.

Danert, S. 1958. Zur Systematik von *Papaver somniferum* L. Kulturpflanze 6: 61-88.

Duke, J.A. 1973. Utilization of *Papaver*. Econ. Bot. 27: 390-400.

Flanderkova, V. 1979. The resistance of poppy to downy mildew of poppy. Rostl. Vyroba 25: 521-527.

Gelin, O., and Schwanbom, N. 1943. Studies on poppy cultivation and breeding. Agric. Hort. Genet. 1: 34-56. (Swedish with German Summary).

Heeger, E.F., and Poethke, W. 1947. *Papaver somniferum* L. The poppy. Cultivation, chemistry, utilization. Pharmazie, 4. Beiheft, 1. Ergänzungsband, Berlin. pp. 235-340.

Iljina, G.M. 1962. The phenology of embryogenesis in poppy *Papaver somniferum* L. Nauczn. Dokl. Vyssz. Szk. Biol. Nauk 1: 116-118.

Incekara, F. 1949. Different Turkish poppies with Respect to their Value for Seeds and Opium. Ph.D. Thesis, Ankara University. (Turkish).

Krzymanski, J., and Przyluska, F. 1967. Preliminary investigations on the influence of maturity grade of blue poppy KM on the morphine content. Biuletyn IHAR 6: 119-122.

Küracay, A. 1946. Opium poppy cultivation. Position and part played by Turkish poppies. Cankaya Matbaasi, Ankara No. 6: 1-48. (Turkish). cited in Pl. Breed. Abstr. 18, abs. 391.

Lööf, B. 1966. Poppy cultivation. Field Crop Abstr. 19: 1-5.

Lörincz, Gy., and Tetenyi, P. 1963. Results of our experiments in inter-specific hybridization in *Papaver*. Herb. Hungar. 2: 127 cited in Pl. Breed. Abstr. 34, No. 3, abs. 4538.

Martinek, V. 1962. The application of heterosis in poppy. Ved. Pr. Vyzk. Ustavu Rostl. Vyroby Praze-Ruzyni 6: 9-25.

Miczulska, I. 1967. Heterosis effect in hybrids of certain varieties of poppy *Papaver somniferum*. Rocz. Nauk Roln. Ser. A Prod. Rosl. 93A: 197-204.

Nikolloff, J. 1939. On the botanical composition of the poppy in the new regions of Bulgaria. Revue Inst. Rech. Agron. Bulg. 9, No. 1: 63-73.

Nyman, U. 1978. Selection for high thebaine/low morphine content in *Papaver somniferum* L. Hereditas 89: 43-50.

——, and Hall, O. 1974. Breeding oil poppy *Papaver somniferum* for low content of morphine. Hereditas 76: 49-54.

——, and Hansson, B. 1978. Morphine content variation in *Papaver somniferum* L. as affected by the presence of some isoquinoline alkaloids. Hereditas 88: 17-26.

Pieper, H. 1939. Comparison of varieties of cultivated poppy. Results from the German expedition to Hindu Kush. Landw. Jbr. 89: 333-392.

Reinmuth, E. 1942. The wilting of the leaves of poppy - a notable fungus pest. Angew. Bot. 24: 273-277.

——. 1943. Further observations on the wilting of the leaves of poppy. Angew. Bot. 25: 300-304.

Romisch, H. 1958. Morphine from the green matter of poppy. Pharmazie 13, No. 12: 769-777.

Tetenyi, P., Lörincz, C., and Szabo, E. 1961. Investigation on infraspecific chemical differences in poppy. Contributions towards the characterization of hybrids of *Papaver somniferum* L. x *Papaver orientale* L. Pharmazie 16: 426-433.

Chapter 20

Niger

K. W. Riley and H. Belayneh

IMPORTANCE AND DISTRIBUTION

Although niger (*Guizotia abyssinica* Cass.) is unknown to most of the world, it is an important oil crop in Ethiopia and parts of India, where it is grown by peasant farmers, in traditional agriculture systems (Fig. 20.1). In Ethiopia, niger, or "noug" as it is known in that country, provides about 50 to 60% of that country's edible oil, while in India, niger accounts for almost 2% of total oilseeds produced.

Historical production statistics for niger are scarce and tend to be unreliable. However, recent surveys have provided estimates of plantings and yields for Ethiopia and India (Table 20.1). It has been reported that niger is grown as a minor oilseed crop in the Sudan, Uganda, Tanzania, and Malawi (Baagoe, 1974; Purseglove, 1979). Fields have also been observed in Nepal. In Zimbabwe the crop has been grown for silage and green manure (Vaughan, 1970).

In both India and Ethiopia, farmers recognize that niger has the ability to produce a crop on waterlogged or infertile soils and is a good precursor for crops following niger. The tolerance of this crop to high salinity, high boron, and low soil oxygen levels have been documented by Abebe (1978).

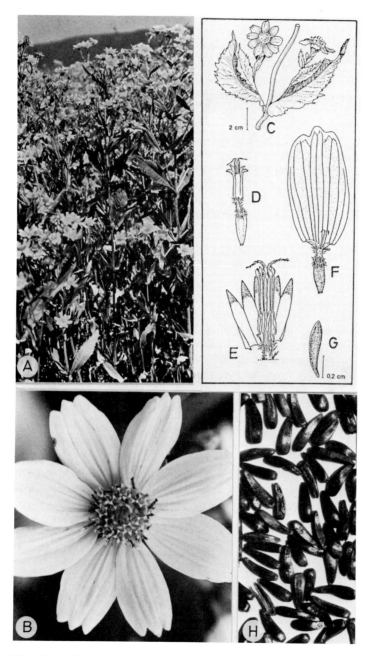

Fig. 20.1 Niger. A - Field stand of flowering niger. B - Yellow flower head.
C - Flowering branch. D - Disk floret. E - Details of a disk floret, the upper part of
the tube laid open. F - Ray floret. G and H - Niger seed.
C - G from Seegler (1983).

Oil Crops of the World

Table 20.1 Estimates of Area,YProduction and Yield of Niger in India and
Ethiopia

Year	India[1]			Ethiopia[2]		
	Area '000ha	Prod. '000t	Yield kg/ha	Area '000ha	Prod. '000t	Yield kg/ha
1978/79	612.1	146.5	239			
1979/80	583.5	105.4	181	112	49.1	438
1980/81	598.7	146.1	244	123.6	64.1	519
1981/82	573.5	152.5	266	151.3	50.2	332
1982/83	500.8	118.1	236	172.6	78.9	457

[1] Directorate of Economics and Statistics. Ministry of Agriculture, Government of India.
1984. New Delhi.
[2] Central Statistics Office, Office of the National Committee for Central Planning. 1984.
Addis Ababa, Ethiopia.

In Ethiopia the crop is grown in the mid-altitude and highland areas (1500 to 2300 m) in the north, central and western regions of the country. It is usually sown on heavy clay soils, although Prinz (1976) reports that the crop grows equally well on either well-drained soils or waterlogged clays. The crop is normally planted in July, about one month after the rains begin, but may be sown anytime between May and September. When the rains cease in early October, flowering begins. The crop matures almost entirely on soil-stored moisture and is harvested in December or January. Generally 150 to 180 days are required from emergence to maturity.

In central India the crop is normally sown on light, gravelly, shallow soils common to the hills of that region. The crop is generally planted after the rainy season is well advanced and matures in 75 to 150 days, depending on the elevation and sowing date. In the Western Ghat region of Maharashtra state a single crop of niger is grown in the short, intense rainy season from June to September when up to 3000 mm of rain is expected. In the hilly areas (400 to 1500 m elevation) niger may be planted as a sequence crop following the June to September harvest of the minor millets *(Panicum miliare* and *P. miliaceum)*.

Niger is usually planted in a pure stand. However, it is sometimes interplanted with teff *(Eragrostis tef)* in northern Ethiopia and finger millet *(Eleucine coracana)* in India (Candussio, 1941; Chavan, 1961), while on the black level vertisols of the Indian states of Maharashtra and Karnataka, intercropping with sorghum *(Sorghum bicolor)* and cotton *(Gossypium hirsutum)* is common.

ORIGIN AND SYSTEMATICS

There is evidence that niger originated in the highlands of Ethiopia, north of 10° N latitude (Baagoe, 1974). Harlan (1975) considers niger to be among the earliest of the domesticated crops in Ethiopia, along with teff, ensete or false banana *(Ensete ventricosum)*, finger millet, and coffee *(Coffee arabica)*. From Ethiopia it is believed to have migrated onto the East African highlands and, during the second millenium B.C., may have moved across to India with other crops, such as finger millet, as part of what Harland describes as the "Savannah complex."

The genus *(Guizotia)*, named in 1829 by Cassini after the French historian Guizot, has been taxonomically revised by Baagoe (1974). Niger is included in the Compositae family, the tribe Helianthoides and the subtribe Verbesininae. The genus Guizotia is a small genus of six species. All species are native to tropical Africa, and five are found in Ethiopia. *G. abyssinica* is almost certainly derived from *G. scabra*, most likely from the subspecies *schimperi*. This has been confirmed by karyomorphological investigations (S. C. Hiremath 1985, personal communication). *G. scabra* spp. *schimperi* is a common Ethiopian weed in niger fields. The weedy and cultivated species are very similar in appearance, but can be distinguished from each other by the shape of the paleae and involucre bracts which are narrow and pointed in *G. scabra* spp. *schimperi* and broadly ovate in *G. abyssinica*. Also the seeds of the wild species are much shorter (1 to 3 mm) compared with those of niger (3.5 to 5 mm). Oil content of *G. scabra* spp. *schimperi* samples ranged from 24 to 35%, while seeds of *G. abyssinica* contained 36 to 42% (Holetta Research Station, unpublished data).

Guizotia abyssinica has a complement of 2n=30 chromosomes. During meiosis, 15 bivalents were generally observed with an occasional trivalent and tetravalent association (Chavan, 1961). Hiremath (personal communication, 1985) has found that niger shows considerable pollen sterility associated with univalent formation and subsequent meiotic abnormalities.

There is evidence that introgression of genes from the weedy species into cultivated niger can occur. Cultivated niger has been reported to hybridize easily with *G. scabra* spp. *schimperi* and sets viable seeds, but rarely with other wild species (Hiremath 1985, personal communication).

In Ethiopia, Candussio (1941) reported a spontaneous hybrid between *G. abyssinica* and *G. scabra* spp. *scabra*, but he was not able to find another such hybrid. Moreover, all crosses between *G. abyssinica* and *G. scabra* ssp. *schimperi* failed to set seed, although crosses between lines of *G. abyssinica* were easily made at Holetta research station (1983, unpublished).

Seegler (1983) and Chavan (1961) were unable to distinguish distinct forms and landraces of niger. However, in a 1982 survey three distinct types were reported to be under cultivation in the Gojjam region of Ethiopia (G. Alemaw, 1982, personal communication). The predominant and main season type, "Abat noug," is grown during the rainy season from June to December, while "Mesno noug" is planted late, about September, and harvested in January. "Mesno noug" is sown where waterlogging of the soil is severe. A third, fast-maturing type, known as "Bunenge noug," is used in the lowlands where rainfall is more limited. It is planted in July and harvested in October.

MODE OF REPRODUCTION

Niger is an annual, highly branched herb, 35 to 200 cm tall, with a well developed root system consisting of a short tap root with may laterals, especially in the top 5 cm of the soil. Branching begins from the upper nodes at the 6 to 8 leaf stage. Plant-to-plant competition usually limits the branches per plant to not more than eight. Two to three buds are formed close together at the tips of the branches, followed by the formation of buds in the axils of the leaves. A single plant often bears 20 to 40 heads. Flowering begins 50 to 110 days after sowing and can continue for 4 to 6 weeks in a field (Fig. 20.1).

The head or inflorescence consists of a receptacle 1 to 2 cm in diameter surrounded by two rows of involucral bracts. Receptacle paleae subtend each floret. Generally eight ray florets form a showy outer whorl, light yellow to orange in color. The ray florets of niger are female and normally produce seeds. The disc florets, up to 60 per head, are usually arranged in three whorls and are hermaphroditic. Each floret consists of a tube of five lobes (fused petals) with a distinct upper section surrounding the style and stamens, and a lower section surrounding the ovary. The style bears a stigma consisting of two hairy arms.

The florets open about two hours after sunrise. The anthers liberate their sticky pollen and the styles elongate bearing the stigma arms well above the anthers, so that there is no contact between pollen and stigma of the same floret. The outer whorl of ray florets flower first, with flowering proceeding concentrically over a period of about eight days. Niger is largely or entirely a cross-pollinated crop and, when in flower, is highly attractive to bees and other insects. Three days after flowering the florets start to dry. The seed (achene) is usually shiny black or dark brown, 3 to 5 mm long and 1.5 to 2 mm wide. Seed weight ranges from 3 to 4.8 g/1000 seeds. Further descriptions can be found in Chavan (1961) and Seegler (1983).

The physical structure of the niger flower forces cross-pollination but this appears to be reinforced by a sporophytic self-incompatibility system. Little or no seedset has been obtained under bagging with muslin bags, even when the bagged heads of the same plant are rubbed together. When pollen from the same plant is applied to stigmas of one-to three-day old buds, seedset is increased over that found in bagged heads, but if the buds are over four days old, no seed is set on selfing. (Naik and Panda 1968; Ramachandran and Menon, 1979). However, some self-compatible plants have been identified. In Ethiopia some thirty plants in a germplasm collection of 600 produced at least 1 gm of self seed under muslin bags. S_4 progenies have been obtained from these plants. Many of these progenies show little or no inbreeding depression.

BREEDING PROCEDURES

Genetic improvement of niger has been limited, mainly due to the crop's self-incompatibility, but also because niger has been regarded as a minor oilseed crop. Testing and selecting plants or accessions from local collections has been the usual method of developing improved varieties. A range of germplasm, from which such varieties can be produced, is available in India (1000 local collections) and in Ethiopia (700 local collections).

Population improvement methods have now been initiated by breeders in Ethiopia as well as in India. In Ethiopia several populations are being improved through simple mass selection. In addition, a half-sib recurrent selection program is being carried out which is more likely to be effective in improving low heritability traits such as yield. This procedure, which is very similar to Pustovoit's "Method of Reserves" used in sunflower (see Chapter 14) involves selection of several hundred single plants from a random mating isolation plot (Fick, 1978). Part of the seed from each selected plant is grown in a two-row plot and part is kept in reserve. Progenies are evaluated for yield, oil content, maturity and seed shattering relative to the check. The best 25 to 30 lines are identified, and equal amounts of the reserve seed of these selections are recombined into another random mating bulk which is planted in isolation the following year. Progenies with improved performance can be retained for evaluation as potential varieties. With this procedure this system requires no selfing and the general combining ability of the selections is assessed in the progeny row trials. Random mating of the best selections is assured by the self-incompatible nature of the crop. Similar methods are being followed by breeders in India.

To produce crossed seed Shrivastava and Shamwanshi (1974) suggested that flowers from the two parent plants be rubbed together. However, rubbing the florets may result in some selfing. Thus it may be preferable to make specific crosses by removing all the disc florets, just as the bud begins to open, but leaving the ray female florets intact. By bagging the emasculated head and pollinating the ray florets the next morning, when the stigma arms have opened, several crossed seed per head can usually be obtained.

Maintenance of pure lines is a problem because of the self-incompatibility of the crop. However, sibbing of the germplasm collections can be carried out by covering 10 to 50 plants within a muslin bag or mosquito netting to exclude insects, and rubbing flowering capitula together two to three times a week. Seed increase of advanced lines can be done in isolated plots, preferably at least 1 km away from any other niger.

The niger gene pools in Ethiopia and India have been separated for several thousand years, and have become adapted to rather different conditions. Prinz (1976) noted that Ethiopian niger has a longer growing period, and was more sensitive to temperature and photoperiod than was Indian niger. A preliminary evaluation of Indian niger at Holetta, Ethiopia (unpublished) indicated that some Indian niger lines have very high 1000 seed weights, but yields of all Indian niger lines were rather low in comparison with Ethiopian niger. The divergence which has occurred between Indian and Ethiopian material might be usefully exploited in a disruptive selection procedure where improved lines or populations from Ethiopia and India are intermated. Rapid advance from selection could be expected in such intercrossed progenies.

BREEDING OBJECTIVES

The primary aim of breeding programs both in India and Ethiopia is to improve yield and oil content. The average yields of niger on farmers' fields are low, ranging from 200 to 400 kg/ha. Maximum yields of 1000 to 1500 kg/ha obtained under research conditions in Ethiopia indicate that other oilseed crops such as sunflower and rapeseed can produce much higher seed yields when conditions are favorable. Niger, however, has proved its ability to tolerate adverse soil conditions, and has the ability to enhance yields of crops which follow niger in the rotation.

A limited number of studies have examined variation, heritability and interrelationships of traits in niger. In a set of eighteen Indian genotypes, Nayaker (1976) found that days to flower and plant height had high variability, high heritability and hence calculated genetic advance from selection was high. Other traits such as number of primary branches, number of capitula per plant, 1000 seed weight and seed yield per plant had low variability and low genetic advance. Sahu and Patnaik (1980) found that a selection index using number of seeds per capitulum and 1000 seed weight, along with selection for late flowering and a longer grain-filling period, might lead to more rapid yield improvement than selecting directly for yield.

Oil content of niger is reported to range from 30 to 50% (Seegler, 1983). Other surveys place the range in Ethiopia at 35 to 42%, while Nema and Singh (1965) report the range in Indian samples to be 39 to 47%. A sharp increase in oil content could probably be achieved through selection for thin hull types, as was successfully done in sunflower and safflower. Reduction in hull thickness could also be expected to reduce fiber levels in the meal, thus making it more desirable as a livestock feed.

Being indeterminate, niger is prone to seed shattering; thus selection for a non-shattering, determinate flowering habit would allow the farmer more flexibility in harvesting his crop.

Niger farmers, both in Ethiopia and India, report that the crop helps to reduce weed infestation in subsequent crops. Preliminary work in Ethiopia (unpublished) indicated that a water-soluble extract from niger plants inhibited the germination of monocots. This raises the possibility of selecting for enhanced allelopathic ability in niger to suppress weeds.

When conditions for vegetative growth are favourable, niger is prone to lodging. Shorter plants with strong stems, possibly with a better harvest index, might be required for these situations.

Fortunately, insects and diseases are not usually serious pests in either major producing country. Thus there appears to be little need to breed for insect or disease resistance at the moment.

Due to the self-incompatible nature of the crop, inbreeding normally results in reduced vigor and seed yield. In India, seed yields of S_1 lines were reduced by about 91%, although one line was found which exhibited no inbreeding depression (Ramachandran and Madhava Menon, 1979). In Ethiopia, little or no inbreeding depression was found among the S_1 and S_2 progenies from self-compatible lines. The development of inbred lines raises the possibility of producing synthetic varieties from inbreds with good combining ability.

HISTORY OF CULTIVAR DEVELOPMENT

In India, selection of improved varieties has been underway for many years. In 1961, Chavan listed eleven improved varieties which were recommended for cultivation in different niger areas of the country. Niger improvement programs are carried out at seven centers in India. Promising lines are tested across India in coordinated trials, and varieties are recommended for each state. A number of varieties such as "Ootacamund," "No. 5" and "IGP 76" are widely adapted and are recommended for cultivation in several states. Other varieties are recommended for cultivation within a single state.

In Ethiopia, plant improvement of niger started only 10 years ago. At the present time, one variety "Sendafa" is recommended for the central highland areas.

UTILIZATION OF PRODUCTS

Niger oil is pale yellow in color with a sweet odour and pleasant "nutty" taste. However, on storage at moderate temperatures for more than six months, the oil may thicken and become rancid(Seegler, 1983).

The fatty acid composition of the oil is similar to that of safflower and sunflower, with a high content of up to 75% linoleic acid, except that it may contain a small amount (2%) of lignoceric acid (Seegler, 1983) (Table 20.2). Indian and Ethiopian oils are reported to differ markedly in linoleic acid content, with the Ethiopian oil averaging 70% and extending up to 85% under cool conditions. Indian oil, ranged from 52 to 74% linoleic, with the difference being made up by oleic acid (Chavan, 1961). It is believed that the temperature under which the seed matures is the major determinant of this variation.

In India the oil is extracted by bullock-powered "ghanis" or in mechanized mills (Chavan, 1961). Usually the oil is sold for edible purposes in the local market in its pure form, but may also be mixed with other oils. Occasionally it is used as an illuminant or in the manufacture of soap or paint.

Table 20.2 Fatty Acid Composition of Niger Seed Oil as Reported by:
(1) Seegler (1983); (2) Grieco and Piepoli (1967); (3) Chavan (1961)

		Fatty acid composition in %		
Fatty Acid	Symbol	1	2	3
Myristic	(14:0)		trace	trace
Palmitic	(16:0)	9.1	9.4	5.0-8.4
Palmitoleic	(16:1)		0.2	
Heptadecanoic	(17:0)		trace	
Stearic	(18:0)	6.8	6.7	2.0-10.6
Oleic	(18:0)	7.7	5.9	6.0-38.9
Linoleic	(18:2)	73.0	76.5	51.6-74.1
Linolenic	(18:3)	trace	0.2	trace
Arachidic	(20:0)	0.5	0.5	trace
Eicosenic	(20:1)		trace	
Behenic	(22:0)	0.4	0.6	
Lignoceric	(24:0)	2.0		

After Seegler (1983)

Most Ethiopian niger is extracted in small mechanical village expeller mills. Such oil is highly prized for edible purposes and usually commands a premium over other available oils. Some oil is extracted in the home by parching the seed, grinding it into a fine powder, adding hot water and stirring. This process allows the oil to float to the surface and be skimmed off. Water may also be added to the parched, ground seed to make a drink. Other minor uses include mixing the parched seed with pulses as a snack food, and making a stew or "wat" with ground seed and spices. Niger flour is also baked into a bread or sprinkled on bread prior to consumption.

Niger expeller cake is normally used as an animal feed, although in Ethiopia it may also be used as a fuel, and in India it is sometimes used as a fertilizer (Seegler, 1983). In general, Ethiopian cake was found to be higher in fiber (24%), lower in protein (24%), and total digestible nutrients than other oilseed cakes (Seegler, 1983; Beyene et al. 1977). Indian niger cake was found to be lower in fiber (14%) and higher in protein (30%) than that reported for Ethiopia (Chavan, 1961). An experimental lipoprotein concentrate was prepared by Eklund (1971) which contained 40% protein. A chemical score of 56 was established, with lysine being the limiting amino acid.

REFERENCES

Abebe, M., Bingham, F.T., and Yermanos, D.M. 1978. The ecophysiology of noog (*Guizotia abyssinica* Cass.) III. Growth, yield and mineral composition under saline conditions. Af. J. Agric. Sci. 5(2): 49-59.

Baagoe, J. 1974. The genus *Guizotia* (Compositae). A taxonomic revision. Bot. Tidsskr. 69: 1-39.

Beyene, C., Coppock, C.E., and McDowell, R.E. 1977. Laboratory evaluation and estimation of nutritive values of some Ethiopian feed stuffs and formula feeds. Afr. J. of Agric. Sci. 4: 9-24.

Candussio, R. 1941. Il miglioramento del "neuk" *(Guizotia abyssinica* Cass). Prime indagini ed osservatzione e direttive del lavoro di selezione. L'Agricoltura Coloniale 35: 347-354.

Chavan, V.M. 1961. *Niger and Sunflower.* Indian Central Oilseeds Committee, Hyderabad.

Eklund, A. 1971. Preparation and chemical analysis of a lipoprotein from niger seed (*Guizotia abyssinica* Cass). Acta Chem. Scand. 25: 2225-2231.

Fick, G.N. 1978. Breeding and genetics, pp. 279-338. *In* J.F. Carter (ed.), *Sunflower Science and Technology.* No. 19. Agronomy Series. Am. Soc. of Agron. Crop Sci. Soc. Madison, Wis.

Grieco, D., and Piepoli, G. 1976. Composition en acides gras des huiles vegetales alimentaires. Oleagineux 22: 611-612.

Harlan, J.R. 1975. *Crops and Man.* Am. Soc. of Agron. Crop Sci. Soc. Madison, Wis.

Naik, S.S., and Panda, B.S. 1968. Time of bud pollination in increasing fertility in self-incompatible niger (*Guizotia abyssinica* Cass). Indian J. Sci. and Ind. 2: 177-180.

Nayakar, N.Y. 1976. Genetic variability and heritability for six quantitative characters in niger. (*Guizotia abyssinica* Cass). Mysore J. Agric. Sci. 10: 553-558.

Nema, N.P., and Singh, L. 1965. Estimates of genotypic and environmental variability in niger. Indian Oilseeds J. 9: 192-194.

Prinz, K.D. 1976. Untersuchungen zur "Okophysiologie von Niger-saat *(Guizotia abyssinica)* " thiopishcer und indischer Herkunft. Ph.D. Thesis, Agr. wiss. F.B., Univ. of Gottingen. 204 pp.

Purseglove, J.W. 1979. *Tropical Crops, Dicotyledons.* Longman, London.

Ramachandran T.K., and Madhava Menon P. 1979. Pollination mechanism and inbreeding depression in niger (*Guizotia abyssinica* Cass). Madras Agric. J. 66: 449-454.

Sahu, D.P., and Patnaik, M.C. 1980. Selection indices in niger *Guizotia abyssinica.* Indian J. Agric. Sci. 50: 914-917.

Seegler, C.J.P. 1983. *Oil Plants in Ethiopia, their Taxonomy and Agricultural Significance.* Center for Agricultural Publishing and Documentation, PUDOC, Wageningen.

Shrivastava, P.S., and Shamwanshi, K.P.S. 1974. Investigation on the extent of cross pollination and selfing, and crossing technique in niger (*Guizotia abyssinica* Cass.). JNKVV (Jawaharlal Nehru Krishi Vishwa Vidyalaya) Res. J. 8: 110-112.

Vaughan, J.G. 1970. *The Structure and Utilization of Oilseeds.* Chapman and Hall, London.

Chapter 21

Cotton

R. J. Kohel

IMPORTANCE AND DISTRIBUTION

Cottonseed is second only to soybean in the amount of oilseed produced worldwide (Anon. 1982). Such a position is unique because cottonseed is a secondary product in the production of cotton fibers. The producer grows cotton plants (Fig. 21.1) for the production of the seed fibers, and the product is sold as seed cotton, seeds with the fibers still attached; as lint, ginned fibers for which the cottonseed is used to defray the cost of ginning; or as lint and cottonseed as separate products. The trend is toward the latter, but all variations still exist throughout the world.

The cottonseed-processing industry originated in the 19th century as an industry utilizing a by-product (Altschul et al. 1958). Overshadowed by the economic value of lint, the cottonseed industry exerted little influence on such things as the genetics research, breeding, and production of cotton. Now, however, cottonseed is gaining the status of an important product, and there exists a need for increased research and development.

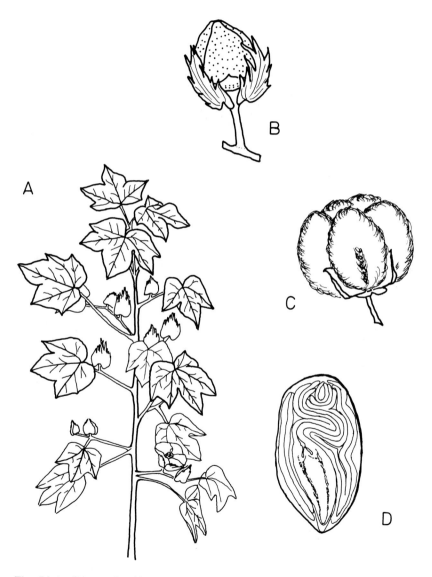

Fig. 21.1 Cotton. A – Young plant. B. – Mature green boll (fruit). C – Open boll.
D. – Cross-section of mature seed showing convoluted cotyledons filling seed.

Table 21.1 World Cotton Production by Region and Major Producing Countries

Region or Country	Production area ('000 ha)			Seed yield (kg/ha)			Seed production ('000 tonnes)		
	1969-71	1979-81	1985	1969-71	1979-81	1985	1969-71	1979-81	1985
World	**32595**	**34523**	**35165**	**638**	**790**	**916**	**22440**	**27267**	**32217**
Africa	**4740**	**3608**	**4017**	**511**	**566**	**596**	**2423**	**2024**	**2395**
Chad	298	163	172	218	294	407	65	48	70
Cote d'Ivoire	40	119	180	500	321	667	20	74	120
Egypt	668	507	425	1349	1611	1765	901	817	750
Kenya	74	110	180	149	182	83	11	20	15
Mali	73	100	110	534	810	1000	39	81	110
Mozambique	360	131	142	233	260	246	84	34	35
Nigeria	405	482	405	304	131	79	123	63	32
South Africa	81	115	110	469	861	673	38	99	74
Sudan	502	407	410	880	538	878	442	219	360
Tanzania	425	430	340	320	265	256	136	114	87
Uganda	923	284	530	187	46	62	173	13	33
Zimbabwe	78	112	150	1077	1054	1187	84	118	178
N. & C. America	**5270**	**6086**	**4623**	**888**	**996**	**987**	**4681**	**6061**	**5463**
Guatemala	77	116	63	1429	2034	1460	110	236	92
Mexico	461	632	205	1308	1525	1634	603	552	335
Nicaragua	112	104	115	1161	1058	852	130	110	98
U.S.A.	4543	5381	4171	824	936	1168	3742	5034	4872

S. America	**3560**	**4833**	**4826**	**516**	**397**	**577**	**1836**	**1918**	**2783**
Argentina	408	506	450	539	500	644	220	253	290
Brazil	2644	3619	3582	453	297	489	1197	1075	1750
Colombia	241	184	223	851	984	973	205	181	217
Paraguay	46	299	350	435	545	886	20	163	310
Peru	150	147	146	987	1272	1164	148	187	170
Asia	**15972**	**16557**	**17940**	**554**	**660**	**846**	**8848**	**10921**	**15186**
Burma	162	167	230	154	234	361	25	39	93
China	4791	4868	5770	830	1079	1438	3977	5255	8300
India	7707	8045	8100	282	328	346	2176	2638	2800
Pakistan	1817	2135	2500	655	684	920	1190	1460	2300
Syria	266	146	170	906	1473	1852	241	215	315
Thailand	62	138	87	1000	826	770	62	114	67
Turkey	608	646	620	1141	1209	1335	705	781	828
Europe	**335**	**237**	**303**	**1090**	**1485**	**1624**	**365**	**352**	**492**
Greece	147	138	209	1544	1681	1766	227	232	369
Oceania	**33**	**68**	**151**	**1364**	**1838**	**2570**	**45**	**125**	**388**
U.S.S.R.	**2685**	**3035**	**3305**	**1580**	**1866**	**1667**	**4241**	**5848**	**5510**

Source: FAO Production Yearbooks 1980 (vol. 34) and 1985 (vol. 39) [seed yield = seed production/production area]

Cotton originates from tropical to subtropical latitudes, but approximately 50% of the production areas are in temperate zones (Waddle, 1984). The People's Republic of China, USSR, USA, India, and Pakistan account for about 80% of the area of production. A listing of major cotton producing countries and their production is provided in Table 21.1.

ORIGIN AND SYSTEMATICS

There are about thirty-nine species of *Gossypium* (Fryxell, 1984). Of these, two diploid species (2n=26), *G. arboreum* L. and *G. herbaceum* L., and two tetraploid species (2n=4x=52), *G. barbadense* L. and *G. hirsutum* L., are cultivated.

The diploid species are placed in genomic groupings and designated A through G. An Asiatic diploid species, A genome, in combination with a diploid of the New World, D genome, are presumed progenitors of the tetraploids. The cultivated diploid species have their center-of-origin in Africa-Asia, and they are referred to as the Asiatic species because it was in this area that domestication and weaving became established. The early cotton textile industry in Europe was based on the Asiatic species.

The tetraploid species have their center-of-origin in Mexico, Central America, and South America. The discovery of cottons in the New World by European explorers further fueled the cotton textile industry and the accompanying industrial revolution. Cotton production expanded in the New World, and the New World tetraploids began to displace the less productive diploids. Upland cotton, *G. hirsutum,* became the predominant species grown. Today it accounts for about 90% of the world cotton production, *G. barbadense* accounts for about 10%, and the Asiatic cotton production remains only in marginal growing areas of India and Pakistan (Lee, 1984).

As the archaeological records continue to push the domestication of cottons to earlier times in both the New World and Asiatic cottons, the case for independent domestication becomes stronger. It has been proposed that Asiatic cottons were domesticated initially for their seed as an animal feed, and that subsequently their seed fibers were incorporated into an existing linen textile industry (Chowdhury and Burth, 1971).

MODE OF REPRODUCTION

Cotton plants are perennials that have indeterminate growth habits, and most of the wild forms are short-day photoperiodic. The cultivated forms are predominantly day-neutral in flowering response, and they are cultivated as annuals. Growth is characterized by a vegetative monopodial main-stem on which the axial buds can produce either monopodial or sympodial, fruiting, branches. Each node of a branch arises from an axillary bud at the terminus. Therefore, continued vegetative plant growth is required to sustain flowering (Mauney, 1984), and the earlier the initiation of sympodial growth, the earlier is the crop production.

The cotton plant has perfect flowers that open in the morning, shed pollen, and wither by nightfall. In cultivated cottons, pollen sheds concurrently with flower opening. The anthers surround the stigma, so self pollination is readily accomplished. The stigmas remain receptive until noon or shortly thereafter, depending on weather conditions. The pollen grains are large and sticky, so no wind pollination occurs, but insects, primarily bees, are capable of effecting cross-pollination. Because insects can cause cross-pollination, the cotton plant is classed as often cross-pollinated. However, cotton is completely self-compatible, and any cross-pollination is a function of the numbers of pollinating insects present. In production fields where frequent applications of insecticides are used to control pests, cross-pollination is from 0 to 10%.

Cotton plants begin to flower about sixty days after planting; flowering continues for about forty-five days, and individual bolls mature in about fifty-five days. Cotton bolls are capsules with 3 to 5 locules, each with 7 to 10 ovules. A boll normally matures 20 to 30 seeds. Variation in the time for each developmental period depends on the genotype of the plant and climatic conditions. Cotton plants are very responsive to stress, and flowers and young bolls are readily shed when plants are subjected to stress. As crop development progresses and bolls are set, the rate of vegetative growth and flowering diminishes and the amount of flower shedding increases. Once a crop of bolls matures sufficiently, cotton plants initiate new growth and flowering activity. If the growing season is long enough, production can be increased by this "second crop." In most production areas, growth and fruiting are limited by temperature and/or moisture, and plants produce only a single crop of bolls.

The bulk of storage reserves of the cottonseed are produced during later stages of seed development (Benedict et al. 1976). In areas of temperate climate, low temperatures at the later stages of seed development have a marked influence on seed oil. As temperatures decrease, the rate of boll development decreases, as does the seed-oil content. Relative amounts of individual fatty acids change in response to temperature, but the pattern of response in cottonseed is not clear (Kohel and Cherry, 1984). This relationship is made even less clear by the differences in developmental age of bolls on a plant at any given time.

The response of seed development and oil content to moisture varies. Chronic moisture stress has not been shown to produce any negative changes on seed-oil content (Cherry et al. 1981). An acute moisture stress at a late stage of boll development may adversely influence seed-oil content because individual seed may be arrested in their development. Stress at early stages of boll development or chronic stress are generally compensated by boll shedding (Kohel and Benedict, 1984).

BREEDING PROCEDURES

Cotton breeding is directed toward enhancing the yield of quality fibers, and because the yield of fiber is directly related to the number of seeds produced, both seed and fiber yield are increased. The lack of specific attention to seed quality has not seemed to result in a change of seed composition. Breeding efforts directed to more efficient production systems and the preservation of fiber quality have a similar positive effect on the production and preservation of seed quality. Some of the new mechanization production systems, which include the use of cotton modules, can affect seed quality negatively, but the effects are more serious on planting seed quality (Cherry and Leffler, 1984).

Breeding methodologies used in cotton are those normally utilized with self-pollinating crops. A recent review of cotton breeding is provided by Niles and Feaster (1984). The discovery of a cytoplasmic-male-sterile (CMS) and restorer factors (Meyer, 1973; 1975) has stimulated interest in producing hybrid planting seed. The CMS system is still under development and evaluation. However, hybrid cotton planting-seed are in limited use in areas of the world where abundant, low cost hand-labor is available for hand cross-pollination, primarily in India and People's Republic of China. There is no reason to assume that changes in cotton breeding methods would result in a change of emphasis on seed quality.

BREEDING OBJECTIVES

As with most crops, the major aim of cotton breeding is to increase production efficiency and total yield. Since the original cottons were slow maturing, short-day photoperiodic perennials, and since cultivated cotton is generally produced as an annual crop, the history of cotton breeding has been directed toward increased earliness (Niles and Feaster, 1984). Originally, earliness was needed to maximize yield of a perennial plant within an annual cropping system. Today earliness is desired to minimize production inputs, avoid hazardous weather, or to facilitate double-cropping systems. Plant breeders have been able to select for increased earliness and restricted plant growth to the point where yield potential is limited. The indeterminate growth habit of the cotton plant requires vegetative plant growth to produce flowering sites. To overcome these limitations, efforts are directed toward increasing the rate of flowering, and this has met with some success. In addition, selection has been practiced to decrease the period of boll development. Success of such selection could influence seed quality if the rates of developmental processes in the boll are not increased to compensate for the shortened period of boll development. There are scattered reports of breeding attempts to improve the compositional quality of cottonseed. The reports are characteristically positive, but do not appear to represent any continuous effort to breed for improved seed quality (Cherry et al. 1981).

Areas of the world suited to cotton production are generally conducive to pests that prey on cotton. Favorable climatic conditions and normally long growing period for cotton plants combine to make insect pests a major problem in cotton production. Sizable breeding efforts are directed toward breeding for pest resistance. Thus far, little success has been realized other than breeding for avoidance through increased earliness. Breeding for long trichomes was successful against the jassid, but resistance to other insects is less dramatic and does not persist under high insect pressures (Ridgway, 1984).

Breeding for disease resistance was successful against bacterial blight. Resistance factors with single gene inheritance were identified and included individually or in combination in cultivars in the problem areas. Other diseases are not so readily controlled because the genetics of resistance is either complex or not known (Bell, 1984).

The discovery of the genes gl_2 and gl_3, which remove the pigment glands from seed and all aerial portions of the plant, has had the greatest impact on seed quality (McMichael, 1960). These glands contain pigments, gossypol, and gossypol precursors that are the greatest quality detriment in cottonseeds. With the discovery of glandless cotton, much breeding effort was directed toward breeding glandless cultivars. The discovery that chewing insects prefer glandless cotton caused a recession of these breeding efforts, and breeding was directed toward increasing the gland content of the cotton plant (Jenkins et al. 1966; Lukefahr et al. 1969).

Breeding to produce glandless cotton has continued in a few programs and is at a maintenance level in others. Glandless plants were discovered in progeny of a cross between Hopi cotton, domesticated by the Hopi Indians, and an Acala type. The original material was very poor agronomically, and breeding efforts were directed toward transferring the glandless genes into well adapted agronomic backgrounds. Because of the very poor agronomic origin of glandless, there was initial concern about possible genetic linkages or pleiotropic associations between the glandless genes and poor agronomic performance.

Evidence does not suggest that glandlessness *per se* contributes to poor performance. However, the present group of glandless cottons are poorer performers than the glanded cottons, probably because the majority of breeding efforts are directed toward the glanded cottons. The performance of glandless cottons will lag behind glanded cottons until a broad base of improved glandless germplasm is developed, and major breeding efforts are directed to breeding cottons with the glandless genotype.

A glandless mutant was discovered in Egyptian cotton, *G. barbadense*. This glandless expression was found to be controlled by an incompletely dominant allele (Gl^e_2) at the Gl^e_2 locus (Kohel and Lee, 1984). The use of a single, incomplete dominant gene that is identifiable as a heterozygote should be easier than using the two recessive genes gl_2 and gl_3 in the development of cultivars.

Despite the limited acceptance of glandless cottons, they have served to focus increased attention on seed quality. A breeding program in California, USA resulted in the release of a cultivar with decreased seed-gossypol and increased seed-oil content, compared to earlier releases. The United States National Cotton Variety Testing program has included seed quality among its evaluations. The author maintains a genetics program for cottonseed quality improvement.

Studies of seed-oil content have revealed that it is controlled by predominantly additive gene variation with sizable environmental variation, which leads to lowered heritabilities (Kohel, 1980). Genetic studies of seed-oil content in Egyptian cultivars have shown larger amounts of non-additive genetic variance, but these materials have a more restrictive genetic base.

Research and breeding efforts to improve seedling vigor and protection against seedling diseases seem to impart better preservation of seed quality. There is no evidence that seed constituents are changed, but rather seed coat changes provide better protection of the embryo.

One of the reasons that integration of seed quality into breeding programs will be slow is the lack of means to make seed quality evaluations. Routine fiber quality evaluations are available through relatively inexpensive service laboratories, and certain large breeding programs have their own laboratories. The evaluation of seed quality, on the other hand, for oil, protein, and gossypol is expensive, and test procedures require large quantities of seed for separate analyses of oil and protein and gossypol that are not available in genetic studies or in early stages of plant breeding. Few breeding programs have the resources available for such determinations. Given the relative lower value of seed, compared to fiber, there exists little incentive to devote limited resources to the evaluation and breeding of cottonseed quality.

HISTORY OF CULTIVAR DEVELOPMENT

The prevalent species of cultivated cotton, *G. hirsutum,* accounts for 90% of the world production. The center-of-origin of this species is in Mexico-Central America, and a home spinning-weaving industry and cotton commerce was practiced by the natives when the European explorers arrived. The Europeans were effective in disseminating seed and establishing production throughout their colonial empires. The large growing area that developed in the southern US resulted in the selection of day-neutral, early maturing, and prolific types, and repeated introductions from the center-of-origin contributed to the US germ pool. The US selections provided a germplasm base for further world expansion, especially in temperate areas. Evidence of early direct dissemination from the center-of-origin is recognizable in cottons of the more tropical regions, because when grown in temperate regions many cultivars display residual photoperiodic and late-maturity traits.

The second most widely grown cultivated species, *G. barbadense,* accounts for about 10% of world production. Its center-of-origin is in South and Central America. It includes the Sea Island type of *G. barbadense* that was grown in the coastal islands of colonial USA. Sea Island cottons were introduced into Egypt and, following hybridization and selection, *G. barbadense* became established as the cotton of Egypt. Later *G. barbadense* was reintroduced into the southwest desert of the USA. Derivatives of this cotton, known as Egyptian, Egyptian-American, and Pima, are known for their long and strong fiber. This fiber characteristic is not known in the native *G. barbadense* cottons, and some regions of the world grow *G. barbadense* that does not have fiber with these quality characteristics.

UTILIZATION OF PRODUCTS

Cottonseed is the second ranking oilseed in the world in production, from which is produced oil (16%), meal (45%), linters (9%), hulls (26%), and the remainder (4%) as waste and processing losses. Refined cottonseed oil is used in the food industry, and in some parts of the world it is the preferred vegetable oil.

The cottonseed meal remaining after oil extraction is used as a protein-rich feed for ruminant animals in most areas of the world. Often the hulls are added to the meal as a roughage. In contrast, the contamination of meal by contents of the pigment glands limits the use of cottonseed meal in non-ruminant feeds since gossypol in the pigment glands is toxic to non-ruminants, such as swine and poultry. Free gossypol is commonly bound by heat treatments, which also binds part of the available lysine.

The Southern Regional Research Center at New Orleans, La., USA, has devoted major efforts toward cottonseed utilization (Cherry and Leffler, 1984). Results have identified the chemical and physical properties of the proteins, described functional properties, and developed potential products. The presence of pigment glands and their undesirable contamination of cottonseed products has remained a deterrent to full utilization of cottonseed. In addition to genetic removal of the pigment glands, methods were developed to physically remove them in processing. One such method was the liquid cyclone process. The liquid cyclone process offers the potential to produce food grade products from glanded cottonseed (Gardner et al. 1976).

From a processing and utilization point of view, glandless cottonseed is highly desirable because it allows the production of traditional products with higher quality and reduced cost and allows expanded uses (Anon. 1977). The incentives to improve cottonseed and its products originate not only from the cotton industry, which would benefit directly, but also from a worldwide perspective that would benefit food and feed resources. Cotton will continue to be produced for its fiber because cotton fibers are a renewable resource that is processed into products with highly desirable textile properties. Given that cottonseeds will be produced in the continued production of cotton fibers, a major goal is to efficiently and effectively utilize the seed. Cottonseeds devoid of pigment glands are highly desirable for their high nutritional value and for their unique protein properties. The physical and functional properties of cottonseed proteins are such that they will not only complement existing vegetable proteins, but they offer unique properties not found in other vegetable proteins (Cherry and Leffler, 1984).

In the seed crushing industry, glandless cottonseeds offer advantages directly related to the absence of pigment glands, and all of these result in more efficient processing and higher quality products. The reduction of gossypol in the system eliminates the need of high energy inputs for heat binding of free gossypol; the oil would require less refining due to the absence of pigments; the meal produced would have a higher lysine value and could be safely fed to both ruminants and non-ruminants.

In the food industry, glandless cottonseed products can range from the full-fat kernel, to defatted flours, to protein concentrates. Traditional vegetable protein products could be produced and new product potentials have been identified, capitalizing on the properties of cottonseed proteins. Given the worldwide distribution of cotton production, advances in glandless cottonseed would provide for a new protein source in areas where protein availability is limited.

REFERENCES

Altschul, A.M., Lyman, C.M., and Thurber, F.H. 1958. Cottonseed Meal, pp. 469-534. *In* A. M. Altschul (ed.), *Processed Plant Protein Foodstuffs*. Academic Press, Inc., New York.

Anonymous. 1977. Glandless cotton: Its significance, status, and prospects. Conf. Proc., Dallas, Tex.

Anonymous. 1982. World forecast: Record oilseed production. J. Am. Oil Chem. Soc. 59: 752A-766A.

Bell, A.A. 1984. Cotton Protection: Diseases, pp. 288-309. *In* R. J. Kohel and C. F. Lewis (eds), *Cotton*. Agronomy Monograph 24. Am. Soc. Agon., Madison, Wis.

Benedict, C.R., Kohel, R.J., and Schubert, A.M. 1976. Transport of ^{14}C-assimilates to cottonseed: Integrity of funiculus during seed filling stage. Crop Sci. 16: 23-27.

Cherry, J.P., and Leffler, H.R. 1984. Seed, pp. 522-567. *In* R. J. Kohel and C. F. Lewis (eds.), *Cotton*. Agronomy Monograph 24. Am. Soc. Agron., Madison, Wis.

——, Kohel, R.J., Jones, L.A., and Powell, W.H. 1981. Cottonseed quality: Factors affecting feed and food uses, pp. 266-283. Proc. Beltwide Cotton Prod. Res. Conf., New Orleans, La.

Chowdhury, K.A., and Burth, G.M. 1971. Cotton seeds from the Neolithic of Egyptian Nubia and the origin of Old World cotton. Linn. Soc. London. Biol. J. 3: 303-312.

Fryxell, P.A. 1984. Taxonomy and Germplasm Resources, pp. 27-57. *In* R. J. Kohel and C. F. Lewis (eds.), *Cotton*. Agronomy Monograph 24. Am. Soc. Agron., Madison, Wis.

Gardner, H.K., Hron, R.J., and Vix, H.L.E. 1976. Removal of pigment glands (gossypol) from cottonseed. Cereal Chem. 53: 549-560.

Jenkins, J.N., Maxwell, F.G., and Lafever, H.N. 1966. The comparative preference of insects for glanded and glandless cottons. J. Econ. Entomol. 59: 352-356.

Kohel, R.J. 1980. Genetic studies of seed oil in cotton. Crop Sci. 20: 784-787.

——, and Benedict, C.R. 1984. Year effects in partitioning of dry matter into cotton boll components. Crop Sci. 24: 268-270.

——, and Cherry, J.P. 1984. Variation of cottonseed quality with stratified harvests. Crop Sci. 23: 1119-1124.

——, and Lee, J.A. 1984. Genetic analysis of Egyptian glandless cotton. Crop Sci. 24: 1119-1121.

Lee, J.A. 1984. Cotton as a World Crop, pp. 1-15. *In* R. J. Kohel and C. F. Lewis (eds.), *Cotton.* Agronomy Monograph 24. Am. Soc. Agron., Madison, Wis.

Lukefahr, M.J., Shaver, T.N., and Parrot, W.L. 1969. Sources and nature of resistance in *Gossypium hirsutum* to bollworm and tobacco budworms, pp. 81-82. Proc. Beltwide Cotton Prod. Res. Conf., New Orleans, La.

Mauney, J.R. 1984. Anatomy and Morphology of Cultivated Cottons, pp. 59-80. *In* R. J. Kohel and C. F. Lewis (eds.), *Cotton.* Agronomy Monograph 24. Am. Soc. Agron., Madison, Wis.

McMichael, S.C. 1960. Combined effects of the glandless genes gl_2 and gl_3 on pigment glands in the cotton plant. Agron. J. 46: 385-386.

Meyer, V.G. 1973. Fertility restorer genes for cytoplasmic male sterility from *Gossypium harknessii*, p. 65. Proc. Beltwide Cotton Prod. Res. Conf., Phoenix, Ariz.

——. 1975. Male sterility from *Gossypium harknessii*. J. Hered. 66: 23-27.

Niles, G.A., and Feaster, C.V. 1984. Breeding, pp. 201-231. *In* R. J. Kohel and C. F. Lewis (eds.), *Cotton.* Agronomy Monograph 24. Am. Soc. Agron., Madison, Wis.

Ridgway, R.L. 1984. Cotton Protection Practices in the USA and World. Insects, pp. 265-287. *In* R. J. Kohel and C. F. Lewis (eds.), *Cotton.* Agronomy Monograph 24. Am. Soc. Agron., Madison Wis.

Waddle, B.A. 1984. Cotton Growing Practices, pp. 233-263. *In* R. J. Kohel and C. F. Lewis (eds.), *Cotton.* Agronomy Monograph 24. Am. Soc. Agron., Madison, Wis.

Chapter 22

Linseed

C. L. Lay and C. D. Dybing

IMPORTANCE AND DISTRIBUTION

Linseed or flax, *Linum usitatissimum* L., is grown either for the oil (linseed) extracted from the seed or for fiber from the stem (Fig. 22.1). Countries where the major production of flaxseed occurs are Argentina, Canada, India, USA and the USSR (Table 22.1). These countries accounted for 87% of the total 2.9 million metric tons produced in 1982. Total production in 1982 was down about 17% from 1969-1971, reflecting a general downward trend in area planted to flax which began shortly after World War II. Highest seed yields are generally found in Canada or Argentina which accounts in part for high overall production in these two countries.

Flax fiber production has declined over the past fourteen years both in tonnes produced and area sown (Table 22.2). The largest producer of fiber flax is the USSR although the highest yields per hectare are found in China and the EEC countries of France, Belgium and the Netherlands.

Fig. 22.1 Linseed. A – Annual plant with a long slender shoot; this is more intensively branched in varities for oil uses than in those for fiber uses. The top carries flowers and seed capsules. B – Flowers of white (upper) or blue color (lower). C – Brown and glossy seeds.
From Severa (1983).

Table 22.1 World Flax (Linseed) Production by Region and Major Producing Countries

Region or Country	Production area ('000 ha)			Seed yield (kg/ha)			Seed production ('000 tonnes)		
	1969-71	1979-81	1985	1969-71	1979-81	1985	1969-71	1979-81	1985
World	**6768**	**5419**	**5033**	**514**	**454**	**500**	**3481**	**2458**	**2518**
Africa	**139**	**82**	**89**	**582**	**734**	**583**	**81**	**60**	**52**
N. and C. America	**1965**	**941**	**986**	**795**	**859**	**1157**	**1563**	**808**	**1141**
Canada	1001	650	740	832	884	1242	833	575	920
U.S.A.	942	286	236	742	801	893	699	229	211
S. America	**832**	**915**	**811**	**759**	**754**	**535**	**632**	**690**	**434**
Argentina	692	841	780	788	764	526	545	643	410
Asia	**1985**	**2019**	**1796**	**256**	**264**	**296**	**508**	**533**	**533**
China	77	108	132	414	723	742	32	78	98
India	1799	1793	1546	236	228	251	424	409	388
Europe	**311**	**270**	**234**	**636**	**511**	**543**	**198**	**138**	**127**
Poland	100	81	50	660	362	400	66	29	20
Romania	78	83	80	587	522	525	46	43	42
Oceania	**42**	**13**	**12**	**892**	**1016**	**957**	**37**	**14**	**11**
U.S.S.R.	**1493**	**1178**	**1105**	**309**	**182**	**199**	**462**	**215**	**220**

Source: FAO Production Yearbooks 1980 (vol. 34) and 1985 (vol. 39).

Table 22.2 World Production of Fiber Flax and Tow by Region and Major Producing Countries

Region or Country[1]	Production area ('000 ha)			Seed yield (kg/ha)			Seed production ('000 tonnes)		
	1969-71	1979-81	1985	1969-71	1979-81	1985	1969-71	1979-81	1985
World	**1654**	**1397**	**1342**	**441**	**449**	**530**	**728**	**628**	**711**
Africa	**11**	**26**	**17**	**783**	**892**	**909**	**9**	**24**	**15**
S. America	**6**	**4**	**4**	**675**	**794**	**800**	**4**	**3**	**3**
Asia	**95**	**79**	**73**	**580**	**1725**	**992**	**55**	**137**	**72**
China	81	71E	65E	652	1907	1092	53E	135E	71E
Europe	**262**	**248**	**226**	**702**	**705**	**923**	**184**	**175**	**208**
Belgium	12	7	9E	1137	1464	1500	14	10	14E
France	41	44	59	1201	1387	1610	49	62	95
German D.R.	11	—	—	521	—	—	6	—	—
Netherlands	7	4	3E	1234	1732	2294	9	6	8E
Poland	100	81	50E	553	611	600	55	49	30E
Romania	37	70	65E	484	332	462	18	23	30E
Oceania	**1**	**2**	**2**	**1006**	**982**	**918**	**1**	**2**	**2**
U.S.S.R.	**1279**	**1037**	**1020**	**372**	**277**	**402**	**476**	**287**	**410E**

[1] N. and C. America figures not available
E - FAO estimate
Source: FAO Production Yearbooks 1980 (vol. 34) and 1985 (vol. 39).

ORIGIN AND SYSTEMATICS

Common flax (*L. usitatissimum* L., n=15) is one of the oldest cultivated plants grown by man for food and fiber. Remains of flax, possibly *L. angustifolium* Huds., have been found associated with the earliest records of civilization in deposits of the Swiss Lake Dwellers (Simmonds, 1976). However, the origin of cultivated flax is not certain. The most likely progenitor is *L. angustifolium*, but other species such as *L. bienne* Mill. may have contributed some germplasm. Most believe that flax originated in an area east of the Mediterranean Sea, near India, because of the great diversity of forms found in this region (Harlan, 1975; Simmonds, 1976; Zeven and Zhukovsky, 1975). From there it apparently spread north and westward. Seed-type flax grown for its oil was developed primarily in southwestern Asia, whereas fiber flax was developed in the Mediterranean region. Selection necessarily would have favored annual plants with indehiscent or semidehiscent capsules suitable for modern methods of agriculture.

By the year 6000 BC domestic flax, grown primarily for its fiber, could be found in the Near East region (Israel, Syria, Jordan, Iraq, Iran) (Harlan, 1975). Linen was worn in ancient Egypt and was used to wrap mummies, while linseed oil was used in the embalming process (Simmonds, 1975). Roman emperors wore linen garments produced in Babylonia, Greece, Egypt and Spain. The Phoenicians used strong coarse linen cloth to make sails for their boats.

Flax production spread to Europe. It was grown extensively as a fiber crop until the end of the 18th century, when cotton, due to the advent of the cotton gin, became more important than flax as a source of fiber (Eastman, 1968). Flaxseed was used as a food during Greek and Roman eras, a practice which continues in India today. However, its use as a food is limited because of the laxative properties of mucilage associated with the seed coat and to the high level of linolenic acid that can oxidize causing off-flavors. The first historical record of the use of linseed oil as a drying oil is in a Roman manuscript dated 230 AD (Eastman, 1968). As demand for flax fiber declined in Europe, more and more flaxseed was used as a source of drying oil. The linseed oil industry in the USA began in 1793 (Eastman, 1968).

Linum is one of nine genera belonging to the family *Linaceae* (Simmonds, 1976). There are over twenty species in *Linum* spread over the warm temperate zones of the northern hemisphere, mostly in Europe and Asia, with about fifty species in America. Basic chromosome numbers are x=8, 9, 10, 12, 14, 15 and 16. Flax has a chromosome number 2n=30 and is the only species with nondehiscent or semidehiscent capsules suitable for commercial farming.

Linum species have been divided into five groups based on chromosome number, cytological studies from crossing experiments, and flower structure (Nagao, 1941). *L. usitatissimum* L., *L. crepitans* Dum., and *L. angustifolium* are the species which comprise Group II. The characteristic which distinguishes this group from the other four is that all species are homostylous.

Gill and Yermanos reported on cytogenetic studies of crosses among nine *Linum* species with a haploid chromosome number of 15 and among six *Linum* species with a haploid number of nine (Gill and Yermanos, 1967a, 1967b). Within the n=15 chromosome *Linum* species, *L. usitatissimum* differed from *L. angustifolium*, *L. africanum* Linn.and *L. decumbens* Desf. by one translocation; *L. angustifolium* differs from *L. africanum*, *L. corymbiferum* Desf. and *L. decumbens* by two translocations. Otherwise, the taxa studied in this group have homologous chromosomes. Chromosome pairing within the group of *Linum* species with n=9 chromosomes indicated that *L. altaicum* Fisch. differs from *L. alpinum* Linn., *L. austriacum* Linn., *L. julicum* Hayek, *L. narbonense* Linn., and *L. perenne* Linn by one reciprocal translocation. *L. austriacum* and *L. narbonense* as well as *L. julicum* and *L. narbonense* also differ by one translocation, while *L. perenne* and *L. narbonense* differed by two translocations. Chromosomes not involved in translocations appear to be homologous. It appears that within *Linum* species with a haploid chromosome number of 15 and within species with a haploid chromosome of nine, speciation occurred as a result of chromosome reorganization. Crosses between *Linum* spp with fifteen chromosomes and *Linum* spp. with nine chromosomes have not been successful (Gill and Yermanos, 1967b).

MODE OF REPRODUCTION

Breeding methods for most sexually propagated crop plants are determined largely by flower structure. Heritabilities and genetic correlations of traits with economic importance are also considered in selecting a breeding method. Flax is a highly self-pollinated species because of its flower structure and because its "sticky pollen" is rarely transferred by insects (Beard and Comstock, 1980). The flax flower is perfect, complete, and pedicellate, with a single flower born terminally on the pedicle in a multiflowered panicle (Lay and Dybing, 1985). In the afternoon of the day prior to flower opening, the petals form a narrow cone with the tips slightly exposed above the sepals. During the night they expand slowly so that by daylight the cone is perceptibly wider than the previous day. On a clear warm day the flowers are fully open approximately thirty minutes after sunrise. The anthers dehisce approximately twenty minutes after the flowers open, and the petals fall by early afternoon. The styles are receptive for nearly two days, from the day prior to anther dehiscence until the morning of the day after pollen shed. The pollen, however, is viable only for a few hours, from anther dehiscence until about the time petals abscise. At the time the anthers dehisce the flower is usually in a semi-opened condition. The anthers are away from, but at the same level as, the twisted stigma. As the flower opens, the anthers come together and form a cap over the stigmatic surface (Kadam and Patel, 1938). Fertilization occurs a few hours after pollination (Dillman, 1938).

BREEDING PROCEDURES

Nearly every seedflax breeding program lists increased seed yield, oil percent and oil yield as its major objectives. However, greatest progress has come from improved disease resistance, notably rust (*Melampsora lini* (Ehrenb.) Lev. and wilt, *Fusarium oxysporum* Schlecht. f. *lini* (Bolley) Snyder & Hansen.

Selection from introduced accessions and pedigree selection following hybridization have been the predominant methods of flax breeding (Culbertson et al. 1954; Kenaschuk, 1975; and Pustovoit, 1973). Although hybridization was practiced prior to 1936, all cultivars then recommended for production in the USA were derived by either mass or single plant selection from introduced accessions (Culbertson et al. 1954). The first cultivar developed by hybridization in the USA probably was "Renew," which was released in 1936. Twenty years later, all of the cultivars recommended, with the exception of "Redwing" and "Punjab" had been developed by hybridization.

A somewhat similar progression of events apparently has occurred in Argentina. The first cultivars resulted from mass selection and single plant selection in two introduced heterogenous populations called "linos" and "linetas" (Dora H. Manfroni de Silvero Sanz, personal communication). A number of additional cultivars were then released via this method of breeding before Professor Klein began his work with flax hybridization. From 1928 to 1935 he developed "Klein 11," "Lineta Klein 10" and "Klein 18."

A typical pedigree breeding procedure for flax begins by making a cross between two genotypes with contrasting characteristics (Culbertson et al. 1954). This can be accomplished in the field or in the greenhouse. The methods used to make a cross and proper greenhouse cultural practices were recently summarized (Beard and Comstock, 1980). Briefly, flowers to be used as females are emasculated the afternoon of the day prior to anthesis or the morning of the day of anthesis. An unopened bud that has the petals protruding about 30 to 60 mm past the sepals is selected as the female. Pollen from the male parent can be transferred as soon as the anthers dehisce. Twenty to thirty pollinations per hour can be made with about 70% of the pollinations resulting in the production of viable F_1 seeds. F_1 plants are usually grown in the greenhouse, but they can also be grown in the field.

In the second year a large number of F_2 plants (2000 to 10,000) are grown on wilt-infested soil and selected on the basis of disease resistance, maturity, plant height, etc. F_3 plants can again be grown on wilt-infested soil, and at the same time screened for rust resistance using seedling tests in a greenhouse or growth chamber. Another possibility for handling the F_3 generation is to omit wilt testing but rust test by growing approximately 25 plants in a 10 cm clay pot. F_3 seedlings are inoculated with rust, preferably more than one race.

Lines breeding true for resistance are retained, while segregating and susceptible lines are discarded. Reserve seeds of those lines saved after rust testing are then tested for oil content and quality. Oil content of one gram samples can be tested using non-destructive NMR analysis or by use of a modified Soxhlet procedure (Dybing, 1963). Oil quality is measured using a refractometer and expressed as iodine number (Hunt et al. 1950). Rust resistant F_3 plants from F_2 seed having high oil content and oil quality are grown to maturity in the greenhouse. This method could require considerable greenhouse space if many individuals or crosses are tested. F_4 and F_5 plants are again planted on wilt-infested soil and again selected for wilt tolerance and agronomic characteristics such as flowering date and plant height. Selection is continued for seedling resistance to rust and for oil quantity, and can begin for oil quality (iodine number) if not already started in an earlier generation. After F_5, uniform rows are bulked, and yield testing begins.

Another breeding method being used to a lesser degree than pedigree selection in some flax breeding programs is single-seed-descent combined with seedling rust testing. Single seed descent is a form of pedigree selection and can be used to rapidly advance germplasm through segregating generations. Basically the procedure consists of harvesting a single boll from each of a large number of F_2 plants. These plants may or may not have been grown on a wilt nursery. Seed from each boll is planted in a 10 cm pot, and plants are inoculated with rust after emergence. Each pot is thinned to one or two resistant plants and grown to maturity. A single boll is again harvested from one of the F_3 plants in a pot, and the process repeated through the F_5 or F_6 generation. With single seed descent, individuals within a population cannot be traced to an identifiable plant in the previous generation as is the case in pedigree selection. However, each F_5 or F_6 line traces to a single F_2 plant. It is possible to get at least three generations per year and possibly four, using greenhouse, growth chamber and field facilities.

The use of backcross breeding has been limited primarily to the transfer of rust-resistant genes to a recurrent parent. Dr. H. H. Flor developed a set of rust differentials by backcrossing individual genes into the cultivar "Bison" (Table 22.3). These lines have been used extensively in genetic studies and as sources of resistance to rust. For example, "Flor" was developed from the cross Bison M^3M^3/Linott//Bison P^3P^3/Linott (Hammond, 1975; Hammond et al. 1983). Bison M^3M^3 and Bison P^3P^3 are near isogenic lines developed by H. H. Flor. "Linott" is a Canadian cultivar carrying the L^6 gene. Flor possesses all three genes (L^6, M^3, and P^3) which confer resistance to naturally occurring races of flax rust in North America.

Early generation yield testing and the release of F_2 and F_2 derived lines as cultivars is also being utilized as a breeding method. Two such cultivars have been released, "Clark" and "Rahab" (Lay et al. 1987; Grady et al. 1987). Both trace to a single F_2 plant from different populations which were advanced without any additional selection. The profusely branched panicle of flax allows for more plant to plant variation without detracting from its field appearance than could be accommodated in other species. This characteristic, plus selection for uniformity, allows for the release of cultivars that appear fairly uniform. A typical procedure consists of making 300 to 500 crosses, selfing the F_1 and growing a single

Table 22.3   Flax Lines Currently Used To Differentiate and Identify Races of Rust (*Melampsora lini*)

Gene C.I. No.	Source name	Gene	No. Bison back-crosses[1]	Gene C.I. No.	Source name	Gene	No. Bison back-crosses[1]
355	Ottawa 770B	L	12	——	Bison	L^9	—
1071	Dakota	M	12	1183	B. Golden Sel	L^{10}	6
42	Bombay	N_2	12	1190	Barnes	L^7	6
708	Stewart	L	12	1136	Bisbee	L^8	12
1182	Cass	M^3	12	1335	Marshall	N^2	8
842	Koto	P	12	1512	Cortland	M^5	8
1188	Clay	K	12	647	Pale Blue Crimped	L^3	8
1191	Polk	N^1	12	1180	Burke	L^1	7
1085	Birio	L^6	12	1181	Ward	M^2	14
709	Kenya	L^4	7	——	Kugler C	Ku	6
515	Akmolinsk Acc.	P^1	10	——	Linore	L_{11}	0
701	Abyssinian Brown	P^2	4	1911	Punjab 53	P_4	0
				2008		M_6	0
836	Leona	P^3	13				
1193	Wilden	L^5	6				
803	Wiliston Brown	M^1	12				
1170	Victory	M^4	12				

[1] Number of backcrosses to the Bison cultivar.

row of F_2 plants. The F_2 population may or may not be grown on a wilt nursery. Selection between populations is on the basis of lodging, uniformity and oil content of the bulk. At maturity, a large volume of bolls are harvested from a portion of each population or row. The remaining portion of the population is harvested, and threshed in bulk to provide seed for yield testing the next year. Unthreshed intact bolls (200 to 300 per cross) are planted, one boll to a hill, on a wilt nursery the following year (F_3). At the same time a replicated yield test consisting of single row plots using F_3 seed harvested the previous year is planted. Populations for further selection are chosen on the basis of seed and oil yield. Thirty to fifty random hills are harvested from selected populations. Oil content is determined for each hill, and the top 20% retained for replanting. No further selection is applied within an F_3 line.

Another breeding method which has received some attention is the hybrid technique (Comstock, 1965). Flax is probably one of the first crops of commercial value in which cytoplasmic male sterility was identified (Bateson and

Gairdner, 1921; Gairdner, 1929). However, this system has not been used to produce commercial hybrid flax seed. The main barrier to its use is pollination since flowers of male sterile plants do not open sufficiently to allow cross-pollination, and also the petals are not retained long enough to attract the natural pollinators needed for cross pollination. Bees usually appear in the field only after 9 to 10 a.m. and the flax petals fall from the flowers by noon. However, male sterile plants with open corollas have been reported (Kumar and Singh, 1970; Thompson, 1977). The most promising of these appear to be in interspecific crosses involving *L. bienne* (Thompson, 1977). Heterosis levels of 25 to 40% have been reported for hybrid flax (Kumar and Singh, 1970).

Plant regeneration utilizing tissue culture techniques has also been used in flax improvement (Murray et al. 1977; McHughen, 1984). McHughen was able to regenerate plants from callus derived from 2 to 3 day old seedlings of "McGregor" grown on cultures containing elevated levels of salt. The salt composition and concentration were similar to "high salt" soils found in Saskatchewan. A salt-tolerant breeding line resulting from this research is currently being field tested for other agronomic traits.

Flax is a renewable resource and is easy to produce commercially. As such, it will play a role in providing raw materials for the oil and textile industries of the future. In order for it to remain economically viable and able to compete with other crops for high quality cropland, it is imperative that oil or fiber yield be increased. This may require the redirection of effort away from disease-resistance breeding, especially in an era of limiting financial resources. Both single gene resistance and field levels of tolerance to flax rust exist in current cultivar or germplasm collections. Breeding for wilt tolerance has been successful so that wilt is seldom observed in commercial fields, even in susceptible cultivars. Thus, while disease resistance remains important, past efforts appear to have already produced maximum results. Unfortunately, breeding for higher yields is more difficult than breeding for the more simply inherited traits because of the large number of genes involved in the control of oil and fiber yields. For this reason there needs to be greater emphasis placed on conventional breeding methodology of flax.

There also needs to be increased emphasis on genetic studies in flax. Again, most genetic information on flax concerns disease resistance. Other studies have been restricted primarily to easily identified traits like flower color, including the petal, anther, style, stigma, and seed color. Studies of the inheritance of oil content and oil quality have also received some attention. However, other agronomically important traits such as seed yield and its components, oil yield, and flowering patterns, for example, have received little research effort. Beard and Comstock (1965) did suggest thirty-five different loci, some of which have several alleles, controlling traits in flax affecting disease resistance, male sterility, seedling lethality, and the color of the plant, petal, stamen, pistil, and seed. Although these studies are significant, they do not compare in number with other important oilseeds such as soybean or sunflower.

The flax plant offers many opportunities for future research. It is a small plant requiring relatively little greenhouse or growth chamber space. The yield components of bolls per acre, seeds per boll and seed weight, are easy to identify and easy to measure which should permit effective genetic and selection studies. The physiological factors limiting seed yield are yet to be identified. However, once this has been done, another avenue of research for increasing seed yields would be opened. The cyclic flowering pattern of flax is unique and can be used as a model for flowering mechanisms in plants. Most importantly it has the potential for providing industrial and food products of the future.

HISTORY OF CULTIVAR DEVELOPMENT

Flax cultivar development in the USA can be divided into two eras, the first involving the development of wilt-resistant varieties which began about 1900 and lasted through the 1930s, and the second, breeding for rust resistance, began in the 1930s and extends through to the present (Lay and Hammond, 1984). The need for wilt-resistant varieties became evident in the early 1890s; the linseed oil industry had matured and flaxseed production had settled into the northcentral states. As farmers began to produce flax on land that had grown flax previously, seed yields declined. Stands were often unsatisfactory, and plants that did survive lacked vigor and often died prematurely. Farmers described this phenomenon as "flax sick" soil, a concept that exists to some degree today. Popular cultivars in the USA at the time were "Primost" and "Frontier," both of which were selected from Russian introductions (Stoa, 1961). European farmers avoided the problem of reduced stand and plant vigor by using a complex rotation where flax was grown once every eight years.

Dr. H. R. Bolley, a plant pathologist at North Dakota State University, was able to demonstrate the cause of this "sickness" in flax as a soil-borne fungus, *Fusarium oxysporium* f. *lini*. None of the cultivars then grown were resistant to this disease. In 1894, Bolley first planted flax on "plot 30" of the North Dakota Agriculture Experiment Station (Thompson and Comstock, 1975). By 1908 he released the first wilt-resistant flax cultivars "NDR No. 52" and "NDR No. 73." In 1912 "NDR No. 114" was released, and in 1925 "Bison" was added to the list of wilt-resistant cultivars. By the mid 1930s Bison was probably the most popular cultivar in flax production, due primarily to its wilt resistance, earliness and larger seed size.

The second period of flax cultivar development began in the late 1930s to early 40s. Flax rust had not been considered a serious problem in the USA prior to this time, though it did occur on occasion. However, the popularity of Bison provided an ideal environment for rust development so that rust and rust damage became increasingly common. For example, from 1940 to 1942 flax rust caused serious losses and sharply reduced the acreage of Bison. As a result of the dangers posed by flax rust, emphasis was placed on development of cultivars with genetic resistance to both wilt and rust. The first cultivar with resistance to both was Renew (Stoa, 1961). Renew was developed at the USDA Northern Plains Field Station at Mandan and released cooperatively with the North Dakota Experiment Station. "Royal," which was developed at Saskatchewan for wilt resistance and had been released earlier, was observed to also have a fairly high level of resistance to rust. For the next few years considerable acreage of these cultivars was grown until better cultivars became available. Changes in races of rust detected in the field by changes in cultivar reaction occurred in 1948, 1963, and in 1972. With each rust race change there was a corresponding shift in cultivars made available to producers.

It was during this period that Dr. Flor developed his theories on rust resistance (Flor, 1946, 1947, 1951, 1955, 1956, and 1971). By means of rather detailed genetic studies of both the flax plant and the disease organism, he found that a plant was resistant only to a pathogen with a corresponding gene for avirulence, and that the pathogen was avirulent only on a plant with a corresponding gene for resistance. This concept has become known as the "gene for gene pattern of resistance" and is the basis for the development of rust-resistant flax cultivars worldwide.

It seems rather remarkable that with all the breeding emphasis being placed on disease resistance, progress in the improvement of other important traits such as seed yield, oil content, and oil quality was possible at the same time. Progress for seed yield due to breeding in the USA has averaged approximately 4.3 kg/ha per year since the release of Bison (Miller and Hammond, 1976). Table 22.4 summarizes these two time periods of flax breeding by listing some of the more important cultivars released in the northcentral USA since about 1908.

UTILIZATION OF PRODUCTS

Flax is grown for either its oil or fiber. The meal which remains after oil extraction is fed to animals as a protein supplement. Linseed oil is unique among the vegetable oils in that it contains more than 50% linolenic acid, the 18-carbon fatty acid with three double bonds. Rapeseed oil contains 10 to 14% linolenic acid, soybean oil 6 to 9%, and some other vegetable fats near 0% linolenic acid. The double bonds react rapidly with oxygen in the air to polymerize into a relatively soft and flexible film. As a result linseed oil has its greatest use in house paints, exterior stains, and industrial coatings. Linseed oil can also be found in printing ink, core oil for sand cores used in metal castings, automobile brake linings, concrete protection and curing, and in many restructured wood products (Formo, 1984). Recent studies by Green and Marshall (1984) have shown that genotypes with very low levels of linolenic acid can be developed. This opens up the possibility of using linseed as a food oil without the problems associated with oxidation.

Table 22.4   Flax Cultivars Released Since 1908 for Commercial Production and Which Were Somewhat Successful in the Northcentral States, Plus Some of the More Recent Releases

Period 1 - Wilt Tolerance			Period 2 - Rust and Wilt Resistance		
Cultivar	Year released	Organ-ization	Cultivar	Year released	Organ-ization
NDR 52	1908	NDSU	Royal	1935	Canada
NDR 73	1908	NDSU	Renew	1942	NPFS-Mandan
NDR 114	1912	NDSU	B-5128	1943	NDSU
Chippewa	1919	Minnesota	Rocket	1947	Canada
Linota	1925	NDSU	Norland	1949	NDSU
Buda	1925	NDSU	Marine	1951	NDSU-USDA
Bison	1926	NDSU	Bolley	1951	NDSU-USDA
Redwing	1928	Minnesota	Redwood	1951	Minnesota-USDA
Winona	1929	Minnesota	Windom	1952	Minnesota-USDA
Walsh	1931	NDSU	Arny	1958	Minnesota-USDA
Bolley Golden	1931	NDSU	Summit	1959	SDSU
			Redwood 65	1961	Canada
			Linott	1966	Canada
			Nored	1968	Minnesota-USDA
			Norstar	1969	Minnesota-USDA
			Culbert	1974	Minnesota-USDA
			Dufferin	1975	Canada
			Culbert 79	1979	SDSU
			Wishek	1979	NDSU-USDA
			Flor	1981	NDSU-USDA
			McGregor	1982	Canada
			Clark	1983	SDSU
			Norlin	1983	Canada

NDSU = North Dakota State University
SDSU = South Dakota State University
USDA = United States Department of Agriculture
NPFS = Northern Plains Field Station - USDA

Fiber from flax is obtained from fibrous bundles, composed primarily of cellulose, running the length of the stem and forming a ring in the cortex. The fiber comes from bundles of overlapping strands averaging 4 cm in length. These fibers are extracted by retting. Flax fibers are stronger, more durable, and more resistant to moisture than cotton or wool. Therefore, it is used in gloves, footwear, netting and sports gear. Fiber-type cultivars have been developed specifically for fiber production. Flax fibers are also extracted from seedflax cultivars, a practice which started in the USA in the 1930s (Dybing and Lay, 1981). These fibers are extracted through mechanical means and are shorter than fiber from fiber cultivars. They are used in paper manufacture and to a lesser degree in the textile industry. These are especially important in the manufacture of cigarette paper. Studies indicated sufficient market potential in the textile field to propose expansion of the USA flax straw processing industry (Bedker and Anderson, 1975).

REFERENCES

Bateson, W., and Gairdner, A.E. 1921. Male sterility in flax. J. Genet. 11: 269-275.

Beard, B.H., and Comstock, V.E. 1965. Flax genetics and gene symbolism. Crop Sci. 5: 151-155.

——, and ——. 1980. Flax, pp. 357-364. *In* W.R. Fehr and H.H. Hadley (eds.), *Hybridization of Crop Plants.* Am. Soc. of Agron., Madison, Wis.

Bedker, G., and Anderson, D. 1975. Flax straw availability in North Dakota. Flax Inst. U.S. Proc., 45: 9.

Comstock, V.E. 1965. Possibilities of hybrid flax production. Flax Inst. U.S. Proc. 34: 24-25.

Culbertson, J.P., Geddes, W.F., Flor, H.H., Christensen, J.J., and Dunham, R.S. 1954. Seed-flax Improvement, pp. 144-178. *In* A.G. Norman (ed.), *Advances in Agronomy* Vol. 6. Academic Press, New York.

Dillman, A.C. 1938. Natural crossing in flax. J. Am. Soc. Agron. 30: 279-286.

Dybing, C.D. 1963. Determination of oil and fatty acid contents of small samples of immature flax seed. Crop Sci. 3: 280-282.

——, and Lay, C.L. 1981. Flax *Linum usitatissimum*, pp. 71-85. *In* T. A. McClure and E.S. Lipinsky (eds.), *Handbook of Biosolar Resources.* Vol. 2. CRC Press Inc., Boca Raton, Fla.

Eastman, W. 1968. *The history of the linseed oil iindustry n the United States.* T.S. Denison and Co. Inc., Minneapolis, Minn.

Flor, H.H. 1946. Genetics of pathogenicity in *Melampsora lini*. J. Agric. Res. 73: 335-357.

——. 1947. Inheritance of reaction to rust in flax. J. Agric. Res. 74: 241-262.

——. 1951. Genes for resistance to rust in Victory flax. Agron. J. 43: 527-531.

——. 1955. Host-parasite interaction in flax rust - its genetics and other implications. Phytopathology 45: 680-685.

——. 1956. Complimentary genic systems in flax rust. Adv. in Genet. 8: 29-54.

——. 1971. Current status of the gene-for-gene concept. Annu. Rev. Phytopathol. 9: 275-296.

Formo, M.W. 1984. The future of linseed oil. Flax Inst. U.S. Proc. 50: 14-22.

Gairdner, A.E. 1929. Male sterility in Flax II. A case of reciprocal crosses differing in F_2. J. Genet. 21: 117-124.

Gill, K.S., and Yermanos, D.M. 1967a. Cytogenetic studies on the Genus *Linum* I. Hybrids among taxa with 15 as the haploid chromosome number. Crop Sci. 7: 623-627.

——, and ——. 1967b. Cytogenetic studies on the Genus *Linum* II. Hybrids among taxa with nine as the haploid chromosome number. Crop Sci. 7: 627-631.

Grady, K., Lay, C., and Ferguson, M. W. 1987. Registration of Rahab Flax. Crop Sci. 27:362-363.

Green, A.G., and Marshall, D.R. 1984. Isolation of induced mutants in linseed (*Linum usitatissimum*) having reduced linolenic acid content. Euphytica 33: 321-328.

Hammond, J.J. 1975. Screening for multiple rust gene flax lines. Flax Inst. U.S. Proc. 45: 14-15.

——, Miller, J.F., Statlee, G.D., and Gulya, T.J. 1983. Registration of Flor Flax. Crop Sci. 23: 401.

Harlan, J.R. 1975. Crops and man. Am. Soc. of Agron., Madison, Wis.

Hunt, W.H., Neustadt, M.H., Shurkus, A.A., and Zeleny, L. 1950. A simple iodine-number refractometer for testing flaxseed and soybean. Am. Oilseed Soc. Proc. 1-3.

Kadam, B.S., and Patel, S.M. 1938. Anthesis in flax. J. Am. Soc. Agron. 30: 932-940.

Kenaschuk, E.O. 1975. Flax Breeding and Genetics. *In Oilseed and Pulse Crops in Western Canada*. Western Co-operative Feritlizers Limited. Calgary, Alta.

Kumar, S., and Singh, S.P. 1970. Inheritance of male sterility in some introduced varieties of linseed (*Linum usitatissimum* L.). Indian J. Agric. Sci. 40: 184-191.

Lay, C.L., and Dybing, C.D. 1985. *Linum usitatissimum*, pp. 302-305. *In* A.H. Halevy (ed.), *Handbook of Flowering*. Vol. 3. CRC Press Inc., Boca Raton, Fla.

——, Grady, K., and Ferguson, M. W. 1987. Registration of Clark Flax. Crop Sci. 27:362

——, and Hammond, J. J. 1984. Highlights of flax breeding and genetics. Flax Inst. U. S. Proc. 50:8-11.

McHughen, A. 1984. The development of saline tolerant flax lines from tissue culture. Flax Inst. U.S. Proc. 50: 84-89.

Miller, J.E., and Hammond, J.J. 1976. Analysis of yield progress in flax breeding. Flax Inst. U.S. Proc. 46: 7-10.

Murray, B., Handyside, R.J., and Keller, W.A. 1977. In vitro regeneration of shoots on stem explants of haploid and diploid flax (*Linum usitatissimum*). Can. J. Genet. Cytol. 19: 177-186.

Nagao, S. 1941. Cytogenetics in the Genus *Linum*. Jpn. J. Genet. 17: 110-116.

Pustovoit, V.S. 1973. Seed Flax. *In* V.S. Pustovoit (ed.), N. Kaner (Transl.), *Handbook of Selection and Seed Growing of Oil Plants*. Israel Program for Scientific Translations Ltd., Keter Press Binding, Wiener Bindery Ltd., Jerusalem, Israel.

Simmonds, N.W. 1976. *Evolution of crop plants*. Langman Inc., New York.

Stoa, T.E. 1961. A brief history - flax variety improvement and preferences on farms in North Dakota. N. Dak. Exp. Stn. Farm Res. 21: 19-25.

Thompson, T.E. 1977. Cytoplasmic male-sterile flax with open corollas. J. Hered. 68: 185-187.

——, and Comstock, V.E. 1975. Plot 30: Proving ground for wilt resist flax varieties. N. Dak. Exp. Stn. Farm Res. 32: 28-29.

Zeven, A.C., and Zhukovsky, P.M. 1975. *Dictionary of Cultivated Plants and Their Centers of Diversity*. Center for Agricultural Publishing and Documentation, Wageningen.

Chapter 23

Maize

D. E. Alexander

IMPORTANCE AND DISTRIBUTION

Maize is possibly the most widely-grown cereal, however wheat and rice produce greater tonnage annually. It is primarily a feed grain and an industrial crop although it is consumed directly by humans in many developing countries. In the USA only 10 to 15% is used in wet and dry milling. Annual exports from the USA are typically 50,000,000 tonnes of grain.

ORIGIN AND SYSTEMATICS

Maize (*Zea mays* L), usually called "corn" in the USA, has been a "companion" of man for at least 8000 years (Fig. 23.1). Modern corns are poorly adapted to survival without man's intervention. Although several proposals have been advanced, it is most appealing that modern corn derived directly from teosinte by selection for more palatable, easily harvestable and productive segregants. Modern maize and teosinte hybridize readily and the F_1 is fertile. Maize also hybridizes, with some difficulty, with certain *Tripsacum* species; hybrid embryos can be cultured in vivo and rescued. The F_1 is vigorous, quite sterile and will produce progeny of vast heterogeneity. However, whether *Tripsacum* entered substantially into the evolution of maize seems marginal.

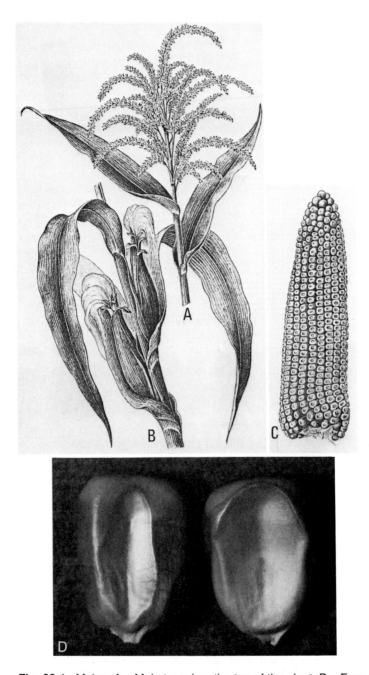

Fig. 23.1 Maize. A – Male tassel on the top of the plant. B – Female ear in the axil of a medium leaf. C – Ripe maize ear. D – Kernel of a standard variety (left) and a high oil genotype (right) . Note the large embryo of the latter.
A – C from Severa.

Botanical and archaeological evidence points to either central or northern South America as the place of origin of modern maize. Diversity is still great although the germplasm resources are being eroded slowly through the loss of local varieties which are replaced by hybrids or improved varieties. More attention is now being paid to the collection and to preservation of land races.

MODE OF REPRODUCTION

Maize is a classical panmictic, monoecious species. Abundant pollen is dispersed by gravity and wind from the male inflorescences (Fig. 23.1A). Pollen shedding usually begins two to three days before silk emergence on the ear (Fig. 23.1B). Self-fertilization occurs at a low frequency, typically less than 5% in dense stands.

Landraces are many and exceptionally varied. For example, selection has produced cultivars that require 11 to 12 months to mature, while others flower 30 days after planting and are harvestable in another 40 days.

BREEDING OBJECTIVES, PROCEDURES AND RESULTS

Maize is not generally considered to be an oil crop, primarily because it is relatively low in oil and secondly, because its oil content is "hidden," i.e. the grain is generally fed to animals without processing, or consumed directly by humans. In the USA, 10 to 15% is processed through wet or dry milling processes which produce "visible" oil that is consumed by humans. Consequently, breeders have largely ignored oil content and have selected for attributes of greater economic value as yield, standability, disease and insect resistance and maturity.

Oil content has not been completely overlooked, however. Beginning in 1896 Burr's White, an open-pollinated variety, was mass selected for both higher and lower percent oil at the Illinois Agricultural Experiment Station (Dudley, 1974). The original level of oil which was 4.7%, reached 20.4% in the 85th generation of selection. The low oil strain has apparently reached the physiological lower limit of approximately 0.5%.

In the Illinois High Oil strain, the increase in percent oil from generation 0 to 40 can be attributed to an increase in embryo to endosperm ratio rather than to an increase in percent oil in the embryo (Leng, 1961) (Fig. 23.1D). He found that the embryo made up 14% of the kernel at generation six, but 21.5% at the 40th. Over the same period oil content of the kernel increased from 6.5 to 12.0%. A similar change occurred in another synthetic (Alexho). In cycle 0, the embryo made up 12%, but in cycle 20, 24% of the weight of the kernel. However, kernel weight declined (from 31 to 24 g/100 kernels), but embryo size nearly doubled from cycle 0 to 20 (3.3 vs 6.3 g).

In 1958, a recurrent selection program was begun at Illinois in a composite of 38 open-pollinated varieties (Alexho Synthetic) (Misevic et al. 1985). Alternate selfing and recombination of the higher oil segregants was carried out for five generations. In the 6th generation, nuclear magnetic resonance spectroscopy was used to analyze non-destructively both bulk and single kernel samples (Alexander et al. 1967). Bulk samples of random-mated ears were analyzed and the highest ear from each of 125 families was selected for single-kernel analysis. As few as 10 to as many as 50 kernels per ear have been analyzed each cycle. The three higher oil kernels from each ear were planted ear-to-row to produce the next random-mated generation. Realized heritability over the 25 cycles was 0.30. However, during the first five generations, that value was 0.54. Mean oil content reached 20.1% in the 26th generation (Fig. 23.2). Progress in selection for higher oil in six populations is summarized in Table 23.1.

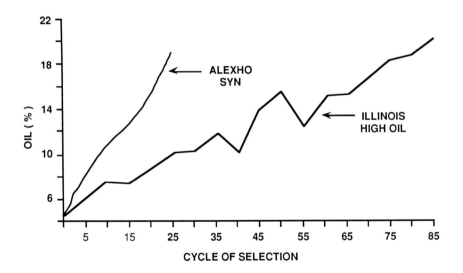

Fig. 23.2　Effect of selection for percent oil in two populations.

Dudley and Lambert (1969) found significant genetic variability in the Illinois High OII strain after 65 generations. Miller et al. (1981) found that additive genetic variance did not diminish during five cycles of high-intensity single-kernel selection for higher oil content in Reid Yellow Dent, an open-pollinated variety. Realized heritability over five cycles amounted to 43%. Oil content increased from 4 to 7.7%.

Table 23.1   Effect of Selection for Increased Percent Oil in Six Populations[1]

Population	No. selected generations	% Oil original	% Oil last gen.	Method of selection
Ill. High Oil	85	4.7	20.4	Mass
Alexho Synthetic	25	4.6	19.1	Single kernel[2]
Synthetic D. O	6	4.2	9.5	Recurrent selection[3]
Reid Yellow Dent	7	4.3	8.9	Single kernel[2]
BS10	4	4.8	7.0	Single kerne[2]
RSSSC	3	4.5	6.1	Single kernel[2]

[1] Unpublished data, University of Illinois
[2] See Alexander et al. 1976
[3] Self fertilization in a random-mated pool followed by recombination of the higher oil segregants.

In cycles five and six of Alexho Synthetic, inbreds were isolated and crossed with elite lines from Iowa Stiff Stalk Synthetic. At least one high oil inbred (R806) from this synthetic is used in commercial hybrid production in the USA.

Higher oil hybrids, and presumably synthetics, tend to be higher in grain moisture at harvest than do lower oil, conventional hybrids. For example, R806 x B73 and Mo17 x B73 flower at the same time, yet moisture levels at harvest are invariably higher in the former.

In the 1940s, an effort was made by Woodworth and Jugenheimer of Illinois to recover higher oil versions of the better inbreds of the time by outcrossing them to Illinois High Oil and backcrossing to the respective inbreds. Production of hybrids from the recovered lines never became important because their performance was inferior. This is understandable because the lines were related. Some private breeding programs in the USA which used similar pedigree schemes were also unsuccessful.

A paramount question facing breeders is whether higher oil maize is intrinsically lower in yield than conventional hybrids. If they produce as much tonnage per hectare as lower oil sorts, obviously calorie production is higher because increased oil content is accompanied by a reduction in the proportion of starch, a lower calorie component. Experience suggests that yields of hybrids with as high as 7% oil can be competitive with those in the 4 to 4.5% oil range. Evidence from performance of cycles of Alexho Synthetic (Table 23.2) clearly demonstrates that the higher oil populations are lower in yield. But it should be noted that the effect of inbreeding is confounded with high oil level; the coefficient of inbreeding of cycle 22 is at least 30%.

Recently acquired data on hybrids in the 8 to 10% range of oil suggest that they may yield well. They have arisen from recurrent selection program for yield and other agronomic properties in Alexho Synthetic cycle 22. The tester parent is an inbred out of Iowa Stiff Stalk Synthetic (B73), which possesses approximately 4% oil.

Table 23.2 Performance of Populations from Different Cycles of Alexho Synthetic in Urbana, II., 1982 (10 replications)

Cycle	Yield	H_2O Grain	Lodged	Oil[1]
	t/ha	(%)	(%)	(%)
0	8.50	30	3	6.2
5	8.38	30	2	8.8
16	6.31	33	0	11.2
22	5.69	34	0	12.9

[1] Samples from performance trial plots. Oil values are distorted by xenia effects.

UTILIZATION OF PRODUCTS

At least 85% of the domestically-consumed USA maize crop is in the form of animal feed. The remaining 10 to 15% is used for wet and dry milling. Since the major portion of the crop is used for animal production, nutritional properties of higher oil corns are of particular interest due to their higher calorie-density and potentially higher protein quantity and quality.

Nordstrom et al. (1972) found that swine fed a diet containing corn with higher levels of oil had superior feed conversion ratios compared to regular corn. He further noted that protein supplementation was reduced, the amount depending on protein level in the corn. Surprisingly, the soybean meal savings were large: "... 22% reduction ... for the 16% protein diets and a ... 41% reduction for the 13% protein diets..."

A. H. Jensen of Illinois has conducted many feeding trials comparing high oil and regular corn in swine diets. He concludes that "... in properly balanced corn-soybean meal diets the high oil corn diet is as efficiently utilized as the energy-equivalent regular-corn-plus-corn-oil diet" (personal communication). D. H. Baker, also of Illinois, has found that "In a ... chick study ... true metabolizable energy value of 3851 ± 32 k cal/kg and 3584 ± 117 k cal/kg were for high oil and conventional corn respectively ... expressed on an air-dry basis" (personal communication). More recent studies by C. Parsons (personal communication) of Illinois, through an 8 to 14 day feeding trial with young chicks, further substantiate the Baker findings. Diets containing corns of 4.5, 6.5, 9, 12, and 14% oil were compared for feed efficiency. Chicks gained 103.9, 107.9, 111.4 and 114.3% respectively, per unit of feed as compared to those on the 4.5% corn diet.

Although higher oil corns have substantial advantage in non-ruminant diets, there are problems with their wide-scale use in wet and dry milling. The production of high fructose sugars by USA wet millers suggests that increases in oil or protein might not be attractive even though corn oil is more valuable by a factor of at least three than starch, the basic raw product of high fructose sugars. Certain dry milling processes excessively damage the larger embryos of higher oil corns causing oil contamination of endosperm starch. Adoption of higher oil types for milling not only will depend on performance of hybrids but on relative value of milled products, and perhaps on costs of adapting milling machinery to accommodate their peculiarities.

REFERENCES

Alexander, D.E., Silvela L., Collins, F.I., and Rodgers, R.C. 1967. Analysis of oil content of maize by wide-line NMR. J. Am. Oil Chem. Soc. 44(10): 555-558.

Dudley, J.W. 1974. Seventy Generations of Selection for Oil and Protein. Crop Science Society, Madison, Wis.

——, and Lambert, R.J. 1969. Genetic variability after 65 generations of selection in Illinois High Oil, Low Oil, High Protein, and Low Protein of *Zea mays* L. Crop Sci. 9: 179-181.

Leng, E.R. 1961. Predicted and actual responses during long-term selection for chemical composition in maize. Euphytica 10(3): 368-378.

Miller, R.L., Dudley, J.W., and Alexander, D.E. 1981. High intensity selection for percent oil in corn. Crop Sci. 21: 433-437.

Misevic, D., Alexander, D.E., Dumanovic, J., and Ratkovic, S. 1985. Recurrent selection for percent oil in corn. Genetika 17(2): 97-106.

Nordstrom, J.W., Behrends, B.R., Meade, R.J., and Thompson, E.H. 1972. Effects of feeding high oil corns to growing-finishing swine. J. Anim. Sci. 35(2): 357-361.

Chapter 24

Castor

D. Atsmon

IMPORTANCE AND DISTRIBUTION

The castor plant (Fig. 24.1) is a minor oil crop, contributing between 0.5 and 1.0% of the total world oilseed production (see Weiss, 1971; Weiss, 1983; and Kulkarni and Ramanamurthy, 1977 for comprehensive reviews). World production of castor beans has been rather stable for the last twenty years, at about one million tonnes annually, despite sharp fluctuations in certain countries (Table 24.1). Since 1970 China has doubled and India nearly quadrupled their production. It is important to note that these data represent estimates based on export and import statistics, rather than farm production in *sensus strictus*. This is due to the fact that much of the harvested crop is derived from beans collected from 'semi-wild' plants, and not from commercially cultivated fields. The main producing countries are India, Brazil, USSR, China and Thailand (Table 24.1), while the main importing countries are the leading industrialized countries; i.e. the USA, the USSR, the EEC and Japan.

438

Fig. 24.1   Castor. A – Normal, monoecious plant, homozygous for the recessive dwarfing gene. B – An inflorescence of a monoecious plant, displaying lower staminate and upper pistillate flowers. The stump at the base belongs to a leaf and branch bud at its axil. C – Seed capsule. D – Seeds of various sizes, colors and patterns.

Table 24.1 World Castor Bean Production by Region and Major Producing Countries

Region or Country	Production area ('000 ha)			Seed yield (kg/ha)			Seed production ('000 tonnes)		
	1969-71	1979-81	1985	1969-71	1979-81	1985	1969-71	1979-81	1985
World	**1434**	**1455**	**1751**	**589**	**579**	**742**	**844**	**842**	**1298**
Africa	**104**	**72**	**74**	**548**	**495**	**503**	**57**	**36**	**37**
Angola	11	12	12	253	250	250	3	3	3
Ethiopia	22	12	12	581	1000	1000	13	13	12
Sudan	16	10	10	1020	448	500	16	4	5
Tanzania	19	10	10	597	508	500	11	5	5
N. and C. America	**23**	**12**	**11**	**691**	**535**	**604**	**16**	**6**	**6**
S. America	**415**	**450**	**525**	**984**	**729**	**845**	**408**	**328**	**444**
Brazil	373	421	495	973	711	840	363	299	416
Paraguay	12	22	20	1249	1026	1000	15	23	20
Asia	**681**	**738**	**986**	**414**	**542**	**752**	**282**	**423**	**742**
China	180	197	220	485	619	795	87	122	175
India	411	462	674	304	477	696	125	220	469
Pakistan	17	23	32	760	778	813	13	18	26
Thailand	39	39	39	1021	914	923	40	35	36
Europe	**21**	**14**	**21**	**726**	**306**	**529**	**15**	**4**	**11**
Romania	19	14	20	663	303	500	13	4	10
Oceania	-	-	-	-	-	-	-	-	-
U.S.S.R.	**191**	**169**	**134**	**349**	**266**	**433**	**67**	**45**	**58**

Source: FAO Production Yearbooks 1980 (vol. 34) and 1985 (vol. 39).

The castor plant is an easily adaptable crop growing successfully in the tropical, sub-tropical and even some temperate zones, but is susceptible to frost particularly in the early growth stages. The plant does not tolerate saline or poorly drained soils and requires 600 to 700 mm of rain or supplemental irrigation during the growing season. Many kinds of pests and diseases have been identified on the castor plant, but only in extreme cases of infestation would chemical control be economical.

Chemical fertilization for castor is not normally recommended. High soil fertility may even be detrimental due to excessive vegetative development which delays flowering and fruit ripening.

The castor plant can be considered an easily cultivated, adaptable cash crop, on well drained soils in frost-free seasons. The crop can be successfully handled manually or mechanically at all farming system levels.

ORIGIN AND SYSTEMATICS

Castor (*Ricinus communis* L.) belongs to the monotypic genus *Ricinus* and to the family *Euphorbiaceae* (spurge family). It has been suggested the species *R. communis* be divided into several sub-species, based on morphology and geographic distribution. However, it is doubtful whether such a classification is justified, since the morphological differences are by and large simply inherited. Moreover, the most distant types are freely intercrossable and their hybrids fully fertile.

Castor plants may differ in color, from extreme red, with even the stamen filaments containing anthocyanin, to pure green, in which even the hypocotyl is devoid of anthocyanin. Stems, leaves and fruits may be covered to a varying extent by a waxy, bluish bloom. The usually three-seeded capsules may be spiny or spineless, or intermediate. The seeds display a great genetic variety in size, shape and color patterns (Fig. 24.1). The plants may be genetically dwarf, semi-dwarf or tall, ranging in height from one to several meters. The plants are usually monoecious, bearing staminate flowers at the base of each inflorescence (raceme) and pistillate ones above them, although genetic deviants are known.

It has been suggested that the castor plant has a polyphyletic origin with four centers of variability. However, the Ethiopian-East African region is considered to be the most probable site of origin. All types of castor have the same number of chromosomes (2n=20). Chromosomal polymorphism has been occasionally reported. Claims have been made that the species is an allopolyploid, with a basic number of x=5.

Its "domestication" is lost to history. The earliest indications of human use were found in Egypt (ca 4000 BC). However, even today it cannot be considered fully domesticated since much of the crop is picked from wild plants on field borders or in uncultivated areas. These 'semi-wild' plants tend to grow tall, nearly 'palm-like' in appearance, with only a few racemes bearing a small number of dehiscing capsules.

MODE OF REPRODUCTION

Castor seeds have a wide range in size and weight (Fig. 24.1D) but normally weigh about 300 mg each (300 g/1000 seeds). The caruncula, which protrudes at the tapering side of the seed, attracts insects (mostly ants), and may help in seed dispersal. In the wild, castor seeds usually shatter and germinate in clusters directly beneath the mother plant.

Unlike the majority of the dicots, most of the seed oil is stored in the endosperm tissue rather than the embryo. Normally seeds will germinate immediately after harvest with no evidence of dormancy although small seeds which have been stressed at filling may germinate poorly.

Genetically inhibited germination, associated with small seed size and low lipase activity, has been reported in isolated cases. Germinability drops drastically after 2 or 3 years, unless the seeds are stored under cool, dry conditions. Germination will not occur or be very slow at temperatures below 15°. Seedlings normally emerge 10 to 12 days after sowing and this long emergence time increases vulnerability to soil-borne fungal rots. Germination is epigeal with the hypocotyl hook breaking through the soil surface first.

The main stem terminates with the primary inflorescence, which is usually the largest. The number of nodes to the primary inflorescence is genetically determined and serves as a good indication of the earliness of any specific genotype. The stem is usually hollow between internodes. At each internode a single palmate leaf is born. Even a mild temporary water stress will result in the shedding of mature leaves and seed which are partially or completely empty. Side branches usually develop from the penultimate internode with each branch terminating in an inflorescence. Thus, the seed bearing racemes develop successively throughout the life of the plant, and the degree of chronological yield concentration is genetically determined by the number of nodes in each branch and the size of each raceme.

Most castor genotypes are monoecious. The relative proportion of the basal staminate, to the upper pistillate zones on the raceme is genetically determined (Fig. 24.1B). However, completely male or female inflorescences have been described in certain genotypes. In some genotypes, and under certain environmental conditions, staminate and pistillate flowers may be interspersed. Hermaphrodite flowers have also been observed, usually at the tip of the inflorescence. Pollen is shed late in the morning in dry weather and is carried both by wind and insects. The capsule is normally triloculate and contains three and occasionally four seeds. The castor plant is both self- and cross-pollinated (see Atsmon, 1985, for a comprehensive review on the biology of flowering and sex expression).

At least two different female genotypes have been described; a stable, monogenic recessive (Katayama, 1948; Claassen and Hoffman, 1950), and the so-called sex reversals (Shifriss, 1956). With the latter type the early inflorescences are strictly female while, at a later stage, normal and regular bi-sexual inflorescences are formed. The process is irreversible. Recurrent selection for the partially dominant late reversion may result in stable femaleness. Low temperatures and/or short days tend to promote maleness, while sprays with gibberellin A3 have been reported to promote femaleness.

Upon ripening, capsules on some plants may explode dropping the seeds to the ground. Other plants may drop the intact capsules which split and release the seeds as the capsule walls decay.

BREEDING PROCEDURES

Self and cross seed is usually produced by bagging the inflorescences. Seed set under bags is lower than under open pollination conditions so it is advisable to bag the large primary inflorescences. The paper bags should be changed to larger sizes as the inflorescence elongates. The bags should be semi-rigid and puffed, so that the paper does not rest on the raceme. The raceme should be kept bagged until harvested, to prevent loss of capsules.

For crossing, young inflorescences are emasculated by removing all staminate buds, then tagged and bagged. A week later staminate flowers of the desired male parent are collected in the morning, when the anthers are about to dehisce. The flowers are kept for about two hours in a fully open paper bag, then the loose pollen is applied with a camel hair brush to the stigmas of the previously emasculated flowers. Pollinations of the same inflorescences are repeated two or three times at 2 to 3 day intervals as pistillate buds open.

For selfing, the inflorescences should be bagged before the most mature buds have opened, or all open flowers should be removed prior to bagging.

The instruments and hands used in pollination, should be wiped with 96% ethanol after each operation in order to avoid contamination.

Commercial F_1 hybrid seed can be produced using a monogenic recessive female parent. Such a male sterile plant can usually be propagated only through pollination by a heterozygote, maintainer line. Such a production system requires roguing of the 50% monoecious segregants in the hybrid production field prior to pollen shedding (Fig. 24.2).

The female lines of the 'sex reversal' type usually contain a gene for interspersed staminate flowering. This gene is expressed under male-enhancing environmental conditions; i.e. short days and/or low temperatures. Thus, under Mediterranean summer conditions these genotypes are strictly female and can be used for hybrid seed production, while under winter conditions under isolation these same genotypes will develop an abundance of interspersed staminate flowers facilitating self- seed production. Isolation distances of several hundred meters to one kilometer, from other pollen sources are used. The production of interspersed staminate flowers may be promoted by pistillate flower abortion when pollen is lacking and fertilization is poor. Seed of the commercial pollen parent is maintained by harvesting the male rows in the hybrid production field.

A. Genotypes grown in maintenance field:

Genotype: ff   x   Ff
Phenotype: strictly female   Monoecious (maintainer line)

B. Hybrid production field:
                 Female parent   Male parent
          50% ff, male sterile   x   100% FF monoecious
          50% Ff, monoecious (to be rogued)

Fig. 24.2 Multiplication and maintenance of recessive stable female lines in castor for F_1 hybrid seed production.

No inbreeding depression has been reported for the castor plant. Hybrid vigor has rarely been observed (Hooks et al. 1971), but the main yield advantage of the F_1 hybrids is their strong female tendency, which increases the number of capsules per inflorescence. Thus the yield of the F_1 may be increased over that of the parents by the compounded effect of arithmetic means of the parent values in the F_1 for two independent yield components, the number of racemes per plant and number of capsules per raceme (H. Stein, personal communication).

The ratio of the pollen parent to the seed parent rows in hybrid seed production fields is usually 1:3 or 4, depending on height, flowering pattern and pollen production of the pollen parent. It is of utmost importance that the pollen parent start flowering earlier than the seed parent, since a shortage of pollen at the beginning of flowering will appreciably reduce the hybrid seed yield due to poor setting in the primary inflorescence which is the main contributor to seed yield. If the F_1 hybrid is characterized by a strong female tendency, due either to its genotypic composition and/or the environment about 10% of a monoecious line is mechanically mixed with the F_1 seed to secure an ample supply of pollen in the commercial production field. There have been several reports on induced mutants of breeding importance (Kulkarni and Ankineedu, 1966; Singh, 1965).

BREEDING OBJECTIVES

Higher seed yield is one of the main breeding objectives. In addition to selecting more vigorous plants, breeding strategies include selection for a higher proportion of female flowers per raceme, greater numbers of racemes per plant and/or increased seed weight. Other objectives include earlier maturity and/or reduced plant height together with indehiscent capsules, all of which will make the crop better adapted to mechanical harvesting.

Reduced plant height can be achieved by using the Brazilian recessive allele for dwarfism, and/or by earlier maturity, through determinate flowering with few nodes (5 to 7) on the primary inflorescence. The dwarfing gene *per se* tends to slow plant development, as measured by primary node number.

Capsule dehiscence occurs along sutures in the middle of each locule's outer wall. Some indehiscent strains have been developed with tightly closed sutures in a very thick, tough capsule wall. Other indehiscent strains have a relatively thin capsule wall which can flex during drying and thus reduce the possibility of the capsule exploding. The latter solution is preferred since thick, tough capsules are difficult to thresh.

Many pests and diseases have been described in connection with the castor plant. Pathogens include *Fusarium, Rhizoctonia* and *Sclerotium* which cause seedling and/or mature plant rot, while *Alternaria* (leaf spot) and *Botrytis* attack the leaves and capsules. Insect pests include the larvae of *Agrotis* (cutworm) and *Heliothis* (bollworm), as well as the pentatomid bug *Nezara*. It has been repeatedly claimed that the waxy bloom coating protects against certain pests, while the anthocyanin of red genotypes increases resistance against fungal diseases. Genetic resistance to certain diseases and pests has been found (i.e. Moshkin and Sviridov, 1975) although, there are few reports of breeding programs designed to improve resistance to pests or diseases.

The variation in oil content within the castor bean germplasm is narrow. Further, since the beans are purchased on a weight rather than oil percentage basis there is little incentive to breed for this characteristic.

The yield potential of the best hybrids of about 3 to 4 t/ha is well above the 1 t/ha best average yields obtained to date. Therefore, yield improvement is more likely to result from better cultural practices rather than from further breeding.

DEVELOPMENT OF CULTIVARS

Genetic variability within the wild populations of castor is vast. Any desirable traits so far sought, such as indehiscence, earliness, profuse branching, slender structure, large seed and two kinds of femaleness, have been found. Rapid improvement of the crop has been possible because of the lack of inbreeding depression, and the relatively simple inheritance of many important economic characteristics.

Since castor is largely cross-pollinated, and shows little inbreeding depression any desirable plant should be selfed for several generations, while selecting for the desired character, in order to fix the characteristic and study its inheritance.

Several criteria are important in developing parental lines for commercial F_1 hybrid production. First, the pollen parent should be somewhat earlier than the seed parent and produce pollen continuously and profusely throughout the seed production season. Second, the seed parent should be strictly female during the hybrid production season, but should be genetically able to produce the interspersed staminate flowers in another environment in order to facilitate self propagation. Third, it is advisable that each parent contain a dominant marker so that the degree of hybridization in the commercial F_1 hybrid can be readily assessed. For instance, the red stem characteristic of one parent may be combined with the waxy bloom of the other, resulting in an F_1 plant different and more desirable than either parent. Some marker characteristics can be identified in the seedling stage, permitting a quick estimate of the percent hybrid seed produced.

Hybrid castor cultivars have been primarily developed and used in the USA and Israel. However, in recent years, no new commercial hybrids have been released. In Israel the hybrids were produced using the sex reversal mechanism. In the USA some hybrid cultivars have been produced using monogenic recessive femaleness. Other hybrids depend on the pollination of the recessive female with pollen from interspersed staminate parents resulting in a strong female tendency in the F_1.

Conventional and mutation breeding approaches have resulted in open pollinated cultivars with improved disease resistance, indehiscence, reduced height and earliness. However, the commercial impact of these improved cultivars is not clear due to the widespread use of semi-wild plants in the major producing countries.

UTILIZATION OF PRODUCTS

In South East Asia and India leaves of the castor plant have been used for feeding silkworms (Reddy and Alfred, 1979) and cattle. Where fresh green food is scarce, castor leaves, mostly in a preserved form, have also been used for human food. The branches and stem can be used for the production of low grade paper and paper-related products, as well as for fuel.

Most producing countries prohibit or discourage export of beans in order to promote the local oil industry. The oil, which forms ca 50% of the shelled beans, is by far the most economically important part of the plant. It is obtained from the seed endosperm by mechanically pressing, straight solvent extraction or by the prepress solvent system. Variation in bean size, common in harvests from semi-wild plants, may cause technical problems in the mills.

There are literally hundreds of different industrial uses for castor oil and its derivatives. Many of them are based on the exceptionally high content (ca 85%) of a unique hydroxy fatty acid, ricinoleic acid. $(C_{17}H_{32}OH.COOH)$. By far the most important uses are; paints and varnishes for surface coatings, nylon type synthetic polymers, resins and lubricants. Significant amounts of oil are also used in the production of cosmetics, textile dyeing, insecticides and the leather industry. The drying oils produced from the castor oil are derived after dehydration. The use of castor oil for medicinal purposes, including its use as a laxative, has declined greatly through the years and is now of little importance.

The residual meal after oil extraction contains between 30 and 45% protein depending on the oil extraction process used. Because of the high toxicity of the endosperm protein, ricin, and an allergenic component found in all castor plant parts, untreated meal can only be used as an organic fertilizer, containing about 5% nitrogen, or as a fish feed. However, if the meal is detoxified by heat or other means it can be fed to farm animals, preferably to ruminants.

REFERENCES

Atsmon, D. 1985. Ricinus Communis L., pp. 204-213. *In* A. H. Halevy (ed.), *Handbook of Flowering*. Vol. 4. CRC Press, Inc., Boca Raton, Fla.

Claassen, C.E., and Hoffman, A. 1950. The inheritance of the pistillate character in castors and its possible utilization in the production of commercial hybrid seed. Agron. J. 42: 79-82.

Hooks, J.A., Williams, J.H., and Gardner, C.O. 1971. Estimates of heterosis from diallel cross of inbred lines of castors *Ricinus communis*. Crop Sci. 11: 651-655.

Katayama, J. 1948. The progeny of female individuals in castorbeans. Jpn. J. Genet. 23: 19.

Kulkarni, L.G., and Ramanamurthy, G.V. 1977. *Castor*. 2nd Ed. Indian Counc. Agric. Res. New Delhi.

——, and Ankineedu, G. 1966. Isolation of pistillate lines in castor for exploitation of hybrid vigour. Indian J. Genet. Plant Breed. 26: 363-365.

Moshkin, V.A., and Sviridov, A.A. 1975. The castor oil plant collection - useful initial material in breeding for resistance to *Fusarium* wilt. Trudy po Prikladnoi Botanike, Genetike i Selektsii 55: 143-150.

Reddy, M.V., and Alfred, J.R.B. 1979. Utilization of castor (*Ricinus communis* L.) leaves by the last instar larvae of the silk moth, *Philosamia ricini* Hutt. (Lepidoptera: Saturniidae). Indian Biol. 11: 36-40.

Shifriss, O. 1956. Sex instability in *Ricinus*. Genetics 41: 265-280.

Weiss, E.A. 1971. *Castor, Sesame and Safflower*. Leonard Hill, London.

——. 1983. *Oilseed Crops*. Longman, London and New York.

Chapter 25

Jojoba

A. Benzioni and M. Forti

IMPORTANCE AND DISTRIBUTION

Jojoba, *Simmondsia chinensis* (Link) Schneider, is a perennial crop that was practically unknown to commercial agriculture as recently as 10 to15 years ago. Today there are plantations on about 17000 ha in the southwestern USA and Mexico, and on smaller areas in Australia and various countries in Latin America, Asia and Africa (Table 25.1). In addition 250,000 ha of wild populations in Mexico (Fig. 25.1A) are thought to be worth economic exploitation.

The jojoba plant has generated worldwide interest as a potential oil crop, as its seeds (Fig. 25.1E) contain a liquid (technically a wax) which is unique in the plant kingdom. It is a straight-chain ester of 20:1, 22:1 and 24:1 fatty acids and fatty alcohols. The wax has an average total carbon chain length of 42 and contains two unsaturated bonds, which are susceptible to such chemical reactions as isomerization, sulfurization, saturation, etc. Those chemical modifications yield a broad spectrum of derivatives that have potential for use in diverse products such as cosmetics, pharmaceuticals, lubricants, electrical insulators, foam control agents, high-pressure oils, plasticizers, fire retardants and transformer oil (Miwa, 1980; United States National Research Council, 1985).

448

Fig. 25. 1 Jojoba. A – Wild, unusually large female shrub. The multi stemmed trunk is the result of animal browsing. B – Male inflorescence at anthesis. C – Female floral bud at anthesis. D – Fully developed fruits on twin inflorescences with hermaphroditic flowers. At the base of the fruit on the right, capsules of undeveloped fruits are still visible, while the remains of dried male flowers are visible at the base of the fruit on the left. E – Seeds and hydrogenated wax of jojoba.

Table 25.1   Area of Cultivated Jojoba by Producing Country, 1983

Country	Area, ha	Country	Area, ha
World	23,516	Argentina	220
USA	15,310	Chile	120
Mexico	2,025	Israel	400
Costa Rica	1,620	Kenya	40
Brazil	1,000	South Africa	344
Paraguay	1,000	Australia	1,437

Sources: J. Wisniak and J. Zabicky (1985) and U.S. National Research Council (1985)

Commercial plantations of jojoba are still young with the oldest established in the late 70s. Their yields and overall performance are not yet indicative of jojoba's agricultural potential, since cultural practices are continually improved and the search for better plant populations or clones is only beginning.

At present jojoba oil production is estimated at a few hundred tons per year, including the oil extracted from seeds collected in the wild. The major oil producers are the USA and Mexico, which export considerable amounts of the oil to Japan and Europe.

Jojoba is being cultivated commercially or experimentally in widely differing environments, from the tropics to the temperate zone. It has not been ascertained as yet how and to what extent the interaction of various ecological factors will affect growth, phenology and productivity, and whether the genetic variability of the species is broad enough to facilitate selection of lines adapted to such a wide range of conditions.

Jojoba is tolerant to drought and salinity. In areas with low precipitation, its drought tolerance permits some flexibility in the amount and distribution of irrigation water to comply with local constraints and the requirements of other crops. For best yields, however, regular irrigation and fertilization are crucial in the dry hot season. Salinity tolerance can permit utilization of marginal water and soils. The extent to which salinity affects growth and yields has not yet been investigated.

The cost of harvesting appears crucial to successful commercialization. Where manpower is inexpensive, wild populations and plantations are hand-picked. In the USA and Israel, mechanical harvesters that were developed for other crops (i.e. grapes, raspberries and nuts) have been modified for use with jojoba. Collecting seed from the ground by vacuum or other means appears the most promising approach and is in an advanced stage of development.

ORIGIN AND SYSTEMATICS

Jojoba is an evergreen perennial shrub (Fig. 25.1A) endemic to the Sonora desert of the southwestern USA, northwestern Mexico and Baja California. In these and adjacent areas it is found in discontinuous populations, between latitudes 23° and 34° north and longitudes 109° and 117° west, at altitudes between sea level and up to 1500 m. The species usually grows in well drained soils and develops well where annual rainfall exceeds 300 mm (Gentry, 1958). Where rainfall is lower than 200 mm, the plant is restricted to beds of temporary water courses. According to Gentry (1958) the phenology of jojoba seems to indicate that it originated in the Mediterranean type of climate along the North American Pacific coast. It flowers after the cool rainy season, and the fruit ripens in the warm season. Jojoba prefers mild climates and open spaces. The cold of the highlands in the east, the close chaparral plant communities of the north west, and the thorn forest in the south have restricted its expansion. The absence of jojoba in environments that seem otherwise suitable to it, is explained by some authors by its palatability and the consequent destructive effect of browsing in ancient periods of very high animal pressure.

Jojoba was first described by H. F. Link in 1822 as *Buxus chinensis*. In 1844 Nuttall classified it into a new genus *Simmondsia* and named it *californica* with reference to its origin. In 1907 Schneider retained the earlier specific name and the plant was designated *Simmondsia chinensis* (Link) Schneider. Early botanists placed the species in the Buxaceae or Euphorbiaceae families, but numerous authors assigned it to a monotypic genus in a separate family, Simmondsiaceae. This classification was recently supported by pollen morphology studies. The chromosome number in male, female and hermaphrodite plants is 2n=52. Sex chromosomes were not found.

MODE OF REPRODUCTION

Jojoba is usually dioecious. In cultivated areas the male:female ratio is approximately 1:1 but more male than female plants were observed in certain wild populations. The flowers are small and born in leaf axils of the previous year's growth (Gentry, 1958). The male flowers occur in inflorescences and are subtended by several bracts. They are up to 4 mm long and consist of 4 to 6 sepals with 8 to 16 stamens each having a short filament and a large erect anther (Fig. 25.1B) (Schmid, 1978). The female flowers are usually solitary and borne on recurved short peduncles, so that inverted flowers (Fig. 25.1C) and fruits (Fig. 25.1D) result. Fascicled and racemose female inflorescences may be found in low amounts on certain shrubs and only seldom characterize entire plants. Both types of flowers originate from apical meristems that develop into dormant flower buds (for detailed description see Moncur, 1978). The buds may remain dormant for periods of several weeks up to two or even three years, until suitable conditions for flowering occur (Gentry, 1958; Benzioni et al. 1983). After dormancy is broken, differentiation of the flowers continues. The stigmas and ovules renew their growth until the stigmas emerge past the bracts and open. In the male buds the anthers develop and extend out of the opening flower.

Clusters of perfect flowers have been reported to occur on plants with otherwise male characteristics at frequencies of about 1:1000. Different degrees of hermaphroditism are expressed by different individuals or by the same plant in different growing seasons. The hermaphroditic flowers usually exhibit poor fruit set, but some (Fig. 25.1D) produce viable seed after selfing or cross pollination (Yermanos, 1982; Milthorpe, personal communication). A normal male can be induced to produce hermaphroditic flowers if subjected to low temperatures (12/7°C day/night) for a period of about two months (Dunstone, 1982). Thus sex expression may be modulated to some extent by environmental factors.

Flower buds usually form under nearly all environmental conditions provided vegetative growth occurs (Gentry, 1958). They usually appear on every second node, but the proportion of nodes that bear flower buds varies with genotype and is also affected by environmental conditions. For example, in the second half of the warm season Forti (unpublished) observed bud formation at every node. High temperatures (30/25°C day/night) enhance flower bud production (Dunstone, 1982).

The breaking of flower bud dormancy is mainly controlled by temperature and the plant's water status. Other factors, including genotypic differences, light intensity, nutrition, and plant hormones, are also involved. Gentry (1958) observed that "drought appears to be one of the strongest factors inhibiting flower buds."

In non-irrigated plantations, shrubs may fail to flower in a drought year. Prolonged periods of low xylem water potential resulted in complete inhibition of flowering in the field (Table 25.2) (Nerd, 1985), and in delayed and decreased percent of flowering in controlled environments (Benzioni and Dunstone, 1985). Under conditions of adequate moisture, temperature is the major factor affecting dormancy. At day/night temperatures of 27/22°C or higher, no flowering occurs (Dunstone, 1980; 1982). As the temperature decreases the percent of buds which break dormancy increases. The longer the period of low temperature, the higher the proportion of buds that flower (Fig. 25.2) (Dunstone, 1986, unpublished).

Table 25.2   Effect of Xylem Water Potential on Percent Flowering

IrIrrigation treatment	Flowering[1] % of total buds	Water potential range, - MPa	
		dawn	noon
Nonirrigated	0	3.7-4.2	4.4-4.7
Nonirrigated	67	2.8-3.4	3.7-4.2
Irrigated	86	1.6-1.7	2.6-2.8

[1]Each value is the mean of four plants, of which 25 pretagged floral buds were followed on each plant.
Source: A. Nerd (1985).

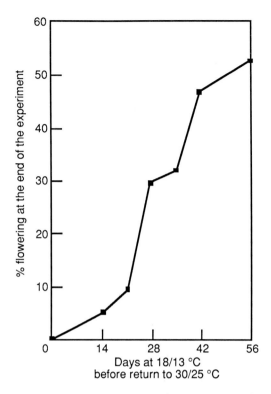

Fig. 25.2 Effect of duration of exposure to low temperature on percent flowering (courtesy R. L. Dunstone, CSIRO, Canberra, unpublished).

Since moisture and low temperatures favor breaking of flower bud dormancy, flowering occurs at the end of the rainy, cold season and is most abundant in years when the spring moisture supply is adequate. Well fertilized plants flower earlier than unfertilized ones. Application of nutrients in late autumn often results in partial out-of-season flowering (Benzioni et al. 1983).

The environmental factors may influence flowering by affecting the production level of one or more growth regulators. For example, abscisic acid (ABA) may play a role in controlling flower bud dormancy, since a negative correlation between flowering response and endogenous ABA levels has been demonstrated in the field and in controlled environments (Benzioni and Dunstone, 1985).

Genotypes differ in their response to environmental conditions, and both "early flowering" and "late flowering" types can be identified. Frequently, the early flowering plants bloom to some extent in autumn and are in full bloom in early spring. The late flowering types bloom mainly in the late spring and rarely out of season. A large proportion of the progeny of a particular mother plant maintains its flowering pattern (Forti et al. 1985).

After anthesis the stigmas remain receptive to pollen and can set fruit for 20 to 25 days. Receptiveness is not completely lost until forty days after anthesis (Fig. 25.3) (Benzioni and Shafat, unpublished). The styles of unpollinated flowers continue to grow and remain long, yellow and turgid for about thirty days after anthesis, and then senesce.

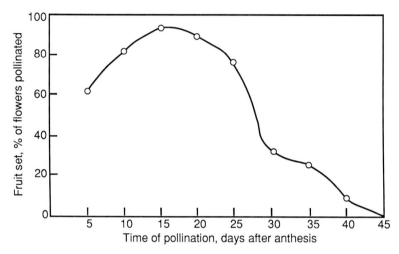

Fig. 25.3 Effect of flower age on fruit set of jojoba (Benzioni and Shafat, unpublished).

Jojoba is wind-pollinated. Its pollen grains are 30 to 35 μm in diameter and have three germination pores and a waxy coat that results in their aggregation. The aerobiology of the pollen, its abundance and dispersion have been described by Niklas and Buchmann (1985). The atmospheric concentration of jojoba pollen is much higher during daylight hours than at night. Even moderate precipitation causes pollen levels to decrease sharply for at least one day, due to the capture of pollen by rain droplets. A high pollen concentration appears to depend on high maximum daily temperature and low relative humidity conditions, which are probably ideal conditions for anther dehiscence.

Germinability and vigor of pollen may vary widely from plant to plant. In some pollen stocks in vitro germination was found to be 80 to 90% and in others less than 10%. In vivo pollination with stored pollen resulted in 60 to 80% fruit set (Benzioni and Shafat, unpublished; Ramonet and Morales, 1985). Pollen can be stored for several weeks without losing germinability if kept at 4°C, and for prolonged periods if kept dry, and frozen at -20°C or below (Lee et al. 1982).

It is not known whether incompatibility between males and females occurs in jojoba. Ramonet and Morales (1985) showed that the highest fruit set was achieved by certain combinations of males and females. Similar results were obtained by Benzioni and Shafat (unpublished), but in their experiments poor fruit set was correlated with pollen sources having low in vitro germinability.

Whenever the pollen germinability was 20% or more, the fruit set was good (60 to 80%). In the field, 70 to 80% of the open flowers set fruit that develop to maturity, 5 to 20% fail to set fruit, and 5 to 10% set fruit that aborts at some stage of fruit filling (Benzioni and Nerd, observations at Beer-Sheva and Omer, Israel, through 1978-1984). Early flowering genotypes usually have a lower percentage fruit set and more abortions than late flowering varieties. In some years, fruit set failure is a serious problem. The use of early flowering varieties in areas susceptible to spring frosts may result in flower loss and reduced yields. Agronomic practices which favor early flowering in such areas, including late fall irrigation and fertilizer application, may also result in yield losses.

After fertilization, the capsule enlarges but the ovule normally does not begin development until 30 to 35 days later. Seed growth is affected by temperature. If day/night temperatures remain low (15/10°C), ovule growth may be delayed up to 106 days, while at higher temperatures (36/31°C) the time lag may be as short as seven days (Wardlaw and Dunstone, 1984; Dunstone et al. 1984). Temperature during seed filling affects not only seed growth and final size, but also wax composition. High temperatures during seed filling interfere with fatty acid elongation from those with twenty carbons to those with 22 and 24. In addition high temperatures also favor the reduction of fatty acids to alcohols. The result is a decrease in C_{22} and longer chain fatty acids and alcohols, as well as a decrease in wax esters with chain lengths over forty carbons (Dunstone et al. 1984; 1985).

The fruit consists of a dehiscent capsule (Fig. 25.1D) containing 1 to 3 ovules attached to the placenta at the capsule apex (Gentry, 1958). The seed contains little or no endosperm and the cotyledons make up most of the seed. The cotyledons are filled with storage organelles of two types; protein bodies surrounded by a unit membrane and wax bodies containing liquid wax (Rost and Paterson, 1978).

BREEDING PROCEDURES

Jojoba is still at a very early stage of domestication and improvement. It contains much genetic variability which is expressed in phenological, morphological, anatomical, physiological and production characteristics, such as overall size and growth habit; leaf size, shape and color; flower morphology; seed size, shape and color; flowering period; cold hardiness; yield potential; earliness of coming into production; determinate bearing, etc. (Gentry, 1958). Because of the crop's dioecious nature, the genotype of every plant originating from seed is different from that of every other sexually produced plant so that a wide range of segregation is obtained in seedlings from a single mother plant. No homozygous plants have yet been bred. The important agronomic characteristics appear to be quantitative and cannot be sharply defined. Environmental conditions such as wind, rainfall, temperature, soil, fire, and browsing may also affect these param-. eters. Thus germplasm collections from wild populations with the aim of obtaining plants with specific characteristics have generally been unsuccessful. Most of the shrubs in the plantations of today were grown from open pollinated seed collected from wild plants and therefore exhibit poor yield potential and enormous segregation for every known parameter, including yield. For example, a frequency distribution from 0 to 2200 g per plant was shown by Palzkill and Hogan (1983) in the yield of six-year-old plants in an experimental plot in Arizona. Such variability emphasizes the need to develop lines or cultivars with predictable performances.

Conventional breeding techniques are not easily applied to jojoba for three reasons. First, the plants require 2 to 4 years to flower, which seriously delays a hybridization program. Second, the dioecious flowering habit slows the development of inbred lines; and third, progeny assessment requires a minimum of 6 to 7 years. The first reliable indications of yield can be obtained only in the fourth year after planting. In addition, yields in subsequent years may fluctuate considerably because of alternate bearing patterns.

Such factors increase costs and breeding time and are expensive. It may be possible to use hermaphrodite plants to produce inbred lines. Some selfing has been done, but the proportion of hermaphrodites in the progeny is not yet known. Milthorpe and Dunstone (personal communication) have found some hermaphrodites among F_1 progenies. In order to test the general and specific combining ability of the inbred lines and to cross the best combiners to produce hybrids with superior qualities, at least five generations of selfing, each requiring 2 to 3 years, will be required. Such a program may take a minimum of twenty years and may still fail to produce the desired results. The process may be shortened by using anther culture as a source of homozygous material, as suggested by Jahuar (1982).

A practical and more immediate approach to jojoba improvement is practiced by growers and involves the cloning of plants with desired traits using tissue culture or rooted cuttings. This approach allows the exploitation of the great genetic variability within a seedling population and the opportunity of utilizing outstanding individuals in production fields. The frequency of relatively high yielding plants (1 to 1.2 kg per plant per year over 15 years) was 1:80 in an introduction plot in Israel, irrigated with up to 200 mm water in addition to an average annual precipitation of 230 mm (Forti, unpublished). Thus, if the population is large enough, plants with a combination of several desirable traits can be identified. The opportunities for improvement can be enhanced if selection is practiced among the F_1 progeny of outstanding plants. For example, progenies from shrubs selected for seed yield and upright growth had a frequency of superior plants of about 1:20 as compared with a 1:80 ratio in the progeny from unselected parents.

Vegetative propagation appears to be the most practical and rapid approach to improve present breeding stocks in the medium term. Although various clones are available, most have not yet been evaluated in valid clone-test experiments. An average yield of 1.2 kg per shrub was recorded in the fourth year after planting for a clone propagated by tissue culture and planted in a small plot in

Beer–Sheva, Israel (Birnbaum et al. 1985). In a test plot at Givat Brenner, Israel, 2.2 and 2.0 kg of seed per plant were produced by the best line, in the third and fourth year after planting, respectively. Selected plants differ in their ability to clone, and some of the best performing shrubs display a very low rooting rate, suggesting that modifications of the basic propagation procedure may be required.

BREEDING OBJECTIVES

At the present very early stage of domestication, selection programs of jojoba are aimed at two main objectives. The first objective is to increase the yield potential by selecting for abundant fruiting, fascicled and nodal fruiting, large seeds, and either no or low alternation in bearing. The second objective is the development of plants suitable for mechanical harvesting which would include the characteristics of upright habit, determinate flowering with ripening concentrated in a short period and a low pull force requirement for fruit removal.

Additional traits which should be considered are ease of vegetative propagation, erect but not brittle stems, short internodes and a high flower bud to node ratio, and dehiscent fruits. Quality factors for selection include seeds with a high wax content but little or no simmondsin content. "Deep" flower bud dormancy is required for climates with cold frosty winters. Plants with very light bud dormancy may prove valuable in tropical climates, where temperatures remain high throughout the year but where a dry season exists. For male plants, abundant pollen production with good pollen germinability and long viability as well as synchronization of pollen dispersal with receptiveness of the female clones in the plantation will be important. Other traits for selection are cold hardiness, resistance to *Verticillium* and other diseases, good response to irrigation and fertilizer application, high water use efficiency, and precocious fruiting. Additional characteristics may become important with time and with the expansion of the crop into new environments.

HISTORY OF CULTIVAR DEVELOPMENT

The history of jojoba as a cultivated plant is still too short to have permitted the development of cultivars. Yermanos (1982) reported the development of both a self-pollinating strain and a high oil line; however, further research is needed to establish their usefulness.

Several germplasm collections in jojoba's natural habitat have been carried out. Seeds from wild plants were used to establish introduction nurseries and follow-up plots in botanical gardens and experimental stations in California, Arizona, and Israel. However, selection of outstanding plants is in its infancy. Several good shrubs were selected in experimental areas in Israel and are now being cloned (Birnbaum et al. 1985). More extensive testing is still required. A large test plot of clones collected in a variety of American environments was established in California by Tenneco Oil Company (Palzkill and Hogan, 1983) and has resulted in the identification of very promising material. In Arizona, H. Purcell (personal communication) has also started a line test plantation. Introduction and preliminary testing is also under way in Costa Rica where results could be relevant to tropical areas having a dry season. Producers are also actively seeking out superior performing shrubs in their groves. The use of such vegetatively propagated material is expanding.

UTILIZATION OF PRODUCTS

The major potential of jojoba as a modern industrial crop is embodied in the liquid wax which makes up about 50% of the seed's dry weight. This liquid, usually referred to as an oil, is similar in composition and properties to sperm whale oil. Unlike other vegetable oils, it is not a triglyceride fat, but a wax composed almost entirely of esters of straight long-chain unsaturated fatty acids and alcohols. More than 87% of the oil is composed of straight-chain C_{20} and C_{22} fatty acids and alcohols (Miwa, 1980; United States National Research Council, 1985).

The oil is extracted by pressing. Solvents may be used to remove the oil remaining in the meal after mechanical processing. The extracted oil is relatively pure, nontoxic, and biodegradable. It is stable and has a long shelf life, probably because the oil contains natural antioxidants. Repeated heating to temperatures above 285°C for four days as well as high pressures do not alter its properties (United States National Research Council, 1985).

The double bonds and ester moieties can be modified to yield new products. When the oil is isomerized at the double bonds, the liquid is transformed to a cream. Depending on the degree of isomerization, a series of waxes with different melting points can be produced. Hydrogenation of jojoba oil produces a crystalline wax (Fig. 25.1E), whose hardness among waxes of plant origin is second only to that of carnauba wax. Incomplete hydrogenation yields a range of products of different degrees of hardness, suitable for use in polishes, coatings, impregnation, carbon paper, etc. When sulfur or radicals containing both sulfur and phosphorus, chlorine, or bromine are incorporated into the oil, its properties as a lubricant additive are remarkably enhanced (Wisniak, 1977; Miwa, 1980).

The main current use of jojoba oil, either unmodified or as one of its soft derivatives, is in cosmetics. As many as 300 cosmetic products containing jojoba oil have appeared in recent years in the USA alone (United States National Research Council, 1985). Relatively large amounts of oil are exported from America to Japan and Europe. Use of jojoba oil as a carrier in the pharmaceutical industry has been proposed. Tests have shown that the oil can be utilized as an antifoam agent during the production of antibiotics and also as a treatment for skin disorders.

Jojoba oil and its sulfurized derivatives are regarded as excellent substitutes for sperm whale oil, even out-performing it as additives in high-quality, high-pressure lubricants (e.g. gear oils and greases), and in cutting and drawing oils. Lubricants containing jojoba oil are advertised in the USA. By blending jojoba oil with other waxes, high-quality candles are being produced. Jojoba oil has been proposed as a source of numerous other derivatives, such as unusual acids and alcohols, plasticizers, detergents, fire retardants, as well as cooking oil, edible oil for dietetic purposes, transformer oil, and use in the leather industry (United States National Research Council, 1985).

The meal remaining after the oil is extracted contains up to 30% protein, with an amino acid composition that is relatively well balanced,except for a low content of methionine (Yermanos, 1974). The meal could therefore serve as an acceptable animal feed. However, toxic compounds (simmondsins) make its direct use hazardous. Methods of detoxification and palatability improvement are being tested (Verbiscar and Banigan, 1983).

The jojoba plant is used on a small scale in gardening and landscaping, and selection of types specifically suitable for this purpose has been recommended. Although jojoba is tolerant to drought and salinity and cattle browse its canopy (Gentry, 1958), its growth appears too slow and its palatability too high to permit its successful establishment and utilization as an evergreen fodder shrub in pasture improvement projects in semi-arid areas.

Some of the potential uses of jojoba mentioned above are contingent upon the outcome of laborious, often very expensive tests such as its use in skin disease treatments and pharmaceuticals as well as in feed and food. Other uses, such as in lubricants and possibly in the leather industry, depend on the oil's availability in large amounts, the reliability of the supply, and the competitiveness with other oils in terms of price, quality, and processing costs. Jojoba is still at the very beginning of its economical development. The price of the oil is still very high, up to US $10 to 15 per liter, depending on quantity and quality. Many seeds are still obtained by harvesting wild populations, making their supply erratic and dependent on environmental and socio-economic factors. Expansion of jojoba cultivation combined with higher yields from the use of advanced technologies and selected plant material should increase the oil supply and its reliability, decrease its price, and permit its industrial utilization for commodities with lower values and much larger markets.

REFERENCES

Benzioni, A., and Dunstone, R.L. 1985. Jojoba flower buds: a possible role for abscisic acid in controlling dormancy in jojoba flower buds. Aust. J. Plant Physiol. 12: 463-470.

——, Nerd, A., and Forti, M. 1983. Effect of Irrigation, Fertilization and Genetic Background on Flowering in Jojoba, pp. 221-227. *In* A. Elias-Cesnik (ed.), *Jojoba and Its Uses Through 1982*. Proc. 5th Intern. Conf. Univ. Arizona, Tucson, Ariz.

Birnbaum, E., Matias, S., and Wenkart, S. 1985. Vegetative Propagation of Jojoba by Tissue Culture, pp. 233-241. *In* J. Wisniak and K. Zabicky (eds.), *Jojoba*. Proc. 6th Intern. Conf. on Jojoba and Its Uses. Ben-Gurion Univ. Negev, Beer-Sheva, Israel.

Dunstone, R.L. 1980. Jojoba flower buds: Temperature and photoperiod effects in breaking dormancy. Aust. J. Agric. Res. 31: 727-737.

——. 1982. Jojoba flower buds: Effect of preconditioning temperature. Aust. J. Agric. Res. 33:649-656.

——, Tonnet, M.L., Wardlaw, I.F., and Shani, A. 1984. The effect of temperature on seed development in jojoba (*Simmondsia chinensis* (Link) Schneider). II. Wax content and composition. Aust. J. Agric. Res. 35: 693-700.

——, Benzioni, A., Tonnet, M.L., Milthorpe, P., and Shani, A. 1985. The effect of temperature on the biosynthesis of jojoba wax. Aust. J. Plant Physiol. 12: 355-362.

Forti, M., Nerd, A., and Benzioni, A. 1985. Effect of the Genetic Background on Flowering Pattern, Growth and Yield of Jojoba, pp. 293-298. *In* J. Wisniak and J. Zabicky (eds.), *Jojoba*. Proc. 6th Intern. Conf. on Jojoba and Its Uses. Ben-Gurion Univ. Negev, Beer-Sheva, Israel.

Gentry, H.S. 1958. The natural history of jojoba (*Simmonsdia chinensis*) and its cultural aspects. Econ. Bot. 12: 261-295.

Jahuar, P.P. 1982. Cytological and Agrobotanical Studies of Hermaphroditic Plants and Their Possible Use in Genetic Improvement of Jojoba, pp. 371-375. *In* M. Puebla (ed.), *Jojoba*. Proc. 4th Intern. Conf. on Jojoba. Intern. Counc. on Jojoba.

Lee, C.W., Anderson, J.O., Palzkill, D.A., and Hogan, L. 1982. In Vitro Germination and Cryogenic Storage of Jojoba Pollen, pp. 347-351. *In* M. Puebla (ed.), *Jojoba*. Proc. 4th Intern. Conf. on Jojoba. Intern. Counc. on Jojoba.

Miwa, T.K. (ed.). 1980. *Jojoba*, Vol. I. Jojoba Plantation Products, Inc., Los Angeles, Calif.

Moncur, M.W. 1978. *Floral Initiation in Field Crops*, pp. 118-121. CSIRO, Div. of Land Use Res., Canberra, Australia.

Nerd, A. 1985. The Effect of Water Regime on Vegetative Growth, Seed Production and Assimilate Partitioning in Jojoba *(Simmondsia chinensis* (Link) Schneider). Ph.D. Thesis (in Hebrew with English summary), Ben-Gurion Univ. Negev, Beer-Sheva, Israel.

Niklas, K.J., and Buchmann, S.L. 1985. Aerodynamics of wind pollination in *Simmondsia chinensis* (Link) Schneider. Am. J. Bot. 72: 530-539.

Palzkill, D.A., and Hogan, L. 1983. Jojoba Seed Yield From a Seedling Planting at Mesa, Arizona and From a Cutting-grown Planting near Bakersfield, California, pp. 231-236. *In* A. Elias-Cesnik (ed.), *Jojoba and Its Uses Through 1982*. Proc. 5th Intern. Conf. Univ. Arizona, Tucson, Ariz.

Ramonet, R.R., and Morales, A.M. 1985. Seed Yield Variability and Selection Criterion of Jojoba Clones in Mexico, pp. 279-285. *In* J. Wisniak and J. Zabicky (eds.), *Jojoba*. Proc. 6th Intern. Conf. on Jojoba and Its Uses. Ben-Gurion Univ. Negev, Beer-Sheva, Israel.

Rost, T.L., and Paterson, K.E. 1978. Structural and histochemical characterization of the cotyledon storage organelles of jojoba (*Simmondsia chinensis*). Protoplasma 95: 1-10.

Schmid, R. 1978. Floral and Fruit Anatomy of Jojoba (*Simmondsia chinensis*), pp. 143-148. *In* W.G. Guzman (ed.), *La Jojoba*. Proc. 2nd Intern. Conf. on Jojoba and Its Uses. National Council for Science and Technology, Mexico City, Mexico.

U.S. National Research Council, 1985. *Jojoba: New Crop for Arid Lands, New Material for Industry*. National Academy Press, Washington, D.C.

Verbiscar, A.J., and Banigan, T.F. 1983. Jojoba Meal as a Livestock Feed, pp. 267-281. *In* A. Elias-Cesnik (ed.), *Jojoba and its Uses Through 1982*. Proc. 5th Intern. Conf. Univ. Arizona, Tucson, Ariz.

Wardlaw, I.F., and Dunstone, R.L. 1984. Effect of temperatures on seed development in jojoba (*Simmondsia chinensis* (Link) Schneider). I. Dry matter changes. Aust. J. Agric. Res. 35: 685-691.

Wisniak, J. 1977. Jojoba oil and derivatives. Prog. Chem. Fats, Other Lipids 15: 167-218.

Yermanos, D.M. 1974. Agronomic survey of jojoba in California. Econ. Bot. 28: 160-174.

———. 1982. Self-pollinating Jojoba, pp. 345-346. *In* M. Puebla (ed.), *Jojoba*. Proc. 4th Intern. Conf. on Jojoba.

Chapter 26

Olive

G. Brousse

IMPORTANCE AND DISTRIBUTION

Through the centuries the olive tree (Fig. 26.1) has been regarded as part of the social and cultural traditions of every country and region in which it has been grown. Because of its long life and hardiness and its adaptation to areas where often it is the only type of tree farming possible, different cultivation techniques, beliefs and traditions have evolved. Such traditions often impede the introduction and acceptance of improved olive tree farm management techniques.

Past civilizations have created an enormous olive grove throughout the Mediterranean basin. There are 805 million registered olive trees in the world which cover a surface area of approximately 9.6 million hectares (Table 26.1). Of the registered trees 97% of them are located in the Mediterranean basin with the remaining 3% grown in the Americas and Oceania.

Although the olive tree is often grown together with other perennial plants and is frequently found as an isolated tree growing in the wild, the majority of the production comes from the homogeneous olive groves. The density of tree plantings in olive groves varies greatly from country to country and even from region to region within the same country. For example, in southern Tunisia the planting density is approximately 17 trees/ha while in central Italy up to 400 trees/ha are planted.

Fig. 26.1 Olive. A – Olive tree viewed in the late nineteenth century. B – Branch laden with fruit. C – Diagram of real size of fruit.
From L Figuier, in "Les merveilles de l'industrie."

Table 26.1 World Olive Production by Region and Major Producing Countries

Region or Country	Olive prod. ('000 tonnes)			Oil prod. ('000 tonnes)		
	1969-71	1979-81	1985	1969-71	1979-81	1985
World	7611	9205	8273	1549	1827	1592
Africa	999	1078	1015	172	174	196
Algeria	150	153	140	21	19	24
Libya	38	139	128	7	26	26
Morocco	329	260	260	41	28	31
Tunisia	476	521	480	103	101	115
N. & C. America	65	94	106	2	2	2
U.S.A.	54	65	90	1	-	-
S. America	94	121	101	18	18	9
Argentina	70	94	78	17	16	9
Asia	668	1128	927	158	206	128
Syria	110	265	185	23	59	38
Turkey	438	727	600	86	129	73
Europe	5783	6782	6122	1228	1428	1257
Greece	876	1465	1420	178	302	290
Italy	2530	2962	2600	553	635	537
Portugal	422	271	215	70	47	33
Spain	1897	2022	1824	419	435	387
Oceania	2	2	2	-	-	-
U.S.S.R.	-	-	-	-	-	-

Source: FAO Production Yearbooks 1980 (vol. 34) and 1985 (vol. 39).

Oil is the main product of the olive tree with more than 93% of the world's olive production of 11 million tonnes being processed into oil. Of the world's total olive oil production 93% originates in the five Mediterranean countries of Italy, Spain, Greece, Turkey, and Tunisia. Spain and Italy alone account for 60.8% of the oil. In addition, the fruit of the olive tree throughout the ages has been used for edible purposes.

ORIGIN AND SYSTEMATICS

The origin of the olive tree *Olea europaea* L. is uncertain but is generally believed to have evolved in the Syro-Iranian regions of Asia Minor. With its westward spread to the shores of the Mediterranean the olive tree species was improved and diversified over time. The Oleaceae family consists of trees and shrubs including such things as the lilac (*Syringa*), forsythia, privets (*Ligustrum*), the jasmine tree (*Jasminium*), the ash (*Fraximus*), *Fhillyrea,* and others.

The *Olea* genus consists of more than thirty different species distributed over five continents. Only *O. europaea* has been domesticated to any extent with the other olive species frequently found growing in the wild. *O. europaea* is also known as *Olea communis* Stend or *Olea polymorpha* Risso. The species *O. europaea* is made up of four subspecies or stocks, namely:

- *sativa* Hoffmg et Link (cultivated olive tree), which consists of a large number of improved cultivars multiplied by cuttings or grafting and which are not found growing in the wild.
- *sylvestris* Mill. or *Olea oleaster* Hoffmg et Link (wild or oleaster olive tree). It is a shrub with thorns and the fruit is usually small.
- *laperrini* Batt. et Trab., which is found in Northern Africa from the Moroccan Atlas Mountains to Libya including the Hoggar Massif and the Tassili of Adjers.
- *ferruginea* Royale or *Olea cuspidata* Vall., Cif., which is found North-West of the Himalayas near Afghanistan.

MODE OF REPRODUCTION

The olive tree is a perennial evergreen. Its dimensions and shape vary with climatic conditions, exposure to the elements, fertility of the soil, and the cultivar grown. Trees growing in the wild exhibit a pyramidal form of growth and can reach a height of 12 to 15 m (Fig. 26.1A). The roots penetrate 50 to 70 cm into the soil and are mainly concentrated directly under the tree. The paniculate inflorescence consists of a long flexible cluster, capable of bearing 4 to 6 secondary branches. The inflorescences are formed in the axils of leaves on the previous year's shoots. The number of flowers per inflorescence will vary from 10 to 40 depending upon the cultivar. The flowers are small, regular and yellowish white in color, consisting of four sepals, four petals, two stamens and two carpels. The calyx has four shallow divisions and is persistent. The corolla to which the petals are attached is three times larger than the calyx and it has four round oval lobes. The two stamens which lie over the corolla have short filaments, and the anthers have two lobes. The ovary is unattached, and has two compartments, each containing two anatropic ovules. The style is short and forked. Olive trees are largely self-pollinated when planted in solid blocks of one cultivar although some spontaneous cross-pollination occurs. For many cultivars fruit set can be increased by cross-pollination with a different cultivar. Yet there are numerous cultivars which show inter-cultivar incompatibility, e.g. Mission x Manzanillo and Barouni x Sevillano. The degree of parthenocarpic seed development is genetically controlled.

The fruit is a fleshy, elliptical drupe with a stone (Fig. 26.1B,C). Its shape varies with the variety but is normally oval-shaped. When ripe, the fruit is brownish-black in color. The endocarp is spindle-shaped and very hard. It is divided into two unequal compartments and contains one seed which has an oily albumen. The epicarp remains firmly attached to the mesocarp (or pulp) and is fleshy when ripe. The epicarp and mesocarp contain the olive oil and form the edible part of the fruit. At maturity the fruit contains 15 to 35% oil, depending upon the cultivar.

The annual development cycle of the olive tree is closely linked to the climatic conditions of the growing area which normally is a Mediterranean type climate (Pansiot and Rebour, 1960; Colbrant and Fabre, in Maillard, 1975). After the winter resting period which lasts from November to February, spring vegetative growth commences and soon thereafter a bud appears in the axil of each leaf. The buds are initially vegetative and can eventually differentiate into flower buds the next growing season depending on growing conditions. As spring temperatures rise and the days become longer, the inflorescences which were formed the same year begin growing and anthesis takes place in May and June. In the July - August period, the endocarp firms up and the fruits continue to grow until they reach full size in late September or October. The length of the maturation period depends upon the cultivar and whether it is harvested for table olives or for oil. Table olives are harvested in the green state for edible purposes. Normally, this picking starts in late September. Oil varieties are not harvested until February of the following year when oil content is maximum. Normally, olives are green before harvesting, but begin to change color at the start of the harvest and turn black when they are fully ripe. Table olives are processed to remove oleaeropea, the bitter principle which makes them otherwise inedible.

Vegetative Propagation

The olive tree can be propagated by cuttings or by grafting seedlings onto root stocks. The propagation methods used vary with the environmental conditions of the country or region in which the crop is grown. Since the olive tree easily develops new roots from its semi-ligneous tissue, cuttings are normally taken from one-year-old branches near the bottom of selected superior trees. In the Mediterranean region these cuttings are normally taken either at the end of the spring period, that is from March to May; and/or at the end of the hot summer period extending from the end of August to the beginning of October.

Cuttings from the base or the middle of the branches can be easily rooted depending on the cultivar. Usually two or three cuttings, 10 to 12 cm long, with 5 to 6 pairs of leaves, are used. The cuttings, in batches of 25 to 50, are dipped into about a 2 cm deep hormone solution (indole butyric acid) for a few seconds and then placed in mist-propagating root trays where they remain for about two months in temperature and humidity- controlled greenhouses. Once the cuttings are well-rooted, they are potted and kept in the greenhouse for an additional 3 to 4 months to induce hardening. At the end of the hardening period, the rooted plants are taken out of the pots and planted in outdoor nursery beds where they will remain for the next 12 to 18 months before being sold. Under intensive management systems the plants might only be kept for 9 to 10 months in the nursery beds before being planted into new olive groves.

The propagation of the olive tree by cuttings is efficient and economical and also reduces the heterogeneity of an olive grove. On the other hand, growers will often graft directly onto trees in the orchard to rapidly change a cultivar and to take advantage of the well developed, large root system of the tree. If one wishes to develop seedling rootstocks this can be accomplished but it is time consuming and expensive. Most olive seeds have very low percent germination and subsequent seedlings grow slowly. At least two additional years will be required to develop a tree from seed as compared to cuttings. Seeds are sown in August or September into boxes or trays at the rate of 2.5 to 3.0 kg of seeds per m^2. The resulting seedlings are transplanted into beds when the seedlings have 6 to 8 leaves. Normally, at this stage, the plants are 13 to 18 months old, and the transplanting takes place between October and March. The following spring the selected cultivar may be grafted on the seedling rootstock. Normally it takes 3 to 4 years to grow an olive tree from a grafted seedling.

BREEDING PROCEDURES

The olive tree is highly heterozygous. Although self-fertilization is the norm in olive groves, cases of self-incompatibility and inter-incompatibility have been noted. The cultivated species is considered to be of alloploid origin with a chromosome number of 2n=46. The successful implementation of a genetic improvement program for olive trees requires a full knowledge of the genetic variability available. However, many of the agronomic and quality characteristics that require improvement are quantitatively inherited. Most of the genetic variability is under the control of additive genes but epistatic effects between different genes are also important (Buiatti and Roselli, 1972). Heritability estimates for the different traits, when available, are important indicators of the difficulties encountered in the selection for a specific trait (Roselli, 1972). Only the heritable part of this variation is available for genetic improvement through plant breeding. In addition to the environmental influences, some phenotypical characteristics cannot be manipulated through crossing and selection since they may be of chimeric origin and not present in the sporogenic tissue.

Some fruit characteristics of the olive tree have high heritabilities (Fanizza, 1982). Research into fruit characteristics suggests that increased fruit weight can be achieved by selecting trees that produce heavy fruit with a small diameter stone. Since much of the genetic variability is additive, the simplest and frequently most effective method of genetic improvement in the olive tree has been that of mass selection. Trees are selected on the basis of their phenotype and cross-pollinations are carried out between selected trees (Fig. 26.2). The offspring from each cross constitute a new population in which superior trees can be identified and cultivars can be developed through phenotypic mass selection of the best trees. Superior individuals identified in the various new populations can also be used as parents to start the next cycle of mass selection.

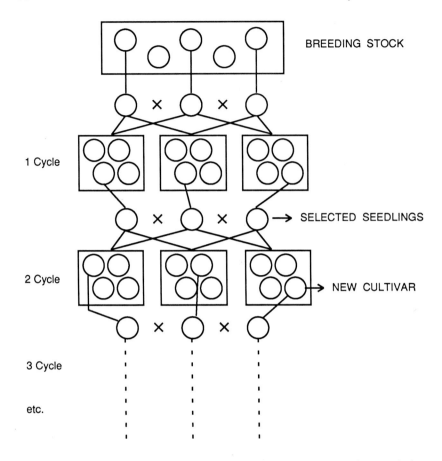

Fig. 26.2 Scheme of breeding by mass selection of parents on phenotypic base.

As with most perennial trees, the main obstacle to the improvement of the olive tree through plant breeding is the large size of the plant and its long juvenile period. The large amount of land required for each plant and the high cost of maintaining a progeny nursery is a major constraint on the evaluation and selection of superior trees since only a limited number of progeny can be assessed from any one cross. The several thousand trees which would be required to increase the probability that the desired combination of quantitatively inherited characters would be present in a single tree cannot be accommodated. The space problem may be alleviated to some extent if dwarf types were developed. Such a dwarf characteristic could be introduced through the use of mutagens (Roselli and Donini, 1982). The long juvenile period of the olive tree also increases the cost of evaluation and reduces the efficiency of the selection process. Although the juvenile period could also be reduced using horticultural techniques, an intensive selection process would have to be utilized as well.

Clonal Selection

The aim of clonal selection is to select the best genotype from among the genetic variability which already exists. Clonal selection consists of identifying single trees with superior phenotypes, vegetatively propagating them, and evaluating the clonal progeny for their agronomic and quality characteristics (Fig. 26.3). The extensive use of clonal selection could be a disadvantage in that the genetic diversity presently available in olive groves could be gradually eroded through the continual cycles of clonal selection resulting in the retention of only a few outstanding individuals. Thus, clonal selection should always be carried out in conjunction with measures to safeguard germplasm resources.

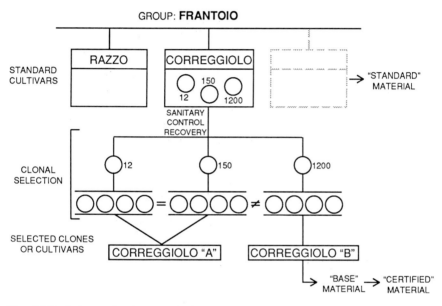

Fig. 26.3 Scheme for the constitution of homogeneous clones ("Base" material) through the clonal selection of a heterogeneous cultivar ("Standard" material).

Induced Mutagenesis

Mutagens have been applied in olive tree breeding to obtain sturdy plants and induce self-compatibility in known cultivars. The mutagenic agents normally used are X-rays or gamma rays at a rate of about 140 to 280 R/h and a total dose of 3000 to 4000 R (30-40 gy). The irradiation is normally applied to single self-rooted plants with the shoot tip being the main target. This tip contains an average of about twenty buds with the center 12 to 14 primordial buds being the most likely to give the highest mutation rates and the least likely to be primary in nature. Following the growth of the irradiated M_1V_1 (the first vegetative "generation" after mutagenic treatment) bud, a section is cut from the plant which is either grafted or self-rooted so that any mutations in the M_1V_2 vegetative generation can be identified. The M_1V_2 can lead to M_1V_3 and later vegetative generations (Fig. 26.4). An alternative propagation method which could reduce or eliminate the incidence of chimeras would be to use in vitro culture of the shoot meristem.

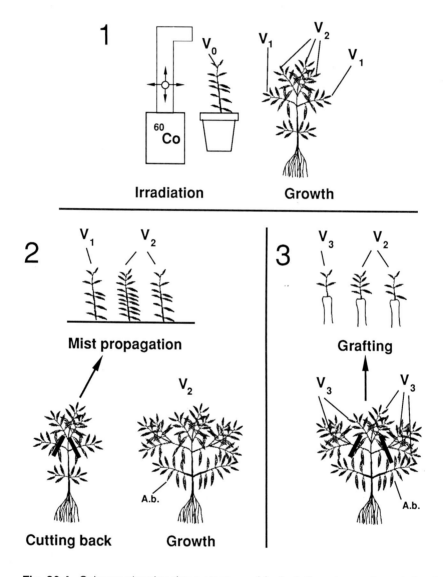

Fig. 26.4 Scheme showing three steps used for isolation of somatic mutation in olive trees.

Although the irradiation and subsequent propagation of the treated material is relatively easy, the identification of true mutants is more difficult. Mutations which affect the base of the plant can be quickly identified visually. For dwarf mutants shoot and internode lengths must be measured, while self-compatible mutants can be detected by bagging the inflorescences. Experience has shown that to establish new, true breeding lines (not chimeras) the material must pass through several vegetative propagation cycles (M_1V_3, M_1V_4 etc.) plus agronomic trials which normally takes some 10 to 12 years.

BREEDING OBJECTIVES

An improvement program requires the development of an ideal ideotype which encompasses all the desired agronomic and quality characteristics sought in an olive tree. One of the first objectives for improvement in olive tree planting stocks is the adaptation and uniformity of the plant material. The cultivars presently grown are heterogeneous and have been derived from individual populations that have been and still are cloned by chance. A good norm for defining the currently grown cultivars usually does not exist and as a result they are perhaps better classified as a group or collection of similar clones (Brickell, 1980). The first step in olive breeding is therefore to identify the various clones making up the cultivar or group and using clonal selection methods to select the best clone.

Some interesting results have been obtained in China using young plants of *O. ferruginae* which are grafted onto *O. europaea* root stocks. Trees from such interspecific grafting are apparently smaller and more productive. Using this technique one could develop olive groves which are homogeneous, well adapted to difficult soil conditions and resistant to certain diseases.

Harvesting of the fruit is the most expensive single management input for growing olives due to the high cost of manpower. Therefore, one of the main breeding objectives is to select for plant characteristics which might facilitate mechanical harvesting. Under favorable growing conditions, trees of the presently cultivated olive cultivars can attain great heights with the branches bending under the weight of the fruit. This type of plant architecture does not lend itself to the use of mechanical vibrating harvesters. The breeding objective is therefore to develop small, straight trees with stiff fruit bearing branches. Such cultivars would also be better adapted to high planting densities. Ionizing radiation has been successfully used to reduce tree size and height as well as vegetative growth (Petruccioli, et al. 1974).

Under the same environmental conditions, some cultivars yield more than others; however, the yield of all cultivars varies widely from year to year. There are many reasons for the wide fluctuation in yield including, failure to fertilize, self-incompatibility, cold requirement for flower induction, ovary failure, variable responses to agronomic practices, and unidentified physiological processes which prevent flowering. A better understanding of fruit set and development requires study in greater detail of the factors affecting olive tree productivity.

The physiology of fruit ripening and abscission has an important bearing on yields obtained. The olive fruit ripens gradually over time and is closely linked to the fruit abscission mechanism and natural fruit abscission from the tree. The abscission mechanism reaches its highest level of expression when the majority of the fruits on a tree have achieved physiological maturity. The practice of harvesting some fruits from a tree prematurely enhances the ripening and abscission of the remaining fruits. However, this can be a hazardous practice since some trees respond more than others and can absciss and drop their fruits prematurely. The breeding objective is therefore to develop cultivars where all the fruits on a tree ripen more or less at the same time and at a period corresponding to the full expression of the abscission mechanism. It would also be advantageous to have certain cultivars or clones which ripen at different intervals during the harvest season so that staggered harvesting and more efficient use of harvest machinery could be achieved. Multiple harvests would also lengthen the marketing period (Fiorino, 1980). In addition, cultivars which ripen early would permit harvesting to be undertaken under more favorable weather conditions (Roselli, 1966). The size of the olive fruit varies greatly and is influenced by many environmental factors as well as genetics and cultural practices. Cultivars used for the production of table olives usually have larger fruits than those used for oil production. However, large-sized fruit is also desirable for oil extraction since large fruits make both manual and mechanical harvesting easier.

The oil content of the olive fruit is important for oil production and varies considerably with the cultivar grown. There are also differences from cultivar to cultivar in the content of saturated and unsaturated fatty acids present in the oil. The fatty acid composition, however, is greatly influenced by the environmental conditions under which the olives develop. As a rule, fruit produced in northern areas has a higher content of saturated fatty acids; whereas oil from southern grown olives tends to have a higher content of unsaturated fatty acids. In the case of green table olives a low oil content is desired in order to improve their preservation characteristics and to reduce the content of sugars so that a good lactic acid fermentation occurs. In table olives the resistance of the fruit to bruising is also important and varies considerably among cultivars as does the flesh to stone ratio. At present the general tendency is to grow dual purpose cultivars so that if there is overproduction of table olives the excess fruit could be allowed to ripen and be sold into the oil market.

Breeding for winter hardiness is important in the northern farming areas. Severe winter weather can cause serious damage to olive groves and it is now known that different cultivars react differently to low winter temperatures. Certain cultivars when used as rootstocks are capable of transferring their frost resistance to the more sensitive grafted cultivars. Many different factors determine the tolerance of olive cultivars to low temperatures, thus the degree of tolerance observed in any one year is only a partial indication of the cultivars true hardiness. In addition, the ability of olive cultivars to recover from low temperature damage is also an important selection criteria. (Scaramuzzi and Andreucci, 1957).

The most damaging insect pests of olives are *Dacus oleae* which attacks only the fruit and *Prays oleae* which attacks not only the fruit but the flowers and leaves as well. All cultivars so far tested are susceptible to the aphid *Saissetia oleae* but to varying degrees. Susceptibility to the diseases *Verticillium dahliae* and *Pseudomonas savastanoi* is widespread. Resistance to *Cycloconium oleaginum* appears to be linked to a very thin septum in the leaf tissue. Thus it should be possible to select for resistance to *C. oleaginum* on this basis. All cultivars tested to date have proved to be sensitive to nematode attack (Morettini, 1954 a,b).

HISTORY OF CULTIVAR DEVELOPMENT

The "domestication" of the *O. europaea* species which resulted in the cultivated olive *O. sativa* is based on vegetative propagations of cuttings, ovules, and grafting from superior clones and has led to the cultivars we know today. The large number of cultivars presently being grown have three different points of origin. A certain proportion of genetic variation in the material has resulted from cross-pollination between cultivated varieties and wild trees. Other cultivars have arisen from empirical selection of superior trees and parents over the centuries of cultivation. Other important clones and cultivars have arisen due to mutations which have occurred over the centuries and selected by man because of their improved yield or quality (Loussert and Brousse, 1978). The taxonomy and/or genetic relationships within the olive tree taxon is extremely complicated because of the large number of named populations or clones which exist in the Mediterranean Basin. The confusion is confounded by giving different names to the same cultivars in various regions or countries.

UTILIZATION OF PRODUCTS

Oil from the olive fruit has been extracted for more than 6000 years by crushing the olives, followed by kneading and pressing of the crushed material. The crushed material is then allowed to settle and the oil is decanted. Today better techniques and modern equipment make it possible to extract a quality oil at a much lower cost. The early extraction methods used millstones and standard presses. These have now given way to mechanical crushers and kneaders as well as to super presses equipped with centrifuges. Oil yield of between 15 to 35% is normally obtained and the amount depends upon the cultivar harvested, the degree of fruit ripeness and the extraction method employed. Olive oils are marketed under different names. For example, virgin olive oil can be extra-fine or semi-fine according to the acidity level of the oil. The virgin olive oil is a natural oil which is obtained using mechanical processes, including pressing, and which is not mixed with oils of a different type or olive oil obtained by any other means.

The term pure olive oil is a mixture of virgin oil and olive oil obtained by refining. Normally when virgin oils have too high an acidity level, they are refined and mixed with olive oil. Each kind of olive oil corresponds to a specific processing technique. A number of cultivars such as green olives "à la Picholine" and Calamata type black olives have lent their name to a particular style of oil preparation.

All the industrial processes involved in preserving green olives are generally divided into three main processing stages or steps; a) soaking the olives in a caustic soda solution to remove their bitterness, b) washing the olives and c) preserving them in brine, with or without fermentation. In the preparation of Mediterranean black olives, the first stage i.e. the removal of bitterness, is omitted. However, black olives like green olives can be preserved in brine as well as a variety of other ways such as in salt, vinegar, oil, etc. The way in which the edible olive is prepared is very much a question of regional preference.

REFERENCES

Brickell, C.D. 1980. International code of nomenclatura for cultivated plants. Regnum Vegetabile 104: 7-32.

Buiatti, M., and Roselli, G. 1979. Variabilita e selezione in piante a propagazione vegetativa. Riv. Ortoflorofrutt. Ital. n. 4-5-6.

Donini, B., and Roselli, G. 1972. Mutazioni indote nell'olivo per irraggiamento di talee autoradicate. Genet. Agrar. 26: 1-2, 149.

Fanizza, F. 1982. Genetic variability and fruit character associations in table olives (*Olea europaea*). Riv. Ortoflorofrutt. Ital. 66: 115-119.

Fiorino, P. 1980. La raccolta meccanica delle olive. Olivicoltura, Elaiotecnica, Olio di Oliva, 1, 22.

Loussert, R., and Brousse, G. 1978. *L'Olivier*. Maisonneuve et Larose, Paris. 465 pp.

Maillard, R. 1975. *L'Olivier*. INVUFLEC, Paris, 146 pp.

Morettini, A. 1954a. Ricerche sull'anatomia delle foglie delle piu note varieta di olivo toscane in relazione alla loro resistenza al Cycloconium oleaginum. Notiziario sulle malattie delle piante, 28 N.S. 7, 1954a.

——. 1954b. Mutazioni gemmarie nell'olivo e loro applicazione per il miglioramento della coltura. Ital. Agric. 12.

Pansiot, F., and Rebour, H. 1960. *Amelioration de la culture de l'olivier*. Et. Agr. FAO, Rome, 50, 252 pp.

Petruccioli, G., Filippucci, B., and Donini, B. 1974. L'impiego della mutagenesi per l'ottenimento di forme nanizzanti nell'olivo. Ann. Ist. Sper. Oliv. 2: 57.

Roselli, G. 1966. Indagine sull'incidenza dell'andamento meteorico sulla raccolta delle olive in Toscana. Atti Acad. Econ. Agr. Georgofili, Suppl. al 142, 53.

——. 1972. Mutazioni spontanee e piante chimeriche nell'olivo. Genet. Agrar. 26: 1-2, 62.

——, and Donini, B. 1982. "Briscola." Nuova cultivar di olivo a sviluppo compatto. Riv. Ortoflorofrutt. Ital. 66: 103-114.

Scaramuzzi, F., and Andreucci, E. 1957. Indagini e osservazioni sui danni provocati dalle minime termiche del febbraio 1956 agli olivi nei vivai di Pescia. Nuovo G. Bot. Ital. (Nuova Ser.) n. 1-2: 19-124.

Chapter 27

Oil Palm

J. P. Gascon, J. M. Noiret and J. Meunier

IMPORTANCE AND DISTRIBUTION

Of all oil-bearing plants, the oil palm (Fig. 27.1) produces the most oil per unit area, with current production amounting to 5 to 7 tonnes of oil per hectare. In 1980, palm oil became the world's second most important vegetable oil after soybean. Production has increased in a spectacular manner, more than doubling during the decade from 1970 to 1980 (Table 27.1). Palm kernels are also an important oil source, with a composition similar to coconut oil.

In 1977, 78% of the palm oil produced came from South-East Asia (Malaysia and Indonesia); 17% from Africa and 5% from South America. The distribution of the planted areas on these three continents is shown in Table 27.2. More recently, Malaysia and Indonesia have accelerated the areas being planted to oil palm. This evolution will result in a distinct increase in palm oil production in the coming years.

Fig. 27.1 Oil Palm. A – Adult oil palm plantation. B – An oil palm crown (tree 21–1) bearing unripe bunches. C – Plantaion of a dwarf variety. D – Young plantlets in a tube for in-vitro mass propagation.

Table 27.1 **World Palm Kernel and Palm Oil Production by Region and Major Producing Countries**

Region or Country	Palm kernels (tonnes)			Palm oil (tonnes)		
	1969-71	1979-81	1985	1969-71	1979-81	1985
World	**1178651**	**1781655**	**2659420**	**1983034**	**5048105**	**7578121**
Africa	**731005**	**724202**	**781570**	**1108647**	**1341362**	**1474900**
Angola	15867	12000	12000	40333	40000	40000
Benin	68652	66667	75000	28349	32000	37000
Cameroon	40737	43773	50000	63400	83667	90000
Cote d'Ivoire	19333	35996	45000	46467	152530	180000
Ghana	36000	30000	30000	19333	21000	25000
Guinea	35000	35000	35000	42600	41333	45000
Nigeria	287100	343333	370000	528333	666667	770000
Sierra Leone	60100	30910	30000	46467	46667	44000
Zaire	99100	68100	75000	232433	167767	150000
N. and C. America	**21464**	**16001**	**15950**	**31037**	**36364**	**46200**
S. America	**249489**	**303711**	**305500**	**46752**	**137285**	**255021**
Colombia	7000	15733	23000	26933	70500	130921
Ecuador	5667	5819	14000	5815	37333	80000
Asia	**177683**	**715922**	**1503000**	**796583**	**3470580**	**5642000**
China	28333	41333	50000	114333	188000	230000
Indonesia	48980	127343	214000	217900	720487	1148000
Malaysia	98996	540587	1210000	457298	2529455	4130000
Thailand	–	4251	20000	–	20221	100000
Europe	**–**	**–**	**–**	**–**	**–**	**–**
Oceania	**10**	**21819**	**53400**	**16**	**62514**	**160000**
Papua New Guinea	10	19229	48800	16	47408	140000
U.S.S.R.	**–**	**–**	**–**	**–**	**–**	**–**

Source: FAO Production Yearbooks 1980 (vol. 34) and 1985 (vol. 39).

Table 27.2 **Development of Oil Palm Plantation Areas in the World (1000 ha) 1960 to 1985**

Region	1960	1970	1980	1985[1]
South East Asia	150	450	1260	2000
Malaysia	55	270	907	1290
Indonesia	104	134	294	600
Africa	40	145	235	260
SouthAmerica	9	46	100	160
TOTAL	358	641	1595	2420

[1] estimated

ORIGIN AND SYSTEMATICS

The oil palm, *Elaeis guineensis* Jacq., (Fig. 27.1) originated in Africa where its natural habitat is in the humid tropics, 15°on either side of the equator. The plant is a monocotyledon of the order Spadiciflorae of the Palmae family, and is a member of the Cocoineae tribe. In addition to the oil palm, the genus *Elaeis* includes two other species of American origin, that of *E. oleifera* (H. B. K.) Cortes. (*E. melanococca*), which is easily crossed with *E. guineensis* in spite of its different origin, and *E. odora* Trail, a less well-known species of secondary importance.

Cytogenetics in the oil palm is hindered by difficulties in observing chromosomes. The chromosome number for both *E. guineensis* and *E. oleifera* is n=16. Normal pairing occurs in both species, while in interspecific F_1 hybrids the pairing is close to normal except for rare unpaired chromosome segments.

MODE OF REPRODUCTION

Vegetative Characters

The oil palm, with its stem or trunk topped by 35 to 60 pinnate leaves and possessing an adventitious root system, is well described by Hartley (1967). The oil palm is one of the larger palm species and has a single stem that can attain a height of 25 to 35 m. The trunk is a mass of vascular bundles distributed within parenchymatous tissue. It grows transversally for 2 to 3 years when young, and then grows longitudinally by 35 to 90 cm each year. The upward growth is in function of the number of leaves produced each year, and the dimensions of nodes and internodes are governed by both genetic and environmental factors. The oil palm has only a single meristem located in a depression at the stem apex but there is a primary stem thickening meristem located below the apical meristem.

On average the leaves are produced at a rate of about two per month in a regular sequence, which is evident in the spiral pattern on the terminal bud. The pinnate leaf is typically about 7 m long and consists of a petiole approximately 150 cm long, and a rachis bearing 250 to 350 leaflets, each of which may be up to 130 cm long. The leaflets are arranged on two lateral planes. Variations in the plane angle as well as the angle of the insertion of the leaves and leaflets determine the general appearance of the tree, and govern, in particular, the penetration of light into the foliage. An inflorescence appears in the axil of each leaf.

The adventitious roots grow from a bole at the base of the stem and number several thousands in the adult palm. Primary roots are about 6 to 10 mm in diameter and 1 to 20 m long, branching into secondaries, tertiaries and quaternaries. The roots spread horizontally or descend at varying angles into the soil.

Flowers and Fruits

An inflorescence is initiated in the axil of each leaf although some may abort at an early age. The inflorescence is enveloped in two inflated bracts or spathes which open shortly before flowering. Initiated at the same time as the leaf (about 33 months before anthesis), the inflorescence bud will become sexually differentiated nine months later (22 to 24 months before anthesis). The process of sexual differentiation is not well understood but it is known to be under genetic control and highly influenced by environment. Favorable conditions induce a higher female sex-ratio. An individual palm will produce, during successive cycles, male and female inflorescences. The length of the male and female cycles vary widely according to genotype and environment. Cycles may sometimes be separated by 1 or 2 hermaphrodite inflorescences, but the pure male and female cycles rarely overlap. In addition, usually only one inflorescence on a tree will be at anthesis at any one time. Thus although the oil palm is a monoecious species, it is considered as strictly allogamous.

The male inflorescence has a peduncle approximately 40 cm long and bears 100 to 300 finger-like spikelets that are 10 to 30 cm long. Each inflorescence produces 10 to 50 g of pollen, i.e. several billion grains. The female inflorescence has about the same number of spikelets as the male, but they are shorter (6 to 15 cm), and bear 5 to 30 flowers which are receptive for 2 to 3 days. After 5.5 to 6 months a fruit bunch, consisting of 1100 to 1500 fruits, is produced (Fig. 27.1B). On an adult tree the bunch may weigh 15 to 20 kg. The number and size of the bunches depends on the age of the tree, the environment and hereditary factors.

The fruit is a sessible drupe which varies in shape and may weigh from 3 to 30 g. At maturity the fruit is reddish-orange to red and consists of the pulp, the shell and the kernel. The pulp or mesocarp is yellowish-orange in color and is rich in oil (40 to 60% of fresh weight). The shell or endocarp consists of black sclerenchyma. Two alleles determine the presence or absence of the shell, and defines the fruit forms *dura* (thick shell), *pisifera* (shell-less), and *tenera* (thin-shelled hybrid). The kernel contains the triploid endosperm and a cylindrical embryo. The dried kernel yields about 50% kernel oil, which is similar in composition to coconut oil, and an oilcake.

Breeding Behavior

The most important characteristics influencing improvement strategy with regard to the oil palm are the size and lifespan of the tree, the type of reproduction, and the duration of an improvement cycle. The lifespan of the oil palm is exceptional. The first palms introduced into Indonesia are now 140 years old and are still producing. This factor facilitates the evaluation of populations and individual trees and is an important aid to the breeder who thus has several generations at his disposal. The duration of one improvement cycle is in the order of twelve years because of the constraints connected with biological features and the development of the plant (Table 27.3).

Table 27.3   Progress Achieved After Two Cycles of Recurrent Reciprocal Selection (RRS) of Oil Palm in the Ivory Coast

Stage	Number of progenies	Total bunch weight (t/ha)	Oil extraction rate(%)	Palm oil (t/ha)	Breeding progress in%
Initial hybrids between ecotypes: 1956	529	15.0	22.0	3.33	100
1st RRS cycle: 1970	74	16.7	23.4	3.93	118
2nd RRS cycle: 1984	14	19.0	24.0	4.55	137

The land area required to evaluate a single progeny is about half a hectare. Normally palms are planted at a density of 143 trees per hectare arranged in a 9 m triangular system.

Genetic Aspects

The long generation time required and the area occupied per tree are major constraints to obtaining genetic information. On the other hand, the length of tree life, abundance of pollen, many seeds per bunch, ease of self- and cross-fertilization and of individual plant observation are advantages which, together with the utilization of specialized techniques, have made it possible to obtain the genetic data for the handling of modern improvement programs.

Genetic Variability

The first observations of the oil palm made in Africa revealed great variation in the shape of fruit, the appearance of the trees and the production of bunches.

The ecotypes, created by the various research centers using local material, display considerable differences. Gascon and de Berchoux (1964) showed that Deli palm (few, large bunches), palms from the Ivory Coast and from Benin (many small bunches) and from Zaire displayed great differences with regard to components of total bunch yield and quality of the bunches. This also applied to the oil content of fruit, characteristics of foliage and growth of the stem. In spite of their narrow genetic base, each of these ecotypes displays considerable variation, i.e. yield variation coefficients of 50% or more are frequent (Hartley, 1967).

Recent exploration has found these wide variations of all characteristics in "natural" populations. However, analyses of the populations in Nigeria show that nearly 80% of overall variation may be caused by differences between individuals, and that effects which can be attributed to location and populations are probably small (Rajanaidu et al. 1981).

Electrophoresis has made a substantial contribution to knowledge of genetic variability. The work carried out by Ghesquiere (1984) on 52 alleles with fifteen loci revealed considerable overall enzymatic polymorphism, allowing preliminary partitioning of genetic variability into two groups; namely, the West and Central Africa palms (to which the Deli palm belongs). A high rate of heterozygosity was shown (up to 0.5 in Angola palms). The distribution of alleles does not appear to be compartmentalized, and allele frequency is the essential factor in variation between populations. Some 75% of the genetic diversity is of the intra-population type.

Monogenically Inherited Traits

A number of simple Mendelian characters, usually involving one major gene, are known in the palm tree and include: coloring of the pericarp, absence of carotene in the mesocarp, existence of supplementary carpels, bonded leaflets, dwarfing, resistance to crown disease, and certain anomalies such as chlorophyll deficiency, vivipary, etc.

The most important feature from the historical and economic point of view is shell thickness, whose heredity was explained in 1941 by Beirnaert and Vanderweyen. In natural palm groves, the most common fruit is of the *dura* type with shells of 2 mm or more in thickness. However, 4 to 6% of trees exhibit *tenera* or thin-shelled fruit having less than 2 mm thickness, and there are other very rare examples which give fruit with no shell at all, the *pisifera* type. Belgian research scientists have shown that *tenera* sh+ sh- is a hybrid of *dura* sh+ sh+ and *pisifera* sh- sh-. Since the *pisifera* variety is usually a sterile female, it is of no interest for production. However, *tenera* fruit bunches contain more oil-bearing pulp than *dura* type plants. The replacement of *dura* by *tenera* in plantations is a rare example of how the use of a single allele has resulted in a 25% yield increase.

Quantitative Traits

Most of the features which are of economic interest are quantitative and display continuous variation. Such characteristics are controlled by numerous genes having additive or dominant effects in varying proportions. Although quantitative traits are difficult to study, recent investigations by several scientists, working with different plant materials and ecologies, point to some general trends.

Narrow sense heritability of bunch or oil characteristics is small or nil (Thomas et al. 1969; Meunier et al. 1970; Van der Vossen, 1974). Genetic variance of these two characteristics is caused above all by the effects of dominance and/or epistasis, and inbreeding affects them considerably (Gascon et al. 1969; Hardon, 1970). The components of the total productivity of bunches, number and average weight, are more heritable than production itself. These two characters display strong negative correlation.

The fact that phenotypic selection for yield is almost impossible has led researchers to investigate physiological components of yield such as Crop Growth Rate (CGR), Leaf Area Ratio (LAR), Bunch Index (BI), and Vegetative Dry Matter Production (VDM) (Hardon et al. 1972). In spite of additive variances which are sometimes significant, these parameters remain difficult to use. However, according to Breure et al. (1982), simultaneous selection of BI and LAR might be effective in view of their correlation and the better heritability of LAR.

As regards the composition of bunches, two characteristics generally possess low heritability; a) the percentage of fruit in the bunch, which is greatly affected by the environment, and particularly by the effectiveness of pollination, and b) the oil content of the pulp. On the other hand, additive variance predominates for the pulp content of the fruit, the quantity of kernel and the average weight of the fruit. These latter characteristics are not independent.

On the other hand, certain important characteristics such as height (Jacquemard et al. 1981), fatty acid composition and iodine value (Wuidart and Gascon, 1975), as well as resistance to vascular wilt disease (Meunier et al. 1979) have a high degree of heritability enabling effective phenotypic selection of the parents. Finally, yield genotype x environmental interactions observed under very different conditions have been unexpectedly insignificant (Gascon et al. 1981; Rosenquist, 1981).

BREEDING PROCEDURES

Before approaching the improvement programs themselves, it is necessary to briefly describe the techniques that have been progressively developed for the observation and evaluation of plant populations.

Methods

All oil palm research centers use more or less standardized methods for the assessment of characters and for artificial fertilization. All the trees are inspected approximately once a week. The ripe bunches are cut and their weight and number recorded. The observation period generally lasts for seven years and covers the start of production, the young tree (3 to 5 years old) and the beginning of the adult stage (6 to 9 years old).

Bunch analysis consists of separating and weighing each of the constituents, i.e. rachis, spikelets, fruit, pulp, shell and kernel. The oil content is determined either by direct extraction using a Soxhlet extractor or by measuring the specific gravity of the mixture obtained by dissolving the oil in orthodichlorobenzene.

As a rule, 40 trees per hybrid combination are analyzed when they are five and six years old to obtain the average extraction rate of a progeny. Evaluation of an individual requires analysis of 16 bunches over a four-year period. The storage and processing of the substantial data are handled by computers, as is the monitoring of the genealogy and pedigree of all the trees.

The artificial fertilization is used for all crosses and is achieved by covering the male and female inflorescences with special bags. This technique was possible only after the development of a reliable process to preserve pollen for up to one year by storing it dry, at a low temperature (-18°C) and under vacuum.

Improvement of Yield

Increase in per hectare oil yield is the main breeding objective but the best breeding methods to achieve this goal are still being discussed. In Malaysia, improvement programs are based on mass selection of individuals and families (Hardon and Thomas, 1968). It is considered that progress can be obtained more easily by exploiting additive genetic variance. Since this variance is small, it is necessary to create new, more variable populations by crossing materials of varied origin (Hardon et al. 1973). In Africa, some research scientists consider that although mass selection is effective for the improvement of characters with higher heritability, it has little effect on yield, whose genetic variance is mainly nonadditive. The choice of parents according to heritable characters must be combined with selection according to progeny testing in order to make the best use of combining ability (Meunier and Gascon, 1972).

This conclusion has led the Institut de Recherches pour les Huiles et Oleagineux (IRHO) to adopt a Recurrent Reciprocal Selection (RRS)scheme in which the initial material is divided into two groups, according to how each group complements the other in terms of yield components (Meunier and Gascon, 1972). Group A may be characterized as having a small number of large bunches while Group B may produce a large number of small bunches. In each group, individuals are chosen for the desired fruit pulp content, vertical growth and oil composition (heritable characters). The selected individuals are crossed with those of the other group in as many combinations as possible.

Progenies obtained are evaluated by comparative trials and the parents which have produced the best progenies are retained and crossed within each group to form the populations for the start of the next cycle. Each group can be enriched by new material obtained by exploration or exchange. (Fig. 27.2).

Some constraints of this scheme are; a) the limited number of parents that can be included in a test, b) the effectiveness of alternate cycles of mass selection and progeny tests for the achievement of steady progress, and c) the narrow choice of parents resulting in inbreeding in the initial populations (Hardon et al. 1973). These disadvantages can easily be overcome by increasing the number of comparative tests and adding to the initial population material obtained from the wild or other base populations.

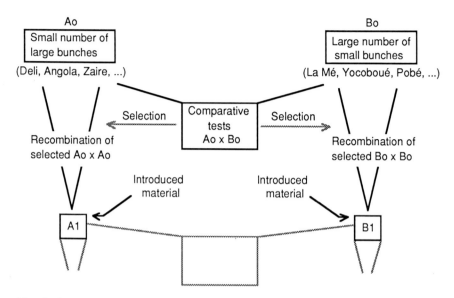

Fig. 27.2   Recurrent Reciprocal Selection scheme employed by the Institut de Recherches de Huiles et Oleagineux.

The great advantage of selection, based on cross performance, is the significant progress obtained in the first cycles (Table 27.3). Planters are supplied with just those few crosses which have proved their superiority in the field. With the perfection of in vitro vegetative multiplication, specific combining ability has also become an important factor in the search for better trees. In practice, however, the management of an improvement program does not appear to be as divergent as might be supposed. All programs attempt to obtain maximum enrichment of base populations, and all programs use progeny tests, at least for *pisifera*, with the only variation being in the relative importance of the phenotype and progeny choices.

The use of early selection tests is important to reduce the duration of the selection cycle and to increase the effectiveness of comparative trials. Vegetative measurements in the nursery have not given significant correlations with yield. However, in 1978 Kouame indicated that the level of heterosis in an oil palm is associated with the plant's mitochondrial activity. Measuring the mitochondrial ADP/O activity, by determining the quantity of oxygen used to phosphorylate a fixed amount of ADP to ATP, and comparing this activity to the bunch production of the corresponding adult trees, Kouame and Noiret (1981) found a close positive correlation of r=0.8 to 0.9. Using this test it is now possible to design early nursery selection tests. The oil palm is the only plant for which such a test is routinely used. Research is being carried out on other early tests, in particular tests of the oil content of the bunch, by studying the enzymes involved in lipogenesis.

Improvement of Other Characters

Vertical growth rate and oil quality are highly heritable and are easily improved by phenotypic selection of parents. A simple iodine value determination of the oil permits preliminary selection of individual palms with a higher level of unsaturated fatty acids (Noiret and Wuidart, 1976). The possibility that unsaturated/saturated ratio in the fruit lipids may be correlated to the ratio found in leaf lipids is under investigation and may lead to a new nursery selection criteria.

Resistance to vascular wilt disease (*Fusarium oxysporum* Schl. f. sp. *elaeidis* Toovey) also has a high heritability. Resistant hybrids are selected through artificial inoculation of progenies in a pre-nursery. Those individuals that survive the pre-nursery inoculation in good health are also used as parents for further improvement (Meunier et al. 1979).

Tolerance to drought is a more complex phenomenon. This is particularly true in a perennial plant in which climatic effects and production in successive years interact and lead to physiological processes that are difficult to evaluate. Genetic control of tolerance to drought exists but it appears to be secondary to such interactions and the environment, as well as stand density, castration, cover, and other cultural practices. The breeding strategy used consists of selecting highly productive plants and discarding the more sensitive material using early physiological stress tests.

Interspecific Hybridization with *Elaeis oleifera*

Although *E. oleifera* (*E. melanococca*) is indigenous to America, it hybridizes easily with *E. guineensis*. This American species is extremely attractive to the breeder because of its low vertical growth rate, its production of excellent quality fluid oil, and as a source of resistance to several serious diseases in oil palms (Meunier, 1975). Thus, *E. oleifera* has been integrated into all oil palm improvement programs. Large collections of wild plants have also been made from its area of natural distribution in the Central America countries of Nicaragua, Costa Rica, and Panama, as well as in the South America countries of Columbia, Brazil and Surinam.

However, F_1 hybrids between *E. oleifera* and *E. guineensis* display partial sterility in male and female flowers which makes direct commercial utilization impossible. This sterility appears to be associated more with gene interaction than with chromosomes pairing. To overcome the sterility problem, backcross and F_2 plants are being evaluated and it may soon be possible to exploit exceptional individuals using in vitro vegetative multiplication.

In Vitro Propagation

The development of oil palm cloning procedures in the 1970s, using in vitro cultivation of tissue, was a major breakthrough in oil palm cultivation (Fig. 27.1D). Using various tissues, research teams in England, France and Malaysia succeeded in obtaining a process of somatic embryogenesis making it possible to obtain millions of identical plantlets from an exceptional tree (Rabechault and Martin, 1976; Corley et al. 1977). From 1980 onwards, several laboratories were set up in the Ivory Coast, Malaysia and Indonesia to expedite the industrial production of plantlets required for 1990 and future plantation programs.

There are many advantages to such multiplication techniques. Since the oil palm is strongly heterozygotic, individual plants in conventional plantations display relatively high variability in numerous characteristics and, in particular, yield. By establishing homogeneous plantations using propagated plantlets from the best trees, a 30% improvement in oil yield seems possible in just the first generation (Corley et al. 1982).

Cloning has opened up new possibilities. The effect of environment can be better assessed and controlled and an outstanding individual progeny within a highly variable cross can be propagated for direct use. Thus, hybrids between exceptional palms with complementary characters such as F_2's from a cross between *E. oleifera* and *E. guineensis* could produce recombined genotypes for plantation use 15 to 20 years ahead of comparable material obtained by sexual propagation.

Uncertainties do remain, particularly with regard to the method of selecting trees for cloning. Thus, the selected clones and their plantlets must first be subjected to a field trial period. The distribution of the best selections about 1990 will mark the beginning of a new stage in the development of the oil palm.

BREEDING OBJECTIVES

All agricultural activity aims at obtaining a better net return per cultivated hectare. Genetic improvement contributes to this objective by breeding for plant characteristics which lead to increased yields and reduced losses, as well as reducing production costs and matching product to market needs.

Increased oil production per hectare has always been, and remains today, the primary aim for oil palm improvement. It is achieved by selecting on the two main oil yield components, bunch yield and extraction rate. Several breeding options are possible. In some situations it may be more efficient to increase the oil content or extraction rate while maintaining the same bunch production. On the other hand, it might be more desirable to produce fewer but larger bunches (to reduce picking cost). Whatever policy is decided, two objectives receive unanimous support; a) higher oil yield, and b) uniformity of production throughout the year. Production uniformity is particularly important in regions with marked seasonal variations. By spreading production over the whole year, factory over-sizing and the resulting underutilization during the small harvest period is avoided.

Other desirable characteristics are a long peduncle to make bunch cutting easier, and homogeneous maturation to reduce fruit fall and loss of oil.

The vertical growth of the trees has a direct effect on the operation costs of a palm grove. Harvesting becomes difficult and expensive when the palms are more than 9 to 10 m high, and impossible when they are more than 14 m. With a generally accepted duration of operation of twenty years, the objective is to develop trees whose height does not rise by more than 65 to 70 cm per year. Slower growth also makes it possible to extend the economic life of plantations (Fig. 27.1C).

Interplant competition is slight or non-existent in young plantings but increases each year as the trees develop. Production of a grove rises steadily at first and then attains a uniform level. However, production may decrease if competition continues to intensify. The competitive ability of a tree will vary from genotype to genotype but the characteristic is not well understood. It is believed that compact trees with decumbent leaves that let the light through and which have a high photosynthesis activity should minimize the competition effect.

The speed with which a palm grove can be brought into production and provide a return to investment is an important breeding consideration. However, the objective is centered more on increasing the productivity of young palms (3 to 5 years old) than to shorten the unproductive phase (2 to 3 years). There appears to be hardly any hope for further shortening of the unproductive phase except if clones are used. However, heavy production in young trees is also associated with vigor and competitiveness in adult trees. Thus a highly productive young tree may contribute to competition and result in a production decline as the grove ages. It is therefore necessary to find a balance between rapid increase in production and a high yield assessed over the total economic lifespan of the grove. Production in the first three years represents only 10 to 15% of the grove's total production.

Palm oil quality is a recent addition to the breeding objectives. The oil consists of equal proportions of saturated fatty acids (palmitic and stearic acids) and unsaturated fatty acids (oleic and linoleic) the proportions of which can be easily modified. The trend in producing countries to use the oil for edible purposes has directed most improvement programs towards increasing the proportion of unsaturated fatty acids for dietetic reasons. The resulting increase in fluidity also makes oil handling and treatment easier. On the other hand, for certain industrial uses an increase in saturated fatty acids such as stearic could be desirable.

Breeding for adaptation to the environment is a general aim which may take several forms, depending on the region concerned. Programs are primarily concerned with resistance to diseases and tolerance to drought. Vascular wilt caused by *Fusarium oxysporum* f. spp. *elaeidis* is a serious disease in Africa where it affects replantation in particular. The selection of resistant crosses is the only economic solution for the control of this disease. In the Far East, several programs are under way to assess the reaction of plant materials to trunk or basal stem rot of palms caused by *Ganoderma* spp., although the incidence of this disease in Africa is less serious than that of vascular wilt.

Tolerance to drought is an important breeding objective since many palm oil producing countries have a marked dry season lasting 2 to 3 months. The palm is also traditionally grown in marginal areas where the annual water deficit can reach 600 mm or more. The search for trees able to produce an economic oil yield without sustaining serious drought damage is a continuing activity in such drought-prone regions.

The uniform and efficient uptake of minerals on a plantation basis is also a desirable objective. However, it is difficult to carry out simultaneous selection for numerous characteristics in a perennial tree such as the oil palm. Such problems may be largely overcome with the introduction and use of vegetative propagation.

HISTORY OF CULTIVAR DEVELOPMENT

The history of oil palm improvement is relatively short. However, such an examination is necessary to understand the different approaches and materials which have resulted in today's selection programs (see Hartley, 1967, for further details).

Early Selection

Although the palm oil originated in Africa, the first plantations were established in the Far East. The palms were all descendants of four trees of unknown origin planted in a botanical garden in Bogor (Indonesia) in 1848. The first selections were made in the early 1920s at the Marihat Baris estate (AVROS = Algemene Vereniging van Rubberplanters ter Oostkust van Sumatra) in Indonesia, and, at the Elmina estate and the Serdang experimental station in Malaysia using seed imported from Indonesia. These were mass selection programs whereby individuals with good production and high quality bunches were selected. The four original trees were all of *dura* type, and an improved *dura* ecotype called Deli resulted. The Deli ecotype is considered to have the best fruit composition available, and as a result this ecotype has served as one of the parents for all of the world's present plantations. New material introduced from Africa in the early years was considered to be disappointing and was discarded. However, some of the African material was used later and now forms the basis of improvement materials in the Far East.

Also in the 1920s, Ringoet and then Beirnaert (1941) in Zaire, realized the value of the *tenera* type fruit. Using the progeny of 10 open-pollinated *tenera* bunches, they determined the heredity of shell thickness and initiated *tenera* type plantations. The program at Yangambi, Zaire, consisted of crossing individual plants which exhibited desirable complementary characteristics. The trees which produced good progeny were used as future parents. Such selection led to the "Yangambi" ecotype which was widely used in later selection programs.

Early work in West Africa was carried out using several locally chosen *tenera* type trees. Such selection led to the development of the Sibiti ecotype in the Congo with the same origin as Yangambi, as well as the Nifor ecotype in Nigeria and La Me ecotype in the Ivory Coast. The Pobe ecotype in Benin (formerly Dahomey) is the only one which originated from a representative sample of a spontaneous palm grove evaluated in 1922.

The Postwar Period

Initially, each organization carried out selection within its local ecotype which frequently had a narrow genetic base. In 1942, IRHO was set up and established research centers in French-speaking African countries including La Me, Pobe and Sibiti in the Ivory Coast, Benin and the Congo. In 1946, IRHO organized an "Experience Internationale" (the International Experiment) and brought into the existing international network the Institut National pour l'Etude Agronomique du Conge Belge (INEAC) at Yangambi and SOCFIN or the Societe Financiere in Malaysia who were working with Deli material. The Experiment called for each center to intercross in all possible combinations what the center considered to be its ten best trees from its ecotype. Pollen was also collected from each of these ten trees and sent to all the other cooperating centers to make cross combinations with other ecotypes. The resulting seeds were exchanged.

Analysis of the experiment carried out mainly in the Ivory Coast indicated that; a) the variation within an ecotype is fairly small but the ecotypes differed considerably in many important characteristics, b) the number and mean weight of bunches are controlled by factors whose effects are generally additive, and c) crosses between different ecotypes gave better results because they tended to complement one another as regards to size and number of bunches (Table 27.4) as well as the elimination of a certain degree of inbreeding within ecotypes. These results together with those concerning heritability of yield led IRHO to adopt reciprocal recurrent selection as the main breeding procedure to improve the oil palm.

Meanwhile, in Zaire INEAC and the West African Institute for Oil Palm Research (WAIFOR) in Nigeria, which had breeding objectives similar to those at IRHO, either had their activities temporarily reduced (WAIFOR) or discontinued (INEAC). In Malaysia the Oil Palm Genetics Laboratory (OPGL) and later the Malaysian Agricultural Research and Development Institute (MARDI) and the Palm Oil Research Institute of Malaysia (PORIM) reorganized their research along distinctly different lines.

Table 27.4   Bunch Yield Improvement Obtained by Crossing Two Complimentary Ecotypes

Ecotype	No. bunches per tree	Mean bunch weight (kg)	Total yield (kg/tree)
Deli ecotype	6.2	14.2	84
La Me ecotype	14.4	7.3	101
Deli x La Me	10.3	11.8	119

Source: Gascon and de Berchoux, 1964

In the years 1960 to 1970, all organizations recognized the narrowness of their genetic base and recommended it be widened by evaluating and collecting in natural populations. In agreement with the International Board for Plant Genetic Resources (IBPGR); IRHO, NIFOR and PORIM carried out a series of exploration operations in the Ivory Coast, Angola, Nigeria, Cameroons and Zaire which led to the establishment of large collections in Malaysia, Indonesia and the Ivory Coast.

SEED AND PLANT MULTIPLICATIONS

The production of selected seed is currently the only source of planting material for plantations. All the seed produced in the world is of the *tenera* type obtained by fertilizing *dura* mother-trees with pollen from *pisifera* trees using artificial fertilization under conditions of strict isolation. A female parent plant can produce 5000 to 15,000 seeds per year. The number of parent plants is adjusted according to plantation requirements. The choice of these parents is periodically re-examined on the basis of the performance of their progenies. Thus, seed production is handled directly by research stations working on the oil palm improvement, and procedures followed will depend on local policies and regulations.

In Malaysia a decree, MS 3.18:1973, specifies the minimal production characteristics of mother-trees despite the preponderant effect of environment on such characteristics. In fact, most Malaysian centers use the Ulu Remis (U.R.) strain of the Deli ecotype as the female parent while the male parents are usually direct or secondary introductions from Zaire. The Zaire source is comprised to a greater or lesser extent of Deli lineage, particularly "Dumpy." Major users of this seed source are large groups, such as Guthrie Research, Harrisons Malaysian Plantations and the Highlands Research Unit which use some 5 million seeds each. United Plantations (1 to 2 million seeds) and above all the Federal Land Development Authority (FELDA) (8 to 10 million seeds) tend to use the method recommended by IRHO which consists of reproducing the best crosses observed during comparative trials. In addition to the material above, these latter organizations have recently introduced *pisifera* from La Me for use in their seed production. Malaysia does not permit the exportation of seed.

In Papua New Guinea, the Dami station (2 million seeds) uses the same type of material as Harrisons Malaysian Plantations and makes an effort to progeny test the parents (Breure et al. 1982).

In Indonesia, large oil palm development projects have given new impetus to research and seed production. Marihat Research Station (30 million seeds) has adopted, in cooperation with IRHO, a system of reproduction of the best performing crosses using a recurrent reciprocal selection method. The material in question arises from crosses between Deli (source: Indonesia) and strains of African *pisifera*, mainly from Zaire (EX5, SP540, L718T, etc.), as well as the Cameroons and the Ivory Coast (Suheimi and Lubis, 1985). In cooperation with IRHO, the SOCFINDO (SOCFIN Indonesia) Station at Bangun Bandar (5 million seeds) also delivers tested crosses of Indonesian Deli with Yangambi, La Me and Nigerian pollinators.

In Africa, the La Me (Ivory Coast, 8 to 10 million seeds), Pobe (Benin, 1.5 million seeds) and Dibamba (Cameroons, 1 million seeds) research stations reproduce fifteen tested crosses, most of which are of the Deli x La Me type (Gascon et al. 1981). These IRHO associates have for many years used the recurrent reciprocal selection system which has already been described. Part of their seed production includes material which is resistant to vascular wilt. The Unilever group plantations supply Deli x Nigeria-Cameroons crosses at Lobe in the Cameroons and Deli x Yangambi seed at Binga in Zaire (1 to 2 million seeds). A proportion of the material is also resistant to vascular wilt. The WAIFOR station in Benin City produces a varying quantity of Deli x Nigeria material which is used by local plantations.

Seed production in South America is relatively limited. In Coto in Costa Rica (5 million seeds), the Compania Bananera de Costa Rica produces hybrids between plants introduced to Honduras about 1926 and parents originating in Zaire but introduced via Malaysia. In Brazil, within the framework of a cooperative program with IRHO, Empresa Brasileira de Pesquisa Agropecuaria (EMBRAPA) has established a large amount of material at the Rio Urubu station near Manaus (potential 6 million seeds).

Thus, some 80 to 100 million seeds are produced annually by about fifteen research stations, enabling the planting or replanting of approximately 300,000 hectares of palm groves each year. The advent of in vitro tissue culture propagation is opening up a new era by producing plant material in the form of cloned plantlets. Full-scale commercial production will only begin in about 1990 after field trials of the clones are complete. A number of laboratories are already operational and ready to start production. Unifield T.C. Ltd. in England and Bakasawit & Co. in Malaysia use the process developed by Unilever. The La Me laboratory in the Ivory Coast, the FELDA laboratory in Malaysia, and the SOCFINDO and Marihat laboratories in Indonesia use the ORSTOM-IRHO method. Most seed-producing bodies have research in progress to prepare for clonal reproduction.

UTILIZATION OF PRODUCTS

One oil palm bunch provides 20 to 24% palm oil and 2 to 3% palm kernel oil. Palm oil, known as "red oil," has always been part of the human diet in West Africa. In the 20th century, use of palm and palm kernel oil has extended world wide.

Palm oil normally has a 50:50 ratio of saturated to unsaturated fatty acids. Thus it consists of a liquid fraction that is clear at 5 to 7°C and a fraction which is solid at that temperature. Because of its tendency to cloud at low temperatures the edible uses of palm oil tend to be restricted to hardened fats such as shortenings, vanaspati, margarines and frying fats. Vanaspati or "vegetable ghee" containing 8 to 10% palm oil is used in India, Pakistan and Iraq. Research is in progress on the utilization of palm oil as a fermentation substrate for the production of proteins and antibiotics. Well known non-food uses are soap and candle manufacture and the tin plate industry. More recently, several countries, particularly Malaysia (PORIM) and Brazil, have shown interest in palm oil as a "fuel." This trend involves the use of palm oil itself or the valorization of its by-products.

Palm kernel oil has a fatty acid make-up similar to that of coconut oil and has a similar use pattern. The same applies to palm kernel cake.

Apart from oil, the fermented sap of the oil palm is used to make wine and alcohol, and the palms themselves are used for fencing and firewood. Unfortunately, these practices are detrimental to producing trees and the maintenance of soil fertility.

REFERENCES

Beirnaert, A., and Vanderweyen, R. 1941. Contribution a l'etude genetique et biomtrique des varietes d'*Elaeis guineensis* Jacq. Publication INEAC. Serie Scientifique n° 27.

Breure, C.J., Konimor, J., and Rosenquist, E.A. 1982. Oil palm selection and seed production at Dami oil palm research station, Papua New Guinea. Oil Palm News 26:2-17.

Corley, R.H.V., Barrett, J.N., and Jones, L.H. 1977. Vegetative propagation of oil palm via tissue culture. Oil Palm News 2: 2-17.

——, Wong, C.Y., and Wooi, K.C. 1982. Early Results from the First Oil Palm Clone Trials, pp. 173-196. *In* E. Pushparajah and P. S. Chew (eds.), *The Oil Palm in Agriculture in the Eighties*. Vol. I. Incorporated Society of Planters (ISP) Kuala Lumpur.

Gascon, J-P., and Berchoux, Ch. de. 1964. Caracteristiques de la production d'*Elaeis guineensis* Jacq. de diverses origines et de leurs croisements. Application a la selection du palmier a huile. Oleagineux 19(2): 75-84.

——, Meunier, J., and Noiret, J-M. 1969. Effets de la consanguinite chez *Elaeis guineensis* Jacq. Oleagineux 24(11): 603-607.

——, Jacquemard, J-C., Houssou, M., Boutin, D., Chaillard, H., and Fondjo, F.K. 1981. Production of selected *Elaeis guineensis* oil palm seeds. Oleagineux 36(10): 475-486.

Ghesquiere, M. 1984. Polymorphisme enzymatique chez le palmier a huile (*Elaeis guineensis* Jacq.) I. Controle genetique de neuf systemes enzymatiques. Oleagineux 39 (12): 561-574.

Hardon, J.J. 1970. Inbreeding in populations of the oil palm (*E. guineensis* Jacq.) and its effect on selection. Oleagineux 25(8-9): 85-90.

——, and Thomas, R.L. 1968. Breeding and selection of the oil palm in Malaya. Oleagineux 23(2): 85-90.

——, Corley, R.H., and Ooi, S.C. 1972. Analysis of growth in the oil palm. II. Estimation of genetic variances of growth parameters and yield of fruit bunches. Euphytica 21: 257-264.

——, Mokhtar, H., and Ooi, S.C. 1973. Oil Palm Breeding: A Review. *In* R. L. Wastie and D. A. Earp (eds.), *Advances in Oil Palm Cultivation.* Incorporated Society of Planters (ISP) Kuala Lumpur.

Hartley, C.W.S. 1967. *The Oil Palm.* Longman, London.

Jacquemard, J-C., Meunier, J., and Bonnot, F. 1981. Genetic study of the reproduction of an *Elaeis guineensis* oil palm cross. Oleagineux 36(7): 343-352.

Kouame, B. 1978. Measurement of mitochondrial activity in the oil palm (*E. guineensis* Jacq.). Demonstration of mitochondrial heterosis and comparison of the mitochondrial activity of several hybrids. Oleagineux 33(6): 267-275.

——, and Noiret, J-M. 1981. A precocious test for productivity in the oil palm (*E. guineensis* Jacq.) by measurement of mitochondrial activities. Oleagineux 36(11): 533-542.

Meunier, J. 1975. Le palmier a huile americain, *Elaeis melanococca.* Oleagineux 30(2): 51-61.

——, and Gascon, J-P. 1972. General schema for oil palm improvement at the IRHO. Oleagineux 27(1): 1-12.

——, ——, and Noiret, J-M. 1970. Heredite des caracteristiques du regime d'*Elaeis guineensis* Jacq. en Cote d'Ivoire. Heritabilite, aptitude a la combinaison. Oleagineux 25 (7): 377-382.

——, Renard, J-L., and Quillec, G. 1979. Heredity of resistance to *Fusarium* wilt in the oil palm *Elaeis guineensis* Jacq. Oleagineux 34(12): 555-561.

Noiret, J-M., and Wuidart, W. 1976. Possibilities of improving the fatty acid composition of palm oil. Results and prospects. Oleagineux 31(11): 465-474.

Rabechault, H., and Martin, J-P. 1976. Multiplication vegetative du palmier a huile (*Elaeis guineensis* Jacq.) a l'aide de cultures de tissus foliaires. C.R. Acad. Sc. Paris 283 serie D, 1735-37.

Rajanaidu, N., Lawrence, M.J., and Ooi, S.C. 1981. Variation in Nigerian Oil Palm Germplasm and its Relevance to Oil Palm Breeding. *In* E. Pushparajah and P. S. Chew (eds.), *The Oil Palm in Agriculture in the Eighties.* Incorporated Society of Planters (ISP) Kuala Lumpur.

Rosenquist, E.A. 1981. Performances of Identical Oil Palm Progenies in Contrasting Environment. *In* E. Pushparajah and P. S. Chew (eds.), *The Oil Palm in Agriculture in the Eighties.* Incorporated Society of Planters (ISP) Kuala Lumpur.

Suheimi, S., and Lubis, A.U. 1985. DxP planting materials of Pusat Penelitian Marihat. Symposium on Oil Palm. Medan Indonesia. March.

Thomas, R.L., Watson, I., and Hardon, J.J. 1969. Inheritance of some components of yield in the Deli dura of oil palm. Euphytica 18: 92-100.

Van der Vossen, H.A.M. 1974. Towards More Efficient Selection for Oil Yield in the Oil Palm, *Elaeis guineensis* Jacqin. Doc. Thesis. Wageningen, Netherlands. 108pp.

Wuidart, W., and Gascon, J-P. 1975. Study of the composition of *Elaeis guineensis* Jacq. oil. Possibilities for improvement. Oleagineux 30(10): 401-408.

Chapter 28

Coconut

K. Satyabalan

IMPORTANCE AND DISTRIBUTION

The coconut palm is grown on some 8.9 million hectares in over eighty countries. The palm is cultivated for the nut it produces (Fig. 28.1 A and C). The dried kernel of the nuts, called copra, contains 65 to 72% oil which is used in a wide range of edible and industrial purposes.

Coconut oil ranks sixth in world vegetable oil production and fourth in international edible oil trade. About 35 million tonnes of coconuts are produced world wide resulting in some 5 million tonnes of copra. Asia produces about 84% of the total world output (Table 28.1). The three main producing countries are the Philippines, Indonesia and India. Oceania, Latin America and Africa together account for about 15% of the world total. The main coconut products traded internationally are coconut oil, copra and the copra cake which remains after oil extraction. World exports of copra and coconut oil amount to some 1.5 million tonnes of oil equivalent. This represents approximately 10 to 11% of the world's total export trade in oils and fats.

Fig. 28.1 Coconut. A – Dwarf x tall hybrid palm tree. B – An inflorescence with female flowers (FF) and male flowers (MF). C – A longitudinal section of a fruit with husk (H), embryo (E), shell (S), testa (T), meat (M) and water (W).

Table 28.1   World Coconut and Copra Production by Region and Major
Producing Countries

Region or Country	Production ('000 tonnes)			Copra production ('000 tonnes)		
	1969-71	1979-81	1985	1969-71	1979-81	1985
World	**27614**	**33233**	**34661**	**3842**	**4510**	**4507**
Africa	**1451**	**1545**	**1567**	**150**	**177**	**198**
Cote d'Ivoire	49	156	300	6	22	44
Ghana	257	160	108	10	7	7
Mozambique	400	453	400	59	72	65
Tanznaia	310	310	320	31	29	29
N. & C. America	**1356**	**1413**	**1203**	**202**	**187**	**166**
Jamaica	150	176	120	17	7	8
Mexico	815	851	655	146	149	120
S. America	**612**	**601**	**687**	**29**	**37**	**28**
Brazil	331	254	284	2	2	3
Venezuela	147	160	164	16	18	9
Asia	**22054**	**27320**	**28752**	**3163**	**3773**	**3754**
Burma	67	95	100	-	-	-
India	4472	4204	4550	359	374	380
Indonesia	5892	9761	10754	753	1049	1160
Malaysia	1039	1625	1721	191	210	216
Philippines	7601	8654	7793	1582	1897	1700
Sri Lanka	1963	1692	2100	209	137	180
Thailand	713	781	1121	31	38	35
Viet Nam	100	329	400	20	55	64
Europe	**-**	**-**	**-**	**-**	**-**	**-**
Oceania	**2142**	**2354**	**2452**	**297**	**335**	**361**
Fiji	260	217	240	30	22	25
F.R. Polynesia	178	132	110	24	17	14
Pacific Is.	101	211	192	12	29	25
Papua New Guinea	741	804	850	131	145	160
Samoa	193	207	200	15	21	23
Solomon Is.	184	234	311	25	32	45
Vanuatu	247	302	326	35	43	47

Source: FAO Production Yearbooks 1980 (vol. 34) and 1985 (vol. 39).

Coconuts are important to the rural economy of producing countries, both as the provider of basic subsistence foods and as a source of useful, nonedible products. It is the only source of livelihood for millions of small farmers in developing countries like Philippines, Indonesia, Malaysia, Sri Lanka and India. In several developing countries copra, coconut oil and copra cake are important sources of export earnings and their contribution to their national economy is significant.

The coconut palm is grown throughout the tropical world between latitudes 22° N and S not only along the sea coasts but in interior areas as well. Child (1974) has indicated the geographical limits of the coconut palm. In Asia it is rarely found to the west of India. In India the palm grows as far north as Lucknow (lat. 26° 24') but does not fruit there. In Africa the northern limits are Cape Verde (15° N) on the west coast and Djibouti (11° 30' N) on the east, while the southern limits are Mossamedes (15° S) on the west coast and the Zambesi river (19° S) on the east. In the Pacific the palm is found as far north as the Bonin Islands (26° N) and as far south as Pitcairn Island (25° S). In South America the palm is found in Brazil at a latitude of 27° S and in North America in Florida and Bahamas at a latitude of 25° N. On the west coast of Central America it is not seen, but in the north it is found in Mexico. The main coconut growing areas are located in Asia, Oceania, West Indies, Central and South America and West and East Africa. Fremond et al. (1966) have summarized the climatic conditions required for raising an economically worthwhile crop.

ORIGIN AND SYSTEMATICS

The antiquity of the coconut palm (*Cocos nucifera* L.), its wide distribution and the absence of wild or spontaneous populations make it difficult to identify the center or centers of origin. One theory is that the coconut palm originated in the northern end of the Andes in tropical America, a second suggests the coast of Central America. A third theory presumes its place of origin to be somewhere in South Asia or the Pacific. It is thought that dispersal from the center(s) of origin occurred by ocean currents and/or explorers. It is in South East Asia that the coconut has attained its highest development in terms of variability, number of local names and uses. Based on the available facts, the weight of evidence supports the theory of a center of origin somewhere in South East Asia. The smaller fruited coconuts identified in the New Hebrides Islands and the fossil palms in New Zealand, led Harries (1978) to suggest that the center of origin was in the region of the submerged continental fragment of the Lord Howe Rise-Norfolk Ridge complex near Australia.

The coconut palm belongs to the palm family *Palmae*, an important member of the monocotyledonous group of angiosperms. It is included in the tribe *Cocoideae* which comprises more than twenty genera. The genus *Cocos* formerly included thirty species, mostly from Central and South America. Beccari (1916) regarded the genus *Cocos* as monotypic containing *Cocos nucifera* as the sole species and assigned the other *Cocos* species to several new genera. Tomlinson (1961) examined the anatomy of some of the genera formerly included in *Cocos* and retained only *Cocos nucifera* in the genus *Cocos*. The various geographical races of the coconut palm fall into two groups; the tall *typica,* which is predominantly cross-pollinated, and the dwarf *nana,* which is predominantly self-pollinated. The cross-pollinated nature of the tall *typica* has resulted in considerable variability, forming diverse panmictic populations. The genetic complexity of the present day populations with pan tropical distribution is not amenable to normal taxonomic methods of classification. Harries (1978) has described a classification system in which the varieties are identified by the degree of introgression, based mainly on fruit component analysis.

MODE OF REPRODUCTION

At present, the coconut palm is propagated only through seed, though recent successful attempts to produce plantlets through tissue culture methods have been reported (Raju et al. 1984). Once the palm begins to bear fruit, it continues to bear the year round throughout its life. The lifespan of a coconut palm can extend for sixty years or more under favorable conditions. Leaves are produced continuously at intervals of about one month. An inflorescence is produced in each new leaf axil and since the coconut palm produces inflorescences throughout the year, one matured bunch of coconuts can be harvested every month.

The coconut inflorescence is a spadix which develops within a double sheath called the spathe. When mature, the spadix breaks through the spathe and opens out its 30 to 35 flower-bearing branches or spikelets (Fig. 28.1B). The coconut palm is monoecious and unisexual. The male flowers, 8,000 to 10,000 per spadix, occur from the tips of the spikelets downwards, while the less numerous female flowers are situated at the base of the spikelets (Fig. 28.1 B). In the tall, cross-pollinated types of palms, there is an interval of 3 to 4 days between the male and female phases. The male phase, measured from the opening of the first to the shedding of the last male flower, lasts about three weeks following the opening of the spathe. The beginning of the female phase is indicated by the secretion of nectar at the three inter-secretory canals, the splitting of the stigmatic end into three lobes and a slight change in color of the stigmatic end. The receptivity period of the female flowers varies with the season but usually lasts 4 to 7 days depending on the number of female flowers. Both wind and insects are considered to be important pollinators in coconut. The floral biology of the coconut palm has been described in detail by Menon and Pandalai (1958).

About 25 to 40% of the female flowers produced develop into mature coconuts. After fertilization the female flowers take about 11 to 12 months to mature into nuts. The fruit of the coconut is botanically known as a fiberous drupe and popularly as the nut. The constituents of the nut are illustrated in Figure 28.1C.

For propagation, open-pollinated, well-matured seednuts are collected from high-yielding selected mother palms. Selection is based on desirable phenotypic characters associated with high yield of nuts and copra output. The seednuts begin to germinate about 2 to 3 months after planting. When the seedlings are about 10 to 12 months old, a rigorous selection is made based on characteristics such as early germination, good girth at collar and a large number of leaves. These indicators identify vigorous seedlings and are correlated with high yield. Early transplanting of seedlings to the field is recommended to avoid transplanting shock and delayed establishment.

BREEDING PROCEDURES

The tall variety of coconut is extensively cultivated for the high yield and quality of its copra, oil and fiber. It is late bearing, requiring 5 to 8 years for initial flowering. It is tall growing, hardy, and long-lived (60 to 80 years or even longer). The dwarf variety of coconut is a delicate palm of short stature. It is precocious and bears fruit in the third or fourth year after planting. It is irregular in coconut production and bears small-sized nuts. The copra obtained from these nuts is leathery and not commercially important. The dwarf palms occur in three color types: green, yellow and red or orange. They are mainly planted for their ornamental nature and their fruits used for drinking purposes. The life span of the dwarf variety is about 35 to 40 years. The following breeding methods are adopted mainly for the improvement of the tall variety of coconut.

Collection, Conservation and Evaluation of Germplasm

Tall and dwarf cultivars of coconut, grown in different regions of the world, are collected and their performance evaluated under local conditions. Promising cultivars are multiplied by *inter se* pollination for multi-location trials. The selected cultivar is evaluated for its yield of nuts and copra output. Its reaction to diseases of unknown origin, and serious pests which threaten coconut production are also observed. Parents are also evaluated in crosses for the production of prolific hybrids. This improvement method is time consuming, but it aids in the conservation of existing germplasm now facing the danger of genetic erosion due to the rapid introduction of superior genotypes.

Selection

The coconut palm is presently propagated only through its seed. Maternal line selection, where only the female is evaluated, has been the traditional practice. However under such a system the male parent is unknown and the female is highly heterozygous. Thus the selected female parent may not transmit its high productivity to its progeny. Indeed, even though rigorous selection standards have been applied to the female parents and their seedlings over many years, little progress in population improvement has been demonstrated.

Progress through selection based on the phenotype of a single maternal plant can be limited by large and undetermined environmental effects which give low heritability values for complex traits such as yield. In addition, the high nut yield of an individual plant may result from a combination of both additive and non-additive gene effects (Harland, 1957). Maternal line selection could not be expected to be highly effective if non-additive gene effects are important in this sexually propagated species. Liyanage and Sakai (1960) reported that the heritability of nut yield is approximately 0.5. Greater response to selection would be expected for traits such as copra yield and weight per husked nut, for which higher heritability values of 0.67 and 0.95 respectively have been observed.

Growth characteristics like collar girth and leaf production in seedlings are genetically correlated with the yield of adult palms (Satyabalan and Mathew, 1983). Hence attempts have been made to identify genetically superior palms in nurseries by comparing a large number of open-pollinated progenies from different families. Highly significant differences in growth rate and vigor of seedlings between families have been found in comparison with limited variation within families. Such findings should lead to a more rapid advance in coconut improvement in the years to come.

Hybridization

In coconut, the manifestation of hybrid vigor was observed in growth as well as yield characteristics. Inter-varietal hybrids obtained between the tall and dwarf varieties are more promising than intra-varietal hybrids. The inter-varietal hybrids with the tall variety as the female parent and the dwarf variety as the pollen parent are precocious, high yielding, and produce nuts with copra quality, equal to the tall parent. There was, however, considerable variation in the yield of hybrids derived from different matings, indicating the need for selection of suitable parents for the production of useful hybrids. The production of a large number of inter-varietal hybrids by artificial pollination is discouraged by several factors; a) the absence of suitable markers to identify the hybrids, b) the inability of the hybrids to perform well except under favorable management conditions and, c) the considerable labor and expenditure involved in the production of hybrids.

The reciprocal hybrid with the yellow or orange dwarf variety as the female parent (Fig. 28.1A) are more promising and superior in yield of nuts and copra outturn. Hybrids can be easily identified in the nursery by the color marker and the vigor of the seedlings when compared to the yellow or orange seedlings resulting from the self or sib pollination of the maternal parent. For controlled pollination, the inflorescence of the selected female parent is emasculated a few days after opening, and the female flowers are bagged to prevent the entry of foreign pollen. In the tall variety, the female flowers become receptive about three weeks after the opening of the inflorescence, while in the dwarf variety they become receptive 7 to 10 days earlier. When there is exudation of nectar from the stigmatic pores, pollen collected from male flowers of the selected pollen parent is dusted on the stigmatic end of the female flower. The inflorescence is kept covered until all the female flowers are pollinated. The bag covering is removed after a week to enable the pollinated flowers to develop into nuts under normal conditions. Thick cloth or polyethylene bags may be used for covering the inflorescence, depending on weather conditions.

For mass production of hybrids under controlled conditions, isolated seed gardens are established wherein selected dwarf and tall palms are planted in alternate rows or in certain ratios. When all the palms are in flower, the dwarf palms are emasculated and left to be pollinated by pollen from the tall palms. Pollen from selected tall type parents can also be dusted onto isolated, emasculated dwarf plants.

BREEDING OBJECTIVES

The objective of coconut breeding programs in all producing countries is the development of improved planting stock which will increase nut, copra and oil production. As the economic tall palm variety is late bearing, a common aim of all the coconut breeders is to produce a variety or a hybrid which is precocious and at the same time resulting in higher yields of nuts, copra and oil per unit area than the local cultivar. In countries where serious diseases of unknown etiology occur, like lethal yellowing in Jamaica, cadang cadang in the Philippines and root wilt in India, breeding programs seek to identify disease-resistant breeding material. Similarly, in countries where coconut production is affected by hurricanes, cyclones and drought, efforts are made to select suitable varieties or hybrids which can withstand these natural calamities. Harries (1979) has given a brief account of the general aims of coconut palm breeding programs worldwide and the specific goals of breeders from some coconut growing countries.

HISTORY OF CULTIVAR DEVELOPMENT

The long generation time of the palm makes coconut breeding a work of generations. The heterogenous nature of the palm, the difficulties in its clonal propagation, the long period of experimentation necessary to obtain results and the large area required for well laid out trials are other factors responsible for the slow progress in coconut breeding work.

A brief description of coconut breeding work in some important coconut-growing countries follows. In Sri Lanka, the local tall female and local green dwarf male (*typica* x *nana* form *pumilla* - CRIC 65) hybrids as well as the San

Ramon (Philippines) x *nana* form *pumilla* hybrids have shown great promise. The tall x tall (*typica* x *typica* - CRIC 60) hybrid, though late flowering, is capable of producing 15,000 nuts per hectare per annum and is suitable for all areas where the crop is now cultivated (Manthriratna, 1978).

In the Philippines, the dwarf x tall hybrids, Catigan x Bago-Oshiro and Tacunan x Bago-Oshiro, showed a total copra yield of 2.5 t/ha and 1.7 tonnes respectively over 2.5 years, while the local tall Bago-Oshiro (control) was barely at the productive stage, producing a mere 0.23 tonnes. Mass production of these hybrids by assisted pollination has been undertaken to allow regional testing (Santos, 1982).

In Malaysia, early results indicate that hybrids Malayan Dwarf x Malayan Tall, Malayan Dwarf x Rennel Tall and Malayan Dwarf x West African Tall are superior to Malayan Tall in earliness of bearing and yield (Chan, 1979). In Indonesia, studies show that hybrids with the local Nias Yellow Dwarf as the female parent and the local Tenga Tall, Bali Tall and Palu Tall as male parents are early flowering and produce nuts with a high copra content. Testing of Dwarf x Tall hybrids is being conducted in six locations where environmental conditions vary from ideal to marginal for coconut (Luntungan, 1982). In Papua, New Guinea, hybrids under trial include those with Malayan Red Dwarf as the female parent and Rennel, Malaysian and Solomon Talls as male parents; a natural hybrid of Malayan Red Dwarf with Gazelle Tall (Papua New Guinea); and the introduced Malayan Yellow Dwarf x West African Tall from the Ivory Coast. The tall varieties under trial include Rennel, Markham, Kar Kar and Gazelle. Among the hybrids, Malayan Red Dwarf x Rennel Tall was the highest yielding, with a yield equivalent to 3.1 t/ha dry copra (Brook, 1982). In Jamaica, the hybrid Maypan (Malayan Dwarf x Panama Tall) is found to be fairly resistant to the lethal yellowing disease of coconut (Harries, 1974). In the Ivory Coast, of 10 dwarf x tall hybrids studied, Port Bouet 121 (Malayan Yellow Dwarf x West African Tall) was always the highest yielding (Nuce de Lamothe et al. 1980). This hybrid has been introduced in some countries to study its performance under different environmental conditions.

In India, evaluation trials of exotic and indigenous cultivars have indicated that certain cultivars like San Ramon (Philippines), Zanzibar Tall (East Africa), Guam Tall (Pacific) and Laccadive Ordinary (Laccadive Islands) are superior to the local West Coast Tall. Among the hybrids tested, the combination of the local Chowghat Dwarf Orange as female parent and local West Coast Tall as male parent is more promising than the reciprocal combination. Investigations to identify the best combiners and to obtain a high percentage of hybrids is in progress (Satyabalan, 1982).

UTILIZATION OF PRODUCTS

Coconut is essentially an oil crop though every part of the palm is useful to mankind in some way. The oil is extracted by crushing the copra in rotary mills, expellers and hydraulic presses. Coconut oil has a high saponification value, a low iodine number, and is used extensively for edible and industrial purposes. Coconut oil is used in the margarine, biscuit and cooking oil industries, and also in the production of toilet articles such as hair oil, shaving creams, shampoos and cosmetics. The major industrial use of coconut oil is in soap manufacturing by saponification. The resulting glycerol is used mainly in the pharmaceutical industry and in nitroglycerine manufacture for explosives. Coconut oil is also used in the production of plasticizers, the manufacture of safety glass, and synthetic resins as well as rubber substitutes and detergents. The oil can also be used as a lubricant and fuel. Production of petrol, heavy oil and kerosene oil substitutes is possible from coconut oil. The cake obtained after oil extraction can be used as fertilizer for field crops or fed to cattle, poultry or young growing swine.

The meat of the ripe coconut is used in cooking, the preparation of sweetmeats and for household oil production. The milk or cream obtained from gratings of the meat is used in the preparation of delicacies and also as a substitute for cow's milk. Coconut syrup and coconut honey, which is an excellent substitute for real honey, are obtained from coconut milk. Extraction of edible quality protein, oil and flour from fresh coconut meats are found to be feasible by different processes. Desiccated coconut, which is the dried shredded coconut meat, is used in the confectionery and food industries. The liquid or coconut water in the tender nut, is a refreshing drink, is often recommended as a medicine in cases of gastroenteritis where it is considered a substitute for saline glucose. Coconut water is also the basic ingredient of Nato De Coco, a delicious Philippino food, as well as coconut vinegar, coconut sauce and coconut lemonade. Industrially coconut water can also be used as a rubber coagulant in the production of high quality rubber. Sweet toddy, obtained by tapping the unopened inflorescence of the palm, is an excellent beverage and palm sugar or jaggery is obtained by boiling and evaporating fresh toddy. An alcoholic drink, arrack is obtained by distillation of fermented toddy. On storage, continued fermentation converts the alcohol into acetic acid or vinegar.

The hard shells of coconut are used in the manufacture of shell charcoal, activated carbon and shell flour. Shell charcoal is used as a refining agent, both as a deodorizer and as a decolorizer. Activated carbon is used for purifying, refining and bleaching of volatile oils and chemical solutions and also as an absorbent of gases. Coconut shell flour is used extensively as a compound filler for synthetic resin glues and as a filler in thermoplastics. It gives a smooth and lustrous finish to moulded articles and improves their resistance to moisture and heat. The fibrous husk of coconut yields a fiber known commercially as coir which is used in making mats, mattings, ropes, cordage, nets and bags as well as hardboard and rubberized coir products. Coir dust is used as an insulating material as it has a low thermal conductivity.

The stem of the palm, after immersion in saline water which increases its durability, is used for the construction of houses and cattle sheds and in the manufacture of particle board. The plaited coconut leaves are used for thatching houses, fencing and for making baskets. Thampan (1981) has described in detail the food and commercial products obtained from the palm.

REFERENCES

Beccari, O. 1916. Note on Palmae. *In* J. F. Rock, *Palmyra Island with a Description of its Flora*. Coll. Hawaii Bull. 4: 44-48.

Brook, R.M. 1982. The hybrid coconut project in Papua New Guinea-its past, present and future. Indian Coconut J. 12(12): 3-8.

Chan, E. 1979. Growth and early yield performance of Malayan Dwarf x Tall coconut hybrids on the coastal clays of Peninsular Malaysia. Oleagineux 34: 65-70.

Child, R. 1974. *Coconuts*. 2nd Ed. Longman, London.

Fremond, Y., Ziller, R., and Nuce de Lamothe, M. de. 1966. *The Coconut Palm*. International Potash Institute. Berne, Switzerland.

Harland, S.C. 1957. The Improvement of Coconut Palm by Breeding and Selection. Bull. No. 15. Coconut Research Institute, Ceylon.

Harries, H.C. 1974. The performance of F_1 hybrid coconuts in Jamaica. J. Plant. Crops 2: 15-20.

——.1978. The evolution, dissemination and classification of *Cocos nucifera* L. Bot. Rev. 44: 265-320.

——. 1979. Targets for Coconut Breeding Programmes, pp. 1-11. Fifth Session of the FAO Technical Working Party on Coconut Production, Protection and Processing. Manilla, Philippines. 3-8 December 1979. (AGP: CNP/79/19).

Liyanage, D.V., and Sakai, K.I. 1960. Heritabilities of certain yield characters of coconut palm. J. Genet. 57: 245-257.

Luntungan, H.T. 1982. Progress Report on Coconut Breeding in Indonesia, pp. 2-3. Yearly Progress Report on Coconut Research and Development 1981. Food and Agriculture Organization of the United Nations, Rome.

Manthriratna, M.A.P.P. 1978. Intra-specific hybridization of the coconut palm (*Cocos nucifera* L.) in Sri Lanka. Philipp. J. Coconut Stud. 3(3): 29-38.

Menon, K.P.V., and Pandalai, K.M. 1958. *The Coconut Palm - A Monograph*. Indian Central Coconut Committee, Ernakulam.

Nuce de Lamothe, M. de, Wuidart, W., and Rognon, F. 1980. Review of 12 years of genetic research on coconut in Ivory Coast. Oleagineux 35: 131-140.

Raju, C.R., Prakash Kumar, P., Chandramohan, M., and Iyer, R.D. 1984. Coconut plantlets from leaf tissue cultures. J. Plant. Crops 12: 75-78.

Santos, G.A. 1982. Progress Report on Coconut Breeding Research at the Philippine Coconut Authority, pp. 8-9. Yearly Progress Report on Coconut Research and Development 1981. Food and Agriculture Organization of the United Nations, Rome.

Satyabalan, K. 1982. The present status of coconut breeding in India. J. Plant. Crops 10: 67-80.

——, and Mathew, J. 1983. Identification of Prepotent Palms in West Coast Tall Coconuts Based on the Early Stages of Growth of the Progeny in the Nursery, pp. 15-22. *In* N. M. Nayar (ed.), *Coconut Research and Development*. Wiley Eastern Ltd., New Delhi.

Thampan, P.K. 1981. *Handbook on Coconut Palm*. Oxford and IBH Publishing Co., New Delhi.

Tomlinson, P.B. 1961. *Anatomy of the Monocotyledons* II. *Palmae*. Clarendon Press, Oxford.

Chapter 29

Neotropical Oil Palms

M. J. Balick

INTRODUCTION

Preceding chapters have discussed cultivated plants domesticated over many years of selection and breeding. The New World oleaginous palms are not cultivated, but rather harvested by the local populace. They occur in the vast belts of tropical forest and other types of native vegetation, particularly in the Amazon Valley. Thus, sections of this chapter, which would otherwise be devoted to breeding and history of cultivation are modified to reflect the potential of domestication and characteristics of wild germplasm advantageous to this process. The harvest of palm products from the wild cannot be expected to continue indefinitely. In some areas and species it involves a destructive process which eliminates the resource upon harvest. Trees too tall to climb might be cut down to collect the fruit and the stem may then be cut open to attract egg laying insects. When the eggs hatch, the resulting larvae are harvested as an edible protein source. Far more serious is the fact that the environments in which these wild oil palms grow are being destroyed at a rapid rate for "development," either for mechanized agriculture, pasture lands, or subsistence farms. Indeed, if these wild palms are to be of service to humankind in the future, then only a decade or two of opportunity remains for their collection, study, and safeguarding of germplasm. Dozens of genera of Neotropical palms, such as *Orbignya* (Fig. 29.1), yield oil-rich fruits; due to space constraints, this chapter considers two in some detail, and mentions a number of others.

Fig. 29.1 The fruits of *Orbignya phalerata* or Babassu form on large panicles in clusters of 100-200.

There is more than just passing academic interest in studying the potential use of Neotropical palms in agriculture. Palms can exploit many of the marginal habitats available to the bulk of the rural tropical population. While mechanized agriculture is developed on the best land, poor farmers must often cultivate the leftover land areas of secondary quality, such as those subject to seasonal inundation. Certain palm species grow, even thrive under such conditions and provide good use for the land. As perennial crops, palms form permanent or semipermanent stands which help to conserve and even rebuild the forest structure and its natural ecosystem. Palm fruits are rich in protein as well as oil, and this is a commodity lacking in the diet of many tropical-dwelling people. Many of the palms are multi-use species, providing food, fiber, shelter, fuel, medicine and other important products in addition to oil for the commercial or subsistence agriculturist. All things considered, it is very worthwhile to include palms in agricultural systems, especially in agroforestry.

GENUS *ORBIGNYA*

Importance and Distribution

In relative terms, the exploitation of *Orbignya* palms, especially in the dry areas of northeastern Brazil, comprises by far the largest such enterprise involving native Neotropical oil palms. It is estimated that perhaps 450,000 families, centered in the Brazilian state of Maranhão, base part of their economic activity on harvesting *Orbignya* or "Babassu" as it is called in Brazil (May et al. 1985). This activity represents the world's largest oilseed industry that is completely dependent on a wild plant. The palms are distributed over a vast area in Brazil (Fig. 29.2) and a portion of northeastern Bolivia. However, economic activity is concentrated in three states: Maranhão, Piauí and Goiás. In 1980, 2,621,000 tonnes of fruit was collected in Maranhão (73% of total collection in three states), 693,000 tonnes in Goiás (19% of total) and 286,000 tonnes in Piauí (8% of total). Minor amounts of fruit were collected in other states but these represented only 2% of total collection (Pick et al. 1985).

Of the fruit harvested, approximately 7% of total weight is kernel, accounting for some 250,000 to 300,000 tonnes of kernel produced per year. Kernels are extracted by hand from the fruits, which is why the industry is so labor-intensive. Individual fruits are put on top of an upturned axe head, secured by hand and hit with a wooden stake to crack them open. Endocarp fragments are then variously split by striking with the stake and individual kernels extracted. From 1 to 8 kernels are found in each fruit, although the usual range is 3 to 6. Great effort is made to crack the fruits in such a manner as to leave the kernels unbroken, as exposure to the air results in rancidity. Although no exact figures are available, it is estimated that 100,000 to 120,000 tonnes of babassu oil are produced each year in Brazil. Babassu oil is similar to coconut oil in physical and chemical composition, with about 44% lauric acid.

Fig. 29.2   Distribution of *Orbignya* in Brazil.
From May et al. 1985.

Systematics

According to Glassman (1977) there are about eighteen species of *Orbignya*, distributed from Mexico through Central America, across much of northern South America to Bolivia and central Brazil. Current research on the systematics of the group has shown that the genus comprises fewer species. The most economically important species is *Orbignya phalerata* Mart., the babassu palm (Fig. 29.1), which is also referred to in the literature as *Orbignya speciosa, O. martiana, O. barbosiana* and by other epithets. Field studies indicate that the palm found in Bolivia is identical to that of northeastern Brazil. Since the earliest description is from Bolivia, that name takes priority (see Anderson et al. 1985 for a discussion of this question). Another species, *O. oleifera* Burret, found in Pirapora in the State of Minas Gerais, produces about five times more fruit each with more kernels (ca 13% vs. 7% in *O. phalerata*) than the common babassu palm. This species has great potential for future utilization. *Orbignya* species, as previously mentioned, are also found in Mexico and Central America (*O. cohune* (Mart.) Dahlgren and *O. guacuyule* (Lieb. ex Mart.) Hernandez x.), Columbia (*O. cuatrecasana* Dugand), Peru (*O. pixuna* Barbosa Rodrigues) and elsewhere. Most of these are valued for their oil-and protein-rich kernels and are harvested for local use. Other palms that have importance for utilization are the hybrid groups within *Orbignya* as well as those crosses found between *Orbignya* and other genera such as *Attalea* and *Maximiliana*. All this diversity is being studied in a multinational effort by the Brazilian National Center for Genetic Resources (CENARGEN/EMBRAPA), State Center for Environmental Research in Teresina, Piauí (UEPAE-Teresina), Institute of Economic Botany of the New York Botanical Garden (IEB/NYBG) as well as other collaborators in a number of Latin American countries. This effort is funded by the USA and Brazilian governments and private foundations.

Mode of Propagation

Babassu is an aggressive species which invades cleared lands and establishes by a specialized system of germination and early growth. The seed germinates and immediately pushes the apical meristem underground, in a system known as cryptogeal germination. The apical meristem stays below ground as the palm develops. Any attempt to weed out the palms by cutting or burning fails as the subterranean meristem continues to produce leaves. One to seven seedlings arise from each fruit, depending on the number of kernels present. Basic research on tissue culture propagation is being carried out at CENARGEN/EMBRAPA, with the ultimate aim of mass propagating unusually productive clones.

Improvement

Two approaches can be taken to fully exploit babassu's bounty. Existing populations can be made more productive through improvements in cultural practices and replanting higher-yielding varieties within present stands. The effects of fertilizer, irrigation, stand thinning, intercropping, mulching and other variables upon fruit yield are being tested in Piauí. Alternatively, plantations of high-yielding varieties could be established within and outside babassu's present production areas. Hypothetical yields of oil, charcoal and meal from managed stands of babassu appear highly economic (Table 29.1) (Pick et al. 1985). Although these purely hypothetical yields need to be verified under plantation conditions, genetically superior material from *O. oleifera* might in fact result in even greater yields and returns.

Table 29.1   Hypothetical Production from Managed and Unmanaged Babassu Stands

| Trees/ha | Fruit per tree, kg | Fruit kg/ha | Product output/ha/year in kg | | | Ann. value[a] per ha |
			Oil	Meal	Charcoal	
Unmanaged[b] stands	20	2,000	80	60	400	US$ 135
100	70	7,000	280	210	1,400	US$ 470
120	100	12,000	480	360	2,400	US$ 810

[a]In final product prices prevailing in the first trimester of 1984 (oil, US $1200/tonne; cake, US $100/tonne; and charcoal, US$ 80/tonne).
[b]Unmanaged stands is the current practice.

Utilization

Babassu is a multi-use species. At the subsistence level, all parts of the plant are used, and in fact the palms are so important that in times of economic instability or drought millions of people depend upon this species for survival. The leaves are used for fiber, fuel, construction material, medicine, and in agriculture. The stems are used for construction, food (palmito, salt, animal feed), and mulch (May et al. 1985). The kernels provide oil and protein-rich meal, the endocarp is made into high-energy, low-polluting charcoal, and the mesocarp into a starchy meal. At the industrial level two forms of utilization are recognized, a very simple crushing technology and a high technology operation known as "integral processing." This simple technology produces a number of products which as a percentage of the whole fruit includes starch (13.8%), fertilizer (9.2%), primary combustion material (11%), charcoal (18.6%), coke (14.7%), oil-soap (4.2%) and feedcake (8.4%) (Anderson and Anderson, 1983). The balance is unusable residue. Integral processing involves a series of systems designed to yield a wealth of products from the entire fruit. The commodities, as a percentage of fruit weight, vary depending on the choices made in the factory, but a list of obtainable products is as follows: ethanol, fertilizer, animal ration, reactivated charcoal, coke, combustible gasses, acetates (acetic acid, acetone), methanol, tar (pitch, phenol, creosol, benzol), edible oil (margarine), soap, and glycerine. While the technology exists to obtain these products from babassu fruit, there are few examples of operational factories other than on an experimental level. For a number of reasons, large scale integral processing projects using babassu have not been successful. Pick et al. (1985) deals with this aspect in detail.

OENOCARPUS-JESSENIA COMPLEX

Importance and Distribution

The *Oenocarpus-Jessenia* complex of palms yield an oil physically and chemically identical to olive oil. The palms are distributed in Costa Rica, Panama and over the northern half of South America. They thrive on waterlogged or seasonally inundated sites, such as along river banks, as well as in upland *terra firme* areas where they grow in combination with primary forest to an altitude of about 1000 m. In wet sites this group forms "monospecific" stands, and can survive in standing water. Distribution of one of the important species, *Jessenia bataua* (Mart.) Burret, is shown in Figure 29.3. Inhabitants of the areas where this palm complex is found have always utilized its products. The fruit is of great

Fig. 29.3 Distribution of two subspecies of *Jessenia bataua*.

importance, both for the oil-rich mesocarp as well as for a beverage obtained by soaking the fruit in water. The protein found in the mesocarp of *Jessenia bataua* fruit is a highly nutritious food with a biological value comparable to animal meat or human milk (Balick and Gershoff, 1981).

Systematics

Balick (1980, 1986) maintained two genera in this complex, *Oenocarpus* and *Jessenia*. Following this taxonomic system, *Oenocarpus* comprises eight species (*Oenocarpus distichus, O. discolor, O. tarampabo, O. bacaba, O. macrocalyx, O. mapora, O. minor* and *O. circumtextus*). Four subspecies are recognized: *O. mapora* subsp. *mapora, O. mapora* subsp. *dryanderae, O. minor* subsp. *minor* and *O. minor* subsp. *intermedius*. The creation of subspecies reflects a conclusion, based on intensive field studies, that two previously existing species (*O. dryanderae* and *O. intermedius*) are not worthy of species status and differ only slightly from other valid species. *Jessenia* is felt to comprise one species, *Jessenia bataua*, divided into two subspecies, *J. bataua* subsp. *bataua* and *J. bataua* subsp. *oligocarpa*; this latter subspecies is confined to the northern edge of South America and in Trinidad.

The palms in this complex are both solitary and caespitose in habit, as massive trees and diminutive understory components, and with leaves either spirally arranged on the stem or two-ranked (distichous). This diversity offers a great deal of material for the genetic manipulations necessary to provide improved plants for cultivation.

Mode of Propagation

At present, the only method of propagation is by seed. The Indians soak *Oenocarpus* and *Jessenia* fruits in warm water to soften the mesocarp, making it easy to remove and process into beverage or oil. The seeds are then discarded, either in the surrounding forests or within the habitation site. This soaking process actually stimulates germination and hastens early growth. Studying a former habitation site about fifteen years after abandonment, one can often observe a large population of *Oenocarpus* and *Jessenia* palms. One of the objectives of the research at IEB/NYBG is the development of tissue culture techniques to propagate superior clones.

Improvement

The palms in this complex have never been cultivated, and thus little is known of their agronomic requirements. In the primary forest, once the tree attains a substantial stature, fruit is born in panicles 5 to 7 m above ground. In open areas which receive ample light and nutrients fruit panicles begin to form between ground level to 1 m up the trunk (Fig. 29.4). The bearing of the fruit at the tree base permits easy harvest and extends the useful life of the tree. It is expected that this natural trait would be maintained in the plantation environment.

Fig. 29.4 Formation of *Jessenia bataua* panicles at a low height, when the palm is grown in an open area. Note that the scars of the first panicles are at about 2m from ground level.

Another important phenomenon observed in the wild is the formation of double-seeded fruit, containing much more mesocarp (and thus more oil) than in the single-seeded fruit. Some trees develop up to 7% double fruits, however the factors controlling this trait are not known. Hybrids between *Oenocarpus* and *Jessenia* have been observed in the forests of Venezuela and Colombia, and the resultant fruits contained a small aborted seed, with a high percentage of mesocarp. These hybrid trees would be of great value in a plantation setting if a technique for cloning the hybrids could be developed. The ideal morphotype for a plantation tree would be a diminutive, caespitose individual with large panicles, large fruit and aborted embryos. Table 29.2 illustrates the range of species in this complex, their distribution and potential value in breeding.

Table 29.2   Agronomic Potential of Palms in the _Oenocarpus-Jessenia_ Complex

Species	Range	Habit	Fruit shape and size	Productivity
Oenocarpus distichus	Brazil	solitary, tall (10-20 m); 2-ranked leaves	± globose; 1.8-2.1 cm long	high
O. discolor	Brazil	solitary, medium (8 m); 2-ranked leaves	unknown	unknown
O. tarampabo	Brazil Bolivia	solitary, medium (8-9 m); 2-ranked leaves	subglobose; ca 1.5 cm diameter	unknown
O. bacaba	Amazon and Orinoco Valley	solitary, tall (8-20 m); spirally arranged leaves	globose; 1.6-2.1 cm long	high
O. macrocalyx	Brazil	solitary (?); tall (30 m); spirally arranged leaves (?)	ellipsoid acute; 1.3-1.7 cm long	medium
O. mapora	Costa Rica Panama and much of northern half of lowland South America	caespitose or solitary short-medium (3-16 m); spirally arranged leaves	ellipsoid to sub-ovoid; 1.8-2.9 cm long	high
O. minor	Brazil	caespitose or solitary short-medium (4-10cm); spirally arranged leaves	globose-ovoid to ellipsoid 1.6-2.3 cm long	low-medium
O. circumtextus	Colombia	solitary (?); short (3-6 m); spirally arranged leaves	oblong-cylindrical 1.7 cm long	unknown
Jessenia bataua	Panama, Trinidad and northern half of South America	solitary; tall (14-25 m); spirally arranged leaves	ovoid-ellipsoid, 2.5-4.0 cm long	high

Utilization

Aside from oil and beverage, the palms provide a wealth of products to the indigenous inhabitants of the Amazon and Orinoco valleys. The protein-rich fruit also serves as an animal feed. Spine-like fibers that develop along the immature trunk and in the leaf sheaths of *Jessenia bataua* are used as blowgun darts, or as kindling for fires and torches. The leaves make an excellent thatch and are woven into pack baskets, wall dividers, mats, animal pens and other important items. The stem is felled to attract and culture weevil larvae prized as food. The wood from some species is used to construct houses. The seedlings are used medicinally and in ritual baths to banish evil spirits.

At the industrial level, a small oilseed industry developed in Brazil around the time of the Second World War when olive oil supplies were cut off from the USA. At its peak in 1944, 214 tonnes of "pataua" oil, as it was called, was exported from Brazil, primarily to the USA for soap manufacture. Unfortunately, the harvest utilized destructive methods substantially reducing the resource base of this palm complex. While there are still huge monospecific pataua stands in Colombia, Brazil, Ecuador, Peru, Venezuela and elsewhere, it is felt that future utilization efforts must be through organized plantations. An experimental pilot plant at Centro "Las Gaviotas," of Colombia, proved the feasibility of mechanical extraction of pataua oil (previous to this all oil was extracted by hand in a simple basket press). The press, developed with the aid of the Dutch Government, uses a modified Stork press similar to that used to process African palm oil. This processing system is quite simple and could be erected near any plantation of *Oenocarpus-Jessenia* palms to be developed.

OTHER GENERA

Of the approximately eighty-one genera and 1147 species of palms found in the New World, a number are used as sources of oil. Utilization ranges from that by subsistence farmers for personal needs to exploiting species for domestic national use and for export. Seven genera of New World palms having potential for greater use (Table 29.3).

A cursory survey of the Neotropical oil palms may not reflect the current importance and future potential of these trees for economic utilization. In South America, millions of people utilize the species on a daily basis, and a significant number depend upon palms for their livelihood or even survival. Products from Brazilian stands of wild palms generate a cash value of about $100 million per year and probably several times that value if their use at the subsistence level is included. Considering the diversity of products, adaptability to marginal environments and perennial nature, this family is of great promise for cultivation throughout the tropics where not only fats and oils but protein, wax, fuel, fiber, medicine and construction materials are desperately needed. Unfortunately, the resource may be destroyed before it can be researched and conserved for full and future utilization.

Table 29.3 Characteristics and Potential of Seven Additional New World Oil Palms

Genus	Number of species	Kernel oil	Mesocarp oil	Native range	Ecology	Uses
Acrocomia	ca 29	Yes	Yes	West Indies, Central America, Northern South America	Dry & moist areas	Oil, food, fuel
Astrocaryum	ca 41	Yes	Yes	Mostly Central America, Amazon and Orinoco Valley	Moist, well drained sites to seasonally inundated areas along river banks	Fruits, oil, palmito, fiber
Bactris	One major economic species *B.gasipaes*	Yes	Yes	Cultivated in the Neotropics	Moist, well-drained sites	Fruits, oil, protein meal, palmito, handcrafts
Manicaria	4	Yes	No	Central America, Amazon and Orinoco Valley	Wet swampy sites, along river banks with seasonal flooding	Fruits, oil, fiber, thatch starch from trunk
Mauritia	3	No	Yes	Northern South America and Trinidad	Moist swampy areas, areas along river banks	Fruits, oil, fiber, cordage thatch, starch from trunk
Maximiliana	1	Yes	Yes	Northern South America	Well drained, moist and drier sites in primary forest and open areas	Fruit, oil, thatch
Scheelea	ca 44	Yes	No	Central and South America and West Indies	Moist and dry areas, open fields, pastures	Oil, thatch fuel

REFERENCES

Anderson, A.B., and Anderson, E.S. 1983. People and the palm forest. Final Report to the USDA Forest Service, Consortium for the Study of Man's Relationship with the Global Environment. Univ. Florida, Gainesville.

——, Balick, M.J., and Pinheiro, C.U.B. 1985. O Que é Babaçu. From Special Palm Symposium presented at the 36th Congresso Nacional de Botanica, Curitiba, Paraná, Brazil. To be published as a symposium volume.

Balick, M.J. 1980. The Biology and Economics of the *Oenocarpus-Jessenia* (Palmae) Complex. Ph.D. Dissertation, Department of Biology, Harvard University.

——. 1986. Systematics and economic botany of the *Oenocarpus-Jessenia* (Palmae) complex. Adv. Econ. Bot. 3:1-140.

——, and Gershoff, S.N. 1981. Nutritional evaluation of the *Jessenia bataua* palm: source of high quality protein and oil from Tropical America. Econ. Bot. 35(3): 261-271.

Glassman, S.F. 1977. Preliminary taxonomic studies in the palm genus *Orbignya* Mart. Phytologia 36(2): 89-115.

May, P.H., Anderson, A.B., Balick, M.J., and Frazão, J.M.F. 1985. Subsistence benefits from the Babassu palm (*Orbignya martiana*). Econ. Bot. 39(2): 113-129.

Pick, P.J., Frazão, J.M.F., Mason, W.P., May, P.H., and Milfont, W. Jr. 1985. Babassu (*Orbignya* spp.): Gradual disappearance vs. slow metamorphosis to integrated agribusiness. Report, New York Botanical Garden Institute of Economic Botany. 56 pp., January.

Chapter 30

New Annual Oil Crops

F. Hirsinger

INTRODUCTION

Commercialization of novel oil bearing plants is a difficult task. Frequently the new crop is not well suited to local agronomic practices or the residue remaining after oil extraction has little or no value. Other plants may produce valuable oils but in quantities either too small or too erratic to make extraction economically viable. Nevertheless plant selection and experimentation can sometimes overcome the plants' initial shortcomings and lead to the development of a new oil crop.

Interest in new oil crops resulted from a research project by the chemists of the United States Department of Agriculture at the Northern Regional Research Center in Peoria, Illinois (Wolff and Jones, 1958) in which the seed oil of some 8000 plant species was chemically analyzed (Princen, 1983). These studies confirmed that the type of oil and fat deposited in plant seeds varied widely, both within and between plant species. Indeed the wide range of fatty acid compositions tolerated in seed storage oils within a single species suggests that the oil composition of the seed is of little consequence to the plant, provided the oil's energy is available for germination and growth (Downey, 1987). A sample of complex chemical structures contained in potential new oil sources is given in Table 30.1.

Fig. 30.1   A - Field experiment with *Euphorbia lathyris* . Ebelsbach, West Germany, 1986. B - Maturing seeds of *E. lathyris* . C - Flower and seed morphology of *Cuphea wrightii* . A zygomorphic (bilateral) symmetry of the flower (left) is characteristic for all *Cuphea* species, normally consisting of a long calyx tube (8 mm in length) and six petals, the two dorsal ones more than twice as long as the four ventral petals. About two weeks after pollination the three seeds have increased in size (about 2.5 x 1 mm; length x width) and are turned together with the placenta through the calyx tube, maturing outside (right). D - Harvesting experiment with *C. wrightii* at Davis, Calif. 1983. A cotton picker, modified for sucking up the seeds from the plant with vacuum overcomes two main wild plant-characteristics of *Cuphea* : seed indehiscence and indeterminate growth. E - Flowering plant of *Crambe abyssinica* . F- A commercial production field of meadowfoam (*Limnanthes alba*). Corvallis, Oreg. 1984.

Table 30.1 Minor Species with Oils Containing a High Content of a Specific Fatty Acid

Genus and species	Fatty acid of interest	Fatty acid carbon number and structure
Cuphea cyanea	caprylic acid	
Cuphea leptopoda	capric acid	
Cuphea laminuligera	lauric acid	
Cuphea aequipetala	myristic acid	
Coriandrum sativum	petroselinic acid	
Euphorbia lathyris	oleic acid	
Euphorbia lagascae	vernolic acid	
Crepis alpina	crepenynic acid	
Dimorphotheca pluvialis	dimorphecolic acid	
Centranthus macrosiphon	α-elaeostearic acid	
Calendula officinalis	calendic acid	
Impatiens balsamina	α-parinaric acid	
Limnanthes alba	cis-5-eicosenoic acid	
Lesquerella fendleri	lesquerolic acid	
Crambe abyssinica	erucic acid	

Although the chemical composition of seed oils and fats can now be quickly and efficiently determined it is much more difficult and time consuming to evaluate the crop's environmental adaptation. Even though a plant may be regionally adapted, long term breeding programs are almost always needed to bring about the domestication process. Modifications needed to adapt wild plants to successful commercial production usually involve plant characteristics such as seed retention, uniform flowering, pattern and habit of growth, resistance to insects and diseases as well as the elimination of toxic byproducts. Since the development of an improved variety of a well established crop normally requires 8 to 10 years it is evident that the development of agronomically acceptable new crops could take significantly longer. In addition to the challenge of domesticating the new crop, the breeder also faces the difficulty of establishing minimum oil and meal quality goals for a largely untried market.

Support for new crop development is usually strong in times of agricultural surpluses since producers are willing to experiment with something new, provided there is a possibility of opening up an additional market outlet for a raw agricultural product. Similarly, primary processors of agricultural produce are usually more willing to experiment with a new product that may utilize idle processing capacity.

Five new annual oil crops with potential for exploration will be examined in this chapter. None of these crops has yet reached major commercial importance but if the market interest in their unique oil composition can be sustained, any or all could be commercialized.

CUPHEA

Importance and Chemical Properties

Agronomic research with *Cuphea* did not begin until the mid 1970s (Hirsinger, 1980a). The species are of interest because the seed oil contains medium chain saturated fatty acids (Wilson et al. 1960) with oil contents ranging between 25 and 43% (Hirsinger, 1980a).

None of the species are ready for commercialization since they are not yet competitive with other sources of medium chain fatty acids such as coconut or palm kernel oil. However, as an annual crop, which could be adapted to southern European countries and the midwestern USA or other similar locations, *Cuphea* has the potential to compete with the perennial tropical palms and its oil characteristics are of superior quality due to higher lauric or capric fatty acid contents. Primary experiments indicate that no toxic byproducts are present in *Cuphea* oil or meal (B. Kleimann, personal communication). Therefore *Cuphea* oil could be utilized in the same areas of nutrition and oleochemistry where coconut and palm kernel oil are now employed, such as the production of soaps, detergents, emulsifiers, surfactants, lubricants, cosmetics, etc. (comp. Henkel KGaA, 1982).

Origin and Systematics

The genus *Cuphea* of the Lythraceae family is widely distributed in Central (Mexico) and South America (Brazil). *Cuphea ignea* A.DC. is a well known ornamental. It is also known as the cigarflower or fire cracker because of its red calyx tube (Fig. 30.1C). Other genera of the family that attracted economic attention are *Woodfordia*, the leaves of which are used for the dyeing agent Henna, and *Lagerstroemia*, a perennial ornamental (crape myrtle). In the latest monograph of the Lythraceae family by Koehne (1903), *Cuphea* and *Pleurophora* are placed as close relatives of *Lythrum*. Chemotaxonomic research indicates that the formation of seed lipids in *Cuphea* is correlated with increased floral specialization. Less developed species tend to form longer-chained fatty acids i.e. linoleic acid, (18:2) whereas more highly developed species tend to form shorter-chained fatty acids like capric (10:0) and caprylic acid (8:0) (Graham et al. 1981).

Mode of Reproduction

The relatively high temperatures (18 to 24 °C) required for *Cuphea* seed germination tend to limit the crop's area of adaptation. *Cuphea* species may be either cross- or self-pollinated. The mode of pollination is correlated with the size of petals. Small petaled species like, *C. wrightii* A. Gray, are self-pollinating whereas large petaled species such as *C. leptopoda* Hemsl. are cross-pollinated. Emasculation is usually performed 1 to 2 days before anthesis by removing the calyx tube, where the eleven stamina are inserted internally (Fig. 30.1C) Pollinations are made 2 to 4 days later.

All *Cuphea* species display the wild plant characteristic of seed dehiscence. Seeds will fall from the calyx tube if they are struck by rain or by strong physical action. On the other hand strong winds are usually not sufficient to cause seed shattering. This seed shattering characteristic prevents the use of the normal combine harvesting methods. However it has been shown that *Cuphea* can be mechanically harvested by vacuuming the seeds from the plants (Fig. 30.1D; Hirsinger, 1985) which also allows multiple harvests of the same field. Vacuum harvesting overcomes the problem of uneven seed ripening due to the plants' indeterminate growth pattern. This non destructive multiple harvesting technique resulted in seed yields of approximately 1 t/ha at Davis, California. This was significantly higher than yields obtained with other harvest methods.

Breeding Goals

Cuphea can be improved by selection in existing germplasm, by hybridization and mutation breeding techniques. In a pilot experiment with the fast growing species *C. aperta* Koehne it was shown that mutation breeding is an efficient way of changing wild plant characteristics of *Cuphea*. In this experiment fasciated mutants with determinate growth patterns were selected as well as mutants that were non-pubescent and even indehiscent (Hirsinger, 1980b).

Four *Cuphea* species of interest vary considerably in both, fatty acid composition and agronomic characteristics (Table 30.2). All four species require the modification or removal of one or more wild traits to make them suitable for commercial cultivation. Sticky glandular hairs characteristic of *C. leptopoda* can be a major problem although in *C. lutea* Rose and Koehne, *C. laminuligera* Koehne, and *C. wrightii* such hairs can be tolerated because they are not as sticky (Hirsinger and Knowles, 1984). Plant height needs to be increased in *C. wrightii* and seed dehiscence is of course a problem in all the *Cuphea* species. However, shattering is of less importance in *C. wrightii* and *C. laminuligera* which produce relatively small seeds that are not shattered as readily as those of *C. lutea* and *C. leptopoda*.

Table 30.2   Some Agronomic and Quality Characteristics of Four *Cuphea* Species

Cuphea Species	Plant height (cm)	Seed weight g/1000	Fatty acid Composition in %			Mode of pollination
			C10:0	C12:0	C14:0	
C. wrightii	60	1.6	30	54	11	Self
C. lutea	105	2.5	30	38	5	Self
C. laminuligera	90	2.1	17	63	10	Cross
C. leptopoda	110	3.7	87	2	—	Cross

History of Cultivars and Species

No cultivars of *Cuphea* have yet been produced and research is still focused on the selection of the best adapted species. *C. lanceolata* Ait. was the first species to be tested in plot experiments in West Germany. An induced non-glabrous line was selected which, however, did not yield as well as the glabrous line. Of the other capric acid species *C. leptopoda* was found to be highest yielding. In 1984 a non-glabrous line was selected in *C. leptopoda*. One line, 651, was selected from nine *C. wrightii* germplasm collections to be best adapted to mechanical harvesting. In field experiments in western Oregon *C. lutea* was chosen because of its larger seeds and higher yield potential as well as its higher lauric acid content as compared with *C. wrightii* and *C. laminuligera* (Hirsinger and Knowles, 1984).

EUPHORBIA

Importance, Utilization, Distribution

Euphorbia lathyris L. (caper spurge) is considered to have potential for the production of industrial hydrocarbons for use as an energy source (Calvin, 1980; Ayerbe et al. 1984a and b). The use of *Euphorbia* as an oil crop is comparatively new. Interest in this crop results from its high oil content of ca. 50% of which oleic acid makes up 80 to 90%. Because of its high oleic acid content the oil has a higher value than today's most common sources of oleic acid such as lard and tallow. The normal method of obtaining oleic acid from tallow is the physical hydrophylization process. For economical reasons the oleic acid content of such oils can not be raised above 70%. With *Euphorbia* oil, however, an oil with up to 90% oleic acid is produced, thus yielding an almost pure chemical. The oil could find direct application in areas where oleic acid is presently used, such as the production of soaps, detergents, lubricants, paints, cosmetics, etc. It is also possible that the high yield of *Euphorbia* oil might allow its utilization as a diesel fuel substitute.

E. lathyris originated in the Mediterranean area, from where it spread throughout Europe and was later introduced to the new world. In the Middle Ages the seed was widely used as a lamp oil and had some importance as an officinal herb.

Systematics and Mode of Reproduction

E. lathyris can be grown either as a winter or spring crop (Fig. 30.1A). However, *Euphorbia* requires a long growing period for seed set thus the development of winter-hardy forms could be beneficial. *Euphorbia* is self-compatible, but plants are frequently visited by insects which carry pollen from plant to plant. Emasculation of *Euphorbia* is complicated by the fact that a milky sap is excreted after the stamens have been removed which can cover the pistil and prevent pollination. For controlled crosses, techniques will have to be developed to overcome both the problem of emasculation and outcrossing. Other related Euphorbiaceae crops of commercial interest are castor (*Ricinus communis* L.), manioc (*Manihot esculenta* Crantz) and the rubber tree (*Hevea brasiliensis* H.B.K.)

Breeding Goals

Breeding work with *Euphorbia* has mainly been done throughout mass selection in wild populations. Because of potential for high rates of outcrossing it is important to isolate plants as early as possible. In *Euphorbia* shattering of the seed has been a serious problem. At full maturity seed pods of the wild species open with an audible snap shattering the seed. Pod shattering results from a differential shrinkage of the pericarp. One line has been selected for shattering resistance (Fig. 30.1B). Other traits that need to be improved are canopy establishment and winter hardiness, as well as early maturity and determinant growth. There is also a need for cultivars free of the cocarcinogenic milky sap, which can upon exposure cause acrid injury to eyes and skin (Adolf et al. 1986; Hecker, 1978). Elimination of the sap should be possible since other species of the Euphorbiaceae family such as *E. pulcherrima* Willd., *Hevea brasiliensis, Manihot esculenta, Ricinus communis, Sapium sebiferum* (L.) Roxb. do not produce such irritants.

Early in 1985 the first non shattering cultivar of *E. lathyris* was given cultivar protection in West Germany under the name of Utopia. In plot experiments with this cultivar seed yields of 2000 kg/ha or more have been reported (v. Rotenhan, private communication), suggesting that one tonne of oil/ha might be obtainable.

Euphorbia lagascae and Other Sources of Epoxy Fatty Acids

Another member of the genus, *E. lagascae* Spreng. is of interest because of its high content (60 to 70%) of epoxy fatty acids in its seed oil. Normally epoxy fatty acids can only be obtained through chemical derivatization of the C18 unsaturated fatty acids. A breeding program to develop non shattering, high yielding *E. lagascae* strains has been initiated at the University of Göttingen, West Germany (Meier zu Beerentrup, 1986).

Other species that have been identified as potential sources of epoxy fatty acids are *Vernonia galamensis* (Cass.) Less., commonly known as ironweed, and *Stokesia laevis* Hill (Greene) or Stokes aster. The epoxy oils produced by these species can be recovered without excessive levels of free fatty acids and appear to be suitable for use in epoxy coatings and resins (Carlson, et al. 1981; Carlson and Chang, 1985). Laboratory extraction trials show that most of the vernolic acid in *V. galamensis* is present as di- and trivernolin and that lipase activity in the seed can be inactivated by steam tempering to maintain oil quality.

LIMNANTHES

Importance and Chemical Properties

Species of the genus *Limnanthes* commonly known as Meadowfoam were first described as having potential as an oil crop by Earle et al. (1959). After twenty-five years of intensive agronomic research about 160 ha/year of *Limnanthes alba* Benth. are being grown in the Willamette Valley in Oregon (Fig. 30.1F) (Jolliff, 1986). The oil content of *L. alba* seed is as high as 29% (Crane et al. 1981). Seed yields of 2500 kg/ha are reported for *L. douglasii* R.Br. and 1800 kg/ha for *L. alba* (Jolliff, 1980).

Meadowfoam has an oil content of 20 to 33%. About 95% of the total fatty acids of *Limnanthes* seed oil have chain lengths greater than C18 with 52 to 77% C20:1 (Table 30.1); 8 to 29% C22:1; and 7 to 20% C22:2 (Miller et al. 1964). Oleochemical products similar to sperm whale oil can be derivatized from meadowfoam oil. Wax esters of meadowfoam fatty acids with meadowfoam fatty alcohols have properties similar to those of jojoba seed oil (*Simmondsia chinensis* (Link) Schneider). The oil is useful for cosmetics and special technical applications (see Chapter 25).

The fact that meadowfoam can be grown as a winter annual crop and harvested with normal farm equipment should enable lower market prices for *Limnanthes* oil as compared to those of jojoba.

Origin and Systematics

Limnanthes is a small herbaceous winter annual crop, native to northern California and southern Oregon and endemic to North America. The genus consists of eight species. There is a botanical relationship between Limnanthaceae and Geraniaceae/Tropaeolaceae and a chemotaxonomical relationship to Cruciferae (Hegnauer, 1966). Because of its superior seed retention and erect growth habit *L. alba* has given the best agronomic performance under experimental conditions in Alaska, California, Maryland and Oregon (Fig. 30.1F) (Higgins et al. 1971).

Breeding Procedures

L. alba is a cross pollinated species that is highly self-compatible. Devine and Johnson (1978) showed that apomixis does not occur in this species. Emasculation is best performed at the immature bud stage when buds are 4 mm in length. The ten anthers are removed with forceps and pollination is done daily after style elongation occurs. For floral isolation glycine bags 3 to 5 cm long can be used (Jolliff et al. 1981).

History of Cultivar Development

Improvement in *Limnanthes* has been made by mass selection and hybridization. The first cultivar, developed in Oregon from a single plant selection, was called Foamore. This cultivar is upright in growth and shows good seed retention for combine harvesting (Calhoun, 1975). The second cultivar Mermaid had much better seed retention with yields equal to Foamore (Jolliff et al. 1981).

Breeding Goals

The most important breeding objectives for meadowfoam are taller and more competitive plants with higher seed yields, higher oil content, better seed retention and a better plant architecture. Other goals include improving meal quality by reducing the amount of glucosinolates present. The production of a self pollinating cultivar might also increase seed set by removing the dependence of the crop on foraging honey bees. Interspecific crosses between *L. alba* and *L. floccosa* (Howell) have been proposed as one means of achieving some of these objectives (Jolliff et al. 1984).

CRAMBE

Chemical Characteristics and Utilization Opportunities

In the USA and Canada *Crambe abyssinica* Hochst. Ex. R.E. Fries, is considered a potential industrial oil crop because of the high level of erucic acid (55 to 60%) contained in its seed oil. The traditional source for erucic acid has been rapeseed oil imported from Europe. As rapeseed growers in western Europe and Canada have changed their production to low-erucic acid type cultivars, the source of this oil has become increasingly scarce. Several thousand hectares of *Crambe* have been grown in extended experimental plots in the Pacific Northwest, Texas, the Midwest, and in the western Canadian provinces. *Crambe* yields up to 2000 kg/ha of seed, with an oil content of 26 to 38% (Lessman and Anderson, 1981). Among other applications *Crambe* oil, due to its good stability at high temperatures, is well suited as a lubricant for steel casting. Derivatives of erucic acid can be used for various chemical applications, such as slip agents, plasticizers, lubricants, antistatics, softeners, antifoamers, fixatives in perfumes, etc. (for more details consult Nieschlag and Wolff, 1971; Princen and Rothfus, 1984). Erucic acid yields pelargonic- and brassylic acid on ozonolysis, and behenic acid through hydrogenation. Liquid wax esters can also be produced from erucic acid.

Origin and Systematics

Crambe is a genus of the Cruciferae family. About twenty different *Crambe* species have been described; most of these originated in the Mediterranean area. The chromosome numbers are reported as n=45 for *C. abyssinica* Hochst., n=30 for *C. hispanica* var. *hispanica*, and n=15 for *C. hispanica* var. *glabrata* (White and Solt, 1978). Different levels of polyploidy tend to mask the variability which may lie within the species (Downey, 1971). Different species have been grown in Europe, Africa, the Near East, Central and West Asia, as well as in North and South America (Mazzani, 1954).

Since about 1932 *Crambe* has been evaluated by numerous countries including Canada, Denmark, Germany, Poland, Russia, Sweden, and Venezuela. In the 1940s seed stocks were first introduced to the USA and agronomic evaluation began in 1958 (White and Higgins, 1966).

Production

In the USA *C. abyssinica* is considered to have potential because it yielded dependably higher levels of erucic acid than rapeseed. Commercial scale production has established processing conditions and proven the efficacy of *Crambe* seed meal as a feed supplement for cattle (Princen and Rothfus, 1984).

Crambe is considered a winter crop for a climate with temperatures not lower than -7°C. In colder climates it should be grown as a spring crop. If the growing season is sufficiently long two crops of *Crambe* may be produced the same year with early spring and mid summer plantings (Christmas et al. 1968; Lessman and Anderson, 1980).

Mode of Reproduction

The inflorescence of *Crambe* is an indeterminate flowering panicle raceme (Fig. 30.1E). The typical cruciferous flowers have four white petals, about 3 mm in length and six stamens. The flowers are primarily self-pollinating with some natural outcrossing (Beck et al. 1975). Only one seed is formed per flower. Each seed is contained in a papery thin pod. The seed pod, however, is easily broken and separated from the mature seed. Emasculation is done by removing the stamens with tweezers from young unopened flower buds similar to procedures used in *Brassica* crops.

Cultivars and Breeding Goals

Three *Crambe* cultivars have been registered in the USA. At the University of Indiana selection work for larger, heavier seed resulted in the cultivar Prophet from *C. abyssinica*. Later the high seed yielding cultivar, Indy, selected within the *C. hispanica* species was released. The third cultivar, Meyer, was developed by selection among progenies of crosses between *C. abyssinica* and *C. hispanica* (Lessman, 1975). A major breeding goal is the reduction or elimination of toxic glucosinolates in *Crambe* seed meal. According to the law of parallel variation it can be speculated that there is a chance to select low glucosinolate strains as they have also been selected in other species of the Cruciferae family. *Crambe* has received GRAS (generally recommended as safe) status in the USA. A high volume to weight ratio in the threshed seed with a husk content of up to 40% (by weight) is considered a limiting factor of *Crambe* development (Downey, 1971).

The husk cannot be easily removed from the seed and must therefore be transported to the extraction mill. Husked seed usually contains 30 to 54% oil and 30 to 50% protein, whereas oil and protein are reduced accordingly if husks are not removed, with fiber content increasing to 16%. Commercial production of *Crambe* in western Canada, which reached several thousand acres in the mid-to late-1960s, was severely affected by the disease *Alternaria brassicicola* (Downey, private communication). Campbell et al. (1986) have registered new *Crambe* germplasm (C-22, C-29, C-37) that are reported as moderately tolerant to *Alternaria*.

Little genetic variability was observed in important agronomic traits of *Crambe* introductions which Lessman and Meier (1982) attributed to either the limited germplasm examined, the non-existence of variation, or experimental errors interfering with the identification of real variation. In hybridization experiments the authors later succeeded in creating more variation in the traits for plant height, primary and secondary branching, pod size, seed weight, and yield.

LESQUERELLA

Lesquerella species were discovered by the Northern Regional Research Center technical screening programs in the 1960s as a natural source of hydroxy-unsaturated fatty acids (Table 30.1) (Smith et al. 1960; Mikolajczak et al. 1962). *Lesquerella* oil should be useful in all those areas of technical application where castor oil is now being used, such as paints, lubricants, hydraulic fluids, linoleum, cosmetics, etc. *Lesquerella* meal does not contain toxic protein such as is found in the castor bean, however glucosinolates can be expected to be present in this cruciferous crop (Princen, 1983).

The genus *Lesquerella* is a member of the Cruciferae family and is native mainly to the arid parts of western North America. It consists of approximately seventy species, of which about 30% are annuals (Payson, 1921). The formation of hydroxy-fatty acids has a significant taxonomic relevance within the genus *Lesquerella* (Hegnauer, 1964).

Very little is known with respect to the genetics and plant breeding of *Lesquerella* because it has not been cultivated for any length of time. *Lesquerella* species appear to be cross pollinated (Rollins, 1957). Emasculation procedures should be similar to those of other cruciferous crops (see "*Crambe* " and Chapter 16).

In the USA the species native to the southwest tend to be adapted to calcareous soils or to rather specific ecological conditions such as the prairies. Plants tend to be adapted to dry conditions, growing contiguously in colonies containing large numbers of individual plants. This is especially true for *Lesquerella fendleri* (Gray) Wats., *L. gracilis* (Hook) Wats., and *L. gordonii* (Gray) Wats. (Rollins and Shaw, 1973).

Gentry and Barclay (1962) reported a wide range of genetic variability in wild stands of *L. fendleri* which they suggest as a prime candidate for domestication. This species grows as a winter annual at elevations from 600 to 1800 m in areas with annual precipitation of 250 to 400 mm such as the southern high plains, southeastern Arizona, southwestern Texas, and the Edwards Plateau of south central Texas (Gentry and Barclay, 1962). A wild stand of *L. fendleri* has been combine harvested yielding ca. 1000 kg/ha. Seeds of this species contain 20 to 28% oil with about 62% lesquerolic acid ((+)-14-hydroxy-cis-11-eicosenoic acid).

L. gordonii occupies many of the same regions as *L. fendleri*, extending further east in the Texas prairies and growing on sandy instead of calcic soils. *L. gracilis* is found on the Texas blackland prairies and grand prairies, as well as on the Cherokee prairies of Kansas and Oklahoma (Rollins and Shaw, 1973).

L. globosa is a perennial species adapted to limestone soils in Kentucky and Tennessee (Rollins and Shaw, 1973). Seeds of this species contain 39% oil with 66% lesquerolic acid. However, *L. globosa* (Desv.) Wats. has been placed on the list of threatened plant species in the USA (Ayensu and Filipps, 1978).

REFERENCES

Adolf, W., Opferkuch, H.J., and Hecker, E. 1987. Systematic screening of 85 species of the plant family Euphorbiaceae for irritants and tumor promoters. Toxicon, In Press.

Ayensu, E.S., and de Filipps, R.A. 1978. Endangered and Threatened Plants of the United States. Smithsonian Institution and World Wildlife Fund, Washington, DC.

Ayerbe, L., Tenorio, J.L., Ventas, P., Funes, E., and Mellado, L. 1984a. *Euphorbia lathyris* as an energy crop. Part I: Vegetative matter and seed productivity. Biomass 4: 283-293.

——, ——, ——, ——, and —— 1984b. *Euphorbia lathyris* as an energy crop. Part II: Hydrocarbon and sugar productivity. Biomass 5: 37-42.

Beck, L.C., Lessman, K.J., and Buker, R.J. 1975. Inheritance of pubescence and its use in outcrossing measurements between a *Crambe hispanica* type and *C. abyssinica* Hochst. Ex. R.E. Fries. Crop Sci. 15: 221-224.

Calhoun, W. 1975. New oil crops for Oregon: Meadowfoam, *Limnanthes*, pp. 74-80. Proc. 26th Annu. Meet. Oreg. Essent. Oil Grow. League.

Calvin, M. 1980. Hydrocarbons from plants: Analytic methods and observations. Naturwissenschaften 67: 525-533.

Campbell, T.A., Crock, J., Williams, J.H., Hang, A.N., Sigafus, R.E., Schneiter, A.A., McClain, E.F., Graves, C.R., Woolley, D.G., Kleiman, R., and Adamson, W.C. 1986. Registration of C-22, C-29, C-37 *Crambe* germplasm. Crop Sci. 26: 1088-1089.

Carlson, K.D., Schneider, W.J., Chang, S.P., and Princen, L.H. 1981. *Vernonia galamensis* Seed Oil: A New Source for Epoxy Coatings, pp. 297-318. *In* E. H. Pryde, L. H. Princen and K. D. Mukherjee (eds.), *New Sources of Fats and Oils*. AOCS Monograph No. 9, Am. Oil Chem. Soc., Champaign, Ill.

——, and Chang, S.P. 1985. Chemical epoxidation of a natural unsaturated epoxy seed oil from *Vernonia galamensis* and a look at epoxy oil markets. J. Am. Oil Chem. Soc. 62: 934-939.

Christmas, E.P., Lessmann, K.J., Southard, C.B., and Phillips, M.W. 1968. *Crambe*: A Potential New Crop for Indiana. Purdue University. Agric. Extension Service Bull. AY-168.

Crane, J.M., Calhoun, W., and Eayres, T.A. 1981. Seed and oil characteristics of nitrogen fertilized meadowfoam. Agronomy J. 83: 255-256.

Devine, M.B., and Johnson, J.W. 1978. Mode of pollination and reproduction of meadowfoam. Crop Sci. 18: 126-128.

Downey, R.K. 1971. Agricultural and genetic potentials of cruciferous oilseed crops. J. Am. Oil Chem. Soc. 48: 718-722.

———. 1987. Genetic Manipulation of Oilseed Quality, pp. 669-676. *In* P. K. Stumpf, J. B. Mudd, and W. D. Nes (eds.), *The Metabolism, Structure, and Function of Plant Lipids*. Plenum Publishing Corp., New York

Earle, F.R., Melvin, E.H., Mason, I.H., Van Etten, C.H., and Wolff, I.A. 1959. Search for new industrial oils. I. Selected oils from 24 plant families. J. Am. Oil Chem. Soc. 36: 304-307.

Gentry, H.S., and Barclay, A.S. 1962. The search for new industrial crops. III. Prospectus of *Lesquerella fendleri*. Econ. Bot. 16: 206-211.

Graham, Shirley A., Hirsinger, F., and Röbbelen, G. 1981. Fatty acids of *Cuphea* seed lipids and their systematic significance. Am. J. Bot. 68: 908-917.

Hecker, E. 1978. Structure-Activity Relationships in Diterpene Esters Irritant and Cocarcinogenic to Mouse Skin, pp. 11-4. *In* T. J. Slaga, A. Sivak, and R. K. Boutwell (eds.), *Carcinogenesis*. Vol. 2. *Mechanism of Tumor Promotion and Cocarcinogenesis*. Raven Press, New York.

Hegnauer, R. 1964. *Chemotaxonomie der Pflanzen*. Vol. 2. Birkhäuser Verlag, Basel and Stuttgart.

———. 1966. *Chemotaxonomie der Pflanzen*. Vol. 4. Birkhäuser Verlag, Basel and Stuttgart.

Henkel KGaA. 1982. *Fatty Alcohols*. Henkel KGaA, Düsseldorf.

Higgins, J.J., Calhoun, W., Willingham, W., Dinkel, D.H., Raisler, W.L., and White, G.A. 1971. Agronomic evaluation of prospective new crops species. II. The American *Limnanthes*. Econ. Bot. 25: 44-54.

Hirsinger, F. 1980a. Untersuchungen zur Beurteilung der Anbauwürdigkeit einer neuen MCT-Ölpflanze *Cuphea* (Lythraceae), Teil I. Natürliche Variabilität in taxonomischen und pflanzenbaulichen Eigenschaften bei *Cuphea* Arten. Angew. Bot. 54: 157-177.

———. 1980b. Untersuchungen zur Beurteilung der Anbauwürdigkeit einer neuen MCT-Ölpflanze *Cuphea* (Lythraceae). 2. Chemische Mutagenese bei *Cuphea aperta* Koehne. Z. Pflanzenzuchtg. 85: 157-169.

———. 1985. Agronomic potential and seed composition of *Cuphea*, an annual crop for lauric and capric seed oils. J. Am. Oil Chem. Soc. 62: 76-80.

———, and Knowles, P.F. 1984. Morphological and agronomic description of selected *Cuphea* germplasm. Econ. Bot. 38: 439-451.

Jolliff, G.D. 1980. Development and Production of Meadowfoam (*L. alba*), p. 269. *In* E. H. Pryde, L. H. Princen, and K. D. Mukherjee (eds.), *New Sources of Fats and Oils*. AOCS Monograph No. 9, Am. Oil Chem. Soc., Champaign, Ill.

———. 1986. The status of Meadowfoam (*Limnanthes*), development of a new industrial oilseed crop. J. Am. Oil Chem. Soc. 63: 404.

———, Tinsley, I.J., Calhoun, W., and Crane, J.M. 1981. Meadowfoam (*Limnanthes alba*): Its Research and Development as a Potential New Oilseed Crop for the Williamette Valley of Oregon. Oreg. Agric. Exp. Stn. Bull. No. 648.

——, Calhoun, W., and Crane, J.M. 1984. Development of a self-pollinated meadowfoam from interspecific hybridization. Crop Sci. 24: 369-370.

Koehne, E. 1903. Lythraceae, p. 216. IV. *In* A. Engler (ed.), *Das Pflanzenreich. Regni vegetabilis conspectus.* Heft 17.

Lessman, K.J. 1975. Variation in *Crambe, Crambe abyssinica* Hochst. J. Am. Oil Chem. Soc. 52: 386-389.

——, and Anderson, W.P. 1980. *Crambe*, pp. 339-346. *In* W. R. Fehr and H. H. Hadley (eds.), *Hybridization of Crop Plants.* Am. Soc. of Agron., and Crop Sci. Soc. America, Madison, Wis.

——, and Meyer, V.D. 1972. Agronomic evaluation of *Crambe* as a source of oil. Crop Sci. 12: 224-227.

Mazzani, B. 1954. Introduction de plantas oleoginosas nuevas para Venezuela, *Crambe abyssinica* Hochst. Agron. Trop. 4: 101-104.

Meier zu Beerentrup, Hanna. 1986. Identifizierung, Erzeugung und Verbesserung von einheimischen Ölsaaten mit ungewöhnlichen Fettsäuren. PhD. Thesis. Univ. Göttingen.

Mikolajczak, K.L., Earle, F.R., and Wolff, J.A. 1962. Search for new industrial oils. VI. Seed oils of the genus *Lesquerella*. J. Am. Oil Chem. Soc. 39: 78-80.

Miller, R.W., Daxenbichler, M.E., Earle, F.R., and Gentry, H.S. 1964. Search for new industrial oils. VIII. The genus *Limnanthes*. J. Am. Oil Chem. Soc. 41: 167-169.

Nieschlag, H.J., and Wolff, I.A. 1971. Industrial uses of high erucic oils. J. Am. Oil Chem. Soc. 48: 723-727.

Payson, E.B. 1921. A monograph of the genus *Lesquerella*. Ann. Mo. Bot. Gard. 8: 103-236.

Princen, L.H. 1983. New oilseed crops on the horizon. Econ. Bot. 37: 478-492.

——, and Rothfus, J.A. 1984. Development of new crops for industrial raw materials. J. Am. Oil Chem. Soc. 61: 281-289.

Röbbelen, G., and Thies, W. 1980. Biosynthesis of Seed Oil and Breeding for Oil Quality, pp. 253-283. *In* S. Tsunoda, K. Hinata, and C. Gomez-Campo (eds.), *Brassica Crops and Wild Allies - Biology and Breeding.* Japan Scient. Soc. Press, Tokyo.

Rollins, R.C. 1957. Interspecific hybridization in *Lesquerella*. Contrib. Gray Herb. Harv. Univ. 181: 1-40.

——, and Shaw, E.A. 1973. The genus *Lesquerella* (Cruciferae) in North America. Harvard University Press, Cambridge, Mass.

Smith, C.R. Jr., Wilson, T.L., Melvin, E.H., and Wolff, I.A. 1960. Dimorphecolic acid - a unique hydroxy fatty acid. J. Am. Chem. Soc. 82: 1417-1421.

White, G.A., and Higgins, J.J. 1966. Culture of *Crambe*. A new industrial oilseed crop. U.S. Dept. Agric., Agric. Res. Service Prod. Res. Rep. No. 95, 22.

——, and Solt, M. 1978. Chromosome numbers in *Crambe, Crambella,* and *Hemicrambe*. Crop Sci. 18: 160-161.

Wilson, T.L., Miwa, T.K., and Smith, C.R. 1960. *Cuphea llavea* seed oil, a good source of capric acid. J. Am. Oil Chem. Soc. 37: 675-676.

Wolff, I.A., and Jones, Q. 1958. Cooperative new crops research - what the program has to involve. Chemurgic Digest 17: 4-8.

Index

H

I

J

ABOUT THE EDITORS

R. Keith Downey is Assistant Director and Head, Oilseeds Section, Agriculture Canada Research Station, Saskatoon, and an Adjunct Professor of the University of Saskatchewan, Canada. He is an Officer of the Order of Canada and a Fellow of the Agricultural Institute and the Royal Society of Canada. He received the American Oil Chemists' Bond Gold Medal in 1963, the Public Service of Canada Merit Award in 1969, the Agricultural Institute Grindley Medal in 1973 and the Royal Bank of Canada Award in 1976. He and his colleagues have made major breakthroughs in rapeseed and mustard improvement. He is past president of the Canadian Society of Agronomy and Chairman of the International Rapeseed Breeders' Committee. He has authored numerous book chapters and over 115 research publications as well as managing oilseed improvement projects in India and China.

Gerhard P. K. Röbbelen is the Director of the Institute of Agronomy and Plant Breeding at the University of Göttingen, Federal Republic of Germany. He is past president of the German Society of Genetics and President of Eucarpia, the European Association for Research in Plant Breeding, as well as the German Association of Fat Sciences (DGF). In 1976 he was awarded an honorary doctorate in Agriculture by the Faculty of Agriculture, University of Kiel, and has been a member of the Academy of Sciences, Göttingen, since 1981. He is managing editor of the Journal, "Plant Breeding" (Zeitschrift für Pflanzenzüchtung). He established the first centre for *Arabidopsis* research in Göttingen and pioneered research on oil crops, such as *Cuphea*, for industrial uses. He is well known for his research in rapeseed improvement and has authored several book chapters and many scientific publications.

Amram Ashri is Professor and Head of the Department of Field and Vegetable Crops and Genetics, and was formerly Dean of Agriculture at the Hebrew University of Jerusalem, Israel. He is internationally known for his research on sesame, peanuts and safflower. He has frequently served as an international consultant on sesame and peanuts for FAO and other organizations and has been a visiting scientist at the International Atomic Energy Agency (IAEA), Vienna. He is well known for his innovative breeding work on oilseeds and has published extensively in the area.